A Retargetable C Compiler: Design and Implementation

A Retargetable C Compiler: Design and Implementation

Christopher W. Fraser

AT&T BELL LABORATORIES

David R. Hanson

PRINCETON UNIVERSITY

Addison-Wesley Publishing Company
Menlo Park, California
Reading, Massachusetts • New York • Don Mills, Ontario • Wokingham, U.K.
Amsterdam • Bonn • Sydney • Singapore • Tokyo • Madrid • San Juan

Acquisitions Editor: John Carter Shanklin
Executive Editor: Dan Joraanstad
Editorial Assistant: Melissa Standen
Production Supervisor: Ray Kanarr
Cover Design and Illustration: Cloyce Wall
Text Designer: Peter Vacek
Copyeditor: Elizabeth Gehrman
Proofreader: Christine Sabooni

Many of the designations used by manufacturers and sellers to distinguish their products are claimed as trademarks. Where those designations appear in this book, and Addison-Wesley was aware of a trademark claim, the designations have been printed in initial caps or in all caps.

Camera-ready copy for this book was prepared using LaTeX, TeX, and Adobe Illustrator.

Instructional Material Disclaimer

The program presented in this book has been included for its instructional value. It has been tested with care but is not guaranteed for any particular purpose. Neither the publisher, AT&T, or the authors offer any warranties or representations, nor do they accept any liabilities with respect to the program.

Library of Congress Cataloging-in-Publication Data

```
Fraser, Chistopher W.
   A retargetable C compiler: design and implementation /
 Christopher W. Fraser, David R. Hanson
      p.   cm.
   Includes index.
   ISBN 0-8053-1670-1
   1. C (Computer program language)  2. Compilers (Computer programs)
 I. Hanson, David R.  II. Title.
 QA76.73.C15F75  1995
 005.4'53--dc20                                    94-24583
                                                   CIP
```

ISBN 0-8053-1670-1

2 3 4 5 6 7 8 9 10 DOC 98 97 96 95

Addison-Wesley Publishing Company
390 Bridge Parkway
Redwood City, CA 94065

To Linda
To Maylee

Contents

Preface

The compiler is the linchpin of the programmer's toolbox. Working programmers use compilers every day and count heavily on their correctness and reliability. A compiler must accept the standard definition of the programming language so that source code will be portable across platforms. A compiler must generate efficient object code. Perhaps more important, a compiler must generate correct object code; an application is only as reliable as the compiler that compiled it.

A compiler is itself a large and complex application that is worthy of study in its own right. This book tours most of the implementation of lcc, a compiler for the ANSI C programming language. It is to compiling what *Software Tools* by B. W. Kernighan and P. J. Plauger (Addison-Wesley, 1976) is to text processing like text editors and macro processors. Software design and implementation are best learned through experience with real tools. This book explains in detail and shows most of the code for a real compiler. The accompanying diskette holds the source code for the complete compiler.

lcc is a production compiler. It's been used to compile production programs since 1988 and is now used by hundreds of C programmers daily. Detailing most of a production compiler in a book leaves little room for supporting material, so we present only the theory needed for the implementation at hand and leave the broad survey of compiling techniques to existing texts. The book omits a few language features — those with mundane or repetitive implementations and those deliberately treated only in the exercises — but the full compiler is available on the diskette, and the book makes it understandable.

The obvious use for this book is to learn more about compiler construction. But only few programmers need to know how to design and implement compilers. Most work on applications and other aspects of systems programming. There are four reasons why this majority of C programmers may benefit from this book.

First, programmers who understand how a C compiler works are often better programmers in general and better C programmers in particular. The compiler writer must understand even the darkest corners of the C language; touring the implementation of those corners reveals much about the language itself and its efficient realization on modern computers.

Second, most texts on programming must necessarily use small examples, which often demonstrate techniques simply and elegantly. Most programmers, however, work on large programs that have evolved — or degenerated — over time. There are few well documented examples of this kind of "programming in the large" that can serve as reference examples. lcc isn't perfect, but this book documents both its good and bad points in detail and thus provides one such reference point.

Third, a compiler is one of the best demonstrations in computer science of the interaction between theory and practice. lcc displays both the places where this interaction is smooth and the results are elegant, as well as where practical demands strain the theory, which shows in the resulting code. Exploring these interactions in a real program helps programmers understand when, where, and how to apply different techniques. lcc also illustrates numerous C programming techniques.

Fourth, this book is an example of a "literate program." Like *TEX: The Program* by D. E. Knuth (Addison-Wesley, 1986), this book is lcc's source code and the prose that describes it. The code is presented in the order that best suits understanding, not in the order dictated by the C programming language. The source code that appears on the diskette is extracted automatically from the book's text files.

This book is well suited for self-study by both academics and professionals. The book and its diskette offer complete documented source code for lcc, so they may interest practitioners who wish to experiment with compilation or those working in application areas that use or implement language-based tools and techniques, such as user interfaces.

The book shows a large software system, warts and all. It could thus be the subject of a postmortem in a software engineering course, for example.

For compiler courses, this book complements traditional compiler texts. It shows *one* way of implementing a C compiler, while traditional texts survey algorithms for solving the broad range of problems encountered in compiling. Limited space prevents such texts from including more than a toy compiler. Code generation is often treated at a particularly high level to avoid tying the book to a specific computer.

As a result, many instructors prepare a substantial programming project to give their students some practical experience. These instructors usually must write these compilers from scratch; students duplicate large portions and have to use the rest with only limited documentation. The situation is trying for both students and instructors, and unsatisfying to boot, because the compilers are still toys. By documenting most of a real compiler and providing the source code, this book offers an alternative.

This book presents full code generators for the MIPS R3000, SPARC, and Intel 386 and successor architectures. It exploits recent research that produces code generators from compact specifications. These methods allow us to present complete code generators for several machines, which no other book does. Presenting several code generators avoids tying the book to a single machine, and helps students appreciate engineering retargetable software.

Assignments can add language features, optimizations, and targets. When used with a traditional survey text, assignments could also replace existing modules with those using alternate algorithms. Such assignments come closer to the actual practice of compiler engineering than assignments that implement most of a toy compiler, where too much time goes to low-level infrastructure and accommodating repetitive language features. Many of the exercises pose just these kinds of engineering problems.

lcc has also been adapted for purposes other than conventional compilation. For example, it's been used for building a C browser and for generating remote-procedure-call stubs from declarations. It could also be used to experiment with language extensions, proposed computer architectures, and code-generator technologies.

We assume readers are fluent in C and assembly language for some computer, know what a compiler is and have a general understanding of what one does, and have a working understanding of data structures and algorithms at the level covered in typical undergraduate courses; the material covered by *Algorithms in C* by R. Sedgewick (Addison-Wesley, 1990), for example, is more than sufficient for understanding lcc.

Acknowledgments

This book owes much to the many lcc users at AT&T Bell Laboratories, Princeton University, and elsewhere who suffered through bugs and provided valuable feedback. Those who deserve explicit thanks include Hans Boehm, Mary Fernandez, Michael Golan, Paul Haahr, Brian Kernighan, Doug McIlroy, Rob Pike, Dennis Ritchie, and Ravi Sethi. Ronald Guilmette, David Kristol, David Prosser, and Dennis Ritchie provided valuable information concerning the fine points of the ANSI Standard and its interpretation. David Gay helped us adapt the PFORT library of numerical software to be an invaluable stress test for lcc's code generators.

Careful reviews of both our code and our prose by Jack Davidson, Todd Proebsting, Norman Ramsey, William Waite, and David Wall contributed significantly to the quality of both. Our thanks to Steve Beck, who installed and massaged the fonts used for this book, and to Maylee Noah, who did the artwork with Adobe Illustrator.

Christopher W. Fraser
David R. Hanson

1
Introduction

A *compiler* translates source code to assembler or object code for a target machine. A *retargetable* compiler has multiple targets. Machine-specific compiler parts are isolated in modules that are easily replaced to target different machines.

This book describes lcc, a retargetable compiler for ANSI C; it focuses on the implementation. Most compiler texts survey compiling algorithms, which leaves room for only a toy compiler. This book leaves the survey to others. It tours most of a practical compiler for full ANSI C, including code generators for three target machines. It gives only enough compiling theory to explain the methods that it uses.

1.1   Literate Programs

This book not only describes the implementation of lcc, it *is* the implementation. The noweb system for "literate programming" generates both the book and the code for lcc from a single source. This source consists of interleaved prose and labelled code *fragments*. The fragments are written in the order that best suits describing the program, namely the order you see in this book, not the order dictated by the C programming language. The program noweave accepts the source and produces the book's typescript, which includes most of the code and all of the text. The program notangle extracts all of the code, in the proper order for compilation.

Fragments contain source code and references to other fragments. Fragment definitions are preceded by their labels in angle brackets. For example, the code

⟨*a fragment label* 1⟩≡   2

```
   sum = 0;
   for (i = 0; i < 10; i++) ⟨increment sum 1⟩
```

⟨*increment* sum 1⟩≡   1

```
   sum += x[i];
```

sums the elements of x. Fragment uses are typeset as illustrated by the use of ⟨*increment* sum⟩ in the example above. Several fragments may have the same name; notangle concatenates their definitions to produce a single fragment. noweave identifies this concatenation by using $+\equiv$ instead of $\equiv$ in continued definitions:

⟨*a fragment label* 1⟩$+\equiv$ $\overset{\blacktriangle}{1}$
  printf("%d\n", sum);

Fragment definitions are like macro definitions; notangle extracts a program by expanding one fragment. If its definition refers to other fragments, they are themselves expanded, and so on.

Fragment definitions include aids to help readers navigate among them. Each fragment name ends with the number of the page on which the fragment's definition begins. If there's no number, the fragment isn't defined in this book, but its code does appear on the companion diskette. Each continued definition also shows the previous definition, and the next continued definition, if there is one. $\overset{\blacktriangle}{14}$ is an example of a previous definition that appears on page 14, and $\underset{\blacktriangledown}{31}$ says the definition is continued on page 31. These annotations form a doubly linked list of definitions; the up arrow points to the previous definition in the list and down arrow points to the next one. The previous link on the first definition in a list is omitted, and the next link on the last definition is omitted. These lists are complete: If some of a fragment's definitions appear on the same page with each other, the links refer to the page on which they appear.

Most fragments also show a list of pages on which the fragment is used, as illustrated by the number 1 to the right of the definition for ⟨*increment* sum⟩, above. These unadorned use lists are omitted for root fragments, which define modules, and for some fragments that occur too frequently, as detailed below.

notangle also implements one extension to C. A long string literal can be split across several lines by ending the lines to be continued with underscores. notangle removes leading white space from continuation lines and concatenates them to form a single string. The first argument to error on page 119 is an example of this extension.

1.2 How to Read This Book

Read this book front-to-back. A few variants are possible.

- Chapter 5 describes the interface between the front end and back ends of the compiler. This chapter has been made as self-contained as possible.

- Chapters 13–18 describe the back ends of the compiler. Once you know the interface, you can read these chapters with few excursions back into their predecessors. Indeed, people have *replaced* the front end and the back ends without reading, much less understanding, the other half.

- Chapters 16-18 describe the modules that capture all information about the three targets — the MIPS, SPARC, and Intel 386 and successor architectures. Each of these chapters is independent, so you may read any subset of them. If you read more than one, you may notice some repetition, but it shouldn't be too irritating because most code common to all three targets has been factored out into Chapters 13-15.

Some parts of the book describe lcc from the bottom up. For example, the chapters on managing storage, strings, and symbol tables describe functions that are at or near the ends of call chains. Little context is needed to understand them.

Other parts of the book give a top-down presentation. For example, the chapters on parsing expressions, statements, and declarations begin with the top-level constructs. Top-down material presents some functions or fragments well after the code that uses them, but material near the first use tells enough about the function or fragment to understand what's going on in the interim.

Some parts of the book alternate between top-down and bottom-up presentations. A less variable explanation order would be nice, but it's unattainable. Like most compilers, lcc includes mutually recursive functions, so it's impossible to describe all callees before all callers or all callers before all callees.

Some fragments are easier to explain before you see the code. Others are easier to explain afterward. If you need help with a fragment, don't struggle before scanning the text just before *and* after the fragment.

Most of the code for lcc appears in the text, but a few fragments are used but not shown. Some of these fragments hold code that is omitted to save space. Others implement language extensions, optional debugging aids, or repetitious constructs. For example, once you've seen the code that handles C's for statement, the code that handles the do-while statement adds little. The only wholesale omission is the explanation of how lcc processes C's initializers, which we skipped because it is long, not very interesting, and not needed to understand anything else. Fragments that are used but not defined are easy to identify: no page number follows the fragment name.

Also omitted are assertions. lcc includes hundreds of assertions. Most assert something that the code assumes about the value of a parameter or data structure. One is `assert(0)`, which guarantees a diagnostic and thus identifies states that are not supposed to occur. For example, if a switch is supposed to have a bona fide case for all values of the switch expression, then the default case might include `assert(0)`.

The companion diskette is complete. Even the assertions and fragments that are omitted from the text appear on the diskette. Many of them are easily understood once the documented code nearby is understood.

A "mini-index" appears in the middle of the outside margin of many pages. It lists each program identifier that appears on the page and the page number on which the identifier is defined in code or explained in text. These indices not only help locate definitions, but highlight circularities: Identifiers that are used before they are defined appear in the mini-indices with page numbers that follow the page on which they are used. Such circularities can be confusing, but they are inevitable in any description of a large program. A few identifiers are listed with more than one definition; these name important identifiers that are used for more than one purpose or that are defined by both code and prose.

1.3   Overview

lcc transforms a source program to an assembler language program. Following a sample program through the intermediate steps in this transformation illustrates lcc's major components and data structures. Each step transforms the program into a different representation: preprocessed source, tokens, trees, directed acyclic graphs, and lists of these graphs are examples. The initial source code is:

```
int round(f) float f; {
        return f + 0.5;   /* truncates */
}
```

round has no prototype, so the argument is passed as a double and round reduces it to a float upon entry. Then round adds 0.5, truncates the result to an integer, and returns it.

The first phase is the C preprocessor, which expands macros, includes header files, and selects conditionally compiled code. lcc now runs under DOS and UNIX systems, but it originated on UNIX systems. Like many UNIX compilers, lcc uses a separate preprocessor, which runs as a separate process and is not part of this book. We often use the preprocessor that comes with the GNU C compiler.

A typical preprocessor reads the sample code and emits:

```
# 1 "sample.c"
int round(f) float f; {
        return f + 0.5;
}
```

The sample uses no preprocessor features, so the preprocessor has nothing to do but strip the comment and insert a # directive to tell the compiler the file name and line number of the source code for use when issuing diagnostics. These sample coordinates are straightforward, but a program with numerous #include directives brackets each included

```
INT       inttype
ID        "round"
'('
ID        "f"
')'
FLOAT     floattype
ID        "f"
','
';'
'{'
RETURN
ID        "f"
'+'
FCON      0.5
';'
'}'
EOI
```

FIGURE 1.1 Token stream for the sample.

file with a pair of # directives, and every other one names a line other than 1.

The compiler proper picks up where the preprocessor leaves off. It starts with the *lexical analyzer* or *scanner*, which breaks the input into the *tokens* shown in Figure 1.1. The left column is the *token code*, which is a small integer, and the right column is the associated value, if there is one. For example, the value associated with the keyword int is the value of inttype, which represents the type integer. The token codes for single-character tokens are the ASCII codes for the characters themselves, and EOI marks the end of the input. The lexical analyzer posts the source *coordinate* for each token, and it processes the # directive; the rest of the compiler never sees such directives. lcc's lexical analyzer is described in Chapter 6.

The next compiler phase *parses* the token stream according to the syntax rules of the C language. It also analyzes the program for *semantic* correctness. For example, it checks that the types of the operands in operations, such as addition, are legal, and it checks for implicit conversions. For example, in the sample's addition, f is a float and 0.5 is a double, which is a legal combination, and the sum is converted from double to int implicitly because round's return type is int.

The outcome of this phase for the sample are the two decorated *abstract syntax trees* shown in Figure 1.2. Each node represents one basic operation. The first tree reduces the incoming double to a float. It assigns a float (ASGN+F) to the cell with the address &f (the left ADDRF+P). It computes the value to assign by converting to float (CVD+F) the double fetched (INDIR+D) from address &f (the right ADDRF+P).

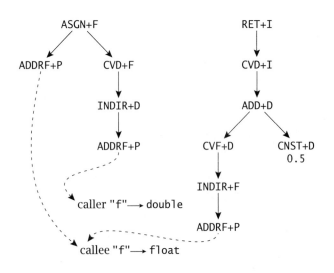

FIGURE 1.2   Abstract syntax trees for the sample.

The second tree implements the sample's lone explicit statement, and returns an int (RET+I). The value is computed by fetching the float (INDIR+F) from the cell with the address &f (ADDRF+P), converting it to double, adding (ADD+D) the double constant 0.5 (CNST+D), and truncating the result to int (CVD+I).

These trees make explicit many facts that are implicit in the source code. For example, the conversions above are all implicit in the source code, but explicit in the ANSI standard and thus in the trees. Also, the trees type all operators explicitly; for example, the addition in the source code has no explicit type, but its counterpart in the tree does. This *semantic analysis* is done as lcc's parser recognizes the input, and is covered in Chapters 7–11.

From the trees shown in Figure 1.2, lcc produces the directed acyclic graphs — *dags* — shown in Figure 1.3. The dags labelled 1 and 2 come from the trees shown in Figure 1.2. The operators are written without the plus signs to identify the structures as dags instead of trees. The transition from trees to dags makes explicit additional implicit facts. For example, the constant 0.5, which appeared in a CNST+D node in the tree, appears as the value of a static variable named 2 in the dag, and the CNST+D operator has been replaced by operators that develop the address of the variable (ADDRGP) and fetch its value (INDIRD).

The third dag, shown in Figure 1.3, defines the label named 1 that appears at the end of round. Return statements are compiled into jumps to this label, and trivial ones are elided.

As detailed in Chapter 12, the transition from trees to dags also eliminates repeated instances of the same expression, which are called *common subexpressions*. Optionally, each multiply referenced dag node can

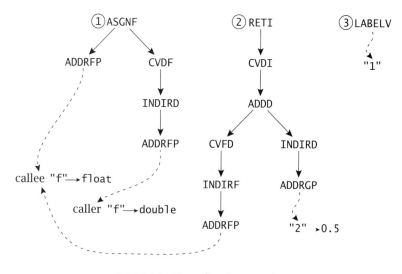

FIGURE 1.3 Dags for the sample.

be eliminated by assigning its value to a temporary and using the temporary in several places. The code generators in this book use this option.

These dags appear in the order that they must execute on the *code list* shown in Figure 1.4. Each entry in this list following the Start entry represents one component of the code for round. The Defpoint entries identify source locations, and the Blockbeg and Blockend entries identify the boundaries of round's one compound statement. The Gen entries carry the dags labelled 1 and 2 in Figure 1.3, and the Label entry carries the dag labelled 3. The code list is described in Chapters 10 and 12.

217	Blockbeg
217	Blockend
217	Defpoint
217	Gen
217	Label
217	Start

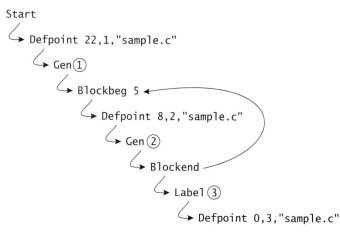

FIGURE 1.4 Code list for the sample.

At this point, the structures that represent the program pass from lcc's machine-independent front end into its back end, which translates these structures into assembler code for the target machine. One can hand-code a back end to emit code for a specific machine; such code generators are often largely machine-specific and must be replaced entirely for a new target.

The code generators in this book are driven by tables and a tree grammar that maps dags to instructions as described in Chapters 13–18. This organization makes the back ends partly independent of the target machine; that is, only part of the back end must be replaced for a new target. The other part could be moved into the front end — which serves all code generators for all target machines — but this step would complicate using lcc with a different kind of code generator, so it has not been taken.

The code generator operates by annotating the dags. It first identifies an assembler-code template — an instruction or operand — that implements each node. Figure 1.5 shows the sample's dags annotated with assembler code for the 386 or compatibles, henceforth termed X86. %*n* denotes the assembler code for child *n* where the leftmost child is numbered 0, and %*letter* denotes one of the symbol-table entries at which the node points. In this figure, the solid lines link instructions, and the dashed lines link parts of instructions, such as addressing modes, to the instructions in which they are used. For example, in the first dag, the ASGNF and INDIRD nodes hold instructions, and the two ADDRGP nodes hold their operands. Also, the CVDF node that was in the right operand of the ASGNF in Figure 1.3 is gone — it's been swallowed by the instruction selection because the instruction associated with the ASGNF does both the conversion and the assignment. Chapter 14 describes the mechanics of instruction selection and lburg, a program that generates selection code from compact specifications.

For those who don't know X86 assembler code, fld loads a floating-point value onto a stack; fstp pops one off and stores it; fistp does likewise but truncates the value and stores the resulting integer instead; fadd pops two values off and pushes their sum; and pop pops an integral value off the stack into a register. Chapter 18 elaborates.

The assembler code is easier to read after the compiler takes its next step, which chains together the nodes that correspond to instructions in the order in which they're to be emitted, and allocates a register for each node that needs one. Figure 1.6 shows the linearized instructions and registers allocated for our sample program. The figure is a bit of a fiction — the operands aren't actually substituted into the instruction templates until later — but the white lie helps here.

Like many compilers that originated on UNIX systems, lcc emits assembler code and is used with a separate assembler and linker. This book's back ends work with the vendors' assemblers on MIPS and SPARC

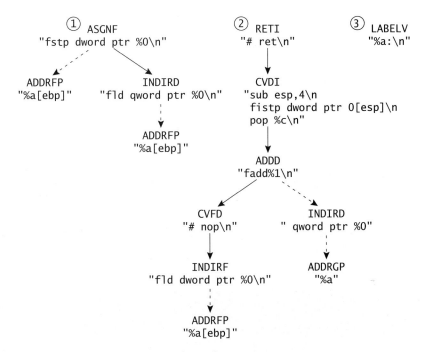

FIGURE 1.5   After selecting instructions.

systems, and with Microsoft's MASM 6.11 and Borland's Turbo Assembler 4.0 under DOS. lcc generates the assembler language shown in Figure 1.7 for our sample program. The lines in this code delimit its major parts. The first part is the boilerplate of assembler directives emitted for every program. The second part is the *entry sequence* for round. The four push instructions save the values of some registers, and the mov instruction establishes the *frame pointer* for this invocation of round.

The third part is the code emitted from the annotated dags shown in Figure 1.5 with the symbol-table data filled in. The fourth part is round's

Register	Assembler Template
	fld qword ptr %a[ebp]\n
	fstp dword ptr %a[ebp]\n
	fld dword ptr %a[ebp]\n
	# nop\n
	fadd qword ptr %a\n
eax	sub esp,4\nfistp dword ptr 0[esp]\npop %c\n
	# ret\n
	%a:\n

FIGURE 1.6   After allocating registers.

```
.486
.model small                        boilerplate
extrn __turboFloat:near
extrn __setargv:near

public _round
_TEXT segment
_round:
push ebx                            entry
push esi                            sequence
push edi
push ebp
mov ebp,esp

fld qword ptr 20[ebp]
fstp dword ptr 20[ebp]
fld dword ptr 20[ebp]               body of
fadd qword ptr L2                   round
sub esp,4
fistp dword ptr 0[esp]
pop eax

L1:
mov esp,ebp
pop ebp                             exit
pop edi                            sequence
pop esi
pop ebx
ret

_TEXT ends
_DATA segment
align 4
L2 label byte                      initialized data
dd 00H,03fe00000H                  & boilerplate
_DATA ends
end
```

FIGURE 1.7 Generated assembler language for the sample.

exit sequence, which restores the registers saved in the entry sequence and returns to the caller. L1 labels the exit sequence. The last part holds initialized data and concluding boilerplate. For round, these data consist only of the constant 0.5; L2 is the address of a variable initialized to $000000003\text{fe}00000_{16}$, which is the IEEE floating-point representation for the 64-bit, double-precision constant 0.5.

1.4 Design

There was no separate design phase for lcc. It began as a compiler for a subset of C, so its initial design goals were modest and focussed on its use in teaching about compiler implementation in general and about code generation in particular. Even as lcc evolved into a compiler for ANSI C that suits production use, the design goals changed little.

Computing costs less and less, but programmers cost more and more. When obliged to choose between two designs, we usually chose the one that appeared to save our time and yours, as long as the quality of the generated code remained satisfactory. This priority made lcc simple, fast, and less ambitious at optimizing than some competing compilers. lcc was to have multiple targets, and it was *overall* simplicity that counted. That is, we wrote extra code in lcc's one machine-independent part to save code in its multiple target-specific parts. Most of the design and implementation effort devoted to lcc has been directed at making it easy to port lcc to new targets.

lcc had to be simple because it was being written by only two programmers with many other demands on their time. Simplicity saved implementation time and saves more when it comes time to change the compiler. Also, we wanted to write this book, and you'll see that it was hard to make even a simple compiler fit.

lcc is smaller and faster than most other ANSI C compilers. Compilation speed is sometimes neglected in compiler design, but it is widely appreciated; users often cite compilation speed as one of the reasons they use lcc. Fast compilation was not a design goal *per se*; it's a consequence of striving for simplicity and of paying attention to those relatively few compiler components where speed really matters. lcc's lexical analysis (Chapter 6) and instruction selection (Chapter 14) are particularly fast, and contribute most to its speed.

lcc generates reasonably efficient object code. It's designed specifically to generate good local code; global optimizations, like those done by optimizing compilers, were not part of lcc's design. Most modern compilers, particularly those written by a CPU vendor to support its machines, must implement ambitious optimizers so that benchmarks put their machines in the best light. Such compilers are complex and typically supported by groups of tens of programmers. Highly optimizing C compilers generate more efficient code than lcc does when their optimization options are enabled, but the hundreds of programmers who use lcc daily as their primary C compiler find that its generated code is fast enough for most applications, and they save another scarce resource — their own time — because lcc runs faster. And lcc is easier to understand when systems programmers find they must change it.

Compilers don't live in a vacuum. They must cooperate with preprocessors, linkers, loaders, debuggers, assemblers, and operating systems, all of which may depend on the target. Handling all of the target-dependent variants of each of these components is impractical. lcc's design minimizes the adverse impact of these components as much as possible. For example, its target-dependent code generators emit assembler language and rely on the target's assembler to produce object code. It also relies on the availability of a separate preprocessor. These design decisions are not without some risk; for example, in vendor-supplied assemblers, we have tripped across several bugs over which we have no control and thus must live with.

A more important example is generating code with calling sequences that are compatible with the target's conventions. It must be possible for lcc to do this so it can use existing libraries. A standard ANSI C library is a significant undertaking on its own, but even if lcc came with its own library, it would still need to be able to call routines in target-specific libraries, such as those that supply system calls. The same constraint applies to proprietary third-party libraries, which are increasingly important and are usually available only in object-code form.

Generating compatible code has significant design consequences on both lcc's target-independent front end and its target-dependent back ends. A good part of the apparent complexity in the interface between the front and back ends, detailed in Chapter 5, is due directly to the tension between this design constraint and those that strive for simplicity and retargetability. The mechanisms in the interface that deal with passing and returning structures are an example.

lcc's front end is roughly 9,000 lines of code. Its target-dependent code generators are each about 700 lines, and there are about 1,000 lines of target-independent back-end code that are shared between the code generators.

With a few exceptions, lcc's front end uses well established compiler techniques. As surveyed in the previous section, the front end performs lexical, syntactic, and semantic analysis. It also eliminates local common subexpressions (Chapter 12), folds constant expressions, and makes many simple, machine-independent transformations that improve the quality of local code (Chapter 9); many of these improvements are simple tree transformations that lead to better addressing code. It also lays down efficient code for loops and switch statements (Chapter 10).

lcc's lexical analyzer and its recursive-descent parser are both written by hand. Using compiler-construction tools, such as parser generators, is perhaps the more modern approach for implementing these components, but using them would make lcc dependent on specific tools. Such dependencies are less a problem now than when lcc was first available, but there's little incentive to change working code. Theoretically, using these kinds of tools simplifies both future changes and fixing errors, but accommodating change is less important for a standardized language like ANSI C, and there have been few lexical or syntactic errors. Indeed, probably less than 15 percent of lcc's code concerns parsing, and the error rate in that code is negligible. Despite its theoretical prominence, parsing is a relatively minor component in lcc and other compilers; semantic analysis and code generation are the major components and account for most of the code — and have most of the bugs.

One of the reasons that lcc's back ends are its most interesting components is because they show the results of the design choices we made to enhance retargetability. For retargeting, future changes — each new target — *are* important, and the retargeting process must make it reasonably easy to cope with code-generation errors, which are certain to occur. There are many small design decisions made throughout lcc that affect retargetability, but two dominate.

First, the back ends use a code-generator generator, lburg, that produces code generators from compact specifications. These specifications describe how dags are mapped into instructions or parts thereof (Chapter 14). This approach simplifies writing a code generator, generates optimal local code, and helps avoid errors because lburg does most of the tedious work. One of the lburg specifications in this book can often be used as a starting point for a new target, so retargeters don't have to start from scratch. To avoid depending on foreign tools, the companion diskette includes lburg, which is written in ANSI C.

Second, whenever practical, the front end implements as much of an apparently target-dependent function as possible. For example, the front end implements switch statements completely, and it implements access to bit fields by synthesizing appropriate combinations of shifting and masking. Doing so precludes the use of instructions designed specifically for bit-field access and switch statements on those increasingly few targets that have them; simplifying retargeting was deemed more important. The front end can also completely implement passing or returning structures, and it does so using techniques that are often used in target-dependent calling conventions. These capabilities are under the control of interface options, so, on some targets, the back end can *ignore* these aspects of code generation by setting the appropriate option.

While lcc's overall design goals changed little as the compiler evolved, the ways in which these goals were realized changed often. Most of these changes swept more functionality into the front end. The switch statement is an example. In earlier versions of lcc, the code-generation interface included functions that the back end provided specifically to emit the selection code for a switch statement. As new targets were added, it became apparent that the new versions of these functions were nearly identical to the corresponding functions in existing targets. This experience revealed the relatively simple design changes that permitted *all* of this code to be moved into the front end. Doing so required changing all of the existing back ends, but these changes *removed* code, and the design changes simplify the back ends on future targets.

The most significant and most recent design change involves the way lcc is packaged. Previously, lcc was configured with one back end; that is, the back end for target X was combined with the front end to form an instance of lcc that ran on X and generated code for X. Most of lcc's back ends generate code for more than one operating system. Its MIPS back end, for example, generates code for MIPS computers that run DEC's Ultrix or SGI's IRIX, so two instances of lcc were configured. N targets and M operating systems required $N \times M$ instances of lcc in order to test them completely, and each one was configured from a slightly different set of source modules depending on the target and the operating system. For even small values of N and M, building $N \times M$ compilers quickly becomes tedious and prone to error.

In developing the current version of lcc for this book, we changed the code-generation interface, described in Chapter 5, so that it's possible to combine *all* of the back ends into a single program. Any instance of lcc is a *cross-compiler*. That is, it can generate code for any of its targets regardless of the operating system on which it runs. A command-line option selects the desired target. This design packages all target-specific data in a structure, and the option selects the appropriate structure, which the front end then uses to communicate with the back end. This change again required modifying all of the existing back ends, but the changes added little new code. The benefits were worth the effort: Only M instances of lcc are now needed, and they're all built from *one* set of source modules. Bugs tend to be easier to decrypt because they can usually be reproduced in all instances of lcc by specifying the appropriate target, and it's possible to include targets whose sole purpose is to help diagnose bugs. It's still possible to build a one-target instance of lcc, when it's important to save space.

lcc's source code documents the results of the hundreds of subordinate design choices that must be made when implementing software of any significance. The source code for lcc and for this book is in noweb files that alternate text and code just as this book does. The code is extracted to form lcc's modules, which appear on the companion diskette. Table 1.1 shows the correspondence between chapters and modules, and groups the modules according to their primary functions. Some correspondences are one-to-one, some chapters generate several small modules, and one large module is split across three chapters.

The modules without chapter numbers are omitted from this book, but they appear on the companion diskette. list.c implements the list-manipulation functions described in Exercise 2.15, output.c holds the output functions, and init.c parses and processes C initializers. event.c implements the event hooks described in Section 8.5, trace.c emits code to trace calls and returns, and prof.c and profio.c emit profiling code.

Function	Chapter	Header	Modules
common definitions	1	c.h	
infrastructure and data structures	2 3 4		alloc.c string.c sym.c types.c list.c
code-generation interface	5	ops.h	bind.c null.c symbolic.c
I/O and lexical analysis	6	token.h	input.c lex.c output.c
parsing and semantic analysis	7 8 9 10 11		error.c expr.c tree.c enode.c expr.c simp.c stmt.c decl.c main.c init.c
intermediate-code generation	12		dag.c
debugging and profiling			event.c trace.c prof.c profio.c
target-independent instruction selection and register management	13 13, 14, 15	config.h	gen.c
code generators	16 17 18		mips.md sparc.md x86.md

TABLE 1.1 Chapters and modules.

By convention, each chapter specifies the implementation of its module by a fragment of the form

⟨*M* 15⟩ ≡
   #include "c.h"
   ⟨*M macros*⟩
   ⟨*M types*⟩
   ⟨*M prototypes*⟩
   ⟨*M data*⟩
   ⟨*M functions*⟩

where *M* is the module name, like alloc.c. ⟨*M macros*⟩, ⟨*M types*⟩, and ⟨*M prototypes*⟩ define macros and types and declare function prototypes that are used only within the module. ⟨*M data*⟩ and ⟨*M functions*⟩ include definitions (not declarations) for both external and static data and functions. Empty fragments are elided. A module is extracted by giving `notangle` a module name, such as `alloc.c`, and it extracts the fragment shown above and all the fragments it uses, which yields the code for the module.

Page numbers are *not* included in the fragments above, and they do not appear in the index; they're used in too many places, and the long lists of page numbers would be useless. Pointers to previous and subsequent definitions are given, however.

1.5 Common Declarations

Each module also specifies what identifiers it *exports* for use in other modules. Declarations for exported identifiers are given in fragments named ⟨*M typedefs*⟩, ⟨*M exported macros*⟩, ⟨*M exported types*⟩, ⟨*M exported data*⟩, and ⟨*M exported functions*⟩, where *M* names a module. The header file `c.h` collects these fragments from *all* modules by defining fragments without the *M*s whose definitions list the similarly named fragments from each module. All modules include `c.h`. These fragments are neither page-numbered nor indexed, just like those in the last section, and for the same reason.

⟨*c.h* 16⟩≡
    ⟨*exported macros*⟩
    ⟨*typedefs*⟩
    `#include "config.h"`
    ⟨*interface* 78⟩
    ⟨*exported types*⟩
    ⟨*exported data*⟩
    ⟨*exported functions*⟩

The include file `config.h` defines back-end-specific types that are referenced in ⟨*interface*⟩, as detailed in Chapter 5. `c.h` defines lcc's global structures and some of its global manifest constants.

lcc can be compiled with pre-ANSI compilers. There are just enough of these left that it seems prudent to maintain compatibility with them. ANSI added prototypes, which are so helpful in detecting errors that we want to use them whenever we can. The following fragments from `output.c` show how lcc does so.

⟨*output.c exported functions*⟩≡   18
    `extern void outs ARGS((char *));`

⟨*output.c functions*⟩≡   18
    `void outs(s) char *s; {`
      `char *p;`

```
    for (p = bp; (*p = *s++) != 0; p++)
        ;
    bp = p;
    if (bp > io[fd]->limit)
        outflush();
}
```

Function *definitions* omit prototypes, so old compilers compile them directly. Function *declarations* precede the definitions and give the entire list of ANSI parameter types as one argument to the macro ARGS. ANSI compilers must predefine __STDC__, so ARGS yields the types if __STDC__ is defined and discards them otherwise.

⟨*c.h exported macros*⟩≡   17

```
    #ifdef __STDC__
    #define ARGS(list) list
    #else
    #define ARGS(list) ()
    #endif
```

A pre-ANSI compiler sees the declaration for outs as

```
    extern void outs ();
```

but lcc and other ANSI C compilers see

```
    extern void outs (char *);
```

Since the declaration for outs appears before its definition, ANSI compilers must treat the definition as if it included the prototype, too, and thus will check the legality of the parameters in all calls to outs.

ANSI also changed variadic functions. The macro va_start now expects the last declared parameter as an argument, and varargs.h became stdarg.h:

⟨*c.h exported macros*⟩+≡   17 18

```
    #ifdef __STDC__
    #include <stdarg.h>
    #define va_init(a,b) va_start(a,b)
    #else
    #include <varargs.h>
    #define va_init(a,b) va_start(a)
    #endif
```

Definitions of variadic functions also differ. The ANSI C definition

```
    void print(char *fmt, ...) { ... }
```

replaces the pre-ANSI C definition

```
void print(fmt, va_alist) char *fmt; va_dcl; { ... }
```

so lcc's macro VARARGS uses the ANSI parameter list or the pre-ANSI parameter list and separate declarations depending on the setting of __STDC__:

⟨*c.h exported macros*⟩+≡   ▲ 17 18 ▼

```
#ifdef __STDC__
#define VARARGS(newlist,oldlist,olddcls) newlist
#else
#define VARARGS(newlist,oldlist,olddcls) oldlist olddcls
#endif
```

The definition of print from output.c shows the use of ARGS, va_init, and VARARGS.

⟨*output.c exported functions*⟩+≡   ▲ 16 97 ▼

```
extern void print ARGS((char *, ...));
```

⟨*output.c functions*⟩+≡   ▲ 16

```
void print VARARGS((char *fmt, ...),
(fmt, va_alist),char *fmt; va_dcl) {
    va_list ap;

    va_init(ap, fmt);
    vprint(fmt, ap);
    va_end(ap);
}
```

ARGS 17
va_init 17

This definition is verbose because it gives the same information in two slightly different formats, but lcc uses VARARGS so seldom that it's not worth fixing.

c.h also includes a few general-purpose macros that fit nowhere else.

⟨*c.h exported macros*⟩+≡   ▲ 18 19 ▼

```
#define NULL ((void*)0)
```

NULL is a machine-independent expression for a null pointer; in environments where integers and pointers aren't the same size, f(NULL) passes a correct pointer where f(0) can pass more bytes or fewer in the absence of a prototype for f. lcc's generated code assumes that pointers fit in unsigned integers. lcc can, however, be *compiled by* other compilers for which this assumption is false, that is, for which pointers are larger than integers. Using NULL in calls avoids these kinds of errors in environments where pointers are wider than unsigned integers, and thus permits lcc to be compiled and used as a cross-compiler in such environments.

⟨*c.h exported macros*⟩+≡   ▲
                                                                            18 97
```
#define NELEMS(a) ((int)(sizeof (a)/sizeof ((a)[0])))
#define roundup(x,n) (((x)+((n)-1))&(~((n)-1)))
```

NELEMS(a) gives the number of elements in array a, and roundup(x,n) returns x rounded up to the next multiple of n, which must be a power of two.

1.6 Syntax Specifications

Grammars are used throughout this book to specify syntax. Examples include C's lexical structure and its syntax and the specifications read by lburg, lcc's code-generator generator.

A *grammar* defines a language, which is a set of sentences composed of symbols from an alphabet. These symbols are called *terminal* symbols or tokens. Grammar rules, or *productions*, define the structure, or *syntax*, of the sentences in the language. Productions specify the ways in which sentences can be produced from *nonterminal* symbols by repeatedly replacing a nonterminal by one of its rules.

A production specifies a sequence of grammar symbols that can replace a nonterminal, and a production is defined by listing the nonterminal, a colon, and nonterminal's replacement. A list of replacements for a nonterminal is given by displaying the alternatives on separate lines or by separating them by vertical bars (|). Optional phrases are enclosed in brackets ([...]), braces ({...}) enclose phrases that can be repeated zero or more times, and parentheses are used for grouping. Nonterminals appear in *slanted* type and terminals appear in a fixed-width typewriter type. The notation "one of ..." is also used to specify a list of alternatives, all of which are terminals. When vertical bars, parentheses, brackets, or braces appear as terminals, they're enclosed in single quotes to avoid confusing their use as terminals with their use in defining productions.

For example, the productions

> *expr:*
>   *term* { (+ | -) *term* }
>
> *term:*
>   *factor* { (* | /) *factor* }
>
> *factor:*
>   ID
>   '(' *expr* ')'

define a language of simple expressions. The nonterminals are *expr*, *term*, and *factor*, and the terminals are ID + - * / ( ). The first production says that an *expr* is a *term* followed by zero or more occurrences of + *term* or - *term*, and the second production is a similar specification for the multiplicative operators. The last two productions specify that a *factor* is an ID or a parenthesized *expr*. These last two productions could also be written more compactly as

>   *factor:* ID | '(' *expr* ')'

Giving some alternatives on separate lines often makes grammars easier to read.

Simple function calls could be added to this grammar by adding the production

>   *factor:* ID '(' *expr* { , *expr* } ')'

which says that a *factor* can also be an ID followed by a parenthesized list of one or more *exprs* separated by commas. All three productions for *factor* could be written as

>   *factor:* ID ['(' *expr* { , *expr* } ')'] | '(' *expr* ')'

which says that a *factor* is an ID optionally followed by a parenthesized list of comma-separated *exprs*, or just a parenthesized *expr*.

This notation for syntax specifications is known as extended Backus-Naur form, or EBNF. Section 7.1 gives the formalities of using EBNF grammars to derive the sentences in a language.

1.7 Errors

1cc is a large, complex program. We find and repair errors routinely. It's likely that errors were present when we started writing this book and that the act of writing added more. If you think that you've found an error, here's what to do.

1. If you found the error by inspecting code in this book, you might not have a source file that displays the error, so start by creating one. Most errors, however, are exposed when programmers try to compile a program they think is valid, so you probably have a demonstration program already.

2. Preprocess the source file and capture the preprocessor output. Discard the original code.

3. Prune your source code until it can be pruned no more without sending the error into hiding. We prune most error demonstrations to fewer than five lines. We need you to do this pruning because there are a lot of you and only two of us.

4. Confirm that the source file displays the error with the *distributed* version of 1cc. If you've changed 1cc and the error appears only in your version, then you'll have to chase the error yourself, even if it turns out to be our fault, because we can't work on your code.

5. Annotate your code with comments that explain why you think that lcc is wrong. If lcc dies with an assertion failure, please tell us where it died. If lcc crashes, please report the last part of the call chain if you can. If lcc is rejecting a program you think is valid, please tell us why you think it's valid, and include supporting page numbers in the ANSI Standard, Appendix A in *The C Programming Language* (Kernighan and Ritchie 1988), or the appropriate section in *C: A Reference Manual* (Harbison and Steele 1991). If lcc silently generates incorrect code for some construct, please include the corrupt assembler code in the comments and flag the bad instructions if you can.

6. Confirm that your error hasn't been fixed already. The latest version of lcc is always available for anonymous ftp in pub/lcc from ftp.cs.princeton.edu. A LOG file there reports what errors were fixed and when they were fixed. If you report an error that's been fixed, you might get a canned reply.

7. Send your program in an electronic mail message addressed to lcc-bugs@cs.princeton.edu. Please send only valid C programs; put all remarks in C comments so that we can process reports semi-automatically.

Further Reading

Most compiler texts survey the breadth of compiling algorithms and do not describe a production compiler, i.e., one that's used daily to compile production programs. This book makes the other trade-off, sacrificing the broad survey and showing a production compiler in-depth. These "breadth" and "depth" books complement one another. For example, when you read about lcc's lexical analyzer, consider scanning the material in Aho, Sethi, and Ullman (1986); Fischer and LeBlanc (1991); or Waite and Goos (1984) to learn more about alternatives or the underlying theory. Other depth books include Holub (1990) and Waite and Carter (1993).

Fraser and Hanson (1991b) describe a previous version of lcc, and include measurements of its compilation speed and the speed of its generated code. This paper also describes some of lcc's design alternatives and its tracing and profiling facilities.

This chapter tells you everything you need to know about noweb to use this book, but if you want to know more about the design rationale or implementation see Ramsey (1994). noweb is a descendant of WEB (Knuth 1984). Knuth (1992) collects several of his papers about literate programming.

   The ANSI Standard (American National Standards Institute, Inc. 1990) is the definitive specification for the syntax and semantics of the C programming language. Unlike some other C compilers, `lcc` compiles only ANSI C; it does not support older features that were dropped by the ANSI committee. After the standard, Kernighan and Ritchie (1988) is the quintessential reference for C. It appeared just before the standard was finalized, and thus is slightly out of date. Harbison and Steele (1991) was published after the standard and gives the syntax for C exactly as it appears in the standard. Wirth (1977) describes EBNF.

2
Storage Management

Complex programs allocate memory dynamically, and lcc is no exception. In C, malloc allocates memory and free releases it. lcc could use malloc and free, but there is a superior alternative that is more efficient, easier to program, and better suited for use in compilers, and it is easily understood in isolation.

Calling malloc incurs the obligation of a subsequent call to free. The cost of this explicit deallocation can be significant. More important, it's easy to forget it or, worse, deallocate something that's still referenced.

In some applications, most deallocations occur at the same time. Window systems are an example. Space for scroll bars, buttons, etc., are allocated when the window is created and deallocated when the window is destroyed. A compiler, like lcc, is another example. lcc allocates memory in response to declarations, statements, and expressions as they occur within functions, but it deallocates memory only at the ends of statements and functions.

Most implementations of malloc use memory-management algorithms that are necessarily based on the sizes of objects. Algorithms based on object *lifetimes* are more efficient — if all of the deallocations can be done at once. Indeed, stacklike allocation would be most efficient, but it can be used only if object lifetimes are nested, which is generally not the case in compilers and many other applications.

This chapter describes lcc's storage management scheme, which is based on object lifetimes. In this scheme, allocation is more efficient than malloc, and the cost of deallocation is negligible. But the real benefit is that this scheme simplifies the code. Allocation is so cheap that it encourages simple applicative algorithms in place of more space-efficient but complex ones. And allocation incurs *no* deallocation obligation, so deallocation can't be forgotten.

2.1 Memory Management Interface

Memory is allocated from *arenas*, and entire arenas are deallocated at once. Objects with the same lifetimes are allocated from the same arena. The arena is identified by an arena identifier — a nonnegative integer — when space from it is allocated or when all of it is deallocated:

⟨*alloc.c exported functions*⟩≡   24
```
extern void  *allocate ARGS((unsigned long n, unsigned a));
extern void deallocate ARGS((unsigned a));
```

Many allocations have the form

```
struct T *p;
p = allocate(sizeof *p, a);
```

for some C structure T and arena a. The use of `sizeof *p` where p is a pointer works for any pointer type. Alternatives that depend on the pointer's referent type are prone to error when the code is changed. For example,

```
p = allocate(sizeof (struct T), a);
```

is correct only if p really is a pointer to a `struct T`. If p is changed to a pointer to another structure and the call isn't updated, `allocate` may allocate too much or too little space. The former is merely inefficient, but the latter is disasterous.

This allocation idiom is so common that it deserves a macro:

⟨*alloc.c exported macros*⟩≡
```
#define NEW(p,a) ((p) = allocate(sizeof *(p), (a)))
#define NEW0(p,a) memset(NEW((p),(a)), 0, sizeof *(p))
```

allocate 26
deallocate 28
newarray 28

`allocate` and thus NEW return a pointer to *uninitialized* space on the grounds that most clients will initialize it immediately. NEW0 is used for those allocations that need the new space cleared, which is accomplished by the C library function `memset`. `memset` returns its first argument. Notice that both NEW and NEW0 evaluate p exactly once, so it's safe to use an expression that has side effects as an actual argument to either macro; e.g., `NEW(a[i++])`.

Incidently, the result of `sizeof` has type `size_t`, which must be an unsigned integral type capable of representing the size of the largest object that can be declared. In practice, `size_t` is either unsigned int or unsigned long. The declaration for `allocate` uses unsigned long so that it can always represent the result of `sizeof`.

Arrays are another common allocation, and `newarray` allocates enough uninitialized space in a given arena for m elements each of size n bytes:

⟨*alloc.c exported functions*⟩+≡   24
```
extern void *newarray
    ARGS((unsigned long m, unsigned long n, unsigned a));
```

2.2 Arena Representation

The implementation of the memory management module is:

⟨*alloc.c* 25⟩≡
```
#include "c.h"
```
⟨*alloc.c types*⟩
```
#ifdef PURIFY
```
⟨*debugging implementation*⟩
```
#else
```
⟨*alloc.c data*⟩
⟨*alloc.c functions*⟩
```
#endif
```

If PURIFY is defined, the implementation is replaced in its entirety by one that uses malloc and free, and is suitable for finding errors. See Exercise 2.1 for details.

As mentioned above, an arena is a linked list of large blocks of memory. Each block begins with a header defined by:

⟨*alloc.c types*⟩≡   26 ▼
```
struct block {
    struct block *next;
    char *limit;
    char *avail;
};
```

The space immediately following the arena structure up to the location given by the limit field is the allocable portion of the block. avail points to the first free location within the block; space below avail has been allocated and space beginning at avail and up to limit is available. The next field points to the next block in the list. The implementation keeps an arena pointer, which points to the first block in the list with available space. Blocks are added to the list dynamically during allocation, as detailed below. Figure 2.1 shows an arena after three blocks have been allocated. Shading indicates allocated space. The unused space at the end of the first full-sized arena in Figure 2.1 is explained below.

26	allocate
28	deallocate
103	limit
28	newarray

There are three arenas known by the integers 0–2; clients usually equate symbolic names to these arena identifiers for use in calls to allocate, deallocate, and newarray; see Section 5.12. The arena identifiers index an array of pointers to one-element lists, each of which holds a zero-length block. The first allocation in each arena causes a new block to be appended to the end of the appropriate list.

⟨*alloc.c data*⟩≡   27 ▼
```
static struct block
    first[] = {  { NULL },  { NULL },  { NULL } },
    *arena[] = { &first[0], &first[1], &first[2] };
```

The initializer for first serves only to provide its size; the omitted initializers cause the remaining fields of each of the three structures to be

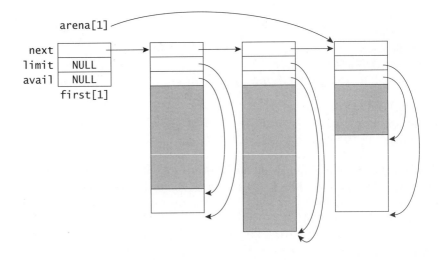

FIGURE 2.1 Arena representation.

initialized to null pointers. While this implementation has only three arenas, it is easily generalized to any number of arenas by changing only the number of initializations for first and arena. Section 5.12 describes how lcc uses the three arenas.

2.3 Allocating Space

Most allocations are trivial: Round the request amount up to the proper alignment boundary, increment the avail pointer by the amount of the rounded request, and return the previous value.

⟨*alloc.c functions*⟩≡   28

```
void *allocate(n, a) unsigned long n; unsigned a; {
    struct block *ap;

    ap = arena[a];
    n = roundup(n, sizeof (union align));
    while (ap->avail + n > ap->limit) {
        ⟨get a new block 27⟩
    }
    ap->avail += n;
    return ap->avail - n;
}
```

⟨*alloc.c types*⟩+≡   25 27

```
union align {
```

```
        long l;
        char *p;
        double d;
        int (*f) ARGS((void));
    };
```

Like malloc, allocate must return a pointer suitably aligned to hold values of any type. The size of the union align gives the minimum such alignment on the host machine. Its fields are those that are most likely to have the strictest alignment requirements.

The while loop in the code above terminates when the block pointed to by ap has at least n bytes of available space. For most calls to allocate, this block is the one pointed to by the arena pointer pointed to by allocate's second argument.

If the request cannot be satisfied from the current block, a new block must be allocated. As shown below, deallocate never frees a block; instead, it keeps the free blocks on a list that emanates from freeblocks. allocate checks this list before getting a new block:

⟨alloc.c data⟩+≡   25
```
    static struct block *freeblocks;
```

⟨get a new block 27⟩≡   26
```
    if ((ap->next = freeblocks) != NULL) {
        freeblocks = freeblocks->next;
        ap = ap->next;
    } else
        ⟨allocate a new block 28⟩
    ap->avail = (char *)((union header *)ap + 1);
    ap->next = NULL;
    arena[a] = ap;
```

| 78 align |
| 26 allocate |
| 25 arena |
| 25 avail |
| 28 deallocate |

⟨alloc.c types⟩+≡   26
```
    union header {
        struct block b;
        union align a;
    };
```

The union header ensures that ap->avail is set to a properly aligned address. Once ap points to a new block, the arena pointer passed to allocate is set to point to this new block for subsequent allocations. If the new block came from freeblocks, it might be too small to hold n bytes, which is why there's a while loop in allocate.

If a new block must be allocated, one is requested that is large enough to hold the block header and n bytes, and have 10K of available space left over:

⟨*allocate a new block* 28⟩≡   27

```
    {
        unsigned m = sizeof (union header) + n + 10*1024;
        ap->next = malloc(m);
        ap = ap->next;
        if (ap == NULL) {
            error("insufficient memory\n");
            exit(1);
        }
        ap->limit = (char *)ap + m;
    }
```

When a request cannot be filled in the current block, the free space at the end of the current block is wasted. This waste is illustrated in the first full-size arena in Figure 2.1.

newarray's implementation simply calls allocate:

⟨*alloc.c functions*⟩+≡   26 28

```
    void *newarray(m, n, a) unsigned long m, n; unsigned a; {
        return allocate(m*n, a);
    }
```

2.4 Deallocating Space

An arena is deallocated by adding its blocks to the free-blocks list and reinitializing it to point to the appropriate one-element list that holds a zero-length block. The blocks are already linked together via their next fields, so the entire list of blocks can be added to freeblocks with simple pointer manipulations:

⟨*alloc.c functions*⟩+≡   28

```
    void deallocate(a) unsigned a; {
        arena[a]->next = freeblocks;
        freeblocks = first[a].next;
        first[a].next = NULL;
        arena[a] = &first[a];
    }
```

2.5 Strings

Strings are created for identifiers, constants, registers, and so on. Strings are compared often; for example, when a symbol table is searched for an identifier.

The most common uses of strings are provided by the functions exported by string.c:

⟨*string.c exported functions*⟩≡
```
extern char * string ARGS((char *str));
extern char *stringn ARGS((char *str, int len));
extern char *stringd ARGS((int n));
```

Each of these functions returns a pointer to a permanently allocated string. string makes a copy of the null-terminated string str, stringn makes a copy of the len bytes in str, and stringd converts n to its decimal representation and returns that string.

These functions save exactly one copy of each distinct string, so two strings returned by these functions can be compared for equality by comparing their addresses. These semantics simplify comparisons and save space, and stringn can handle strings with embedded null characters.

The function string calls stringn and provides an example of its use:

⟨*string.c functions*⟩≡   29
```
char *string(str) char *str; {
   char *s;

   for (s = str; *s; s++)
      ;
   return stringn(str, s - str);
}
```

30 stringn

stringd converts its argument n into a string in a private buffer and calls stringn to return the appropriate distinct string.

⟨*string.c functions*⟩+≡   29 30
```
char *stringd(n) int n; {
   char str[25], *s = str + sizeof (str);
   unsigned m;

   if (n == INT_MIN)
      m = (unsigned)INT_MAX + 1;
   else if (n < 0)
      m = -n;
   else
      m = n;
   do
      *--s = m%10 + '0';
   while ((m /= 10) != 0);
   if (n < 0)
      *--s = '-';
   return stringn(s, str + sizeof (str) - s);
}
```

The code uses unsigned arithmetic because ANSI C permits different machines to treat signed modulus on negative values differently. The code starts by assigning the absolute value of n to m; no two's complement signed integer can represent the absolute value of the most negative number, so this value is special-cased. The string is built backward, last digit first. Exercise 2.10 explores why the local array str has 25 elements. INT_MIN is defined in the standard header limits.h.

stringn maintains the set of distinct strings by saving them in a *string table*. It saves exactly one copy of each distinct string, and it never removes any string from the table. The string table is an array of 1,024 hash buckets:

⟨*string.c data*⟩≡
```
static struct string {
    char *str;
    int len;
    struct string *link;
} *buckets[1024];
```

Each bucket heads a list of strings that share a hash value. Each entry includes the length of the string (in the len field) because strings can include null bytes.

stringn adds a string to the table unless it's already there, and returns the address of the string.

29

⟨*string.c functions*⟩+≡
NELEMS 19
string 29
```
char *stringn(str, len) char *str; int len; {
    int i;
    unsigned int h;
    char *end;
    struct string *p;

    ⟨h ← hash code for str, end ← 1 past end of str 31⟩
    for (p = buckets[h]; p; p = p->link)
        if (len == p->len) {
            char *s1 = str, *s2 = p->str;
            do {
                if (s1 == end)
                    return p->str;
            } while (*s1++ == *s2++);
        }
    ⟨install new string str 31⟩
}
```

h identifies the hash chain for str. stringn loops down this chain and compares str with strings of equal length. end points to the character one past the end of str.

An ideal hash function would distribute strings uniformly from 0 to NELEMS(buckets)-1, which would give hash chains of equal length. The code

⟨h ← *hash code for* str, end ← *1 past end of* str 31⟩≡   30
```
    for (h = 0, i = len, end = str; i > 0; i--)
        h = (h<<1) + scatter[*(unsigned char *)end++];
    h &= NELEMS(buckets)-1;
```

is a good approximation. scatter is a static array of 256 random numbers, which helps distribute the hash values. Using the character pointed to by end as an index runs the risk that the character will be sign-extended and become a negative integer; casting end to a pointer to an unsigned character avoids this possibility. This fragment also leaves end pointing just past str's last character, which is used when comparing and copying the string as shown above.

Conventional wisdom recommends that hash table sizes should be primes. Using a power of two makes lcc faster, because masking is faster than modulus.

stringn stores new strings in chunks of permanently allocated memory of at least 4K bytes. PERM identifies the permanent storage arena.

⟨*install new string* str 31⟩≡   30
```
    {
        static char *next, *strlimit;
        if (next + len + 1 >= strlimit) {
            int n = len + 4*1024;
            next = allocate(n, PERM);
            strlimit = next + n;
        }
        NEW(p, PERM);
        p->len = len;
        for (p->str = next; str < end; )
            *next++ = *str++;
        *next++ = 0;
        p->link = buckets[h];
        buckets[h] = p;
        return p->str;
    }
```

26	allocate
19	NELEMS
24	NEW
97	PERM
30	stringn

The static variable next points to the next free byte in the current chunk, and strlimit points one past the end of the chunk. The code allocates a new chunk, if necessary, and a new table entry. It copies str, which incidentally allocates space for it as it is copied by incrementing next, and links the new entry into the appropriate hash chain.

Further Reading

Storage management is a busy area of research; Section 2.5 in Knuth (1973a) is the definitive reference. There is a long list of techniques that are designed both for general-purpose use and for specific application areas, including the design described in this chapter (Hanson 1990). A competitive alternative is "quick fit" (Weinstock and Wulf 1988). Quick-fit allocators maintain *N* free lists for the *N* block sizes requested most frequently. Usually, these sizes are small and contiguous; e.g., 8–128 bytes in multiples of eight bytes. Allocation is easy and fast: Take the first block from the appropriate free list. A block is deallocated by adding it to the head of its list. Requests for sizes other than one of the *N* favored sizes are handled with other algorithms, such as first fit (Knuth 1973a).

One of the advantages of lcc's arena-based algorithm is that allocations don't have to be paired with individual deallocations; a single deallocation frees the memory acquired by many allocations, which simplifies programming. Garbage collection takes this advantage one step further. A garbage collector periodically finds all of the storage that is in use and frees the rest. It does so by following all of the accessible pointers in the program. Appel (1991) and Wilson (1994) survey garbage-collection algorithms. Garbage collectors usually need help from the programming language, its compiler, and its run-time system in order to locate the accessible memory, but there are algorithms that can cope without such help. Boehm and Weiser (1988) describe one such algorithm for C. It takes a conservative approach: Anything that looks like a pointer is taken to be one. As a result, the collector identifies some inaccessible memory as accessible and thus busy, but that's better than making the opposite decision.

allocate 26
deallocate 28

Storing all strings in a string table and using hashing to keep only one copy of any string is a scheme that's been used for years in compilers and related programming-language implementations, but it's rarely documented. It's used in SNOBOL4 (Griswold 1972), for example, to make comparison fast and to make it easy to use strings as keys in associative tables. Related techniques store strings in a separate string space, but don't bother to avoid storing multiple copies of the same string to simplify some string operations, such as substring and concatenation (Hansen 1992; Hanson 1974; McKeeman, Horning, and Wortman 1970).

Knuth (1973b) is the definitive exposé on hashing. Section 7.6 of Aho, Sethi, and Ullman (1986) describes hash functions and their use in compilers.

Exercises

2.1 Revise `allocate` and `deallocate` to use the C library functions `malloc` and `free`.

2.2 The only objective way to make decisions between competitive algorithms and designs in lcc is to implement them and measure their performance. lcc compiling itself is a reasonable benchmark. Measure the performance of the arena-based algorithm against malloc and free as implemented in the previous exercise.

2.3 Redefine NEW so that it does most allocations inline, i.e., so that it calls allocate only when there isn't enough space in the arena. Measure the benefit. You'll need to export the arena data structures to implement inline allocation.

2.4 When allocate creates a new block, there's a good chance that this block is adjacent to the previous one for the arena and that they can be merged into one larger block. Implement this and measure the improvement.

2.5 When allocate takes a block from freeblocks, it's possible that the block is too small. Instrument the allocator and find out how often this situation occurs. Is it worth fixing?

2.6 Show that deallocate works correctly when the arena list holds only the zero-length block.

2.7 deallocate never frees blocks, for example, by calling free. For some inputs, lcc's arenas will balloon temporarily, but the blocks allocated will never be reused. Revise deallocate to free blocks instead of adding them onto freeblocks. Does this change make lcc run faster?

2.8 Implement a conservative garbage collector for lcc or modify lcc to use an existing one. The collector described by Boehm and Weiser (1988) is publicly available. Most such allocators initiate a collection or a partial collection at every allocation, so you can simply gut deallocate, or make it a null macro and revise allocate to call the appropriate allocation function.

2.9 Strings installed in the string table by stringn are never discarded. Is this feature a problem? Instrument stringn to measure the distribution of the size of the string table. Suppose it gets too big; how would you revise the string interface to permit strings to be deleted?

2.10 stringd formats its argument into str, which is an array of 25 characters. Explain why 25 is large enough for all modern computers on which lcc runs or for which it generates code.

2.11 Many of the integers passed to stringd are small; say, in the range −100 to 100. Strings for these integers could be preallocated at compile time, and stringd and stringn could return pointers to them and thereby avoid allocations. Implement this optimization. Does it make lcc run faster?

2.12 `stringn` allocates memory in big chunks to hold the characters in a string instead of calling `allocate` for each string. Revise `stringn` so that it calls `allocate` for each string and measure the differences in both time and space. Explain any differences you find.

2.13 The size of `stringn`'s hash table is a power of two, which is often deprecated. Try a prime and measure the results. Try to design a better hash function and measure the results.

2.14 `stringn` compares strings with inline code instead of, for example, calling `memcmp`. Replace the inline code with a call to `memcmp` and measure the result. Why was our decision to inline justified?

2.15 `lcc` makes heavy use of circularly linked lists of pointers, and the implementation of the module `list.c` exemplifies the use of the allocation macros. `list.c` exports a list element type and three list-manipulation functions:

⟨*list.c typedefs*⟩≡
```
typedef struct list *List;
```

⟨*list.c exported types*⟩≡
```
struct list {
    void *x;
    List link;
};
```

⟨*list.c exported functions*⟩≡
```
extern List append ARGS((void *x, List list));
extern int  length ARGS((List list));
extern void *ltov  ARGS((List *list, unsigned a));
```

A `List` holds zero or more elements stored in the x fields of the list structures. A `List` points to the *last* `struct list` in a list, and a null `List` is the empty list by definition. append adds a node containing x onto the end of `list` and returns `list`. `length` returns the number of elements in `list`. `ltov` copies the n elements in `list` into a null-terminated array of pointers in the arena indicated by a, deallocates the list structures, and returns the array. The array has $n + 1$ elements including the terminating null element. Implement the list module.

3
Symbol Management

The symbol tables are the central repository for all information within the compiler. All parts of the compiler communicate through these tables and access the data — symbols — in them. For example, the lexical analyzer adds identifiers to the identifier table, and the parser adds type information to these identifiers. The code generators add target-specific data to symbol-table entries; for example, register assignments for locals and parameters. Symbol tables are also used to hold labels, constants, and types.

Symbol tables map names into sets of symbols. Constants, identifiers, and label numbers are examples of names. Different names have different attributes. For example, the attributes for the identifier that names a local variable might include the variable's type, its location in a stack frame for the procedure in which it is declared, and its storage class. Identifiers that name members of a structure have a very different set of attributes, including the members' types, the structures in which they appear, and their locations within those structures.

Symbols are collected into *symbol tables*. The symbol-table module manages symbols and symbol tables.

Symbol management must deal not only with the symbols themselves, but must also handle the *scope* or *visibility* rules imposed by the ANSI C standard. The scope of an identifier is that portion of the program text in which the identifier is visible; that is, where it may be used in expressions, and so forth. In C, scopes nest. An identifier is visible at the point of its declaration until the end of the compound statement or parameter list in which it is declared. An identifier declared outside of any compound statement or parameter list has *file scope*; it is visible from the point of its declaration to the end of the source file in which it appears.

A declaration for an identifier X hides a visible identifier X declared at an outer level. The following program illustrates this effect; the line numbers are for explanatory purposes and are not part of the program.

```
1   int x, y;
2   f(int x, int a) {
3       int b;
4       y = x + a*b;
5       if (y < 5) {
6           int a;
7               y = x + a*b;
8       }
9       y = x + a*b;
10  }
```

Line 1 declares the globals x and y, whose scopes begin at line 1 and extend through line 10. But the declaration of the parameter x in line 2 interrupts the scope of the global x. The scopes of the parameters x and a begin at line 2 and extend through line 9. The scope of a is interrupted by the declaration of the local a in line 6. Each identifier in the expression on line 4 is bound to a specific declaration, and these bindings are specified by C's scope rules. Using $x{:}n$ to denote the identifier x declared at line n, y is bound to y:1, x to x:2, a to a:2, and b to b:3. The bindings for the expression in line 7 are the same, except that a is bound to a:6.

Declarations like those for x in line 2 and a in line 6 create a hole in the scopes of similarly named identifiers declared in outer scopes. For example, the scope of a:6 is lines 6–8, which is the hole in the scope of a:2, whose scope is lines 2–5 and 9–10. The symbol-management functions must accommodate this and similar situations.

In most languages, like Pascal, there is one *name space* for identifiers. That is, there is a single set of identifiers for all purposes and, at any point in the program, there can be only one visible identifier of a given name.

The name spaces in ANSI C categorize identifiers according to use: Statement labels, tags, members, and ordinary identifiers. Tags identify structures, unions, and enumerations. There are three separate name spaces for labels, tags, and identifiers, and, for each structure or union, there is a separate name space for its members.

For each name space, there can be only one visible identifier of a given name at any point in the program. There can, however, be more than one visible identifier at any point in the program if each such identifier is in a different name space. The following artificial and confusing program illustrates this effect.

```
1  struct list { int x; struct list *list; } *list;
2  walk(struct list *list) {
3      list:
4          printf("%d\n", list->x);
5          if ((list = list->list) != NULL)
6              goto list;
7  }
8  main() { walk(list); }
```

Line 1 declares three identifiers named list, all of which are visible after the declaration. list is a structure tag, a field name, and a variable. The tag and the variable have file scope; technically, so does the field name, but it can be used only with the field reference operators . and ->. Line 2 declares a parameter list whose scope is lines 2–7. Line 3 declares the label list, which has *function scope*; it is visible anywhere in the function walk. The uses of list in lines 4–8 determines which name space is used; line 4 uses ordinary identifiers, line 5 uses ordinary identifiers for the first two occurrences of list and members of struct list for the rightmost occurrence of list, line 6 consults the label name space, and line 8 again uses the ordinary identifiers.

Roughly speaking, there is a separate symbol table for each name space, and symbol tables themselves handle scope. lcc also uses separate symbol tables for unscoped collections, like constants.

```
38 Coordinate
34 List
422 uses
```

3.1 Representing Symbols

The memory-allocation and string modules could be used outside of lcc, but the symbol-table module is specific to lcc. It manages lcc-specific symbols and symbol tables, and it implements the scope rules and name spaces specified by ANSI C.

There is little about symbols themselves that is relevant to the symbol-table module, which needs only those attributes, like names, that relate to scope. It's simplest, however, to collect the name and all of the other attributes into a single symbol structure:

⟨*sym.c typedefs*⟩≡   38 ▼
```
typedef struct symbol *Symbol;
```

⟨*sym.c exported types*⟩≡   38 ▼
```
struct symbol {
    char *name;
    int scope;
    Coordinate src;
    Symbol up;
    List uses;
```

```
int sclass;
⟨symbol flags 50⟩
Type type;
float ref;
union {
    ⟨labels 46⟩
    ⟨struct types 65⟩
    ⟨enum constants 69⟩
    ⟨enum types 68⟩
    ⟨constants 47⟩
    ⟨function symbols 290⟩
    ⟨globals 265⟩
    ⟨temporaries 346⟩
} u;
Xsymbol x;
⟨debugger extension⟩
};
```

The fields above the union u apply to all kinds of symbols in all tables.
Most of the symbol-table functions read and write only the name, scope,
src, up, and uses fields. Those specific to constants and labels also rely
on some of the fields in the union u and some of the ⟨symbol flags⟩ as
detailed below. The remaining fields implement attributes that are associated with specific kinds of symbols, and are initialized and modified
by clients of the symbol-table module.

file 104
uses 422
Xsymbol 362

   The name field is usually the symbol-table key. For identifiers and
keywords that name types, it holds the name used in the source code.
For generated identifiers, such as structures without tags, name is a digit
string.

   The scope field classifies each symbol as a constant, label, global, parameter, or local:

⟨*sym.c exported types*⟩+≡   37
```
enum { CONSTANTS=1, LABELS, GLOBAL, PARAM, LOCAL };
```

A local declared at nesting level k has a scope equal to LOCAL+k.

   The src field is the point in the source code that defines the symbol,
as in a variable declaration. Its Coordinate value pinpoints the symbol's
definition:

⟨*sym.c typedefs*⟩+≡   37 39
```
typedef struct coord {
    char *file;
    unsigned x, y;
} Coordinate;
```

The file field is the name of the file that contains the definition, and
y and x give the line number and character position within that line at
which the definition occurs.

The up field chains together all symbols in a symbol table, starting with the last one installed. Traversing up this chain reveals all of the symbols that are in scope at the time of the traversal, as well as those hidden by declarations of the same identifiers in nested scopes. This facility may help back ends emit debugger symbol-table information, for example.

lcc has an option that causes it to keep track of every use of every symbol. When this option is specified, the uses field holds a list of Coordinates that identify these uses. If the option is not specified, uses is null. See Exercise 3.4.

The sclass field is the symbol's extended storage class, which may be AUTO, REGISTER, STATIC, or EXTERN. sclass is TYPEDEF for typedefs and ENUM for enumeration constants, and it's unused and thus zero for constants and labels.

The type field holds the Type for variables, functions, constants, and structure, union, and enumeration types.

For variables and labels, the ref field is an approximation of the number of times that variable is referenced. Section 10.3 explains how this approximation is computed.

The u field is a union that supplies additional data for labels, structure and union types, enumeration identifiers, enumeration types, constants, functions, global and static variables, and temporary variables. The ⟨symbol flags⟩ are one-bit attribute flags for each symbol. The x field and the ⟨debugger extension⟩ collect fields that are manipulated only by back ends, such as the register assigned to a variable or the information necessary to generate data for a debugger.

The typedefs for Symbol and Coordinate illustrate a convention used throughout lcc: Capitalized type names refer to structures with the simpler lowercase tag, or to pointers to such structures. Thus, the typedef Coordinate names the type struct coord and Symbol names the type struct symbol *.

80	AUTO
40	constants
38	Coordinate
109	ENUM
40	externals
80	EXTERN
41	globals
41	identifiers
80	REGISTER
38	sclass
80	STATIC
37	Symbol
41	table
54	Type
422	uses

3.2 Representing Symbol Tables

Symbol tables are manipulated only by the symbol-table module. It exports an opaque type for tables and the tables themselves:

⟨sym.c typedefs⟩+≡   38 47
```
    typedef struct table *Table;
```

⟨sym.c exported data⟩≡   42
```
    extern Table constants;
    extern Table externals;
    extern Table globals;
    extern Table identifiers;
```

```
extern Table labels;
extern Table types;
```

Subsets of these tables implement three of the name spaces in ANSI C. identifiers holds the ordinary identifiers. externals holds the subset of identifiers that have been declared extern; it is used to warn about conflicting declarations of external identifiers. globals is the part of the identifiers table that holds identifiers with file scope.

Compiler-defined internal labels are stored in labels, and type tags are stored in types.

The tables themselves are lists of hash tables, one for each scope:

⟨*sym.c types*⟩≡

```
struct table {
    int level;
    Table previous;
    struct entry {
        struct symbol sym;
        struct entry *link;
    } *buckets[256];
    Symbol all;
};
#define HASHSIZE NELEMS(((Table)0)->buckets)
```

A Table value, like identifiers, points to a table structure that holds a hash table for the symbols at one scope, specifically the scope given by the value of the level field. The buckets field is an array of pointers to the hash chains. The previous field points to the table for the enclosing scope.

Entries in the hash chains hold a symbol structure and a pointer to the next entry on the chain. Looking up a symbol involves hashing the key to pick a chain and walking down the chain to the appropriate symbol. If the symbol isn't found, following the previous field exposes entries in the next enclosing scope.

In each table structure, all heads a list of all symbols in this and enclosing scopes. This list is threaded through the up fields of the symbols.

The symbol-table module initializes all but one of the Tables it exports:

⟨*sym.c data*⟩≡   42

```
static struct table
    cns = { CONSTANTS },
    ext = { GLOBAL },
    ids = { GLOBAL },
    tys = { GLOBAL };
Table constants  = &cns;
Table externals  = &ext;
```

```
Table identifiers = &ids;
Table globals     = &ids;
Table types       = &tys;
Table labels;
```

globals always points to the identifier table at scope GLOBAL, while identifiers points to the table at the current scope. types is described in Chapter 4. funcdefn creates a new labels table for each function.

Tables for nested scopes are created dynamically and linked into the appropriate enclosing table:

⟨sym.c functions⟩≡   41

```
Table table(tp, level) Table tp; int level; {
    Table new;

    NEW0(new, FUNC);
    new->previous = tp;
    new->level = level;
    if (tp)
        new->all = tp->all;
    return new;
}
```

All dynamically allocated tables are discarded after compiling each function, so they are allocated in the FUNC arena.

Figure 3.1 shows the four tables that emanate from identifiers when lcc is compiling line 7 of the example at the top of page 36. The figure's entry structures show only the name and up fields of their symbols and their link fields. The solid lines show the previous fields, which connect tables; the elements of buckets and the link fields, which connect entries; and the name fields. The dashed lines emanate from the all fields in tables and from the up fields of symbols.

The all field is initialized to the enclosing table's list so that it is possible to visit *all* symbols in *all* scopes by following the symbols beginning at a table's all. This capability is used by foreach to scan a table and apply a given function to all symbols at a given scope.

⟨sym.c functions⟩+≡   41 42

```
void foreach(tp, lev, apply, cl) Table tp; int lev;
    void (*apply) ARGS((Symbol, void *)); void *cl; {
    while (tp && tp->level > lev)
        tp = tp->previous;
    if (tp && tp->level == lev) {
        Symbol p;
        Coordinate sav;
        sav = src;
        for (p = tp->all; p && p->scope == lev; p = p->up) {
```

```
                    src = p->src;
                    (*apply)(p, cl);
                }
                src = sav;
            }
        }
```

The while loop finds the table with the proper scope. If one is found, `foreach` sets the global variable `src` to each symbol's definition coordinate and calls `apply` with the symbol. `cl` is a pointer to call-specific data — a *closure* — supplied by callers of `foreach`, and this closure is passed along to `apply` so that it can access those data, if necessary. `src` is set so that diagnostics that might be issued by `apply` will refer to a meaningful source coordinate.

The for loop traverses the table's `all` and stops when it encounters the end of the list or a symbol at a lower scope. `all` is not strictly necessary because `foreach` could traverse the hash chains, but presenting the symbols to `apply` in an order independent of hash addresses makes the order of the emitted code machine-independent.

3.3 Changing Scope

The value of the global variable `level` and the corresponding tables represent a scope.

⟨*sym.c exported data*⟩+≡   39 52

```
    extern int level;
```

⟨*sym.c data*⟩+≡   40

```
    int level = GLOBAL;
```

There are more scopes than source-code compound statements because scopes are used to partition symbols for other purposes. For example, there are separate scopes for constants and for parameters.

`level` is incremented upon entering a new scope.

⟨*sym.c functions*⟩+≡   41 42

```
    void enterscope() {
        ++level;
    }
```

At scope exit, `level` is decremented, and the corresponding `identifiers` and `types` tables are removed.

⟨*sym.c functions*⟩+≡   42 44

```
    void exitscope() {
        rmtypes(level);
```

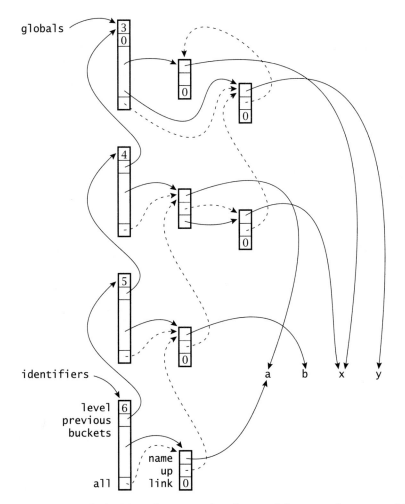

FIGURE 3.1 Symbol tables when compiling line 7 of the example on page 36.

```
    if (types->level == level)
        types = types->previous;
    if (identifiers->level == level) {
        ⟨warn if more than 127 identifiers⟩
        identifiers = identifiers->previous;
    }
    --level;
}
```

Tables at the current scope are created only if necessary. Few scopes in C declare new symbols, so lazy table allocation saves time, but exitscope must check levels to see if there is a table to remove. rmtypes removes from the type cache types with tags defined in the vanishing scope; see Section 4.2.

3.4   Finding and Installing Identifiers

install allocates a symbol for name and adds it to a given table at a specific scope level, allocating a new table if necessary. It returns a symbol pointer.

⟨*sym.c functions*⟩+≡   42 45

```
    Symbol install(name, tpp, level, arena)
    char *name; Table *tpp; int level, arena; {
        Table tp = *tpp;
        struct entry *p;
        unsigned h = (unsigned)name&(HASHSIZE-1);

        if (level > 0 && tp->level < level)
            tp = *tpp = table(tp, level);
        NEW0(p, arena);
        p->sym.name = name;
        p->sym.scope = level;
        p->sym.up = tp->all;
        tp->all = &p->sym;
        p->link = tp->buckets[h];
        tp->buckets[h] = p;
        return &p->sym;
    }
```

name is a saved string, so its address can be its hash value.

tpp *points* to a table pointer. If *tpp is a table with scopes, like identifiers, and there is not yet a table corresponding to the scope indicated by the argument level, install allocates a table for the scope indicated by level and updates *tpp. It then allocates and zeroes a symbol-table entry, initializes some fields of the symbol itself, and adds the entry to the hash chain. `level` must be zero or at least as large as the table's scope level; a zero value for `level` indicates that `name` should be installed in `*tpp`. `install` accepts an argument that specifies the appropriate arena because function prototypes and thus the symbols in them are retained forever, even if they're declared in a nested scope.

`lookup` searches a table for a name; it handles lookups where the search key is the `name` field of a symbol. It returns a symbol pointer if it succeeds and the null pointer otherwise.

⟨*sym.c functions*⟩+≡   44 45

```
Symbol lookup(name, tp) char *name; Table tp; {
    struct entry *p;
    unsigned h = (unsigned)name&(HASHSIZE-1);

    do
        for (p = tp->buckets[h]; p; p = p->link)
            if (name == p->sym.name)
                return &p->sym;
    while ((tp = tp->previous) != NULL);
    return NULL;
}
```

The inner loop scans a hash chain, and the outer loop scans enclosing scopes. Comparing two strings is trivial because the string module guarantees that two strings are identical if and only if they are the same string.

---
40 HASHSIZE
44 install
39 Table

3.5 Labels

The symbol-table module also exports functions to manage labels and constants. These are similar to `lookup` and `install`, but there is no scope management for these tables, and looking up a label or constant installs it if necessary and thus always succeeds. Also, the search key is a field in the union u that is specific to labels or constants.

Compiler-generated labels and the internal counterparts of source-language labels are named by integers. `genlabel` generates a run of these integers by incrementing a counter:

⟨*sym.c functions*⟩+≡   45 46

```
int genlabel(n) int n; {
    static int label = 1;

    label += n;
    return label - n;
}
```

genlabel is also used whenever a unique, anonymous name is needed, such as for generated identifiers like temporaries.

A symbol is allocated for each label, and u.l.label holds its label number:

⟨*labels* 46⟩≡   38
```
struct {
    int label;
    Symbol equatedto;
} l;
```

When two or more internal labels are found to label the same location, the equatedto fields of such label symbols point to one of them.

There is an internal label for each source-language label. These and other compiler-generated labels are kept in labels. This table is created once for each function (see Section 11.6) and is managed by findlabel, which takes a label number and returns the corresponding label symbol, installing and initializing it, and announcing it to the back end, if necessary.

⟨*sym.c functions*⟩+≡   ▲ 45 47 ▼
```
Symbol findlabel(lab) int lab; {
    struct entry *p;
    unsigned h = lab&(HASHSIZE-1);

    for (p = labels->buckets[h]; p; p = p->link)
        if (lab == p->sym.u.l.label)
            return &p->sym;
    NEW0(p, FUNC);
    p->sym.name = stringd(lab);
    p->sym.scope = LABELS;
    p->sym.up = labels->all;
    labels->all = &p->sym;
    p->link = labels->buckets[h];
    labels->buckets[h] = p;
    p->sym.generated = 1;
    p->sym.u.l.label = lab;
    (*IR->defsymbol)(&p->sym);
    return &p->sym;
}
```

defsymbol	89
(MIPS) "	457
(SPARC) "	491
(X86) "	520
FUNC	97
generated	50
genlabel	45
HASHSIZE	40
IR	306
LABELS	38
labels	41
NEW0	24
scope	37
stringd	29

generated is one of the one-bit ⟨*symbol flags*⟩, and it identifies a generated symbol. Some back ends use specific formats for the names of generated symbols to avoid, for example, cluttering linker tables.

3.6 Constants

A reference to a compile-time constant as an operand in an expression is made by pointing to a symbol for the constant. These symbols reside in the constants table. Like labels, this table is not scoped; all constants have a scope field equal to CONSTANTS.

The actual value of a constant is represented by instances of the union

⟨*sym.c typedefs*⟩+≡   ▲39

```
typedef union value {
    /* signed */ char sc;
    short ss;
    int i;
    unsigned char uc;
    unsigned short us;
    unsigned int u;
    float f;
    double d;
    void *p;
} Value;
```

The value is stored in the appropriate field according to its type, e.g., integers are stored in the i field, unsigned characters are stored in the uc field, etc.

When a constant is installed in constants, its Type is stored in the symbol's type field; Types encode C's data types and are described in Chapter 4. The value is stored in u.c.v:

⟨*constants* 47⟩≡   38

```
struct {
    Value v;
    Symbol loc;
} c;
```

On some targets, some constants — floating-point numbers — cannot be stored in instructions, so the compiler generates a static variable and initializes it to the value of the constant. For these, u.c.loc points to the symbol for the generated variable. Taken together, the type and u.c fields represent all that is known about a constant.

Only one instance of any given constant appears in the constants table, e.g., if the constant "hello world" appears three times in a program, all three references point to the same symbol. constant searches the constant table for a given value of a given type, installing it if necessary, and returns the symbol pointer. Constants are never removed from the table.

⟨*sym.c functions*⟩+≡   ▲46 49▼

```
Symbol constant(ty, v) Type ty; Value v; {
```

```
                    struct entry *p;
                    unsigned h = v.u&(HASHSIZE-1);

                    ty = unqual(ty);
                    for (p = constants->buckets[h]; p; p = p->link)
                       if (eqtype(ty, p->sym.type, 1))
                          ⟨return the symbol if p's value == v 48⟩
                    NEW0(p, PERM);
                    p->sym.name = vtoa(ty, v);
                    p->sym.scope = CONSTANTS;
                    p->sym.type = ty;
                    p->sym.sclass = STATIC;
                    p->sym.u.c.v = v;
                    p->link = constants->buckets[h];
                    p->sym.up = constants->all;
                    constants->all = &p->sym;
                    constants->buckets[h] = p;
                    ⟨announce the constant, if necessary 49⟩
                    p->sym.defined = 1;
                    return &p->sym;
            }
```

unqual returns the unqualified version of a Type, namely without const or volatile, and eqtype tests for type equality (see Section 4.7). If v appears in the table, its symbol pointer is returned. Otherwise, a symbol is allocated and initialized. The name field is set to the string representation returned by vtoa.

This value is useful only for the integral types and constant pointers; for the other types, the string returned by vtoa may not reliably depict the value. Constants are found by comparing their actual values, not their string representations, because some floating-point constants have no natural string representations. For example, the constant expression (double)(float)0.3 truncates 0.3 to a machine-dependent value. The effect of the casts cannot be captured by a valid string constant.

The type operator determines which union fields to compare.

⟨*sym.c macros*⟩≡

```
    #define equalp(x) v.x == p->sym.u.c.v.x
```

⟨*return the symbol if* p's *value* == v 48⟩≡   48

```
    switch (ty->op) {
    case CHAR:     if (equalp(uc)) return &p->sym; break;
    case SHORT:    if (equalp(ss)) return &p->sym; break;
    case INT:      if (equalp(i))  return &p->sym; break;
    case UNSIGNED: if (equalp(u))  return &p->sym; break;
    case FLOAT:    if (equalp(f))  return &p->sym; break;
```

```
case DOUBLE:   if (equalp(d))  return &p->sym; break;
case ARRAY: case FUNCTION:
case POINTER:  if (equalp(p))  return &p->sym; break;
}
```

constant calls defsymbol to announce to the back end those constants
that might appear in dags:

⟨*announce the constant, if necessary* 49⟩ ≡   48
```
    if (ty->u.sym && !ty->u.sym->addressed)
      (*IR->defsymbol)(&p->sym);
```

The primitive types, like the integers and floating-point types, appear in
dags only if lcc is so configured, which is what the addressed flag tests.
See Sections 4.2 and 5.1.

    Integer constants abound in both the front and back ends. intconst
encapsulates the idiom for installing and announcing an integer constant:

⟨*sym.c functions*⟩+≡   ▲ 47 49 ▼
```
    Symbol intconst(n) int n; {
      Value v;

      v.i = n;
      return constant(inttype, v);
    }
```

3.7   Generated Variables

The front end generates local variables for many purposes. For example,
it generates static variables to hold out-of-line constants like strings and
jump tables for switch statements. It generates locals to pass and return
structures to functions and to hold the results of conditional expressions and switch values. genident allocates and initializes a generated
identifier of a specific type, storage class, and scope:

⟨*sym.c functions*⟩+≡   ▲ 49 50 ▼
```
    Symbol genident(scls, ty, lev) int scls, lev; Type ty; {
      Symbol p;

      NEW0(p, lev >= LOCAL ? FUNC : PERM);
      p->name = stringd(genlabel(1));
      p->scope = lev;
      p->sclass = scls;
      p->type = ty;
      p->generated = 1;
      if (lev == GLOBAL)
```

```
        (*IR->defsymbol)(p);
    return p;
}
```

⟨*symbol flags* 50⟩≡   50   38

```
    unsigned temporary:1;
    unsigned generated:1;
```

The names are digit strings, and the generated flag is set. Parameters and locals are announced to the back end elsewhere; generated globals are announced here by calling the back end's defsymbol interface function. IR points to a data structure that connects a specific back end with the front; Section 5.11 explains how this binding is initialized.

Temporaries are another kind of generated variable, and are distinguished by a lit temporary flag:

⟨*sym.c functions*⟩+≡   49 50

```
    Symbol temporary(scls, ty, lev) Type ty; int scls, lev; {
        Symbol p = genident(scls, ty, lev);

        p->temporary = 1;
        return p;
    }
```

Back ends must also generate temporary locals to spill registers, for example. They cannot call temporary directly because they do not know about the type system. newtemp accepts a type suffix, calls btot to map this suffix into a representative type, and calls temporary with that type.

⟨*sym.c functions*⟩+≡   50

```
    Symbol newtemp(sclass, tc) int sclass, tc; {
        Symbol p = temporary(sclass, btot(tc), LOCAL);

        (*IR->local)(p);
        p->defined = 1;
        return p;
    }
```

btot	74
defsymbol	89
(MIPS) "	457
(SPARC) "	491
(X86) "	520
genident	49
IR	306
LOCAL	38
local	90
(MIPS) "	447
(SPARC) "	483
(X86) "	518

⟨*symbol flags* 50⟩+≡   50 179   38

```
    unsigned defined:1;
```

Calls to newtemp occur during code generation, which is too late for new temporaries to be announced like front-end temporaries. So newtemp calls local to announce them. The flag defined is lit after the symbol has been announced to the back end.

Further Reading

lcc's symbol-table module implements only what is necessary for C. Other languages need more; for example, in block-structured languages — those with nested procedures — more than one set of parameters and locals are visible at the same time. Newer object-oriented languages and languages with explicit scope directives have more scopes; some need many separate symbol tables to exist at the same time.

Fraser and Hanson (1991b) describe the evolution of lcc's symbol-table module.

Knuth (1973b), Section 6.4, gives a detailed analysis of hashing and describes the characteristics of good hashing functions. Suggestions for good hash functions abound; the one in Aho, Sethi, and Ullman (1986), Section 7.6 is an example.

Exercises

3.1 Try a better hash function for hashing entries in symbol tables; for example, try the one in Aho, Sethi, and Ullman (1986), Section 7.6. Does it make lcc run faster?

3.2 lcc never removes entries from the `constants` table. When might this approach be a problem? Propose and implement a fix, and measure the benefit. Is the benefit worth the effort?

40	constants
38	Coordinate
42	enterscope
42	exitscope
90	global
458	" (MIPS)
492	" (SPARC)
524	" (X86)
44	install
34	List
45	lookup
422	uses

3.3 Originally, lcc used a single hash table for its symbol tables (Fraser and Hanson 1991b). In this approach, hash chains held *all* of the symbols that hashed to that bucket, and the chains were ordered in decreasing order of scope values. lookup simply searched a single hash table. install and enterscope were easy using this approach, but exitscope was more complicated because it had to scan the chains and remove the symbols at the current scope level. The present design ran faster on some computers, but it might not be faster than the original design on other computers. Implement the original design; make sure you handle accesses to global correctly. Which design is easier to understand? Which is faster?

3.4 sym.c exports data and functions that help generate cross-reference lists for identifiers and symbol-table information for debuggers. The -x option causes lcc to set the uses field of a symbol to a List of pointers to Coordinates that identify each use of the symbol. sym.c exports

⟨*sym.c exported functions*⟩≡   52
```
    extern void use ARGS((Symbol p, Coordinate src));
```

which appends src to p->uses. It also exports

⟨*sym.c exported data*⟩+≡   ▲
                                                                      42
    `extern List loci, symbols;`

⟨*sym.c exported functions*⟩+≡   ▲
                                                                      51
    `extern void locus ARGS((Table tp, Coordinate *cp));`

`loci` and `tables` hold pointers to `Coordinates` and `Symbols`. An entry in `symbols` is the tail end of a list of symbols that are visible from the corresponding source coordinate in `loci`. Following the up field in this symbol visits all of the symbols visible from this point in the source program. `locus` appends `tp->all` and `cp` to `symbols` and `loci`. `tp->all` points to the symbol most recently added to the table `*tp`, and is thus the current tail of the list of visible symbols. Implement `use` and `locus`; both take fewer than five lines.

4
Types

Types abound in C programs. These include the types given explicitly in declarations and those derived as intermediate types in expressions. For example, the assignment in

```
int *p, x;
*p = x;
```

involves three different types. x is the address of a cell that holds an int, so the type of the address of x — its *lvalue* — is "pointer to an int." The type of the value of x — its *rvalue* — is int, as expected from the declaration. Similarly, the type of p's lvalue is pointer to pointer to an int, the type of p's rvalue is pointer to an int, and the type of *p is int. lcc must deal with all of these types when it compiles the assignment.

lcc implements a representation for types and a set of functions on that representation, which are described in this chapter. The functions include *type constructors*, which build types, and *type predicates*, which test facts about types. lcc must also implement *type checking*, which ensures that declarations and expressions adhere to the rules dictated by the language. Type checking uses the predicates described here and is detailed in Chapters 9 and 11.

4.1 Representing Types

As suggested above, C types are usually rendered in English in a prefix form in which a type operator is followed by its operand. For example, the C declarator int *p declares p to be a pointer to an int, which is a prefix rendition of the C type int * where pointer to is the operator and an int is the operand. Similarly, char *(*strings)[10] declares strings to be a

> pointer to
> > an array of 10
> > > pointers to
> > > > char,

where operands are indented under their operators.

There are many ways to represent this kind of prefix type specification. For example, some older C compilers used bit strings in which the type operators and the basic type were each encoded with a few bits. Bit-string representations are compact and easy to manipulate, but they usually limit the number of basic types, the number of operators that can be applied, and may not be able to carry size data, which are needed for arrays, for example.

lcc represents types by linked structures that mirror their prefix specifications. Type nodes are the building blocks:

⟨*types.c typedefs*⟩≡   66

```
typedef struct type *Type;
```

⟨*types.c exported types*⟩≡   66

```
struct type {
    int op;
    Type type;
    int align;
    int size;
    union {
        ⟨types with names or tags 55⟩
        ⟨function types 63⟩
    } u;
    Xtype x;
};
```

The op field holds an integer operator code, and the type field holds the operand. The operators are the values of the global enumeration constants:

CHAR	LONG	ARRAY	FUNCTION
INT	ENUM	STRUCT	CONST
UNSIGNED	FLOAT	UNION	VOLATILE
SHORT	DOUBLE	POINTER	VOID

The CHAR, INT, UNSIGNED, SHORT, LONG, and ENUM operators define the *integral types*, and the FLOAT and DOUBLE operators define the *floating types*. Together, these types are known as the *arithmetic types*. Except for ENUM types, these types have no operands. The operand of an ENUM type is its compatible integral type, i.e., the type of the enumeration identifiers. For lcc, this type is always int, as explained in Section 4.6.

The ARRAY, STRUCT, and UNION operators identify the *aggregate types*. STRUCT and UNION do not have operands; their fields are stored in an auxiliary symbol-table entry for the structure or union tag. ARRAY's operand is the *element type*. The POINTER and FUNCTION operators define *pointer types* and *function types*. They take operands that give the *referenced type* and the *return type*. The CONST and VOLATILE operators specify *qualified types*; their operands are the unqualified versions of the types. The sum CONST+VOLATILE is also a type operator, and it specifies a type that is both constant and volatile. The VOID operator identifies the void type; it has no operand.

The align and size fields give the type's alignment and the size of objects of that type in bytes. As specified by the code-generation interface in Chapter 5, the size must be a multiple of the alignment. The back end must allocate space for a variable so that its address is a multiple of its type's alignment.

The x field plays the same role for types as it does in symbols; back ends may define Xtype to add target-specific fields to the type structure. This facility is most often used to support debuggers.

The innards of Types are revealed by exporting the declaration so that back ends may read the size and align fields and read and write the x fields; by convention, these are the only fields the back ends are allowed to inspect. The front end, however, may access all of the fields.

The op, type, size, and align fields give most of the information needed for dealing with a type. For unqualified types with names or tags — the built-in types, structure and union types, and enumeration types — the u.sym fields point to symbol-table entries that give more information about the types:

⟨*types with names or tags* 55⟩≡   54
    Symbol sym;

The symbol-table entry gives the name of the type, and the value of u.sym->addressed is zero if constants of the type can be included as parts of instructions. u.sym->type points back to the type itself; this pointer is used to map tags to types, for example. There is one symbol-table entry for each structure, union, and enumeration type, one for each basic type, and one for all pointer types. These entries appear in the types table, as detailed below in Section 4.2. This representation is used so that the functions in sym.c can be used to manage types.

Types can be depicted in a parenthesized prefix form that follows closely the English prefix form introduced above. For example, the type int on the MIPS is:

    (INT 4 4 ["int"])

The first 4 is the alignment, the second 4 is the size, and the ["int"] denotes a pointer to a symbol-table entry for the type name int. Other types are depicted similarly, for example

    (POINTER 4 4 (INT 4 4 ["int"]) ["T*"])

is the type pointer to an int. The type name T* represents the single symbol-table entry that is used for all pointer types.

The alignments, sizes, and symbol-table pointers are omitted from explanations (but not from the code) when they're not needed to understand the topic at hand. For instance, the types given at the beginning of this section are:

37 symbol
54 Type
41 types
109 VOID

```
(INT)
(POINTER (INT))
(POINTER (ARRAY 10 (POINTER (CHAR))))
```

The last line, which depicts the type pointer to an array of 10 pointers to char, illustrates the convention for array types in which the number of elements is given instead of the size of the array. This convention is only a notational convenience; the `size` field of the array type always holds the actual size of the array. The number of elements can be computed by dividing that size by the size of the element type. Thus, the type array of 10 ints is more accurately depicted as

```
(ARRAY 40 4 (INT 4 4 ["int"]))
```

but, by convention, is usually depicted as (ARRAY 10 (INT)). An *incomplete type* is one whose size is unknown and that thus has a `size` field equal to zero. These arise from declarations that omit sizes, such as

```
int a[];
extern struct table *identifiers;
```

Opaque pointers, such as pointers to lcc's `table` structures, are incomplete types. Sizes for incomplete types are sometimes shown when it's important to indicate that they are incomplete.

align 78
NELEMS 19
stringn 30

4.2 Type Management

One of the basic operations in type checking is determining whether two types are equivalent. This test can simplified if there is only one copy of any type, much the same way that string comparison is simplified by keeping only one copy of any string.

type does for types what `stringn` does for strings. type manages typetable:

⟨*types.c data*⟩≡   59
```
    static struct entry {
        struct type type;
        struct entry *link;
    } *typetable[128];
```

Each `entry` structure in `typetable` holds a type. The function type searches `typetable` for the desired type, or constructs a new type:

⟨*types.c functions*⟩≡   58
```
    static Type type(op, ty, size, align, sym)
        int op, size, align; Type ty; void *sym; {
        unsigned h = ⟨hash op and ty 57⟩&(NELEMS(typetable)-1);
        struct entry *tn;
```

```
      if (op != FUNCTION && (op != ARRAY || size > 0))
         ⟨search for an existing type 57⟩
      NEW(tn, PERM);
      tn->type.op = op;
      tn->type.type = ty;
      tn->type.size = size;
      tn->type.align = align;
      tn->type.u.sym = sym;
      memset(&tn->type.x, 0, sizeof tn->type.x);
      tn->link = typetable[h];
      typetable[h] = tn;
      return &tn->type;
  }
```

type always builds new types for function types and for incomplete array types. When type builds a new type, it initializes the fields specified by the arguments, clears the x field, adds the type to the appropriate hash chain, and returns the new Type.

type searches typetable by using the exclusive OR of the type operator and the address of the operand as the hash value, and searching the appropriate chain for a type with the same operator, operand, size, alignment, and symbol-table entry:

⟨hash op and ty 57⟩≡   56
    (op^((unsigned)ty>>3))

⟨search for an existing type 57⟩≡   57
    for (tn = typetable[h]; tn; tn = tn->link)
        if (tn->type.op   == op && tn->type.type == ty
        && tn->type.size == size && tn->type.align == align
        && tn->type.u.sym == sym)
            return &tn->type;

typetable is initialized with the built-in types and the type for void*. These types are also the values of 14 global variables:

⟨types.c exported data⟩≡
    extern Type chartype;
    extern Type doubletype;
    extern Type floattype;
    extern Type inttype;
    extern Type longdouble;
    extern Type longtype;
    extern Type shorttype;
    extern Type signedchar;
    extern Type unsignedchar;
    extern Type unsignedlong;

```
extern Type unsignedshort;
extern Type unsignedtype;
extern Type voidptype;
extern Type voidtype;
```

The front end uses these variables to refer to specific types, and can thus avoid searching `typetable` for types that are known to exist. These variables and `typetable` are initialized by `typeInit`:

⟨*types.c functions*⟩+≡   56 59

```
void typeInit() {
    ⟨typeInit 58⟩
}
```

As detailed in Section 5.1, each basic type is characterized by its *type metric*, which is a triple that gives the type's size and minimum alignment, and tells whether constants of the type can appear in dags. These triples are structures with `size`, `align`, and `outofline` fields.

⟨typeInit 58⟩≡   59   58

```
#define xx(v,name,op,metrics) { \
    Symbol p = install(string(name), &types, GLOBAL, PERM);\
    v = type(op, 0, IR->metrics.size, IR->metrics.align, p);\
    p->type = v; p->addressed = IR->metrics.outofline; }
xx(chartype,     "char",         CHAR,     charmetric);
xx(doubletype,   "double",       DOUBLE,   doublemetric);
xx(floattype,    "float",        FLOAT,    floatmetric);
xx(inttype,      "int",          INT,      intmetric);
xx(longdouble,   "long double",  DOUBLE,   doublemetric);
xx(longtype,     "long int",     INT,      intmetric);
xx(shorttype,    "short",        SHORT,    shortmetric);
xx(signedchar,   "signed char",  CHAR,     charmetric);
xx(unsignedchar, "unsigned char", CHAR,    charmetric);
xx(unsignedlong, "unsigned long", UNSIGNED,intmetric);
xx(unsignedshort,"unsigned short",SHORT,   shortmetric);
xx(unsignedtype, "unsigned int",  UNSIGNED,intmetric);
#undef xx
```

The unsigned integral types have the same operators, sizes, and alignments as their signed counterparts, but they have different symbol-table entries, so distinct types are constructed for them. Similarly, lcc assumes that long and int, and long double and double, have the same structure, but each has a distinct type. Comparing a type to `longtype` suffices to test if it represents the type long. IR points to the interface record supplied by the back end; see Section 5.11. The type void has no metrics:

```
⟨typeInit 58⟩+≡                                                    58 61    58
    {
        Symbol p;
        p = install(string("void"), &types, GLOBAL, PERM);
        voidtype = type(VOID, NULL, 0, 0, p);
        p->type = voidtype;
    }
```

typeInit installs the symbol-table entries into the `types` table defined in Section 3.2. This table holds entries for all types that are
named by identifiers or tags. The basic types are installed by `typeInit`
and are never removed. But the types associated with structure, union,
and enumeration tags must be removed from `typetable` when their associated symbol-table entries are removed from `types` by `exitscope`.
`exitscope` calls `rmtypes(lev)` to remove from `typetable` any types
whose `u.sym->scope` is greater than or equal to `lev`:

```
⟨types.c data⟩+≡                                                   56 61
    static int maxlevel;
```

```
⟨types.c functions⟩+≡                                              58 61
    void rmtypes(lev) int lev; {
        if (maxlevel >= lev) {
            int i;
            maxlevel = 0;
            for (i = 0; i < NELEMS(typetable); i++) {
                ⟨remove types with u.sym->scope >= lev 59⟩
            }
        }
    }
```

42	exitscope
109	FUNCTION
38	GLOBAL
44	install
19	NELEMS
97	PERM
37	scope
29	string
58	typeInit
41	types
56	typetable
109	VOID
58	voidtype

The value of `maxlevel` is the largest value of `u.sym->scope` for any type
in `typetable` that has an associated symbol-table entry. `rmtypes` uses
`maxlevel` to avoid scanning `typetable` in the frequently occurring case
when none of the symbol-table entries have `scopes` greater than or equal
to `lev`. Removing the types also recomputes `maxlevel`:

```
⟨remove types with u.sym->scope >= lev 59⟩≡                                59
    struct entry *tn, **tq = &typetable[i];
    while ((tn = *tq) != NULL)
        if (tn->type.op == FUNCTION)
            tq = &tn->link;
        else if (tn->type.u.sym && tn->type.u.sym->scope >= lev)
            *tq = tn->link;
        else {
            ⟨recompute maxlevel 60⟩
            tq = &tn->link;
        }
```

⟨*recompute* maxlevel 60⟩≡   59
```
if (tn->type.u.sym && tn->type.u.sym->scope > maxlevel)
    maxlevel = tn->type.u.sym->scope;
```

Function types are treated specially because they have fields that overlap
u.sym but themselves have no u.sym. Arrays and qualified types have no
u.sym fields, so the last clause handles them.

4.3   Type Predicates

The global variables initialized by typeInit can be used to specify a
particular type and to test for a particular type. For example, if the type
ty is equal to inttype, ty is type int. The is... predicates listed below,
implemented as macros, test for sets of types by checking for specific
operators. Most operate on *unqualified* types, which are obtained by
calling unqual:

⟨*types.c exported macros*⟩≡   60
```
#define isqual(t)      ((t)->op >= CONST)
#define unqual(t)      (isqual(t) ? (t)->type : (t))
```

⟨*types.c exported macros*⟩+≡   60 66
```
#define isvolatile(t) ((t)->op == VOLATILE \
                      || (t)->op == CONST+VOLATILE)
#define isconst(t)    ((t)->op == CONST \
                      || (t)->op == CONST+VOLATILE)
#define isarray(t)    (unqual(t)->op == ARRAY)
#define isstruct(t)   (unqual(t)->op == STRUCT \
                      || unqual(t)->op == UNION)
#define isunion(t)    (unqual(t)->op == UNION)
#define isfunc(t)     (unqual(t)->op == FUNCTION)
#define isptr(t)      (unqual(t)->op == POINTER)
#define ischar(t)     (unqual(t)->op == CHAR)
#define isint(t)      (unqual(t)->op >= CHAR \
                   && unqual(t)->op <= UNSIGNED)
#define isfloat(t)    (unqual(t)->op <= DOUBLE)
#define isarith(t)    (unqual(t)->op <= UNSIGNED)
#define isunsigned(t) (unqual(t)->op == UNSIGNED)
#define isdouble(t)   (unqual(t)->op == DOUBLE)
#define isscalar(t)   (unqual(t)->op <= POINTER \
                      || unqual(t)->op == ENUM)
#define isenum(t)     (unqual(t)->op == ENUM)
```

The values of the type operators are defined in token.h so that the comparisons made in the macros above yield the desired result.

4.4   Type Constructors

type constructs an arbitrary type. Other functions encapsulate calls to type to construct specific types. For example, ptr builds a pointer type:

⟨*types.c functions*⟩+≡   59 61

```
Type ptr(ty) Type ty; {
    return type(POINTER, ty, IR->ptrmetric.size,
        IR->ptrmetric.align, pointersym);
}
```

which, given a type ty, returns (POINTER ty). The symbol-table entry associated with pointer types is assigned to pointersym during initialization, and the type for void* is initialized by calling ptr:

⟨*types.c data*⟩+≡   59

```
static Symbol pointersym;
```

⟨*typeInit* 58⟩+≡   59   58

```
pointersym = install(string("T*"), &types, GLOBAL, PERM);
pointersym->addressed = IR->ptrmetric.outofline;
voidptype = ptr(voidtype);
```

While ptr builds a pointer type, deref dereferences it; that is, it returns the reference type. Given a type (POINTER ty), deref returns ty:

⟨*types.c functions*⟩+≡   61 61

```
Type deref(ty) Type ty; {
    if (isptr(ty))
        ty = ty->type;
    else
        error("type error: %s\n", "pointer expected");
    return isenum(ty) ? unqual(ty)->type : ty;
}
```

deref, like some of the other constructors below, issues errors for invalid operands. Technically, these kinds of tests are part of type-checking, not type construction, but putting these tests in the constructors simplifies the type-checking code and avoids oversights. The last line of deref handles pointers to enumerations: dereferencing a pointer to an enumeration must return its associated unqualified integral type. unqual is described above.

array(ty, n, a) builds the type (ARRAY n ty). It also arranges for the resulting type to have alignment a or, if a is 0, the alignment of ty. array also checks for illegal operands.

⟨*types.c functions*⟩+≡   61 62

```
Type array(ty, n, a) Type ty; int n, a; {
```

```
            if (isfunc(ty)) {
                error("illegal type 'array of %t'\n", ty);
                return array(inttype, n, 0);
            }
            if (level > GLOBAL && isarray(ty) && ty->size == 0)
                error("missing array size\n");
            if (ty->size == 0) {
                if (unqual(ty) == voidtype)
                    error("illegal type 'array of %t'\n", ty);
                else if (Aflag >= 2)
                    warning("declaring type 'array of %t' is _
                        undefined\n", ty);
            } else if (n > INT_MAX/ty->size) {
                error("size of 'array of %t' exceeds %d bytes\n",
                    ty, INT_MAX);
                n = 1;
            }
            return type(ARRAY, ty, n*ty->size,
                a ? a : ty->align, NULL);
        }
```

C does not permit arrays of functions, arrays of void, or incomplete arrays (those with zero length) at any scope level except GLOBAL. array also forbids arrays whose size is greater than INT_MAX bytes, because it cannot represent their sizes, and warns about declaring incomplete arrays of incomplete types if lcc's (fussy) double -A option, which sets Aflag to 2, indicating that lcc should warn about non-ANSI usage. The format code %t prints an English description of the corresponding type argument; see Exercise 4.4.

Array types "decay" into pointers to their element types in many contexts, such as when an array is the type of a formal parameter. atop implements this decay:

⟨*types.c functions*⟩+≡   61 62

```
    Type atop(ty) Type ty; {
        if (isarray(ty))
            return ptr(ty->type);
        error("type error: %s\n", "array expected");
        return ptr(ty);
    }
```

qual and unqual, shown above, respectively construct and deconstruct qualified types. Given a type ty, qual checks for illegal operands and builds (CONST ty), (VOLATILE ty), or (CONST+VOLATILE ty).

⟨*types.c functions*⟩+≡   62 64

```
    Type qual(op, ty) int op; Type ty; {
```

```
    if (isarray(ty))
        ty = type(ARRAY, qual(op, ty->type), ty->size,
            ty->align, NULL);
    else if (isfunc(ty))
        warning("qualified function type ignored\n");
    else if (isconst(ty)    && op == CONST
    ||        isvolatile(ty) && op == VOLATILE)
        error("illegal type '%k %t'\n", op, ty);
    else {
        if (isqual(ty)) {
            op += ty->op;
            ty = ty->type;
        }
        ty = type(op, ty, ty->size, ty->align, NULL);
    }
    return ty;
}
```

If ty is the type (ARRAY ety), the qualification applies to the element type, so qual(op, ty) builds (ARRAY (op ety)). If ty is already qualified, it's either (CONST ty->type) or (VOLATILE ty->type), and op is the other qualifier. In this case, qual builds (CONST+VOLATILE ty->type). This convention complicates the code for qual, but makes it possible to describe qualified types with only one type node instead of one or two type nodes, thus simplifying isqual.

4.5 Function Types

The type field of a function type gives the type of the value returned by the function, and the u union holds a structure that gives the types of the arguments:

⟨*function types* 63⟩≡   54
```
    struct {
        unsigned oldstyle:1;
        Type *proto;
    } f;
```

The f.oldstyle flag distinguishes between the two kinds of function types: A one indicates an old-style type, which may omit the argument types of the arguments, and a zero indicates new-style function, which always includes the argument types. f.proto points to a null-terminated array of Types; f.proto[i] is the type of argument $i+1$. The f.oldstyle flag is needed because old-style function types may carry prototypes, but, as dictated by the ANSI Standard, those prototypes are not used to type-check actual arguments that appear in calls to such functions. This anomaly appears when an old-style definition is followed by a new-style declaration; for example,

```
int f(x,y) int x; double y; { ... }
extern int f(int, double);
```

defines f as an old-style function and subsequently declares a prototype for f. The prototype must be compatible with the definition, but it's not used to type-check calls to f.

func builds the type (FUNCTION ty {proto}), where ty is the type of the return value and the braces enclose the prototype, and it initializes the prototype and old-style flag:

⟨*types.c functions*⟩+≡   62 64

```
Type func(ty, proto, style) Type ty, *proto; int style; {
    if (ty && (isarray(ty) || isfunc(ty)))
        error("illegal return type '%t'\n", ty);
    ty = type(FUNCTION, ty, 0, 0, NULL);
    ty->u.f.proto = proto;
    ty->u.f.oldstyle = style;
    return ty;
}
```

freturn is to function types what ptr is to pointer types. It takes a type (FUNCTION ty) and dereferences it to yield ty, the type of the return value.

⟨*types.c functions*⟩+≡   64 65

```
Type freturn(ty) Type ty; {
    if (isfunc(ty))
        return ty->type;
    error("type error: %s\n", "function expected");
    return inttype;
}
```

ANSI C supports functions with *no* arguments; such a function is declared with void as the argument list. For example,

```
void f(void);
```

declares f to be a function that takes no arguments and returns no value. Internally, the prototype for functions with no arguments is not empty; it consists of a void type and the terminating null. Thus, the type of f is depicted as

```
(FUNCTION (VOID) {(VOID)})
```

ANSI C also supports functions with a variable number of arguments. sprintf is an example; it's declared as

```
int sprintf(char *, char *, ...);
```

where the ellipsis denotes the variable portion of the argument list. The prototype for a variable number of arguments consists of the types of the declared arguments, a void type, and the terminating null. sprintf's type is thus

```
(FUNCTION (INT)
   {(POINTER (CHAR))
    (POINTER (CHAR))
    (VOID)})
```

The predicate variadic tests whether a function type has a variable-length argument list by looking for the type void at the end of its prototype:

⟨*types.c functions*⟩+≡   64 67

```
int variadic(ty) Type ty; {
    if (isfunc(ty) && ty->u.f.proto) {
        int i;
        for (i = 0; ty->u.f.proto[i]; i++)
            ;
        return i > 1 && ty->u.f.proto[i-1] == voidtype;
    }
    return 0;
}
```

66 Field
60 isfunc
37 symbol
58 voidtype

A function with a variable number of arguments always has at least one declared argument, followed by one or more optional arguments, so the void at the end of the prototype can't be confused with the prototype for a function with no arguments, which has the one-element prototype {(VOID)}.

4.6 Structure and Enumeration Types

Structure and union types are identified by tags, and the u.sym fields of these types point to the symbol-table entries for these tags. The fields are stored in these symbol-table entries, not in the types themselves. The relevant field of the symbol structure is u.s:

⟨struct *types* 65⟩≡   38

```
struct {
    unsigned cfields:1;
    unsigned vfields:1;
    Field flist;
} s;
```

cfields and vfields are both one if the structure or union type has any const-qualified or volatile-qualified fields. flist points to a list of field structures threaded through their link fields:

⟨*types.c typedefs*⟩+≡   54

```
typedef struct field *Field;
```

⟨*types.c exported types*⟩+≡   54

```
struct field {
    char *name;
    Type type;
    int offset;
    short bitsize;
    short lsb;
    Field link;
};
```

name holds the field name, type is the field's type, and offset is the byte offset to the field in an instance of the structure.

When a field describes a bit field, the type field is either inttype or unsignedtype, because those are the only two types allowed for bit fields. The lsb field is nonzero and the following macros apply. lsb is the number of the least significant bit in the bit field plus one, where bit numbers start at zero with the least significant bit.

⟨*types.c exported macros*⟩+≡   60 74

```
#define fieldsize(p)   (p)->bitsize
#define fieldright(p)  ((p)->lsb - 1)
#define fieldleft(p)   (8*(p)->type->size - \
                            fieldsize(p) - fieldright(p))
#define fieldmask(p)   (~(~(unsigned)0<<fieldsize(p)))
```

fieldsize returns the bitsize field, which holds the size of the bit field in bits. fieldright is the number of bits to the right of a bit field, and is used to shift the field over to the least significant bits of a signed or unsigned integer. Likewise, fieldleft is the number of bits to the left of a field; it is used when a signed bit field must be sign-extended. fieldmask is a mask of bitsize ones and is used to clear the extraneous bits when a bit field is extracted. Notice that this representation for bit fields does not depend on the target's endianness; the same representation is used for both big and little endians.

newstruct creates a new type, (STRUCT ["tag"]) or (UNION ["tag"]), where tag is the tag. It's called by structdcl whenever a new structure or union type is declared or defined, with or without a field list. When a new structure or union type is created, its tag is installed in the types table. Tags are generated for anonymous structures and unions; that is, those without tags:

⟨*types.c functions*⟩+≡ 65 68

```
Type newstruct(op, tag) int op; char *tag; {
   Symbol p;

   if (*tag == 0)
      tag = stringd(genlabel(1));
   else
      ⟨check for redefinition of tag 67⟩
   p = install(tag, &types, level, PERM);
   p->type = type(op, NULL, 0, 0, p);
   if (p->scope > maxlevel)
      maxlevel = p->scope;
   p->src = src;
   return p->type;
}
```

Installing a new tag in types might create an entry with a scope that exceeds maxlevel, so maxlevel is adjusted if necessary. Structure types point to their symbol-table entries, which point back to the type, so that tags can be mapped to types and vice versa. Tags are mapped to types when they are used in declarators, for example; see structdcl. Types are mapped to tags when rmtypes removes them from the typetable.

It's illegal to define the same tag more than once in the same scope, but it is legal to *declare* the same tag more than once. Giving a structure declaration with fields declares and defines a structure tag; using a structure tag without giving its fields declares the tag. For example,

```
struct employee {
   char *name;
   struct date *hired;
   char ssn[9];
}
```

declares and defines employee but only declares date. When a tag is defined, its defined flag is lit, and defined is examined to determine if the tag is being redefined:

⟨*check for redefinition of tag* 67⟩≡ 67

```
if ((p = lookup(tag, types)) != NULL && (p->scope == level
|| p->scope == PARAM && level == PARAM+1)) {
   if (p->type->op == op && !p->defined)
      return p->type;
   error("redefinition of '%s' previously defined at %w\n",
      p->name, &p->src);
}
```

Arguments and argument types have scope PARAM, and locals have scopes beginning at PARAM+1. ANSI C specifies that arguments and top-level locals are in the same scope, so the scope test must test for a local tag that redefines a tag defined by an argument. This division is not mandated by the ANSI C Standard; it's used internally by lcc to separate parameters and locals so that foreach can visit them separately.

newfield adds a field with type fty to a structure type ty by allocating a field structure and appending it to the field list in ty's symbol-table entry:

⟨*types.c functions*⟩+≡   67 69

```
Field newfield(name, ty, fty) char *name; Type ty, fty; {
    Field p, *q = &ty->u.sym->u.s.flist;

    if (name == NULL)
        name = stringd(genlabel(1));
    for (p = *q; p; q = &p->link, p = *q)
        if (p->name == name)
            error("duplicate field name '%s' in '%t'\n",
                name, ty);
    NEW0(p, PERM);
    *q = p;
    p->name = name;
    p->type = fty;
    return p;
}
```

If name is null, newfield generates a name; this capability is used by fields for unnamed bit fields. Field lists are searched by fieldref; see Exercise 4.6.

Enumeration types are like structure and union types, except that they don't have fields, and their type fields give their associated integral type, which for lcc is always inttype. The standard permits compilers to use any integral type that can hold all of the enumeration values, but many compilers always use ints; lcc does likewise to maintain compability. Enumeration types have a type field so that lcc could use different integral types for different enumerations. Enumeration types are created by calling newstruct with the operator ENUM, and newstruct returns the type (ENUM ["tag"]).

Like a structure or union type, the u.sym field of an enumeration type points to a symbol-table entry for its tag, but it uses a different component of the symbol structure:

⟨*enum types* 68⟩≡   38

```
Symbol *idlist;
```

idlist points to a null-terminated array of Symbols for the enumeration constants associated with the enumeration type. These are installed in the identifiers table, and each one carries its value:

⟨enum *constants* 69⟩≡   38
   int value;

The enumeration constants are not a part of the enumeration type. They are created, initialized, and packaged in an array as they are parsed; see Exercise 11.9.

4.7 Type-Checking Functions

Determining when two types are compatible is the crux of type checking, and the functions described here help to implement ANSI C's type-checking rules.

   eqtype returns one if two types are compatible and zero otherwise.

⟨*types.c functions*⟩+≡   ▲ 68 71
                                                            ▼

```
int eqtype(ty1, ty2, ret) Type ty1, ty2; int ret; {
    if (ty1 == ty2)
        return 1;
    if (ty1->op != ty2->op)
        return 0;
    switch (ty1->op) {
    case CHAR: case SHORT: case UNSIGNED: case INT:
    case ENUM: case UNION: case STRUCT:    case DOUBLE:
        return 0;
    case POINTER:   ⟨check for compatible pointer types 70⟩
    case VOLATILE: case CONST+VOLATILE:
    case CONST:     ⟨check for compatible qualified types 70⟩
    case ARRAY:     ⟨check for compatible array types 70⟩
    case FUNCTION: ⟨check for compatible function types 70⟩
    }
}
```

The third argument, ret, is the value returned when either ty1 or ty2 is an incomplete type.

   A type is always compatible with itself. type ensures that there is only one instance of most types, so many tests of compatible types pass the first test in eqtype. Likewise, many tests of incompatible types test types with different operators, which are never compatible and cause eqtype to return zero.

   If two different types have the same operator CHAR, SHORT, UNSIGNED, or INT, the two types represent different types, such as unsigned short and signed short, and are incompatible. Similarly, two enumeration, structure, or union types are compatible only if they are the same type.

   The remaining cases traverse the type structures to determine compatibility. For example, two pointer types are compatible if their referenced types are compatible:

⟨*check for compatible pointer types* 70⟩≡   69
```
return eqtype(ty1->type, ty2->type, 1);
```

Two similarly qualified types are compatible if their unqualified types are compatible.

⟨*check for compatible qualified types* 70⟩≡   69
```
return eqtype(ty1->type, ty2->type, 1);
```

An incomplete type is one that does not include the size of the object it describes. For example, the declaration

```
int a[];
```

declares an array in which the size is unknown. The type is given by (ARRAY 0 (INT)); a `size` of zero identifies an incomplete type. Two array types are compatible if their element types are compatible and if their sizes, if given, are equal:

⟨*check for compatible array types* 70⟩≡   69
```
if (eqtype(ty1->type, ty2->type, 1)) {
    if (ty1->size == ty2->size)
        return 1;
    if (ty1->size == 0 || ty2->size == 0)
        return ret;
}
return 0;
```

---
eqtype 69
---

eqtype returns `ret` if *one* of the array types is incomplete but they are otherwise compatible. `ret` is always one when eqtype calls itself, and is usually one when called from elsewhere. Some operators, such as pointer comparison, insist on operands that are both incomplete types or both complete types; `ret` is 0 for those uses of eqtype. The first test handles the case when both arrays have unknown sizes.

Two function types are compatible if their return types are compatible and if their prototypes are compatible:

⟨*check for compatible function types* 70⟩≡   69
```
if (eqtype(ty1->type, ty2->type, 1)) {
    Type *p1 = ty1->u.f.proto, *p2 = ty2->u.f.proto;
    if (p1 == p2)
        return 1;
    if (p1 && p2) {
        ⟨check for compatible prototypes 71⟩
    } else {
        ⟨check if prototype is upward compatible 71⟩
    }
}
return 0;
```

The easy case is when both functions have a prototype. The prototypes must both have the same number of argument types, and the unqualified versions of the types in each prototype must be compatible.

⟨*check for compatible prototypes* 71⟩≡   70
```
    for ( ; *p1 && *p2; p1++, p2++)
        if (eqtype(unqual(*p1), unqual(*p2), 1) == 0)
            return 0;
    if (*p1 == NULL && *p2 == NULL)
        return 1;
```

The other case is more complicated. Each argument type in the one function type that has a prototype must be compatible with the type that results from applying the *default argument promotions* to the unqualified version of the type itself. Also, if the function type with a prototype has a variable number of arguments, the two function types are incompatible.

⟨*check if prototype is upward compatible* 71⟩≡   70
```
    if (variadic(p1 ? ty1 : ty2))
        return 0;
    if (p1 == NULL)
        p1 = p2;
    for ( ; *p1; p1++) {
        Type ty = unqual(*p1);
        if (promote(ty) != ty || ty == floattype)
            return 0;
    }
    return 1;
```

69	eqtype
57	floattype
60	isenum
60	isint
60	isunsigned
57	longtype
60	unqual
65	variadic

The default argument promotions stipulate that floats are promoted to doubles and that small integers and enumerations are promoted to ints or unsigneds. The code above checks the float promotion explicitly, and calls promote for the others. promote implements the *integral promotions*:

⟨*types.c functions*⟩+≡   ▲69 72▼
```
    Type promote(ty) Type ty; {
        ty = unqual(ty);
        if (isunsigned(ty) || ty == longtype)
            return ty;
        else if (isint(ty) || isenum(ty))
            return inttype;
        return ty;
    }
```

Two compatible types can be combined to form a new, *composite type.* This operation occurs, for example, in the C fragment

```
int x[];
int x[10];
```

The first declaration associates the type (ARRAY 0 (INT)) with x. The second declaration forms the new type (ARRAY 10 (INT)). These two types are combined to form the type (ARRAY 10 (INT)), which becomes the type of x. Combining these two types uses the size of the second type in the composite type. Another example is combining a function type with a prototype with a function type without one.

compose accepts two compatible types and returns the composite type. compose is similar in structure to eqtype and the easy cases are similar.

⟨*types.c functions*⟩+≡   71 73

```
Type compose(ty1, ty2) Type ty1, ty2; {
    if (ty1 == ty2)
        return ty1;
    switch (ty1->op) {
    case POINTER:
        return ptr(compose(ty1->type, ty2->type));
    case CONST+VOLATILE:
        return qual(CONST, qual(VOLATILE,
            compose(ty1->type, ty2->type)));
    case CONST: case VOLATILE:
        return qual(ty1->op, compose(ty1->type, ty2->type));
    case ARRAY:    { ⟨compose two array types 72⟩    }
    case FUNCTION: { ⟨compose two function types 72⟩ }
    }
}
```

Two compatible array types form a new array whose size is the size of the complete array, if there is one.

⟨*compose two array types* 72⟩≡   72

```
Type ty = compose(ty1->type, ty2->type);
if (ty1->size && ty1->type->size && ty2->size == 0)
    return array(ty, ty1->size/ty1->type->size, ty1->align);
if (ty2->size && ty2->type->size && ty1->size == 0)
    return array(ty, ty2->size/ty2->type->size, ty2->align);
return array(ty, 0, 0);
```

The composite type of two compatible function types has a return type that is the composite type of the two return types, and argument types that are the composite types of the corresponding argument types. If one function type does not have a prototype, the composite type has the prototype from the other function type.

⟨*compose two function types* 72⟩≡   72

```
Type *p1  = ty1->u.f.proto, *p2 = ty2->u.f.proto;
```

```
Type ty    = compose(ty1->type, ty2->type);
List tlist = NULL;
if (p1 == NULL && p2 == NULL)
    return func(ty, NULL, 1);
if (p1 && p2 == NULL)
    return func(ty, p1, ty1->u.f.oldstyle);
if (p2 && p1 == NULL)
    return func(ty, p2, ty2->u.f.oldstyle);
for ( ; *p1 && *p2; p1++, p2++) {
    Type ty = compose(unqual(*p1), unqual(*p2));
    if (isconst(*p1)    || isconst(*p2))
        ty = qual(CONST, ty);
    if (isvolatile(*p1) || isvolatile(*p2))
        ty = qual(VOLATILE, ty);
    tlist = append(ty, tlist);
}
return func(ty, ltov(&tlist, PERM), 0);
```

This code uses the list functions append and ltov to manipulate Lists, which are lists of pointers.

4.8 Type Mapping

The type representation and type functions described in this chapter are used primarily by the front end. Back ends may inspect the size and align fields, but must not rely on the other fields.

They may, however, have to map Types to type suffixes, which are used to form type-specific operators as described in Chapter 5. The type suffixes are a subset of the type operators. ttob maps a type to its corresponding type suffix:

⟨*types.c functions*⟩+≡   72 74

```
int ttob(ty) Type ty; {
    switch (ty->op) {
    case CONST: case VOLATILE: case CONST+VOLATILE:
        return ttob(ty->type);
    case CHAR: case INT:   case SHORT: case UNSIGNED:
    case VOID: case FLOAT: case DOUBLE:  return ty->op;
    case POINTER: case FUNCTION:         return POINTER;
    case ARRAY: case STRUCT: case UNION: return STRUCT;
    case ENUM:                           return INT;
    }
}
```

widen is similar, but widens all integral types to int:

⟨*types.c exported macros*⟩+≡   66
```
#define widen(t) (isint(t) || isenum(t) ? INT : ttob(t))
```

btot is the opposite of `ttob`; it maps an operator or type suffix op to some Type such that `optype(op) == ttob(btot(op))`.

⟨*types.c functions*⟩+≡   73
```
Type btot(op) int op; {
    switch (optype(op)) {
    case F: return floattype;
    case D: return doubletype;
    case C: return chartype;
    case S: return shorttype;
    case I: return inttype;
    case U: return unsignedtype;
    case P: return voidptype;
    }
}
```

The enumeration identifiers F, D, C, ..., defined on page 82, are abbreviations for the corresponding type operators.

Further Reading

lcc's type representation is typical for languages in which types can be specified by grammars and hence represented by linked structures that amount to abstract syntax trees for expressions derived from those grammars. Aho, Sethi, and Ullman (1986) describe this approach in more detail and illustrate how type checking is done not only for languages like C but also for functional languages, such as ML (Ullman 1994). Section 6.3, particularly Exercise 6.13, in Aho, Sethi, and Ullman (1986) describes how PCC, the Portable C Compiler (Johnson 1978), represented types with the bit strings.

Exercises

4.1 Give the parenthesized prefix form for the types in the following declarations.
```
long double d;
char ***p;
const int *const volatile *q;
int (*r)[10][4];
struct tree *(*s[])(int, struct tree *, struct tree *);
```

4.2 Give an example of a C structure definition that draws the tag re-definition diagnostic described in Section 4.6.

4.3 Implement the predicate

⟨*types.c exported functions*⟩≡   75

```
extern int hasproto ARGS((Type));
```

which returns one if ty includes no function types or if all of the function types it includes have prototypes, and zero otherwise. hasproto is used to warn about missing prototypes. It doesn't warn about missing prototypes in structure fields that are function pointers, because it's called explicitly with the types of the fields as the structure is parsed.

4.4 lcc prints an English rendition of types in diagnostics. For example, the types of sprintf, shown in Section 4.5, and of

```
char *(*strings)[10]
```

are printed as

```
int function(char *, char *, ...)
pointer to array 10 of pointer to char
```

54 Type

The output functions interpret the printf-style code %t to print the next Type argument, and call

⟨*types.c exported functions*⟩+≡   75 75

```
extern void outtype ARGS((Type));
```

to do so. Implement outtype.

4.5 types.c exports three other functions that format and print types.

⟨*types.c exported functions*⟩+≡   75 76

```
extern void printdecl  ARGS((Symbol p, Type ty));
extern void printproto ARGS((Symbol p, Symbol args[]));
extern char *typestring ARGS((Type ty, char *id));
```

typestring returns a C declaration that specifies ty to be the type of the identifier id. For example, if ty is

```
(POINTER (ARRAY 10 (POINTER (CHAR))))
```

and id is "strings", typestring returns "char *(*strings)[10]". lcc's -P option helps convert pre-ANSI code to ANSI C by printing new-style prototypes for functions and globals on the standard error output. printdecl prints a declaration for p assuming it has type ty (ty is usually p->type), and `printproto` prints a declaration for a function p that has parameters given by the symbols in args. `printproto` uses args to build a function type and then calls `printdecl`, which calls `typestring`. Implement these functions.

4.6 The function

⟨*types.c exported functions*⟩+≡   75

```
extern Field fieldref ARGS((char *name, Type ty));
```

searches ty's field list for the field given by name, and returns a pointer to the `field` structure. It returns NULL if ty doesn't have a field name. Implement `fieldref`.

4.7 Explain why lcc diagnoses that the operands of the assignment in the C program below have illegal types.

```
struct { int x, y; } *p;
struct { int x, y; } *q;
main() { p = q; }
```

4.8 Explain why lcc complains that the argument to f is an illegal type in the C program below.

```
void f(struct point { int x, y; } *p) {}
struct { int x, y; } *origin;
main() { f(origin); }
```

4.9 Explain why lcc insists that the definition of `isdigit` in the C program below conflicts with the external declaration of `isdigit`.

```
extern int isdigit(char c);
int isdigit(c) char c; { return c >= '0' && c <= '9'; }
```

4.10 Measurements show that the if statement in type's ⟨*search for an existing type*⟩ is one of lcc's hot spots. Instrument lcc to determine the order of the tests in this conditional that gives the best execution time. Once you've found the best order, measure the improvement of lcc's execution time when compiling itself. Was the change worthwhile?

4.11 Structure types point to symbols that hold their field lists, and those symbols point back to the types. Redesign this apparently awkward data structure so that types are completely independent of symbol tables. For example, structure types could carry their field lists in one of the u fields, and types with tags could use another field to store the scope level at which they're defined. You'll need to revise functions like `newstruct` to initialize these fields, and to provide functions for mapping tags to types and perhaps vice versa. The basic types need the data that's in their symbol-table entries, such as the `addressed` flag. Compare your revised design; is it obviously superior to the present one? Does your implementation duplicate functionality provided elsewhere, such as in the symbol-table module?

179 addressed
67 newstruct

5
Code Generation Interface

This chapter defines the interface between the target-independent front end and the target-dependent back ends. Good code-generation interfaces are hard to design. An inadequate interface may force each back end to do work that could otherwise be done once in the front end. If the interface is too small, it may encode too little information to exploit new machines thoroughly. If the interface is too large, the back ends may be needlessly complicated. These competing demands require careful engineering and re-engineering as new targets expose flaws.

lcc's interface consists of a few shared data structures, 18 functions, most of which are simple, and a 36-operator language, which encodes the executable code from a source program in directed acyclic graphs, or dags. The front and back ends share some fields of the shared data structures, but other fields are private to the front or back end.

Two of the shared data structures are described in previous chapters: symbol in Chapter 3 and type in Chapter 4. Back ends are able to examine any field in either structure, but by convention they don't. This chapter lists the fields that back ends may examine and, to describe the entire interface in one place, it reviews what they represent. It omits fields that are logically private to the front (or back) end.

symbol 37
type 56

5.1   Type Metrics

A *type metric* specifies the size and alignment for a primitive type:

⟨*interface* 78⟩ ≡   79   16
```
typedef struct metrics {
    unsigned char size, align, outofline;
} Metrics;
```

The outofline flag controls the placements of constants of the associated type. If outofline is one, constants cannot appear in dags; such constants are placed in anonymous static variables and their values are accessed by fetching the variables. Each primitive type has a metric:

⟨*metrics* 78⟩ ≡   79
```
Metrics charmetric;
Metrics shortmetric;
Metrics intmetric;
```

```
Metrics floatmetric;
Metrics doublemetric;
Metrics ptrmetric;
Metrics structmetric;
```

ptrmetric describes pointers of all types. The alignment of a structure
is the maximum of the alignments of its fields and structmetric.align,
which thus gives the minimum alignment for structures; structmetric's
size field is unused. Back ends usually set outofline to zero only for
those types whose values can appear as immediate operands of instructions.

The size and alignment for characters must be one. The front end
correctly treats signed and unsigned integers and longs as distinct types,
but it assumes that they all share intmetric. Likewise for doubles and
long doubles. Each pointer must fit in an unsigned integer.

5.2 Interface Records

A cross-compiler produces code for one machine while running on another. lcc can be linked with code generators for several targets, so it
can be used as either a native compiler or a cross-compiler. lcc's *interface record* captures everything that its front end needs to know about a
target machine, including pointers to the interface routines, type metrics,
and interface flags. The interface record is defined by:

⟨*interface* 78⟩+≡   ▲ 78 96   16
    typedef struct interface {   ▼
        ⟨*metrics* 78⟩
        ⟨*interface flags* 87⟩
        ⟨*interface functions* 80⟩
        Xinterface x;
    } Interface;

lcc has a distinct instance of the interface record for each target. The x
field is an extension in which the back end stores target-specific interface
data and functions. The x field is private to the back end and is defined
in config.h.

The interface records hold pointers to the 18 interface functions described in the following sections. The functions defined in this chapter
by ⟨*interface functions*⟩ are often denoted by just their name. For example, gen is used instead of the more accurate but verbose "the function
pointed to by the gen field of the interface record."

The interface record also holds pointers to some functions that the
front end calls to emit symbol tables for debuggers:

⟨*interface functions* 80⟩≡   89   79

```
void (*stabblock) ARGS((int, int, Symbol*));
void (*stabend)   ARGS((Coordinate *, Symbol, Coordinate **,
                        Symbol *, Symbol *));
void (*stabfend)  ARGS((Symbol, int));
void (*stabinit)  ARGS((char *, int, char *[]));
void (*stabline)  ARGS((Coordinate *));
void (*stabsym)   ARGS((Symbol));
void (*stabtype)  ARGS((Symbol));
```

To save space, this book does not describe these stab functions. The companion diskette shows them, though some are just stubs for some targets.

5.3 Symbols

A `symbol` represents a variable, label, or constant; the `scope` field tells which. For variables and constants, the back end may query the `type` field to learn the data type suffix of the item. For variables and labels, the floating-point value of the `ref` field approximates the number of times that variable or label is referenced; a nonzero value thus indicates that the variable or label is referenced at least once. For labels, constants, and some variables, a field of the union u supplies additional data.

Variables have a `scope` equal to GLOBAL, PARAM, or LOCAL+k for nesting level k. `sclass` is STATIC, AUTO, EXTERN, or REGISTER. The name of most variables is the name used in the source code. For temporaries and other generated variables, `name` is a digit sequence. For global and static variables, `u.seg` gives the logical segment in which the variable is defined. If the interface flag `wants_dag` is zero, the front end generates explicit temporary variables to hold common subexpressions — those used more than once. It sets the `u.t.cse` fields of these symbols to the dag nodes that compute the values stored in them.

The flags `temporary` and `generated` are set for temporaries, and the flag `generated` is set for labels and other generated variables, like those that hold string literals. `structarg` identifies structure parameters when the interface flag `wants_argb` is set; the material below on `wants_argb` elaborates.

Labels have a `scope` equal to LABELS. The `u.l.label` field is a unique numeric value that identifies the label, and `name` is the string representation of that value. Labels have no `type` or `sclass`.

Constants have a `scope` equal to CONSTANTS, and an `sclass` equal to STATIC. For an integral or pointer constant, `name` is its string representation as a C constant. For other types, `name` is undefined. The actual value of the constant is stored in the `u.c.v` field, which is defined on page 47. If a variable is generated to hold the constant, u.c.loc points to the symbol-table entry for that variable.

Symbols have an x field with type Xsymbol, defined in config.h. It's an extension in which the back end stores target-specific data for the symbol, like the stack offset for locals. The x field is private to the back end, and thus its contents are not part of the interface. Chapter 13 elaborates.

5.4 Types

Symbols have a type field. If the symbol represents a constant or variable, the type field points to a structure that describes the type of the item. Back ends may read the size and align fields of this structure to learn the size and alignment constraints of the type in bytes. Back ends may also pass the type pointer itself to predicates like isarray and ttob to learn about the type without examining other fields.

5.5 Dag Operators

Executable code is specified by dags. A function body is a sequence, or *forest*, of dags, each of which is passed to the back end via gen. Dag nodes, sometimes called *nodes*, are defined by:

⟨*c.h typedefs*⟩ ≡
```
typedef struct node *Node;
```

⟨*c.h exported types*⟩ ≡   82 ▼
```
struct node {
    short op;
    short count;
    Symbol syms[3];
    Node kids[2];
    Node link;
    Xnode x;
};
```

The elements of kids point to the operand nodes. Some dag operators also take one or two symbol-table pointers as operands; these appear in syms. The back end may use the third syms for its own purposes; the front end uses it, too, but its uses are temporary and occur before dags are passed to the back end, as detailed in Section 12.8. link points to the root of the next dag in the forest.

count records the number of times the value of this node is used or referred to by others. Only references from kids count; link references don't count because they don't represent a use of the value of the node. Indeed, link is meaningful only for root nodes, which are executed for side effect, not value. If the interface flag wants_dag is zero, roots always have a zero count. The generated code for shared nodes — those whose count exceed one — must evaluate the node only once; the value is used count times.

The x field is the back end's extension to nodes. The back end defines the type Xnode in config.h to hold the per-node data that it needs to generate code. Chapter 13 describes the fields.

The op field holds a dag operator. The last character of each is a *type suffix* from the list in the type definition:

⟨*c.h exported types*⟩+≡   ▲81 82▼

```
enum {
    F=FLOAT,
    D=DOUBLE,
    C=CHAR,
    S=SHORT,
    I=INT,
    U=UNSIGNED,
    P=POINTER,
    V=VOID,
    B=STRUCT
};
```

For example, the generic operator ADD has the variants ADDI, ADDU, ADDP, ADDF, and ADDD. These suffixes are defined so that they have the values 1–9.

The operators are defined by

⟨*c.h exported types*⟩+≡   ▲82 91▼

```
enum { ⟨operators 82⟩ };
```

⟨*operators* 82⟩≡   82

```
CNST=1<<4,
    CNSTC=CNST+C,
    CNSTD=CNST+D,
    CNSTF=CNST+F,
    CNSTI=CNST+I,
    CNSTP=CNST+P,
    CNSTS=CNST+S,
    CNSTU=CNST+U,
ARG=2<<4,
    ARGB=ARG+B,
    ARGD=ARG+D,
    ARGF=ARG+F,
```

```
ARGI=ARG+I,
ARGP=ARG+P,
```

The rest of ⟨operators⟩ defines the remaining operators. Table 5.1 lists each generic operator, its valid type suffixes, and the number of kids and syms that it uses; multiple values for kids indicate type-specific variants, which are described below. The notations in the syms column give the number of syms values and a one-letter code that suggests their uses: 1V indicates that syms[0] points to a symbol for a variable, 1C indicates that syms[0] is a constant, and 1L indicates that syms[0] is a label. For 1S, syms[0] is a constant whose value is a size in bytes; 2S adds syms[1], which is a constant whose value is an alignment. For most operators, the type suffix denotes the type of operation to perform and the type of the result. Exceptions are ADDP, in which an integer operand in kids[0] is added to a pointer operand in kids[1], and SUBP, which subtracts an integer in kids[1] from a pointer in kids[0]. The operators for assignment, comparison, arguments, and some calls return no result; their type suffixes denote the type of operation to perform.

The leaf operators yield the address of a variable or the value of a constant. syms[0] identifies the variable or constant. The unary operators accept and yield a number, except for INDIR, which accepts an address and yields the value at that address. There is no BCOMI; signed integers are complemented using BCOMU. The binary operators accept two numbers and yield one.

81 kids
81 syms

The type suffix for a conversion operator denotes the type of the result. For example, CVUI converts an unsigned (U) to a signed integer (I). Conversions between unsigned and short and between unsigned and character are unsigned conversions; those between integer and short and between integer and character are signed conversions. For example, CVSU converts an unsigned short to an unsigned, and thus clears the high-order bits. CVSI converts a signed short to a signed integer, and thus propagates the short's sign to fill the high-order bits.

The front end builds dags or otherwise composes conversions to form those not in the table. For example, it converts a short to a float by first converting it to an integer and then to a double. The 16 conversion operators are represented by arrows in Figure 5.1. Composed conversions follow the path from the source type to the destination type.

ASGN stores the value of kids[1] into the cell addressed by kids[0]. syms[0] and syms[1] point to symbol-table entries for integer constants that give the size of the value and its alignment. These are most useful for ASGNB, which assigns structures and initializes automatic arrays.

JUMPV is an unconditional jump to the address computed by kids[0]. For most jumps, kids[0] is a constant ADDRGP node, but switch statements compute a variable target, so kids[0] can be an arbitrary computation. LABEL defines the label given by syms[0], and is otherwise a no-op. For the comparisons, syms[0] points to a symbol-table entry for

syms	kids	Operator	Type Suffixes	Operation
1V	0	ADDRF	P	address of a parameter
1V	0	ADDRG	P	address of a global
1V	0	ADDRL	P	address of a local
1C	0	CNST	CSIUPFD	constant
	1	BCOM	U	bitwise complement
	1	CVC	IU	convert from char
	1	CVD	I F	convert from double
	1	CVF	D	convert from float
	1	CVI	CS U D	convert from int
	1	CVP	U	convert from pointer
	1	CVS	IU	convert from short
	1	CVU	CSI P	convert from unsigned
	1	INDIR	CSI PFDB	fetch
	1	NEG	I FD	negation
	2	ADD	IUPFD	addition
	2	BAND	U	bitwise AND
	2	BOR	U	bitwise inclusive OR
	2	BXOR	U	bitwise exclusive OR
	2	DIV	IU FD	division
	2	LSH	IU	left shift
	2	MOD	IU	modulus
	2	MUL	IU FD	multiplication
	2	RSH	IU	right shift
	2	SUB	IUPFD	subtraction
2S	2	ASGN	CSI PFDB	assignment
1L	2	EQ	I FD	jump if equal
1L	2	GE	IU FD	jump if greater than or equal
1L	2	GT	IU FD	jump if greater than
1L	2	LE	IU FD	jump if less than or equal
1L	2	LT	IU FD	jump if less than
1L	2	NE	I FD	jump if not equal
2S	1	ARG	I PFDB	argument
1	1 or 2	CALL	I FDBV	function call
	1	RET	I FD	return from function
	1	JUMP	V	unconditional jump
1L	0	LABEL	V	label definition

TABLE 5.1 Node operators.

the label to jump to if the comparison is true. Signed comparisons are used for unsigned equals and not equals, since equality tests needn't special-case the sign bit.

Function calls have a CALL node preceded by zero or more ARG nodes. The front end unnests function calls — it performs the inner call first, assigns its value to a temporary, and uses the temporary henceforth — so ARG nodes are always associated with the next CALL node in the forest. If wants_dag is one, CALL nodes always appear as roots in the forest. If wants_dag is zero, only CALLV nodes appear as roots; other CALL nodes appear as right operands to ASGN nodes, which are roots.

A CALL node's syms[0] points to a symbol whose only nonnull field is type, which is the function type of the callee.

ARG nodes establish the value computed by kids[0] as the next argument. syms[0] and syms[1] point to symbol-table entries for integer constants that give the size and alignment of the argument.

In CALL nodes, kids[0] computes the address of the callee. CALLB nodes are used for calls to functions that return structures; kids[1] computes the address of a temporary local variable to hold the returned value. The CALLB code and the function prologue must collaborate to store the CALLB's kids[1] into the callee's first local. The SPARC interface procedures function and local, and the CALLB emitter illustrate such collaboration. CALLB nodes have a count of zero because the front end references the temporary wherever the returned value is referenced. There is no RETB; the front end uses an ASGNB to the structure addressed by the first local. CALLB nodes appear only if the interface flag wants_callb is one; see Section 5.6. In RET nodes, kids[0] computes the value returned.

Character and short-integer actual arguments are always promoted to the corresponding integer type even in the presence of a prototype, because most machines must pass at least integers as arguments. Upon entry to the function, the promoted values are converted back to the type declared for the formal parameter. For example, the body of

```
f(char c) { f(c); }
```

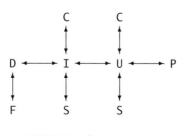

FIGURE 5.1 Conversions.

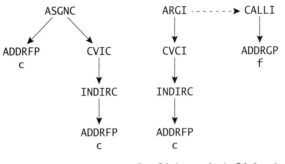

FIGURE 5.2 Forests for `f(char c) { f(c); }`

becomes the two forests shown in Figure 5.2. The solid lines are `kids` pointers and the dashed line is the `link` pointer. The left forest holds one dag, which narrows the widened actual argument to the type of the formal parameter. In the left dag, the left `ADDRFP c` refers to the formal parameter, and the one under the `INDIRC` refers to the actual argument. The right forest holds two dags. The first widens the formal parameter `c` to pass it as an integer, and the second calls `f`.

Unsigned variants of `ASGN`, `INDIR`, `ARG`, `CALL`, and `RET` were omitted as unnecessary. Signed and unsigned integers have the same size, so the corresponding signed operator is used instead. Likewise, there is no `CALLP` or `RETP`. A pointer is returned by using `CVPU` and `RETI`. A pointer-valued function is called by using `CALLI` and `CVUP`.

In Table 5.1, the operators listed at and following `ASGN` are used for their side effects. They appear as roots in the forest, and their reference counts are zero. `CALLD`, `CALLF`, and `CALLI` may also yield a value, in which case they appear as the right-hand side of an `ASGN` node and have a reference count of one. With this lone exception, all operators with side effects always appear as roots in the forest of dags, and they appear in the order in which they must be executed. The front end communicates all constraints on evaluation order by ordering the dags in the forest. If ANSI specifies that x must be evaluated before y, then x's dag will appear in the forest before y's, or they will appear in the same dag with x in the subtree rooted by y. An example is

```
int i, *p; f() { i = *p++; }
```

The code for the body of `f` generates the forest shown in Figure 5.3. The `INDIRP` fetches the value of `p`, and the `ASGNP` changes `p`'s value to the sum computed by this `INDIRP` and 4. The `ASGNI` sets `i` to the integer pointed to by the original value of `p`. Since the `INDIRP` appears in the forest *before* `p` is changed, the `INDIRI` is guaranteed to use the original value of `p`.

kids 81

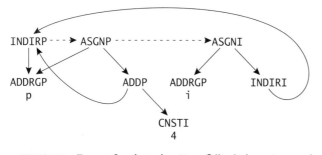

FIGURE 5.3 Forest for int i, *p; f() { i = *p++; }

5.6 Interface Flags

The interface flags help configure the front end for a target.

⟨*interface flags* 87⟩≡   87   79
```
unsigned little_endian:1;
```

should be one if the target is a little endian and zero if it's a big endian. A computer is a *little endian* if the least significant byte in each word has the smallest address of the bytes in the word. For example, little endians lay out the word with the 32-bit unsigned value 0xAABBCCDD thus:

where the addresses of the bytes increase from the right to the left.

    A computer is a *big endian* if the least significant byte in each word has the largest address of the bytes in the word. For example, big endians lay out the word with the unsigned value 0xAABBCCDD thus:

In other words, lcc's front end lays out a list of bit fields in the addressing order of the bytes in an unsigned integer: from the least significant byte to the most significant byte on little endians and vice versa on big endians. ANSI permits either order, but following increasing addresses is the prevailing convention.

⟨*interface flags* 87⟩+≡   87 88   79
```
unsigned mulops_calls:1;
```

should be zero if the hardware implements multiply, divide, and remainder. It should be one if the hardware leaves these operations to library routines. The front end unnests nested calls, so it needs to know which operators are emulated by calls. It might become necessary to generalize this feature to handle other emulated instructions, but no target so far has needed more.

⟨*interface flags* 87⟩+≡   ▲87 88   79
```
unsigned wants_callb:1;
```

tells the front end to emit CALLB nodes to invoke functions that return
structures. If wants_callb is zero, the front end generates no CALLB
nodes but implements them itself, using simpler operations: It passes
an extra, leading, hidden argument that points to a temporary; it ends
each structure function with an ASGNB dag that copies the return value
to this temporary; and it has the caller use this temporary when it needs
the structure returned. When wants_callb is one, the front end generates CALLB nodes. The kids[1] field of a CALLB computes the address
of the location at which to store the return value, and the first local of
any function that returns a structure is assumed to hold this address.
Back ends that set wants_callb to one must implement this convention
by, for example, initializing the address of the first local accordingly. If
wants_callb is zero, the back end cannot control the code for functions
that return structure arguments, so it cannot, in general, mimic an existing calling convention. In this book, the MIPS and X86 code generators
initialize wants_callb to zero; the front end's implementation of CALLB
happens to be compatible with the calling conventions for the MIPS.

⟨*interface flags* 87⟩+≡   ▲88 88   79

structarg 292

```
unsigned wants_argb:1;
```

tells the front end to emit ARGB nodes to pass structure arguments. If
wants_argb is zero, the front end generates no ARGB nodes but implements structure arguments itself using simpler operations: It builds an
ASGNB dag that copies the structure argument to a temporary; it passes a
pointer to the temporary; it adds an extra indirection to references to the
parameter in the callee; and it changes the types of the callee's formals
to reflect this convention. It also sets structarg for these parameters
to distinguish them from bona fide structure pointers. If wants_argb is
zero, the back end cannot control the code for structure arguments, so
it cannot, in general, mimic an existing calling convention. In this book,
the SPARC code generator initializes wants_argb to zero; the others initialize it to one. The front end's implementation of ARGB is compatible
with the SPARC calling convention.

⟨*interface flags* 87⟩+≡   ▲88 89   79
```
unsigned left_to_right:1;
```

tells the front end to evaluate and to present the arguments to the back
end left to right. That is, the ARG nodes that precede the CALL appear in
the same order as the arguments in the source code. If left_to_right is
zero, arguments are evaluated and presented right to left. ANSI permits
either order.

⟨*interface flags* 87⟩ +≡   ▲ 79
                                                88
    unsigned wants_dag:1;

tells the front end to pass dags to the back end. If it's zero, the front end undags all nodes with reference counts exceeding one. It creates a temporary, assigns the node to the temporary, and uses the temporary wherever the node had been used. When wants_dag is zero, all reference counts are thus zero or one, and only trees, which are degenerate dags, remain; there are no general dags. The code generators in this book generate code using a method that requires trees, so they initialize wants_dag to zero, but other code generators for lcc have generated code from dags.

5.7 Initialization

During initialization, the front end calls

⟨*interface functions* 80⟩ +≡   ▲ 89   79
                                                80 89 ▼
    void (*progbeg) ARGS((int argc, char *argv[]));

argv[0..argc-1] point to those program arguments that are not recognized by the front end, and are thus deemed target-specific. progbeg processes such options and initializes the back end.

    At the end of compilation, the front end calls

⟨*interface functions* 80⟩ +≡   ▲ 89   79
                                                89 89 ▼
    void (*progend) ARGS((void));

to give the back end an opportunity to finalize its output. On some targets, progend has nothing to do and is empty.

5.8 Definitions

Whenever the front end defines a new symbol with scope CONSTANTS, LABELS, or GLOBAL, or a static variable, it calls

⟨*interface functions* 80⟩ +≡   ▲ 90   79
                                                89 90 ▼
    void (*defsymbol) ARGS((Symbol));

to give the back end an opportunity to initialize its Xsymbol field. For example, the back end might want to use a different name for the symbol. The conventions on some targets in this book prefix an underscore to global names. The Xsymbol fields of symbols with scope PARAM are initialized by function, those with scope LOCAL+*k* by local, and those that represent address computations by address.

    A symbol is *exported* if it's defined in the module at hand and used in other modules. It's *imported* if it's used in the module at hand and defined in some other module. The front end calls

⟨*interface functions* 80⟩+≡ 　　　　　　　　　　　　　　▲89 90　79
```
void (*export) ARGS((Symbol));
void (*import) ARGS((Symbol));
```

to announce an exported or imported symbol. Only nonstatic variables and functions can be exported. The front end always calls export *before* defining the symbol, but it may call import at any time, before or after the symbol is used. Most targets require export to emit an assembler directive. Some require nothing from import; the MIPS back end, for example, has an empty import.

⟨*interface functions* 80⟩+≡ 　　　　　　　　　　　　　　▲90 90　79
```
void (*global) ARGS((Symbol));
```

emits code to define a global variable. The front end will already have called segment, described below, to direct the definition to the appropriate logical segment, and it will have set the symbol's u.seg to that segment. It will follow the call to global with any appropriate calls to the data initialization functions. global must emit the necessary alignment directives and define the label.

The front end announces local variables by calling

⟨*interface functions* 80⟩+≡ 　　　　　　　　　　　　　　▲90 90　79
```
void (*local) ARGS((Symbol));
```

It announces temporaries likewise; these have the symbol's temporary flag set. local must initialize the Xsymbol field, which holds data like the local's stack offset or register number.

The front end calls

⟨*interface functions* 80⟩+≡ 　　　　　　　　　　　　　　▲90 91　79
```
void (*address) ARGS((Symbol p, Symbol q, int n));
```

to initialize q to a symbol that represents an address of the form x+n, where x is the address represented by p and n is positive or negative. Like defsymbol, address initializes q's Xsymbol, but it does so based on the values of p's Xsymbol and n. A typical address adds p's stack offset to n for locals and parameters, and sets q's x.name to p's x.name concatenated with +n or –n for other variables. For example, if n is 40 and p points to a symbol with the source name array, and if the back end forms names by prefixing an underscore, then address will create the name _array+40, so that the addition can be done by the assembler instead of at run time. address accepts globals, parameters, and locals, and is called only after these symbols have been initialized by defsymbol, function, or local.

When the front end announces a symbol by calling one of the interface procedures above, it sets the symbol's defined flag after the call. This flag prevents the front end from announcing a symbol more than once.

lcc's front end manages four logical segments that separate code, data, and literals:

⟨*c.h exported types*⟩+≡   82 97
```
enum { CODE=1, BSS, DATA, LIT };
```

The front end emits executable code into the CODE segment, defines uninitialized variables in the BSS segment, and it defines and initializes initialized variables in the DATA segment and constants in the LIT segment. The front end calls

⟨*interface functions* 80⟩+≡   90 91   79
```
void (*segment) ARGS((int));
```

to announce a segment change. The argument is one of the segment codes above. segment maps the logical segments onto the segments provided by the target machine.

CODE and LIT can be mapped to read-only segments; BSS and DATA must be mapped to segments that can be read and written. The CODE and LIT segments can be mapped to the same segment and thus combined. Any combination of BSS, DATA, and LIT can be combined likewise. CODE would be combined with them only on single-segment targets.

5.9   Constants

The interface functions

47 Value

⟨*interface functions* 80⟩+≡   91 92   79
```
void (*defaddress) ARGS((Symbol));
void (*defconst)   ARGS((int ty, Value v));
```

initialize constants. defconst emits directives to define a cell and initialize it to a constant value. v is the value, and ty encodes its type and thus which element of the Value v to access, as shown in the following table.

ty	v *Field*	*Type*
C	v.uc	character
S	v.us	short
I	v.i	int
U	v.u	unsigned
P	v.p	any pointer type
F	v.f	float
D	v.d	double

The codes C, S, I, ... are identical to the type suffixes used for the operators. The signed fields v.sc and v.ss can be used instead of v.uc and v.us, but defconst must initialize only the specified number of bits. If ty is P, v.p holds a numeric constant of some pointer type. These originate in declarations like char *p=(char*)0xF0. defaddress initializes pointer constants that involve symbols instead of numbers.

The defconst functions in Chapters 16–18 permit cross-compilation, so they compensate for different representations and byte orders. For example, they swap the two halves of a double if compiling for a big endian on a little endian or vice versa.

In general, ANSI C compilers can't leave the encoding of floating-point constants to the assembler, because few assemblers implement C's casts. For example, the correct initialization for

```
double x = (float)0.3;
```

has zeros in the least significant bits. Typical assembler directives like

```
.double 0.3
```

can't implement casts and thus erroneously initialize x without zeros in the least significant bits, so most defconsts must initialize doubles by emitting two unsigneds.

⟨*interface functions* 80⟩+≡   91 92   79
```
    void (*defstring) ARGS((int n, char *s));
```

emits code to initialize a string of length len to the characters in s. The front end converts escape sequences like \000 into the corresponding ASCII characters. Null bytes can be embedded in s, so they can't flag its end, which is why defstring accepts not just s but also its length.

⟨*interface functions* 80⟩+≡   92 92   79
```
    void (*space) ARGS((int));
```

emits code to allocate n zero bytes.

5.10 Functions

The front end compiles functions into private data structures. It completely consumes each function before passing any part of the function to the back end. This organization permits certain optimizations. For example, only by processing complete functions can the front end identify the locals and parameters whose address is not taken; only these variables may be assigned to registers.

Three interface functions and two front-end functions collaborate to compile a function.

⟨*interface functions* 80⟩+≡   92 95   79
```
    void (*function) ARGS((Symbol, Symbol[], Symbol[], int));
    void (*emit)     ARGS((Node));
    Node (*gen)      ARGS((Node));
```

⟨*dag.c exported functions*⟩≡   311

```
extern void emitcode ARGS((void));
extern void gencode  ARGS((Symbol[], Symbol[]));
```

At the end of each function, the front end calls `function` to generate and emit code. The typical form of `function` is

⟨*typical* `function` 93⟩≡

```
void function(Symbol f, Symbol caller[], Symbol callee[],
    int ncalls) {
    ⟨initialize⟩
    gencode(caller, callee);
    ⟨emit prologue⟩
    emitcode();
    ⟨emit epilogue⟩
}
```

`gencode` is a front-end procedure that traverses the front end's private structures and passes each forest of dags to the back end's `gen`, which selects code, annotates the dag to record its selection, and returns a dag pointer. `gencode` also calls `local` to announce new locals, `blockbeg` and `blockend` to announce the beginning and end of each block, and so on. `emitcode` is a front-end procedure that traverses the private structures again and passes each of the pointers from `gen` to `emit` to emit the code.

This organization offers the back-end flexibility in generating function prologue and epilogue code. Before calling `gencode`, `function` initializes the Xsymbol fields of the function's parameters and does any other necessary per-function initializations. After calling `gencode`, the size of the procedure activation record, or *frame*, and the registers that need saving are known; this information is usually needed to emit the prologue. After calling `emitcode` to emit the code for the body of the function, `function` emits the epilogue.

The argument `f` to `function` points to the symbol for the current function, and `ncalls` is the number of calls to other functions made by the current function. `ncalls` helps on targets where *leaf* functions — those that make no calls — get special treatment.

`caller` and `callee` are arrays of pointers to symbols; a null pointer terminates each. The symbols in `caller` are the function parameters as passed by a caller; those in `callee` are the parameters as seen within the function. For many functions, the symbols in each array are the same, but they can differ in both `sclass` and `type`. For example, in

```
single(x) float x; { ... }
```

a call to `single` passes the actual argument as a double, but `x` is a float within `single`. Thus, `caller[0]->type` is `doubletype`, the front-end global that represents doubles, and `callee[0]->type` is `floattype`. And in

```
int strlen(register char *s) { ... }
```

caller[0]->sclass is AUTO and callee[0]->sclass is REGISTER. Even without register declarations, the front end assigns frequently referenced parameters to the REGISTER class, and sets callee's sclass accordingly. To avoid thwarting the programmer's intentions, this assignment is made only when there are no explicit register locals.

caller and callee are passed to gencode. If caller[i]->type differs from callee[i]->type, or the value of caller[i]->sclass differs from callee[i]->sclass, gencode generates an assignment of caller[i] to callee[i]. If the types are not equal, this assignment may include a conversion; for example, the assignment to x in single includes a truncation of a double to a float. For parameters that include register declarations, function must assign a register and initialize the x field accordingly, or change the callee's sclass to AUTO to prevent an unnecessary assignment of caller[i] to callee[i].

function could also change the value of callee[i]->sclass from AUTO to REGISTER if it wished to assign a register to that parameter. The MIPS calling convention, for example, passes some arguments in registers, so function assigns those registers to the corresponding callees in leaf functions. If, however, callee[i]->addressed is set, the address of the parameter is taken in the function body, and it must be stored in memory on most machines.

Most back ends define for each function activation an *argument-build area* to store the arguments to outgoing calls. The front end unnests calls, so the argument-build area can be used for all calls. The back end makes the area big enough to hold the largest argument list. When a function is called, the caller's argument-build area becomes the callee's actual arguments.

Calls are unnested because some targets pass some arguments in registers. If we try to generate code for a nested call like f(a,g(b)), and if arguments are evaluated and established left to right, it is hard not to generate code that loads a into the first argument register and then destroys it by loading b into the same register, because both a and b belong in the first argument register, but a belongs there later.

Some calling conventions push arguments on a stack. They can handle nested calls, so an argument-build area is not always necessary. Unnesting has the advantage that stack overflow can occur only at function entry, which is useful on targets that require explicit prologue code to detect stack overflow.

For each block, the front end first announces locals with explicit register declarations, in order of declaration, to permit programmer control of register assignment. Then it announces the rest, starting with those that it estimates to be most frequently used. It assigns REGISTER class to even these locals if their addresses are not taken and if they are estimated to be used more than twice. This announcement order and sclass override collaborate to put the most promising locals in registers even if no registers were declared.

If p's sclass is REGISTER, local may decline to allocate a register and may change sclass to AUTO. The back end has no alternative if it has already assigned all available registers to more promising locals. As with parameters, local could assign a register to a local with sclass equal to AUTO and change sclass to REGISTER, but it can do so only if the symbol's addressed is zero.

Source-language blocks bracket the lifetime of locals. gencode announces the beginning and end of a block by calling:

⟨interface functions 80⟩+≡   92   79
```
void (*blockbeg) ARGS((Env *));
void (*blockend) ARGS((Env *));
```

Env, defined in config.h, is target-specific. It typically includes the data necessary to reuse that portion of the local frame space associated with the block and to release any registers assigned to locals within the block. For example, blockbeg typically records in an Env the size of the frame and the registers that are busy at the beginning of the block, and blockend restores the register state and updates the stack if the new block has pushed deeper than the maximum depth seen so far. Chapter 13 elaborates.

The front end calls gen to select code. It passes gen a forest of dags. For example, Figure 5.3 on page 87 shows the forest for

```
int i, *p; f() { i = *p++; }
```

A postorder traversal of this forest yields the linearized representation shown in the table below.

Node #	op	count	kids	syms
1	ADDRGP	2		p
2	INDIRP	2	1	
3	CNSTI	1		4
4	ADDP	1	2, 3	
5	ASGNP	0	1, 4	
6	ADDRGP	1		i
7	INDIRI	1	2	
8	ASGNI	0	6, 7	

This forest consists of three dags, rooted at nodes 2, 5, and 8. The INDIRP node, which fetches the value of p, comes before node 5, which changes p, so the original value of p is available for subsequent use by node 7, which fetches the integer pointed to by that value.

gen traverses the forest and selects code, but it emits nothing because it may be necessary to determine, for example, the registers needed before the function prologue can be emitted. So gen merely annotates the nodes in their x fields to identify the code selected, and returns a pointer that is ultimately passed to the back end's emit to output the code. Once the front end calls gen, it does not inspect the contents of the nodes again, so gen may modify them freely.

emit emits a forest. Typically, it traverses the forest and emits code by switching on the opcode or some related value stored in the node by gen.

5.11   Interface Binding

The compiler option -target=*name* identifies the desired target. The name-interface pairs for the available targets are stored in

⟨*interface* 78⟩+≡   ▲ 79 96   16
```
typedef struct binding {
    char *name;
    Interface *ir;
} Binding;

extern Binding bindings[];
```

The front end identifies the one in the -target and stores a pointer to its interface record in

⟨*interface* 78⟩+≡   ▲ 96   16
```
extern Interface *IR;
```

Whenever the front end needs to call an interface function, or read a type metric or an interface flag, it uses IR.

Back ends must define and initialize bindings, which associates names and interface records. For example, the back ends in this book define bindings in bind.c:

⟨*bind.c* 96⟩≡
```
#include "c.h"
extern Interface nullIR,   symbolicIR;
extern Interface mipsebIR, mipselIR;
extern Interface sparcIR,  solarisIR;
extern Interface x86IR;
Binding bindings[] = {
    "symbolic",      &symbolicIR,
    "mips-irix",     &mipsebIR,
    "mips-ultrix",   &mipselIR,
    "sparc-sun",     &sparcIR,
    "sparc-solaris", &solarisIR,
    "x86-dos",       &x86IR,
```

```
    "null",           &nullIR,
    NULL,             NULL
  };
```

The MIPS, SPARC, and X86 interfaces are described in Chapters 16, 17, and 18. The interfaces null and symbolic are described in Exercises 5.2 and 5.1.

5.12 Upcalls

The front and back ends are clients of each other. The front end calls on the back end to generate and emit code. The back end calls on the front end to perform output, allocate storage, interrogate types, and manage nodes, symbols, and strings. The front-end functions that back ends may call are summarized below. Some of these functions are explained in previous chapters, but are included here to make this summary complete.

void *allocate(int n, int a) permanently allocates n bytes in the arena a, which can be one of

⟨*c.h exported types*⟩+≡   ▲91
```
  enum { PERM=0, FUNC, STMT };
```

and returns a pointer to the first byte. The space is guaranteed to be aligned to suit the machine's most demanding type. Data allocated in PERM are deallocated at the end of compilation; data allocated in FUNC and STMT are deallocated after compiling functions and statements.

⟨*input.c exported data*⟩≡   103
```
  extern char *bp;
```
                                                                    ▼

points to the next character in the output buffer. The idiom *bp++ = c thus appends c to the output as shown in outs on page 16. One of the other output functions, described below, must be called at least once every 80 characters.

⟨*output.c exported functions*⟩+≡   ▲18 98
```
  extern void fprint ARGS((int fd, char *fmt, ...));
```
                                                                    ▼

prints its third and following arguments on the file descriptor fd. See print for formatting details. If fd is not 1 (standard output), fprint calls outflush to flush the output buffer for fd.

Type freturn(Type ty) is the type of the return value for function type ty.

⟨*c.h exported macros*⟩+≡   ▲19 98
```
  #define generic(op) ((op)&~15)
```
                                                                    ▼

is the generic version of the type-specific dag operator op. That is, the expression generic(op) returns op without its type suffix.

int genlabel(int n) increments the generated-identifier counter by n and returns its old value.

int is*type*(Type ty) are type predicates that return nonzero if type ty is a type shown in the table below.

Predicate	Type
isarith	arithmetic
isarray	array
ischar	character
isdouble	double
isenum	enumeration
isfloat	floating
isfunc	function
isint	integral
isptr	pointer
isscalar	scalar
isstruct	structure or union
isunion	union
isunsigned	unsigned

Node newnode(int op, Node l, Node r, Symbol sym) allocates a dag node; initializes the op field to op, kids[0] to l, kids[1] to r, and syms[0] to sym; and returns a pointer to the new node.

Symbol newconst(Value v, int t) installs a constant with value v and type suffix t into the symbol table, if necessary, and returns a pointer to the symbol-table entry.

Symbol newtemp(int sclass, int t) creates a temporary with storage class sclass and a type with type suffix t, and returns a pointer to the symbol-table entry. The new temporary is announced by calling local.

opindex(op) is the operator number, for operator op:

⟨*c.h exported macros*⟩+≡   97 98
```
#define opindex(op) ((op)>>4)
```

opindex is used to map the generic operators into a contiguous range of integers.

⟨*c.h exported macros*⟩+≡   98
```
#define optype(op) ((op)&15)
```

is the type suffix for the dag operator op.

⟨*output.c exported functions*⟩+≡   97 99
```
extern void outflush ARGS((void));
```

writes the current output buffer to the standard output, if it's not empty.

void outs(char *s) appends string s to the output buffer for standard output, and calls outflush if the resulting buffer pointer is within 80 characters of the end of the buffer.

void print(char *fmt, ...) prints its second and following arguments on standard output. It is like printf but supports only the formats %c, %d, %o, %x, and %s, and it omits precision and field-width specifications. print supports four lcc-specific format codes. %S prints a string of a specified length; the next two arguments give the string and its length. %k prints an English rendition of the integer token code given by the corresponding argument, and %t prints an English rendition of a type. %w prints the source coordinates given by its corresponding argument, which must be a pointer to a Coordinate. print calls outflush if it prints a newline character from fmt within 80 characters of the end of the output buffer. Each format except %c does the actual output with outs, which may also flush the buffer.

int roundup(int n, int m) is n rounded up to the next multiple of m, which must be a power of two.

char *string(char *s) installs s in the string table, if necessary, and returns a pointer to the installed copy.

char *stringd(int n) returns the string representation of n; stringd installs the returned string in the string table.

⟨*output.c exported functions*⟩+≡   98
    extern char *stringf ARGS((char *, ...));

formats its arguments into a string, installs that string to the string table, and returns a pointer to the installed string. See print for formatting details.

int ttob(Type ty) is the type suffix for type ty.

int variadic(Type ty) is true if type ty denotes a variadic function.

Further Reading

Fraser and Hanson (1991a and 1992) describe the earlier versions of lcc's code generation interface. This chapter is more detailed, and corresponds to version 3.1 and above of lcc.

Some compiler interfaces emit *abstract machine code*, which resembles an assembler code for a fictitious machine (Tanenbaum, van Staveren, and Stevenson 1982). The front end emits code for the abstract machine, which the back end reads and translates to target code. Abstract machines decouple the front and back ends, and make it easy to insert extra optimization passes, but the extra I/O and structure allocation and initialization take time. lcc's tightly coupled interface yields efficient, compact compilers, but it can complicate maintenance because changes to the front end may affect the back ends. This complication is less important for standardized languages like ANSI C because there will be few changes to the language.

Exercises

5.1 lcc can be turned into a syntax and semantics checker by writing a null code generator whose interface record points to functions that do nothing. Implement this interface.

5.2 Implement a symbolic back end that generates a trace of the interface functions as they are called and a readable representation of their arguments. As an example, the output of the symbolic back end that comes with lcc for

```
int i, *p; f() { i = *p++; }
```

is

```
export f
segment text
function f type=int function(void) class=auto ...
maxoffset=0
node#2 ADDRGP count=2 p
node'1 INDIRP count=2 #2
node#5 CNSTI count=1 4
node#4 ADDP count=1 #1 #5
node'3 ASGNP count=0 #2 #4 4 4
node#7 ADDRGP count=1 i
node#8 INDIRI count=1 #1
node'6 ASGNI count=0 #7 #8 4 4
1:
end f
segment bss
export p
global p type=pointer to int class=auto ...
space 4
export i
global i type=int class=auto scope=GLOBAL ref=1000
space 4
```

emit	92
emit	393
function	92
(MIPS) "	448
(SPARC) "	484
(X86) "	518
gen	92
gen	402

All of the interface routines in this back end echo their arguments and some provide additional information. For example, function computes a frame size, which it prints as the value of maxoffset as shown above. gen and emit collaborate to print dags as shown above. gen numbers the nodes in each forest (by annotating their x fields), and emit prints these numbers for node operands. emit also identifies roots by prefixing their numbers with accents graves, as shown for nodes 1, 3, and 6 in the first forest above. For a LABELV node, emit prints a line with just the label number and a colon. Compare this output with the linearized representation shown on page 95.

5.3 Write a code generator that simply emits the names of all identifiers visible to other modules, and reports those imported names that are *not* used.

5.4 When lcc's interface was designed, 32-bit integers were the norm, so nothing was lost by having integers and longs share one metric. Now, many machines support 32-bit and 64-bit integers, and our shortcut complicates using both data types in the same code generator. How would adding two new type suffixes — L for long and O for unsigned long — change lcc's interface? Consider the effect on the type metrics, the node operators in general, and the conversion operators in particular. Redraw Figure 5.1. Which interface functions would have to change? How?

5.5 Design an abstract machine consistent with lcc's interface, and use it to separate lcc's front end from its back end. Write a code generator that emits code for your abstract machine. Adapt lcc's back end to read your abstract machine code, rebuild the data structures that the back end uses now, and call the existing back end to generate code. This exercise might take a month or so, but the flexibility to read abstract-machine code, optimize it, and write it back out would simplify experimenting with optimizers.

92	emit
393	emit
92	gen
402	gen

6
Lexical Analysis

The *lexical analyzer* reads source text and produces *tokens*, which are the basic lexical units of the language. For example, the expression *ptr = 56; contains 10 characters or five tokens: *, ptr, =, 56, and ;. For each token, the lexical analyzer returns its *token code* and zero or more *associated values*. The token codes for single-character tokens, such as operators and separators, are the characters themselves. Defined constants (with values that do not collide with the numeric values of significant characters) are used for the codes of the tokens that can consist of one or more characters, such as identifiers and constants.

For example, the statement *ptr = 56; yields the token stream shown on the left below; the associated values, if there are any, are shown on the right.

```
'*'
ID      "ptr"    symbol-table entry for "ptr"
'='
ICON    "56"     symbol-table entry for 56
```

stringn 30

The token codes for the operators * and = are the operators themselves, i.e., the numeric values of * and =, respectively, and they do not have associated values. The token code for the identifier ptr is the value of the defined constant ID, and the associated values are the saved copy of the identifier string itself, i.e., the string returned by stringn, and a symbol-table entry for the identifier, if there is one. Likewise, the integer constant 56 returns ICON, and the associated values are the string "56" and a symbol-table entry for the integer constant 56.

Keywords, such as "for," are assigned their own token codes, which distinguish them from identifiers.

The lexical analyzer also tracks the *source coordinates* for each token. These coordinates, defined in Section 3.1, give the file name, line number, and character index within the line of the first character of the token. Coordinates are used to pinpoint the location of errors and to remember where symbols are defined.

The lexical analyzer is the only part of the compiler that looks at each character of the source text. It is not unusual for lexical analysis to account for half the execution time of a compiler. Hence, speed is important. The lexical analyzer's main activity is moving characters, so minimizing the amount of character movement helps increase speed. This is done by dividing the lexical analyzer into two tightly coupled modules.

The input module, input.c, reads the input in large chunks into a buffer, and the recognition module, lex.c, examines the characters to recognize tokens.

6.1 Input

In most programming languages, input is organized in lines. Although in principle, there is rarely a limit on line length, in practice, line length is limited. In addition, tokens cannot span line boundaries in most languages, so making sure complete lines are in memory when they are being examined simplifies lexical analysis at little expense in capability. String literals are the one exception in C, but they can be handled as a special case.

The input module reads the source in large chunks, usually much larger than individual lines, and it helps arrange for complete tokens to be present in the input buffer when they are being examined, except identifiers and string literals. To minimize the overhead of accessing the input, the input module exports pointers that permit direct access to the input buffer:

⟨*input.c exported data*⟩+≡   ▲ 97 104
    extern unsigned char *cp;   ▼
    extern unsigned char *limit;

106 fillbuf
106 nextline

cp points to the current input character, so *cp is that character. limit points one character past the end of the characters in the input buffer, and *limit is always a newline character and acts as a sentinel. These pointers reference unsigned characters so that *cp, for example, won't sign-extend a character whose value is greater than 127.

The important consequence of this design is that most of the input characters are accessed by *cp, and many characters are never moved. Only identifiers (excluding keywords) and string literals that appear in executable code are copied out of the buffer into permanent storage. Function calls are required only at line boundaries, which occur infrequently when compared to the number of characters in the input. Specifically, the lexical analyzer can use *cp++ to read a character and increment cp. If *cp++ is a newline character, however, it must call nextline, which might reset cp and limit. After calling nextline, if cp is equal to limit, the end of file has been reached.

Since *limit is always a newline, and nextline must be called after reading a newline, it is rarely necessary for the lexical analyzer to check if cp is less than limit. nextline calls fillbuf when the newline is the character pointed to by limit. The lexical analyzer can also call fillbuf explicitly if, for example, it wishes to ensure that an entire token is present in the input buffer. Most tokens are short, less than 32 characters, so the lexical analyzer might call `fillbuf` whenever `limit-cp` is less than 32.

This protocol is necessary in order for `fillbuf` to properly handle lines that span input buffers. In general, each input buffer ends with a partial line. To maintain the illusion of contiguous lines, and to reduce unnecessary searching, `fillbuf` moves the `limit-cp` characters of the partial line to the memory locations *preceding* the characters in the input buffer so that they will be concatenated with the characters in the trailing portion of the line when the input buffer is refilled. An example clarifies this process: Suppose the state of the input buffer is

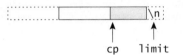

where shading depicts the characters that have yet to be consumed and \n represents the newline. If `fillbuf` is called, it slides the unconsumed tail of the input buffer down and refills the buffer. The resulting state is

where the darker shading differentiates the newly read characters from those moved by `fillbuf`. When a call to `fillbuf` reaches the end of the input, the buffer's state becomes

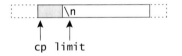

Finally, when `nextline` is called for the last sentinel at `*limit`, `fillbuf` sets `cp` equal to `limit`, which indicates end of file (after the first call to `nextline`). This final state is

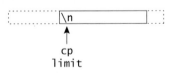

The remaining global variables exported by `input.c` are:

⟨*input.c exported data*⟩+≡   ▴
                                                                             103

```
extern int infd;
extern char *firstfile;
extern char *file;
extern char *line;
extern int lineno;
```

Input is read from the file descriptor given by infd; the default is zero,
which is the standard input. file is the name of the current input file;
line gives the location of the beginning of the current line, if it were
to fit in the buffer; and lineno is the line number of the current line.
The coordinates f, x, y of the token that begins at cp, where f is the file
name, are thus given by file, cp-line, and lineno, where characters in
the line are numbered beginning with zero. line is used only to compute
the x coordinate, which counts tabs as single characters. firstfile
gives the name of the first source file encountered in the input; it's used
in error messages.

The input buffer itself is hidden inside the input module:

⟨*input.c exported macros*⟩≡
```
#define  MAXLINE   512
#define  BUFSIZE 4096
```

⟨*input.c data*⟩≡
```
static int bsize;
static unsigned char buffer[MAXLINE+1 + BUFSIZE+1];
```

BUFSIZE is the size of the input buffer into which characters are read,
and MAXLINE is the maximum number of characters allowed in an unconsumed tail of the input buffer. fillbuf must not be called if limit-cp
is greater than MAXLINE. The standard specifies that compilers need not
handle lines that exceed 509 characters; lcc handles lines of arbitrary
length, but, except for identifiers and string literals, insists that tokens
not exceed 512 characters.

The value of bsize encodes three different input states: If bsize is less
than zero, no input has been read or a read error has occurred; if bsize
is zero, the end of input has been reached; and bsize is greater than
zero when bsize characters have just been read. This rather complicated
encoding ensures that lcc is initialized properly and that it never tries
to read past the end of the input.

inputInit initializes the input variables and fills the buffer:

⟨*input.c functions*⟩≡   106
```
void inputInit() {
    limit = cp = &buffer[MAXLINE+1];
    bsize = -1;
    lineno = 0;
    file = NULL;
    ⟨refill buffer 106⟩
    nextline();
}
```

nextline is called whenever *cp++ reads a newline. If cp is greater than
or equal to limit, the input buffer is empty.

⟨*input.c functions*⟩+≡   1̂05 106
```
void nextline() {
    do {
        if (cp >= limit) {
            ⟨refill buffer 106⟩
            if (cp == limit)
                return;
        } else
            lineno++;
        for (line = (char *)cp; *cp==' ' || *cp=='\t'; cp++)
            ;
    } while (*cp == '\n' && cp == limit);
    if (*cp == '#') {
        resynch();
        nextline();
    }
}
```

If cp is still equal to limit after filling the buffer, the end of the file has been reached. The do-while loop advances cp to the first nonwhite-space character in the line, treating sentinel newlines as white space. The last four lines of nextline check for resynchronization directives emitted by the preprocessor; see Exercise 6.2. inputInit and nextline call fillbuf to refill the input buffer:

⟨*refill buffer* 106⟩≡   105 106
```
fillbuf();
if (cp >= limit)
    cp = limit;
```

If the input is exhausted, cp will still be greater than or equal to limit when fillbuf returns, which leaves these variables set as shown in the last diagram on page 104. fillbuf does all of the buffer management and the actual input:

⟨*input.c functions*⟩+≡   1̂06
```
void fillbuf() {
    if (bsize == 0)
        return;
    if (cp >= limit)
        cp = &buffer[MAXLINE+1];
    else
        ⟨move the tail portion 107⟩
    bsize = read(infd, &buffer[MAXLINE+1], BUFSIZE);
    if (bsize < 0) {
        error("read error\n");
        exit(1);
```

```
    }
    limit = &buffer[MAXLINE+1+bsize];
    *limit = '\n';
}
```

`fillbuf` reads the `BUFSIZE` (or fewer) characters into the `buffer` beginning at position `MAXLINE+1`, resets `limit`, and stores the sentinel newline.
If the input buffer is empty when `fillbuf` is called, `cp` is reset to point
to the first new character. Otherwise, the tail `limit-cp` characters are
moved so that the last character is in `buffer[MAXLINE]`, and is thus adjacent to the newly read characters.

⟨*move the tail portion* 107⟩≡   106
```
    {
        int n = limit - cp;
        unsigned char *s = &buffer[MAXLINE+1] - n;
        line = (char *)s - ((char *)cp - line);
        while (cp < limit)
            *s++ = *cp++;
        cp = &buffer[MAXLINE+1] - n;
    }
```

Notice the computation of `line`: It accounts for the portion of the current
line that has already been consumed, so that `cp-line` gives the correct
index of the character `*cp`.

6.2 Recognizing Tokens

There are two principal techniques for recognizing tokens: building a
finite automaton or writing an ad hoc recognizer by hand. The lexical
structure of most programming languages can be described by regular
expressions, and such expressions can be used to construct a *determin-
istic finite automaton* that recognizes and returns tokens. The advantage
of this approach is that it can be automated. For example, LEX is a program that takes a lexical specification, given as regular expressions, and
generates an automaton and an appropriate interpreting program.

The lexical structure of most languages is simple enough that lexical
analyzers can be constructed easily by hand. In addition, automatically
generated analyzers, such as those produced by LEX, tend to be large
and slower than analyzers built by hand. Tools like LEX are very useful, however, for one-shot programs and for applications with complex
lexical structures.

For C, tokens fall into the six classes defined by the following EBNF
grammar:

token:
   keyword
   identifier
   constant
   string-literal
   operator
   punctuator

punctuator:
   one of [ ] ( ) { } * , : = ; ...

White space — blanks, tabs, newlines, and comments — separates some tokens, such as adjacent identifiers, but is otherwise ignored except in string literals.

The lexical analyzer exports two functions and four variables:

⟨*lex.c exported functions*⟩ ≡
```
extern int getchr ARGS((void));
extern int gettok ARGS((void));
```

⟨*lex.c exported data*⟩ ≡
```
extern int t;
extern char *token;
extern Symbol tsym;
extern Coordinate src;
```

gettok returns the next token. getchr returns, but does not consume, the next nonwhite-space character. The values returned by gettok are the characters themselves (for single-character tokens), enumeration constants (such as IF) for the keywords, and the following defined constants for the others:

ID	identifiers
FCON	floating constants
ICON	integer constants
SCON	string constants
INCR	++
DECR	--
DEREF	->
ANDAND	&&
OROR	||
LEQ	<=
EQL	==
NEQ	!=
GEQ	>=
RSHIFT	>>
LSHIFT	<<
ELLIPSIS	...
EOI	end of input

These constants are defined by

⟨*lex.c exported types*⟩≡
```
enum {
#define xx(a,b,c,d,e,f,g) a=b,
#define yy(a,b,c,d,e,f,g)
#include "token.h"
    LAST
};
```

where `token.h` is a file with 256 lines like

⟨*token.h* 109⟩≡   109 ▾
```
yy(0,         0, 0,  0,   0,    0,      0)
xx(FLOAT,     1, 0,  0,   0,    CHAR,   "float")
xx(DOUBLE,    2, 0,  0,   0,    CHAR,   "double")
xx(CHAR,      3, 0,  0,   0,    CHAR,   "char")
xx(SHORT,     4, 0,  0,   0,    CHAR,   "short")
xx(INT,       5, 0,  0,   0,    CHAR,   "int")
xx(UNSIGNED,  6, 0,  0,   0,    CHAR,   "unsigned")
xx(POINTER,   7, 0,  0,   0,    0,      0)
xx(VOID,      8, 0,  0,   0,    CHAR,   "void")
xx(STRUCT,    9, 0,  0,   0,    CHAR,   "struct")
xx(UNION,    10, 0,  0,   0,    CHAR,   "union")
xx(FUNCTION, 11, 0,  0,   0,    0,      0)
xx(ARRAY,    12, 0,  0,   0,    0,      0)
xx(ENUM,     13, 0,  0,   0,    CHAR,   "enum")
xx(LONG,     14, 0,  0,   0,    CHAR,   "long")
xx(CONST,    15, 0,  0,   0,    CHAR,   "const")
xx(VOLATILE, 16, 0,  0,   0,    CHAR,   "volatile")
```

⟨*token.h* 109⟩+≡   ▴ 109
```
yy(0,        42, 13, MUL,  multree,ID,       "*")
yy(0,        43, 12, ADD,  addtree,ID,       "+")
yy(0,        44, 1,  0,    0,      ',',      ",")
yy(0,        45, 12, SUB,  subtree,ID,       "-")
yy(0,        46, 0,  0,    0,      '.',      ".")
yy(0,        47, 13, DIV,  multree,'/',      "/")
xx(DECR,     48, 0,  SUB,  subtree,ID,       "--")
xx(DEREF,    49, 0,  0,    0,      DEREF,    "->")
xx(ANDAND,   50, 5,  AND,  andtree,ANDAND,   "&&")
xx(OROR,     51, 4,  OR,   andtree,OROR,     "||")
xx(LEQ,      52, 10, LE,   cmptree,LEQ,      "<=")
```

`token.h` uses macros to collect everything about each token or symbolic constant into one place. Each line in `token.h` gives seven values of interest for the token as arguments to either `xx` or `yy`. The token codes are given by the values in the second column. `token.h` is read to define symbols, build arrays indexed by token, and so forth, and using it guarantees that such definitions are synchronized with one another. This technique is common in assembler language programming.

Single-character tokens have yy lines and multicharacter tokens and other definitions have xx lines. The first column in xx is the enumeration identifier. The other columns give the identifier or character value, the precedence if the token is an operator (Section 8.3), the generic operator (Section 5.5), the tree-building function (Section 9.4), the token's set (Section 7.6), and the string representation.

These columns are extracted for different purposes by defining the xx and yy macros and including `token.h` *again*. The enumeration definition above illustrates this technique; it defines xx so that each expansion defines one member of the enumeration. For example, the xx line for DECR expands to

    DECR=48,

and thus defines DECR to an enumeration constant with the value 48. yy is defined to have no replacement, which effectively ignores the yy lines.

The global variable `t` is often used to hold the current token, so most calls to `gettok` use the idiom

    t = gettok();

`token`, `tsym`, and `src` hold the values associated with the current token, if there are any. `token` is the source text for the token itself, and `tsym` is a `Symbol` for some tokens, such as identifiers and constants. `src` is the source coordinate for the current token.

`gettok` could return a structure containing the token code and the associated values, or a pointer to such a structure. Since most calls to `gettok` examine only the token code, this kind of encapsulation does not add significant capability. Also, `gettok` is the most frequently called function in the compiler; a simple interface makes the code easier to read.

`gettok` recognizes a token by switching on its first character, which classifies the token, and consuming subsequent characters that make up the token. For some tokens, these characters are given by one or more of the sets defined by `map`. `map[c]` is a mask that classifies character `c` as a member of one or more of six sets:

⟨*lex.c types*⟩ ≡
```
    enum { BLANK=01,  NEWLINE=02, LETTER=04,
           DIGIT=010, HEX=020,    OTHER=040 };
```

⟨*lex.c data*⟩ ≡   117
```
    static unsigned char map[256] = { ⟨map initializer⟩ };
```

`map[c]&BLANK` is nonzero if `c` is a white-space character other than a newline. Newlines are excluded because hitting one requires `gettok` to call `nextline`. The other values identify other subsets of characters: `NEWLINE` is the set consisting of just the newline character, `LETTER` is the set of upper- and lowercase letters, `DIGIT` is the set of digits 0–9, `HEX` is the set of digits 0–9, a–f, and A–F, and `OTHER` is the set that holds the rest of the ASCII characters that are in the source and execution character sets specified by the standard. If `map[c]` is zero, `c` is not guaranteed to be acceptable to all ANSI C compilers, which, somewhat surprisingly, is the case for $, @, and '.

`gettok` is a large function, but the switch statement that dispatches on the token's first character divides it into manageable pieces:

⟨*lex.c macros*⟩≡
```
#define MAXTOKEN 32
```

⟨*lex.c functions*⟩≡   1̲1̲7̲
                                                                                        ▼
```
int gettok() {
    for (;;) {
        register unsigned char *rcp = cp;
        ⟨skip white space 112⟩
        if (limit - rcp < MAXTOKEN) {
            cp = rcp;
            fillbuf();
            rcp = cp;
        }
        src.file = file;
        src.x = (char *)rcp - line;
        src.y = lineno;
        cp = rcp + 1;
        switch (*rcp++) {
        ⟨gettok cases 112⟩
        default:
            if ((map[cp[-1]]&BLANK) == 0)
                ⟨illegal character⟩
        }
    }
}
```

110	BLANK
110	DIGIT
104	file
106	fillbuf
110	HEX
110	LETTER
103	limit
104	line
104	lineno
110	map
110	NEWLINE
106	nextline
110	OTHER

`gettok` begins by skipping over white space and then checking that there is at least one token in the input buffer. If there isn't, calling `fillbuf` ensures that there is. `MAXTOKEN` applies to all tokens except identifiers, string literals, and numeric constants; occurrences of these tokens that are longer than `MAXTOKEN` characters are handled explicitly in the code for those tokens. The standard permits compilers to limit string literals to 509 characters and identifiers to 31 characters. `lcc` increases these limits to 4,096 (BUFSIZE) and 512 (MAXLINE) to accommodate *programs* that emit C programs, because these emitted programs may contain long identifiers.

Instead of using cp as suggested in Section 6.1, gettok copies cp to the register variable rcp upon entry, and uses rcp in token recognition. gettok copies rcp back to cp before it returns, and before calls to nextline and fillbuf. Using rcp improves performance and makes scanning loops compact and fast. For example, white space is elided by

⟨*skip white space* 112⟩≡   111
```
    while (map[*rcp]&BLANK)
        rcp++;
```

Using a register variable to index map generates efficient code where it counts. These kinds of scans examine every character in the input, and they examine characters by accessing the input buffer directly. Some optimizing compilers can make similar improvements locally, but not across potentially aliased assignments and calls to other, irrelevant functions.

Each of the sections below describes one of the cases in ⟨gettok cases⟩. The cases omitted from this book are

⟨gettok *cases* 112⟩≡   112   111
```
    case '/': ⟨comment or /⟩
    case 'L': ⟨wide-character constants⟩
    ⟨cases for two-character operators⟩
    ⟨cases for one-character operators and punctuation⟩
```

gettok calls nextline when it trips over a newline or one of its synonyms:

⟨gettok *cases* 112⟩+≡   112 113   111
```
    case '\n': case '\v': case '\r': case '\f':
        nextline();
        if (⟨end of input 112⟩) {
            tsym = NULL;
            return EOI;
        }
        continue;
```

⟨*end of input* 112⟩≡   112 124
```
    cp == limit
```

When control reaches this case, cp points to the character that *follows* the newline; when nextline returns, cp still points to that character, and cp is less than limit. End of file is the exception: here, cp equals limit. Testing for this condition is rarely needed, because *cp will always be a newline, which terminates the scans for most tokens.

The sections below describe the remaining cases. Recognizing the tokens themselves is relatively straightforward; computing the associated values for some token is what complicates each case.

6.3 Recognizing Keywords

There are 28 keywords:

keyword: one of

auto	double	int	struct
break	else	long	switch
char	extern	return	union
const	float	short	unsigned
continue	for	signed	void
default	goto	sizeof	volatile
do	if	static	while

Keywords could be recognized through a look-up in a table in which each keyword entry carries its token code and each built-in type entry carries its type. Instead, keywords are recognized by a hard-coded decision tree, which is faster than searching a table and nearly as simple. The cases for the lowercase letters that begin keywords make explicit tests for the keywords, which are possible because the entire token must appear in the input buffer. For example, the case for i is

⟨gettok *cases* 112⟩+≡   112 114   111

```
case 'i':
    if (rcp[0] == 'f'
    && !(map[rcp[1]]&(DIGIT|LETTER))) {
        cp = rcp + 1;
        return IF;
    }
    if (rcp[0] == 'n'
    &&  rcp[1] == 't'
    && !(map[rcp[2]]&(DIGIT|LETTER))) {
        cp = rcp + 2;
        tsym = inttype->u.sym;
        return INT;
    }
    goto id;
```

110	DIGIT
109	INT
110	LETTER
110	map
111	rcp
108	tsym

id labels the code in the next section that scans identifiers. If the token is if or int, cp is updated and the appropriate token code is returned; otherwise, the token is an identifier. For int, tsym holds the symbol-table entry for the type int. The cases for the characters abcdefglrsuvw are similar, and were generated automatically by a short program.

The code generated for these fragments is short and fast. For example, on most machines, int is recognized by less than a dozen instructions, many fewer than are executed when a table is searched for keywords, even if perfect hashing is used.

6.4   Recognizing Identifiers

The syntax for identifiers is

> *identifier:*
>   *nondigit { nondigit | digit }*
>
> *digit:*
>   one of 0 1 2 3 4 5 6 7 8 9
>
> *nondigit:*
>   one of _
>   a b c d e f g h i j k l m
>   n o p q r s t u v w x y z
>   A B C D E F G H I J K L M
>   N O P Q R S T U V W X Y Z

The code echoes this syntax, but must also cope with the possibility of identifiers that are longer than MAXTOKEN characters and thus might be split across input buffers.

⟨gettok *cases* 112⟩+≡   113 116   111

```
case 'h': case 'j': case 'k': case 'm': case 'n': case 'o':
case 'p': case 'q': case 'x': case 'y': case 'z':
case 'A': case 'B': case 'C': case 'D': case 'E': case 'F':
case 'G': case 'H': case 'I': case 'J': case 'K':
case 'M': case 'N': case 'O': case 'P': case 'Q': case 'R':
case 'S': case 'T': case 'U': case 'V': case 'W': case 'X':
case 'Y': case 'Z': case '_':
id:
    ⟨ensure there are at least MAXLINE characters 115⟩
    token = (char *)rcp - 1;
    while (map[*rcp]&(DIGIT|LETTER))
        rcp++;
    token = stringn(token, (char *)rcp - token);
    ⟨tsym ← type named by token 115⟩
    cp = rcp;
    return ID;
```

All identifiers are saved in the string table. At the entry to this and all cases, both cp and rcp have been incremented past the first character of the token. If the input buffer holds less than MAXLINE characters, cp is backed up one character to point to the identifier's first character, fillbuf is called to replenish the input buffer, and cp and rcp are adjusted to point to the identifier's second character as before:

⟨*ensure there are at least* MAXLINE *characters* 115⟩≡   114 116 120
```
if (limit - rcp < MAXLINE) {
    cp = rcp - 1;
    fillbuf();
    rcp = ++cp;
}
```

A typedef makes an identifier a synonym for a type, and these names are installed in the identifiers table. gettok thus sets tsym to the symbol-table entry for token, if there is one:

⟨tsym ← *type named by* token 115⟩≡   114
```
tsym = lookup(token, identifiers);
```

If token names a type, tsym is set to the symbol-table entry for that type, and tsym->sclass will be equal to TYPEDEF. Otherwise, tsym is null or the identifier isn't a type name. The macro

⟨*lex.c exported macros*⟩≡
```
#define istypename(t,tsym) (kind[t] == CHAR \
    || t == ID && tsym && tsym->sclass == TYPEDEF)
```

encapsulates testing if the current token is a type name: A type name is either one of the keywords that names a type, such as int, or an identifier that is a typedef for a type. The global variables t and tsym are the only valid arguments to istypename.

109	CHAR
106	fillbuf
111	gettok
41	identifiers
143	kind
103	limit
45	lookup
105	MAXLINE
111	rcp
108	token
108	tsym

6.5 Recognizing Numbers

There are four kinds of numeric constants in ANSI C:

> *constant:*
>> *floating-constant*
>> *integer-constant*
>> *enumeration-constant*
>> *character-constant*
>
> *enumeration-constant:*
>> *identifier*

The code for identifiers shown in the previous section handles enumeration constants, and the code in Section 6.6 handles character constants. The lexical analyzer returns the token code ID and sets tsym to the symbol-table entry for the enumeration constant. The caller checks for an enumeration constant and uses the appropriate integer in its place; the code in Section 8.8 is an instance of this convention.

There are three kinds of integer constants:

> *integer-constant:*
> > *decimal-constant* [*integer-suffix*]
> > *octal-constant* [*integer-suffix*]
> > *hexadecimal-constant* [*integer-suffix*]
>
> *integer-suffix:*
> > *unsigned-suffix* [*long-suffix*]
> > *long-suffix* [*unsigned-suffix*]
>
> *unsigned-suffix:* u | U
>
> *long-suffix:* 1 | L

The first few characters of the integer constant help identify its kind.

⟨gettok *cases* 112⟩+≡   114 119   111

```
case '0': case '1': case '2': case '3': case '4':
case '5': case '6': case '7': case '8': case '9': {
    unsigned int n = 0;
    ⟨ensure there are at least MAXLINE characters 115⟩
    token = (char *)rcp - 1;
    if (*token == '0' && (*rcp == 'x' || *rcp == 'X')) {
        ⟨hexadecimal constant⟩
    } else if (*token == '0') {
        ⟨octal constant⟩
    } else {
        ⟨decimal constant 117⟩
    }
    return ICON;
}
```

MAXLINE 105
rcp 111
token 108

As for identifiers, this case begins by insuring that the input buffer holds at least MAXLINE characters, which permits the code to look ahead, as the test for hexadecimal constants illustrates.

The fragments for the three kinds of integer constant set n to the value of the constant. They must not only recognize the constant, but also ensure that the constant is within the range of representable integers.

Recognizing decimal constants illustrates this processing. The syntax for decimal constants is:

> *decimal-constant:*
> > *nonzero-digit* { *digit* }
>
> *nonzero-digit:*
> > one of 1 2 3 4 5 6 7 8 9

The code accumulates the decimal value in n by repeated multiplications:

⟨*decimal constant* 117⟩≡   116
```
    int overflow = 0;
    for (n = *token - '0'; map[*rcp]&DIGIT; ) {
        int d = *rcp++ - '0';
        if (n > ((unsigned)UINT_MAX - d)/10)
            overflow = 1;
        else
            n = 10*n + d;
    }
    ⟨check for floating constant 117⟩
    cp = rcp;
    tsym = icon(n, overflow, 10);
```

At each step, overflow will occur if $10*n+d >$ UINT_MAX, where UINT_MAX is the value of the largest representable unsigned number. Rearranging this equation gives the test shown above, which looks before it leaps into computing the new value of n. overflow is set to one if the constant overflows. icon handles the optional suffixes.

A decimal constant is the prefix of a floating constant if the next character is a period or an exponent indicator:

⟨*check for floating constant* 117⟩≡   117
```
    if (*rcp == '.' || *rcp == 'e' || *rcp == 'E') {
        cp = rcp;
        tsym = fcon();
        return FCON;
    }
```

110	DIGIT
120	fcon
111	gettok
110	map
111	rcp
37	symbol
108	token
108	tsym
57	unsignedlong

fcon is similar to icon; it recognizes the suffix of a floating constant. overflow will be one when a floating constant has a whole part that exceeds UINT_MAX, but neither n nor overflow is passed to fcon, which reexamines token to check for *floating* overflow.

icon recognizes the optional U and L suffixes (in either case), warns about values that overflow, initializes a symbol to the appropriate type and value, and returns a pointer to the symbol

⟨*lex.c data*⟩+≡   110
```
    static struct symbol tval;
```

tval serves only to provide the type and value of a constant to gettok's caller. The caller must lift the relevant data before the next call to gettok.

⟨*lex.c functions*⟩+≡   111 119
```
    static Symbol icon(n, overflow, base)
    unsigned n; int overflow, base; {
        if ((*cp=='u'||*cp=='U') && (cp[1]=='l'||cp[1]=='L')
        ||  (*cp=='l'||*cp=='L') && (cp[1]=='u'||cp[1]=='U')) {
            tval.type = unsignedlong;
```

```
            cp += 2;
        } else if (*cp == 'u' || *cp == 'U') {
            tval.type = unsignedtype;
            cp += 1;
        } else if (*cp == 'l' || *cp == 'L') {
            if (n > (unsigned)LONG_MAX)
                tval.type = unsignedlong;
            else
                tval.type = longtype;
            cp += 1;
        } else if (base == 10 && n > (unsigned)LONG_MAX)
            tval.type = unsignedlong;
        else if (n > (unsigned)INT_MAX)
            tval.type = unsignedtype;
        else
            tval.type = inttype;
        if (overflow) {
            warning("overflow in constant '%S'\n", token,
                (char*)cp - token);
            n = LONG_MAX;
        }
        ⟨set tval's value 118⟩
        ppnumber("integer");
        return &tval;
    }
```

If both U and L appear, n is an unsigned long, and if only U appears, n is an unsigned. If only L appears, n is a long unless it's too big, in which case it's an unsigned long. n is also an unsigned long if it's an unsuffixed decimal constant and it's too big to be a long. Unsuffixed octal and hexadecimal constants are ints unless they're too big, in which case they're unsigneds. The format code %S prints a string like printf's %s, but consumes an additional argument that specifies the length of the string. It can thus print strings that aren't terminated by a null character.

The types int, long, and unsigned are different types, but lcc insists that they all have the same size. This constraint simplifies the tests shown above and the code that sets tval's value:

⟨*set* tval*'s value* 118⟩≡   118
```
    if (isunsigned(tval.type))
        tval.u.c.v.u = n;
    else
        tval.u.c.v.i = n;
```

Relaxing this constraint would complicate this code and the tests above. For example, the standard specifies that the type of an unsuffixed decimal constant is int, long, or unsigned long, depending on its value. In lcc, ints and longs can accommodate the same range of integers, so an unsuffixed decimal constant is either int or unsigned.

A numeric constant is formed from a *preprocessing number*, which is the numeric constant recognized by the C preprocessor. Unfortunately, the standard specifies preprocessing numbers that are a superset of the integer and floating constants; that is, a valid preprocessing number may *not* be a valid numeric constant. 123.4.5 is an example. The preprocessor deals with such numbers too, but it may pass them on to the compiler, which must treat them as single tokens and thus must catch preprocessing numbers that aren't valid constants.

The syntax of a preprocessing number is

>*pp-number:*
>   [.] *digit* { *digit* | . | *nondigit* | E *sign* | e *sign* }
>
>*sign:* - | +

Valid numeric constants are prefixes of preprocessing numbers, so the processing in icon and fcon might conclude successfully without consuming the complete preprocessing number, which is an error. ppnumber is called from icon, and fcon and checks for this case.

⟨*lex.c functions*⟩+≡   117 120 ▼

```
static void ppnumber(which) char *which; {
    unsigned char *rcp = cp--;

    for ( ; (map[*cp]&(DIGIT|LETTER)) || *cp == '.'; cp++)
        if ((cp[0] == 'E' || cp[0] == 'e')
        &&  (cp[1] == '-' || cp[1] == '+'))
            cp++;
    if (cp > rcp)
        error("'%S' is a preprocessing number but an _
            invalid %s constant\n", token,
            (char*)cp-token, which);
}
```

ppnumber backs up one character and skips over the characters that may comprise a preprocessing number; if it scans past the end of the numeric token, there's an error.

fcon recognizes the suffix of floating constants and is called in two places. One of the calls is shown above in ⟨*check for floating constant*⟩. The other call is from the gettok case for '.':

⟨gettok *cases* 112⟩+≡   116 122 ▼   111

```
case '.':
    if (rcp[0] == '.' && rcp[1] == '.') {
        cp += 2;
        return ELLIPSIS;
```

```
    }
    if ((map[*rcp]&DIGIT) == 0)
        return '.';
    ⟨ensure there are at least MAXLINE characters 115⟩
    cp = rcp - 1;
    token = (char *)cp;
    tsym = fcon();
    return FCON;
```

The syntax for floating constants is

> *floating-constant:*
>   *fractional-constant* [*exponent-part*] [*floating-suffix*]
>   *digit-sequence exponent-part* [*floating-suffix*]
>
> *fractional-constant:*
>   [*digit-sequence*] . *digit-sequence*
>   *digit-sequence* .
>
> *exponent-part:*
>   e [*sign*] *digit-sequence*
>   E [*sign*] *digit-sequence*
>
> *digit-sequence:*
>   *digit* { *digit* }
>
> *floating-suffix:*
>   one of f l F L

fcon recognizes a *floating-constant*, converts the token to a double value, and determines tval's type and value:

⟨*lex.c functions*⟩+≡   119

```
    static Symbol fcon() {
        ⟨scan past a floating constant 121⟩
        errno = 0;
        tval.u.c.v.d = strtod(token, NULL);
        if (errno == ERANGE)
            ⟨warn about overflow 120⟩
        ⟨set tval's type and value 121⟩
        ppnumber("floating");
        return &tval;
    }
```

⟨*warn about overflow* 120⟩≡   120 121

```
    warning("overflow in floating constant '%S'\n", token,
        (char*)cp - token);
```

strtod is a C library function that interprets its first string argument as a floating constant and returns the corresponding double value. If the constant is out of range, strtod sets the global variable errno to ERANGE as stipulated by the ANSI C specification for the C library.

A floating constant follows the syntax shown above, and is recognized by:

⟨*scan past a floating constant* 121⟩≡   120
```
    if (*cp == '.')
        ⟨scan past a run of digits 121⟩
    if (*cp == 'e' || *cp == 'E') {
        if (*++cp == '-' || *cp == '+')
            cp++;
        if (map[*cp]&DIGIT)
            ⟨scan past a run of digits 121⟩
        else
            error("invalid floating constant '%S'\n", token,
                (char*)cp - token);
    }
```

⟨*scan past a run of digits* 121⟩≡   121
```
    do
        cp++;
    while (map[*cp]&DIGIT);
```

As dictated by the syntax, an exponent indicator must be followed by at least one digit.

A floating constant may have an F or L suffix (but not both); these specify the types float and long double, respectively.

⟨*set* tval*'s type and value* 121⟩≡   120
```
    if (*cp == 'f' || *cp == 'F') {
        ++cp;
        if (tval.u.c.v.d > FLT_MAX)
            ⟨warn about overflow 120⟩
        tval.type = floattype;
        tval.u.c.v.f = tval.u.c.v.d;
    } else if (*cp == 'l' || *cp == 'L') {
        cp++;
        tval.type = longdouble;
    } else
        tval.type = doubletype;
```

110	DIGIT
57	doubletype
57	floattype
57	longdouble
110	map
108	token
117	tval

6.6 Recognizing Character Constants and Strings

Recognizing character constants and string literals is complicated by escape sequences like \n, \034, \xFF, and \", and by wide-character constants. lcc implements so-called wide characters as normal ASCII characters, and thus uses unsigned char for the type wchar_t. The syntax is

> *character-constant:*
>   [L] '*c-char* { *c-char* }'
>
> *c-char:*
>   any character except ', \, or newline
>   *escape-sequence*
>
> *escape-sequence:*
>   one of \' \" \? \\ \a \b \f \n \r \t \v
>   \ *octal-digit* [*octal-digit* [*octal-digit*]]
>   \x *hexadecimal-digit* { *hexadecimal-digit* }
>
> *string-literal:*
>   [L] "{ *s-char* }"
>
> *s-char:*
>   any character except ", \, or newline
>   *escape-sequence*

String literals can span more than one line if a backslash immediately precedes the newline. Adjacent string literals are automatically concatenated together to form a single literal. In a proper ANSI C implementation, this line splicing and string literal concatenation is done by the preprocessor, and the compiler sees only single, uninterrupted string literals. lcc implements line splicing and concatenation for string literals anyway, so that it can be used with pre-ANSI preprocessors.

Implementing these features means that string literals can be longer than MAXLINE characters, so ⟨*ensure there are at least* MAXLINE *characters*⟩ cannot be used to ensure that a sequence of adjacent entire string literals appears in the input buffer. Instead, the code must detect the newline at limit and call nextline explicitly, and it must copy the literal into a private buffer.

⟨gettok *cases* 112⟩+≡   ▲
119   111

```
  scon:
  case '\'': case '"': {
    static char cbuf[BUFSIZE+1];
    char *s = cbuf;
    int nbad = 0;
    *s++ = *--cp;
    do {
      cp++;
      ⟨scan one string literal 123⟩
      if (*cp == cbuf[0])
        cp++;
      else
```

```
            error("missing %c\n", cbuf[0]);
        } while (cbuf[0] == '"' && getchr() == '"');
        *s++ = 0;
        if (s >= &cbuf[sizeof cbuf])
            error("%s literal too long\n",
                cbuf[0] == '"' ? "string" : "character");
        ⟨warn about non-ANSI literals⟩
        ⟨set tval and return ICON or SCON 123⟩
}
```

The outer do-while loop gathers up adjacent string literals, which are
identified by their leading double quote character, into cbuf, and reports
those that are too long. The leading character also determines the type
of the associated value and gettok's return value:

⟨*set* tval *and return* ICON *or* SCON 123⟩≡   123
```
    token = cbuf;
    tsym = &tval;
    if (cbuf[0] == '"') {
        tval.type = array(chartype, s - cbuf - 1, 0);
        tval.u.c.v.p = cbuf + 1;
        return SCON;
    } else {
        if (s - cbuf > 3)
            warning("excess characters in multibyte character _
                literal '%S' ignored\n", token, (char*)cp-token);
        else if (s - cbuf <= 2)
            error("missing '\n'");
        tval.type = inttype;
        tval.u.c.v.i = cbuf[1];
        return ICON;
    }
```

String literals can contain null characters as the result of the escape sequence \0, so the length of the literal is given by its type: An n-character
literal has the type (ARRAY n (CHAR)) (n does not include the double
quotes). gettok's callers, such as primary, call stringn when they want
to save the string literal referenced by tval.

The code below, which scans a string literal or character constant,
copes with four situations: newlines at limit, escape sequences, non-
ANSI characters, and literals that exceed the size of cbuf.

⟨*scan one string literal* 123⟩≡   122
```
    while (*cp != cbuf[0]) {
        int c;
        if (map[*cp]&NEWLINE) {
            if (cp < limit)
```

```
            break;
        cp++;
        nextline();
        if (⟨end of input 112⟩)
            break;
        continue;
    }
    c = *cp++;
    if (c == '\\') {
        if (map[*cp]&NEWLINE) {
            if (cp < limit)
                break;
            cp++;
            nextline();
        }
        if (limit - cp < MAXTOKEN)
            fillbuf();
        c = backslash(cbuf[0]);
    } else if (map[c] == 0)
        nbad++;
    if (s < &cbuf[sizeof cbuf] - 2)
        *s++ = c;
}
```

If *limit is a newline, it serves only to terminate the buffer, and is thus ignored unless there's no more input. Other newlines (those for which cp is less than limit) and the one at the end of file terminate the while loop without advancing cp. backslash interprets the escape sequences described above; see Exercise 6.10. nbad counts the number of non-ANSI characters that appear in the literal; lcc's -A -A option causes warnings about literals that contain such characters or that are longer than ANSI's 509-character guarantee.

Further Reading

The input module is based on the design described by Waite (1986). The difference is that Waite's algorithm moves one partial line instead of potentially several partial lines or tokens, and does so after scanning the *first* newline in the buffer. But this operation overwrites storage before the buffer when a partial line is longer than a fixed maximum. The algorithm above avoids this problem, but at the per-token cost of comparing limit-cp with MAXTOKEN.

Lexical analyzers can be generated from a regular-expression specification of the lexical structure of the language. LEX (Lesk 1975), which is available on UNIX, is perhaps the best known example. Schreiner and

Friedman (1985) use LEX in their sample compilers, and Holub (1990) details an implementation of a similar tool. More recent generators, such as `flex`, `re2c` (Bumbulis and Cowan 1993), and ELI's scanner generator (Gray et al. 1992; Heuring 1986), produce lexical analyzers that are much faster and smaller than those produced by LEX. On some computers, ELI and `re2c` produce lexical analyzers that are faster than `lcc`'s. ELI originated some of the techniques used in `lcc`'s `gettok`.

A "perfect" hash function is one that maps each word from a known set into a different hash number (Cichelli 1980; Jaeschke and Osterburg 1980; Sager 1985). Some compilers use perfect hashing for keywords, but the hashing itself usually takes more instructions than `lcc` uses to recognize keywords.

`lcc` relies on the library function `strtod` to convert the string representation of a floating constant to its corresponding double value. Doing this conversion as accurately as possible is complicated; Clinger (1990) shows that it may require arithmetic of arbitrary precision in some cases. Many implementations of `strtod` are based on Clinger's algorithm. The opposite problem — converting a double to its string representation — is just as laborious. Steele and White (1990) give the gory details.

Exercises

6.1 What happens if a line longer than BUFSIZE characters appears in the input? Are zero-length lines handled properly?

6.2 The C preprocessor emits lines of the form

```
#  n "file"
#line n "file"
#line n
```

These lines are used to reset the current line number and file name to *n* and *file*, respectively, so that error messages refer to the correct file. In the third form, the current file name remains unchanged. `resynch`, called by `nextline`, recognizes these lines and resets `file` and `lineno` accordingly. Implement `resynch`.

6.3 In many implementations of C, the preprocessor runs as a separate program with its output passed along as the input to the compiler. Implement the preprocessor as an integral part of `input.c`, and measure the resulting improvement. Be warned: Writing a preprocessor is a big job with many pitfalls. The only definitive specification for the preprocessor is the ANSI standard.

6.4 Implement the fragments omitted from `gettok`.

6.5 What happens when `lcc` reads an identifier longer than `MAXLINE` characters?

6.6 Implement `int getchr(void)`.

6.7 Try perfect hashing for the keywords. Does it beat the current implementation?

6.8 The syntax for octal constants is

> *octal-constant:*
>   0 { *octal-digit* }
>
> *octal-digit:*
>   one of 0 1 2 3 4 5 6 7

Write ⟨*octal constant*⟩. Be careful; an octal constant is a valid prefix of a floating constant, and octal constants can overflow.

6.9 The syntax for hexadecimal constants is

> *hexadecimal-constant:*
>   (0x | 0X) *hexadecimal-digit* { *hexadecimal-digit* }
>
> *hexadecimal-digit:*
>   one of 0 1 2 3 4 5 6 7 a b c d e f A B C D E F

Write ⟨*hexadecimal constant*⟩. Don't forget to handle overflow.

6.10 Implement

⟨*lex.c prototypes*⟩≡
```
static int backslash ARGS((int q));
```

which interprets a single escape sequence beginning at `cp`. `q` is either a single or double quote, and thus distinguishes between character constants and string literals.

6.11 Implement the code for ⟨*wide-character constants*⟩. Remember that `wchar_t` is unsigned char, so the value of the constant `L'\377'` is 255, not −1.

6.12 Reimplement the lexical analyzer using LEX or an equivalent program generator, and compare the two implementations. Which is faster? Smaller? Which is easier to understand? Modify?

6.13 How many instructions is ⟨*skip white space*⟩ on your machine? How many would it be if it used `cp` instead of `rcp`?

6.14 Write a program to generate the ⟨`gettok` *cases*⟩ for the C keywords.

6.15 `lcc` assumes that int and long (signed and unsigned) have the same size. Revise `icon` to remove this regrettable assumption.

7
Parsing

The lexical analyzer described in Chapter 6 provides a stream of tokens to the parser. The parser confirms that the input conforms to the syntax of the language, and builds an internal representation of the input source program. Subsequent phases of 1cc traverse this representation to generate code for a specific target machine.

1cc uses a *recursive-descent* parser. It's a straightforward application of classical parsing techniques for constructing parsers by hand. This approach produces a small and efficient compiler, and is suitable for languages as simple as C or Pascal. Indeed, many commercial compilers are constructed using these techniques.

For more complex languages, however, techniques that use parser generators might be preferable. For example, C is in the class of languages that can be recognized by recursive-descent parsers, but other languages, like ADA, are not. For those languages, more powerful parsers, such as bottom-up parsers, must be used. Construction of these kinds of parsers by hand is too difficult; automatic methods must be used.

The remainder of this chapter lays the groundwork in formal language theory, syntax-directed translation, and error handling that the code in subsequent chapters implements.

7.1 Languages and Grammars

EBNF grammars, like those shown in the previous chapters, are used to define languages. Most languages of any interest, such as programming languages, are infinite. Grammars are a way to define infinite sets with finite specifications.

Productions give the rules for producing the sentences in a language by repeatedly replacing a nonterminal with the right-hand side of one of its productions. For example, the EBNF grammar

> *expr:*
>   *expr + expr*
>   `ID`

defines a language of simple expressions. The nonterminal *expr* is the *start* nonterminal. Sentences in this language are derived by starting with *expr* and replacing a nonterminal by the right-hand side of one of the rules for the selected nonterminal. In this example, there are only two rules, so one possible replacement is

$$expr \implies expr + expr$$

This operation is a *derivation step*, and a sequence of such steps that ends in a sentence is a *derivation*. At each step, one nonterminal is replaced by one of its right-hand sides. For example, the sentence ID+ID+ID can be obtained by the following derivation.

$$
\begin{aligned}
expr &\implies expr + expr \\
&\implies expr + \text{ID} \\
&\implies expr + expr + \text{ID} \\
&\implies \text{ID} + expr + \text{ID} \\
&\implies \text{ID} + \text{ID} + \text{ID}
\end{aligned}
$$

In the first step, the production

$$expr:\ expr + expr$$

is applied to replace *expr* by the right-hand side of this rule. In the second step, the rule *expr:* ID is applied to the rightmost occurrence of *expr*. The next three steps apply these rules to arrive at the sentence ID+ID+ID. Each of the steps in a derivation yields a *sentential form*, which is a string of terminals and nonterminals. Sentential forms differ from sentences in that they can include both terminals and nonterminals; sentences contain just terminals.

At each step in a derivation, any of the nonterminals in the sentential form can be replaced by the right-hand side of one of its rules. If, at each step, the leftmost nonterminal is replaced, the derivation is a *leftmost derivation*. For example,

$$
\begin{aligned}
expr &\implies expr + expr \\
&\implies \text{ID} + expr \\
&\implies \text{ID} + expr + expr \\
&\implies \text{ID} + \text{ID} + expr \\
&\implies \text{ID} + \text{ID} + \text{ID}
\end{aligned}
$$

is a leftmost derivation for the sentence ID+ID+ID. Parsers reconstruct a derivation for a given sentence, i.e., the input C program. lcc's parser is a *top-down parser* that reconstructs the leftmost derivation of its input.

7.2 Ambiguity and Parse Trees

Consider the language defined by the following grammar.

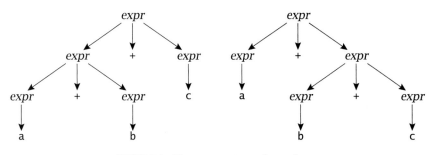

FIGURE 7.1   Two parse trees for a+b+c.

expr:
    expr + expr
    *expr * expr*
    ID

Assuming a, b, and c are identifiers, a+b, a+b+c, and a+b*c are sentences in this language.

A derivation can be written as described above or shown pictorially by a *parse tree.* For example, a leftmost derivation for a+b+c is

$$
\begin{aligned}
expr &\implies expr + expr \\
&\implies expr + expr + expr \\
&\implies a + expr + expr \\
&\implies a + b + expr \\
&\implies a + b + c
\end{aligned}
$$

and the corresponding parse tree is the one on the left in Figure 7.1. A parse tree is a tree with its nodes labelled with nonterminals and its leaves labelled with terminals; the root of the tree is labelled with the start symbol. If a node is labelled with nonterminal A and its immediate offspring are labelled, left to right, with $X_1, X_2, \ldots, X_n$, then $A: X_1 X_2 \ldots X_n$ is a production.

If a sentence has more than one parse tree, which is equivalent to having more than one leftmost derivation, the language is *ambiguous.* For example, a+b+c has another leftmost derivation in addition to the one shown above, and the resulting parse tree is the one shown on the right in Figure 7.1.

The problem in this example is that the normal left-associativity of + is not captured by the grammar. The correct interpretation, which corresponds to (a+b)+c, is given by the derivation above, and is shown in Figure 7.1's left tree.

This problem can be solved by rewriting the grammar to use EBNF's repetition construct so that a+b+c has only one derivation, which can be interpreted as (a+b)+c:

expr:
   expr { + *expr* }
   expr { * *expr* }
   ID

With this change, there is only one leftmost derivation for a+b+c, but understanding that derivation requires understanding how to apply EBNF productions involving repetitions. A production of the form

A: β { α }

says that *A* derives β followed by zero or more occurrences of α. This language is also specified by the grammar

A: β X

X: ϵ | αX

X derives the empty string, denoted by ϵ, or α followed by *X*. One application of *A*'s production followed by repeated applications of *X*'s productions thus derives β followed by zero or more occurrences of α. EBNF's repetition construct is an abbreviation for a hidden nonterminal like *X*, but these nonterminals must be included in parse trees. It's easiest to do so by rewriting the grammar to include them. Adding them to the expression grammar yields

expr:
   expr X
   expr Y
   ID

X: ϵ | + expr X

*Y: ϵ | * expr Y*

With this change, there's only one leftmost derivation for a+b+c:

$$
\begin{aligned}
expr &\Rightarrow & expr\ X \\
&\Rightarrow & a\ X \\
&\Rightarrow & a + expr\ X \\
&\Rightarrow & a + b\ X \\
&\Rightarrow & a + b + expr\ X \\
&\Rightarrow & a + b + c\ X \\
&\Rightarrow & a + b + c\ \epsilon
\end{aligned}
$$

The parser can interpret this derivation as is appropriate for the operators involved; here, it would choose the left-associative interpretation, but it could also choose the other interpretation for right-associative operators.

The operator * has the same problem, which can be fixed in a way similar to that suggested above. In addition, * typically has a higher precedence than +, so the grammar should help arrive at the correct interpretation for sentences like a+b*c. For example, the revised grammar given above does not work; the derivation for a+b*c is

$$
\begin{aligned}
expr &\implies expr\ X \\
&\implies a\ X \\
&\implies a + expr\ Y \\
&\implies a + b\ Y \\
&\implies a + b * expr\ Y \\
&\implies a + b * c\ Y \\
&\implies a + b * c\ \epsilon
\end{aligned}
$$

The fourth derivation step can cause the expression to be interpreted as (a+b)*c instead of a+(b*c).

The higher precedence of * can be accommodated by introducing a separate nonterminal that derives sentences involving *, and arranging for occurrences of this nonterminal to appear as the operands to +:

expr: term X

term: ID Y

X: ε | + term X

Y: ε | * ID Y

With this grammar, the only leftmost derivation for a+b*c is

$$
\begin{aligned}
expr &\implies term\ X \\
&\implies a\ Y\ X \\
&\implies a\ \epsilon\ X \\
&\implies a\ \epsilon + term\ X \\
&\implies a\ \epsilon + b\ Y\ X \\
&\implies a\ \epsilon + b * c\ Y\ X \\
&\implies a\ \epsilon + b * c\ \epsilon\ X \\
&\implies a\ \epsilon + b * c\ \epsilon\ \epsilon
\end{aligned}
$$

term derives a sentential form that includes b*c, which can be interpreted as the right-hand operand of the sum. As detailed in Chapter 8, this approach can be generalized to handle an arbitrary number of precedence levels and both right- and left-associative operators.

The grammar manipulations described above are usually omitted, and the appropriate EBNF grammar is written directly. For example, the expression grammar shown in Section 1.6 completes the expression grammar shown here.

Other ambiguities can be handled by rewriting the grammar, but it's often easier to resolve them in an ad hoc fashion by simply choosing one of the possible interpretations and writing the code to treat other interpretations as errors. An example is the dangling-else ambiguity in the if statement:

stmt:
    if (*expr*) *stmt*
    if (*expr*) *stmt* else *stmt*

Nested if statements have two derivations: one in which the else part is associated with the outermost if, and one in which the else is associated with the innermost if, which is the usual interpretation. As shown in Chapter 10, this ambiguity is handled by parsing the else part as soon as it's seen, which has the effect of choosing the latter interpretation.

7.3   Top-Down Parsing

Grammars define the rules for generating the sentences in a language. These rules can also be used to recognize sentences. As suggested above, a parser is a program that recognizes a sentence in a given language by reconstructing the derivation for the sentence. During the recognition process, the parser reconstructs the parse tree for the sentence, which is equivalent to recognizing the derivation. In practice, most parsers do not construct an explicit tree. Instead, they construct an equivalent internal representation or simply perform some *semantic processing* at the points at which a node would have otherwise been created.

    All practical parsers read their input from left to right, but different kinds of parsers construct parse trees differently. Top-down parsers reconstruct a leftmost derivation for a sentence by beginning with the start nonterminal and guessing at the next derivation step. The next token in the input is used to help select the production to apply as the next derivation step. For example, the grammar

    S: c *A* d

    A: a b
          a

defines the language {cabd, cad}. Suppose a parser for this language is presented with the input cad. The c suggests the application of the (one and only) production for *S*, and the initial step in the derivation is

    $S \implies$ c *A* d

and, since the token c matches the first symbol in the selected production, the input is advanced by one token. For the next step, the parser must choose and apply a production for *A*. The next input token is a, so the first production for *A* is a plausible choice, and the derivation becomes

    $S \implies$ c *A* d
       $\implies$ c a b d

Again, the input is advanced since the input a matches the a in the production for *A*. At this point, the parser is stuck because the next input token, d, does not match the next symbol in the current derivation step, b. The problem is that the wrong production for *A* was chosen. The parser backs up to the previous step, backing up the input that was consumed in the erroneous step, and applies the other production for *A*:

$$S \implies c\,A\,d$$
$$ \implies c\ a\ d$$

The input, which was backed up to the a, matches the remainder of the symbols in the derivation step, and the parser announces success.

As illustrated by this simple example, a top-down parser uses the next input token to select an applicable production, and consumes input tokens as long as they match terminals in the derivation step. When a nonterminal is encountered in the right-hand side of a derivation, the next derivation step is made. This example also illustrates a pitfall of top-down parsing: applying the wrong production and having to backtrack to a previous step. For even a moderately complicated language, such backtracking could cause many steps to be reversed. More important, most of the side effects that can occur in derivation steps are difficult and costly to undo. Backing up the input an arbitrary distance and undoing symbol-table insertions are examples. Also, such backtracking can make recognition very slow; in the worst case, the running time can be exponential in the number of tokens in the input.

Top-down parsing techniques are practical only in cases where backtracking can be avoided completely. This constraint restricts top-down parsers to languages in which the appropriate production for the next derivation step can be chosen correctly by looking at just the next token in the input. Fortunately, many programming languages, including C, satisfy this constraint.

A common technique for implementing top-down parsers is to write a *parsing function* for each nonterminal in the grammar, and to call that function when a production for the nonterminal is to be applied. Naturally, parsing functions must be recursive, since they might be applied recursively. That is, there might be a derivation of the form

$$A \implies \ldots \implies \alpha A \beta \implies \ldots$$

where α and β are strings of grammar symbols. Top-down parsers written using this strategy are called *recursive-descent* parsers because they emulate a descent of the parse tree by calling recursive functions at each node.

The derivation is not constructed explicitly. The call stack that handles the calls to recursive functions records the state of the derivation implicitly. For each nonterminal, the corresponding function encodes the right-hand side of each production as a sequence of comparisons and calls. Terminals appearing in a production become comparisons of the token expected with the current input token, and nonterminals in the production become calls to the corresponding functions. For example, assuming that gettok returns the appropriate tokens for the language above, the function for the production *S:* c *A* d is

```
int S(void) {
    if (t == 'c') {
        t = gettok();
        if (A() == 0)
            return 1;
        if (t == 'd') {
            t = gettok();
            return 1;
        } else
            return 0;
    } else
        return 0;
}
```

A and *S* return one if they recognize sentences derivable from *A* and *S*, and they return zero otherwise. Parsing is initiated by main calling gettok to get the first token, and then calling S:

gettok 111

```
int t;
void main(void) {
    t = gettok();
    if (S() == 0)
        error("syntax error\n");
    if (t != EOI)
        error("syntax error\n");
}
```

EOI is the token code for the end of input; the input is valid only if *all* of it is a sentence in the language.

7.4   FIRST and FOLLOW Sets

In order to write the parsing functions for each nonterminal in a grammar, it must be possible to select the appropriate production by looking at just the next token in the input. Given a string of grammar symbols α, *FIRST*(α) is the set of terminals that begin all sentences derived from α. The *FIRST* sets help select the appropriate production in a derivation step.

Suppose the grammar contains the productions *A:* α and *A:* β, and the next derivation step is the replacement of *A* by the right-hand side of one of its productions. The parsing function for A is called, and it must select the appropriate production. If the next token is in $FIRST(\alpha)$, the production $A: \alpha$ is selected, and if the next token is in $FIRST(\beta)$, $A: \beta$ is selected. If the next token is not in $FIRST(\alpha) \cup FIRST(\beta)$, there is a syntax error. Clearly, $FIRST(\alpha)$ and $FIRST(\beta)$ cannot intersect.

When α is simply a nonterminal, $FIRST(\alpha)$ is the set of terminals that begin sentences derivable from that nonterminal. Given a grammar, $FIRST$ sets for each grammar symbol X can be computed by inspecting the productions. This inspection is an iterative process; it is repeated until nothing new is added to any of the $FIRST$ sets.

If X is a terminal a, $FIRST(X)$ is {a}. If X is a nonterminal and there is a production $X: a\alpha$, where a is a terminal, a is added to $FIRST(X)$. If there are productions of the form $X: [\alpha]$ or $X: \{\alpha\}$, ϵ and $FIRST(\alpha)$ are added to $FIRST(X)$; ϵ is added because these ϵ-productions can derive the empty string. If there are productions of the form

$$
\begin{array}{ll}
X: & \alpha_1 \\
 & \alpha_2 \\
 & \vdots \\
 & \alpha_k
\end{array}
$$

then

$$FIRST(\alpha_1) \cup FIRST(\alpha_2) \cup \ldots \cup FIRST(\alpha_k)$$

is added to $FIRST(X)$. If there is a production of the form $X: Y_1 Y_2 \ldots Y_k$, where Y_i are grammar symbols, then $FIRST(Y_1 Y_2 \ldots Y_k)$ is added to $FIRST(X)$.

$FIRST(Y_1 Y_2 \ldots Y_k)$ depends on the $FIRST$ sets for Y_1 through Y_k. All of the elements of $FIRST(Y_1)$ except ϵ are added to $FIRST(Y_1 Y_2 \ldots Y_k)$, which is initially empty. If $FIRST(Y_1)$ contains ϵ, all of the elements of $FIRST(Y_2)$ except ϵ are also added. This process is repeated, adding all of the elements of $FIRST(Y_i)$ except ϵ if $FIRST(Y_{i-1})$ contains ϵ. The resulting effect is that $FIRST(Y_1 Y_2 \ldots Y_k)$ contains the elements of the $FIRST$ sets for the transparent Y_is, where a $FIRST$ set is transparent if it contains ϵ. If all of the $FIRST$ sets for Y_1 through Y_k contain ϵ, ϵ is added to $FIRST(Y_1 Y_2 \ldots Y_k)$.

Consider the grammar for simple expressions given in Section 1.6:

expr:
    term { + *term* }
    term { - *term* }

term:
    factor { * *factor* }
    factor { / *factor* }

factor:
    ID

```
ID '(' expr { , expr } ')'
'(' expr ')'
```

This grammar has been rewritten to express alternatives as separate productions given on separate lines. $FIRST(expr)$ is equal to

$$FIRST(term \{ + term \}) \cup FIRST(term \{ - term \})$$

which cannot be computed until the value of $FIRST(term)$ is known. Likewise, $FIRST(term)$ is

$$FIRST(factor \{ * factor \}) \cup FIRST(factor \{ / factor \})$$

$FIRST(factor)$, however, is easy to compute because all of the productions for *factor* start with terminals:

$$
\begin{aligned}
FIRST(factor) \quad &= \quad FIRST(\text{ID}) \cup FIRST(\text{ID '(' } expr \{ , expr \} \text{ ')')} \\
&\quad \cup FIRST(\text{'(' } expr \text{ ')')} \\
&= \quad \{\text{ID (}\}
\end{aligned}
$$

Now $FIRST(term)$ can be computed and is {ID (}; $FIRST(expr)$ is also {ID (}.

There is one case in which the *FIRST* sets are not enough to determine which production to apply. Suppose a grammar contains the productions

```
X:  A B
    C
```

Normally, the appropriate production would be selected depending on whether the next token is in $FIRST(AB)$ or $FIRST(C)$. Suppose, however, that $FIRST(AB)$ contains ϵ, meaning that AB can derive the empty sentence. Then selecting the appropriate production depends not only on $FIRST(AB)$ and $FIRST(C)$, but also on the tokens that can *follow* X. This set of tokens is the *FOLLOW* set for X; that is, $FOLLOW(X)$ is the set of terminals that can immediately follow nonterminal X in any sentential form. The *FOLLOW* sets give the "right context" for the non-terminal symbols, and are used in error detection as well as in structuring the grammar so that it is suitable for recursive-descent parsing. In this example, the first production is selected if the next token is in $FIRST(AB) \cup FOLLOW(X)$, and second production is selected if the next token is in $FIRST(C)$. Of course, $FIRST(AB) \cup FOLLOW(X)$ must be disjoint from $FIRST(C)$.

FOLLOW sets are harder to compute than *FIRST* sets, primarily because it is necessary to inspect all productions in which a nonterminal is *used* instead of just the productions that *define* the nonterminal. For all productions of the form $X: \alpha Y \beta$, $FIRST(\beta) - \{\epsilon\}$ is added to $FOLLOW(Y)$. If $FIRST(\beta)$ is transparent — if it contains ϵ — $FOLLOW(X)$ is added to *FOLLOW(Y)*. For all productions of the form *X: αY*, *FOLLOW(X)* is added to *FOLLOW(Y)*. As for computing *FIRST* sets, computing *FOLLOW* sets is an iterative process; it is repeated until nothing new is added to any *FOLLOW* set. The end-of-file marker, ⊣, is included in the *FOLLOW* set of the start symbol.

Here's how the *FOLLOW* sets are computed for the expression grammar. Since *expr* is the start symbol, *FOLLOW(expr)* contains ⊣. *expr* appears in only the productions for *factor*, so

$$FOLLOW(expr) = \{⊣\} \cup FIRST(\{ , expr \} ')') \cup FIRST(')')$$
$$= \{,) ⊣\}$$

FIRST(')') contributes) to *FOLLOW(expr)*, but *FIRST({ , expr })* contains ε, so *FIRST({ , expr } ')')* contributes) as well.

term appears in two places in the two productions for *expr*, so

$$FOLLOW(term) = FOLLOW(expr)$$
$$\cup FIRST(\{ + term \}) \cup FIRST(\{ - term \})$$
$$= \{,) ⊣ + -\}$$

Similarly, *factor* appears twice in each of the productions for *term*:

$$FOLLOW(factor) = FOLLOW(term)$$
$$\cup FIRST(\{ * factor \}) \cup FIRST(\{ / factor \})$$
$$= \{,) ⊣ + - * /\}$$

7.5 Writing Parsing Functions

Equipped with an EBNF grammar for a language and the *FIRST* and *FOL-LOW* sets for each nonterminal, writing parsing functions amounts to translating the productions for each nonterminal into executable code. The idea is to write a function X for each nonterminal *X*, using the productions for *X* as a guide to writing the code for X.

The rules for this translation are derived from the possible forms for the productions in the grammar. For each form of production, *α*, *T(α)* denotes the translation — the code — for *α*. At any point during parsing, the global variable t contains the current token as read by the lexical analyzer. Input is advanced by calling `gettok`.

Given the production, *X: α*, X is

```
X() { T(α) }
```

The right column of Table 7.1 gives *T(α)* for each form of production component *α* listed in the left column where

$$D(α) = \begin{cases} (FIRST(α) - \{ε\}) \cup FOLLOW(X) & \text{if } ε \in FIRST(α) \\ FIRST(α) & \text{otherwise} \end{cases}$$

α	$T(\alpha)$
terminal A	```if (t == A) t = gettok();``` ```else``` *error*
nonterminal X	```X();```

$\alpha_1 \mid \alpha_2 \mid \cdots \mid \alpha_k$	```if``` $(t \in D(\alpha_1))$ $T(\alpha_1)$
	```else if``` $(t \in D(\alpha_2))$ $T(\alpha_2)$
	$\ldots$
	```else if``` $(t \in D(\alpha_k))$ $T(\alpha_k)$
	```else``` *error*

$\alpha_1 \alpha_2 \cdots \alpha_k$	$T(\alpha_1)$ $T(\alpha_2)$ $\cdots$ $T(\alpha_k)$
$[\alpha]$	```if``` $(t \in D(\alpha))$ $T(\alpha)$
$\{\alpha\}$	```while``` $(t \in D(\alpha))$ $T(\alpha)$

TABLE 7.1 Parsing function translations.

There are, of course, other code sequences that are equivalent to those given in Table 7.1. For example, a switch statement is often used for $T(\alpha_1 \mid \alpha_2 \mid \cdots \mid \alpha_k)$. Also, rote application of the sequences given in Table 7.1 sometimes leads to redundant code, which can be improved by simple transformations. For example, the body of the parsing function for

> *parameter-list:* [ID { , ID }]

is derived by applying the rules in Table 7.1 in the following seven steps.

1. $T(parameter\text{-}list)$

2. $T([$ ID $\{$, ID $\}$ $])$

3. ```if (t == ID) {``` $T($ ID $\{$, ID $\})$ ```}```

4. ```if (t == ID) {```
   ```   if (t == ID) t = gettok();```
   ```   else error("missing identifier\n");```
   ``` ``` $T(\{$, ID $\})$
   ```}```

5. ```if (t == ID) {```
   ```   if (t == ID) t = gettok();```
   ```   else error("missing identifier\n");```
   ```   while (t == ',') {``` $T($, ID $)$ ```}```
   ```}```

6. ```if (t == ID) {```
   ```   if (t == ID) t = gettok();```
   ```

```
            else error("missing identifier\n");
            while (t == ',') {
                if (t == ',') t = gettok();
                else error("missing ,\n");
                T(ID)
            }
        }
    }
7. if (t == ID) {
        if (t == ID) t = gettok();
        else error("missing identifier\n");
        while (t == ',') {
            if (t == ',') t = gettok();
            else error("missing ,\n");
            if (t == ID)  t = gettok();
            else error("missing identifier\n");
        }
    }
}
```

The test in the second if statement in step 4, t == ID, is redundant; it must be true if control reaches that if statement. Similarly, the test for a comma in the first if statement in the while loop in step 6 is unnecessary. This function can be simplified to

```
void parameter_list(void) {
    if (t == ID) {
        t = gettok();
        while (t == ',') {
            t = gettok();
            if (t == ID) t = gettok();
            else error("missing identifier\n");
        }
    }
}
```

Left factoring is often taken into account when the parsing function is written instead of rewriting the grammar and adding new nonterminals as described above. For example, A: $\alpha\beta \mid \alpha\gamma$ is equivalent to A: $\alpha(\beta \mid \gamma)$, so the code for $T(\alpha\beta \mid \alpha\gamma)$ can be written directly as

$T(\alpha)\ T(\beta \mid \gamma)$

In a few cases, α appears as a common prefix in several productions, and involves significant semantic processing. In such cases, introducing a new nonterminal and left factoring the relevant productions encapsulates that processing in a single parsing function.

7.6 Handling Syntax Errors

The *FIRST* and *FOLLOW* sets and subsets thereof are used not only to guide parsing decisions but also for detecting errors. There are two major types of errors: *syntax errors* and *semantic errors.* The former occur when the input is not a sentence in the language. The latter occur when the input is a sentence, but is meaningless. For example, the expression x = 6 is syntactically correct, but if x is not declared, the expression is semantically incorrect.

Semantic errors are detected and handled by each parsing function in accordance with the semantics of the specific construct. Such errors are described along with the implementation of the functions.

Syntax errors can be handled in a systematic fashion regardless of the context in which they occur. Detecting syntax errors is relatively easy; such errors occur at the *error* indications in the translations shown in Table 7.1. Recovering from syntax errors is more difficult, however. Since it is unreasonable to stop parsing after the first syntax error, most of the effort in error handling is devoted to recovering from errors so that parsing can continue.

A syntax error indicates the presence of a sentence that is not in the language. Recovering from a syntax error is possible only if the erroneous input can be converted to a sentence by making appropriate assumptions about missing tokens or by ignoring some of the input. Unfortunately, choosing the appropriate course of action is nontrivial. Poor choices may cause the parser to get completely out of step and cause syntax errors to cascade even if the subsequent input is syntactically correct. Even worse, naive error recovery may fail to make forward progress through the input.

The structure of recursive-descent parsers assists in choosing the appropriate error-recovery strategy. The parser is composed of many parsing functions, each of which contributes a small part to the overall goal of parsing the input. Thus the major goal is split into many subgoals, each handled by calling on other parsing functions. In order to continue parsing, each function is written to guarantee that the next token in the input can legally follow its nonterminal in a sentential form. If an error is detected, the parsing function reports the error and discards tokens until it encounters one that can legally follow its nonterminal.

One approach to implementing this technique is to have X, the parsing function for the nonterminal X, ignore input until it encounters a token in $FOLLOW(X)$. The goal is to resynchronize the parser at a point in the input from which it can continue. After advancing to a token in $FOLLOW(X)$, it will appear that all is well to X's caller. One problem with this naive approach is that it doesn't account for the particular sentential form in which this occurrence of X appears. When X appears in the sentential form $\alpha X \beta$, X should ignore tokens in $D(\beta)$, which is often smaller than $FOLLOW(X)$. If X stops discarding tokens when it finds one in $FOLLOW(X)$ but not in $D(\beta)$, it is stopping too early and its caller will announce another syntax error unnecessarily. Thus, parsing functions use sets like $D(\beta)$ whenever they are readily known, and use $FOLLOW(X)$ otherwise. For example, when expr0, one of the parsing functions for expressions, is called to parse the third expression in the for statement, the set {;)} is used when it recovers from a syntax error in the expression.

This strategy is encapsulated in the functions exported by error.c.

⟨*error.c exported functions*⟩≡   141

```
extern void test ARGS((int tok, char set[]));
```

checks if the next token is equal to tok; if it isn't, a message is issued and tokens are skipped until one in {tok} ∪ set is encountered. set is the set of tokens that should *not* be skipped, and ensures that the amount of input skipped is limited. A set is simply a null-terminated array of token codes.

⟨*error.c functions*⟩≡   142

```
void test(tok, set) int tok; char set[]; {
    if (t == tok)
        t = gettok();
    else {
        expect(tok);
        skipto(tok, set);
        if (t == tok)
            t = gettok();
    }
}
```

142	expect
156	expr0
361	set
144	skipto

test issues messages by calling expect and skips tokens by calling skipto, both of which are described below.

The strategy embodied in test works well when the compiler is faced with errors for which skipping some of the input is an appropriate action. It does not work well, however, when an expected token is *missing* from the input. In those cases, a more effective strategy is to issue a message, pretend the expected token was present, and continue parsing. This scheme effectively inserts missing tokens, and it works well because such errors are almost always caused by the omission of tokens that have only simple syntactic functions, such as semicolons and commas. This strategy is implemented by

⟨*error.c exported functions*⟩+≡   141 143

```
extern void expect ARGS((int tok));
```

which checks if the next token, which is the current value of t, is equal to tok and, if so, advances the input.

⟨*error.c functions*⟩+≡   141 142

```
void expect(tok) int tok; {
    if (t == tok)
        t = gettok();
    else {
        error("syntax error; found");
        printtoken();
        fprint(2, " expecting '%k'\n", tok);
    }
}
```

The first test is, of course, never true when `expect` is called from `test`; that call is made to issue the diagnostic. `expect` is also called from other parsing functions whenever a specific token is expected, and it consumes that token. If the expected token is missing, `expect` issues a diagnostic and returns without advancing the input, as if the expected token had been present.

   `expect` calls `error` to begin the message, and it calls the static function `printtoken` to print the current token (i.e., the token given by `t` and `token`), and `fprint` to conclude the message. As an example of `expect`'s effect, the input "int x[5;" draws the diagnostic

```
syntax error; found ';' expecting ']'
```

Error messages are initiated by calling `error`, which is called with a printf-style format string and arguments. In addition to the message, `error` prints the coordinates of the current token set by `gettok` and keeps a count of the number of error messages issued in `errcnt`.

⟨*error.c functions*⟩+≡   142 144

```
void error VARARGS((char *fmt, ...),
(fmt, va_alist),char *fmt; va_dcl) {
    va_list ap;

    if (errcnt++ >= errlimit) {
        errcnt = -1;
        error("too many errors\n");
        exit(1);
    }
    va_init(ap, fmt);
    if (firstfile != file && firstfile && *firstfile)
        fprint(2, "%s: ", firstfile);
    fprint(2, "%w: ", &src);
    vfprint(2, fmt, ap);
    va_end(ap);
}
```

⟨*error.c data*⟩≡   143
```
int errcnt   = 0;
int errlimit = 20;
```

If errcnt gets too big, error terminates execution. warning, which issues warning diagnostics, is similar, but it doesn't increment errcnt. fatal is similar to error, but terminates compilation after issuing the error message. fatal is called only for bona fide compiler bugs.

The last error-handling function is

⟨*error.c exported functions*⟩+≡   141
```
extern void skipto ARGS((int tok, char set[]));
```

which discards tokens until a token t is found that is equal to tok or for which kind[t] is in the null-terminated array set. The array

⟨*error.c exported data*⟩≡
```
extern char kind[];
```

is indexed by token codes, and partitions them into sets. It's defined by including token.h and extracting its sixth column, as described on page 109:

⟨*error.c data*⟩+≡   143
```
char kind[] = {
#define xx(a,b,c,d,e,f,g) f,
#define yy(a,b,c,d,e,f,g) f,
#include "token.h"
};
```

142	error
361	set
144	skipto
109	token.h

kind[t] is a token code that denotes a set of which t is a member. For example, the code ID is used to denote the set *FIRST*(*expression*) for the *expression* defined in Section 8.3. Thus, kind[t] is equal to ID for every t ∈ *FIRST*(*expression*). The test kind[t]==ID determines if the token t is in *FIRST*(*expression*), so passing the array {ID,0} as the second argument to skipto causes it to skip tokens until it finds one in *FIRST*(*expression*).

The following table summarizes the values in kind. The token code on the left denotes the set composed of itself and the tokens on the right.

```
ID       FCON ICON SCON SIZEOF & ++ -- * + - ~ ( !
CHAR     FLOAT DOUBLE SHORT INT UNSIGNED SIGNED
         VOID STRUCT UNION ENUM LONG CONST VOLATILE
STATIC   EXTERN AUTO REGISTER TYPEDEF
IF       BREAK CASE CONTINUE DEFAULT DO ELSE
         FOR GOTO RETURN SWITCH WHILE {
```

For tokens not mentioned in this table, kind[t] is equal to t; for example, kind['}'] is equal to '}'. The sets defined by kind are related to *FIRST* sets described in Section 7.4 as follows.

$$
\begin{array}{lll}
\texttt{kind[ID]} & = & FIRST\,(expression) \\
\texttt{kind[ID]} \cup \texttt{kind[IF]} & = & FIRST\,(statement) \\
\texttt{kind[CHAR]} \cup \texttt{kind[STATIC]} & \subset & FIRST\,(declaration) \\
\texttt{kind[STATIC]} & \subset & FIRST\,(parameter)
\end{array}
$$

The nonterminals listed above are defined in Chapters 8, 10, and 11.

Since `skipto`'s second argument is an array, it can represent supersets of these sets when the additional tokens have `kind` values equal to themselves, as exemplified above by }. These supersets are related to *FOLLOW* sets in some cases. For example, a *statement* must be followed by a } or a token in *FIRST*(*statement*). The parsing function for *statement* thus passes `skipto` an array that holds IF, ID, and }.

As `skipto` discards tokens, it announces the first eight and the last one it discards:

⟨*error.c functions*⟩+≡   142

```
void skipto(tok, set) int tok; char set[]; {
    int n;
    char *s;

    for (n = 0; t != EOI && t != tok; t = gettok()) {
        for (s = set; *s && kind[t] != *s; s++)
            ;
        if (kind[t] == *s)
            break;
        if (n++ == 0)
            error("skipping");
        if (n <= 8)
            printtoken();
        else if (n == 9)
            fprint(2, " ...");
    }
    if (n > 8) {
        fprint(2, " up to");
        printtoken();
    }
    if (n > 0)
        fprint(2, "\n");
}
```

`skipto` discards nothing and issues no diagnostic if t is equal to tok or is in `kind[t]`. Suppose `bug.c` holds *only* the one line

```
fprint(2, " expecting '%k'\n", tok);
```

The syntax error in this example is that this line must be inside a function. The call to `fprint` looks like the beginning of a function definition, but lcc soon discovers the error. `test` calls `expect` and `skipto` to issue the diagnostic

```
bug.c:1: syntax error; found '2' expecting ')'
bug.c:1: skipping '2' ',' " expecting '%k'\12" ',' 'tok'
```

Notice that the right parenthesis was not discarded.

Further Reading

There are many books that describe the theory and practice of compiler construction, including Aho, Sethi, and Ullman (1986), Fischer and LeBlanc (1991), and Waite and Goos (1984). Davie and Morrison (1981) and Wirth (1976) describe the design and implementation of recursive-descent compilers.

A bottom-up parser reconstructs a rightmost derivation of its input, and builds parse trees from the leaves to the roots. Bottom-up parsers are often used in compilers because they accept a larger class of languages and because the grammars are sometimes easier to write. Most bottom-up parsers use a variant of LR parsing, which is surveyed by Aho and Johnson (1974) and covered in detail by Aho, Sethi, and Ullman (1986). In addition, many parser generators have been constructed. These programs accept a syntactic specification of the language, usually in a form like that shown in Exercise 7.2, and produce a parsing program. YACC (Johnson 1975) is the parser generator used on UNIX. YACC and LEX work together, often simplifying compiler implementation considerably. Aho, Sethi, and Ullman (1986), Kernighan and Pike (1984), and Schreiner and Friedman (1985) contain several examples of the use of YACC and LEX. Holub (1990) describes the implementation of another parser generator.

142 expect
144 skipto
141 test

Other parser generators are based on attribute grammars; Waite and Goos (1984) describe attribute grammars and related parser generators.

The error-handling techniques used in lcc are like those advocated by Stirling (1985) and used by Wirth (1976). Burke and Fisher (1987) describe perhaps the best approach to handling errors for LR and LL parser tables.

Exercises

7.1 Using the lexical-analyzer and the symbol-table modules from the previous chapters, cobble together a parser that recognizes expressions defined by the grammar below and prints their parse trees.

expr:
 term { + *term* }
 term { - *term* }

term:
 factor { * *factor* }
 factor { / *factor* }

factor:
 `ID`
 `ID '(' ` *expr* { , *expr* } ` ')'`
 `'(' ` *expr* ` ')'`

7.2 Write a program that computes the *FIRST* and *FOLLOW* sets for an EBNF grammar and reports conflicts that interfere with recursive-descent parsing of the language. Design an input representation for the grammar that is close in the form to EBNF. For example, suppose grammars are given in free format where nonterminals are in lowercase with embedded - signs, terminals are in uppercase or enclosed in single or double quotes, and productions are terminated by semicolons. For example, the grammar in the previous exercise could appear as

```
expr    : term { ( '+' | '-' ) term } ;

term    : factor { ( '*' | '/' ) term } ;

factor  : ID [ '(' expr { , expr } ')' ]
        | '(' expr ')'
        ;
```

Give an EBNF specification for the syntax of the input, and write a recursive-descent parser to recognize it using the techniques described in this chapter.

8
Expressions

C expressions form a sublanguage for which the parsing functions are relatively straightforward to write. This makes them a good starting point for describing lcc's eight modules that collaborate to parse and analyze the input program. These functions build an internal representation for the input program that consists of the abstract syntax trees and the code lists described in Section 1.3.

Four of these modules cooperate in parsing, analyzing, and representing expressions. expr.c implements the parsing functions that recognize and translate expressions. tree.c implements low-level functions that manage trees, which are the internal, intermediate representation for expressions. enode.c implements *type-checking* functions that ensure the semantic validity of expressions, and it exports functions that build and manipulate trees. simp.c implements functions that perform tree transformations, such as *constant folding*.

Broadly speaking, this chapter focuses on tree.c and expr.c, and it describes the shape of the abstract syntax trees used to represent expressions. Much of this explanation is a top-down tour of the parsing functions that build trees. Chapter 9 describes the meaning of these trees as they relate to the semantics of C; most of that explanation is a bottom-up tour of the semantics functions that type-check trees as they are built. This chapter's last section is the exception to this general structure; the functions it describes handle both the shape and meaning of the leaf nodes in abstract syntax trees, which are the nodes for constants and identifiers.

8.1 Representing Expressions

In addition to recognizing and analyzing expressions, the compiler must build an intermediate representation of them from which it can check their validity and generate code. *Abstract syntax trees*, or simply trees, are often used to represent expressions. Abstract syntax trees are parse trees without nodes for the nonterminals and nodes for useless terminals. In such trees, nodes represent operators and their offspring represent the operands. For example, the tree for (a+b)+b*(a+b) is shown in Figure 8.1. There are no nodes for the nonterminals involved in parsing this expression, and there are no nodes for the tokens (and). There are no nodes for the tokens + and * because the nodes contain operators

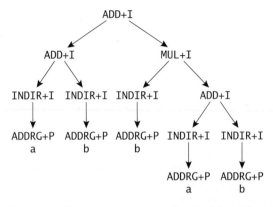

FIGURE 8.1   Abstract syntax tree for (a+b)+b*(a+b).

(ADD+I and MUL+I) that represent operator-specific information. Nodes labelled with the operator ADDRG+P represent computing the address of the identifier given by their operands.

Trees often contain operators that do not appear in the source language. The INDIR+I nodes, for example, fetch the integers at the addresses specified by their operands, but there's no explicit "fetch" operator in C. Other examples include conversion operators, which arise because of implicit conversions, and operators that are introduced as the result of semantic rules. Some of these operators do not have any corresponding operation at runtime; they are introduced only to facilitate compilation.

tree 150

Like types, trees can be written in a parenthesized prefix notation; for example, the tree for the expression (a+b)+b*(a+b) shown in Figure 8.1 can be written as

```
(ADD+I
    (ADD+I (INDIR+I (ADDRG+P a)) (INDIR+I (ADDRG+P b)))
    (MUL+I
        (INDIR+I (ADDRG+P b))
        (ADD+I (INDIR+I (ADDRG+P a)) (INDIR+I (ADDRG+P b)))
    )
)
```

Parsing an expression yields a tree whose nodes are defined by

⟨*tree.c typedefs*⟩≡
```
typedef struct tree *Tree;
```

⟨*tree.c exported types*⟩≡
```
struct tree {
    int op;
    Type type;
```

```
    Tree kids[2];
    Node node;
    union {
        ⟨u fields for Tree variants 168⟩
    } u;
};
```

The op field holds a code for the operator, the type field points to a Type
for the type of the result computed by the node at runtime, and kids
point to the operands. The node field is used to build dags from trees
as detailed in Section 12.2. Trees for some operators have additional
information tucked away in the fields of their u unions.

The operators form a superset of the node operators described in
Chapter 5 and listed in Table 5.1 (page 84), but they are written differently to emphasize their use in trees. An operator is formed by adding
a type suffix to a *generic* operator; for example, ADD+I denotes integer
addition. The + is omitted when referring to the corresponding node
operator ADDI; this convention helps distinguish between trees and dags
in figures and in prose. The type suffixes are listed in Section 5.5, and
Table 5.1 gives the allowable suffixes for each operator.

Table 8.1 lists the six operators that appear in trees in addition to
those shown in Table 5.1. AND, OR, and NOT represent expressions involv-
ing the &&, ||, and ! operators. Comma expressions yield RIGHT trees;
by definition, RIGHT evaluates its arguments left to right, and its value
is the value of its rightmost operand. RIGHT is also used to build trees
that logically have more than two operands, such as the COND operator,
which represents conditional expressions of the form c ? e_1 : e_2. The
first operand of a COND tree is c and the second is a RIGHT tree that holds
e_1 and e_2. RIGHT trees are also used for expressions such as e++. These
operators are used only by the front end and thus do not need — and
must not have — type suffixes. The FIELD operator identifies a reference
to a bit field.

While trees and dags share many of the same operators, the rules concerning the number of operands and symbols, summarized in Table 5.1,
apply only to dags. The front end is *not* constrained by these rules when

81	kids
315	node
54	Type

syms	kids	Operator	Operation
	2	AND	logical And
	2	OR	logical Or
	1	NOT	logical Not
1V	2	COND	conditional expression
	1 or 2	RIGHT	composition
	1	FIELD	bit-field access

TABLE 8.1 Tree operators.

it builds trees, and it often uses additional operands and symbols in trees that do not appear in dags. For example, when it builds the tree for the arguments in a function call, it uses the kids[1] fields in ARG nodes to build what amounts to a list of arguments, the trees for which are stored in the kids[0] fields.

A tree is allocated, initialized, and returned by

⟨*tree.c functions*⟩≡   150

```
Tree tree(op, type, left, right)
int op; Type type; Tree left, right; {
    Tree p;

    NEW0(p, where);
    p->op = op;
    p->type = type;
    p->kids[0] = left;
    p->kids[1] = right;
    return p;
}
```

⟨*tree.c data*⟩≡   155

```
static int where = STMT;
```

NEW0 24
STMT 97

Trees are allocated in the allocation arena indicated by where, which is almost always the STMT arena. Data allocated in STMT is deallocated most frequently, possibly after every statement is parsed. In some cases, however, an expression's tree must be saved beyond the compilation of the current statement. The increment expression in a for loop is an example. These expressions are parsed by calling texpr with an argument that specifies the allocation arena:

⟨*tree.c functions*⟩+≡   150 155

```
Tree texpr(f, tok, a) Tree (*f) ARGS((int)); int tok, a; {
    int save = where;
    Tree p;

    where = a;
    p = (*f)(tok);
    where = save;
    return p;
}
```

texpr saves where, sets it to a, calls the parsing function (*f)(tok), restores the saved value of where, and returns the tree returned by *f.

The remaining functions in tree.c construct, test, or otherwise manipulate trees and operators. These are all applicative — they build new trees instead of modifying existing ones, which is necessary because the front end builds dags for a few operators instead of trees. rightkid(p) returns the rightmost non-RIGHT operand of a nested series of RIGHT trees. retype(p,ty) returns p if p->type == ty or a copy of p with type ty. hascall(p) is one if p contains a CALL tree and zero otherwise.

generic(op) returns the generic flavor of op, optype(op) returns op's type suffix, and opindex(op) returns op's operator index, which is the generic operator mapped into a contiguous range of integers suitable for use as an index.

8.2 Parsing Expressions

C has 41 operators distributed in 15 levels of precedence. Beginning with an EBNF grammar that contains a nonterminal for each precedence level, as suggested in Section 7.2, and deriving the parsing functions is a correct approach, but cumbersome at best. There is an important simplification to this process that reduces the size of both the grammar and the resulting code.

Consider the following simplification of the grammar from Section 7.4, which is for a small subset of C expressions.

> *expr: term { + term }*
>
> *term: factor { * factor }*
>
> *factor:* ID | '(' *expr* ')'

Parsing functions can be written directly from this grammar using the translations given in Table 7.1. For example, the steps in deriving and simplifying the body of the parsing function expr (without semantics) for *expr* are

```
T(expr)
T(term { + term })
T(term) T({ + term })
term(); T({ + term })
term(); while (t == '+') { T(+ term) }
term(); while (t == '+') { T(+) T(term) }
term(); while (t == '+') { t = gettok(); T(term) }
term(); while (t == '+') { t = gettok(); term(); }
```

Likewise, the body of the parsing function term for *term* is

```
factor(); while (t == '*') { t = gettok(); factor(); }
```

factor is the basis case, and it handles the elementary expressions:

```
void factor(void) {
    if (t == ID)
```

```
        t = gettok();
    else if (t == '(') {
        t = gettok();
        expr();
        expect(')');
    } else
        error("unrecognized expression\n");
}
```

There are two precedence levels in this example. In general, for n precedence levels there are $n+1$ nonterminals; one for each level and one for the basis case in which further division is impossible. Consequently, there are $n + 1$ functions — one for each nonterminal. If the binary operators are all left-associative, these functions are very similar. As illustrated by the bodies for expr and term above, the only essential differences are the operators expected and the function to be called; function k calls function $k + 1$.

This similarity can be exploited to replace functions 1 through n by a single function and a table of operators ordered according to increasing precedence. lcc stores the precedences in an array indexed by token code; Table 8.2 lists the precedence and associativity for all of the C operators. prec[t] is the precedence of the operator with token code

prec 155

t; for example, prec['+'] is 12 and prec[LEQ] is 10. Using prec and assuming that the only operators are +, -, *, /, and %, then expr and term given above can be replaced by the single function

```
void expr(int k) {
    if (k > 13)
        factor();
    else {
        expr(k + 1);
        while (prec[t] == k) {
            t = gettok();
            expr(k + 1);
        }
    }
}
```

The 13 comes from Table 8.2; the binary operators + and - have precedence 12 and *, /, and % each have precedence 13. When k exceeds 13, expr calls factor to parse the productions for *factor*. Expression parsing for this restricted grammar begins by calling expr(12), and the call to expr in factor must be changed to expr(12).

expr and factor can be used for any expression grammar of the form

expr: expr ⊗ expr | factor

Precedence	Associativity	Operators	Purpose	Parsed By
1	left	,	composition	expr
2	right	= += -= *= /= %= &= ^= |= <<= >>=	assignment	expr1
3	right	? :	conditional	expr2
4	left	||	logical or	expr3
5	left	&&	logical and	expr3
6	left	|	bitwise OR	expr3
7	left	^	bitwise XOR	expr3
8	left	&	bitwise AND	expr3
9	left	== !=	equality	expr3
10	left	< > <= >=	relational	expr3
11	left	<< >>	shifting	expr3
12	left	+ -	additive	expr3
13	left	* / %	multiplicative	expr3
14		* & - + ! ~ ++ -- sizeof *type-cast*	unary prefix	unary
15		++ --	unary suffix	postfix

TABLE 8.2 Operator precedences, associativities, and parsing functions.

where ⊗ denotes binary, left-associative operators. Adding operators is accomplished by appropriately initializing prec.

The while loop in expr handles left-associative operators, which are specified in EBNF by productions like those for *expr* and *term*. Right-associative operators, like assignment, are specified in EBNF by productions like

> *asgn: expr = asgn*

They can also be handled using this approach by simply calling expr(k) instead of expr(k + 1) in the while loop in expr. Assuming all operators at each precedence level have the same associativity, the decision of whether to call expr with k or k + 1 can be encoded in a table, handled by writing separate parsing functions for left- and right-associative operators, or making explicit tests for each kind of operator.

Unary operators can also be handled using this technique. Fortunately, the unary operators in C have the highest precedence, so they appear in function $n + 1$, as does factor in the example above. Otherwise, upon entry, expr would have to check for the occurrence of unary operators at the *k*th level.

Using this technique also simplifies the grammar for expressions, because most of the nonterminals for the intermediate precedence levels can be omitted.

8.3   Parsing C Expressions

The complete syntax for C expressions is

expression:
    assignment-expression { , *assignment-expression* }

assignment-expression:
    conditional-expression
    unary-expression assign-operator assignment-expression

assign-operator:
    one of = += -= *= /= %= <<= >>= &= ^= |=

conditional-expression:
    binary-expression [? *expression* : *conditional-expression*]

binary-expression:
    unary-expression { *binary-operator unary-expression* }

binary-operator:
    one of || && '|' ^ & == != < > <= >= << >> + - * / %

unary-expression:
    postfix-expression
    unary-operator unary-expression
    '(' *type-name* ')' *unary-expression*
    sizeof *unary-expression*
    sizeof '(' *type-name* ')'

unary-operator:
    one of ++ -- & * + - ~ !

postfix-expression:
    primary-expression { *postfix-operator* }

postfix-operator:
    '[' *expression* ']'
    '(' [*assignment-expression* { , *assignment-expression* }] ')'
    . *identifier*
    -> *identifier*
    ++
    --

primary-expression:
    identifer
    constant
    string-literal
    '(' *expression* ')'

There are seven parsing functions for expressions corresponding to the
expression nonterminals in this grammar. The parsing function for

binary-expression uses the techniques described in Section 8.2 to handle all the binary operators, which have precedences between 4 and 13 inclusive (see Table 8.2).

Each of these functions parses the applicable expression, builds a tree to represent the expression, type-checks the tree, and returns it. Three arrays, each indexed by token code, guide the operation of these functions. `prec[t]`, mentioned in Section 8.2, gives the precedence of the operator denoted by token code `t`. `oper[t]` is the generic tree operator that corresponds to token `t`, and `optree[t]` points to a function that builds a tree for the operator denoted by `t`. For example, `prec['+']` is 12, `oper['+']` is ADD, and `optree['+']` is addtree, which, like most of the functions referred to by `optree` and like `optree` itself, is in `enode.c`. `prec` and `oper` are defined by including `token.h` and extracting its third and fourth columns:

⟨*tree.c data*⟩+≡   ▲150 169▼

```
static char prec[] = {
#define xx(a,b,c,d,e,f,g) c,
#define yy(a,b,c,d,e,f,g) c,
#include "token.h"
};
static int oper[] = {
#define xx(a,b,c,d,e,f,g) d,
#define yy(a,b,c,d,e,f,g) d,
#include "token.h"
};
```

`token.h` is described in Section 6.2.

Each function is derived using the rules described in Section 7.5. Code to build and check the trees is interleaved with the parsing code. The code for *expression* is typical and is also the simplest:

⟨*tree.c functions*⟩+≡   ▲150 156▼

```
Tree expr(tok) int tok; {
    static char stop[] = { IF, ID, '}', 0 };
    Tree p = expr1(0);

    while (t == ',') {
        Tree q;
        t = gettok();
        q = pointer(expr1(0));
        p = tree(RIGHT, q->type, root(value(p)), q);
    }
    ⟨test for correct termination 156⟩
    return p;
}
```

expr begins by calling `expr1`, which parses an *assignment-expression* and returns the tree; it's described in Section 8.4. The while loop corresponds to the

> { , *assignment-expression* }

portion of the production for *assignment-expression*, and it builds a RIGHT tree for each comma operator. The functions `pointer` and `value` check for semantic correctness or return transformations of their argument trees, and are described below. Exercise 12.9 describes `root`, which is called with trees that will be executed only for their side effect.

expr's argument, if nonzero, is the code for the token that should follow this occurrence of an *expression*.

⟨*test for correct termination* 156⟩≡   155 157
```
if (tok)
    test(tok, stop);
```

If `tok` is nonzero, but the expression is followed by something else, `test` skips input up to the next occurrence of `tok` or a token in `stop`, which is the set tok∪{ IF ID '}' } (see Section 7.6). This convention, which is used by several parsing functions, helps detect and handle errors. An *expression* must be followed by one of the tokens in its *FOLLOW* set. But for most uses, there's only one token that can follow *expression*. For example, the increment expression in a for loop must be followed by a right parenthesis. So, instead of checking for *any* token in the *FOLLOW* set, expr checks for *one* of the tokens in the *FOLLOW* set, which is more precise. In contexts where more than one token can follow *expression*, expr(0) is used and the caller checks the legality of the next token.

Statement-level expressions, such as assignments and function calls, are executed for their side effects:

⟨*tree.c functions*⟩+≡   155 157
```
Tree expr0(tok) int tok; {
    return root(expr(tok));
}
```

expr0 calls expr to parse the expression, and passes the resulting tree to `root`, which returns only the tree that has a side effect. For example, the statement a + f() includes a useless addition, which lcc is free to eliminate (even if the addition would overflow). Given the tree for this expression, `root` returns the tree for f(). `root` is described in Exercise 12.9.

8.4   Assignment Expressions

The right recursion in the second production for *assignment-expression* makes assignment right-associative; multiple assignments like a = b = c are interpreted as a = (b = c). Using the production

> *assignment-expression:*
>> *unary-expression { assign-operator conditional-expression }*

instead would be incorrect because it leads to a left-associative interpretation of multiple assignments like (a = b) = c. This interpretation is incorrect because the result of an assignment is not an lvalue.
   expr1 parses assignments.

⟨*tree.c functions*⟩+≡   156 158

```
Tree expr1(tok) int tok; {
    static char stop[] = { IF, ID, 0 };
    Tree p = expr2();

    if (t == '='
    || (prec[t] >=  6 && prec[t] <=  8)
    || (prec[t] >= 11 && prec[t] <= 13)) {
        int op = t;
        t = gettok();
        if (oper[op] == ASGN)
            p = asgntree(ASGN, p, value(expr1(0)));
        else
            ⟨augmented assignment 158⟩
    }
    ⟨test for correct termination 156⟩
    return p;
}
```

197	asgntree
159	expr2
155	oper
155	prec
164	unary
160	value

expr2 parses *conditional-expressions*:

> *conditional-expression:*
>> *binary-expression [? expression : conditional-expression]*

The code for expr1 doesn't follow the grammar precisely; expr2 is called for *both* productions, even though unary should be called for the second production. expr2 ultimately calls unary, so the code above recognizes all correct expressions, but it also recognizes incorrect ones. Incorrect expressions are caught by the semantic analysis in asgntree. The advantage of this approach is that it handles errors more gracefully. For example, in a + b = c, a + b is not a *unary-expression*, so a more strict parser would signal an error at the + and might signal other errors because it didn't parse the expression completely. lcc will accept the expression with no syntax errors, but will complain that the left-hand side of the assignment isn't an lvalue.
   The first if statement in expr1 tests for an assignment (=) or the initial character of the augmented-assignment operators (see Table 8.2).

oper[op] will be the corresponding generic tree operator for these characters, for example, oper['+'] is ADD. expr1 handles augmented assignments, such as +=, by recognizing the two tokens that make up the augmented assignment operator:

⟨*augmented assignment* 158⟩≡   157

```
{
    expect('=');
    p = incr(op, p, expr1(0));
}
```

Each augmented assignment operator is *one* token, but this code appears to treat them as two tokens; expr3, described below, avoids this erroneous interpretation by recognizing tokens like + as binary operators only when they aren't immediately followed by an equals sign. Thus, expr1 correctly interprets a += b as an augmented assignment and lets expr3 discover the error in a + = b.

incr builds trees for expressions of form $v \otimes= e$ for any binary operator $\otimes$, lvalue v, and rvalue e.

⟨*tree.c functions*⟩+≡   157 159

```
Tree incr(op, v, e) int op; Tree v, e; {
    return asgntree(ASGN, v, (*optree[op])(oper[op], v, e));
}
```

incr is one place where the front end builds a dag instead of a tree. For example, Figure 8.2 shows the tree returned by incr for *f() += b. *f() must be evaluated only once, but the lvalue it computes is used twice — once for the rvalue and once as the target of the assignment. Building only one tree for *f() reflects these semantics. Ultimately, these kinds of trees require temporaries, which are generated when the trees are converted into nodes; Chapter 12 explains.

These dags could have been avoided by using additional tree operators for augmented assignments. Doing this would increase the number

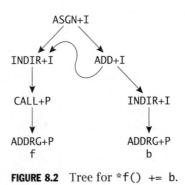

FIGURE 8.2 Tree for *f() += b.

of tree operators, and it might complicate the semantic analyses for the binary operators involved. For example, addtree, the function that performs the semantic analysis for +, might have to cope with both + and +=. There are several other situations in which it's useful to permit dags; an example occurs in dealing with nested functions, which is described in Section 9.3.

8.5 Conditional Expressions

The syntax of conditional expressions is

> *conditional-expression:*
> *binary-expression* [? *expression* : *conditional-expression*]

The value of a conditional expression is the value of *expression* if *binary-expression* is nonzero; otherwise it's the value of the third operand, which itself can be a *conditional-expression*. expr2 does the parsing:

⟨*tree.c functions*⟩+≡   ▲ 158 160 ▼

```
   static Tree expr2() {
      Tree p = expr3(4);

      if (t == '?') {
         Tree l, r;
         Coordinate pts[2];
         if (Aflag > 1 && isfunc(p->type))
            warning("%s used in a conditional expression\n",
               funcname(p));
         p = pointer(p);
         t = gettok();
         pts[0] = src;
         l = pointer(expr(':'));
         pts[1] = src;
         r = pointer(expr2());
         p = condtree(p, l, r);
         if (events.points)
            ⟨plant event hooks for ?:⟩
      }
      return p;
   }
```

192	addtree
62	Aflag
149	COND
200	condtree
38	Coordinate
162	expr3
155	expr
60	isfunc
174	pointer

expr2 begins by calling expr3 to parse a *binary-expression* beginning at precedence level 4, and concludes by calling condtree to build the COND tree (shown in Figure 9.6).

A common error in both if statements and conditional expressions is to use a function name instead of a function call; for example, using the expression test ? a : b instead of test(a,b) ? a : b. Both of these expressions are legal, but the first one is rarely what the programmer intended. lcc's -A option causes lcc to warn about this and similarly suspicious usage. Aflag records the number of -A options specified; multiple occurrences elicit more warnings.

lcc includes facilities for executing event hooks at various points in the source program that correspond to branches in the flow of control. This facility is used, for example, to inject trees that implement expression-level profiling, and to inject data for source-level debuggers. The operator ?: is one of the three that alter flow of control. The parameters to the functions that plant hooks include the source coordinates of the then and else parts of the expression, which is why these coordinates are saved in pts[0] and pts[1] in the code above.

Conditional expressions are also used to convert a relational, which is represented only by flow of control, to a value. For example, a = b < c sets a to one if b < c and to zero otherwise. This conversion is implemented by value, which builds a COND tree corresponding to the expression c ? 1 : 0.

⟨*tree.c functions*⟩+≡   159 162

```
Tree value(p) Tree p; {
    int op = generic(rightkid(p)->op);

    if (op==AND || op==OR || op==NOT || op==EQ || op==NE
    || op== LE || op==LT || op== GE || op==GT)
        p = condtree(p, consttree(1, inttype),
            consttree(0, inttype));
    return p;
}
```

lcc's interface could have specified two flavors of comparison operators: one that's used in conditional contexts, in which there is always a jump, and one that's used in value contexts like a = b < c, and yields a zero or one. An advantage of this design is that lcc could then use instructions that capture the outcome of a comparison and avoid the jumps implied in c ? 1 : 0. But only those targets that have these instructions and that penalize jumps severely would benefit from this alternative, and the rest would pay for the increased operator vocabulary. Specifying only the conditional form of the comparison operators is an example of favoring retargetability over flexibility.

8.6 Binary Expressions

Expressions involving all the binary operators with precedences 4–13 (see Table 8.2) are defined by the productions

binary-expression:
    unary-expression { *binary-operator unary-expression* }

binary-operator:
    one of || && '|' ∧ & == != < > <= >= << >> + - * / %

and are parsed by one function, as described in Section 8.2. Using that approach, the parsing function — without its tree-building code — for *binary-expression* is

```
void expr3(k) int k; {
    if (k > 13)
        unary();
    else {
        expr3(k + 1);
        while (prec[t] == k) {
            t = gettok();
            expr3(k + 1);
        }
    }
}
```

where unary is the parsing function for *unary-expression*. This function parses *binary-expression* correctly, but does more work than is necessary. The call expr3(4) in expr2 is the only external call to expr3 outside of expr3 itself. Thus, there are 10 recursive calls to expr3(5) through expr3(14) before the first call to unary. These 10 calls unwind from highest to lowest precedence as the source expression is parsed. The while loop is not entered until the call with a k equal to prec[t], where t is the token that *follows* the expression parsed by unary. Many of the recursive calls to expr3 serve only to test if their k is equal to prec[t]; only one succeeds.

For example, here's the sequence of calls for the expression a|b:

```
expr3(4)
 expr3(5)
  expr3(6)
   expr3(7)
    expr3(8)
     expr3(9)
      expr3(10)
       expr3(11)
        expr3(12)
         expr3(13)
          expr3(14)
           unary()
 expr3(7)
    . . .
```

```
    expr3(14)
    unary()
```

Of the calls leading up the first call to unary (which parses the a), only
expr3(6) does useful work after unary returns. And none of the recursive calls from within the while loop leading to the second call to unary
(which parses b) do useful work.

This sequence reveals the overall effect of the calls to expr3: parse
a *unary-expression*, then parse *binary-expression*s at precedence levels
13, 12, …, 4. The recursion can be replaced by counting from 14 down
to k. Since nothing interesting happens until the precedence is equal to
prec[t], counting can begin there:

```
void expr3(k) int k; {
    int k1;
    unary();
    for (k1 = prec[t]; k1 >= k; k1--)
        while (prec[t] == k1) {
            t = gettok();
            expr3(k1 + 1);
        }
}
```

This transformation also benefits the one remaining recursive call to
expr3 by eliminating most of the recursion in *that* call. Now, the se-
quence of calls for a|b is

```
expr3(4)
 unary()
 expr3(7)
 unary()
```

Adding the code to validate and build the trees and to solve two remain-
ing minor problems (augmented assignments and the && and || opera-
tors) yields the final version of expr3:

⟨*tree.c functions*⟩+≡   160 164

```
static Tree expr3(k) int k; {
    int k1;
    Tree p = unary();

    for (k1 = prec[t]; k1 >= k; k1--)
        while (prec[t] == k1 && *cp != '=') {
            Tree r, l;
            Coordinate pt;
            int op = t;
            t = gettok();
            pt = src;
```

```
            p = pointer(p);
            if (op == ANDAND || op == OROR) {
                r = pointer(expr3(k1));
                if (events.points)
                    ⟨plant event hooks for && ||⟩
            } else
                r = pointer(expr3(k1 + 1));
            p = (*optree[op])(oper[op], p, r);
        }
    return p;
}
```

Like conditional expressions, the && and || operators alter flow of control and thus must provide for event hooks.

Technically, the && and || operators are left-associative, and their right operands are evaluated only if necessary. It simplifies node generation if they are treated as right-associative during parsing. Each operator is the sole occupant of its precedence level, so, for example, making && right associative simply yields a right-heavy ANDAND tree instead of a left-heavy one. As detailed in Section 12.3, this apparent error is not only repaired during node generation, but leads to better code for the short-circuit evaluation of && and || than left-heavy trees. Making || right-associative requires calling expr3(4) instead of expr3(5) in the while loop. For &&, expr3(5) must be called instead of expr3(6). Calling expr3(k1) instead of expr3(k1+1) for these two operators makes the appropriate calls.

The last problem is augmented assignment. expr1 recognizes the augmented-assignment operators by recognizing two-token sequences. But these operators are single tokens, not two-token sequences; for example, += is the token for additive assignment, and + = is a syntax error. expr1's approach is correct only if + = is never recognized as +=. expr3 guarantees this condition by doing just the opposite: a binary operator is recognized only when it is *not* followed immediately by an equals sign. Thus, the + in a + = b is not recognized as a binary operator, and lcc detects the syntax error.

8.7   Unary and Postfix Expressions

The remaining functions handle the productions

unary-expression:
  postfix-expression
  unary-operator unary-expression
  '(' *type-name* ')' *unary-expression*
  sizeof *unary-expression*
  sizeof '(' *type-name* ')'

unary-operator:
　　one of ++ -- & * + - ~ !

postfix-expression:
　　primary-expression { *postfix-operator* }

postfix-operator:
　　'[' *expression* ']'
　　'(' [*assignment-expression* { , *assignment-expression* }] ')'
　　. *identifier*
　　-> *identifier*
　　++
　　--

and the productions for *primary-expression*, which are given in the next
section. The parsing components of these functions are simple because
these productions are simple. The parsing function for *unary-expression*
is an example: most of the unary operators are parsed by consuming the
operator, parsing the operand, and building the tree.

⟨*tree.c functions*⟩+≡   162 166

```
    static Tree unary() {
        Tree p;
```

```
        switch (t) {
        case '*':    ⟨p ← unary 165⟩ ⟨indirection 179⟩ break;
        case '&':    ⟨p ← unary 165⟩ ⟨address of 179⟩ break;
        case '+':    ⟨p ← unary 165⟩ ⟨affirmation⟩ break;
        case '-':    ⟨p ← unary 165⟩ ⟨negation 178⟩ break;
        case '~':    ⟨p ← unary 165⟩ ⟨complement⟩ break;
        case '!':    ⟨p ← unary 165⟩ ⟨logical not⟩ break;
        case INCR:   ⟨p ← unary 165⟩ ⟨preincrement 165⟩ break;
        case DECR:   ⟨p ← unary 165⟩ ⟨predecrement⟩ break;
        case SIZEOF: t = gettok(); { ⟨sizeof 165⟩ } break;
        case '(':
            t = gettok();
            if (istypename(t, tsym)) {
                ⟨type cast 180⟩
            } else
                p = postfix(expr(')'));
            break;
        default:
            p = postfix(primary());
        }
        return p;
    }
```

⟨p ← *unary* 165⟩≡   164
```
t = gettok(); p = unary();
```

Most of the fragments perform semantic checks, which are described in the next chapter. Three are simple enough to dispose of here. The expression ++*e* is semantically equivalent to the augmented assignment *e* += 1, so incr can build the tree for unary ++:

⟨*preincrement* 165⟩≡   164
```
p = incr(INCR, pointer(p), consttree(1, inttype));
```

Predecrement is similar.

sizeof '(' *type-name* ')' is a constant of type size_t that gives the number of bytes occupied by an instance of *type-name*. In lcc, size_t is unsigned. Similarly, the *unary-expression* in sizeof *unary-expression* serves only to provide a type whose size is desired; the *unary-expression* is *not* evaluated at runtime. Most of the effort in parsing sizeof goes into distinguishing between these two forms of sizeof and finding the appropriate type. Notice that the parentheses are required if the operand is a *type-name*.

⟨*sizeof* 165⟩≡   164
```
Type ty;
p = NULL;
if (t == '(') {
    t = gettok();
    if (istypename(t, tsym)) {
        ty = typename();
        expect(')');
    } else {
        p = postfix(expr(')'));
        ty = p->type;
    }
} else {
    p = unary();
    ty = p->type;
}
if (isfunc(ty) || ty->size == 0)
    error("invalid type argument '%t' to 'sizeof'\n", ty);
else if (p && rightkid(p)->op == FIELD)
    error("'sizeof' applied to a bit field\n");
p = consttree(ty->size, unsignedtype);
```

As the code suggests, sizeof cannot be applied to functions, incomplete types, or those derived from bit fields.

In unary and in ⟨*sizeof*⟩, a left parenthesis is a *primary-expression* or, if the next token is a type name, the beginning of a type cast.

If a left parenthesis does *not* introduce a type cast, it's too late to let primary parse the parenthesized expression, so unary must handle it. This is why postfix expects its *caller* to call primary and pass it the resulting tree instead of calling primary itself:

⟨*tree.c functions*⟩+≡   164 167

```
static Tree postfix(p) Tree p; {
    for (;;)
        switch (t) {
        case INCR:   ⟨postincrement 166⟩ break;
        case DECR:   ⟨postdecrement⟩ break;
        case '[':    ⟨subscript 181⟩ break;
        case '(':    ⟨calls 186⟩ break;
        case '.':    ⟨struct.field⟩ break;
        case DEREF:  ⟨pointer->field 182⟩ break;
        default:
            return p;
        }
}
```

Again, most of the fragments in postfix check the semantics of the operand and build the appropriate tree as detailed in the next chapter, but the tree for postincrement (and postdecrement) can be built by incr:

⟨*postincrement* 166⟩≡   166

```
p = tree(RIGHT, p->type,
    tree(RIGHT, p->type,
        p,
        incr(t, p, consttree(1, inttype))),
    p);
t = gettok();
```

The tree for postfix ++ is a dag because it must increment the operand but return the *previous* value. For example, the expression i++ builds the tree shown in Figure 8.3. The two RIGHT operators in this tree ensure the proper order of evaluation. The value of the entire expression is the rvalue of i, and the lower RIGHT tree ensures that this value is computed and saved *before* i is incremented by the ASGN+I tree. The construction is identical for p++ where p is a pointer — the addition takes care of incrementing p by the size of its referent.

8.8 Primary Expressions

The last parsing function for expressions is primary. It parses

primary-expression:
    identifier

> *constant*
> *string-literal*
> '(' *expression* ')'

which is analogous to *factor* in the simple expression grammars described in Section 8.2. All that's left to handle are constants and identifiers:

⟨*tree.c functions*⟩+≡   166 168

```
static Tree primary() {
    Tree p;

    switch (t) {
    case ICON:
    case FCON: ⟨numeric constants 167⟩ break;
    case SCON: ⟨string constants 168⟩ break;
    case ID:   ⟨an identifier 170⟩ break;
    default:
        error("illegal expression\n");
        p = consttree(0, inttype);
    }
    t = gettok();
    return p;
}
```

CNST trees hold the values of integer and floating constants in their u.v fields:

⟨*numeric constants* 167⟩≡   167

```
p = tree(CNST + ttob(tsym->type), tsym->type, NULL, NULL);
p->u.v = tsym->u.c.v;
```

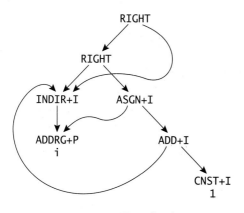

FIGURE 8.3 Tree for i++.

⟨u *fields for* Tree *variants* 168⟩ ≡   168   149
```
    Value v;
```

String constants are abbreviations for read-only variables initialized to the value of the string constant:

⟨*string constants* 168⟩ ≡   167
```
    tsym->u.c.v.p = stringn(tsym->u.c.v.p, tsym->type->size);
    tsym = constant(tsym->type, tsym->u.c.v);
    if (tsym->u.c.loc == NULL)
        tsym->u.c.loc = genident(STATIC, tsym->type, GLOBAL);
    p = idtree(tsym->u.c.loc);
```

The generated variable and its initialization are emitted at the end of the compilation by finalize. The tree for strings is the tree for the generated identifier.

idtree(p) builds a tree for accessing the identifier indicated by the symbol-table entry p. Identifiers are categorized by their scopes and lifetimes (parameters, automatic locals, and statics, including globals) and their types (arrays, functions, and nonarray objects). idtree uses an identifier's scope and storage class to determine its addressing operator, then uses its type to determine the shape of the tree that accesses it, and stores a pointer to the symbol-table entry in the tree's u.sym field:

⟨u *fields for* Tree *variants* 168⟩ +≡   168 183   149
```
    Symbol sym;
```

⟨*tree.c functions*⟩ +≡   167 169
```
    Tree idtree(p) Symbol p; {
        int op;
        Tree e;
        Type ty = p->type ? unqual(p->type) : voidtype;

        p->ref += refinc;
        if (p->scope   == GLOBAL
        ||  p->sclass == STATIC || p->sclass == EXTERN)
            op = ADDRG+P;
        else if (p->scope == PARAM) {
            op = ADDRF+P;
            if (isstruct(p->type) && !IR->wants_argb)
                ⟨return a tree for a struct parameter 170⟩
        } else
            op = ADDRL+P;
        if (isarray(ty) || isfunc(ty)) {
            e = tree(op, p->type, NULL, NULL);
            e->u.sym = p;
        } else {
```

```
    e = tree(op, ptr(p->type), NULL, NULL);
    e->u.sym = p;
    e = rvalue(e);
  }
  return e;
}
```

⟨*tree.c data*⟩+≡   155
```
float refinc = 1.0;
```

p->ref is an estimate of the number of references to the identifier described by p; other functions can adjust the weight of one reference to p by changing refinc. All external, static, and global identifiers are addressed with ADDRG operators; parameters are addressed with ADDRF; and locals are addressed with ADDRL.

Arrays and functions cannot be used as lvalues or rvalues, so references to them have only the appropriate addressing operators. Trees for other types refer to the identifiers' rvalues; an example is the tree for i's rvalue in Figure 8.3. rvalue adds the INDIR:

⟨*tree.c functions*⟩+≡   168 169
```
Tree rvalue(p) Tree p; {
  Type ty = deref(p->type);

  ty = unqual(ty);
  return tree(INDIR + (isunsigned(ty) ? I : ttob(ty)),
    ty, p, NULL);
}
```

61	deref
60	isunsigned
61	ptr
150	tree
73	ttob
60	unqual
160	value
58	voidtype
88	wants_argb

rvalue can be called with any tree that represents a pointer value. lvalue, however, must be called with only trees that represent an rvalue — the contents of an addressable location. The INDIR tree added by rvalue also signals that a tree is a valid lvalue, and the address is exposed by tearing off the INDIR. lvalue implements this check and transformation:

⟨*tree.c functions*⟩+≡   169 173
```
Tree lvalue(p) Tree p; {
  if (generic(p->op) != INDIR) {
    error("lvalue required\n");
    return value(p);
  } else if (unqual(p->type) == voidtype)
    warning("'%t' used as an lvalue\n", p->type);
  return p->kids[0];
}
```

The tree for a structure parameter also depends on the value of the interface field wants_argb. If wants_argb is 1, the code shown above

builds the appropriate tree, which has the form (INDIR+B (ADDRF+P x))
for parameter x. If wants_argb is zero, the front end implements structure arguments by copying them at a call and passing pointers to the
copies. Thus, a reference to a structure parameter needs another indirection to access the structure itself:

⟨*return a tree for a struct parameter* 170⟩≡   168

```
    {
        e = tree(op, ptr(ptr(p->type)), NULL, NULL);
        e->u.sym = p;
        return rvalue(rvalue(e));
    }
```

For a parameter x, this code builds the tree

```
    (INDIR+B (INDIR+P (ADDRF+P x)))
```

idtree is used wherever a tree for an identifier is needed, such as for
string constants (above) and for identifiers:

⟨*an identifier* 170⟩≡   167
```
    if (tsym == NULL)
        ⟨undeclared identifier⟩
    if (xref)
        use(tsym, src);
    if (tsym->sclass == ENUM)
        p = consttree(tsym->u.value, inttype);
    else {
        if (tsym->sclass == TYPEDEF)
            error("illegal use of type name '%s'\n", tsym->name);
        p = idtree(tsym);
    }
```

If tsym is null, the identifier is undeclared, which draws a diagnostic
unless it's a function call (see Exercise 8.5). Enumeration identifiers are
synonyms for constants and yield trees for the constants, not for the
identifiers.

Further Reading

Handling n levels of precedence with one parsing function instead of
n parsing functions is well known folklore in compiler circles, but there
are few explanations of the technique. Hanson (1985) describes the technique as it is used in lcc. Holzmann (1988) used a similar technique
in his image manipulation language, *pico*. The technique is technically
equivalent to the one used in BCPL (Richards and Whitby-Strevens 1979),
but the operators and their precedences and associativities are spread
throughout the BCPL code instead of being encapsulated in tables.

Exercises

8.1 Implement

⟨*tree.c exported functions*⟩≡   171
```
extern Tree retype ARGS((Tree p, Type ty));
```

which returns p if p->type == ty or a copy of p with type ty. Recall that all tree-manipulation functions are applicative.

8.2 Implement

⟨*tree.c exported functions*⟩+≡   171 171
```
extern Tree rightkid ARGS((Tree p));
```

which returns the rightmost non-RIGHT operand of a nested series of RIGHT trees rooted at p. Don't forget that RIGHT nodes can have one or two operands (but not zero).

8.3 Implement

⟨*tree.c exported functions*⟩+≡   171
```
extern int hascall ARGS((Tree p));
```

which returns one if p contains a CALL tree and zero otherwise. Don't forget about the interface flag mulops_calls.

162	expr3
40	externals
158	incr
318	listnodes
87	mulops_calls
149	RIGHT

8.4 Reimplement expr3 the straightforward way shown at the beginning of Section 8.6, and measure its performance. Is the savings gained by removing the recursive calls worth the effort?

8.5 Complete the code for ⟨*undeclared identifier*⟩ used on page 170. If the identifier is used as a function, which is legal, supply an implicit declaration for the identifier at the current scope *and* in the externals table. Otherwise, the undeclared identifier is an error, but it's useful to supply an implicit declaration for it anyway so that compilation can proceed.

8.6 As explained in Section 8.4, the trees returned by incr are dags. Add new tree operators for the augmented assignment operators and rewrite incr to use them and thus avoid the dags. You'll need to change listnodes, and you might have to change the semantics functions in enode.c.

9
Expression Semantics

Expressions must be both syntactically and semantically correct. The parsing functions described in the previous chapter handle the syntactic issues and some of the simpler semantic issues, such as building the trees for constants and identifiers. This chapter describes the semantic analyses that must be done to build trees for expressions. These analyses must deal with three separate subproblems of approximately equal difficulty: implicit conversions, type checking, and order of evaluation.

Implicit conversions are conversions that do not appear in the source program and that must be added by the compiler in order to adhere to the semantic rules of the standard. For example, in a + b, if a is an int and b is a float, a + b is semantically correct, but an implicit conversion must be added to convert a's value to a float.

Type-checking confirms that the types of an operator's operands are legal, determines the type of the result, and computes the type-specific operator that must be used. For example, type checking a + b verifies that the types of a and b are legal combinations of the arithmetic types, and uses the types of a and b to determine the type of the result, which is one of numeric types. It also determines which type-specific addition is required. In the a + b example, type checking is handed the equivalent of (float)a + b, and determines that floating addition is required.

expr 155
promote 71

The compiler must generate trees that obey the standard's rules for the *order of evaluation*. For many operators, the order of evaluation is unspecified. For example, in a[i++] = i, it is unspecified whether i is incremented before or after the assignment. The order of evaluation is specified for a few operators; for example, in f() && g(), f must be called before g; if f returns zero, g must not be called. Similarly, f must be called before g in (f(), g()). As suggested in expr, RIGHT trees have a well defined order of evaluation and can be used to force a specific order of evaluation.

9.1 Conversions

Conversion functions accept one or more types and return a resulting type, or accept a tree and perhaps a type and return a tree with the appropriate conversion. promote(Type ty) is an example of the former kind of conversion: It implements the integral promotions. It widens an integral type ty to int, unsigned, or long, if necessary. As stipulated by the standard, the integral promotions preserve value, including sign. They are *not* unsigned preserving. For example, an unsigned char is promoted to an int, not an unsigned int. A small integral type (or a bit field) is promoted to int if int can represent all the values of the smaller type. Otherwise, the small integral type is promoted to unsigned int. In lcc, int must always represent the values of the smaller integral types, which is why the final if statement in promote returns inttype.

binary implements the *usual arithmetic conversions*; it takes two arithmetic types and returns the type of the result for any binary arithmetic operator:

⟨*tree.c functions*⟩+≡   1̂69 1̲7̲4̲

```
Type binary(xty, yty) Type xty, yty; {
    if (isdouble(xty) || isdouble(yty))
        return doubletype;
    if (xty == floattype || yty == floattype)
        return floattype;
    if (isunsigned(xty) || isunsigned(yty))
        return unsignedtype;
    return inttype;
}
```

lcc assumes that doubles and long doubles are the same size and that longs and ints (both unsigned and signed) are also the same size. These assumptions simplify the standard's specification of the usual arithmetic conversions and thus simplify binary. The list below summarizes the standard's specification in the more general case, when a long double is bigger than a double, and a long is bigger than an unsigned int:

> long double
> double
> float
> unsigned long int
> long int
> unsigned int
> int

The type of the operand that appears highest in this list is the type to which the other operand is converted. If none of these types apply, the operands are converted to ints. lcc's assumptions collapse the first two types to the first if statement in binary, and the second if statement handles floats. The third if statement handles the four integer types because lcc's signed long cannot represent all unsigned values.

pointer is an example of the second kind of conversion function that takes a tree and returns a tree, possibly converted. Array and function types decay into pointers when used in expressions: (ARRAY *T*) and (POINTER *T*) decay into (FUNCTION *T*) and (POINTER (FUNCTION *T*)).

⟨*tree.c functions*⟩+≡   173 174

```
Tree pointer(p) Tree p; {
    if (isarray(p->type))
        p = retype(p, atop(p->type));
    else if (isfunc(p->type))
        p = retype(p, ptr(p->type));
    return p;
}
```

rvalue, lvalue, and value can also be viewed as conversions. cond is
the inverse of value; it takes a tree that might represent a value and
turns it into a tree for a conditional by adding a comparison with zero:

⟨*tree.c functions*⟩+≡   174 175

```
Tree cond(p) Tree p; {
    int op = generic(rightkid(p)->op);

    if (op == AND || op == OR || op == NOT
    ||  op == EQ  || op == NE
    ||  op == LE  || op == LT || op == GE || op == GT)
        return p;
    p = pointer(p);
    p = cast(p, promote(p->type));
    return (*optree[NEQ])(NE, p, consttree(0, inttype));
}
```

A conditional has no value; it's used only in a context in which its outcome affects the flow of control, such as in an if statement. cond returns
a tree whose outcome is true when the value is nonzero.

cond calls cast to convert its argument to the basic type given by its
promoted type. cast implements the conversions depicted in Figure 9.1.
Each arrow in Figure 9.1 represents one of the conversion operators. For
example, the arrow from I to D represents conversion from integer to
double, CVI+D, and the opposite arrow represents conversion from double to integer, CVD+I. The C above the I denotes signed characters and
the C above the U denotes unsigned characters; similar comments apply
to the two occurrences of S.

Conversions that don't have arrows are implemented by combining the
existing operators. For example, a signed short integer *s* is converted to
a float by converting it to an integer, then to a double, and finally to float.
The tree is (CVD+F (CVI+D (CVS+I *s*))). Conversions between unsigned
and double are handled differently, as described below.

cast has three parts that correspond to the steps just outlined. First,
p is converted to its supertype, which is D, I, or U. Then, it's converted to
the supertype of the destination type, if necessary. Finally, it's converted
to the destination type.

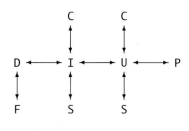

FIGURE 9.1 Conversions.

⟨*tree.c functions*⟩+≡   174 182

```
Tree cast(p, type) Tree p; Type type; {
    Type pty, ty = unqual(type);

    p = value(p);
    if (p->type == type)
        return p;
    pty = unqual(p->type);
    if (pty == ty)
        return retype(p, type);
    ⟨convert p to super(pty) 175⟩
    ⟨convert p to super(ty) 176⟩
    ⟨convert p to ty 177⟩
    return p;
}
```

As shown, these conversions are done with the unqualified versions of the types involved. super returns its argument's supertype.

The first step makes all signed integers ints, floats doubles, and pointers unsigneds:

⟨*convert p to* super(pty) 175⟩≡   175

```
switch (pty->op) {
case CHAR:    p = simplify(CVC, super(pty), p, NULL); break;
case SHORT:   p = simplify(CVS, super(pty), p, NULL); break;
case FLOAT:   p = simplify(CVF, doubletype, p, NULL); break;
case INT:     p = retype(p, inttype);           break;
case DOUBLE:  p = retype(p, doubletype);        break;
case ENUM:    p = retype(p, inttype);           break;
case UNSIGNED:p = retype(p, unsignedtype);      break;
case POINTER:
    if (isptr(ty)) {
        ⟨pointer-to-pointer conversion 176⟩
    } else
        p = simplify(CVP, unsignedtype, p, NULL);
```

```
        break;
    }
```

simplify builds trees just like tree, but folds constants, if possible, and, if a generic operator is given as its first argument, simplify forms the type-specific operator from its first and second arguments. lcc insists that pointers fit in unsigned integers, so that they can be carried by un-signed operators, which reduces the operator vocabulary. There's one special case: the CVP+U is eliminated for pointer-to-pointer conversions because it's always useless there.

⟨*pointer-to-pointer conversion* 176⟩≡   175
```
    if (isfunc(pty->type) && !isfunc(ty->type)
    || !isfunc(pty->type) &&  isfunc(ty->type))
        warning("conversion from '%t' to '%t' is compiler _
            dependent\n", p->type, ty);
    return retype(p, type);
```

lcc warns about conversions between *object pointers* and function point-ers because the standard permits these different kinds of pointers to have different sizes. lcc, however, insists that they have the same sizes.

The second step converts p, which is now a double, int, or unsigned, to whichever one of these three types is ty's supertype, if necessary:

⟨*convert* p *to* super(ty) 176⟩≡   175
```
    {
        Type sty = super(ty);
        pty = p->type;
        if (pty != sty)
            if (pty == inttype)
                p = simplify(CVI, sty, p, NULL);
            else if (pty == doubletype)
                if (sty == unsignedtype) {
                    ⟨double-to-unsigned conversion⟩
                } else
                    p = simplify(CVD, sty, p, NULL);
            else if (pty == unsignedtype)
                if (sty == doubletype) {
                    ⟨unsigned-to-double conversion 177⟩
                } else
                    p = simplify(CVU, sty, p, NULL);
    }
```

Notice that there are no arrows directly between D and U in Figure 9.1. Most machines have instructions that convert between *signed* integers and doubles, but few have instructions that convert between unsigneds and doubles, so there is no CVU+D or CVD+U. Instead, the front end builds

trees that implement these conversions, assuming that integers and unsigneds are the same size.

An unsigned u can be converted to a double by constructing an expression equivalent to

```
2.*(int)(u>>1) + (int)(u&1)
```

u>>1 vacates the sign bit so that the shifted result, which is equal to
u/2, can be converted to a double with an integer-to-double conversion.
The floating-point multiplication and addition compute the value desired.
The code builds the tree for this expression:

⟨*unsigned-to-double conversion* 177⟩ ≡   176
```
    Tree two = tree(CNST+D, doubletype, NULL, NULL);
    two->u.v.d = 2.;
    p = (*optree['+'])(ADD,
        (*optree['*'])(MUL,
            two,
            simplify(CVU, inttype,
                simplify(RSH, unsignedtype,
                    p, consttree(1, inttype)), NULL)),
        simplify(CVU, inttype,
            simplify(BAND, unsignedtype,
                p, consttree(1, unsignedtype)), NULL));
```

Notice that this tree is a dag: It contains two references to p. The optree
functions are used for the multiplication and addition so that the integer-
to-double conversions will be included.

The front end implements double-to-unsigned conversions by constructing a tree for the appropriate expression. Exercise 9.2 explores
how.

The tree now represents a value whose type is the supertype of ty,
and the third step in cast converts the tree to the destination type. This
step is essentially the inverse of super:

⟨*convert* p *to* ty 177⟩ ≡   175
```
    if (ty == signedchar || ty == chartype || ty == shorttype)
        p = simplify(CVI, type, p, NULL);
    else if (isptr(ty)
    || ty == unsignedchar || ty == unsignedshort)
        p = simplify(CVU, type, p, NULL);
    else if (ty == floattype)
        p = simplify(CVD, type, p, NULL);
    else
        p = retype(p, type);
```

9.2   Unary and Postfix Operators

The conversion functions described above provide the machinery needed to implement the semantic checking for each of the operators. The constraints on the operands, such as their types, and the semantics of the operator, such as its result type, are defined in the standard. The prose for unary - is typical:

> The operand of the unary - operator shall have arithmetic type.
> The result of the unary - operator is the negative of its operand. The integral promotion is performed on the operand, and the result has the promoted type.

The code for each operator implements these kinds of specifications; it checks that the operand trees meet the constraints and it builds the appropriate tree for the result. For example, the code for unary - is

⟨*negation* 178⟩ ≡   164

```
p = pointer(p);
if (isarith(p->type)) {
    p = cast(p, promote(p->type));
    if (isunsigned(p->type)) {
        warning("unsigned operand of unary -\n");
        p = simplify(NEG, inttype, cast(p, inttype), NULL);
        p = cast(p, unsignedtype);
    } else
        p = simplify(NEG, p->type, p, NULL);
} else
    typeerror(SUB, p, NULL);
```

cast 175
isarith 60
isunsigned 60
lvalue 169
pointer 174
promote 71
simplify 203
unsignedtype 58

typeerror issues a diagnostic for illegal operands to a unary or binary operator. For example, if pi is an int *, -pi is illegal because pi is not an arithmetic type, and typeerror issues

```
operand of unary - has illegal type 'pointer to int'
```

Warning about using unsigned operands to unary - is not required by the standard, but helps pinpoint probable errors. This warning would be appropriate even if lcc supported a signed long type that could hold all negated unsigneds, because the integral promotions do *not* yield any of the long types.

For unary &, the standard says

> The operand of the unary & operator shall be either a function designator or an lvalue that designates an object that is not a bit-field and not declared with the register storage-class specifier.

Unary & takes an operand of type *T* and returns its address, which has type (POINTER *T*). In most cases, the semantics above are provided by lvalue, which exposes the addressing tree under an INDIR. The exceptions are arrays and functions, which have no INDIRs:

⟨*address of* 179⟩≡   164
```
    if (isarray(p->type) || isfunc(p->type))
        p = retype(p, ptr(p->type));
    else
        p = lvalue(p);
    if (isaddrop(p->op) && p->u.sym->sclass == REGISTER)
        error("invalid operand of unary &; '%s' is declared _
            register\n", p->u.sym->name);
    else if (isaddrop(p->op))
        p->u.sym->addressed = 1;
```

⟨*tree.c exported macros*⟩≡
```
    #define isaddrop(op) \
        ((op)==ADDRG+P || (op)==ADDRL+P || (op)==ADDRF+P)
```

⟨*symbol flags* 50⟩+≡   50̂ 211̲   38
```
    unsigned addressed:1;
```

As specified above, unary & cannot be applied to register variables or to
bit fields. Trees for bit fields don't have INDIRs, so lvalue catches them.
The front end changes the storage class of frequently referenced locals
and parameters to REGISTER before it passes them to the back end. But
it must not change the storage class of variables whose addresses are
taken, which are those symbols with addressed lit.

Unary * is the inverse of unary &; it takes an operand with the type
(POINTER *T*) and wraps it in an INDIR tree to represent an rvalue of type
T. Again, most of the work is done by rvalue, and pointers to arrays
and functions need special treatment.

⟨*indirection* 179⟩≡   164
```
    p = pointer(p);
    if (isptr(p->type)
    && (isfunc(p->type->type) || isarray(p->type->type)))
        p = retype(p, p->type->type);
    else {
        if (YYnull)
            p = nullcheck(p);
        p = rvalue(p);
    }
```

Exercise 9.5 explains YYnull and nullcheck, which help catch null-
pointer errors.

Type casts specify explicit conversions. Some casts, such as pointer-
to-pointer casts, generate no code, but simply specify the type of an expression. Other casts, such as int-to-float, generate code that effects the
conversion at runtime. The code below and the code in cast implement
the rules specified by the standard.

The standard stipulates that the target type specified in a cast must be a qualified or unqualified scalar type or void, and the type of the operand — the source type — must be a scalar type. The semantic analysis of casts divides into computing and checking the target type, parsing the operand, and computing and checking the source type. typename parses a type declarator and returns the resulting Type, and thus does most of the work of computing the target type, except for qualified enumerations:

⟨*type cast* 180⟩≡   180   164

```
Type ty, ty1 = typename(), pty;
expect(')');
ty = unqual(ty1);
if (isenum(ty)) {
    Type ty2 = ty->type;
    if (isconst(ty1))
        ty2 = qual(CONST, ty2);
    if (isvolatile(ty1))
        ty2 = qual(VOLATILE, ty2);
    ty1 = ty2;
    ty = ty->type;
}
```

This code computes the target type ty1 and its unqualified variant ty. The target type for a cast that specifies an enumeration type is the enumeration's underlying integral type (which for lcc is always int), not the enumeration. Thus, ty1 and ty must be recomputed before parsing the operand.

⟨*type cast* 180⟩+≡   180 180   164

```
p = pointer(unary());
pty = p->type;
if (isenum(pty))
    pty = pty->type;
```

This tree is cast to the unqualified type, ty, if the target and source types are legal: arithmetic and enumeration types can be cast to each other; pointers can be cast to other pointers; pointers can be cast to integral types and vice versa, but the result is undefined if the sizes of the types differ; and any type can be cast to void.

⟨*type cast* 180⟩+≡   180 181   164

```
if (isarith(pty) && isarith(ty)
|| isptr(pty)    && isptr(ty))
    p = cast(p, ty);
else if (isptr(pty) && isint(ty)
||        isint(pty) && isptr(ty)) {
    if (Aflag >= 1 && ty->size < pty->size)
```

```
      warning("conversion from '%t' to '%t' is compiler _
         dependent\n", p->type, ty);
   p = cast(p, ty);
} else if (ty != voidtype) {
   error("cast from '%t' to '%t' is illegal\n",
      p->type, ty1);
   ty1 = inttype;
}
```

Recall that cast warns about casts between object and function pointers.

The final step is to annotate p with the possibly qualified type:

⟨*type cast* 180⟩+≡   180   164
```
p = retype(p, ty1);
if (generic(p->op) == INDIR)
   p = tree(RIGHT, ty, NULL, p);
```

A cast is not an lvalue, so if p is an INDIR tree, it's hidden under a RIGHT tree, which keeps lvalue from accepting it as an lvalue.

The standard stipulates that an expression of the form $e[i]$ be treated as equivalent to $*(e+i)$. One of the operands must be a pointer and the other must be an integral type. The semantics function for addition does most of the work once e and i are recognized:

⟨*subscript* 181⟩≡   166

```
   {
      Tree q;
      t = gettok();
      q = expr(']');
      if (YYnull)
         if (isptr(p->type))
            p = nullcheck(p);
         else if (isptr(q->type))
            q = nullcheck(q);
      p = (*optree['+'])(ADD, pointer(p), pointer(q));
      if (isptr(p->type) && isarray(p->type->type))
         p = retype(p, p->type->type);
      else
         p = rvalue(p);
   }
```

175	cast
155	expr
60	isarray
60	isptr
169	lvalue
215	nullcheck
191	optree
174	pointer
171	retype
149	RIGHT
169	rvalue
150	tree
58	voidtype

The last if statement handles n-dimensional arrays; for example, if x is declared int x[10][20], x[i] refers to the ith row, which is has type (ARRAY 20 (INT)), but x[i] is not an lvalue. Similar comments apply to i[x], which is a bit peculiar but equivalent nonetheless.

References to fields are similar to subscripting; they yield trees that refer to the rvalue of the indicated field and are thus lvalues, or, for array fields, trees that refer to the address of the field. The parsing is straightforward:

⟨*pointer->field* 182⟩≡   166
```
    t = gettok();
    p = pointer(p);
    if (t == ID) {
        if (isptr(p->type) && isstruct(p->type->type)) {
            if (YYnull)
                p = nullcheck(p);
            p = field(p, token);
        } else
            error("left operand of -> has incompatible _
                type '%t'\n", p->type);
        t = gettok();
    } else
        error("field name expected\n");
```

field calls fieldref, which returns the Field that gives the type and
location of the field.

⟨*tree.c functions*⟩+≡   1̂75
```
    Tree field(p, name) Tree p; char *name; {
        Field q;
        Type ty1, ty = p->type;

        if (isptr(ty))
            ty = deref(ty);
        ty1 = ty;
        ty = unqual(ty);
        if ((q = fieldref(name, ty)) != NULL) {
            ⟨access the field described by q 182⟩
        } else {
            error("unknown field '%s' of '%t'\n", name, ty);
            p = rvalue(retype(p, ptr(inttype)));
        }
        return p;
    }
```

field must cope with qualified structure types. If a structure type is
declared const or volatile, references to its fields must be similarly qualified even though the qualifiers are not permitted in field declarators.
q->type is the type of the field and q->offset is the byte offset to the
field.

⟨*access the field described by* q 182⟩≡   183   182
```
    if (isarray(q->type)) {
        ty = q->type->type;
        ⟨qualify ty, when necessary 183⟩
        ty = array(ty, q->type->size/ty->size, q->type->align);
```

```
    } else {
        ty = q->type;
        ⟨qualify ty, when necessary 183⟩
        ty = ptr(ty);
    }
    p = simplify(ADD+P, ty, p, consttree(q->offset, inttype));
```

⟨*qualify* ty, *when necessary* 183⟩≡   182 183
```
    if (isconst(ty1) && !isconst(ty))
        ty = qual(CONST, ty);
    if (isvolatile(ty1) && !isvolatile(ty))
        ty = qual(VOLATILE, ty);
```

simplify returns a tree for the address of the field, or the address of the unsigned that holds a bit field. A nonzero q->lsb gives the position plus one of a bit field's least significant bit, and serves to identify a field as a bit field. Bit fields are referenced via FIELD trees, and are not lvalues.

⟨*access the field described by* q 182⟩+≡   182▲   182
```
    if (q->lsb) {
        p = tree(FIELD, ty->type, rvalue(p), NULL);
        p->u.field = q;
    } else if (!isarray(q->type))
        p = rvalue(p);
```

⟨u *fields for* Tree *variants* 168⟩+≡   168▲   149
```
    Field field;
```

The u.field field in a FIELD tree points to the Field structure, defined in Section 4.6, that describes the bit field.

The expression *e*.*name* is equivalent to (&*e*)->*name*, so field is also called by the fragment ⟨*struct*.*field*⟩. That code builds a tree for the address of .'s left operand, and passes it to field.

9.3 Function Calls

Function calls are easy to parse but difficult to analyze. The analysis must cope with calls to both new-style and old-style functions in which the semantics imposed by the standard affect the conversions and argument checking. Semantic analysis must also handle the order of evaluation of the arguments (which depends on the interface flag left_to_right), passing and returning structures by value (which depends on the interface flags wants_argb and wants_callb), and actual arguments that include other calls. All these variants are caused by lcc's interface, not by rules in the standard, and all of them could be eliminated. Doing so, however, would make it impossible for lcc to generate

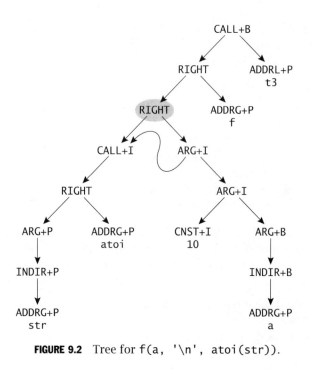

FIGURE 9.2 Tree for `f(a, '\n', atoi(str))`.

code that mimics the established calling sequences on one or more of its targets. These complexities are the price of compatibility with existing calling conventions.

The meaningless program

```
char *str;
struct node { ... } a;
struct node f(struct node x, char c, int i) { ... }
main () { f(a, '\n', atoi(str)); }
```

illustrates almost all these complexities. The tree for the call to f is shown in Figure 9.2, which assumes that wants_argb is one. The CALL+B's right operand is described below. The RIGHT trees in this figure collaborate to achieve the desired evaluation order. A CALL's left operand is a RIGHT tree that evaluates the arguments (the ARG trees) and the function itself. The leftmost RIGHT tree in Figure 9.2 is an example. The tree whose root is the shaded RIGHT in Figure 9.2 occurs because of the nested call to atoi. When this tree is traversed, code is generated so that the call to atoi occurs *before* the arguments to f are evaluated. In general, there's one RIGHT tree for each argument that includes a call, and one if the function name is itself an expression with a call.

The actual arguments are represented by ARG trees, rightmost argument first; their right operands are the trees for the evaluation of the rest of the actual arguments. Recall that ARG trees can have two operands.

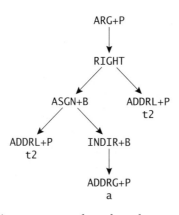

FIGURE 9.3 Passing a structure by value when `wants_argb` is zero.

The topmost ARG+I is for the argument `atoi(str)`, and its left operand points to the CALL+I described above. The presence of the RIGHT tree will cause the back end to store the value returned by `atoi` in a temporary, and the reference from the ARG+I to the CALL+I for `atoi` will pass that value to `f`.

The second ARG+I is for the newline passed as the second argument. `f` has a prototype and is thus a new-style function, so it might be expected that the integer constant `'\n'` would be converted to and passed as a character. Most machines have constraints, such as stack alignment, that force subword types to be passed as words. Even without such constraints, passing subword types as words is usually more efficient. So lcc generates code to widen short arguments and character arguments to integers when they are passed, and code to narrow them upon entry for new-style functions. If the global char `ch` was passed as `f`'s second argument, the tree would be

```
(ARG+I (CVC+I (INDIR+C (ADDRG+P ch))))
```

The bottom ARG+B tree passes the structure `a` to `f` by value. ARG+B is provided so that back ends can use target-specific calling sequences; Chapter 16 shows how it's used on the MIPS. If `wants_argb` is zero, the front end completely implements value transmission for structures. It copies the actual argument to a local temporary in the caller, and passes the address of that temporary. As detailed in `idtree`, references to the actual argument in the callee use an extra indirection to fetch the structure. Figure 9.3 shows the ARG tree for passing `a` to `f` when `wants_argb` is zero. The RIGHT tree generates code to assign `a` to the temporary, `t2`, followed by passing the address of `t2`.

The right operand of CALL+B is the address of a temporary in the caller to which the return value is assigned; `t3` in Figure 9.2, for example. When the interface flag `wants_callb` is one, the back end must arrange to pass this address to the caller. When `wants_callb` is zero, the front end arranges to pass this address as a hidden first argument, and it *changes* the CALL+B to a CALL+V; in this case, the back end never sees CALLB nodes. This change is made by `listnodes` when the tree for a call is converted to a forest of nodes for the back end.

`listnodes` also inspects the interface flag `left_to_right` as it traverses a call tree. If `left_to_right` is one, the argument subtree is traversed by visiting the right operands of ARG trees first, which generates code that evaluates the arguments from the left to the right. If `left_to_right` is zero, the left operands are visited first, which evaluates the arguments from the right to the left.

The case in `postfix` checks the type of the function expression and lets `call` do most of the work:

⟨*calls* 186⟩≡   166

```
{
    Type ty;
    Coordinate pt;
    p = pointer(p);
    if (isptr(p->type) && isfunc(p->type->type))
        ty = p->type->type;
    else {
        error("found '%t' expected a function\n", p->type);
        ty = func(voidtype, NULL, 1);
    }
    pt = src;
    t = gettok();
    p = call(p, ty, pt);
}
```

`call` dedicates locals to deal with each of the semantic issues described above. n counts the number of actual arguments. `args` is the root of the argument tree, and r is the root of the RIGHT tree that holds arguments or function expressions that include calls. For the example shown in Figure 9.2, r points to the CALL+I tree. After parsing the arguments, if r is nonnull, it and `args` are pasted together in a RIGHT tree, which is the subtree rooted at the shaded RIGHT in Figure 9.2. `hascall` returns a nonzero value if its argument tree includes a CALL, and `funcname` returns the name buried in f or the string "a function" if f computes a function address.

⟨*enode.c functions*⟩≡   189

```
Tree call(f, fty, src) Tree f; Type fty; Coordinate src; {
    int n = 0;
    Tree args = NULL, r = NULL;
    Type *proto, rty = unqual(freturn(fty));
    Symbol t3 = NULL;
```

```
    if (fty->u.f.oldstyle)
        proto = NULL;
    else
        proto = fty->u.f.proto;
    if (hascall(f))
        r = f;
    if (isstruct(rty))
        ⟨initialize for a struct function 187⟩
    if (t != ')')
        for (;;) {
            ⟨parse one argument 188⟩
            if (t != ',')
                break;
            t = gettok();
        }
    expect(')');
    if ((⟨still in a new-style prototype? 187⟩))
        error("insufficient number of arguments to %s\n",
            funcname(f));
    if (r)
        args = tree(RIGHT, voidtype, r, args);
    if (events.calls)
        ⟨plant an event hook for a call⟩
    return calltree(f, rty, args, t3);
}
```

f is the expression for the function, rty is the return type, and proto is either null for an old-style function (even if it has a prototype; see Section 4.5) or walks along the function prototype for a new-style function. A nonnull proto is incremented for each actual argument that corresponds to a formal parameter in a new-style prototype, and

⟨still in a new-style prototype? 187⟩≡   187 188
```
    proto && *proto && *proto != voidtype
```

tests if proto points to a formal parameter type, when there *is* a prototype. Reaching the end of a prototype is different from reaching the end of the actual arguments; for example, excess arguments are permitted in new-style functions with a variable number of arguments.

If the function returns a structure, t3 is the temporary that's generated to hold the return value:

⟨initialize for a struct function 187⟩≡   187
```
    {
        t3 = temporary(AUTO, unqual(rty), level);
        if (rty->size == 0)
            error("illegal use of incomplete type '%t'\n", rty);
    }
```

t3 is the temporary shown in Figure 9.2. This initialization could be done after parsing the arguments, but it's done before so that the source coordinate in the diagnostic shown above pinpoints the beginning of the argument list.

An actual argument is an *assignment-expression*:

⟨*parse one argument* 188⟩≡   187
```
Tree q = pointer(expr1(0));
if ((⟨still in a new-style prototype? 187⟩))
    ⟨new-style argument 188⟩
else
    ⟨old-style argument 189⟩
if (!IR->wants_argb && isstruct(q->type))
    ⟨pass a structure directly 191⟩
if (q->type->size == 0)
    q->type = inttype;
if (hascall(q))
    r = r ? tree(RIGHT, voidtype, r, q) : q;
args = tree(ARG + widen(q->type), q->type, q, args);
n++;
if (Aflag >= 2 && n == 32)
    warning("more than 31 arguments in a call to %s\n",
        funcname(f));
```

The if statement at the beginning of this fragment distinguishes between new-style and old-style function types, and handles calls to new-style functions that have a varying number of arguments, such as `printf`, or that have excess arguments. If a prototype specifies a variable length argument list (by ending in `,...`), there are at least two types in the prototype array and the last one is `voidtype`. Actual arguments beyond the last explicit argument are passed in the same way as arguments to old-style functions are passed.

New-style arguments are passed as if the actual argument were assigned to the formal parameter. No assignment is actually made because the argument is carried by an ARG tree, but the argument can be type-checked with `assign`, which type-checks assignments:

⟨*new-style argument* 188⟩≡   188
```
{
    Type aty;
    q = value(q);
    aty = assign(*proto, q);
    if (aty)
        q = cast(q, aty);
    else
        error("type error in argument %d to %s; found '%t' _
            expected '%t'\n", n + 1, funcname(f),
```

```
            q->type, *proto);
    if ((isint(q->type) || isenum(q->type))
    && q->type->size != inttype->size)
        q = cast(q, promote(q->type));
    ++proto;
}
```

The second call to `cast` widens subinteger arguments as described above.

Old-style arguments suffer the *default argument promotions.* The integral promotions are performed and floats are promoted to doubles.

⟨*old-style argument* 189⟩≡   188
```
    {
        if (!fty->u.f.oldstyle && *proto == NULL)
            error("too many arguments to %s\n", funcname(f));
        q = value(q);
        if (q->type == floattype)
            q = cast(q, doubletype);
        else if (isarray(q->type) || q->type->size == 0)
            error("type error in argument %d to %s; '%t' is _
                illegal\n", n + 1, funcname(f), q->type);
        else
            q = cast(q, promote(q->type));
    }
```

The first test in this fragment checks `f.oldstyle` because it's not enough to just check for nonnull `f.proto`: as mentioned in Section 4.5, old-style functions can carry prototypes, but these prototypes cannot be used to type-check actual arguments.

The actual CALL tree is built by `calltree`, which is presented with the tree for the function expression, the return type, the argument tree, and the temporary if the function returns a structure. It combines the trees to form the CALL+B tree shown in Figure 9.2:

⟨*enode.c functions*⟩+≡   186 191
```
    Tree calltree(f, ty, args, t3)
    Tree f, args; Type ty; Symbol t3; {
        Tree p;

        if (args)
            f = tree(RIGHT, f->type, args, f);
        if (isstruct(ty))
            p = tree(RIGHT, ty,
                tree(CALL+B, ty, f, addrof(idtree(t3))),
                idtree(t3));
        else {
            Type rty = ty;
```

```
            if (isenum(ty))
                rty = unqual(ty)->type;
            else if (isptr(ty))
                rty = unsignedtype;
            p = tree(CALL + widen(rty), promote(rty), f, NULL);
            if (isptr(ty) || p->type->size > ty->size)
                p = cast(p, ty);
        }
        return p;
}
```

The operator CALL+I is used for integers, unsigneds, and pointers, so much of `calltree` is devoted to getting the types correct. A CALL+B tree is always tucked under a RIGHT tree that returns the *address* of the temporary that holds the return value. Figure 9.2 omits this RIGHT tree; the tree actually built by `calltree` and thus returned by `call` begins

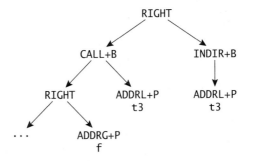

CALL+B itself returns no value; it exists only to permit back ends to generate target-specific calling sequences for these functions.

addrof is an internal version of lvalue that doesn't insist on an INDIR tree (although there *is* an INDIR tree in calltree's use of addrof). addrof follows the operands of RIGHT, COND, and ASGN, and the INDIR trees to find the tree that computes the address specified by its argument. It returns a RIGHT tree representing the original tree and that address, if necessary. For example, if α is the operand tree buried in p that computes the address, addrof(p) returns (RIGHT root(p) α); if p itself computes the address, addrof(p) returns p.

Structures are always passed by value, but if wants_argb is zero and the argument is a structure, it must be copied to a temporary as explained above. There's one optimization that improves the code for passing structures that are returned by functions. For example, in

```
    f(f(a, '\n', atoi(str)), '0', 1);
```

the node returned by the inner call to f is passed to the outer call. In this and similar cases, copying the actual argument can be avoided because it already resides in a temporary. The pattern that must be detected is

```
(RIGHT
    (CALL+B ... )
    (INDIR+B (ADDRL+P temp))
)
```

where *temp* is a temporary. `iscallb` looks for this pattern:

⟨*enode.c functions*⟩+≡   189 192
```
    int iscallb(e) Tree e; {
        return e->op == RIGHT && e->kids[0] && e->kids[1]
            && e->kids[0]->op == CALL+B
            && e->kids[1]->op == INDIR+B
            && isaddrop(e->kids[1]->kids[0]->op)
            && e->kids[1]->kids[0]->u.sym->temporary;
    }
```

⟨*pass a structure directly* 191⟩≡   188
```
    if (iscallb(q))
        q = addrof(q);
    else {
        Symbol t1 = temporary(AUTO, unqual(q->type), level);
        q = asgn(t1, q);
        q = tree(RIGHT, ptr(t1->type),
            root(q), lvalue(idtree(t1)));
    }
```

`asgn(Symbol t, Tree e)` is an internal form of assignment that builds and returns a tree for assigning e to the symbol t.

9.4 Binary Operators

As the indirect call through `optree` in `expr3` suggests, a semantics function for a binary operator takes a generic operator and the trees for the two operands, and returns the tree for the binary expression. Table 9.1 lists the functions and the operators they handle. The operators are grouped as shown in this table because the operators in each group have similar semantics.

`optree` is defined by including `token.h` (see Section 6.2) and extracting its fifth column, which holds the names of the tree-building functions:

⟨*enode.c data*⟩≡
```
    Tree (*optree[]) ARGS((int, Tree, Tree)) = {
    #define xx(a,b,c,d,e,f,g) e,
    #define yy(a,b,c,d,e,f,g) e,
    #include "token.h"
    };
```

Function	Operators
incr	+= -= *= /= %=
	<<= >>= &= ^= |=
asgntree	=
condtree	? :
andtree	|| &&
bittree	| ^ & %
eqtree	== !=
cmptree	< > <= >=
shtree	<< >>
addtree	+
subtree	–
multree	* /

TABLE 9.1   Operator semantics functions.

The function for addition typifies these semantics functions. It must type-check the operands and form the appropriate tree depending on their types. The easy case is when both operands are arithmetic types:

⟨*enode.c functions*⟩+≡   191 193

```
static Tree addtree(op, l, r) int op; Tree l, r; {
    Type ty = inttype;

    if (isarith(l->type) && isarith(r->type)) {
        ty = binary(l->type, r->type);
        ⟨cast l and r to type ty 192⟩
    } else if (isptr(l->type) && isint(r->type))
        return addtree(ADD, r, l);
    else if (  isptr(r->type) && isint(l->type)
    && !isfunc(r->type->type))
        ⟨build an ADD+P tree 193⟩
    else
        typeerror(op, l, r);
    return simplify(op, ty, l, r);
}
```

⟨*cast l and r to type* ty 192⟩≡   192 193 194 195
```
l = cast(l, ty);
r = cast(r, ty);
```

Addition can also take a pointer and an integer in either order. The recursive call to addtree above switches the arguments so the next clause can handle both orders. The front end always puts the integer operand on the left in ADD dags because that order helps back ends implement some additions with addressing modes.

The standard distinguishes between pointers to objects and pointers to functions; most operators, such as addition, that take pointers accept only object pointers. Integers may be added to object pointers, but the addition implies a multiplication by the size of the object:

⟨*build an* ADD+P *tree* 193⟩≡   192
```
{
    int n;
    ty = unqual(r->type);
    ⟨n ← *ty's size 193⟩
    l = cast(l, promote(l->type));
    if (n > 1)
        l = multree(MUL, consttree(n, inttype), l);
    return simplify(ADD+P, ty, l, r);
}
```

⟨n ← *ty's *size* 193⟩≡   193
```
    n = ty->type->size;
    if (n == 0)
        error("unknown size for type '%t'\n", ty->type);
```

consttree builds a tree for a constant of any type that has an associated integer or an unsigned value:

⟨*enode.c functions*⟩+≡   192 193
```
    Tree consttree(n, ty) unsigned n; Type ty; {
        Tree p;

        if (isarray(ty))
            ty = atop(ty);
        p = tree(CNST + ttob(ty), ty, NULL, NULL);
        p->u.v.u = n;
        return p;
    }
```

The relational comparison operators also accept only object pointers and return integers, but they accept more relaxed constraints on their pointer operands.

⟨*enode.c functions*⟩+≡   193 194
```
    static Tree cmptree(op, l, r) int op; Tree l, r; {
        Type ty;

        if (isarith(l->type) && isarith(r->type)) {
            ty = binary(l->type, r->type);
            ⟨cast l and r to type ty 192⟩
        } else if (compatible(l->type, r->type)) {
```

```
      ty = unsignedtype;
      ⟨cast l and r to type ty 192⟩
   } else {
      ty = unsignedtype;
      typeerror(op, l, r);
   }
   return simplify(op + ttob(ty), inttype, l, r);
}
```

The two pointers must point to qualified or unqualified versions of compatible object types or compatible incomplete types. In other words, any const and volatile qualifiers must be ignored when type-checking the objects, which is exactly what `compatible` does:

⟨*enode.c functions*⟩+≡   ▲193 194▼

```
   static int compatible(ty1, ty2) Type ty1, ty2; {
      return isptr(ty1) && !isfunc(ty1->type)
         && isptr(ty2) && !isfunc(ty2->type)
         && eqtype(unqual(ty1->type), unqual(ty2->type), 0);
   }
```

The third argument of zero to `eqtype` causes `eqtype` to insist that its two type arguments are object types or incomplete types.

The equality comparison operators are similar to the relationals but are fussier about pointer operands. These and other operators distinguish between *void pointers*, which are pointers to qualified or unqualified versions of void, and *null pointers*, which are integral constant expressions with the value zero or one of these expressions cast to void *. These definitions are encapsulated in

⟨*enode.c macros*⟩≡

```
   #define isvoidptr(ty) \
      (isptr(ty) && unqual(ty->type) == voidtype)
```

⟨*enode.c functions*⟩+≡   ▲194 195▼

```
   static int isnullptr(e) Tree e; {
      return (isint(e->type) && generic(e->op) == CNST
            && cast(e, unsignedtype)->u.v.u == 0)
         || (isvoidptr(e->type) && e->op == CNST+P
            && e->u.v.p == NULL);
   }
```

In addition to the arithmetic types, which are handled by calling `cmptree`, `eqtree` accepts a pointer and a null pointer, an object pointer and a void pointer, or two pointers to qualified or unqualified versions of compatible types. The leading if statement in `eqtree` tests for just these three combinations for the left and right operands, and the recursive call repeats the test for the right and left operands, when appropriate.

⟨*enode.c functions*⟩+≡   194 195

```
   Tree eqtree(op, l, r) int op; Tree l, r; {
      Type xty = l->type, yty = r->type;

      if (isptr(xty) && isnullptr(r)
      ||  isptr(xty) && !isfunc(xty->type) && isvoidptr(yty)
      ||  ⟨xty and yty point to compatible types 195⟩) {
         Type ty = unsignedtype;
         ⟨cast l and r to type ty 192⟩
         return simplify(op + U, inttype, l, r);
      }
      if (isptr(yty) && isnullptr(l)
      ||  isptr(yty) && !isfunc(yty->type) && isvoidptr(xty))
         return eqtree(op, r, l);
      return cmptree(op, l, r);
   }
```

⟨xty *and* yty *point to compatible types* 195⟩≡   195 196 201

```
   (isptr(xty) && isptr(yty)
   && eqtype(unqual(xty->type), unqual(yty->type), 1))
```

The third argument of 1 to eqtype causes eqtype to permit its two type
arguments to be any combinations of compatible object or incomplete
types. Given the declaration

```
   int (*p)[10], (*q)[];
```

eqtype's third argument is what permits p == q but disallows p < q.

9.5 Assignments

The legality of an assignment expression, a function argument, a return
statement, or an initialization depends on the legality of an assignment
of an rvalue to the location denoted by an lvalue. assign(xty, e) performs the necessary type-checking for any assignment. It checks the
legality of assigning the tree e to an lvalue that holds a value of type
xty, and returns xty if the assignment is legal or null if it's illegal. The
return value is also the type to which e must be converted before the
assignment is made.

⟨*enode.c functions*⟩+≡   195 197

```
   Type assign(xty, e) Type xty; Tree e; {
      Type yty = unqual(e->type);

      xty = unqual(xty);
      if (isenum(xty))
```

193 cmptree
 69 eqtype
 60 isenum
 60 isfunc
194 isnullptr
 60 isptr
194 isvoidptr
203 simplify
 60 unqual
 58 unsignedtype

```
                    xty = xty->type;
                if (xty->size == 0 || yty->size == 0)
                    return NULL;
                ⟨assign 196⟩
            }
```

The body of `assign` tests the five constraints imposed on assignments by the standard. The first two permit assignment of arithmetic and structure types:

⟨*assign* 196⟩≡   196   196

```
    if ( isarith(xty) && isarith(yty)
    || isstruct(xty) && xty == yty)
        return xty;
```

The other three cases involve pointers. The null pointer may be assigned to any pointer:

⟨*assign* 196⟩+≡   196 196   196

```
    if (isptr(xty) && isnullptr(e))
        return xty;
```

Any pointer may be assigned to a void pointer or vice versa, provided the type pointed to by the left pointer operand has at least all the qualifiers carried by the type pointed to by the right operand:

⟨*assign* 196⟩+≡   196 196   196

```
    if ((isvoidptr(xty) && isptr(yty)
        || isptr(xty)      && isvoidptr(yty))
    && ⟨*xty has all of *yty's qualifiers 196⟩)
        return xty;
```

⟨*xty *has all of *yty's qualifiers* 196⟩≡   196

```
    (   (isconst(xty->type)      || !isconst(yty->type))
    && (isvolatile(xty->type) || !isvolatile(yty->type)))
```

A pointer can be assigned to another pointer if they both point to compatible types and the lvalue has all the qualifiers of the rvalue, as above.

⟨*assign* 196⟩+≡   196 196   196

```
    if (⟨xty and yty point to compatible types 195⟩
    && ⟨*xty has all of *yty's qualifiers 196⟩)
        return xty;
```

Finally, if none of the cases above apply, the assignment is an error, and `assign` returns the null pointer:

⟨*assign* 196⟩+≡   196   196

```
    return NULL;
```

`assign` is used in `asgntree` to build a tree for an assignment:

⟨*enode.c functions*⟩+≡   19̇5 2̱0̱0̱
```
    Tree asgntree(op, l, r) int op; Tree l, r; {
        Type aty, ty;

        r = pointer(r);
        ty = assign(l->type, r);
        if (ty)
            r = cast(r, ty);
        else {
            typeerror(ASGN, l, r);
            if (r->type == voidtype)
                r = retype(r, inttype);
            ty = r->type;
        }
        if (l->op != FIELD)
            l = lvalue(l);
```
        ⟨*asgntree* 197⟩
```
        return tree(op + (isunsigned(ty) ? I : ttob(ty)),
            ty, l, r);
    }
```

When the assignment is illegal, `assign` returns null and `asgntree` must choose a type for the result of the assignment. It uses the type of the right operand, unless that type is void, in which case `asgntree` uses int. This code exemplifies what's needed to recover from semantic errors so that compilation can continue.

The body of `asgntree`, revealed by ⟨*asgntree*⟩, below, detects attempts to change the value of a const location, changes the integral rvalue of assignments to bit fields to meet the specifications of the standard, and transforms some structure assignments to yield better code.

An lvalue denotes a const location if the type of its referent is qualified by const or is a structure type that is const-qualified. A structure type so qualified has its `u.sym->u.s.cfields` flag set.

⟨*asgntree* 197⟩≡   1̱9̱8̱   197
```
    aty = l->type;
    if (isptr(aty))
        aty = unqual(aty)->type;
    if ( isconst(aty)
    ||   isstruct(aty) && unqual(aty)->u.sym->u.s.cfields)
        if (isaddrop(l->op)
        && !l->u.sym->computed && !l->u.sym->generated)
            error("assignment to const identifier '%s'\n",
                l->u.sym->name);
        else
            error("assignment to const location\n");
```

aty is set to the type of the value addressed by the lvalue. The assignment is illegal if aty has a const qualifier or if it's a structure type with one or more const-qualified fields. The gymnastics for issuing the diagnostic are used to cope with lvalues that don't have source-program names.

The result of an assignment is the value of the left operand, and the type is the *qualified* version of the left operand. The cast at the beginning of asgntree sets r to the correct tree and ty to the correct type for r and ty to represent the result, so the result of ASGN is its right operand. Unfortunately, this scheme doesn't work for bit fields. The result of an assignment to a bit field is the value that would be extracted from the field after the assignment, which might differ from the value represented by r. So, for assignments to bit fields that occupy less than a full unsigned, asgntree must change r to a tree that computes just this value.

⟨*asgntree* 197⟩+≡   197̲ 199   197

```
    if (l->op == FIELD) {
        int n = 8*l->u.field->type->size - fieldsize(l->u.field);
        if (n > 0 && isunsigned(l->u.field->type))
            r = bittree(BAND, r,
                consttree(fieldmask(l->u.field), unsignedtype));
        else if (n > 0) {
            if (r->op == CNST+I)
                r = consttree(r->u.v.i<<n, inttype);
            else
                r = shtree(LSH, r, consttree(n, inttype));
            r = shtree(RSH, r, consttree(n, inttype));
        }
    }
```

If the bit field is unsigned, the result is r with its excess most significant bits discarded. If the bit field is signed and has m bits, bit $m - 1$ is the sign bit and it must be used to sign-extend the value, which can be done by arithmetically shifting r left to bring bit m into the sign bit, and then shifting right by the same amount, dragging the sign bit along in the process. For example, Figure 9.4 shows the trees assigned to r for the two assignments in

```
struct { int a:3; unsigned b:3; } x;
x.a = e;
x.b = e;
```

In the assignment x.a = e, r is assigned a tree that uses shifts to sign-extend the rightmost 3 bits of e; for x.b = e, r is assigned a tree that ANDs e with 7. If r is constant, the left shift is done explicitly to keep the constant folder from shouting about overflow.

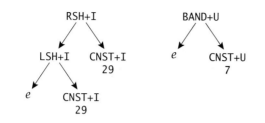

FIGURE 9.4 Trees for the results of x.a = *e* and x.b = *e*.

Back ends typically generate block moves for structure assignments. The job of generating good code for these assignments falls mostly on back ends, but there is an opportunity to reduce the number of useless block moves, and it's similar to the optimization done by call for structure arguments described on page 190. In x = f(), where f returns a structure, a temporary is generated in the caller to hold f's return value, and the temporary is copied to x after the call returns. The left side of Figure 9.5 shows the resulting tree; *x* stands for the tree for x. This copy can be avoided by using x in place of the temporary.

This improvement can be made when x addresses a location directly and there's a temporary that holds the value returned by f:

⟨*asgntree* 197⟩+≡   198   197
```
if (isstruct(ty) && isaddrop(l->op) && iscallb(r))
    return tree(RIGHT, ty,
        tree(CALL+B, ty, r->kids[0]->kids[0], 1),
        idtree(l->u.sym));
```

186	call
168	idtree
179	isaddrop
191	iscallb
60	isstruct
149	RIGHT
150	tree

The right side of Figure 9.5 shows the tree returned by this transformation.

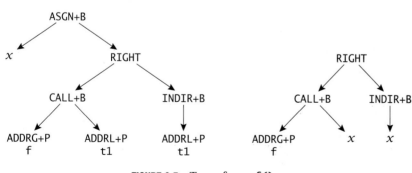

FIGURE 9.5 Trees for x=f().

9.6 Conditionals

The complex semantics of the conditional expression combines parts of
the semantics of comparisons, of the binary operators, of assignment,
and of casts. The COND operator is the only one that takes three operands:
The expression *e* ? *l* : *r* yields the tree shown in Figure 9.6, which is
built by condtree:

⟨*enode.c functions*⟩+≡   197

```
Tree condtree(e, l, r) Tree e, l, r; {
    Symbol t1;
    Type ty, xty = l->type, yty = r->type;
    Tree p;

    ⟨condtree 200⟩
    p = tree(COND, ty, cond(e),
        tree(RIGHT, ty, root(l), root(r)));
    p->u.sym = t1;
    return p;
}
```

t1, carried in the u.sym field of a COND tree, is a temporary that holds
the result of the conditional expression at runtime. t1 is omitted if the
result is void.

The call cond(e) in the code above type-checks the first operand,
which must have a scalar type. There are six legal combinations for the
types of second and third operands. The three easy cases are when both
have arithmetic types, both have compatible structure types, or both have
void type. All three of these cases are covered by the two if statements:

⟨*condtree* 200⟩≡   201   200

```
if (isarith(xty) && isarith(yty))
    ty = binary(xty, yty);
else if (eqtype(xty, yty, 1))
    ty = unqual(xty);
```

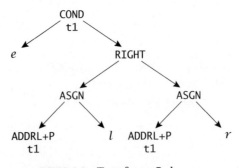

FIGURE 9.6 Tree for *e* ? *l* : *r*.

The first if statement handles the arithmetic types, and the second handles structure types and void.

The remaining three cases involve pointers. If one of the operands is a null pointer and the other is a pointer, the resulting type is the nonnull pointer type:

⟨*condtree* 200⟩+≡   200 201   200

```
else if (isptr(xty)    && isnullptr(r))
    ty = xty;
else if (isnullptr(l) && isptr(yty))
    ty = yty;
```

If one of the operands is a void pointer and the other is a pointer to an object or incomplete type, the result type is the void pointer:

⟨*condtree* 200⟩+≡   201 201   200

```
else if (isptr(xty) && !isfunc(xty->type) && isvoidptr(yty)
||         isptr(yty) && !isfunc(yty->type) && isvoidptr(xty))
    ty = voidptype;
```

If both operands are pointers to qualified or unqualified versions of compatible types, either can serve as the result type:

⟨*condtree* 200⟩+≡   201 201   200

```
else if (⟨xty and yty point to compatible types 195⟩)
    ty = xty;
else {
    typeerror(COND, 1, r);
    return consttree(0, inttype);
}
```

The type-checking code above ignores qualifiers on pointers to qualified types. The resulting pointer type, however, must include *all* of the qualifiers of the referents of both operand types; so if ty is a pointer, it's rebuilt with the appropriate qualifiers:

⟨*condtree* 200⟩+≡   201 202   200

```
if (isptr(ty)) {
    ty = unqual(unqual(ty)->type);
    if (isptr(xty) && isconst(unqual(xty)->type)
    ||  isptr(yty) && isconst(unqual(yty)->type))
        ty = qual(CONST, ty);
    if (isptr(xty) && isvolatile(unqual(xty)->type)
    ||  isptr(yty) && isvolatile(unqual(yty)->type))
        ty = qual(VOLATILE, ty);
    ty = ptr(ty);
}
```

If the conditional, e, is a constant, the result of the conditional expression is one of the other operands:

⟨*condtree* 200⟩ +≡   201 202   200

```
if (e->op == CNST+D || e->op == CNST+F) {
    e = cast(e, doubletype);
    return cast(e->u.v.d != 0.0 ? 1 : r, ty);
}
if (generic(e->op) == CNST) {
    e = cast(e, unsignedtype);
    return cast(e->u.v.u ? 1 : r, ty);
}
```

This constant folding is not just an optimization; it's mandatory because
conditional expressions can be used in contexts that require constant
expressions.

Finally, if the result type isn't void, the temporary is generated and 1
and r are changed to assignments to that temporary:

⟨*condtree* 200⟩ +≡   202   200

```
if (ty != voidtype && ty->size > 0) {
    t1 = temporary(REGISTER, unqual(ty), level);
    1 = asgn(t1, 1);
    r = asgn(t1, r);
} else
    t1 = NULL;
```

9.7 Constant Folding

Constant expressions are permitted wherever a constant is required. Array sizes, case labels, bit-field widths, and initializations are examples.

   constant-expression: conditional-expression

Constant expressions are parsed by

⟨*simp.c functions*⟩ ≡   203

```
Tree constexpr(tok) int tok; {
    Tree p;

    needconst++;
    p = expr1(tok);
    needconst--;
    return p;
}
```

⟨*simp.c data*⟩ ≡

```
int needconst;
```

expr1 parses *assignment-expressions*. Technically, constexpr should
call expr2, which parses *conditional-expressions*, but legal assignments
are never constants, and will always cause semantic errors. Calling expr1
handles syntax errors more gracefully because expr1 consumes an entire assignment and thus avoids multiple diagnostics from the cascading
syntax errors. Callers to constexpr report an error if the tree returned
is not a CNST tree and if it's used in a context that requires a constant.
An example is intexpr, which parses integer constant expressions:

⟨*simp.c functions*⟩+≡   202 203

```
int intexpr(tok, n) int tok, n; {
    Tree p = constexpr(tok);

    needconst++;
    if (generic(p->op) == CNST && isint(p->type))
        n = cast(p, inttype)->u.v.i;
    else
        error("integer expression must be constant\n");
    needconst--;
    return n;
}
```

needconst is a global variable that controls the constant folding done
by simplify, as detailed below. If it's nonzero, simplify warns about
constant expressions that overflow and folds them anyway. Otherwise,
it doesn't fold them.

175	cast
202	constexpr
157	expr1
159	expr2
60	isint
202	needconst
98	optype
150	tree
73	ttob

   Constant folding is not simply an optimization. The standard makes it
required by defining constructs in which the value of a constant expression must be computed during compilation. Array sizes and bit-field
widths are examples. simplify returns the tree specified by its arguments, which are the same as tree's:

⟨*simp.c functions*⟩+≡   203 205

```
Tree simplify(op, ty, l, r) int op; Type ty; Tree l, r; {
    int n;
    Tree p;

    if (optype(op) == 0)
        op += ttob(ty);
    switch (op) {
        ⟨simplify cases 204⟩
    }
    return tree(op, ty, l, r);
}
```

simplify does three things that tree does not: it forms a type-specific
operator if it's passed a generic one, it evaluates operators when both

operands are constants, and it transforms some trees into simpler ones that yield better code as it constructs the tree requested.

Each of the cases in the body of simplify's switch statement handles one type-specific operator. If the operands are both constants, the code builds and returns a CNST tree for the resulting value; otherwise, it breaks to the end of the switch statement, which builds and returns the appropriate tree. The code that checks for constant operands and builds the resulting CNST tree is almost the same for every case; only the type suffix, Value field name, operator, and return type vary in each case, so the code is buried in a set of macros. The case for unsigned addition is typical:

⟨simplify *cases* 204⟩≡   205   203

```
    case ADD+U:
        foldcnst(U,u,+,unsignedtype);
        commute(r,1);
        break;
```

This case implements the transformation

$$(\text{ADD+U} \ (\text{CNST+U} \ c_1) \ (\text{CNST+U} \ c_2)) \quad \Rightarrow \quad (\text{CNST+U} \ c_1 + c_2)$$

This use of foldcnst checks whether both operands are CNST+U trees, and, if so, returns a new CNST+U tree whose u.v.u field is the sum of l->r.v.u and r->r.v.u:

⟨*simp.c macros*⟩≡   204

```
    #define foldcnst(TYPE,VAR,OP,RTYPE) \
        if (l->op == CNST+TYPE && r->op == CNST+TYPE) {\
            p = tree(CNST+ttob(RTYPE), RTYPE, NULL, NULL);\
            p->u.v.VAR = l->u.v.VAR OP r->u.v.VAR;\
            return p; }
```

For commutative operators, commute ensures that if one of the operands is a constant, it's the one given as commute's first argument. This transformation reduces the case analyses that back ends must perform, allowing back ends to count on constant operands of commutative operators being in specific sites.

⟨*simp.c macros*⟩+≡   204 205

```
    #define commute(L,R) \
        if (generic(R->op) == CNST && generic(L->op) != CNST) {\
            Tree t = L; L = R; R = t; }
```

commute swaps its arguments, if necessary, to make L refer to the constant operand. For example, the commute(r,1) in the case for ADD+U above ensures that if one of the operands is a constant, r refers to that operand. This transformation also makes some of simplify's transformations easier, as shown below.

Unsigned addition is easy because the standard dictates that unsigned operators do not overflow. Signed operations, however, must cope with overflow. For example, if the operands to ADD+I are constants, but their sum overflows, the expression is not a constant expression unless it's used in a context that demands one. The signed operators use xfoldcnst, which is like foldcnst, but also checks for overflow.

⟨simplify *cases* 204⟩+≡   204 206   203

```
case ADD+I:
    xfoldcnst(I,i,+,inttype,add,INT_MIN,INT_MAX,needconst);
    commute(r,l);
    break;
```

implements the transformation

$$(\text{ADD+I } (\text{CNST+I } c_1) \ (\text{CNST+I } c_2)) \quad \Rightarrow \quad (\text{CNST+I } c_1 + c_2)$$

but only if $c_1 + c_2$ doesn't overflow or if needconst is 1. xfoldcnst has four additional arguments: A function, the minimum and maximum allowable values for the result, and a flag that is nonzero if a constant is required.

⟨*simp.c macros*⟩+≡   204 206

```
#define xfoldcnst(TYPE,VAR,OP,RTYPE,FUNC,MIN,MAX,needconst)\
    if (l->op == CNST+TYPE && r->op == CNST+TYPE\
    && FUNC((double)l->u.v.VAR,(double)r->u.v.VAR,\
        (double)MIN,(double)MAX, needconst)) {\
        p = tree(CNST+ttob(RTYPE), RTYPE, NULL, NULL);\
        p->u.v.VAR = l->u.v.VAR OP r->u.v.VAR;\
        return p; }
```

204	commute
204	foldcnst
97	FUNC
202	needconst
150	tree
73	ttob

The function takes doubles because lcc assumes that a double has enough bits in its significand to represent all of the integral types. Testing for constant operands and building the resulting CNST tree are identical to the code in foldcnst, but the function is called to check the validity of the operation; it returns zero if the operation will overflow, and one otherwise. The function is passed the values, the minimum and maximum, and the flag. All but the flag are converted to doubles. For integer addition, the test for overflow is simple; $x + y$ overflows if it is less than INT_MIN or greater than INT_MAX, where INT_MIN and INT_MAX are the ANSI values for the smallest and largest signed integers. The function, add, handles all the types, so it must not compute $x + y$ because the addition might overflow. Instead, it tests the conditions under which overflow will occur:

⟨*simp.c functions*⟩+≡   203 210

```
static int add(x, y, min, max, needconst)
double x, y, min, max; int needconst; {
```

```
int cond = x == 0 || y == 0
|| x < 0 && y < 0 && x >= min - y
|| x < 0 && y > 0
|| x > 0 && y < 0
|| x > 0 && y > 0 && x <= max - y;
if (!cond && needconst) {
    warning("overflow in constant expression\n");
    cond = 1;
}
return cond;
}
```

As shown, needconst forces add to return 1 after issuing a warning. sub, mul, and div are similar.

The conversions also divide into those that must check for overflow and those that can ignore it. Conversions from a smaller to a larger type, between unsigned types, between unsigned and pointer types, and from integer to unsigned can ignore overflow. The conversions below exemplify these four cases. They implement transformations like

$$(\text{CVC+I } (\text{CNST+C } c)) \quad \Rightarrow \quad (\text{CNST+I } c')$$

where c' is the possibly sign-extended value of c. For the unsigned conversions, $c' = c$.

⟨simplify *cases* 204⟩+≡   205 207   203

```
case CVC+I:
    cvtcnst(C,inttype, p->u.v.i =
        (l->u.v.sc&0200 ? (~0<<8) : 0)|(l->u.v.sc&0377));
    break;
case CVU+S:
    cvtcnst(U,unsignedshort,p->u.v.us = l->u.v.u); break;
case CVP+U:
    cvtcnst(P,unsignedtype, p->u.v.u  = (unsigned)l->u.v.p);
    break;
case CVI+U:
    cvtcnst(I,unsignedtype, p->u.v.u  = l->u.v.i); break;
```

⟨*simp.c macros*⟩+≡   205 207

```
#define cvtcnst(FTYPE,TTYPE,EXPR) \
    if (l->op == CNST+FTYPE) {\
        p = tree(CNST+ttob(TTYPE), TTYPE, NULL, NULL);\
        EXPR;\
        return p; }
```

The assignment in the CVC+I case must sign-extend the sign bit of the character operand manually, because the compiler cannot count on chars being signed when it's compiled by another C compiler. It's tempting to replace the assignment passed to cvtconst by something like

```
((int)l->u.v.sc<<(8*sizeof(int) - 8))>>(8*sizeof(int) - 8)
```

but whether or not >> replicates the sign bit depends on the compiler that *compiles* lcc.

The four conversions from larger to smaller types must check for overflow. They implement transformations like

$$(CVI{+}C \ (CNST{+}I \ c)) \quad \Rightarrow \quad (CNST{+}C \ c)$$

if c fits in the smaller type or if needconst is one.

⟨simplify *cases* 204⟩+≡   ▲206 207   203

```
case CVI+C:
    xcvtcnst(I, chartype,l->u.v.i,SCHAR_MIN,SCHAR_MAX,
        p->u.v.sc = l->u.v.i); break;
case CVD+F:
    xcvtcnst(D,floattype,l->u.v.d, -FLT_MAX,FLT_MAX,
        p->u.v.f  = l->u.v.d); break;
case CVD+I:
    xcvtcnst(D,  inttype,l->u.v.d,  INT_MIN,INT_MAX,
        p->u.v.i  = l->u.v.d); break;
case CVI+S:
    xcvtcnst(I,shorttype,l->u.v.i, SHRT_MIN,SHRT_MAX,
        p->u.v.ss = l->u.v.i); break;
```

⟨*simp.c macros*⟩+≡   ▲206 208

```
#define xcvtcnst(FTYPE,TTYPE,VAR,MIN,MAX,EXPR) \
    if (l->op == CNST+FTYPE) {\
        if (needconst && (VAR < MIN || VAR > MAX))\
            warning("overflow in constant expression\n");\
        if (needconst || VAR >= MIN && VAR <= MAX) {\
            p = tree(CNST+ttob(TTYPE), TTYPE, NULL, NULL);\
            EXPR;\
            return p; } }
```

57	chartype
204	commute
327	cvtconst
57	floattype
204	foldcnst
208	identity
202	needconst
57	shorttype
203	simplify
150	tree
73	ttob
58	unsignedtype

In addition to evaluating constant expressions, simplify transforms the trees for some operators to help generate better code. Some of these transformations remove identities and other simple cases. For example:

⟨simplify *cases* 204⟩+≡   ▲207 208   203

```
case BAND+U:
    foldcnst(U,u,&,unsignedtype);
    commute(r,l);
    identity(r,l,U,u,(~(unsigned)0));
    if (r->op == CNST+U && r->u.v.u == 0)
```

```
        return tree(RIGHT, unsignedtype, root(l),
            consttree(0, unsignedtype));
    break;
```

⟨*simp.c macros*⟩+≡   207 209
```
    #define identity(X,Y,TYPE,VAR,VAL) \
        if (X->op == CNST+TYPE && X->u.v.VAR == VAL)\
            return Y
```

The use of `identity` and the if statement that follows implement the transformations

$$\text{(BAND+U } e \text{ (CNST+U } \sim 0\text{))} \quad \Rightarrow \quad e$$
$$\text{(BAND+U } e \text{ (CNST+U } 0\text{))} \quad \Rightarrow \quad (e, \text{ (CNST+U } 0\text{))}$$

In the second case, *e* cannot be discarded because it might have side effects. `commute(r,1)` makes it necessary to check only if r is a constant.

`simplify` also implements *strength reduction* for some operators. This transformation replaces an operator by a less expensive one that computes the same value. For example, an unsigned multiplication by a power of two can be replaced by a left shift:

$$\text{(MUL+U (CNST+U } 2^k\text{) } e\text{)} \quad \Rightarrow \quad \text{(LSH+U } e \text{ (CNST+I } k\text{))}$$

The code also uses `foldcnst` to check for constant operands.

⟨*simplify cases* 204⟩+≡   207 208   203
```
    case MUL+U:
        commute(l,r);
        if (l->op == CNST+U && (n = ispow2(l->u.v.u)) != 0)
            return simplify(LSH+U, unsignedtype, r,
                consttree(n, inttype));
        foldcnst(U,u,*,unsignedtype);
        break;
```

`ispow2(u)` returns *k* if u is equal to 2^k for $k > 0$.

Bit fields are often tested by expressions such as p->x != 0, which leads to a NE tree with FIELD and CNST trees as operands. Extracting the bit field, which involves shifting and masking in general, and testing it can be easily replaced by simpler code that fetches the word that contains the field, ANDs it with a properly positioned bit mask, and tests the outcome:

⟨*simplify cases* 204⟩+≡   208 209   203
```
    case NE+I:
        cfoldcnst(I,i,!=,inttype);
        commute(r,l);
        zerofield(NE,I,i);
        break;
```

⟨*simp.c macros*⟩+≡   ▲ 208 209 ▼

```
#define zerofield(OP,TYPE,VAR) \
    if (l->op == FIELD\
    &&  r->op == CNST+TYPE && r->u.v.VAR == 0)\
        return eqtree(OP, bittree(BAND, l->kids[0],\
            consttree(\
                fieldmask(l->u.field)<<fieldright(l->u.field),\
                unsignedtype)), r);
```

This case implements the transformation

$$(\text{NE+I} \ (\text{FIELD} \ e) \ (\text{CNST+I} \ 0)) \quad \Rightarrow$$
$$(\text{NE+I} \ (\text{BAND+U} \ (e \ (\text{CNST+U} \ M))) \ (\text{CNST+I} \ 0))$$

where M is a mask of s bits shifted m bits left, and s is size of the bit field that lies m bits from the least significant end of the unsigned or integer in which it appears. cfoldcnst is a version of foldcnst that's specialized for the relational operators:

⟨*simp.c macros*⟩+≡   ▲ 209 209 ▼

```
#define cfoldcnst(TYPE,VAR,OP,RTYPE) \
    if (l->op == CNST+TYPE && r->op == CNST+TYPE) {\
        p = tree(CNST+ttob(RTYPE), RTYPE, NULL, NULL);\
        p->u.v.i = l->u.v.VAR OP r->u.v.VAR;\
        return p; }
```

Pointer addition is the most interesting and complex case in simplify because it implements many transformations that yield better code. Generating efficient addressing is the linchpin of generating efficient code, so effort in this case pays off on all targets. The easy cases handle constants and identities:

⟨*simplify cases* 204⟩+≡   ▲ 208   203

```
case ADD+P:
    foldaddp(l,r,I,i);
    foldaddp(l,r,U,u);
    foldaddp(r,l,I,i);
    foldaddp(r,l,U,u);
    commute(r,l);
    identity(r,retype(l,ty),I,i,0);
    identity(r,retype(l,ty),U,u,0);
    ⟨ADD+P transformations 210⟩
    break;
```

⟨*simp.c macros*⟩+≡   ▲ 209

```
#define foldaddp(L,R,RTYPE,VAR) \
    if (L->op == CNST+P && R->op == CNST+RTYPE) {\
        p = tree(CNST+P, ty, NULL, NULL);\
```

```
p->u.v.p = (char *)L->u.v.p + R->u.v.VAR;\
return p; }
```

Four uses of `foldaddp` are required because of the asymmetry of ADD+P's operands: one is a pointer and the other is an integer or an unsigned. These uses of `foldaddp` implement transformations like

$$(\text{ADD+P } (\text{CNST+P } c_1) (\text{CNST+I } c_2)) \quad \Rightarrow \quad (\text{CNST+P } c_1 + c_2)$$

The uses of `identity` implement

$$(\text{ADD+P } e (\text{CNST+I } 0)) \quad \Rightarrow \quad e$$

and the similar transformation for unsigned constants.

The remaining transformations of ADD+P trees either produce simpler and thus better trees or feed another transformation. The transformation

⟨*ADD+P transformations* 210⟩≡   211   209
```
  if (isaddrop(l->op)
  && (r->op == CNST+I || r->op == CNST+U))
      return addrtree(l, cast(r, inttype)->u.v.i, ty);
```

eliminates indexed addressing of a known location by a constant, which occurs in array references such as a[5] and in field references such as x.name. These expressions yield trees of the form

$$(\text{ADD+P } n (\text{CNST+}x \; c))$$

where n denotes a tree for the address of an identifier, x is U or I, and c is a constant. This tree can be transformed to n', a tree for an identifier that is bound to the addressed location. `addrtree` creates a new identifier whose address is the location addressed by l plus the constant offset, and builds a tree for the address of this identifier.

⟨*simp.c functions*⟩+≡   205
```
  static Tree addrtree(e, n, ty) Tree e; int n; Type ty; {
      Symbol p = e->u.sym, q;

      NEW0(q, FUNC);
      q->name = stringd(genlabel(1));
      q->sclass = p->sclass;
      q->scope = p->scope;
      q->type = ty;
      q->temporary = p->temporary;
      q->generated = p->generated;
      q->addressed = p->addressed;
      q->computed = 1;
      q->defined = 1;
```

```
        q->ref = 1;
        ⟨announce q 211⟩
        e = tree(e->op, ty, NULL, NULL);
        e->u.sym = q;
        return e;
}
```

⟨*symbol flags* 50⟩+≡   179 292   38
```
   unsigned computed:1;
```

As for other identifiers, the front end must announce this new identifier to the back end. Since its address is based on the address of another identifier, represented by p, it's announced by calling the interface function `address`, and its `computed` flag identifies it as a symbol based on another symbol. But there's a phase problem: p must be announced before q, but if p is a local or a parameter, it has not yet been passed to the back end via `local` or `function`. `addrtree` thus calls `address` only for globals and statics, and delays the call for locals and parameters:

⟨*announce* q 211⟩≡   211
```
   if (p->scope  == GLOBAL
   || p->sclass == STATIC || p->sclass == EXTERN) {
      if (p->sclass == AUTO)
         q->sclass = STATIC;
      (*IR->address)(q, p, n);
   } else {
      Code cp;
      addlocal(p);
      cp = code(Address);
      cp->u.addr.sym = q;
      cp->u.addr.base = p;
      cp->u.addr.offset = n;
   }
```

The code-list entry `Address` is described in Section 10.1. lcc can't delay the call to `address` for globals and statics because expressions like &a[5] are constants and can appear in, for example, initializers.

The next transformation improves expressions like b[i].name, which yields a tree of the form (ADD+P (ADD+P i n) (CNST+x c)), where i is a tree for an integer expression and n and c are defined above. This tree can be transformed into (ADD+P i (ADD+P n (CNST+x c))) and the inner ADD+P tree will be collapsed to a simple address by the transformation above to yield (ADD+P i n').

⟨*ADD+P transformations* 210⟩+≡   210 212   209
```
   if (l->op == ADD+P && isaddrop(l->kids[1]->op)
   && (r->op == CNST+I || r->op == CNST+U))
```

```
         return simplify(ADD+P, ty, l->kids[0],
             addrtree(l->kids[1], cast(r, inttype)->u.v.i, ty));
```

Technically, this transformation is safe only when $(i + n) + c$ is equal to $i + (n + c)$, which is known only at runtime, but the standard permits these kinds of rearrangements to be made at compile time.

Similarly, the tree (ADD+P (ADD+I i (CNST+x c)) n) can be transformed to (ADD+P i n'); this transformation also applies if SUB+I appears in place of the ADD+I:

⟨ADD+P *transformations* 210⟩+≡ $\overset{\blacktriangle}{211}$ $\underset{\blacktriangledown}{212}$ 209

```
    if ((l->op == ADD+I || l->op == SUB+I)
    && l->kids[1]->op == CNST+I && isaddrop(r->op))
        return simplify(ADD+P, ty, l->kids[0],
            simplify(generic(l->op)+P, ty, r, l->kids[1]));
```

The following cases combine constants and implement the transformations

$$(\text{ADD+P} \ (\text{ADD+P} \ x \ (\text{CNST} \ c_1)) \ (\text{CNST} \ c_2)) \qquad\qquad \Rightarrow$$
$$(\text{ADD+P} \ x \ (\text{CNST} \ c_1 + c_2))$$
$$(\text{ADD+P} \ (\text{ADD+I} \ x \ (\text{CNST} \ c_1)) \ (\text{ADD+P} \ y \ (\text{CNST} \ c_2))) \quad \Rightarrow$$
$$(\text{ADD+P} \ x \ (\text{ADD+P} \ y \ (\text{CNST} \ c_1 + c_2)))$$

These transformations trigger others when x or y are identifier trees.

⟨ADD+P *transformations* 210⟩+≡ $\overset{\blacktriangle}{212}$ $\underset{\blacktriangledown}{212}$ 209

```
    if (l->op == ADD+P && generic(l->kids[1]->op) == CNST
    && generic(r->op) == CNST)
        return simplify(ADD+P, ty, l->kids[0],
            (*optree['+'])(ADD, l->kids[1], r));
    if (l->op == ADD+I && generic(l->kids[1]->op) == CNST
    &&  r->op == ADD+P && generic(r->kids[1]->op) == CNST)
        return simplify(ADD+P, ty, l->kids[0],
            simplify(ADD+P, ty, r->kids[0],
                (*optree['+'])(ADD, l->kids[1], r->kids[1])));
```

The last transformation reaches into RIGHT trees to apply ADD+P transformations to their operands.

⟨ADD+P *transformations* 210⟩+≡ $\overset{\blacktriangle}{212}$ 209

```
    if (l->op == RIGHT && l->kids[1])
        return tree(RIGHT, ty, l->kids[0],
            simplify(ADD+P, ty, l->kids[1], r));
    else if (l->op == RIGHT && l->kids[0])
        return tree(RIGHT, ty,
            simplify(ADD+P, ty, l->kids[0], r), NULL);
```

These tests implement

```
(ADD+P (RIGHT x y) e)    ⇒    (RIGHT x (ADD+P y e))
(ADD+P (RIGHT x) e)      ⇒    (RIGHT (ADD+P x e))
```

The first test applies to trees formed by expressions such as f().x; the call returns a temporary, so referencing a field of that temporary will benefit from the first ADD+P transformation described above. The second test applies to expressions that are wrapped in a RIGHT as the result of a conversion.

Table 9.2 lists the remaining transformations in ⟨simplify *cases*⟩.

149 RIGHT

(AND+I (CNST+I 0) e)	⇒	(CNST+I 0)
(AND+I (CNST+I 1) e)	⇒	e
(OR+I (CNST+I 0) e)	⇒	e
(OR+I (CNST+I c) e), $c \neq 0$	⇒	(CNST+I 1)
(BCOM+U (BCOM+U e))	⇒	e
(BOR+U (CNST+U 0) e)	⇒	e
(BXOR+U (CNST+U 0) e)	⇒	e
(DIV+I e (CNST+I 1))	⇒	e
(DIV+U e (CNST+U c)), $c = 2^k$	⇒	(RSH+U e (CNST+I k))
(GE+U e (CNST+U 0))	⇒	(e, (CNST+I 1))
(GE+U (CNST+U 0) e)	⇒	(EQ+I e (CNST+I 0))
(GT+U (CNST+U 0) e)	⇒	(e, (CNST+I 0))
(GT+U e (CNST+U 0))	⇒	(NE+I e (CNST+I 0))
(LE+U (CNST+U 0) e)	⇒	(e, (CNST+I 1))
(LE+U e (CNST+U 0))	⇒	(EQ+I e (CNST+I 0))
(LT+U e (CNST+U 0))	⇒	(e, (CNST+I 0))
(LT+U (CNST+U 0) e)	⇒	(NE+I e (CNST+I 0))
(LSH+I e (CNST+I 0))	⇒	e
(LSH+U e (CNST+I 0))	⇒	e
(MOD+I e (CNST+I 1))	⇒	(e, (CNST+I 0))
(MOD+U e (CNST+I c)), $c = 2^k$	⇒	(BAND+U e (CNST+U $c-1$))
(MUL+I (CNST+I c_1) (ADD+I e (CNST+I c_2)))	⇒	
(ADD+I (MUL+I (CNST+I c_1) e) (CNST+I $c_1 \times c_2$))		
(MUL+I (CNST+I c_1) (SUB+I e (CNST+I c_2)))	⇒	
(SUB+I (MUL+I (CNST+I c_1) e) (CNST+I $c_1 \times c_2$))		
(MUL+I (CNST+I c) e), $c = 2^k$	⇒	(LSH+I e (CNST+I k))
(NEG+D (NEG+D e))	⇒	e
(NEG+F (NEG+F e))	⇒	e
(NEG+I (NEG+I e)), $e \neq$ (CNST+I INT_MIN)	⇒	e
(RSH+I e (CNST+I 0))	⇒	e
(RSH+U e (CNST+I 0))	⇒	e
(SUB+P e (CNST+I c))	⇒	(ADD+P e (CNST+I $-c$))
(SUB+P e (CNST+U c))	⇒	(ADD+P e (CNST+U $-c$))
(SUB+P e_1 (ADD+I e_2 (CNST+I c)))	⇒	
(SUB+P (SUB+P e_1 (CNST+I c)) e_2)		

TABLE 9.2 Remaining simplify transformations.

Further Reading

lcc's approach to type checking is similar to the one outlined in Chapter 6 of Aho, Sethi, and Ullman (1986). simplify's transformations are similar to those described by Hanson (1983). Similar transformations can be done, often more thoroughly, by other kinds of optimizations or during code generation, but usually at additional cost. simplify implements only those that are likely to benefit almost all programs. A more systematic approach is necessary to do a more thorough job; see Exercise 9.8.

Exercises

9.1 Implement Type super(Type ty), which is shown in Figure 9.1. Don't forget about enumerations and the types long, unsigned long, and long double.

9.2 How can a double be converted to an unsigned using only double-to-signed integer conversion? Use your solution to implement cast's fragment ⟨*double-to-unsigned conversion*⟩.

9.3 In lcc, all enumeration types are represented by integers because that's what most other C compilers do, but the standard permits each enumeration type to be represented by any of the integral types, as long it the type chosen can hold all the values. For example, unsigned characters could be used for enumeration types with enumeration values in the range 0–255. Explain how cast must be changed to accommodate this scheme. Earlier versions of lcc implemented this scheme.

9.4 Implement the omitted fragments for unary and postfix.

9.5 Dereferencing null pointers is a common programming error in C programs. lcc's -n option catches these errors. With -n, lcc generates code for

```
static char *_YYfile = "file";
static void _YYnull(int line) {
    char buf[200];
    sprintf(buf,"null pointer dereferenced @%s:%d\\n",
        _YYfile, line);
    write(2, buf, strlen(buf));
    abort();
}
```

at the end of each source file; *file* is the name of the source file. It also arranges for its global YYnull to point to the symbol-table entry for the function _YYnull. Whenever it builds a tree to defer-ence a pointer p, if YYnull is nonnull, it calls nullcheck to build a tree that is equivalent to ((t1 = p) || _YYnull(*lineno*), t1), where t1 is a temporary, and *lineno* is a constant that gives the source-code line at which the dereference appears and is the value of the global lineno. Thus, attempts to dereference a null pointer at runtime result in calls to _YYnull. Implement nullcheck.

9.6 bittree builds the trees for & | ^ %, multree for * /, shtree for << >>, and subtree for binary -. Implement these functions. The pointer subtraction code in subtree and the code in bittree for the modulus operator % are the most subtle. subtree takes about 25 lines, and the others each take less than 20.

9.7 Given the following file-scope declarations, what ADD+P tree is built for the expression x[10].table[i].count? Don't forget to apply simplify's transformations.

```
int i;
struct list {
    char *name;
    struct entry table {
        int age;
        int count;
    } table[10];
} x[100];
```

---
104 lineno
203 simplify

9.8 simplify uses ad hoc techniques to implement constant folding, and it implements only some of the transformations possible. Ex-plore the possibilities of using lburg, which is described in Chap-ter 14, to implement constant folding and a complete set of trans-formations.

10
Statements

The syntax of C statements is

statement:
   ID : *statement*
   case *constant-expression* : *statement*
   default : *statement*
   [*expression*] ;
   if '(' *expression* ')' *statement*
   if '(' *expression* ')' *statement* else *statement*
   switch '(' *expression* ')' *statement*
   while '(' *expression* ')' *statement*
   do *statement* while '(' *expression* ')' ;
   for '(' [*expression*] ; [*expression*] ; [*expression*] ')'
      statement
   break ;
   continue ;
   goto ID ;
   return [*expression*] ;
   compound-statement

compound-statement:
   '{' { *declaration* } { *statement* } '}'

function	92
(MIPS) "	448
(SPARC) "	484
(X86) "	518
gencode	337

compound-statement is implemented in Section 11.7. Some languages, such as Pascal, use semicolons to separate statements. In C, semicolons terminate statements, which is why they appear in the productions for the expression, do-while, break, continue, goto, and return statements, and they do not appear in the production for compound statements.

10.1   Representing Code

The semantics of statements consist of the evaluation of expressions, perhaps intermixed with jumps and labels, which implement transfer of control. Expressions are compiled into trees and then converted to dags, as suggested in Section 1.3 and detailed in Chapter 12. Jumps and labels are also represented by dags. For each function, these dags are strung together in a *code list*, which represents the code for the function. The front end builds the code list for a function and calls the interface function function. As described in Section 11.6, back ends call gencode and `emitcode` to generate and emit code; these functions traverse the code list.

The code list is a doubly linked list of typed code structures:

⟨*stmt.c typedefs*⟩≡   231
```
typedef struct code *Code;
```

⟨*stmt.c exported types*⟩≡
```
struct code {
    enum { Blockbeg, Blockend, Local, Address, Defpoint,
           Label,    Start,    Gen,   Jump,    Switch
    } kind;
    Code prev, next;
    union {
        ⟨Blockbeg 219⟩
        ⟨Blockend 220⟩
        ⟨Local 219⟩
        ⟨Address 219⟩
        ⟨Defpoint 220⟩
        ⟨Label, Gen, Jump 220⟩
        ⟨Switch 242⟩
    } u;
};
```

Each of the fields of u correspond to one of the values of `kind` enumerated above except for `Start`, which needs no u field. `Blockbeg` and `Blockend` entries identify the boundaries of compound statements. `Local` and `Address` identify local variables that must be announced to the back end by the `local` and `address` interface functions. `Defpoint` entries define the locations of execution points, which are the places in the program at which debuggers might plant breakpoints, for example. `Label`, `Gen`, and `Jump` entries carry dags for expressions, labels, and jumps. `Switch` entries carry the data needed to generate code for a switch statement.

The code list begins with a `Start` entry. `codelist` always points to the last entry on the list:

⟨*stmt.c data*⟩≡   238
```
struct code codehead = { Start };
Code codelist = &codehead;
```

The top diagram in Figure 10.1 shows the initial state of the code list. As statements in a function are compiled, the code list grows as entries are appended to it. `code` allocates an entry, links it to the entry pointed to by `codelist`, and advances `codelist` to point to the new entry, which is now the last one on the code list. `code` returns a pointer to the new entry:

⟨*stmt.c functions*⟩≡   219▾

```
    Code code(kind) int kind; {
        Code cp;

        ⟨check for unreachable code 218⟩
        NEW(cp, FUNC);
        cp->kind = kind;
        cp->prev = codelist;
        cp->next = NULL;
        codelist->next = cp;
        codelist = cp;
        return cp;
    }
```

The bottom diagram in Figure 10.1 shows the code list after two entries have been appended.

The values of the enumeration constants that identify code-list entries are important. Those greater than Start generate executable code; those less than Label do not generate code, but serve only to declare information of interest to the back end. Thus, code can detect entries that will generate unreachable code if it appends one with kind greater than Start after an unconditional jump:

⟨*check for unreachable code* 218⟩≡   218

```
    if (kind > Start) {
        for (cp = codelist; cp->kind < Label; )
            cp = cp->prev;
        if (cp->kind == Jump || cp->kind == Switch)
            warning("unreachable code\n");
    }
```

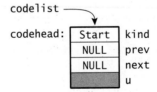

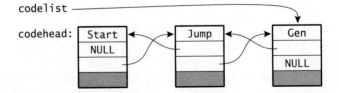

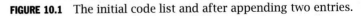

FIGURE 10.1 The initial code list and after appending two entries.

As detailed in Section 10.7, control doesn't "fall through" switch statements; they're like unconditional jumps.

addlocal appends a Local entry for a local variable, unless it's already been defined:

⟨Local 219⟩≡   217
```
Symbol var;
```

⟨*stmt.c functions*⟩+≡   218 220
```
void addlocal(p) Symbol p; {
    if (!p->defined) {
        code(Local)->u.var = p;
        p->defined = 1;
        p->scope = level;
    }
}
```

addrtree illustrates the use of addlocal and the use of code to append an Address entry. Address entries carry the data necessary for gencode to make a call to the interface function address.

⟨Address 219⟩≡   217
```
struct {
    Symbol sym;
    Symbol base;
    int offset;
} addr;
```

When gencode processes this entry, it uses the values of the sym, base, and offset fields as the three arguments to address.

Blockbeg entries store the data necessary to compile a compound statement:

⟨Blockbeg 219⟩≡   217
```
struct {
    int level;
    Symbol *locals;
    Table identifiers, types;
    Env x;
} block;
```

level is the value of level associated with the block, and locals is a null-terminated array of symbol-table pointers for the locals declared in the block. x is back end's Env value for this block. identifiers and types record the identifiers and types tables when the block was compiled; they're used in code omitted from this book to generate debugger symbol-table information when the option -g is specified. Blockend entries just point to their matching Blockbeg:

⟨Blockend 220⟩≡   217
    Code begin;

Label, Gen, and Jump entries all carry a pointer to a forest:

⟨Label, Gen, Jump 220⟩≡   217
    Node forest;

Each of these entries is identified by its own enumeration constant so that its purpose can be determined without inspecting its dag. This capability is used above in code to identify jumps, and it's used in Section 10.9 to eliminate jumps to jumps and unreachable jumps.

10.2 Execution Points

Execution points occur before every *expression* in the grammar at the beginning of this chapter, before the operands of && and ||, before the second and third operands of ?:, at the beginning and end of every compound statement, and at the entry and exit to every function. They give back ends that implement the stab interface functions mentioned in Section 5.2 the opportunity to generate code and symbol-table information for debuggers. For example, debuggers permit breakpoints to be set at execution points.

Execution points and events are also used to implement lcc's profiling facility. The option -b causes lcc to generate code to count the number of times each execution point is executed and to write those counts to a file. The -a option causes that file to be read during compilation and used to compute values of refinc that give *exact* execution frequencies instead of estimates.

An execution-point entry records the source coordinates and a unique number that identifies the execution point:

⟨Defpoint 220⟩≡   217
    struct {
        Coordinate src;
        int point;
    } point;

definept appends a Defpoint entry to the code list and fills in either an explicit coordinate or the current value of src:

⟨*stmt.c functions*⟩+≡   219 221
    void definept(p) Coordinate *p; {
        Code cp = code(Defpoint);

        cp->u.point.src = p ? *p : src;
        cp->u.point.point = npoints;

```
⟨reset refinc if -a was specified⟩
if (events.points)
    ⟨plant event hook⟩
}
```

Usually, definept is called with a null pointer, but the loop and switch statements generate tests and assignments at the ends of their statements, so the execution points are in a different order in the generated code than they appear in the source code. For these, the relevant coordinate is saved when the expression is parsed, and is passed to definept when the code for the expression is generated; the calls to definept in forstmt are examples.

10.3   Recognizing Statements

The parsing function for *statement* uses the current token to identify the kind of statement, and switches to statement-specific code:

⟨*stmt.c functions*⟩+≡   220 224

```
void statement(loop, swp, lev) int loop, lev; Swtch swp; {
    float ref = refinc;

    if (Aflag >= 2 && lev == 15)
        warning("more than 15 levels of nested statements\n");
    switch (t) {
    case IF:        ⟨if statement 224⟩ break;
    case WHILE:     ⟨while statement⟩ break;
    case DO:        ⟨do statement⟩ ⟨semicolon 222⟩
    case FOR:       ⟨for statement 228⟩ break;
    case BREAK:     ⟨break statement 232⟩ ⟨semicolon 222⟩
    case CONTINUE:  ⟨continue statement 228⟩ ⟨semicolon 222⟩
    case SWITCH:    ⟨switch statement 232⟩ break;
    case CASE:      ⟨case label 234⟩ break;
    case DEFAULT:   ⟨default label 234⟩ break;
    case RETURN:    ⟨return statement 243⟩ ⟨semicolon 222⟩
    case '{':       compound(loop, swp, lev + 1); break;
    case ';':       definept(NULL); t = gettok(); break;
    case GOTO:      ⟨goto statement 227⟩ ⟨semicolon 222⟩
    case ID:        ⟨statement label or fall thru to default 226⟩
    default:        ⟨expression statement 222⟩ ⟨semicolon 222⟩
    }
    ⟨check for legal statement termination 222⟩
    refinc = ref;
}
```

62	Aflag
293	compound
220	definept
228	forstmt
38	ref
169	refinc
231	Swtch

⟨*semicolon* 222⟩≡   221
```
expect(';');
break;
```

⟨*check for legal statement termination* 222⟩≡   221
```
if (kind[t] != IF && kind[t] != ID
&& t != '}' && t != EOI) {
    static char stop[] = { IF, ID, '}', 0 };
    error("illegal statement termination\n");
    skipto(0, stop);
}
```

statement takes three arguments: loop is the label number for the inner-most for, while, or do-while loop, swp is a pointer to the swtch structure that carries all of the data pertaining to the innermost switch statement (see Section 10.7), and lev tells how deeply statements are currently nested. If the current statement is not nested in any loop, loop is zero; if it's not nested in any switch statement, swp is null. loop is needed to generate code for break and continue statements, swp is needed to gen-erate code for switch statements, and lev is needed only for the warning shown above at the beginning of statement. The code for each kind of statement passes these values along to nested calls to statement, modi-fying them as appropriate.

Labels, like those used for loop, are *local labels*, and they're gener-ated by genlabel(n), which returns the first of n labels. findlabel(n) returns the symbol-table entry for label n.

For every reference to an identifier, idtree increments that identifier's ref field by refinc. This value is approximately proportional to the num-ber of times the identifier is referenced. statement and its descendants change refinc to weight each reference to an identifier that is appropri-ate for the statement in which it appears. For example, refinc is divided by 2 for the arms of an if statement, and it's multiplied by 10 for the body of a loop. The value of the ref field helps identify those locals and parameters that might profitably be assigned to registers, and locals are announced to the back end in decreasing order of their ref values.

The default case handles *expressions* that are statements:

⟨*expression statement* 222⟩≡   221
```
definept(NULL);
if (kind[t] != ID) {
    error("unrecognized statement\n");
    t = gettok();
} else {
    Tree e = expr0(0);
    listnodes(e, 0, 0);
    if (nodecount == 0 || nodecount > 200)
```

```
        walk(NULL, 0, 0);
     deallocate(STMT);
   }
```

listnodes and walk are the two functions that generate dags from trees. Chapter 12 explains their implementations, but their usage must be explained now in order to understand how the front end implements the semantics of statements.

listnodes takes a tree as its first argument, generates the dag for that tree as described in Chapter 5, and appends the dag to a growing forest of dags that it maintains. Thus, the call to listnodes above generates the dag for the tree returned by expr0, and appends that dag to the forest. For the input

```
   c = a + b;
   a = a/2;
   d = a + b;
```

the fragment ⟨*expression statement*⟩ is executed three times, once for each statement, and thus listnodes is called three times. The first call appends the dag for c = a + b to the initially empty forest, and the next two calls grow that forest by appending the dags for the second and third assignments. As detailed in Section 12.1, listnodes reuses common subexpressions when possible; for example, in the assignment d = a + b, it reuses the dags for the lvalue of a and the rvalue of b formed for the first assignment. It can't reuse the rvalue of a because the second assignment changes a.

The second and third arguments are label numbers, and their purpose is explained in the next section; the zeros shown in the call to listnodes above specify no labels. listnodes also accepts the null tree for which it simply returns.

listnodes keeps the forest to itself until walk is called, which accepts the same arguments as listnodes. walk takes two steps: First, it passes its arguments to listnodes, so a call to walk has the same effect as a call to listnodes. Second, and most important, walk allocates a Gen code-list entry, stores the forest in that entry, appends the entry to the code list, and clears the forest. Once a forest is added to the code list, its dags are no longer available for reuse by listnodes.

The call walk(NULL, 0, 0) effectively executes just the second step, and it has the effect of adding the current forest to the code list, if there is a nonempty forest. This call is made whenever the current forest must be appended to the code list either because some other executable code-list entry must be appended or because two or more separate flows of control merge. In the code above, this call is made when nodecount is zero or when it exceeds 200. nodecount is the number of nodes in the forest that are available for reuse. walk is called when the forest has no nodes that can be reused or when the forest is getting large. The former condition puts dags that do not share common subexpressions into separate forests, and the latter one limits the sizes of forests; both consequences may help back ends.

The call to `deallocate` frees all the space in the STMT arena, which is where trees are allocated. `walk` also deallocates the STMT arena.

10.4   If Statements

The generated code for an if statement has the form

$$
\begin{array}{ll}
& \texttt{if } expression \texttt{ == 0 goto } L \\
& statement_1 \\
& \texttt{goto } L + 1 \\
L\texttt{:} & statement_2 \\
L + 1\texttt{:} &
\end{array}
$$

If the else part is omitted, the `goto` $L + 1$ is omitted. The code is

⟨*if statement* 224⟩≡   221
```
ifstmt(genlabel(2), loop, swp, lev + 1);
```

⟨*stmt.c functions*⟩+≡   221 225

```
static void ifstmt(lab, loop, swp, lev)
int lab, loop, lev; Swtch swp; {
    t = gettok();
    expect('(');
    definept(NULL);
    walk(conditional(')'), 0, lab);
    refinc /= 2.0;
    statement(loop, swp, lev);
    if (t == ELSE) {
        branch(lab + 1);
        t = gettok();
        definelab(lab);
        statement(loop, swp, lev);
        if (findlabel(lab + 1)->ref)
            definelab(lab + 1);
    } else
        definelab(lab);
}
```

The first argument to `ifstmt` is L; `genlabel(2)` generates two labels for use in the if statement. `ifstmt`'s other three arguments echo `statement`'s arguments. `conditional` parses an *expression* by calling `expr`, and ensures that the resulting tree is a conditional, which is an expression whose value is used only to alter flow of control. The root of the tree for a conditional has one of the comparison operators, AND, OR, NOT, or a constant. conditional's argument is the token that should follow the expression in the context in which conditional is called.

⟨*stmt.c functions*⟩+≡   2̂24 2̲2̲6▾

```
static Tree conditional(tok) int tok; {
    Tree p = expr(tok);

    if (Aflag > 1 && isfunc(p->type))
        warning("%s used in a conditional expression\n",
            funcname(p));
    return cond(p);
}
```

The second and third arguments to listnodes and walk are labels that specify true and false targets. walk(e, tlab, flab) passes its arguments to listnodes, which generates a dag from e and adds it to the forest, and appends a Gen entry carrying the forest to the code list, as explained in the previous section. When e is a tree for a conditional expression, either tlab or flab is nonzero. If tlab is nonzero, listnodes generates a dag that transfers control to tlab if the result of e is nonzero; likewise, listnodes generates a dag that jumps to flab if e evaluates to zero. listnodes and walk can be called with a nonzero value for only one of tlab or flab; control always "falls through" for the other case.

For the if statement, walk is called with a nonzero flab corresponding to *L* in the generated code shown above. definelab and branch generate code-list items for label definitions and jumps. *L* + 1 is defined only if it's needed; a label's ref field is incremented each time it's used as the target of a branch. For example, *L* + 1 isn't needed if the branch to it is eliminated, which occurs in code like

```
if (...)
    return;
else
    ...
```

62	Aflag
149	AND
247	branch
174	cond
246	definelab
155	expr
217	Gen
168	idtree
224	ifstmt
60	isfunc
318	listnodes
149	NOT
149	OR
169	refinc
221	statement
311	walk

The return statement acts like an unconditional jump, so the call to branch(lab + 1) doesn't emit the branch.

Recall that refinc is the amount added to each reference to an identifier in idtree. Estimating that each arm of an if statement is executed approximately the same number of times, refinc is halved before they are parsed. The result is that a reference to an identifier in one of the arms counts half as much as a reference before or after the if statement. ifstmt doesn't have to restore refinc because statement does.

10.5   Labels and Gotos

For statements that begin with an identifier, the identifier is a label if it is followed by a colon; otherwise, it begins an expression.

⟨*statement label or fall thru to default* 226⟩≡   221
```
    if (getchr() == ':') {
        stmtlabel();
        statement(loop, swp, lev);
        break;
    }
```

getchr advances the input to just before the initial character of the next token and returns that character. It is used to 'peek' at the next character to check for a colon. Since an identifier can be both a label and a variable, a separate table, stmtlabs, holds source-language labels:

⟨*stmt.c exported data*⟩≡
```
    extern Table stmtlabs;
```

Like other tables, stmtlabs is managed by lookup and install. It maps source-language labels to internal label numbers, which are stored in the symbols' u.1.label fields.

⟨*stmt.c functions*⟩+≡   225 228
```
    static void stmtlabel() {
        Symbol p = lookup(token, stmtlabs);

        ⟨install token in stmtlabs, if necessary 226⟩
        if (p->defined)
            error("redefinition of label '%s' previously _
                defined at %w\n", p->name, &p->src);
        p->defined = 1;
        definelab(p->u.1.label);
        t = gettok();
        expect(':');
    }
```

definelab(n) builds a LABELV dag that defines the label n, allocates a Label code-list entry to hold that dag, and appends the Label entry to the code list.

Labels can be defined before they are referenced and vice versa, so they can be installed either when they label a statement or when they appear in a goto statement.

⟨*install* token *in* stmtlabs, *if necessary* 226⟩≡   226 227
```
    if (p == NULL) {
        p = install(token, &stmtlabs, 0, FUNC);
```

```
        p->scope = LABELS;
        p->u.1.label = genlabel(1);
        p->src = src;
    }
```

A label's `ref` field counts the number of references to the label and is initialized to zero by `install`. Each reference to the label increments the `ref` field:

⟨*goto statement* 227⟩≡   221
```
    walk(NULL, 0, 0);
    definept(NULL);
    t = gettok();
    if (t == ID) {
        Symbol p = lookup(token, stmtlabs);
        ⟨install token in stmtlabs, if necessary 226⟩
        use(p, src);
        branch(p->u.1.label);
        t = gettok();
    } else
        error("missing label in goto\n");
```

`branch(n)` builds a JUMPV dag for a branch to the label n, allocates a Jump code-list entry to hold that dag, and appends the Jump entry to the code list. It also increments n's ref field.

Undefined labels — those referenced in goto statements but never defined — are found and announced when `funcdefn` calls `checklab` at the end of a function definition.

10.6 Loops

The code for all three kinds of loops has a similar structure involving three labels: L is the top of the loop, $L + 1$ labels the test portion of the loop, and $L + 2$ labels the loop exit. For example, the generated code for a while loop is

```
            goto L + 1
L:          statement
L + 1:      if expression != 0 goto L
L + 2:
```

This layout is better than

```
L:
L + 1:      if expression != 0 goto L + 2
            statement
            goto L
L + 2:
```

because the former executes $n + 2$ branch instructions when the loop body is executed n times; the more obvious layout executes $2n + 1$ branches.

The code for continue statements jumps to $L + 1$, and the code for break statements jumps to $L + 2$. L is the *loop handle*, and is passed to statement and the functions it calls, as illustrated by ifstmt. A continue statement, for example, is legal only if there's a loop handle:

⟨*continue statement* 228⟩ ≡   221
```
walk(NULL, 0, 0);
definept(NULL);
if (loop)
    branch(loop + 1);
else
    error("illegal continue statement\n");
t = gettok();
```

The first three of the four labels in a for loop have the same meanings as in the while loop; the layout of the generated code when all three *expressions* are present is

$$
\begin{array}{ll}
& expression_1 \\
& \texttt{goto } L + 3 \\
L\colon & statement \\
L + 1\colon & expression_3 \\
L + 3\colon & \texttt{if } expression_2 \texttt{ != 0 goto } L \\
L + 2\colon &
\end{array}
$$

$expression_1$, $expression_2$, and $expression_3$ are called the initialization, test, and increment, respectively.

Most of the complexity in the parsing function is in coping with the optional expressions, announcing the execution points in the right places, and implementing an optimization for loops that always execute their bodies at least once.

⟨*for statement* 228⟩ ≡   221
```
forstmt(genlabel(4), swp, lev + 1);
```

⟨*stmt.c functions*⟩ +≡   226 233
```
static void forstmt(lab, swp, lev)
int lab, lev; Swtch swp; {
    int once = 0;
    Tree e1 = NULL, e2 = NULL, e3 = NULL;
    Coordinate pt2, pt3;

    t = gettok();
    expect('(');
```

```
        definept(NULL);
        ⟨forstmt 229⟩
    }
```

First, the initialization is parsed and appended to the code list:

⟨*forstmt* 229⟩≡   229   229

```
    if (kind[t] == ID)
        e1 = texpr(expr0, ';', FUNC);
    else
        expect(';');
    walk(e1, 0, 0);
```

Next, the test is parsed, but it cannot be passed to walk until *after* the body of the loop has been compiled. The assignment to pt2 saves the source coordinate of the test for a call to defpoint just before the tree for the test is passed to walk.

⟨*forstmt* 229⟩+≡   229 229   229

```
    pt2 = src;
    refinc *= 10.0;
    if (kind[t] == ID)
        e2 = texpr(conditional, ';', FUNC);
    else
        expect(';');
```

walk has an important side effect: it deallocates the STMT arena from which trees are allocated by tree. texpr causes the trees for the test to be allocated in the FUNC arena, so they survive the calls to walk that are made when the loop body is compiled. texpr is also used for the increment:

⟨*forstmt* 229⟩+≡   229 230   229

```
    pt3 = src;
    if (kind[t] == ID)
        e3 = texpr(expr0, ')', FUNC);
    else {
        static char stop[] = { IF, ID, '}', 0 };
        test(')', stop);
    }
```

225	conditional
220	definept
142	expect
156	expr0
97	FUNC
143	kind
169	refinc
97	STMT
141	test
150	texpr
150	tree
311	walk

pt3 holds the source coordinate for the increment expression for a later call to defpoint.

Multiplying refinc by 10 estimates that loop bodies are executed 10 times more often than statements outside of loops, and weights references to identifiers used in loops accordingly.

Many for loops look like the one in the following code:

```
sum = 0;
for (i = 0; i < 10; i++)
    sum += x[i];
```

The loop bodies in these kinds of loops are always executed at least once and the leading goto $L + 3$ could be omitted, which is accomplished by

⟨*forstmt* 229⟩ +≡   229 230   229

```
if (e2) {
    once = foldcond(e1, e2);
    if (!once)
        branch(lab + 3);
}
```

foldcond inspects the trees for the initialization and for the test to determine if the loop body will be executed at least once; see Exercise 10.3. e1 is passed to foldcond, which is why it was parsed with texpr above.

The rest of forstmt compiles the loop body and lays down the labels and expressions as described above.

⟨*forstmt* 229⟩ +≡   230   229

```
definelab(lab);
statement(lab, swp, lev);
definelab(lab + 1);
definept(&pt3);
if (e3)
    walk(e3, 0, 0);
if (e2) {
    if (!once)
        definelab(lab + 3);
    definept(&pt2);
    walk(e2, lab, 0);
} else {
    definept(&pt2);
    branch(lab);
}
if (findlabel(lab + 2)->ref)
    definelab(lab + 2);
```

Symbol-table entries for generated labels are installed in the labels table by findlabel. Like other labels, the ref field of a generated label is nonzero only if the label is the target of a jump.

10.7 Switch Statements

The C switch statement differs significantly from, for example, the Pascal case statement. *Any* statement can follow the switch clause; the placement of the case and default labels is not specified by the syntax of the

switch statement. In addition, after executing the statement associated
with a case label, control falls through to the next statement, which might
be labelled by another case label. Case and default labels are simply labels, and have no additional semantics. For example, the intent of the
code

```
switch (n%4)
    while (n > 0) {
    case 0: *x++ = *y++; n--;
    case 3: *x++ = *y++; n--;
    case 2: *x++ = *y++; n--;
    case 1: *x++ = *y++; n--;
    }
```

is to copy n values from y to x where n ≥ 1. The loop is unrolled so
that each iteration copies four values. The switch statement copies the
first n%4 values and the n/4 iterations copy the rest. This example is
somewhat contrived but legal nonetheless.

The generated code for a switch statement with n cases and a default
looks like:

$$t1 \leftarrow expression$$
$$\text{select and jump to } L_1, \ldots, L_n, L$$
$$\text{code for } statement$$
$$L + 1:$$

where t1 is a temporary associated with the switch statement, and $L + 1$
is the exit label. Each case label generates a definition for its generated
label, L_i, a default label generates a definition for L, and each break inside
a switch generates a jump to the exit label:

$$\text{goto } L + 1$$

If there's no default, L labels the same location as $L + 1$.

Parsing the switch statement, the case and default labels, and the
break statement are easy; the hard part is generating good code for the
select and jump fragment. Each case label is associated with an integer
value. These value-label pairs are used to generate the code that selects
and jumps to the appropriate case depending on the value of *expression*.
These and other data are stored in a swtch structure associated with the
switch statement during parsing:

⟨*stmt.c typedefs*⟩+≡   217
```
typedef struct swtch *Swtch;
```

⟨*stmt.c types*⟩≡
```
struct swtch {
    Symbol sym;
```

```
        int lab;
        Symbol deflab;
        int ncases;
        int size;
        int *values;
        Symbol *labels;
    };
```

sym holds the temporary, t1, lab holds the value of *L*, and deflab points to the symbol-table entry for the default label, if there is one. values and labels point to arrays that store the value-label pairs. These arrays have size elements, ncases of which are occupied, and these ncases are kept in ascending order of values. A pointer to the swtch structure for the current switch statement — the *switch handle* — is passed to statement and its descendants.

Case and default labels are handled much like break and continue statements: They refer to the innermost, or current, switch statement, and case and default labels that appear outside of switch statements, which is when the switch handle is null, are erroneous. The code for the break statement determines whether it is associated with a loop or a switch by examining both the loop handle and the switch handle:

⟨*break statement* 232⟩≡   221
```
    walk(NULL, 0, 0);
    definept(NULL);
    if (swp && swp->lab > loop)
        branch(swp->lab + 1);
    else if (loop)
        branch(loop + 2);
    else
        error("illegal break statement\n");
    t = gettok();
```

Since the values of labels increase as they are generated, a break refers to a switch statement if there's a switch handle and its *L* is greater than the loop handle.

Parsing switch statements involves parsing and type-checking the *expression*, generating a temporary, appending a Switch placeholder on the code list, initializing a new switch handle and passing it to statement, and generating the closing labels and the selection code.

⟨*switch statement* 232⟩≡   221
```
    swstmt(loop, genlabel(2), lev + 1);
```

⟨*stmt.c macros*⟩≡   239
```
    #define SWSIZE 512
```

⟨*stmt.c functions*⟩+≡   2̂28 235
                                                                               ▾
```
    static void swstmt(loop, lab, lev) int loop, lab, lev; {
        Tree e;
        struct swtch sw;
        Code head, tail;

        t = gettok();
        expect('(');
        definept(NULL);
        e = expr(')');
```
⟨*type-check* e 233⟩
⟨*generate a temporary to hold* e, *if necessary* 233⟩
```
        head = code(Switch);
        sw.lab = lab;
        sw.deflab = NULL;
        sw.ncases = 0;
        sw.size = SWSIZE;
        sw.values = newarray(SWSIZE, sizeof *sw.values, FUNC);
        sw.labels = newarray(SWSIZE, sizeof *sw.labels, FUNC);
        refinc /= 10.0;
        statement(loop, &sw, lev);
```
⟨*define L, if necessary, and L* + 1 236⟩
⟨*generate the selection code* 236⟩
```
    }
```

The placeholder Switch entry in the code list will be replaced by one or
more Switch entries when the selection code is generated. The switch
expression must have integral type, and it's promoted:

⟨*type-check* e 233⟩≡   233
```
    if (!isint(e->type)) {
        error("illegal type '%t' in switch expression\n",
            e->type);
        e = retype(e, inttype);
    }
    e = cast(e, promote(e->type));
```

The temporary also has type e->type, but the temporary can be avoided
in some cases. If the switch expression is simply an identifier, and it's
the right type and is not volatile, then it can be used instead. Otherwise,
the expression is assigned to a temporary:

⟨*generate a temporary to hold* e, *if necessary* 233⟩≡   233
```
    if (generic(e->op) == INDIR && isaddrop(e->kids[0]->op)
    && e->kids[0]->u.sym->type == e->type
    && !isvolatile(e->kids[0]->u.sym->type)) {
        sw.sym = e->kids[0]->u.sym;
```

```
        walk(NULL, 0, 0);
    } else {
        sw.sym = genident(REGISTER, e->type, level);
        addlocal(sw.sym);
        walk(asgn(sw.sym, e), 0, 0);
    }
```

Once the switch handle is initialized, case and default labels simply add data to the handle. For example, a default label fills in the deflab field, unless it's already filled in:

⟨*default label* 234⟩ ≡   221

```
    if (swp == NULL)
        error("illegal default label\n");
    else if (swp->deflab)
        error("extra default label\n");
    else {
        swp->deflab = findlabel(swp->lab);
        definelab(swp->deflab->u.l.label);
    }
    t = gettok();
    expect(':');
    statement(loop, swp, lev);
```

Case labels are similar: The label value is converted to the promoted type of the switch expression, and a label associated with that value is generated and defined:

⟨*case label* 234⟩ ≡   221

```
    {
        int lab = genlabel(1);
        if (swp == NULL)
            error("illegal case label\n");
        definelab(lab);
        while (t == CASE) {
            static char stop[] = { IF, ID, 0 };
            Tree p;
            t = gettok();
            p = constexpr(0);
            if (generic(p->op) == CNST && isint(p->type)) {
                if (swp) {
                    needconst++;
                    p = cast(p, swp->sym->type);
                    needconst--;
                    caselabel(swp, p->u.v.i, lab);
                }
            } else
```

```
            error("case label must be a constant _
                integer expression\n");
        test(':', stop);
    }
    statement(loop, swp, lev);
}
```

needconst is incremented before that call to cast so that simplify will fold the conversion even if it overflows. For example, the input

```
int i;
switch (i)
case 0xffffffff: ;
```

elicits the diagnostic

```
warning: overflow in constant expression
```

because the case value is an unsigned that can't be represented by an integer. Notice that a case label is processed even if it appears outside a switch statement; this prevents the case label from causing additional syntax errors.

caselabel appends the value and the label to the values and labels arrays in the switch handle. It also detects duplicate labels.

⟨*stmt.c functions*⟩+≡   233 239

```
    static void caselabel(swp, val, lab)
    Swtch swp; int val, lab; {
        int k;

        if (swp->ncases >= swp->size)
            ⟨double the size of values and labels⟩
        k = swp->ncases;
        for ( ; k > 0 && swp->values[k-1] >= val; k--) {
            swp->values[k] = swp->values[k-1];
            swp->labels[k] = swp->labels[k-1];
        }
        if (k < swp->ncases && swp->values[k] == val)
            error("duplicate case label '%d'\n", val);
        swp->values[k] = val;
        swp->labels[k] = findlabel(lab);
        ++swp->ncases;
        if (Aflag >= 2 && swp->ncases == 258)
            warning("more than 257 cases in a switch\n");
    }
```

The for loop inserts the new label and value into the right place in the values and labels arrays so that these arrays are sorted in ascending order of values, which helps both to detect duplicate case values and to generate good selection code. If necessary, these arrays are doubled in size to accommodate the new value-label pair.

After the return from statement to swstmt, a default label is defined, if there was no explicit default, and the exit label, $L + 1$, is defined, if it was referenced:

⟨*define L, if necessary, and L + 1* 236⟩ ≡   233
```
    if (sw.deflab == NULL) {
        sw.deflab = findlabel(lab);
        definelab(lab);
        if (sw.ncases == 0)
            warning("switch statement with no cases\n");
    }
    if (findlabel(lab + 1)->ref)
        definelab(lab + 1);
```

The default label is defined even if it isn't referenced, because it will probably be referenced by the selection code.

The selection code can't be generated until all the cases have been examined. Compiling *statement* appends entries to the code list, but the entries for the selection code need to appear just after those for *expression* and before those for *statement*. The selection code could appear after *statement* if branches were inserted so the selection code was *executed* before *statement*. But there's a solution to this problem that's easier and generates better code: rearrange the code list.

The top diagram in Figure 10.2 shows the code list after the exit label has been defined. The solid circle represents the entry for *expression*, the open circle is the Switch placeholder, and the open squares are the entries for *statement*, including the definitions for the case and default labels and the jumps generated by break statements. head points to the placeholder and codelist to the last *statement* entry.

The first step in generating the selection code is to make the solid circle the end of the code list:

⟨*generate the selection code* 236⟩ ≡   236   233
```
    tail = codelist;
    codelist = head->prev;
    codelist->next = head->prev = NULL;
```

The second diagram in Figure 10.2 shows the outcome of these statements. head and tail point to the entries for the placeholder and for *statement*, and codelist points to the entry for *expression*. As the selection code is generated, its entries are appended in the right place:

⟨*generate the selection code* 236⟩ +≡   236 237   233
```
    if (sw.ncases > 0)
```

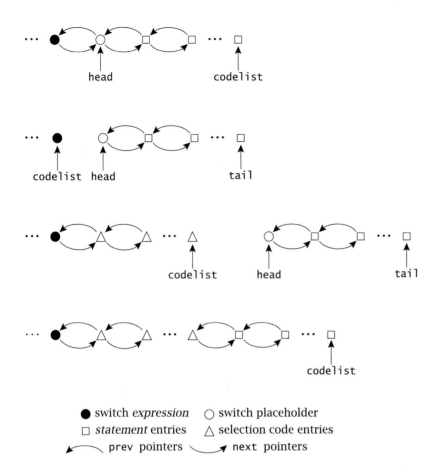

● switch *expression*   ○ switch placeholder
□ *statement* entries   △ selection code entries
prev pointers   next pointers

FIGURE 10.2   Code-list manipulations for generating switch selection code.

```
    swgen(&sw);
  branch(lab);
```

Figure 10.2's third diagram shows the code list after entries for the selection code, which are shown in open triangles, have been added. The
last step is to append the entire list held by head and tail to the code
list and set codelist back to tail:

⟨*generate the selection code* 236⟩+≡   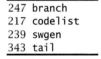   236   233
```
  head->next->prev = codelist;
  codelist->next = head->next;
  codelist = tail;
```

The last diagram in Figure 10.2 shows the result, which omits the placeholder.

The fastest selection code when there are more than three cases is a
branch table: The value of *expression* is used as an index to this table,

and the ith entry holds L_i, or L if i is not a case label. For this organization, selection takes constant time. This table takes space proportional
to $u - l + 1$ where l and u are the minimum and maximum case values.
For n case values, the *density* of the table — the fraction occupied by
nondefault destination labels — is $n/(u - l + 1)$. If the density is too low,
this organization wastes space. Worse, there are legal switch statements
for which it is impractical:

```
switch (i) {
case INT_MIN: ...; break;
case INT_MAX: ...; break;
}
```

At the other extreme, a linear search — a sequence of n comparisons —
is compact but slow. It takes only $O(n)$ space for any set of case labels,
but selection takes $O(n)$ time. Using a binary search would reduce the
time to $O(\log n)$ and increase the space by $O(\log n)$.

lcc combines branch tables and binary search: It generates a binary
search of dense branch tables. If there are m tables, selection takes
$O(\log m)$ time and space that is proportional to $n + \log m$. Generating
the selection code for this approach involves three steps: partitioning
the value-label pairs into dense tables, arranging these tables into a tree
that mirrors the binary search, and traversing this tree to generate code.

An example helps describe the code for these steps. Suppose the case
values are

i	0	1	2	3	4	5	6	7	8	9
$v[i]$	21	22	23	27	28	29	36	37	38	39

v is the values array, and the numbers above the line are the indices into
v. The density, $d(i, j)$, for the subset of values $v[i..j]$ is the number of
values divided by the range of those values:

$$d(i, j) = (j - i + 1)/(v[j] - v[i] + 1).$$

For example,

$$
\begin{aligned}
d(0, 9) &= (9 - 0 + 1)/(39 - 21 + 1) &= 10/19 &= 0.53 \\
d(0, 5) &= (5 - 0 + 1)/(29 - 21 + 1) &= 6/9 &= 0.67 \\
d(6, 9) &= (9 - 6 + 1)/(39 - 36 + 1) &= 4/4 &= 1.0
\end{aligned}
$$

The value of density is the minimum density for branch tables:

⟨*stmt.c data*⟩+≡   217
   `float density = 0.5;`

As shown, the default density is 0.5, which results in a single table for the
example above because $d(0, 9) > 0.5$. lcc's -dx option changes density
to x. If density is 0.66, the example generates two tables ($v[0..5]$

and $v[6..9]$), and three tables if density is 0.75 ($v[0..2]$, $v[3..5]$, and $v[6..9]$). If density exceeds 1.0, there are n one-element tables, which corresponds to a binary search.

A simple greedy algorithm implements partitioning: If the current table is $v[i..j]$ and $d(i, j + 1) \geq$ density, extend the table to $v[i..j + 1]$. Whenever a table is extended, it's merged with its predecessor if the density of the combined table is greater than density. swgen does both of these steps at once by treating the single element $v[j + 1]$ as the table $v[j + 1..j + 1]$ and merging it with its predecessor, if possible. In the code below, buckets[k] is the index in v of the first value in the kth table, i.e., table k is $v[buckets[k]..buckets[k + 1] - 1]$. For n case values, there can be up to n tables, so buckets can have $n + 1$ elements.

⟨*stmt.c macros*⟩+≡   ▲ 232
```
#define den(i,j) ((j-buckets[i]+1.0)/(v[j]-v[buckets[i]]+1))
```

⟨*stmt.c functions*⟩+≡   ▲ 235 240 ▼
```
static void swgen(swp) Swtch swp; {
    int *buckets, k, n, *v = swp->values;

    buckets = newarray(swp->ncases + 1,
        sizeof *buckets, FUNC);
    for (n = k = 0; k < swp->ncases; k++, n++) {
        buckets[n] = k;
        while (n > 0 && den(n-1, k) >= density)
            n--;
    }
    buckets[n] = swp->ncases;
    swcode(swp, buckets, 0, n - 1);
}
```

When swgen calls swcode, there are n tables, buckets[0..n-1] holds the indices into v for the first value in each table, and buckets[n] is equal to n, which is the index of a fictitious n+1st table.

The display below illustrates how swgen partitions the example from above when density is 0.66. The first iteration of the for loop ends with:

$v[i]$ |21 22 23 27 28 29 36 37 38 39

The vertical bars appear to the left of the first element of a table and thus represent the values of buckets. The rightmost bar is the value of buckets[n]. The value associated with k is underlined. So, at the end of the first iteration, k is zero and refers to the value 21, and the one table is $v[0..0]$. The next two iterations set buckets[1] to 1 and 2, and in each case combine the single-element tables $v[1..1]$ and $v[2..2]$ with their predecessors $v[0..0]$ and $v[0..1]$. At the end of the third iteration, the state is

$$v[i] \quad |21 \quad 22 \quad \underline{23} \quad 27 \quad 28 \quad 29 \quad 36 \quad 37 \quad 38 \quad 39$$

and the only table is $v[0..2]$. The fourth iteration cannot merge $v[3..3]$, which holds just 27, with $v[0..2]$ because the density $d(0, 3) = 4/7 = 0.57$ is too low, so the state becomes

$$v[i] \quad |21 \quad 22 \quad 23 \quad |27 \quad 28 \quad 29 \quad 36 \quad 37 \quad 38 \quad 39$$

Next, $v[4..4]$ (28) can be merged with $v[3..3]$, but $v[3..4]$ cannot be merged with $v[0..3]$ because $d(0, 4) = 5/8 = 0.63$.

The iteration that examines 29 is the interesting one. Just before the while loop, n is 2 and the state is

$$v[i] \quad |21 \quad 22 \quad 23 \quad |27 \quad 28 \quad |\underline{29} \quad 36 \quad 37 \quad 38 \quad 39$$

The while loop merges $v[3..4]$ with $v[5..5]$ and decrements n to 1; since $d(0, 5) = 6/9 = 0.67$, it also merges $v[0..2]$ with the just-formed $v[3..5]$ and decrements n to 0. The state after the while loop is

$$v[i] \quad |21 \quad 22 \quad 23 \quad 27 \quad 28 \quad \underline{29} \quad 36 \quad 37 \quad 38 \quad 39$$

This process ends with two tables; the state just before calling swcode is

i	0	1	2	3	4	5	6	7	8	9
$v[i]$	|21	22	23	27	28	29	|36	37	38	39|

and n is 2 and buckets holds the indices 0, 6, and 10.

swgen 239
Swtch 231

The last two steps arrange the tables described by buckets into a tree and traverse this tree generating the selection code for each table. swcode uses a divide-and-conquer algorithm to do both steps at the same time. swgen calls swcode with the switch handle, buckets, the lower and upper bounds of buckets, and the number of tables. buckets also has a sentinel after its last element, which simplifies accessing the last case value in the last table.

swcode generates code for the ub-lb+1 tables given by b[lb..ub]. It picks the middle table as the root of the search tree, generates code for it, and calls itself recursively for the tables on either side of the root table.

⟨*stmt.c functions*⟩+≡ 239 242

```
static void swcode(swp, b, lb, ub)
Swtch swp; int b[]; int lb, ub; {
    int hilab, lolab, l, u, k = (lb + ub)/2;
    int *v = swp->values;

    ⟨swcode 241⟩
}
```

When there's only one table, switch expressions whose value is not within the range covered by the table cause control to be transferred to the default label. For a binary search of tables, control needs to flow to the appropriate subtable when the switch expression is out of range.

⟨*swcode* 241⟩≡   241   240

```
if (k > lb && k < ub) {
   lolab = genlabel(1);
   hilab = genlabel(1);
} else if (k > lb) {
   lolab = genlabel(1);
   hilab = swp->deflab->u.l.label;
} else if (k < ub) {
   lolab = swp->deflab->u.l.label;
   hilab = genlabel(1);
} else
   lolab = hilab = swp->deflab->u.l.label;
```

`lolab` and `hilab` are where control should be transferred to if the switch expression is less than the root's smallest value or greater than the root's largest value. If the search tree has both left and right subtables, `lolab` and `hilab` will label their code sequences. The default label is used for `hilab` when there's no right subtable and for `lolab` when there's no left subtable. If the root is the only table, the default label is used for both `lolab` and `hilab`.

Finally, the code for the root table is generated:

⟨*swcode* 241⟩+≡   ▲241 241   240

246 definelab
45 genlabel
240 swcode

```
l = b[k];
u = b[k+1] - 1;
if (u - l + 1 <= 3)
   ⟨generate a linear search⟩
else {
   ⟨generate an indirect jump and a branch table 242⟩
}
```

and `swcode` is called recursively to generate the left and right subtables.

⟨*swcode* 241⟩+≡   ▲241   240

```
if (k > lb) {
   definelab(lolab);
   swcode(swp, b, lb, k - 1);
}
if (k < ub) {
   definelab(hilab);
   swcode(swp, b, k + 1, ub);
}
```

A branch table takes two comparisons and an indirect jump — at least three instructions. For most targets, this overhead makes a branch table suitable only if there are more than three values in the table. Otherwise, a short linear search is better; see Exercise 10.8.

The code generated for an indirect jump through a branch table has the form:

```
if t1 < v[l] goto lolab
if t1 > v[u] goto hilab
goto *table[t1-v[l]]
```

where `v[l]`, `v[u]`, `lolab`, and `hilab` are replaced by the corresponding values computed by swcode. The branch table is a static array of pointers, and the tree for the target of an indirect jump is the same one that's built for indexing an array:

⟨*generate an indirect jump and a branch table* 242⟩≡   243   241

```
Symbol table = genident(STATIC,
    array(voidptype, u - l + 1, 0), LABELS);
(*IR->defsymbol)(table);
cmp(LT, swp->sym, v[l], lolab);
cmp(GT, swp->sym, v[u], hilab);
walk(tree(JUMP, voidtype,
    rvalue((*optree['+'])(ADD, pointer(idtree(table)),
        (*optree['-'])(SUB,
            cast(idtree(swp->sym), inttype),
            consttree(v[l], inttype)))), NULL), 0, 0);
```

cmp builds the tree for the comparison

$$\text{if } p \otimes n \text{ goto } L$$

and converts it to a dag. p is an identifier, $\otimes$ is a relational operator, and n is an integer constant:

⟨*stmt.c functions*⟩+≡   240 244

```
static void cmp(op, p, n, lab) int op, n, lab; Symbol p; {
    listnodes(eqtree(op,
            cast(idtree(p), inttype),
            consttree(n, inttype)),
        lab, 0);
}
```

cmp is also used to generate a linear search; see Exercise 10.8.

The branch table is generated by defining the static variable denoted by `table` and calling the interface function `defaddress` for each of the labels in the table. But this process cannot be done until the generated code is emitted, so the relevant data are saved on the code list in a `Switch` entry:

⟨`Switch` 242⟩≡   217

```
struct {
    Symbol sym;
```

```
        Symbol table;
        Symbol deflab;
        int size;
        int *values;
        Symbol *labels;
    } swtch;
```

⟨*generate an indirect jump and a branch table* 242⟩+≡   242   241

```
    code(Switch);
    codelist->u.swtch.table = table;
    codelist->u.swtch.sym = swp->sym;
    codelist->u.swtch.deflab = swp->deflab;
    codelist->u.swtch.size = u - 1 + 1;
    codelist->u.swtch.values = &v[1];
    codelist->u.swtch.labels = &swp->labels[1];
    if (v[u] - v[1] + 1 >= 10000)
        warning("switch generates a huge table\n");
```

The table is emitted by emitcode.

10.8   Return Statements

Return statements without an *expression* appear in void functions, and returns with *expression*s appear in all other functions. An extraneous expression is an error, and a missing expression draws only a warning:

⟨*return statement* 243⟩≡   221

```
    {
        Type rty = freturn(cfunc->type);
        t = gettok();
        definept(NULL);
        if (t != ';')
            if (rty == voidtype) {
                error("extraneous return value\n");
                expr(0);
                retcode(NULL);
            } else
                retcode(expr(0));
        else {
            if (rty != voidtype
            && (rty != inttype || Aflag >= 1))
                warning("missing return value\n");
            retcode(NULL);
        }
        branch(cfunc->u.f.label);
    }
```

62	Aflag
247	branch
290	cfunc
218	code
217	codelist
220	definept
341	emitcode
155	expr
64	freturn
41	labels
244	retcode
217	Switch
41	table
58	voidtype

retcode type-checks its argument tree and calls walk to build the corresponding RET dag, as detailed below. This dag is followed by a jump to cfunc->u.f.label, which labels the end of the current function; cfunc points to the symbol-table entry for the current function. (This jump may be discarded by branch.) The back end must finish a function with the *epilogue* — the code that restores saved values, if necessary, and transfers from the function to its caller.

The code above doesn't warn about missing return values for functions that return ints unless lcc's -A option is specified, because it's common to use int functions for void functions; i.e., to use

```
f(double x) { ... return; }
```

instead of the more appropriate

```
void f(double x) { ... return; }
```

For many programs, warnings about missing int return values would drown out the more important warnings about the other types.

For void functions, retcode has nothing to do except perhaps plant an event hook:

⟨*stmt.c functions*⟩+≡   242 246

```
void retcode(p) Tree p; {
    Type ty;

    if (p == NULL) {
        if (events.returns)
            ⟨plant event hook for return⟩
        return;
    }
    ⟨retcode 244⟩
}
```

For types other than void, retcode builds and walks a RET tree. The RET operator simply identifies the return value so that the back end can put it in the appropriate place specified by the target's calling conventions, such as a specific register.

When there's an expression, retcode type-checks it, converts it to the return type of the function as if it were assigned to a variable of that type, and wraps it in the appropriate RET tree:

⟨*retcode* 244⟩≡   245   244

```
p = pointer(p);
ty = assign(freturn(cfunc->type), p);
if (ty == NULL) {
    error("illegal return type; found '%t' expected '%t'\n",
        p->type, freturn(cfunc->type));
```

```
      return;
   }
   p = cast(p, ty);
```

Integers, unsigneds, floats, and doubles are returned as is. Characters and shorts are converted to the promoted type of the return type just as they are in argument lists. Since there's no RET+P, pointers are converted to unsigneds and returned by RET+I. Calls to such functions are made with CALL+I, and their values are converted back to pointers with CVU+P.

⟨*retcode* 244⟩+≡   244   244

```
   if (retv)
      ⟨return a structure 245⟩
   if (events.returns)
      ⟨plant an event hook for return p⟩
   p = cast(p, promote(p->type));
   if (isptr(p->type)) {
      ⟨warn if p denotes the address of a local⟩
      p = cast(p, unsignedtype);
   }
   walk(tree(RET + widen(p->type), p->type, p, NULL), 0, 0);
```

Returning the address of a local variable is a common programming error, so lcc detects and warns about the easy cases; see Exercise 10.9.

There is no RET+B. Structures are returned by assigning them to a variable. As described in Section 9.3, if wants_callb is one, this variable is the second operand to CALL+B in the caller and the first local in the callee, and the back end must arrange to pass its address according to target-specific conventions. If wants_callb is zero, the front end passes the address of this variable as a hidden first argument, and never presents the back end with a CALL+B. In both cases, compound, which implements *compound-statement*, arranges for retv to point to the symbol-table entry for a pointer to this variable. Returning a structure is an assignment to *retv:

⟨*return a structure* 245⟩≡   245

```
   {
      if (iscallb(p))
         p = tree(RIGHT, p->type,
            tree(CALL+B, p->type,
               p->kids[0]->kids[0], idtree(retv)),
            rvalue(idtree(retv)));
      else
         p = asgntree(ASGN, rvalue(idtree(retv)), p);
      walk(p, 0, 0);
      if (events.returns)
         ⟨plant an event hook for a struct return⟩
```

```
        return;
    }
```

As for ASGN+B (see Section 9.5) and ARG+B (see Section 9.3), there's an opportunity to reduce copying for

```
    return f();
```

f returns the same structure returned by the current function, so the current function's retv can be used as the temporary for the call to f. If the call to iscallb in the code above identifies this idiom, the CALL+B tree is rebuilt using retv in place of the temporary.

10.9 Managing Labels and Jumps

Labels are defined by definelab, and jumps to labels are made by branch. These functions also collaborate to remove dead jumps, i.e., those that follow an unconditional jump or a switch, to avoid jumps to jumps, and to avoid jumps to immediately following labels. They do so using a scheme similar to the one used in code to detect unreachable code.

definelab appends a label definition to the code list and then checks if the preceding executable entry is a jump to the new label:

⟨*stmt.c functions*⟩+≡   244 247

```
    void definelab(lab) int lab; {
        Code cp;
        Symbol p = findlabel(lab);

        walk(NULL, 0, 0);
        code(Label)->u.forest = newnode(LABELV, NULL, NULL, p);
        for (cp = codelist->prev; cp->kind <= Label; )
            cp = cp->prev;
        while (⟨cp points to a Jump to lab 247⟩) {
            p->ref--;
            ⟨remove the entry at cp 247⟩
            while (cp->kind <= Label)
                cp = cp->prev;
        }
    }
```

newnode builds a dag for LABELV with a sym[0] equal to p. The for loop walks cp backward in the code list to the first entry that represents executable code, and the while loops remove one or more jumps to lab. cp is a jump to lab if *cp is a Jump entry, and its node computes the address of lab:

⟨cp *points to a* Jump *to* lab 247⟩≡   246
```
    cp->kind == Jump
 && cp->u.forest->kids[0]
 && cp->u.forest->kids[0]->op == ADDRGP
 && cp->u.forest->kids[0]->syms[0] == p
```

Dropping the Jump out of the code list removes the useless jump:

⟨*remove the entry at* cp 247⟩≡   246 247
```
    cp->prev->next = cp->next;
    cp->next->prev = cp->prev;
    cp = cp->prev;
```

When definelab removes a jump, it decrements the label's ref field. It does so because building a jump dag increments the target label's ref field:

⟨*stmt.c functions*⟩+≡   246 247
```
    Node jump(lab) int lab; {
       Symbol p = findlabel(lab);

       p->ref++;
       return newnode(JUMPV, newnode(ADDRGP, NULL, NULL, p),
          NULL, NULL);
    }
```

jump is called by branch, which stores the JUMPV dag in a Jump entry and appends it to the code list.

branch also eliminates jumps to jumps and dead jumps. It begins by appending the jump to the code list using a Label placeholder. The jump is *not* a label, but Label is used so that ⟨*check for unreachable code*⟩ in code won't bark, which it would do if the last executable entry on the code list were an unconditional jump.

⟨*stmt.c functions*⟩+≡   247 248
```
    static void branch(lab) int lab; {
       Code cp;
       Symbol p = findlabel(lab);

       walk(NULL, 0, 0);
       code(Label)->u.forest = jump(lab);
       for (cp = codelist->prev; cp->kind < Label; )
          cp = cp->prev;
       while (⟨cp points to a Label ≠ lab 248⟩) {
          equatelab(cp->u.forest->syms[0], p);
          ⟨remove the entry at cp 247⟩
          while (cp->kind < Label)
             cp = cp->prev;
```

```
        }
        ⟨eliminate or plant the jump 249⟩
    }
```

branch's for loop backs up to the first executable or Label entry before the placeholder. The while loop looks for definitions of labels L' that form the pattern

$$L':$$
```
        goto L
```

where goto L is the jump in the placeholder.

⟨cp *points to a* Label $\neq$ lab 248⟩≡   247
```
        cp->kind == Label
    && cp->u.forest->op == LABELV
    && !equal(cp->u.forest->syms[0], p)
```

If $L' \neq L$, L' is equivalent to L; jumps to L' can go to L instead, and the Label entry for L' can be removed.

⟨*stmt.c functions*⟩+≡   ▲247 248▼
```
        void equatelab(old, new) Symbol old, new; {
            old->u.l.equatedto = new;
            new->ref++;
        }
```

makes new a synonym for old. During code generation, references to old are replaced by the label at the end of the list formed by the equatedto fields. These fields form a list because it's possible that new will be equated to another symbol *after* old is equated to new. The ref field counts the number of references to a label from jumps and from the u.l.equated fields of other labels, so equatelab increments new->ref.

These synonyms complicate testing when two labels are equal. The fragment ⟨cp *points to a* Label $\neq$ lab⟩ must fail when L' is equal to the destination of the jump so code such as

```
    top:
        goto top;
```

is not erroneously eliminated, no matter how nonsensical it seems. Just testing whether L' is equal to the destination, p, isn't enough; the two labels are equivalent if L' is equal to p or to *any* label for which p is a synonym. equal implements this more complicated test:

⟨*stmt.c functions*⟩+≡   ▲248
```
        static int equal(lprime, dst) Symbol lprime, dst; {
            for ( ; dst; dst = dst->u.l.equatedto)
                if (lprime == dst)
```

```
        return 1;
    return 0;
}
```

If `cp` ends on a `Jump` or `Switch`, the branch is unreachable, and the placeholder can be deleted. Otherwise, the placeholder becomes a `Jump`:

⟨*eliminate or plant the jump* 249⟩≡   248
```
    if (cp->kind == Jump || cp->kind == Switch) {
        p->ref--;
        codelist->prev->next = NULL;
        codelist = codelist->prev;
    } else {
        codelist->kind = Jump;
        if (cp->kind == Label
        &&  cp->u.forest->op == LABELV
        &&  equal(cp->u.forest->syms[0], p))
            warning("source code specifies an infinite loop");
    }
```

The warning exposes infinite loops like the one shown above.

Further Reading

Baskett (1978) describes the motivations for the layout of the generated code for the loops.

lcc's execution points have been used for generating debugger symbol tables and for profiling. Ramsey and Hanson (1992) describe how the retargetable debugger ldb uses execution points to locate breakpoints and to provide starting points for searching the debugger's symbol table. Ramsey (1993) details the use of the stab interface functions to generate symbol-table data, and describes how lcc itself can be used to evaluate C expressions entered during debugging. Fraser and Hanson (1991b) describe the implementation of lcc's machine-independent profiling enabled by its -b option.

Many papers and compiler texts describe how to generate selection code for switch statements. Hennessy and Mendelsohn (1982) and Bernstein (1985) describe techniques similar to the one used in lcc. The greedy algorithm groups the case values into dense tables in linear time, but not into the *minimum* number of such tables. The one-page paper by Kannan and Proebsting (1994) gives a simple quadratic algorithm for doing so.

Exercises

10.1 Implement the do statement.

10.2 Implement the while statement.

10.3 Implement

⟨*stmt.c prototypes*⟩≡
```
    static int foldcond ARGS((Tree e1, Tree e2));
```

which is called by forstmt. Hint: Build a tree that conditionally substitutes e1 for the left operand of the test e2, when appropriate. If the operands of this tree are constants, simplify will return a CNST tree that determines whether the loop body will be executed at least once.

10.4 There's a while loop in ⟨*case label*⟩, but there's no repetitive construct in the grammar for case labels. Explain.

10.5 Prove that the execution time of the partitioning algorithm in swgen is linear in n, the number of case values.

10.6 Here's another implementation of swgen's partitioning algorithm (suggested by Arthur Watson).

```
    while (n > 0) {
        float d = den(n-1, k);
        if (d < density
        || k < swp->ncases - 1 && d < den(n, k+1))
            break;
        n--;
    }
```

The difference is that a table and its predecessor are not combined if the table and v[k+1] would form a denser table. For example, with density equal to 0.5, the greedy algorithm partitions the values 1, 6, 7, 8, 11, and 15 into the three tables (1, 6–8), (11), and (15), and this lookahead variant gives the two tables (1) and (6–8, 11, 15). Analyze and explain this variant. Can you prove under what conditions it will give fewer tables than the greedy algorithm?

10.7 Change swgen to use the optimal partitioning algorithm described by Kannan and Proebsting (1994). With density equal to 0.5, the optimal algorithm partitions the values 1, 6, 7, 8, 9, 10, 15, and 19 into the two tables (1) and (6–10, 15, 19); the greedy algorithm and its lookahead variant described in the previous exercise generate the three tables (1, 6–10), (15), and (19). Can you find real programs on which the optimal algorithm gives fewer tables than the greedy algorithm? Can you detect the differences in execution times?

10.8 Implement swcode's ⟨*generate a linear search*⟩. The generated code has the form

> if t1 = $v[l]$ goto L_l
>
> $\vdots$
>
> if t1 = $v[u]$ goto L_u
> if t1 < $v[l]$ goto lolab
> if t1 > $v[u]$ goto hilab

Use cmp to do the comparisons, and avoid generating unnecessary jumps to lolab and hilab.

10.9 Implementing ⟨*warn if* p *denotes the address of a local*⟩ involves examining p to see if it's the address of a local or a parameter. This test catches some, but not all, of these kinds of programming errors. Give an example of an error that this approach cannot detect. Is there a way to catch *all* such errors at compile-time? At run-time?

10.10 swcode is passed ub-lb+1 tables in b[lb..ub], and picks the middle table at b[(lb+ub)/2] as the root of the tree from which it generates a binary search. Other choices are possible; it may, for instance, choose the largest table, or profiling data could supply the frequency of occurrence for each case value, which could pinpoint the table that's most likely to cover the switch value. Alternatively, we could assume a specific probability distribution for the case values. Suppose *all* values in the range $v[b[lb]..b[ub+1]-1]$ — even those for which there are no case labels — are equally likely to occur. For this distribution, the root table should be the one with a case value closest to the middle value in this range. Implement this strategy by computing swcode's k appropriately. Be careful; it's possible that *no* table will cover the middle value, so pick the one that's *closest*.

242	cmp
91	defaddress
456	" (MIPS)
490	" (SPARC)
523	" (X86)
240	swcode

10.11 Some systems support dynamic linking and loading. When new code is loaded, the dynamic linker must identify and update all relocatable addresses in it. This process takes time, so dynamically linked code benefits from *position-independent* addresses, which are relative to the value that the program counter will have during the execution of the instruction that uses the address. For example, if the instruction at location 200 jumps to location 300, conventional relocatable code stores the address 300 in the instruction, but position-independent code stores 300 − 200 or 100 instead. Extend lcc's interface so that it can emit position-independent code for switch statements. The interface defined in Chapter 5 can't do so because it uses the same defaddress for switch statements that it uses to initialize pointer data, which mustn't be position-independent.

11

Declarations

Declarations specify the types of identifiers, define structure and union types, and give the code for functions. Parsing declarations can be viewed as converting the textual representation of types to the corresponding internal representations described in Chapter 4 and generating the code list decribed in Section 1.3.

Declarations are the most difficult part of C to parse. There are two main sources of this difficulty. First, the syntax of declarations is designed to illustrate the *use* of an identifier. For example, the declaration int *x[10] declares x to be an array of 10 pointers to ints. The idea is that the declaration illustrates the use of x; for example, the type of *x[i] is int. Unfortunately, distributing the type information throughout the declaration complicates parsing it.

The other difficulty comes from the restrictions on the declarations for globals, locals, and parameters. For example, locals and globals can be declared static, but parameters cannot. Likewise, both function declarations and function definitions may appear at file scope, but only function declarations may appear at a local scope. It is possible to write a syntax specification that embodies these kinds of restrictions, but the result is a set of repetitious productions that vary slightly in detail. An alternative, illustrated by the declaration syntax given throughout this chapter, is to specify the syntax of the most general case and use semantic checks during parsing to enforce the appropriate restrictions depending on context. Since the rules concerning redeclaration vary among the three kinds of identifiers, such checks are necessary in any case.

The text and the code in this chapter reflect these difficulties: This chapter is the longest one in this book, and some of its code is intricate and complex because it must cope with many, sometimes subtle, details. Some of the functions are mutually recursive or are used for several purposes, so circularities in their explanations are unavoidable.

The first five sections describe how declarations are parsed and are internalized in the front end's data structures described in previous chapters. The last four sections cover function definitions, compound statements, finalization, and 1cc's main program. These sections are perhaps the more important because they contribute most to understanding the interaction between the front end and the back ends. Section 11.6, for example, is where the front end calls the back ends' function interface routine, and Section 11.9 reveals how the interface record for a specific target is bound to the front end.

function	92
(MIPS) "	448
(SPARC) "	484
(X86) "	518

11.1 Translation Units

A C translation unit consists of one or more declarations or function definitions:

> *translation-unit:*
>   *external-declaration { external-declaration }*

> *external-declaration:*
>   *function-definition*
>   *declaration*

`program` is the parsing function for *translation-unit* and one of the five functions exported by `decl.c`, which processes all declarations. It actually parses *translation-unit* as if it permitted empty input, and only warns about that case:

⟨*decl.c functions*⟩≡   255
```
  void program() {
    int n;

    level = GLOBAL;
    for (n = 0; t != EOI; n++)
      if (kind[t] == CHAR || kind[t] == STATIC
      || t == ID || t == '*' || t == '(') {
        decl(dclglobal);
        ⟨deallocate arenas 254⟩
      } else if (t == ';') {
        warning("empty declaration\n");
        t = gettok();
      } else {
        error("unrecognized declaration\n");
        t = gettok();
      }
    if (n == 0)
      warning("empty input file\n");
  }
```

109	CHAR
260	dclglobal
298	dcllocal
274	dclparam
258	decl
38	GLOBAL
143	kind
42	level
80	STATIC

`decl` is the parsing function for both *function-definition* and *declaration*, because a *function-definition* looks like a *declaration* followed by a *compound-statement*. `decl`'s argument is `dclglobal`, `dcllocal`, or `dclparam`. After `decl` and its collaborators have digested a complete declaration for an identifier, they call a `dclX` function to validate the identifier and install it in the appropriate symbol table. These `dclX` functions enforce the semantic differences between globals, locals, and parameters mentioned above.

The two else arms in the loop body above handle two error conditions. The standard insists that a declaration declare at least an identifier, a structure or enumeration tag, or one or more enumeration members. The first else warns about declarations that don't, and the second diagnoses declarations with syntax errors.

Declarations can allocate space in any arena. Function definitions allocate space in the PERM and FUNC arenas, and variable declarations use space in the STMT arena for the trees that represent initializers. Thus, both the FUNC and STMT arenas are deallocated at the ends of declarations and definitions:

⟨*deallocate arenas* 254⟩≡   253
```
    deallocate(STMT);
    deallocate(FUNC);
```

11.2   Declarations

The syntax for declarations is

> *declaration:*
>   *declaration-specifiers init-declarator* { , *init-declarator* } ;
>   *declaration-specifiers* ;
>
> *init-declarator:*
>   *declarator*
>   *declarator* = *initializer*
>
> *initializer:*
>   *assignment-expression*
>   '{' *initializer* { , *initializer* } [,] '}'
>
> *declaration-specifiers:*
>   *storage-class-specifier* [*declaration-specifiers*]
>   *type-specifier* [*declaration-specifiers*]
>   *type-qualifier* [*declaration-specifiers*]
>
> *storage-class-specifier:*
>   typedef | extern | static | auto | register
>
> *type-specifier:*
>   void
>   char | float | short | signed
>   int | double | long | unsigned
>   *struct-or-union-specifier*
>   *enum-specifier*
>   *identifier*
>
> *type-qualifier:* const | volatile

A *declaration* specifies the type of an identifier and its other attributes, such as its storage class. A *definition* declares an identifier and causes storage for it to be reserved. Declarations with initializers are definitions; those without initializers are *tentative definitions*, which are covered in Section 11.8.

A declaration begins with one or more specifiers in any order. For example, all the declarations

```
short const x;
const short x;
const short int x;
int const short x;
```

declare x to be short integer that cannot be modified. *storage-class-specifiers*, *type-specifiers*, and *type-qualifiers* can appear in any order, but only one of each kind of specifier can appear. This flexibility complicates specifier, the parsing function for *declaration-specifiers*.

⟨*decl.c functions*⟩+≡   253 258

```
static Type specifier(sclass) int *sclass; {
    int cls, cons, sign, size, type, vol;
    Type ty = NULL;

    cls = vol = cons = sign = size = type = 0;
    if (sclass == NULL)
        cls = AUTO;
    for (;;) {
        int *p, tt = t;
        switch (t) {
        ⟨set p and ty 256⟩
        default: p = NULL;
        }
        if (p == NULL)
            break;
        ⟨check for invalid use of the specifier 256⟩
        *p = tt;
    }
    if (sclass)
        *sclass = cls;
    ⟨compute ty 257⟩
    return ty;
}
```

80 AUTO

If specifier's argument, sclass, is nonnull, it points to the variable to which the token code for the storage class should be assigned. The locals cls, vol, cons, sign, size, and type record the appearance of the similarly named specifiers by being assigned the token code for their specifier:

⟨*set* p *and* ty 256⟩≡   256 255

```
   case AUTO:
   case REGISTER: if (level <= GLOBAL && cls == 0)
                        error("invalid use of '%k'\n", t);
                     p = &cls;  t = gettok();      break;
   case STATIC: case EXTERN:
   case TYPEDEF:  p = &cls;  t = gettok();        break;
   case CONST:    p = &cons; t = gettok();        break;
   case VOLATILE: p = &vol;  t = gettok();        break;
   case SIGNED:
   case UNSIGNED: p = &sign; t = gettok();        break;
   case LONG:
   case SHORT:    p = &size; t = gettok();        break;
   case VOID: case CHAR: case INT: case FLOAT:
   case DOUBLE:   p = &type; ty = tsym->type;
                             t = gettok();        break;
   case ENUM:     p = &type; ty = enumdcl();      break;
   case STRUCT:
   case UNION:    p = &type; ty = structdcl(t); break;
```

These variables are initialized to zero and change only when their corresponding specifier is encountered. Thus, a nonzero value for any of these variables indicates that their specifier has already appeared, which helps detect errors:

⟨*check for invalid use of the specifier* 256⟩≡   255

```
   if (*p)
      error("invalid use of '%k'\n", tt);
```

Once all the *declaration-specifiers* have been consumed, the values of sign, size, and type encode the specified type. enumdcl and structdcl parse *enum-specifier* and *struct-or-union-specifier*.

If sclass is null, then a storage class must *not* appear, so cls is initialized as if one did occur, which catches errors. This flexibility is needed because specifier is called when parsing *abstract-declarators*, which do not have storage classes; see Section 11.3 and Exercise 11.3.

The body of the switch statement shown above points p to the appropriate local variable, and sets ty to a Type if the token is a *type-specifier*. A typedef name, which arrives as an ID token, can appear with only a storage class or a qualifier:

⟨*set* p *and* ty 256⟩+≡   ▲
                                                                     256 255

```
   case ID:
      if (istypename(t, tsym) && type == 0
      && sign == 0 && size == 0) {
         use(tsym, src);
         ty = tsym->type;
```

```
        p = &type;
        t = gettok();
    } else
        p = NULL;
    break;
```

All that remains after parsing *declaration-specifiers* is to determine the appropriate Type, which is encoded in the values of `sign`, `size`, and `type`. This Type is `specifier`'s return value. The default

⟨*compute* ty 257⟩≡   257   255
```
if (type == 0) {
    type = INT;
    ty = inttype;
}
```

is what makes `short const x` declare `x` a short integer. The remaining cases inspect `sign`, `size`, and `type` to determine the appropriate type:

⟨*compute* ty 257⟩+≡   257 257   255
```
if (size == SHORT && type != INT
||  size == LONG  && type != INT && type != DOUBLE
||  sign && type != INT && type != CHAR)
    error("invalid type specification\n");
if (type == CHAR && sign)
    ty = sign == UNSIGNED ? unsignedchar : signedchar;
else if (size == SHORT)
    ty = sign == UNSIGNED ? unsignedshort : shorttype;
else if (size == LONG && type == DOUBLE)
    ty = longdouble;
else if (size == LONG)
    ty = sign == UNSIGNED ? unsignedlong : longtype;
else if (sign == UNSIGNED && type == INT)
    ty = unsignedtype;
```

The explicit inclusion of `sign` in the test for CHAR is needed to distinguish signed and unsigned chars from plain chars, which are a distinct type. The resulting Type, computed by the code above, `enumdcl` or `structdcl`, can be qualified by const or volatile qualifiers, or both:

⟨*compute* ty 257⟩+≡   257   255
```
if (cons == CONST)
    ty = qual(CONST, ty);
if (vol  == VOLATILE)
    ty = qual(VOLATILE, ty);
```

`decl`, the parsing function for *declaration*, starts by calling `specifier`:

⟨*decl.c functions*⟩+≡   ▲255 260
                                                                                                         ▼

```
static void decl(dcl)
Symbol (*dcl) ARGS((int, char *, Type, Coordinate *)); {
    int sclass;
    Type ty, ty1;
    static char stop[] = { CHAR, STATIC, ID, 0 };

    ty = specifier(&sclass);
    if (t == ID || t == '*' || t == '(' || t == '[') {
        char *id;
        Coordinate pos;
        ⟨id, ty1 ← the first declarator 258⟩
        for (;;) {
            ⟨declare id with type ty1 260⟩
            if (t != ',')
                break;
            t = gettok();
            ⟨id, ty1 ← the next declarator 258⟩
        }
    } else if (ty == NULL
    || !⟨ty is an enumeration or has a tag⟩)
        error("empty declaration\n");
    test(';', stop);
}
```

dclr, described in the next section, parses a *declarator*. The easy case is the one for the second and subsequent *declarators*:

⟨id, ty1 ← *the next declarator* 258⟩≡   258
```
    id = NULL;
    pos = src;
    ty1 = dclr(ty, &id, NULL, 0);
```

dclr accepts a base type — the result of specifier — and returns a Type, an identifier, and possibly a parameter list. The base type, ty in the code above, is dclr's first argument, and its next two arguments are the addresses of the variables to assign the identifier and parameter list, if they appear. It returns the complete Type. Passing a null pointer as dclr's third argument specifies that parameter lists may *not* appear in this context. As detailed in Section 11.3, a nonzero fourth argument causes dclr to parse an *abstract-declarator*. pos saves the source coordinate of the beginning of a declarator for use when the identifier is declared.

The first declarator is treated differently than the rest because decl also recognizes *function-definitions*, which can be confused with only the first declarator at file scope:

⟨id, ty1 ← *the first declarator* 258⟩≡   258
```
    id = NULL;
```

```
pos = src;
if (level == GLOBAL) {
    Symbol *params = NULL;
    ty1 = dclr(ty, &id, &params, 0);
    if ((⟨function definition? 259⟩)) {
        ⟨define function id 259⟩
        return;
    } else if (params)
        exitparams(params);
} else
    ty1 = dclr(ty, &id, NULL, 0);
```

Since the first declarator might be a function definition, a nonnull location for the parameter list is passed as `dclr`'s third argument. If the declarator includes a function and its parameter list, `params` is set to an array of symbol-table entries. When there is a parameter list, but it's not part of a function definition, `exitparams` is called to close the scope opened by that list. This scope isn't closed when the end of the list is reached because the parsing function for parameter lists can't differentiate between a function declaration and a function definition. Section 11.4 elaborates.

A *declaration* is really a *function-definition* if the first declarator specifies a function type and includes an identifier, and the next token begins either a compound statement or a list of parameter declarations:

⟨*function definition?* 259⟩≡   259

```
params && id && isfunc(ty1)
&& (t == '{' || istypename(t, tsym)
|| (kind[t] == STATIC && t != TYPEDEF))
```

`decl` calls `funcdefn` to handle function definitions:

⟨*define function* id 259⟩≡   259

```
if (sclass == TYPEDEF) {
    error("invalid use of 'typedef'\n");
    sclass = EXTERN;
}
if (ty1->u.f.oldstyle)
    exitscope();
funcdefn(sclass, id, ty1, params, pos);
```

The call to `exitscope` closes the scope opened in `parameters` because that scope will be reopened in `funcdefn` when the declarations for the parameters are parsed.

The semantics part of `decl` amounts to declaring the identifier given in the *declarator*. As described above, `decl`'s argument is a `dclX` function that does this semantic processing, except for typedefs.

⟨*declare* id *with type* ty1 260⟩≡   258
```
    if (Aflag >= 1 && !hasproto(ty1))
        warning("missing prototype\n");
    if (id == NULL)
        error("missing identifier\n");
    else if (sclass == TYPEDEF)
        ⟨declare id a typedef for ty1 260⟩
    else
        (void)(*dcl)(sclass, id, ty1, &pos);
```

Typedefs are the easy case. The semantic processing simply checks for redeclaration errors, installs the identifier id into the identifiers table, and fills in its type and storage class attributes.

⟨*declare* id *a typedef for* ty1 260⟩≡   260
```
    {
        Symbol p = lookup(id, identifiers);
        if (p && p->scope == level)
            error("redeclaration of '%s'\n", id);
        p = install(id, &identifiers, level,
            level < LOCAL ? PERM : FUNC);
        p->type = ty1;
        p->sclass = TYPEDEF;
        p->src = pos;
    }
```

The three dclX functions are more complicated. Each copes with a slightly different declaration semantics, and dclglobal and dcllocal also parse initializers. dclglobal is the most complicated of the three functions because it must cope with valid redeclarations. For example,

```
    extern int x[];
    int x[10];
```

validly declares x twice. The second declaration also changes x's type from (ARRAY (INT)) to (ARRAY 40 4 (INT)).

⟨*decl.c functions*⟩+≡   258 264
```
    static Symbol dclglobal(sclass, id, ty, pos)
    int sclass; char *id; Type ty; Coordinate *pos; {
        Symbol p, q;

        ⟨dclglobal 261⟩
        return p;
    }
```

decl accepts any set of specifiers and declarators that are syntactically legal, so the dclX functions must check for the specifiers that are illegal in their specific semantic contexts, and must also check for redeclarations. dclglobal, for example, insists that the storage class be extern, static, or omitted:

⟨dclglobal 261⟩≡   261   260
```
    if (sclass == 0)
        sclass = AUTO;
    else if (sclass != EXTERN && sclass != STATIC) {
        error("invalid storage class '%k' for '%t %s'\n",
            sclass, ty, id);
        sclass = AUTO;
    }
```

Globals that have no storage class or an illegal one are given storage class AUTO so that all identifiers have nonzero storage classes, which simplifies error checking elsewhere.

dclglobal next checks for redeclaration errors.

⟨dclglobal 261⟩+≡   261 262   260
```
    p = lookup(id, identifiers);
    if (p && p->scope == GLOBAL) {
        if (p->sclass != TYPEDEF && eqtype(ty, p->type, 1))
            ty = compose(ty, p->type);
        else
            error("redeclaration of '%s' previously declared _
                at %w\n", p->name, &p->src);
        if (!isfunc(ty) && p->defined && t == '=')
            error("redefinition of '%s' previously defined _
                at %w\n", p->name, &p->src);
        ⟨check for inconsistent linkage 262⟩
    }
```

80	AUTO
72	compose
260	dclglobal
50	defined
69	eqtype
80	EXTERN
38	GLOBAL
41	identifiers
60	isfunc
45	lookup
37	scope
80	STATIC

A redeclaration is legal if the types on both declarations are compatible, which is determined by eqtype, and the resulting type is the composite of the two types. Forming this composite is how the type of x, illustrated above, changed from (ARRAY (INT)) to (ARRAY 40 4 (INT)). Some redeclarations are legal, but redefinitions — indicated by a nonzero defined flag and an approaching initializer — are never legal.

An identifier has one of three kinds of *linkage*. Identifiers with *external linkage* can be referenced from other separately compiled translation units. Those with *internal linkage* can be referenced only within the translation unit in which they appear. Parameters and locals have *no* linkage.

A global with no storage class or declared extern in its first declaration has external linkage, and those declared static have internal linkage. On subsequent declarations, an omitted storage class or extern has a slightly different interpretation. If the storage class is omitted, it has external linkage, but if the storage class is extern, the identifier has the same linkage as a previous file-scope declaration for the identifier. Thus,

```
static int y;
extern int y;
```

is legal and y has internal linkage, but

```
extern int y;
static int y;
```

is illegal because the second declaration demands that y have internal linkage when it already has external linkage. Multiple declarations that all have external or internal linkage are permitted.

The table below summarizes these rules in terms of p->sclass, the storage class of an existing declaration, and sclass, the storage class for the declaration in hand. AUTO denotes no storage class.

		sclass		
		EXTERN	STATIC	AUTO
	EXTERN	√	×	√
p->sclass	STATIC	√	√	×
	AUTO	√	×	√

√ marks the legal combinations, and × marks the combinations that are linkage errors. The code use in dclglobal above is derived from this table:

⟨*check for inconsistent linkage* 262⟩≡   261
```
    if (p->sclass == EXTERN && sclass == STATIC
    ||  p->sclass == STATIC && sclass == AUTO
    ||  p->sclass == AUTO   && sclass == STATIC)
        warning("inconsistent linkage for '%s' previously _
            declared at %w\n", p->name, &p->src);
```

This if statement prints its warning for the second of the two examples shown above.

Next, the global is installed in the globals table, if necessary, and its attributes are initialized or overwritten.

⟨dclglobal 261⟩+≡   261 263   260
```
    if (p == NULL || p->scope != GLOBAL) {
        p = install(id, &globals, GLOBAL, PERM);
        p->sclass = sclass;
        if (p->sclass != STATIC) {
            static int nglobals;
            nglobals++;
            if (Aflag >= 2 && nglobals == 512)
                warning("more than 511 external identifiers\n");
```

```
    }
    (*IR->defsymbol)(p);
  } else if (p->sclass == EXTERN)
    p->sclass = sclass;
  p->type = ty;
  p->src = *pos;
```

New globals are passed to the back end's defsymbol interface function to initialize their x fields. If an existing global has storage class extern, and this declaration has no storage class or specifies static, the global's sclass is changed to either STATIC or AUTO to ensure that it's defined in finalize. If this declaration specifies extern, the assignment to sclass is made but has no effect. lcc's -A option enables warnings about non-ANSI usage. For example, the standard doesn't require an implementation to support more that 511 external identifiers in one compilation unit, so lcc warns about too many externals when -A -A is specified.

The standard permits compilers to accept

```
f() { extern float g(); ... }
int g() { ... }
h() { extern double g(); ... }
```

without diagnosing that the first declaration for g conflicts with its definition (which is also a declaration), or that the last declaration conflicts with the first two. Technically, each declaration for g introduces a different identifier with a scope limited to the compound statement in which the declaration appears. But all three g's have external linkage and must refer to the same function at execution time. lcc uses the externals table to warn about these kinds of errors. dcllocal adds identifiers with external linkage to externals, and both dcllocal and dclglobal check for inconsistencies:

⟨dclglobal 261⟩+≡   262 263   260

```
  {
      Symbol q = lookup(p->name, externals);
      if (q && (p->sclass == STATIC
              || !eqtype(p->type, q->type, 1)))
          warning("declaration of '%s' does not match previous _
              declaration at %w\n", p->name, &q->src);
  }
```

dclglobal concludes by parsing an initializer, if there's one coming and it's appropriate.

⟨dclglobal 261⟩+≡   263   260

```
  if (t == '=' && isfunc(p->type)) {
      error("illegal initialization for '%s'\n", p->name);
      t = gettok();
```

```
        initializer(p->type, 0);
    } else if (t == '=')
        initglobal(p, 0);
    else if (p->sclass == STATIC && !isfunc(p->type)
    && p->type->size == 0)
        error("undefined size for '%t %s'\n", p->type, p->name);
```

The last else if clause above tests for declarations of identifiers with internal linkage and incomplete types, which are illegal; an example would be:

```
    static int x[];
```

initglobal parses an initializer if one is approaching or if its second argument is nonzero, and defines the global given by its first argument. initglobal announces the global in the proper segment, parses its initializer, adjusts its type, if appropriate, and marks the global as defined.

⟨*decl.c functions*⟩+≡   260 265

```
    static void initglobal(p, flag) Symbol p; int flag; {
        Type ty;

        if (t == '=' || flag) {
            if (p->sclass == STATIC) {
                for (ty = p->type; isarray(ty); ty = ty->type)
                    ;
                defglobal(p, isconst(ty) ? LIT : DATA);
            } else
                defglobal(p, DATA);
            if (t == '=')
                t = gettok();
            ty = initializer(p->type, 0);
            if (isarray(p->type) && p->type->size == 0)
                p->type = ty;
            if (p->sclass == EXTERN)
                p->sclass = AUTO;
            p->defined = 1;
        }
    }
```

initializer is the parsing function for *initializer*, and is omitted from this book. If p's type is an array of unknown size, the initialization specifies the size and thus completes the type. An initialization is always a definition, in which case an extern storage class is equivalent to no storage class, so sclass is changed, if necessary. This change prevents doextern from calling the back end's import for p at the end of compilation.

defglobal announces the definition of its argument by calling the appropriate interface functions.

⟨*decl.c functions*⟩+≡   264 265

```
void defglobal(p, seg) Symbol p; int seg; {
    p->u.seg = seg;
    swtoseg(p->u.seg);
    if (p->sclass != STATIC)
        (*IR->export)(p);
    (*IR->global)(p);
}
```

⟨*globals* 265⟩≡   38

```
int seg;
```

Identifiers with external linkage are announced by calling the `export` interface function, and `global` proclaims the actual definition. `swtoseg(n)` switches to segment n (one of BSS, LIT, CODE, or DATA) by calling the `segment` interface function, but it avoids the calls when the current segment is n. `defglobal` records the segment in the global's `u.seg` field.

11.3 Declarators

Treating ⟨*parse the first declarator*⟩ as a special case in `decl` is one of the messy spots in recognizing declarations. Parsing a *declarator*, which is defined below, is worse. The difficulty is that the base type occurs before its modifiers. For example, `int *x` specifies the type (POINTER (INT)), but building the type left-to-right as the declarator is parsed leads to the meaningless type (INT (POINTER)). The precedence of the operators [] and () cause similar difficulties, as illustrated by

```
int *x[10], *f();
```

The types of x and f are

```
(ARRAY 10 (POINTER (INT)))
(POINTER (FUNCTION (INT)))
```

The * appears in the same place in the token stream but in different places in the type representation.

As these examples suggest, it's easier to build a temporary *inverted type* during parsing, which is what `dclr` does, and then traverse the inverted type building the appropriate Type structure afterward. `dclr`'s first argument is the base type, which is the type returned by `specifier`.

⟨*decl.c functions*⟩+≡   265 266

```
static Type dclr(basety, id, params, abstract)
Type basety; char **id; Symbol **params; int abstract; {
    Type ty = dclr1(id, params, abstract);
```

```
    for ( ; ty; ty = ty->type)
        switch (ty->op) {
        case POINTER:
            basety = ptr(basety);
            break;
        case FUNCTION:
            basety = func(basety, ty->u.f.proto,
                ty->u.f.oldstyle);
            break;
        case ARRAY:
            basety = array(basety, ty->size, 0);
            break;
        case CONST: case VOLATILE:
            basety = qual(ty->op, basety);
            break;
        }
    if (Aflag >= 2 && basety->size > 32767)
        warning("more than 32767 bytes in '%t'\n", basety);
    return basety;
}
```

dclr1 parses a *declarator* and returns its inverted type, from which dclr builds and returns a normal Type. The id and param arguments are set to the identifier and parameter list in a *declarator*. Exercise 11.3 describes the abstract argument. dclr1 uses Type structures for the elements of an inverted type, and calls tnode to allocate an element and initialize it:

⟨*decl.c functions*⟩+≡   265 267

```
    static Type tnode(op, type) int op; Type type; {
        Type ty;

        NEWO(ty, STMT);
        ty->op = op;
        ty->type = type;
        return ty;
    }
```

dclr1 is the parsing function for *declarator*; the syntax is

declarator:
   pointer direct-declarator { suffix-declarator }

direct-declarator:
   identifier
   '(' *declarator* ')'

suffix-declarator:
   '[' [*constant-expression*] ']'
   '(' [*parameter-list*] ')'

> *pointer:* { * { *type-qualifier* } }

Parsing declarators is similar to parsing expressions. The tokens *, (, and [are operators, and the identifiers and parameter lists are the operands. Operators yield inverted type elements and operands set id or params.

⟨*decl.c functions*⟩+≡   266 271

```
static Type dclr1(id, params, abstract)
char **id; Symbol **params; int abstract; {
    Type ty = NULL;

    switch (t) {
    case ID:                   ⟨ident 267⟩ break;
    case '*': t = gettok(); ⟨pointer 268⟩ break;
    case '(': t = gettok(); ⟨abstract function 270⟩ break;
    case '[': break;
    default:  return ty;
    }
    while (t == '(' || t == '[')
        switch (t) {
        case '(': t = gettok(); { ⟨concrete function 268⟩ }
                  break;
        case '[': t = gettok(); { ⟨array 268⟩ } break;
        }
    return ty;
}
```

----
108 token

If id is nonnull it points to the location at which to store the identifier. If it is null, it also indicates that the declarator must *not* include an identifier.

⟨*ident* 267⟩≡   267

```
if (id)
    *id = token;
else
    error("extraneous identifier '%s'\n", token);
t = gettok();
```

Pointers may be intermixed with any number of const and volatile qualifiers. For example,

```
int *const *const volatile *p;
```

declares p to be a "pointer to a constant volatile pointer to a constant pointer to an integer." p and ***p can be changed, but *p and **p cannot, and *p may be changed by some external means because it's volatile. dclr1 returns the inverted type

```
[POINTER [CONST [POINTER [VOLATILE [CONST [POINTER]]]]]]
```

where brackets denote inverted type elements. The type ultimately re-turned by dclr is

    (POINTER (CONST+VOLATILE (POINTER (CONST POINTER (INT))))))

The code for parsing *pointer* is

⟨*pointer* 268⟩≡   267
```
    if (t == CONST || t == VOLATILE) {
        Type ty1;
        ty1 = ty = tnode(t, NULL);
        while ((t = gettok()) == CONST || t == VOLATILE)
            ty1 = tnode(t, ty1);
        ty->type = dclr1(id, params, abstract);
        ty = ty1;
    } else
        ty = dclr1(id, params, abstract);
    ty = tnode(POINTER, ty);
```

The recursive calls to dclr1 make it unnecessary for the other fragments in dclr1 to append their inverted types to a pointer type, if there is one. Exercise 11.2 elaborates.

Control emerges from dclr1's switch statement with ty equal to the inverted type for a pointer or a function or null. The suffix type operators [and (wrap ty in the appropriate inverted type element. The case for arrays is

⟨*array* 268⟩≡   267
```
    int n = 0;
    if (kind[t] == ID) {
        n = intexpr(']', 1);
        if (n <= 0) {
            error("'%d' is an illegal array size\n", n);
            n = 1;
        }
    } else
        expect(']');
    ty = tnode(ARRAY, ty);
    ty->size = n;
```

Parentheses either group declarators or specify a function type. Their appearance in *suffix-declarator* always specifies a function type:

⟨*concrete function* 268⟩≡   267
```
    Symbol *args;
    ty = tnode(FUNCTION, ty);
    ⟨open a scope in a parameter list 269⟩
    args = parameters(ty);
```

```
if (params && *params == NULL)
    *params = args;
else
    exitparams(args);
```

⟨*open a scope in a parameter list* 269⟩ ≡   268 270
```
enterscope();
if (level > PARAM)
    enterscope();
```

A parameter list in a function type opens a new scope; hence the call to `enterscope` in this case. The second call to `enterscope` handles an implementation anomaly that occurs when a parameter list itself includes another scope. For example, in the declaration

```
void f(struct T { int (*fp)(struct T { int m; }); } x) {
    struct T { float a; } y;
}
```

the parameter list for `f` opens a new scope and introduces the structure tag `T`. The structure's lone field, `fp`, is a pointer to a function, and the parameter list for *that* function opens another new scope and defines a *different* tag `T`. This declaration is legal. The declaration on the second line is an error because it redefines the tag `T` — `f`'s parameter `x`, its tag `T`, `f`'s local `y`, and `y`'s tag `T` are all in the same scope.

    `lcc` uses scope `PARAM` for identifiers declared at the top-level parameter scope and `LOCAL` for identifiers like `y`; `LOCAL` is equal to `PARAM+1`. This division is only a convenience; `foreach` can visit just the parameters, for example. Redeclaration tests, however, must check for `LOCAL` identifiers that erroneously redeclare `PARAM` identifiers.

    The example above is the one case where redeclaration tests must *not* make this check. The code above arranges for a nested parameter list to have a scope of at least `PARAM+2`. Leaving this "hole" in the scope numbers avoids erroneous redeclaration diagnostics. For example, the tag `T` in `fp`'s parameter has scope `PARAM+2`, and thus does not elicit a redeclaration error because the `x`'s tag `T` has scope `PARAM`.

    At some point, the scope opened by the call or calls to `enterscope` must be closed by a matching call to `exitscope`. The parameter list may be part of a function definition or just part of a function declaration. If the list might be in a function definition, `params` is nonnull and not previously set, and `dclr`'s caller must call `exitscope` when it's appropriate. The call to `exitparams` in `decl`'s ⟨id, ty1 ← *the first declarator*⟩ is an example. `exitparams` checks for old-style parameter lists that are used erroneously, and calls `exitscope`. If `params` is null or already holds a parameter list, then `exitscope` can be called immediately because the parameter list can't be part of a function definition.

*abstract-declarator*s, described in Exercise 11.3, complicate the use of parentheses for grouping.

⟨*abstract function* 270⟩≡   267
```
   if (abstract
   && (t == REGISTER || istypename(t, tsym) || t == ')')) {
       Symbol *args;
       ty = tnode(FUNCTION, ty);
       ⟨open a scope in a parameter list 269⟩
       args = parameters(ty);
       exitparams(args);
   } else {
       ty = dclr1(id, params, abstract);
       expect(')');
       if (abstract && ty == NULL
       && (id == NULL || *id == NULL))
           return tnode(FUNCTION, NULL);
   }
```

If `dclr` is called to parse an *abstract-declarator*, which is indicated by a nonzero fourth argument, a `(` signals a parameter list if it's followed by a new-style parameter list or by a nonempty declarator and a matching `)`. Since *abstract-declarator*s do not appear in function definitions, `exitparams` can be called immediately after parsing the parameter list.

11.4   Function Declarators

The standard permits function declarations and definitions to include old-style and new-style parameter lists. The syntax is

> *parameter-list:*
>   *parameter* { , *parameter* } [, ...]
>   *identifier* { , *identifier* }

> *parameter:*
>   *declaration-specifiers declarator*
>   *declaration-specifiers* [*abstract-declarator*]

An old-style list is just a list of identifiers. A new-style list is a list of declarators, one for each parameter, or at least one parameter followed by a comma and ellipsis (, ...), which specifies a function with a variable number of parameters, or the single type specifier `void`, which specifies a function with no parameters. These two styles and their interaction in declarations and definitions are what contributes most to the complexity of recognizing and analyzing them.

`parameters` parses both styles. It installs each of the parameters in the `identifiers` table at the current scope level, which is established by parameters caller by calling enterscope, as illustrated in the previous section. It returns a pointer to a null-terminated array of symbols, one for each parameter. The first token of a parameter list identifies the style:

⟨*decl.c functions*⟩+≡   267 272

```
static Symbol *parameters(fty) Type fty; {
    List list = NULL;
    Symbol *params;

    if (kind[t] == STATIC || istypename(t, tsym)) {
        ⟨parse new-style parameter list 273⟩
    } else {
        ⟨parse old-style parameter list 271⟩
    }
    if (t != ')') {
        static char stop[] = { CHAR, STATIC, IF, ')', 0 };
        expect(')');
        skipto('{', stop);
    }
    if (t == ')')
        t = gettok();
    return params;
}
```

parameters also annotates the function type, fty, with parameter information, as described below.

Old-style parameters are simply gathered up into a List, which is converted to a null-terminated array after the parameters are recognized.

⟨*parse old-style parameter list* 271⟩≡   271

```
if (t == ID)
    for (;;) {
        Symbol p;
        if (t != ID) {
            error("expecting an identifier\n");
            break;
        }
        p = dclparam(0, token, inttype, &src);
        p->defined = 0;
        list = append(p, list);
        t = gettok();
        if (t != ',')
            break;
        t = gettok();
    }
params = ltov(&list, FUNC);
```

34	append
109	CHAR
274	dclparam
50	defined
42	enterscope
142	expect
97	FUNC
115	istypename
143	kind
34	List
321	list
34	ltov
144	skipto
80	STATIC
108	token
108	tsym

```
fty->u.f.proto = NULL;
fty->u.f.oldstyle = 1;
```

The parameters are installed in `identifiers` by calling `dclparam`. Their types are unknown, so they're installed with the type integer. If the parameter list is part of function definition (which it must be), these symbols will be discarded and reinstalled when the declarations are processed by `funcdefn`. They're installed here only to detect duplicate parameters. Setting the `defined` bit to zero identifies old-style parameters. The function type, `fty`, is edited to record that it's old-style.

At the end of a parameter list that is *not* part of a function definition, new-style parameters can simply go out of scope after using them to build a prototype, as shown below. But it's an error to use an old-style parameter list in such a context. For example, in

```
int (*f)(int a, float b);
int (*g)(a, b);
```

the first line is a legal new-style declaration for the type

```
(POINTER (FUNCTION (INT) {(INT) (FLOAT)}))
```

but the second line is an illegal old-style declaration of the type

```
(POINTER (FUNCTION (INT)))
```

because it includes a parameter list in a context other than a function definition. `exitparams` squawks about this error:

⟨*decl.c functions*⟩+≡   271 274

```
static void exitparams(params) Symbol params[]; {
    if (params[0] && !params[0]->defined)
        error("extraneous old-style parameter list\n");
    ⟨close a scope in a parameter list 272⟩
}
```

⟨*close a scope in a parameter list* 272⟩≡   272

```
if (level > PARAM)
    exitscope();
exitscope();
```

As mentioned in Exercise 2.15, the array returned by `ltov` always has at least the null terminating element, so if `params` comes from `parameters`, it will always be nonnull.

New-style parameter lists are more complicated because they have several variants. A list may or may not contain identifiers depending on whether or not it is part of a function definition. Either variant can end in `,...`, and a list consisting of just `void` is legal in both definitions and declarations. Also, a new-style declaration provides a prototype for the function type, which must be retained for checking calls, other declarations of the same function, and the definition, if one appears. As described in Section 4.5, a new-style function with no arguments has a zero-length prototype; a function with a variable number of arguments has a prototype with at least two elements, the last of which is the type for void. The use of void to identify a variable number of arguments is an encoding trick (of perhaps dubious value); it doesn't appear in the source code and can't be confused with voids that do, because they never appear in prototypes.

⟨*parse new-style parameter list* 273⟩≡   271

```
   int n = 0;
   Type ty1 = NULL;
   for (;;) {
      Type ty;
      int sclass = 0;
      char *id = NULL;
      if (ty1 && t == ELLIPSIS) {
         ⟨terminate list for a varargs function 274⟩
         t = gettok();
         break;
      }
      if (!istypename(t, tsym) && t != REGISTER)
         error("missing parameter type\n");
      n++;
      ty = dclr(specifier(&sclass), &id, NULL, 1);
      ⟨declare a parameter and append it to list 273⟩
      if (ty1 == NULL)
         ty1 = ty;
      if (t != ',')
         break;
      t = gettok();
   }
   ⟨build the prototype 274⟩
   fty->u.f.oldstyle = 0;
```

265	dclr
115	istypename
63	oldstyle
80	REGISTER
255	specifier
108	tsym
58	voidtype

ty1 is the Type of the first parameter, and it's used to detect invalid use of void and, as shown above, of ellipses. Each parameter is a *declarator*, so parsing one uses the machinery embodied in specifier and dclr, but, as shown above, permits only the storage class register. If the type void appears, it must appear alone and first:

⟨*declare a parameter and append it to* list 273⟩≡   273

```
   if ( ty == voidtype && (ty1 || id)
   ||  ty1 == voidtype)
      error("illegal formal parameter types\n");
   if (id == NULL)
```

```
        id = stringd(n);
    if (ty != voidtype)
        list = append(dclparam(sclass, id, ty, &src), list);
```

Omitted identifiers are given integer names; dclparam will complain
about these missing identifiers if the declaration is part of a function
definition.

Variable length parameter lists cause the evolving list of parameters
to be terminated by a statically allocated symbol with a null name and
the type void.

⟨*terminate* list *for a varargs function* 274⟩≡   273
```
    static struct symbol sentinel;
    if (sentinel.type == NULL) {
        sentinel.type = voidtype;
        sentinel.defined = 1;
    }
    if (ty1 == voidtype)
        error("illegal formal parameter types\n");
    list = append(&sentinel, list);
```

After the new-style parameter list has been parsed, list holds the symbols in the order they appeared. These symbols form the params array
returned by parameters, and their types form the prototype for the function type:

⟨*build the prototype* 274⟩≡   273
```
    fty->u.f.proto = newarray(length(list) + 1,
        sizeof (Type *), PERM);
    params = ltov(&list, FUNC);
    for (n = 0; params[n]; n++)
        fty->u.f.proto[n] = params[n]->type;
    fty->u.f.proto[n] = NULL;
```

dclparam declares both old-style and new-style parameters. dclparam
is called twice for each parameter: The first call is from parameters
and the second is from funcdefn. If the parameter list is not part of
a definition, the call to exitscope (in exitparams) discards the entries
made by dclparam.

⟨*decl.c functions*⟩+≡   272 277
```
    static Symbol dclparam(sclass, id, ty, pos)
    int sclass; char *id; Type ty; Coordinate *pos; {
        Symbol p;

        ⟨dclparam 275⟩
        return p;
    }
```

Declaring parameters is simpler than and different from declaring globals. First, the types (ARRAY *T*) and (FUNCTION *T*) decay to (POINTER *T*) and (POINTER (FUNCTION *T*)):

⟨dclparam 275⟩≡   275   274
```
    if (isfunc(ty))
        ty = ptr(ty);
    else if (isarray(ty))
        ty = atop(ty);
```

The only explicit storage class permitted is register, but lcc uses auto internally to identify nonregister parameters.

⟨dclparam 275⟩+≡   275 275   274
```
    if (sclass == 0)
        sclass = AUTO;
    else if (sclass != REGISTER) {
        error("invalid storage class '%k' for '%t%s\n",
            sclass, ty, ⟨id 275⟩);
        sclass = AUTO;
    } else if (isvolatile(ty) || isstruct(ty)) {
        warning("register declaration ignored for '%t%s\n",
            ty, ⟨id 275⟩);
        sclass = AUTO;
    }
```

⟨id 275⟩≡   275
```
    stringf(id ? " %s'" : "' parameter", id)
```

Parameters may be declared only once, which makes checking for redeclaration easy:

⟨dclparam 275⟩+≡   275 275   274
```
    p = lookup(id, identifiers);
    if (p && p->scope == level)
        error("duplicate declaration for '%s' previously _
            declared at %w\n", id, &p->src);
    else
        p = install(id, &identifiers, level, FUNC);
```

dclparam concludes by initializing p's remaining fields and checking for and consuming illegal initializations.

⟨dclparam 275⟩+≡   275   274
```
    p->sclass = sclass;
    p->src = *pos;
    p->type = ty;
    p->defined = 1;
```

```
if (t == '=') {
    error("illegal initialization for parameter '%s'\n", id);
    t = gettok();
    (void)expr1(0);
}
```

Parameters are considered defined when they are declared because they are announced to the back end by the interface procedure `function`, as described in Section 11.6.

11.5   Structure Specifiers

Syntactically, structure, union, and enumeration specifiers are the same as the types specified by the keywords int, float, etc. Semantically, however, they define new types. A structure or union specifier defines an aggregate type with named fields, and an enumeration specifier defines a type and an associated set of named integral constants. Exercise 11.9 describes enumeration specifiers. The syntax for structure and union specifiers is:

> *struct-or-union-specifier:*
>   *struct-or-union* [*identifier*] '{' *fields* { *fields* } '}'
>   *struct-or-union identifier*

> *struct-or-union:* struct | union

> *fields:*
>   { *type-specifier* | *type-qualifier* } *field* { , *field* } ;

> *field:*
>   *declarator*
>   [*declarator*] : *constant-expression*

expr1 157
function 92
(MIPS) "   448
(SPARC) "   484
(X86) "   518

The *identifier*, which is the *tag* of the structure or union, is optional only if the specifier includes a list of *fields*. A *struct-or-union-specifier* defines a new type if it includes *fields* or if it appears alone in a declaration and there is no definition of a structure, union, or enumeration type with the same tag in the same scope. This last kind of definition caters to mutually recursive structure declarations. For example, the intent of

```
struct head { struct node *list; ... };
struct node { struct head *hd; struct node *link; ... };
```

is for the `list` field in an instance of `head` to point to the `nodes` in a linked list, and for each `node` to point to the `head` of the list. The list is threaded through the `link` fields. But if `node` has already been declared as a structure or union tag in an enclosing scope, the `list` field is a pointer to *that* type, not to the `node` declared here. Subsequent assignments of pointers to nodes to `list` fields will be diagnosed as errors.

Exchanging the two lines fixes the problem for list, but exposes head to the same problem. The solution is to define the new type *before* defining head:

```
struct node;
struct head { struct node *list; ... };
struct node { struct head *hd; struct node *link; ... };
```

The lone struct node defines a new incomplete structure type with the tag node in the scope in which it appears, and hides other tags named node defined in enclosing scopes, if there are any. If there is a structure tag node in the same scope as the struct node, the latter declaration has no effect.

The parsing function for *struct-or-union-specifier*, structdcl, deals with tags and their definition, and calls fields to parse *fields* and to assign field offsets. Unions and structures are handled identically, except for assigning field offsets.

⟨*decl.c functions*⟩+≡   274 280

```
static Type structdcl(op) int op; {
    char *tag;
    Type ty;
    Symbol p;
    Coordinate pos;

    t = gettok();
    pos = src;
    ⟨structdcl 277⟩
    return ty;
}
```

38 Coordinate
280 fields
67 newstruct
108 token

structdcl begins by consuming the tag or using the empty string for omitted tags:

⟨structdcl 277⟩≡   277   277

```
if (t == ID) {
    tag = token;
    t = gettok();
} else
    tag = "";
```

If the tag is followed by a field list, this specifier defines a new tag:

⟨structdcl 277⟩+≡   277 278   277

```
if (t == '{') {
    static char stop[] = { IF, ',', 0 };
    ty = newstruct(op, tag);
    ty->u.sym->src = pos;
```

```
            ty->u.sym->defined = 1;
            t = gettok();
            if (istypename(t, tsym))
                fields(ty);
            else
                error("invalid %k field declarations\n", op);
            test('}', stop);
        }
```

newstruct checks for redeclaration of the tag and defines the new type. If the tag is empty, newstruct calls genlabel to generate one. newstruct is also used for enumeration specifiers; see Exercise 11.9.

If the *struct-or-union-specifier* doesn't have *fields* and the tag is already in use for the type indicated by op, the specifier refers to that type.

⟨structdcl 277⟩+≡   277 278   277

```
    else if (*tag && (p = lookup(tag, types)) != NULL
    && p->type->op == op) {
        ty = p->type;
        if (t == ';' && p->scope < level)
            ty = newstruct(op, tag);
    }
```

This case also handles the exception described above: If the tag is defined in an enclosing scope and the specifier appears alone in a declaration, the specifier defines a new type. As described in Chapter 3, tags have their own name space, which is managed in the types table.

If the cases above don't apply, there must be a tag, and the specifier defines a new type:

⟨structdcl 277⟩+≡   278   277

```
    else {
        if (*tag == 0)
            error("missing %k tag\n", op);
        ty = newstruct(op, tag);
    }
    if (*tag && xref)
        use(ty->u.sym, pos);
```

The last else clause handles the case when a specifier appears alone in a declaration and the tag is already defined in an enclosing scope for a *different* purpose. An example is:

```
    enum node { ... };
    f(void) {
        struct node;
        struct head { struct node *list; ... };
```

```
        struct node { struct head *hd; struct node *link; ... };
        ...
    }
```

The else clause above handles the `struct node` on the third line.

Most of the complexity of processing structure and union specifiers is in analyzing the fields and computing their offsets, particularly specifiers involving bit fields. Fields must be laid out in the order they appear in *fields*; their offsets depend on their types and the alignment constraints of those types. Bit fields are allocated in addressable storage units and when *N* bit fields fit in a storage unit, they must be laid out in the order in which they are declared, but that order can be from least to most significant bit or vice versa. It's conventional to use the order that follows increasing addresses: least to most significant bit (right to left) on little-endian targets, and most to least significant bit (left to right) on big endians. A compiler is not obligated to split bit fields across storage units, and it may choose any storage unit for bit fields. lcc uses unsigned integers so that bit fields can be fetched and stored using integer loads, stores, and masking operations.

Figure 11.1 shows a structure definition and its layout on a little-endian MIPS. Unsigneds are 32 bits, and integers and unsigneds must be aligned on 4-byte boundaries. Addresses increase from right to left as suggested by the numbering of a's elements, and from top to bottom as suggested by the offsets on the right side of the figure. The shading depicts holes that result from alignment constraints, and the darker shading is the hole specified by the 26-bit unnamed bit field. This example helps explain the intricacies of `fields`, the parsing function for *fields*.

`fields` parses the field list and builds a list of `field` structures emanating from `ty->u.sym->u.s.flist`. The `field` structure is described in Section 4.6. Its `name`, `type`, and `offset` fields give the field's name, its Type, and its offset in bytes from the beginning of the structure, respec-

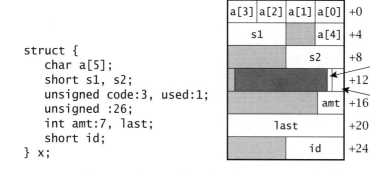

```
struct {
    char a[5];
    short s1, s2;
    unsigned code:3, used:1;
    unsigned :26;
    int amt:7, last;
    short id;
} x;
```

FIGURE 11.1 Little-endian structure layout example.

tively. For bit fields, `bitsize` gives the number of bits in the bit field, and `lsb` gives the number of the bit field's least significant bit plus one, where bits are numbered starting at zero with the least significant bit on all targets. A bit field is identified by a nonzero `lsb`. The list of `field` structures is threaded through the `link` fields. For the example shown in Figure 11.1, this list holds the fields shown in the following table.

name	type	offset	bitsize	lsb
a	chartype	0		
s1	shorttype	6		
s2	shorttype	8		
code	unsignedtype	12	3	1
used	unsignedtype	12	1	4
amt	inttype	16	7	1
last	inttype	20		
id	shortype	24		

`fields` first builds the list of `fields`, then traverses this list computing offsets and bit-field positions:

⟨*decl.c functions*⟩+≡   277 286

```
static void fields(ty) Type ty; {
    { ⟨parse fields 280⟩ }
    { ⟨assign field offsets 282⟩ }
}
```

A list of *fields* is parsed by calling `specifier` to consume the field's specifiers, then parsing each *field*:

⟨*parse fields* 280⟩≡   280

```
int n = 0;
while (istypename(t, tsym)) {
    static char stop[] = { IF, CHAR, '}', 0 };
    Type ty1 = specifier(NULL);
    for (;;) {
        Field p;
        char *id = NULL;
        ⟨parse one field 281⟩
        n++;
        if (Aflag >= 2 && n == 128)
            warning("more than 127 fields in '%t'\n", ty);
        if (t != ',')
            break;
        t = gettok();
    }
    test(';', stop);
}
```

n counts the number of fields, and is used only for the warning about declaring more fields than the maximum specified by the standard, which lcc's -A option enables.

Parsing a *field* is similar to parsing the declarator in a *declaration*, and dclr does most of the work:

⟨*parse one field* 281⟩≡   281   280
```
    p = newfield(id, ty, dclr(ty1, &id, NULL, 0));
```

newfield allocates a field structure, initializes its name and type fields to the value of id and the Type returned by dclr, clears the other fields, and appends it to ty->u.sym->u.s.flist. As it walks down the list to its end, newfield also checks for duplicate field names.

An oncoming colon signifies a bit field, and fields must check the field's type, parse its field width, and check that the width is legal:

⟨*parse one field* 281⟩+≡   281 282   280
```
    if (t == ':') {
        if (unqual(p->type) != inttype
        &&  unqual(p->type) != unsignedtype) {
            error("'%t' is an illegal bit-field type\n",
                p->type);
            p->type = inttype;
        }
        t = gettok();
        p->bitsize = intexpr(0, 0);
        if (p->bitsize > 8*inttype->size || p->bitsize < 0) {
            error("'%d' is an illegal bit-field size\n",
                p->bitsize);
            p->bitsize = 8*inttype->size;
        } else if (p->bitsize == 0 && id) {
            warning("extraneous 0-width bit field '%t %s' _
                ignored\n", p->type, id);
            p->name = stringd(genlabel(1));
        }
        p->lsb = 1;
    }
```

265	dclr
182	field
280	fields
45	genlabel
203	intexpr
68	newfield
29	stringd
60	unqual
58	unsignedtype

As shown, a bit field must be a qualified or unqualified version of int or unsigned. Compilers are permitted to treat plain int bit fields as either signed or unsigned; lcc treats them as signed. An unnamed bit field specifies padding; for now, it's appended to the list like other fields with a unique integer name, but it's removed when offsets are assigned. Similarly, the lsb field is set to one for now to identify the field as a bit field; it's changed to the correct value when its offset is assigned.

newfield has done all of the work for normal fields except to check for missing field names and illegal types:

⟨*parse one field* 281⟩+≡ $\overset{\blacktriangle}{281}$ 282   280

```
else {
    if (id == NULL)
        error("field name missing\n");
    else if (isfunc(p->type))
        error("'%t' is an illegal field type\n", p->type);
    else if (p->type->size == 0)
        error("undefined size for field '%t %s'\n",
            p->type, id);
}
```

If a field or bit field is declared const, assignments to that field are forbidden. Structure assignments must also be forbidden. For example, given the definition

```
struct { int code; const int value; } x, y;
```

x.code and y.code can be changed, but x.value and y.value cannot. Assignments like x = y are also illegal, and they're caught in asgntree by inspecting the structure type's cfields flag, which is set here, along with the vfields flag, which records volatile fields:

⟨*parse one field* 281⟩+≡ $\overset{\blacktriangle}{282}$ 280

```
if (isconst(p->type))
    ty->u.sym->u.s.cfields = 1;
if (isvolatile(p->type))
    ty->u.sym->u.s.vfields = 1;
```

align	78
asgntree	197
cfields	65
Field	66
field	182
IR	306
isconst	60
isfunc	60
isvolatile	60
structmetric	79
vfields	65

At this point, the field list for Figure 11.1's example has nine elements: the eight shown in the table on page 280 plus one between used and amt that has a bitsize equal to 26. The lsb fields of the elements for code, used, and amt are all equal to one, and all offset fields are zero.

Next, field makes a pass over the field list computing offsets. It also computes the alignment of the structure, and rebuilds the field list omitting those field structures that represent padding, which are those with integer names.

⟨*assign field offsets* 282⟩≡ $\underset{\blacktriangledown}{285}$ 280

```
int bits = 0, off = 0, overflow = 0;
Field p, *q = &ty->u.sym->u.s.flist;
ty->align = IR->structmetric.align;
for (p = *q; p; p = p->link) {
    ⟨compute p->offset 283⟩
    if (p->name == NULL
    || !('1' <= *p->name && *p->name <= '9')) {
        *q = p;
        q = &p->link;
    }
```

```
    }
  *q = NULL;
```

off is the running total of the number of bytes taken by the fields up
to but not including the one pointed to by p. bits is the number of
bits plus one taken by bit fields *beyond* off by the sequence of bit fields
immediately preceding p. Thus, bits is nonzero if the previous field is
a bit field, and it never exceeds unsignedtype->size. fields must also
cope with offset computations that overflow. It uses the macro add to
increment off:

⟨*decl.c macros*⟩≡   283
```
  #define add(x,n) (x > INT_MAX-(n) ? (overflow=1,x) : x+(n))
  #define chkoverflow(x,n) ((void)add(x,n))
```

chkoverflow uses add to set overflow if x + n overflows. If overflow is
one at the end of fields, the structure is too big.
    If the fields appear in a union, all the offsets are zero by definition:

⟨*compute* p->offset 283⟩≡   283   282
```
  int a = p->type->align ? p->type->align : 1;
  if (p->lsb)
      a = unsignedtype->align;
  if (ty->op == UNION)
      off = bits = 0;
```

The value of a is the field's alignment; it's used below to increase the
structure's alignment, ty->align, if necessary. It's also used to round
up off to the appropriate alignment boundary:

205	add
78	align
280	fields
364	offset
19	roundup
109	UNION
58	unsignedtype

⟨*compute* p->offset 283⟩+≡   283 284   282
```
  else if (p->bitsize == 0 || bits == 0
  || bits - 1 + p->bitsize > 8*unsignedtype->size) {
      off = add(off, bits2bytes(bits-1));
      bits = 0;
      chkoverflow(off, a - 1);
      off = roundup(off, a);
  }
  if (a > ty->align)
      ty->align = a;
  p->offset = off;
```

⟨*decl.c macros*⟩+≡   283
```
  #define bits2bytes(n) (((n) + 7)/8)
```

off must be rounded up if p isn't a bit field, isn't preceded by fields that
ended in the middle of an unsigned, or is a bit field that's too big to fit
in the unsigned partially consumed by previous bit fields. Before off is

rounded up, it must be incremented past the bits occupied by previous
bit fields in the unsigned at the current value of `off`. This space isn't
accounted for until a normal field is encountered or the end of the list
is reached. `bits` is this space in bits *plus* one, so it's converted to bytes
by computing the ceiling of `bits-1` divided by eight. This computation
is correct even when `bits` is zero.

When the field `s1` from Figure 11.1 is processed, `off` is 5, and `bits`
is 0. `s1`'s alignment is 2, so the code above sets `off` to 6, which becomes
the offset for `s1`. When `amt` is processed, `off` is 12, which is the unsigned
that holds `code` and `used`, and `bits` is $3 + 1 + 26 + 1 = 31$. `amt` needs 7
bits, which won't fit, so `off` is set to $12 + ((31 - 1) + 7)/8 = 16$, which
is on a four-byte boundary as dictated by the alignment `a`, and `bits` is
reset to zero. Next, `last` is processed; `off` is 16 and `bits` is $7 + 1 = 8$.
Since `last` isn't a bit field, `off` is set to $16 + ((8 - 1) + 7)/8 = 17$, then
rounded up to 20.

Once the offset to `p` is computed and stored, `off` is incremented by
the size of `p`'s type, except for bit fields. If `p` is a bit field, `p->lsb` is
computed and `bits` is incremented by the bit-field width:

⟨*compute* p->offset 283⟩+≡   ▲
                                                           283   282

```
    if (p->lsb) {
        if (bits == 0)
            bits = 1;
        if (IR->little_endian)
            p->lsb = bits;
        else
            p->lsb = 8*unsignedtype->size - bits + 1
                - p->bitsize + 1;
        bits += p->bitsize;
    } else
        off = add(off, p->type->size);
    if (off + bits2bytes(bits-1) > ty->size)
        ty->size = off + bits2bytes(bits-1);
```

`bits` is the bit offset plus one in addressing order, but `lsb` is the number
of bits plus one to the right of the bit field regardless of addressing order.
On a little endian, `bits` and `lsb` are the same. But on a big endian with
32-bit unsigneds, for example, the number of bits to the right of an m-bit
field is $32 - (\text{bits} - 1) - m$, where `bits` $- 1$ is the number of bits used
for previous bit fields. The last statement in the code above updates
`ty->size`. This code works for both structures and unions because `off`
is reset to zero for union fields. For unions, including the additional
space given by `bits` is crucial; if it's omitted, the size of

```
    union { int x; int a:31, b:4; };
```

would end up being 4 instead of 8 because the 4 bits for `b`, which are
recorded only in `bits`, wouldn't get counted.

When code is processed, off is 10 and bits is zero. The round-up code shown above bumps off to 12 and becomes code's offset, because bit fields must start on a boundary suitable for an unsigned. bits and code's lsb are set to 1. If Figure 11.1's example is compiled on a 32-bit big endian, code's lsb is $32 - 1 + 1 - 3 + 1 = 30$; i.e., there are 29 bits to the right of code on a big endian. used is reached with off still equal to 12 and bits equal to 4. used fits in the unsigned at offset 12, so its lsb becomes 4 and bits becomes 5. The padding between used and code causes bits to be incremented to $5 + 26 = 31$. There isn't room in the unsigned at offset 12 for amt, so off and bits get changed to 16 and zero, as described above, and amt's lsb becomes one.

Structures can appear in arrays: A structure must end on an address boundary that is a multiple of the alignment of the field with the strictest alignment, so that incrementing a pointer to element n advances the pointer to element $n + 1$. For example, if a structure contains a double and doubles have an alignment of 8, then the structure must have an alignment of 8. As shown above, fields keeps a structure's alignment, ty->align, greater than or equal to the alignments of its fields, but it must pad the structure to a multiple of this alignment, if necessary:

⟨*assign field offsets* 282⟩+≡   282   280

```
chkoverflow(ty->size, ty->align - 1);
ty->size = roundup(ty->size, ty->align);
if (overflow) {
    error("size of '%t' exceeds %d bytes\n", ty, INT_MAX);
    ty->size = INT_MAX&(~(ty->align - 1));
}
```

78	align
258	decl
280	fields
286	funcdefn
19	roundup

For the example in Figure 11.1, the loop in ⟨*assign field offsets*⟩ ends with ty->size equal to 26, the last value of off, which is not a multiple of 4, the value of ty->align, so this concluding code bumps ty->size to 28.

11.6 Function Definitions

A function definition is a *declaration* without its terminating semicolon followed by a *compound-statement*. In a definition of an old-style function, an optional list of *declarations* intervenes.

> *function-definition:*
>   *declaration-specifiers declarator* { *declaration* }
>   *compound-statement*

The parsing function is funcdefn, which is called from decl when it realizes that a function definition is approaching.

⟨*decl.c functions*⟩ += ≡   280 288

```
static void funcdefn(sclass, id, ty, params, pt) int sclass;
char *id; Type ty; Symbol params[]; Coordinate pt; {
    int i, n;
    Symbol *callee, *caller, p;
    Type rty = freturn(ty);

    ⟨funcdefn 286⟩
}
```

funcdefn has much to do. It must parse the optional *declaration*s for old-style functions, reconcile new-style declarations with old-style definitions and vice versa, and initialize the front end in preparation for parsing *compound-statement*, which contributes to the code list for the function. Once the *compound-statement* is consumed, funcdefn must finalize the code list for traversal when the back end calls gencode and emitcode, arrange the correct arguments to the interface procedure function, and re-initialize the front end once code for the function has been generated.

funcdefn's sclass, id, and ty parameters give the storage class, function name, and function type gleaned from the declarator parsed by decl. pt is the source coordinate of the beginning of that declarator. params is the array of symbols built by parameters — one for each parameter, and an extra unnamed one if the parameter list ended with an ellipsis. funcdefn starts by removing this extra symbol because it's used only in prototypes, and it checks for illegal return types:

⟨funcdefn 286⟩ ≡   286   286

```
if (isstruct(rty) && rty->size == 0)
    error("illegal use of incomplete type '%t'\n", rty);
for (n = 0; params[n]; n++)
    ;
if (n > 0 && params[n-1]->name == NULL)
    params[--n] = NULL;
```

params helps funcdefn build two parallel arrays of pointers to symbol-table entries. callee is an array of entries for the parameters as seen by the function itself, and caller is an array of entries for the parameters as seen by callers of the function. Usually, the corresponding entries in these arrays are the same, but they can differ when argument promotions force the type of a caller parameter to be different than the type of the corresponding callee parameter, as shown in Section 1.3. The storage classes of the caller and callee parameters can also be different when, for example, a parameter is declared register by the callee but is passed on the stack by the caller. The details of building callee and caller depend on whether the definition is old-style or new-style:

⟨funcdefn 286⟩ += ≡   286 290   286

```
if (ty->u.f.oldstyle) {
```

```
    ⟨initialize old-style parameters 287⟩
  } else {
    ⟨initialize new-style parameters 287⟩
  }
  for (i = 0; (p = callee[i]) != NULL; i++)
    if (p->type->size == 0) {
      error("undefined size for parameter '%t %s'\n",
          p->type, p->name);
      caller[i]->type = p->type = inttype;
    }
```

New-style definitions are the easier of the two because `parameters` has already done most of the work, so params can be used as `callee`. The caller parameters are copies of the corresponding callee parameters, except that their types are promoted and they have storage class `AUTO` to indicate that they're passed in memory.

⟨*initialize new-style parameters* 287⟩≡   287

```
  callee = params;
  caller = newarray(n + 1, sizeof *caller, FUNC);
  for (i = 0; (p = callee[i]) != NULL && p->name; i++) {
    NEW(caller[i], FUNC);
    *caller[i] = *p;
    caller[i]->type = promote(p->type);
    caller[i]->sclass = AUTO;
    if ('1' <= *p->name && *p->name <= '9')
      error("missing name for parameter %d to _
          function '%s'\n", i + 1, id);
  }
  caller[i] = NULL;
```

Recall that `parameters` uses the parameter number for a missing parameter identifier, so `funcdefn` must check for such identifiers. Identifiers can be omitted in declarations but not in function definitions.

For old-style definitions, `parameters` has simply collected the identifiers in the parameter list and checked for duplicates. `funcdefn` must parse their declarations and match the resulting identifiers with the ones in params. It uses params for the `caller`, makes a copy for use as `callee`, and calls `decl` to parse the declarations.

⟨*initialize old-style parameters* 287⟩≡   288   287

```
  caller = params;
  callee = newarray(n + 1, sizeof *callee, FUNC);
  memcpy(callee, caller, (n+1)*sizeof *callee);
  enterscope();
  while (kind[t] == STATIC || istypename(t, tsym))
    decl(dclparam);
```

Parsing the parameter declarations adds a symbol-table entry for each identifier to the `identifiers` table. These declarations may omit integer parameters and they might declare identifiers that are not in `callee`. `funcdefn` checks for the second condition by visiting every symbol with scope `PARAM` and changing `callee` to point to that symbol:

⟨*initialize old-style parameters* 287⟩+≡   287 288   287
```
    foreach(identifiers, PARAM, oldparam, callee);
```

⟨*decl.c functions*⟩+≡   286 293
```
    static void oldparam(p, cl) Symbol p; void *cl; {
        int i;
        Symbol *callee = cl;

        for (i = 0; callee[i]; i++)
            if (p->name == callee[i]->name) {
                callee[i] = p;
                return;
            }
        error("declared parameter '%s' is missing\n", p->name);
    }
```

After processing the old-style declarations, *some* of the entries in `callee` now point to bonafide parameter symbols. Others point to the placeholder symbols created by `parameters`. These symbols, which have their `defined` flags equal to zero, can now be initialized as if they were explicitly declared integers. At the same time, the corresponding `caller` symbols can be overwritten by the bonafide symbols in `identifiers`.

⟨*initialize old-style parameters* 287⟩+≡   288 289   287
```
    for (i = 0; (p = callee[i]) != NULL; i++) {
        if (!p->defined)
            callee[i] = dclparam(0, p->name, inttype, &p->src);
        *caller[i] = *p;
        caller[i]->sclass = AUTO;
        if (unqual(p->type) == floattype)
            caller[i]->type = doubletype;
        else
            caller[i]->type = promote(p->type);
    }
```

Arguments in calls to old-style functions suffer the default argument promotions, so the types of the `caller` symbols are modified accordingly. For example, in

```
    f(c,x) char c; float x; { ... }
```

`callee`'s two symbols have types (CHAR) and (FLOAT), but `caller`'s symbols have types (INT) and (DOUBLE). As shown in Section 1.3, these differences cause assignments of the caller values to the callee values at the entry to f.

The standard permits mixing old-style definitions and new-style declarations, as the code in this book illustrates, but the definitions must agree with the declarations and vice versa. If a new-style declaration precedes an old-style definition, the function is deemed to be a new-style function, and the old-style definition must provide a parameter list whose types are compatible with the declaration.

⟨*initialize old-style parameters* 287⟩+≡   2̂88 289▾   287

```
    p = lookup(id, identifiers);
    if (p && p->scope == GLOBAL && isfunc(p->type)
    && p->type->u.f.proto) {
        Type *proto = p->type->u.f.proto;
        for (i = 0; caller[i] && proto[i]; i++)
            if (eqtype(unqual(proto[i]),
                unqual(caller[i]->type), 1) == 0)
                break;
        if (proto[i] || caller[i])
            error("conflicting argument declarations for _
                function '%s'\n", id);
    }
```

The new-style declaration cannot end in `,...` because there's no compatible old-style definition. The code above checks that `caller`'s types are compatible with the corresponding types in the new-style declaration. Thus, the only compatible declaration for f above is

```
    extern int f(int, double);
```

The declaration

```
    extern int f(char, float);
```

looks compatible because its types are the same as those for c and x in the definition above, but for compability purposes, it's the promoted types that matter.

If a new-style declaration follows an old-style definition, the function remains an old-style function, but the declaration must be compatible, as above. lcc implements this check by building a prototype for the old-style function and changing the function's type to include this prototype. The function type's `oldstyle` flag is 1, so this prototype is used only by eqtype for these kinds of checks.

⟨*initialize old-style parameters* 287⟩+≡   289▴   287

```
    else {
```

```
Type *proto = newarray(n + 1, sizeof *proto, PERM);
if (Aflag >= 1)
    warning("missing prototype for '%s'\n", id);
for (i = 0; i < n; i++)
    proto[i] = caller[i]->type;
proto[i] = NULL;
ty = func(rty, proto, 1);
}
```

When a subsequent new-style declaration appears, redeclaration code will call eqtype and will use this prototype to check for compatibility.

Once the caller and callee are built, funcdefn can define the symbol for the function itself, because other functions, such as statement and retcode, need access to the current function. This symbol is posted in a global variable:

⟨*decl.c exported data*⟩≡   291

```
    extern Symbol cfunc;
```

Additional information for a function is carried in the symbol's u.f field:

⟨*function symbols* 290⟩≡   38

```
    struct {
        Coordinate pt;
        int label;
        int ncalls;
        Symbol *callee;
    } f;
```

pt is the source coordinate for the function's entry point, label is the label for the exit point, ncalls is the number of calls made by the function, and the field callee is a copy of funcdefn's local variable callee.

⟨*funcdefn* 286⟩+≡   286 291   286

```
    p = lookup(id, identifiers);
    if (p && isfunc(p->type) && p->defined)
        error("redefinition of '%s' previously defined at %w\n",
            p->name, &p->src);
    cfunc = dclglobal(sclass, id, ty, &pt);
    cfunc->u.f.label = genlabel(1);
    cfunc->u.f.callee = callee;
    cfunc->u.f.pt = src;
    cfunc->defined = 1;
    if (xref)
        use(cfunc, cfunc->src);
```

At this point, funcdefn is finally ready to parse the function's body. It initializes the symbol tables for internal labels and statement labels, initializes refinc to one, sets the code list to the single Start entry, appends

an execution point for the function's entry point, and calls compound,
which is described in the next section.

⟨funcdefn 286⟩+≡   ▲290 291   286
   labels   = table(NULL, LABELS);   ▼
   stmtlabs = table(NULL, LABELS);
   refinc = 1.0;
   regcount = 0;
   codelist = &codehead;
   codelist->next = NULL;
   definept(NULL);
   if (!IR->wants_callb && isstruct(rty))
      retv = genident(AUTO, ptr(rty), PARAM);
   compound(0, NULL, 0);

```
⟨decl.c data⟩≡                                                           294
    static int regcount;                                                 ▼
```

```
⟨decl.c exported data⟩+≡                                                 ▲290
    extern Symbol retv;
```

regcount is the number of locals explicitly declared register. As detailed
in Section 10.8, if the interface flag wants_callb is zero, the front end
completely implements functions that return structures. To do so, it
creates a hidden parameter that points to the location at which to store
the return value and posts the symbol for this parameter in retv. It also
arranges to pass the values for this parameter in calls; see Section 9.3.

The code list grows as the *compound-statement* is parsed and ana-
lyzed. When compound returns, funcdefn adds a tree for a return statement to the code list, if necessary. The code is similar to adding a jump:
The return is needed only if control can flow into the end of the function.

⟨funcdefn 286⟩+≡   ▲291 292   286
```
    {                                                                    ▼
        Code cp;
        for (cp = codelist; cp->kind < Label; cp = cp->prev)
            ;
        if (cp->kind != Jump) {
            if (rty != voidtype
            && (rty != inttype || Aflag >= 1))
                warning("missing return value\n");
            retcode(NULL);
        }
    }
    definelab(cfunc->u.f.label);
    definept(NULL);
```

The call to definelab adds the exit-point label, and definept plants the accompanying execution point. lcc warns about the possibility of an implicit return for functions that return values other than integers, or for all nonvoid functions if its -A option is specified. The final steps in parsing the function are to close the scope opened by compound and check for unreferenced parameters:

⟨funcdefn 286⟩+≡   291 292   286
```
    exitscope();
    foreach(identifiers, level, checkref, NULL);
```

checkref is described in the next section.

The code list for the function is now complete (except for the changes made in gencode), and funcdefn is almost ready to call the interface procedure function. Before doing so, however, it may have to make two transformations to the caller and callee, depending on the values of the interface flags wants_callb and wants_argb. If wants_callb is zero, the hidden argument, pointed to by retv, must be inserted at the beginning of callee and a copy of it must be inserted at the beginning of caller:

⟨funcdefn 286⟩+≡   292 292   286
```
    if (!IR->wants_callb && isstruct(rty)) {
        Symbol *a;
        a = newarray(n + 2, sizeof *a, FUNC);
        a[0] = retv;
        memcpy(&a[1], callee, (n+1)*sizeof *callee);
        callee = a;
        a = newarray(n + 2, sizeof *a, FUNC);
        NEW(a[0], FUNC);
        *a[0] = *retv;
        memcpy(&a[1], caller, (n+1)*sizeof *callee);
        caller = a;
    }
```

If wants_argb is zero, the front end completely implements structure parameters, as described in Sections 8.8 and 9.3. idtree, for example, generates an extra indirection for structure parameters when wants_argb is zero because the parameters are really the *addresses* of the structures. This lie must be corrected for the back end, however, which is done by changing the types of the caller and callee parameters and by lighting structarg to identify the identifiers so changed.

⟨*symbol flags* 50⟩+≡   211   38
```
    unsigned structarg:1;
```

⟨funcdefn 286⟩+≡   292 293   286
```
    if (!IR->wants_argb)
```

```
    for (i = 0; caller[i]; i++)
        if (isstruct(caller[i]->type)) {
            caller[i]->type = ptr(caller[i]->type);
            callee[i]->type = ptr(callee[i]->type);
            caller[i]->structarg = callee[i]->structarg = 1;
        }
```

Finally, funcdefn exports the function, if necessary, and passes control to the back end:

⟨funcdefn 286⟩+≡   292 293   286
```
    if (cfunc->sclass != STATIC)
        (*IR->export)(cfunc);
    swtoseg(CODE);
    (*IR->function)(cfunc, caller, callee, cfunc->u.f.ncalls);
```

funcdefn concludes by flushing the output, checking for undefined statement labels, optionally planting an end-of-function event hook, closing the PARAM scope, and consuming the closing brace on the function's *compound-statement*.

⟨funcdefn 286⟩+≡   293   286
```
    outflush();
    foreach(stmtlabs, LABELS, checklab, NULL);
    exitscope();
    expect('}');
```

checklab is similar to checkref; see Exercise 11.4.

11.7 Compound Statements

The syntax of compound statements is

> *compound-statement:*
>   '{' { *declaration* } { *statement* } '}'

and compound is the parsing function. It appends a Blockbeg entry to the code list, opens a new scope, parses the optional *declaration*s and *statement*s, and appends a Blockend entry to the code list. compound's arguments are the loop handle, the switch handle, and the structured statement nesting level.

⟨decl.c functions⟩+≡   288 296
```
    void compound(loop, swp, lev)
    int loop, lev; struct swtch *swp; {
        Code cp;
        int nregs;
```

```
        walk(NULL, 0, 0);
        cp = code(Blockbeg);
        enterscope();
        ⟨compound 294⟩
        cp->u.block.level = level;
        cp->u.block.identifiers = identifiers;
        cp->u.block.types = types;
        code(Blockend)->u.begin = cp;
        if (level > LOCAL) {
            exitscope();
            expect('}');
        }
    }
```

compound is called from statement and from funcdefn. The only difference between these two calls is that the scope is closed only on the
call from statement. As shown above, funcdefn closes the scope that
compound opens on its behalf so that it can call the interface procedure
function before doing so.

Most of compound's semantic processing concerns the locals declared
in the block. dcllocal processes each local and appends it to one of the
lists

⟨decl.c data⟩+≡   ▲
    static List autos, registers;   291

depending on its explicit storage class. Locals with no storage class are
appended to autos, and static locals are handled like globals.

If compound is called from funcdefn, it must cope with the interface
flag wants_callb. When this flag is one, the back end handles the transmission of the return value for functions that return structures. The
front end generates space for this value in the caller, but it doesn't know
how to transmit the address of this space to the callee. It assumes that
the back end will arrange to pass this address in a target-dependent way
and to store it in the first local. So, compound generates the first local
and saves its symbol-table entry in retv:

⟨compound 294⟩≡   295   294
    autos = registers = NULL;   ▼
    if (level == LOCAL && IR->wants_callb
    && isstruct(freturn(cfunc->type))) {
        retv = genident(AUTO, ptr(freturn(cfunc->type)), level);
        retv->defined = 1;
        retv->ref = 1;
        registers = append(retv, registers);
    }
```
```

retv is appended to registers even though it's an AUTO to ensure that it's passed to the back end as the first local; this order is arranged below.

The front end uses retv in one of two ways depending on the value of wants_callb. When wants_callb is one, retv is the symbol-table entry for the *local* that holds the address at which to store the return value, as just described. When wants_callb is zero, there is no such local because the front end arranges to pass this address as the value of the hidden first *parameter*; in this case, retv is the symbol-table entry for that parameter. As far as retcode is concerned, retv is the symbol-table entry for the variable that carries the address, regardless of how it got there.

Next, compound parses the optional block-level declarations:

⟨compound 294⟩+≡   294 295   294

```
    expect('{');
    while (kind[t] == CHAR || kind[t] == STATIC
    || istypename(t, tsym) && getchr() != ':')
        decl(dcllocal);
```

The call to getchr checks for the rare but legal code exemplified by

```
    typedef int T;
    f() { T: ...; goto T; }
```

istypename(t) says T is a typedef, but inside f, T is a label. Peeking at the next input character avoids the misinterpretation.

Once the locals are consumed, those on the autos list are appended to the registers list, which is then converted to a null-terminated array and assigned to the u.block.locals field of the Blockbeg code-list entry.

⟨compound 294⟩+≡   295 295   294

```
    {
        int i;
        Symbol *a = ltov(&autos, STMT);
        nregs = length(registers);
        for (i = 0; a[i]; i++)
            registers = append(a[i], registers);
        cp->u.block.locals = ltov(&registers, FUNC);
    }
```

cp->u.block.locals[0..nregs-1] are the register locals, and the automatic locals begin at cp->u.block.locals[nregs]. This ordering ensures that the register locals are announced to the back end before the automatic locals.

Next, the *statements* are processed:

⟨compound 294⟩+≡   295 296   294

```
    while (kind[t] == IF || kind[t] == ID)
        statement(loop, swp, lev);
```

```
walk(NULL, 0, 0);
foreach(identifiers, level, checkref, NULL);
```

As the statements are compiled, idtree increments the ref fields of the identifiers they use. Thus, at the end of *statements*, the ref fields identify the most frequently accessed variables. checkref, described below, changes the storage class of any scalar variable referenced at least three times to REGISTER, unless its address is taken. compound sorts the locals beginning at cp->u.block.locals[nregs] in decreasing order of ref values.

⟨compound 294⟩+≡   295   294

```
    {
        int i = nregs, j;
        Symbol p;
        for ( ; (p = cp->u.block.locals[i]) != NULL; i++) {
            for (j = i; j > nregs
                && cp->u.block.locals[j-1]->ref < p->ref; j--)
                cp->u.block.locals[j] = cp->u.block.locals[j-1];
            cp->u.block.locals[j] = p;
        }
    }
```

Some of these locals now have REGISTER storage class, and sorting them on their estimated frequency of use permits the back end to assign registers to those that are used most often without having it do its own analysis. The locals in cp->u.block.locals[0..nregs-1] may be less frequently referenced than the others, but they're presented to the back end first because the programmer explicitly declared them as registers.

checkref is called at the ends of compound statements for every symbol in the identifiers table, and it does more than change storage classes.

⟨decl.c functions⟩+≡   293 298

```
    static void checkref(p, cl) Symbol p; void *cl; {
        ⟨checkref 296⟩
    }
```

It also prevents volatile locals and parameters from landing in registers by lighting their addressed flags:

⟨checkref 296⟩≡   297   296

```
    if (p->scope >= PARAM
    && (isvolatile(p->type) || isfunc(p->type)))
        p->addressed = 1;
```

checkref warns about unreferenced statics, parameters, and locals when lcc's -A option appears twice:

⟨checkref 296⟩+≡   296 297   296

```
if (Aflag >= 2 && p->defined && p->ref == 0) {
    if (p->sclass == STATIC)
        warning("static '%t %s' is not referenced\n",
            p->type, p->name);
    else if (p->scope == PARAM)
        warning("parameter '%t %s' is not referenced\n",
            p->type, p->name);
    else if (p->scope >= LOCAL && p->sclass != EXTERN)
        warning("local '%t %s' is not referenced\n",
            p->type, p->name);
}
```

There's more to changing a parameter's or local's storage class from AUTO
to REGISTER than is suggested above. A parameter's storage class is
changed only if there are no explicitly declared register locals. To do
otherwise risks using the registers for parameters instead of for locals
as was intended.

⟨checkref 296⟩+≡   297 297   296

```
if (p->sclass == AUTO
&& (p->scope  == PARAM && regcount == 0
 || p->scope  >= LOCAL)
&& !p->addressed && isscalar(p->type) && p->ref >= 3.0)
    p->sclass = REGISTER;
```

dcllocal increments regcount for each local explicitly declared register
in *any* block.

checkref also helps manage the externals table. As shown below,
dcllocal installs locals that are declared extern in externals as well as
in identifiers. When the local goes out of scope, checkref adds the
value of the ref field in its identifiers symbol to the ref field of its
externals symbol:

⟨checkref 296⟩+≡   297 297   296

```
if (p->scope >= LOCAL && p->sclass == EXTERN) {
    Symbol q = lookup(p->name, externals);
    q->ref += p->ref;
}
```

A ref value for an identifier in the externals table thus accumulates the
references from *all* functions that reference that identifier.

Finally, checkref is also called at the end of compilation to check
for undefined static variables and functions. It tests for this call, which
comes from finalize, by inspecting the current scope level:

⟨checkref 296⟩+≡   297   296

```
if (level == GLOBAL && p->sclass == STATIC && !p->defined
```

```
        && isfunc(p->type) && p->ref)
            error("undefined static '%t %s'\n", p->type, p->name);
```

lcc doesn't complain about unreferenced static functions that are declared but never defined because the standard doesn't say that such declarations are errors.

decl calls the last of the dclX functions, dcllocal, when it's called from compound for each local.

⟨*decl.c functions*⟩+≡   ▲296 303▼

```
        static Symbol dcllocal(sclass, id, ty, pos)
        int sclass; char *id; Type ty; Coordinate *pos; {
            Symbol p, q;

            ⟨dcllocal 298⟩
            return p;
        }
```

Like dclglobal and dclparam, dcllocal starts by checking for an invalid storage class:

⟨dcllocal 298⟩≡   298   298▼

```
        if (sclass == 0)
            sclass = isfunc(ty) ? EXTERN : AUTO;
        else if (isfunc(ty) && sclass != EXTERN) {
            error("invalid storage class '%k' for '%t %s'\n",
                sclass, ty, id);
            sclass = EXTERN;
        } else if (sclass == REGISTER
        && (isvolatile(ty) || isstruct(ty) || isarray(ty))) {
            warning("register declaration ignored for '%t %s'\n",
                ty, id);
            sclass = AUTO;
        }
```

Local variables may have any storage class, but functions must have no storage class or extern. Volatile locals and those with aggregate types may be declared register, but lcc treats them as automatics.

Next, dcllocal checks for redeclarations:

⟨dcllocal 298⟩+≡   ▲298 299▼   298

```
        q = lookup(id, identifiers);
        if (q && q->scope >= level
        || q && q->scope == PARAM && level == LOCAL)
            if (sclass == EXTERN && q->sclass == EXTERN
            && eqtype(q->type, ty, 1))
                ty = compose(ty, q->type);
            else
```

```
        error("redeclaration of '%s' previously _
            declared at %w\n", q->name, &q->src);
```

lcc uses different scopes for parameters and for the locals in a function's *compound-statement*, but the standard treats these scopes as one. Thus, a local declaration is a redeclaration if there's already an identifier at the same scope or if a parameter has the same name and the local has scope LOCAL. The code

```
    f() { extern int x[]; extern int x[10]; ... }
```

illustrates the one case when more than one declaration for a local is permitted: when they're extern declarations. Here, the second extern declaration contributes more information about x's type — namely, its size.

dcllocal next installs the identifier, initializes its fields, and switches on its storage class, which dictates subsequent processing.

⟨dcllocal 298⟩+≡   298 301   298
```
    p = install(id, &identifiers, level, FUNC);
    p->type = ty;
    p->sclass = sclass;
    p->src = *pos;
    switch (sclass) {
    case EXTERN:   ⟨extern local 300⟩ break;
    case STATIC:   ⟨static local 300⟩ break;
    case REGISTER: ⟨register local 299⟩ break;
    case AUTO:     ⟨auto local 299⟩ break;
    }
```

Automatic and register locals are the easy ones; they're simply appended to the appropriate list:

⟨*register local* 299⟩≡   299
```
    registers = append(p, registers);
    regcount++;
    p->defined = 1;
```

⟨*auto local* 299⟩≡   299
```
    autos = append(p, autos);
    p->defined = 1;
```

regcount is the number of locals explicitly declared register anywhere in a function, and is used in checkref, above. Unlike globals, a local's defined flag is lit when it's declared, *before* it's passed to the back end, which occurs in gencode. Locals are treated this way because they can be declared only once (in a given scope), and their declarations are always definitions.

Most of the work for static locals is in dealing with the optional initialization, which is the same as what initglobal does for globals:

⟨*static local* 300⟩ ≡   299
```
  (*IR->defsymbol)(p);
  initglobal(p, 0);
  if (!p->defined)
     if (p->type->size > 0) {
        defglobal(p, BSS);
        (*IR->space)(p->type->size);
     } else
        error("undefined size for '%t %s'\n",
           p->type, p->name);
  p->defined = 1;
```

If there's no initialization, p->defined is zero when initglobal returns, and dcllocal must allocate space for the static local. Like uninitialized globals, uninitialized statics are defined in the BSS segment.

Locals declared extern suffer the rules summarized by the column labelled EXTERN in the table on page 262: If there's a visible file-scope declaration for the identifier, the local refers to that declaration. In any case, the local is announced via the interface function defsymbol since it's like a global except for scope.

⟨*extern local* 300⟩ ≡   300   299
```
  if (q && q->scope == GLOBAL && q->sclass == STATIC) {
     p->sclass = STATIC;
     p->scope = GLOBAL;
     (*IR->defsymbol)(p);
     p->sclass = EXTERN;
     p->scope = level;
  } else
     (*IR->defsymbol)(p);
```

As this code suggests, the presence of a visible file-scope declaration for a static identifier by the same name needs special treatment. A back end's defsymbol might treat statics and externs differently, for example, by using different conventions for their target-dependent names. So, dcllocal changes the storage class and scope for duration of the defsymbol call. This code also fails to check that the two identifiers have compatible types, because that check is made below.

Extern locals are also installed in the externals table that, as described in Section 11.2, is used to detect inconsistencies in block-level extern declarations.

⟨*extern local* 300⟩ +≡   300   299
```
  {
     Symbol r = lookup(id, externals);
     if (r == NULL) {
        r = install(p->name, &externals, GLOBAL, PERM);
```

```
            r->src = p->src;
            r->type = p->type;
            r->sclass = p->sclass;
            q = lookup(id, globals);
            if (q && q->sclass != TYPEDEF && q->sclass != ENUM)
                r = q;
        }
        if (r && !eqtype(r->type, p->type, 1))
            warning("declaration of '%s' does not match previous _
                declaration at %w\n", r->name, &r->src);
    }
```

If there's already a symbol for the identifier in externals, it must have a compatible type. Otherwise, the identifier is installed in externals. There's a tricky case that's not covered by dcllocal's redeclaration code shown on page 298. In

```
int x;
f(int x) { ... { extern float x; ... } }
```

the extern declaration in f for x conflicts with the file-scope declaration for x, because they specify different types for the same x. The lookup call in the redeclaration code returns a pointer to the symbol for the *parameter* x and assigns that pointer to q. It's this value that's used at the beginning ⟨extern local⟩ to check for file-scope identifiers; the parameter x hides the file-scope x, but the latter is the one that's needed to check for these kinds of conflicts. Thus, dcllocal looks up the identifier in globals and, if one is found, uses it to check for compatible types. When there's no intervening declaration that hides the file-scope identifier, this second call to lookup sets q to its existing value, which is the common case. The example above is rare, but occurs nonetheless, particularly in large programs.

dcllocal concludes by parsing the optional initialization. Unlike in initglobal, the initial value may be an arbitrary expression in some cases. If the local has a scalar type, its initializer may be an expression or an expression enclosed in braces. If the local is a structure or union, its initializer can be a single expression or a brace-enclosed list of constant expressions. If the local is an array, its initializer can only be a brace-enclosed list of constant expressions. An array must either have an explicit size or an initializer that determines its size. dcllocal handles all of these cases by generating an assignment to the local:

298	dcllocal
109	ENUM
69	eqtype
40	externals
80	EXTERN
41	globals
264	initglobal
45	lookup

⟨dcllocal 298⟩+≡   299   298

```
    if (t == '=') {
        Tree e;
        if (sclass == EXTERN)
            error("illegal initialization of 'extern %s'\n", id);
```

```
t = gettok();
definept(NULL);
if (isscalar(p->type)
|| isstruct(p->type) && t != '{') {
    if (t == '{') {
        t = gettok();
        e = expr1(0);
        expect('}');
    } else
        e = expr1(0);
} else {
    ⟨generate an initialized static t1 302⟩
    e = idtree(t1);
}
walk(root(asgn(p, e)), 0, 0);
p->ref = 1;
}
if (!isfunc(p->type) && p->defined && p->type->size <= 0)
    error("undefined size for '%t %s'\n", p->type, id);
```

For a local that has a scalar type, a structure type, or a union type, and whose initializer is a single expression, the initialization is an assignment of the initializer to the local. For a local that has an aggregate type and a brace-enclosed initializer, lcc generates an anonymous static variable, and initializes it as specified by the initializer. A single structure assignment initializes the local, even for arrays.

⟨*generate an initialized static* t1 302⟩≡   302
```
Symbol t1;
Type ty = p->type, ty1 = ty;
while (isarray(ty1))
    ty1 = ty1->type;
if (!isconst(ty) && (!isarray(ty) || !isconst(ty1)))
    ty = qual(CONST, ty);
t1 = genident(STATIC, ty, GLOBAL);
initglobal(t1, 1);
if (isarray(p->type) && p->type->size == 0
&& t1->type->size > 0)
    p->type = array(p->type->type,
        t1->type->size/t1->type->type->size, 0);
```

This static will never be modified, so a const qualifier is added to its type, which causes initglobal to define it in the LIT segment.

11.8 Finalization

As suggested in the previous section, checkref is also called at the end of compilation for each file-scope identifier, i.e., those with scope GLOBAL. This call comes from finalize, which also processes externals and globals.

⟨*decl.c functions*⟩+≡   ▲298 303▼

```
void finalize() {
    foreach(externals,   GLOBAL,    doextern, NULL);
    foreach(identifiers, GLOBAL,    doglobal, NULL);
    foreach(identifiers, GLOBAL,    checkref, NULL);
    foreach(constants,   CONSTANTS, doconst,  NULL);
}
```

Each of finalize's four lines processes a set of symbols in the tables shown in the calls to foreach. The first line processes the identifiers in externals. Recall that dcllocal installs locals that are declared extern in this table. Some of these declarations refer to identifiers that are also declared at file scope and thus have entries in identifiers. Some, however, refer to identifiers declared in other translation units, and these must be imported by the translation unit in which the extern declarations occur. doextern imports just these identifiers by calling the interface function import:

⟨*decl.c functions*⟩+≡   ▲303 304▼

```
static void doextern(p, cl) Symbol p; void *cl; {
    Symbol q = lookup(p->name, identifiers);

    if (q)
        q->ref += p->ref;
    else {
        (*IR->defsymbol)(p);
        (*IR->import)(p);
    }
}
```

296 checkref
 38 CONSTANTS
 40 constants
298 dcllocal
 89 defsymbol
457 " (MIPS)
491 " (SPARC)
520 " (X86)
305 doconst
304 doglobal
 40 externals
 41 foreach
 38 GLOBAL
 41 identifiers
 90 import
457 " (MIPS)
491 " (SPARC)
523 " (X86)
306 IR
 45 lookup
 38 ref

import cannot be called when dcllocal encounters an extern declaration because the local declaration can appear *before* the file-scope definition, and import must not be called for those identifiers.

The second call to foreach finalizes *tentative definitions* and file-scope extern declarations. A file-scope declaration of an object without an initializer that has no storage class or has the storage class static is a tentative definition. There may be more than one such declaration for an identifier, as long as the declarations specify compatible types. For example, the input

```
int x;
int x;
int x;
```

is valid and each declaration is a tentative definition for x. A file-scope declaration *with* an initializer is an *external definition*, and there may be only one such definition.

At the end of a translation unit, those file-scope identifiers that have only tentative definitions must be finalized; this is accomplished by assuming that the translation unit includes a file-scope external definition for the identifier with an initializer equal to zero. For example, x is finalized by assuming

```
int x = 0;
```

Uninitialized file-scope objects are thus initialized to zero by definition.
doglobal processes each identifier in identifiers.

⟨*decl.c functions*⟩+≡   303 305
```
static void doglobal(p, cl) Symbol p; void *cl; {
    if (!p->defined && (p->sclass == EXTERN
    || isfunc(p->type) && p->sclass == AUTO))
        (*IR->import)(p);
    else if (!p->defined && !isfunc(p->type)
    && (p->sclass == AUTO || p->sclass == STATIC)) {
        if (isarray(p->type)
        && p->type->size == 0 && p->type->type->size > 0)
            p->type = array(p->type->type, 1, 0);
        if (p->type->size > 0) {
            defglobal(p, BSS);
            (*IR->space)(p->type->size);
        } else
            error("undefined size for '%t %s'\n",
                p->type, p->name);
        p->defined = 1;
    }
    ⟨print an ANSI declaration for p 305⟩
}
```

array 61
AUTO 80
BSS 91
defglobal 265
defined 50
EXTERN 80
identifiers 41
import 90
(MIPS) " 457
(SPARC) " 491
(X86) " 523
IR 306
isarray 60
isfunc 60
space 92
(MIPS) " 459
(SPARC) " 492
(X86) " 524
STATIC 80

If an extern identifier or nonstatic function is undefined, it's imported, because it refers to a definition given in some other translation unit. Undefined objects — those with only tentative definitions — are defined in the BSS segment. Back ends must ensure that this segment is cleared before execution. Arrays receive special treatment: If the array's size is unspecified, it's defined as if it were declared with one element.

lcc's -P option causes doglobal to print an ANSI-style declaration on the standard error output.

⟨*print an ANSI declaration for* p 305⟩≡   304
```
    if (Pflag
    && !isfunc(p->type)
    && !p->generated && p->sclass != EXTERN)
        printdecl(p, p->type);
```

For functions, this output includes prototypes even if the functions are specified with old-style definitions. Editing this output helps convert old programs to ANSI C. See Exercise 4.5.

During compilation, most constants end up in dags and thus embedded in machine instructions. As specified by the configuration metrics shown in Section 5.1, some constants cannot appear in instructions, and string literals never appear in instructions. For each such constant, an anonymous static variable is generated, and doconst arranges to initialize that variable to the value of the constant.

⟨*decl.c functions*⟩+≡   ▲304
```
    void doconst(p, cl) Symbol p; void *cl; {
        if (p->u.c.loc) {
            defglobal(p->u.c.loc, LIT);
            if (isarray(p->type))
                (*IR->defstring)(p->type->size, p->u.c.v.p);
            else
                (*IR->defconst)(ttob(p->type), p->u.c.v);
            p->u.c.loc->defined = 1;
            p->u.c.loc = NULL;
        }
    }
```

The u.c.loc fields of symbols in the constants table point to the symbol for the anonymous static.

11.9   The Main Program

The function main, in main.c, calls program and finalize to initiate and conclude compilation, and it calls the interface functions progbeg and progend to let a back end do its initialization and finalization.

⟨*main.c functions*⟩≡
```
    int main(argc, argv) int argc; char *argv[]; {
        ⟨main 306⟩
        return errcnt > 0;
    }
```

errcnt is the number of errors detected during compilation, so lcc returns one when there are errors. On most systems, this exit code stops the compilation system from running subsequent processors, such as the assembler and linker.

Before `main` calls the initialization functions, it must point IR to the appropriate interface record, as specified in Section 5.11. The back end initializes the array `bindings` to pairs of names and pointers to their associated interface records. `main` uses its rightmost `-target=`*name* option to select the desired interface record:

⟨*main.c data*⟩≡   307

```
Interface *IR = NULL;
```

⟨main 306⟩≡   306   305

```
{
    int i, j;
    for (i = argc - 1; i > 0; i--)
        if (strncmp(argv[i], "-target=", 8) == 0)
            break;
    if (i > 0) {
        for (j = 0; bindings[j].name; j++)
            if (strcmp(&argv[i][8], bindings[j].name) == 0)
                break;
        if (bindings[j].ir)
            IR = bindings[j].ir;
        else {
            fprint(2, "%s: unknown target '%s'\n", argv[0],
                &argv[i][8]);
            exit(1);
        }
    }
}
if (!IR) {
    int i;
    fprint(2, "%s: must specify one of\n", argv[0]);
    for (i = 0; bindings[i].name; i++)
        fprint(2, "\t-target=%s\n", bindings[i].name);
    exit(1);
}
```

bindings 96
fprint 97
Interface 79
main 305
typeInit 58

If no `-target` option is given, lcc lists the available targets and exits. Once IR points to an interface record, the front end is *bound* to a target and this binding cannot be changed for the duration of translation unit.

Next, `main` initializes the front end's type system and parses its other options:

⟨main 306⟩+≡   306 307   305

```
typeInit();
argc = doargs(argc, argv);
```

In addition to processing the arguments the front end understands, doargs sets `infile` and `outfile` to the first and second nonoption arguments. These values name the source-file input file and the assembler language output file. If one or both of these files is specified, `main` opens the file and sets the appropriate file descriptor.

⟨*main.c data*⟩+≡   ▲306

```
static char *infile, *outfile;
```

⟨main 306⟩+≡   ▲306 307   305

```
if (infile && strcmp(infile, "-") != 0)
    if ((infd = open(infile, 0)) < 0) {
        fprint(2, "%s: can't read '%s'\n",
            argv[0], infile);
        exit(1);
    }
if (outfile && strcmp(outfile, "-") != 0)
    if ((outfd = creat(outfile, 0666)) < 0) {
        fprint(2, "%s: can't write '%s'\n",
            argv[0], outfile);
        exit(1);
    }
inputInit();
outputInit();
```

Once the descriptors are initialized, the input and output modules are initialized by the Init functions shown above, and the back end is initialized:

⟨main 306⟩+≡   ▲307 307   305

```
t = gettok();
(*IR->progbeg)(argc, argv);
```

doargs changes `argv` to hold just those options that it doesn't understand, which are assumed to be back-end options. doargs returns the number of these options, which is assigned to `argc` above. `program` compiles the source code

⟨main 306⟩+≡   ▲307 307   305

```
program();
```

and `main` concludes by calling `finalize` and the interface procedure `progend`, and by flushing the output:

⟨main 306⟩+≡   ▲307   305

```
finalize();
(*IR->progend)();
outflush();
```

Further Reading

Ritchie (1993) gives a detailed history of C's development and describes the origins and peculiarities of its declaration syntax, which is one of C's distinguishing characteristics and the one that is most often criticized. Sethi (1981) summarizes the ramifications of those design decisions, and proposes an alternative syntax for declarators in which pointers are denoted by the suffix ∧ as in Pascal instead of C's prefix *. If his alternative had been adopted, dclr and dclr1 would be much simpler.

Like most high-level languages, C demands that identifiers be declared before they are used (functions are the lone exception). This rule forces language designers to permit multiple declarations and induces rules such as those for C's tentative definitions. Much of the code in dcl*X*, doglobal, and doextern is devoted to dealing with these design decisions. Modula-3 (Nelson 1991) is one of the few languages that permits declarations and uses to appear in *any* order and avoids ordering rules altogether, which is simpler to understand. This design decision does have its own impact on the compiler, but that impact is no greater than the impact of C's rules governing multiple declarations.

Exercises

11.1 dclr1 accepts the erroneous declaration int *const const *p, yet lcc issues the expected diagnostic

```
illegal type 'const const pointer to int'
```

Where and how is this error detected?

11.2 dclr1's implementation looks peculiar. The syntax specification on page 266 suggests that dclr1 begin with a loop that consumes *pointer* followed by parsing the rest of *declarator*. Rewrite dclr1 using this approach. You'll find that you'll need to append the pointer portion of the inverted type to the inverted type constructed by parsing the rest of *declarator*. Change your implementation into one similar to dclr1's by applying program transformations.

11.3 Type names are used in casts and as operands to sizeof (see ⟨*type cast*⟩ and ⟨*sizeof*⟩). The syntax for type definitions is

> *type-name:*
>   { *type-specifier* | *type-qualifier* } [*abstract-declarator*]
>
> *abstract-declarator:*
>   * { *type-qualifier* }
>   *pointer* '(' *abstract-declarator* ')'

> { *suffix-abstract-declarator* }
> *pointer* { *suffix-abstract-declarator* }

suffix-abstract-declarator:
'[' [*constant-expression*] ']'
'(' *parameter-list* ')'

An *abstract-declarator* is a *declarator* without an embedded identifier. Implement

⟨*main.c exported functions*⟩≡   309
```
extern Type typename ARGS((void));
```

which parses *type-name*. dclr parses an *abstract-declarator* when its abstract argument is one, so typename can get dclr to do most of the work and takes less than 10 lines.

11.4 Implement

⟨*main.c exported functions*⟩+≡   309 310
```
extern void checklab ARGS((Symbol p, void *cl));
```

which is called for each symbol in stmtlabs. checklab issues an error if p is an undefined label.

11.5 dcllocal calls initglobal to parse the initialization for a static local, but it also parses an optional initialization. Nevertheless, lcc correctly rejects input such as

```
f() { static int x = 2  = 3; }
g() { static int y = 2; = 3; }
```

Explain how.

11.6 In fields, the field with the *largest* alignment determines the alignment of the entire structure, which is correct only because the sizes and alignments of the basic types must be powers of two. Revise fields so that it is correct for *any* positive values for the sizes and alignments of the basic types.

11.7 A bit field declaration like unsigned:0 causes subsequent bit fields to be placed in the next addressable storage unit, even if there's room in the current one. For example, if the declaration in Figure 11.1 is rewritten as

```
struct {
    char a[5];
    short s1, s2;
    unsigned code:3, :0, used:1;
```

```
    int amt:7, last;
    short id;
}
```

the code field stays in the unsigned at offset 12, and used lands to the right of amt in the unsigned at 16. Explain how fields handles this case.

11.8 Reading fields is excruciating. Write a new — presumably better — version and compare the two versions side-by-side. Is your version easier to understand? Do you have more confidence in its correctness?

11.9 The syntax for enumeration specifiers is

> *enum-specifier:*
>   enum [*identifier*] '{' *enumerator* { , *enumerator* } '}'
>   enum *identifier*
>
> *enumerator:*
>   *identifier*
>   *identifier = constant-expression*

Implement the parsing function for *enum-specifier*

⟨*main.c exported functions*⟩+≡   309
```
    extern Type enumdcl ARGS((void));
```

enumdcl is similar to structdcl, but much simpler, and there's no special rule about *enum-specifiers* appearing alone in declarations because there are no mutually recursive enumeration definitions. So an *enum-specifier* with *enumerators* must not refer to an existing enumeration type. enumdcl can use newstruct to define a new enumeration type, and it installs the enumeration constants in identifiers with storage class ENUM. The integer value of an enumeration constant is stored in the symbol's u.value field.

12

Generating Intermediate Code

The remaining missing pieces of lcc's front end are those that convert trees to dags and append them to the code list, and the functions gencode and emitcode, which back ends call from their function interface procedures to traverse code lists. These pieces appear in dag.c, which exports gencode and emitcode (see Section 5.10) and

⟨*dag.c exported functions*⟩+≡   93

```
extern void walk     ARGS((Tree e, int tlab, int flab));
extern Node listnodes ARGS((Tree e, int tlab, int flab));
extern Node newnode   ARGS((int op, Node left, Node right,
                            Symbol p));
```

walk and listnodes manipulate the forest of dags defined in Section 5.5. A sequence of forests represents the code for a function. The sequence is formed by the Gen, Jump, and Label entries in a code list. As outlined in Section 10.3, listnodes constructs a sequence incrementally; it converts the tree e to a dag and appends that dag to the forest. Figures 5.2 and 5.3 (pages 86 and 87) show examples of forests.

    walk converts the tree e to a dag by calling listnodes. It appends the forest to the code list in a Gen entry, and reinitializes the front end for a new forest. listnodes bears the complexity of converting trees to dags, so walk is easy:

⟨*dag.c functions*⟩≡   315

```
void walk(tp, tlab, flab) Tree tp; int tlab, flab; {
    listnodes(tp, tlab, flab);
    if (forest) {
        code(Gen)->u.forest = forest->link;
        forest->link = NULL;
        forest = NULL;
    }
    reset();
    deallocate(STMT);
}
```

⟨*dag.c data*⟩≡   314

```
static Node forest;
```

forest points to the last node in the current forest, which, while it's under construction, is a circularly linked list threaded through the link fields of nodes, so `forest->link` is the first node in the forest. `walk` turns this list into a noncircular linked list as it appends the forest to the code list.

The values of `tlab` and `flab` passed to `listnodes` and `walk` are label numbers and are used when `e` is a conditional expression, like a comparison. If `tlab` is nonzero, `listnodes` generates code that jumps to `tlab` when `e` is nonzero. If `flab` is nonzero, `listnodes` generates code that jumps to `flab` when `e` is zero. Section 10.4 shows how these labels are used in generating code for if statements. Only one of `tlab` or `flab` can be nonzero.

`newnode` allocates a node and initializes its fields with the values of its arguments. `newnode` is called by `definelab` and `jump` in the front end, and by back ends that must build dags to spill registers, for example.

`listnodes` also eliminates *common subexpressions* — expressions that compute redundant values. For example, Figure 8.1 (page 148) shows the tree for the expression `(a+b)+b*(a+b)`. The value of `a+b` is computed twice. The rvalue of `b` is also computed twice: once in `a+b` and again in the multiplication. The rvalue of `b` is a trivial computation, but a redundant one nonetheless. Eliminating these common subexpressions yields the dag shown in Figure 12.1. Lvalues can also be common expressions; `p`'s lvalue in the forest shown in Figure 5.3 (page 87) is an example. In these and other figures that depict dags, the operators are shown as they appear in Table 5.1. Omitting the + before suffixes distinguishes trees from dags.

Some trees built by the front end are really dags because they mirror the dags implicit in the source language by the augmented assignment and postfix operators. The trees for `a += b`, shown in Figure 8.2 and for `i++`, shown in Figure 8.3, are examples. `listnodes` must detect such idioms in order to generate intermediate code that evaluates the operands of these operators as dictated by the standard, which says that the operands of the prefix, suffix, and augmented assignment operators must be evaluated only once.

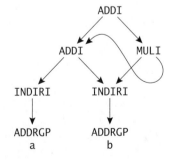

FIGURE 12.1 Dag for `(a+b)+b*(a+b)`.

Trees contain operators that are not part of the interface repertoire listed in Table 5.1. listnodes eliminates all occurrences of these operators, which are listed in Table 8.1, by generating code that implements them. For example, it implements AND by annotating nodes for the comparison operators with labels and by inserting jumps and defining labels where necessary. Similarly, it implements FIELD, which specifies bit-field extraction or assignment, by appropriate combinations of shifting and masking.

A *basic block* is a sequence of instructions that have a single entry and a single exit with straight-line code in between; if one instruction in the block is executed, all the instructions are executed. Instructions that are targets of jumps and that follow a conditional or unconditional jump begin basic blocks. Compilers often use a *flow graph* to represent a function. The nodes in a flow graph are basic blocks and the directed arcs indicate the possible flow of control between basic blocks. lcc's code list is not a flow graph, and the forests in Gen entries do not represent basic blocks because they can include jumps and labels. They represent what might be called *expanded basic blocks*: They do have single entry points, but they can have multiple exits and multiple internal execution paths. As the implementation of listnodes below reveals, this design makes common expressions available across entire expanded basic blocks in some cases. It thus extends the lifetimes of these subexpressions beyond basic blocks with little extra effort.

12.1 Eliminating Common Subexpressions

listnodes takes a Tree t and builds the corresponding Node n. Trees are defined in Section 8.1, and nodes are defined in Section 5.5. n->op comes from t->op, and the elements of n->syms come from t->u.sym, or from installing t->u.v in the constants table, or are fabricated from other constants by listnodes. The elements of n->kids come from the nodes for the corresponding elements of t->kids. n also has a count field, which is the number of nodes that reference n as an operand.

Nodes are built from the bottom up: n is built by traversing t in post-order with the equivalent of

```
l = listnodes(t->kids[0], 0, 0);
r = listnodes(t->kids[1], 0, 0);
n = node(t->op, l, r, t->u.sym);
```

node allocates a new node and uses its arguments to initialize the fields. To eliminate common subexpressions, node must determine if the requested node has already been built; that is, if there's a node with the same fields that can be used instead of building a new one.

node keeps a table of available nodes and consults this table before allocating a new node. When it does allocate a new node, it adds that

Called With			Builds	Returns
ADDRG+P		a	1=(ADDRGP a)	1
INDIR+I	1		2=(INDIRI 1)	2
ADDRG+P		b	3=(ADDRGP b)	3
INDIR+I	3		4=(INDIRI 3)	4
ADD+I	2	4	5=(ADDI 2 4)	5
ADDRG+P		b		3
INDIR+I	3			4
ADDRG+P		a		1
INDIR+I	1			2
ADDRG+P		b		3
INDIR+I	3			4
ADD+I	2	4		5
MUL+I	3	5	6=(MULI 3 5)	6
ADD+I	5	6	7=(ADDI 5 6)	7

TABLE 12.1　Calls to node for (a+b)+b*(a+b).

node to the table. Building the dag shown in Figure 12.1 from the tree shown in Figure 8.1 (page 148) illustrates how this table is constructed and used. Table 12.1 shows the sequence of calls to node, the node each builds, if any, and the value returned. The middle column shows the evolution of the table consulted by node. The nodes are denoted by numbers. The first call is for the ADDRG+P tree in the lower left corner of Figure 8.1; node's table is empty, so it builds a node for the ADDRG+P and returns it. The next four calls, which traverse the remainder of the tree for a+b, are similar; each builds the corresponding node and returns it. As nodes are returned, they're used as operands in other nodes. When node is called for the ADDRG+P node at the leaf of the left operand of the MUL+I, it finds that node in the table (node 3) and returns it. Similarly, it also finds that node 4 corresponds to (INDIRI 3). node continues to find nodes in the table, including the node for the commmon subexpression a+b.

The nodes depicted in the second column of the table above are stored in a hash table:

node 315

⟨*dag.c data*⟩+≡　　　　　　　　　　　　　　　　　　　▲
311 333
▼
```
static struct dag {
    struct node node;
    struct dag *hlink;
} *buckets[16];
int nodecount;
```

dag structures hold a node and a pointer to another dag in the same hash bucket. nodecount is the total number of nodes in buckets. The hash table rarely has more than a few tens of nodes, which is why it has only 16 buckets. node searches buckets for a node with the same operator, operands, and symbol and returns it if it's found; otherwise, it builds a new node, adds it to buckets, and returns it.

⟨*dag.c functions*⟩+≡   311 315

```
static Node node(op, l, r, sym)
int op; Node l, r; Symbol sym; {
    int i;
    struct dag *p;

    i = (opindex(op)^((unsigned)sym>>2))&(NELEMS(buckets)-1);
    for (p = buckets[i]; p; p = p->hlink)
        if (p->node.op      == op && p->node.syms[0] == sym
        &&  p->node.kids[0] == l  && p->node.kids[1] == r)
            return &p->node;
    p = dagnode(op, l, r, sym);
    p->hlink = buckets[i];
    buckets[i] = p;
    ++nodecount;
    return &p->node;
}
```

dagnode allocates and initializes a new dag and its embedded node. It also increments the count fields of the operand nodes, if there are any.

⟨*dag.c functions*⟩+≡   315 315

```
static struct dag *dagnode(op, l, r, sym)
int op; Node l, r; Symbol sym; {
    struct dag *p;

    NEWO(p, FUNC);
    p->node.op = op;
    if ((p->node.kids[0] = l) != NULL)
        ++l->count;
    if ((p->node.kids[1] = r) != NULL)
        ++r->count;
    p->node.syms[0] = sym;
    return p;
}
```

listnodes calls node to use a node for a common subexpression or to allocate a new node. It calls newnode to bypass the search and build a new node that is *not* added to buckets:

⟨*dag.c functions*⟩+≡   315 316

```
Node newnode(op, l, r, sym) int op; Node l, r; Symbol sym; {
    return &dagnode(op, l, r, sym)->node;
}
```

Only newnode can be used by back ends to build nodes for their own uses, such as generating code to spill registers.

Nodes appear in buckets as long as the values they represent are valid. Assignments and function calls can invalidate some or all nodes in buckets. For example, in

```
c = a + b;
a = a/2;
d = a + b;
```

the value of a+b computed in the third line isn't the same as the value computed in the first line. The second line's assignment to a invalidates the node (INDIRI a) where a is the node for the lvalue of a. Operators with side effects, such as ASGN and CALL, must remove the nodes that they invalidate. While these nodes are different for each such operator, lcc handles only two cases: Assignments to an identifier remove nodes for its rvalue, and all other operators with side effects remove *all* nodes. kill handles assignments:

⟨*dag.c functions*⟩+≡   315 317

```
static void kill(p) Symbol p; {
    int i;
    struct dag **q;

    for (i = 0; i < NELEMS(buckets); i++)
        for (q = &buckets[i]; *q; )
            if (⟨*q represents p's rvalue 316⟩) {
                *q = (*q)->hlink;
                --nodecount;
            } else
                q = &(*q)->hlink;
}
```

The obvious rvalue of p is a dag of the form (INDIR (ADDRxP p)), where the ADDRxP is any of the address operators. The less obvious case is a dag of the form (INDIR α) where α is an arbitrary address computation, which *might* compute the address of p. Both cases are detected by

⟨*q represents p's rvalue 316⟩≡   316

```
generic((*q)->node.op) == INDIR &&
(!isaddrop((*q)->node.kids[0]->op)
 || (*q)->node.kids[0]->syms[0] == p)
```

Only the INDIR nodes must be removed, because that's enough to make subsequent searches fail. For example, after the assignment a = a/2, the node for a+b remains in buckets. But the a+b in the assignment to d won't find it because the reference to the rvalue of a builds a new node, which causes a new node to be built for a+b. The sequence of calls to

Called With			Builds	Kills	Returns
ADDRG+P		c	1=(ADDRGP c)		1
ADDRG+P		a	2=(ADDRGP a)		2
INDIR+I	2		3=(INDIRI 2)		3
ADDRG+P		b	4=(ADDRGP b)		4
INDIR+I	4		5=(INDIRI 4)		5
ADD+I	3	5	6=(ADDI 3 5)		6
ASGN+I	1	6			7
ADDRG+P		a			2
INDIR+I	2				3
CNST+I		2	8=(CNSTI 2)		8
DIV+I	3	8	9=(DIVI 3 8)		9
ASGN+I	2	9		3	10
ADDRG+P		d	11=(ADDRGP d)		11
ADDRG+P		a			2
INDIR+I	2		12=(INDIRI 2)		12
ADDRG+P		b			4
INDIR+I	4				5
ADD+I	12	5	13=(ADDI 12 5)		13
ASGN+I	11	13			14

TABLE 12.2 Calls to node for c = a + b; a = a/2; d = a + b.

node for this example appears in Table 12.2. The rvalue of a in d = a + b reuses the lvalue but builds a new INDIRI node because the assignment a = a/2 killed node 3. Assignments build nodes by calling newnode, so they don't appear in buckets.

reset removes all nodes in buckets by clearing both buckets and nodecount:

⟨*dag.c functions*⟩+≡   316 318

```
static void reset() {
    if (nodecount > 0)
        memset(buckets, 0, sizeof buckets);
    nodecount = 0;
}
```

12.2 Building Nodes

listnodes builds a node for its argument tree by calling itself recursively on the tree's operands, calling node or newnode depending on the operator, and calling kill or reset when necessary.

317 321

⟨*dag.c functions*⟩+≡

```
Node listnodes(tp, tlab, flab) Tree tp; int tlab, flab; {
    Node p = NULL, l, r;

    if (tp == NULL)
        return NULL;
    if (tp->node)
        return tp->node;
    switch (generic(tp->op)) {
    ⟨listnodes cases 318⟩
    }
    tp->node = p;
    return p;
}
```

tp->node points to the node for the tree tp. This field marks the tree as visited by listnodes, and ensures that listnodes returns the correct node for trees that are really dags, such as those shown in Figures 8.2 and 8.3 (pages 167 and 158). The multiply referenced subtrees in these idioms are visited more than once; the first visit builds the node and the subsequent visits simply return it.

The switch statement in listnodes collects the operators into groups that have the same traversal and node-building code:

⟨listnodes *cases* 318⟩≡   318

```
case AND:   { ⟨AND 323⟩ } break;
case OR:    { ⟨OR⟩ } break;
case NOT:   { ⟨NOT 322⟩ }
case COND:  { ⟨COND 325⟩ } break;
case CNST:  { ⟨CNST 327⟩ } break;
case RIGHT: { ⟨RIGHT 335⟩ } break;
case JUMP:  { ⟨JUMP 321⟩ } break;
case CALL:  { ⟨CALL 332⟩ } break;
case ARG:   { ⟨ARG 334⟩ } break;
case EQ:  case NE: case GT: case GE: case LE:
case LT:    { ⟨EQ..LT 321⟩ } break;
case ASGN:  { ⟨ASGN 328⟩ } break;
case BOR: case BAND: case BXOR:
case ADD: case SUB:  case RSH:
case LSH:   { ⟨ADD..RSH 319⟩ } break;
case DIV: case MUL:
case MOD:   { ⟨DIV..MOD⟩ } break;
case RET:   { ⟨RET⟩ } break;
case CVC: case CVD: case CVF: case CVI:
case CVP: case CVS: case CVU: case BCOM:
case NEG:   { ⟨CV𝑥,NEG,BCOM 319⟩ } break;
```

```
case INDIR: { ⟨INDIR 319⟩ } break;
case FIELD: { ⟨FIELD 320⟩ } break;
case ADDRG:
case ADDRF: { ⟨ADDRG,ADDRF 319⟩ } break;
case ADDRL: { ⟨ADDRL 319⟩ } break;
```

The largest operator group is the one for the unary operators. The traversal code visits the lone operand and builds the node:

⟨CV*x*,NEG,BCOM 319⟩≡   318
```
l = listnodes(tp->kids[0], 0, 0);
p = node(tp->op, l, NULL, NULL);
```

The traversal code for the binary operators is similar:

⟨ADD..RSH 319⟩≡   318
```
l = listnodes(tp->kids[0], 0, 0);
r = listnodes(tp->kids[1], 0, 0);
p = node(tp->op, l, r, NULL);
```

DIV, MUL, and MOD aren't included in this case because they must be treated as calls if the interface flag mulops_calls is set; see Exercise 12.5.

The three address operators build nodes for the lvalues of the symbols they reference:

⟨ADDRG,ADDRF 319⟩≡   319
```
p = node(tp->op, NULL, NULL, tp->u.sym);
```

⟨ADDRL 319⟩≡   319
```
if (tp->u.sym->temporary)
    addlocal(tp->u.sym);
p = node(tp->op, NULL, NULL, tp->u.sym);
```

If a local is a temporary, it may not yet appear on the code list. addlocal adds a Local code list entry for the temporary, if necessary. These entries are not made earlier because some temporaries are never used and thus need never be announced. Waiting until the last possible moment to generate Local code-list entries effectively discards unused temporaries.

INDIR trees build nodes for rvalues, but locations declared volatile demand special treatment:

⟨INDIR 319⟩≡   319
```
Type ty = tp->kids[0]->type;
l = listnodes(tp->kids[0], 0, 0);
if (isptr(ty))
    ty = unqual(ty)->type;
if (isvolatile(ty)
|| (isstruct(ty) && unqual(ty)->u.sym->u.s.vfields))
```

```
        p = newnode(tp->op, 1, NULL, NULL);
    else
        p = node(tp->op, 1, NULL, NULL);
```

If the lvalue has a type (POINTER T), INDIR is treated like the other unary operators. But if the lvalue has a type (POINTER (VOLATILE T)), every read of the rvalue that appears in the source code must actually read the rvalue at execution. This constraint means that the rvalue must not be treated as a common subexpression, so the node is built by newnode. This constraint also applies to lvalues with types (POINTER (STRUCT ...)) and (POINTER (UNION ...)) where one or more fields of the structure or union are declared volatile.

Bit fields are referenced by FIELD trees. An assignment to a bit field appears as an ASGN tree with a FIELD tree as its left operand; the case for ASGN, described in Section 12.4, detects this idiom. Appearances of FIELD in other trees denote the rvalue of the bit field. FIELD operators can appear only in trees, so listnodes must synthesize bit-field extraction from other operations, such as shifting and masking.

There are two cases for extracting a bit field of s bits that lies m bits from the right of the unsigned or integer in which it appears. If the field is unsigned, it could be extracted by shifting it to the right m bits then ANDing it with a mask of s ones. If the field is signed, however, its most significant bit is treated as a sign bit and must be extended when the field is fetched. Thus, a signed field can be extracted by code like

$$((\text{int})((*p)<<(32 - m)))>>(32 - s)$$

assuming a 32-bit word and that p points to the word that holds the field. This expression shifts the word left so the field's most significant bit is in the sign bit, then shifts it right arithmetically, which drags the sign bit into the vacated bits. This expression also works for the unsigned case by replacing the cast to an int with a cast to an unsigned, which is what listnodes uses for both cases.

⟨FIELD 320⟩ ≡   319
```
    Tree q = shtree(RSH,
        shtree(LSH, tp->kids[0],
            consttree(fieldleft(tp->u.field), inttype)),
        consttree(8*tp->type->size - fieldsize(tp->u.field),
            inttype));
    p = listnodes(q, 0, 0);
```

fieldleft is $32 - m$ and the first argument to consttree is $32 - s$. The type of the tree built by the inner call to shtree depends on the type of tp->kids[0] and will be int or unsigned, which causes the outer shtree to generate an RSH+I or an RSH+U.

12.3 Flow of Control

The unary and binary operators described in the previous section contribute nodes to the node table, and they're referenced by other nodes,
but, except for INDIR nodes, they never appear as roots in the forest. A
node appears as a root if it has a side effect or if it must be evaluated
before the nodes in the dags further down the forest. The appearance of
the INDIRP node as a root in Figure 5.3 on page 87 is an example of this
second case. Assignments, calls, returns, labels, jumps, and conditional
jumps are examples of the first case. Some of these operators also affect the node table because they can alter flow of control. Jumps are the
simplest:

⟨JUMP 321⟩≡   318
```
    l = listnodes(tp->kids[0], 0, 0);
    list(newnode(JUMPV, l, NULL, NULL));
    reset();
```

The node table must be reset at jumps since none of the expressions in
the table can be used in the code that follows the jump. The JUMPV node
is *listed* — appended to the forest as a root — by list:

⟨dag.c functions⟩+≡   ▲318 323▼
```
    static void list(p) Node p; {
        if (p && p->link == NULL) {
            if (forest) {
                p->link = forest->link;
                forest->link = p;
            } else
                p->link = p;
            forest = p;
        }
    }
```

311	forest
318	listnodes
315	newnode
317	reset

forest is a circularly linked list, so it points to the *last* node on the list,
unless it's null, which causes list to initialize forest. The link field
also marks the node as a root, and list won't list roots more than once.

The comparison operators illustrate the use of the arguments tlab
and flab to listnodes. Only one of tlab or flab can be nonzero. The
operator jumps to tlab if the outcome of the comparison is true and to
flab if the outcome is false. Nodes for comparison operators carry the
destination as a label symbol in their syms[0] fields. This symbol is the
destination when the comparison is true; there is no way to specify a
destination for a false outcome. The case for the comparison operators
thus uses the inverse operator when flab is nonzero:

⟨EQ..LT 321⟩≡   318
```
    Node p;
```

```
l = listnodes(tp->kids[0], 0, 0);
r = listnodes(tp->kids[1], 0, 0);
if (tlab)
    list(newnode(tp->op, l, r, findlabel(tlab)));
else if (flab) {
    int op = generic(tp->op);
    switch (generic(op)) {
    case EQ: op = NE + optype(tp->op); break;
    case NE: op = EQ + optype(tp->op); break;
    case GT: op = LE + optype(tp->op); break;
    case LT: op = GE + optype(tp->op); break;
    case GE: op = LT + optype(tp->op); break;
    case LE: op = GT + optype(tp->op); break;
    }
    list(newnode(op, l, r, findlabel(flab)));
}
if (forest && forest->syms[0])
    forest->syms[0]->ref++;
```

listnodes also handles the control-flow operators that appear only in trees: AND, OR, NOT, and COND. NOT is handled by simply reversing the true and false labels in a recursive call to listnodes:

⟨NOT 322⟩ ≡   318
```
    return listnodes(tp->kids[0], flab, tlab);
```

AND and OR use *short-circuit evaluation*: They must stop evaluating their arguments as soon as the outcome is known. For example, in

```
if (i >= 0 && i < 10 && a[i] > max) max = a[i];
```

a[i] must not be evaluated if i is less than zero or greater than or equal to 10. The operands of AND and OR are always conditional expressions or constants (andtree calls cond for each operand), so the cases for these operators need only define the appropriate true and false labels and pass them to the calls on listnodes for the operands.

Suppose tlab is zero and flab is L; the short-circuit code generated for e_1 && e_2 has the form

```
    if e₁ == 0 goto L
    if e₂ == 0 goto L
```

In other words, if e_1 is zero, execution continues at L and e_2 is not evaluated. Otherwise, e_2 is evaluated and execution continues at L if e_1 is nonzero but e_2 is zero. Control falls through only when both e_1 and e_2 are nonzero. When tlab is L and flab is zero, control falls through when e_1 *or* e_2 is zero, and execution continues at L only when e_1 and e_2 are both nonzero. The generated code has the form

```
        if e₁ == 0 goto L'
        if e₂ != 0 goto L
   L':
```

In this case, if e_1 is zero, control falls through *without* evaluating e_2. The
listnodes code for AND is thus

⟨AND 323⟩≡   318
```
   if (depth++ == 0) reset();
   if (flab) {
      listnodes(tp->kids[0], 0, flab);
      listnodes(tp->kids[1], 0, flab);
   } else {
      listnodes(tp->kids[0], 0, flab = genlabel(1));
      listnodes(tp->kids[1], tlab, 0);
      labelnode(flab);
   }
   depth--;
```

The code for OR is similar; see Exercise 12.2. Exercise 12.15 explains the
purpose of the static integer depth and the call to reset.
    labelnode appends a LABELV node to the forest:

⟨dag.c functions⟩+≡   ▲ 321 327
                                                                            ▼
```
   static void labelnode(lab) int lab; {
      if (forest && forest->op == LABELV)
         equatelab(findlabel(lab), forest->syms[0]);
      else
         list(newnode(LABELV, NULL, NULL, findlabel(lab)));
      reset();
   }
```

If the last node in the forest *is* a label, there's no reason to append another one; the new label, lab, is made a synonym for the existing label
as described in Section 10.9. Common subexpressions in the node table
must be discarded at a label because there can be more than one path
to the subsequent code, so labelnode calls reset.
    As detailed in Section 8.6, OR and AND are treated as right-associative
operators, so expressions such as e_1 && e_2 && ... && e_n build right-heavy
trees, as depicted in Figure 12.2.
    This arrangement guarantees that the recursive calls to listnodes in
the code above visit the expressions e_i in the correct order to yield short-
circuit evaluation. It also helps eliminate common subexpressions that
appear in the e_i. For example, in

```
   if (a[i] && a[i]+b[i] > 0 && a[i]+b[i] < 10) ...
```

where a and b are integer arrays, the address computation 4*i, the rvalues of a[i] and b[i], and the sum a[i]+b[i] are each computed once

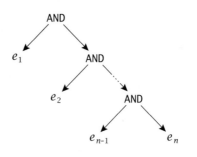

FIGURE 12.2 Tree for e_1 && e_2 && ... && e_n.

and reused as necessary. The AND tree is passed to listnodes with flab equal to, say, 2, and the recursive calls descend the tree passing 2 as flab. There are no intervening calls to reset, so the second and third subexpressions can reuse values computed in first and second subexpressions. The forest for this statement is shown in Figure 12.3. The 2s under the comparison operators and under the LABELV denote the symbol-table pointers to the label 2 in their syms[0] fields.

The expression e ? l : r yields the COND tree shown in Figure 12.4. The RIGHT tree serves only to carry the two assignment trees. The generated code is similar to the code for an if statement:

```
        if e == 0 goto L
        t1 = l
        goto L + 1
L:      t1 = r
L + 1:
```

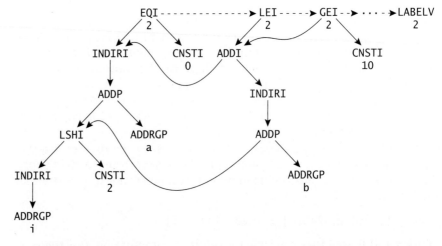

FIGURE 12.3 Forest for a[i] && a[i]+b[i] > 0 && a[i]+b[i] < 10.

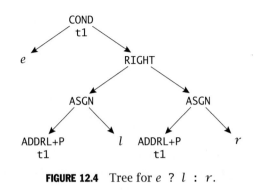

FIGURE 12.4 Tree for *e* ? *l* : *r*.

The rvalue of t1 is the result of the COND expression. The assignments to
t1 are omitted if the value of the conditional expression is not used or
if both *l* and *r* are void expressions. The code for COND begins by adding
a LOCAL code list entry for t1, if it's present; generating L and $L + 1$; and
traversing the conditional expression *e* with L as the false label.

⟨COND 325⟩≡   325   318
```
  Tree q = tp->kids[1];
  if (tp->u.sym)
     addlocal(tp->u.sym);
  flab = genlabel(2);
  listnodes(tp->kids[0], 0, flab);
  reset();
```

Next, the code for this case generates nodes for first assignment, the
jump, L, the second assignment, and $L + 1$:

⟨COND 325⟩+≡   325 326   318
```
  listnodes(q->kids[0], 0, 0);
  ⟨equate LABEL to L + 1 325⟩
  list(jump(flab + 1));
  labelnode(flab);
  listnodes(q->kids[1], 0, 0);
  ⟨equate LABEL to L + 1 325⟩
  labelnode(flab + 1);
```

⟨*equate* LABEL *to* $L + 1$ 325⟩≡   325
```
  if (forest->op == LABELV) {
     equatelab(forest->syms[0], findlabel(flab + 1));
     unlist();
  }
```

If the last node in either arm is a label, it can be equated to $L + 1$ and
removed from the forest, which is what unlist does. Removing this label
in the first arm can eliminate a branch to a branch; see Exercise 12.7.

The value of the conditional expression, if there is one, is in the temporary t1. The COND tree has contributed the nodes that generate the assignments to t1, but the COND tree itself has no value. The node that's returned — and that annotates the COND tree — is the result of generating a node for the rvalue of t1:

⟨COND 325⟩+≡   325   318

```
if (tp->u.sym)
    p = listnodes(idtree(tp->u.sym), 0, 0);
```

The call to reset after traversing tp->kids[0], the tree for *e*, discards common subexpressions before traversing *l* or *r*, because conditional operands may be evaluated before other operands in subexpressions. For example, in the assignment

```
n = a[i] + (i>0?a[i]:0);
```

the conditional is evaluated before the addition's left operand even though the left operand's tree is traversed first. Without the call to reset, the node for the common subexpression a[i] would appear in the node table when the tree for (i>0?a[i]:0) is traversed, and the generated code would be equivalent to

$$
\begin{aligned}
&\text{if i} <= 0 \text{ goto } L_1 \\
&\text{t2 = a[i]} \\
&\text{t1 = t2} \\
&\text{goto } L_2 \\
L_1:\quad &\text{t1 = 0} \\
L_2:\quad &\text{n = t2 + t1}
\end{aligned}
$$

where t1 holds the value of the conditional, and t2 holds the value of a[i]. t2 is computed only in the then arm of the conditional, but is used to compute the sum. reset must be called whenever the evaluation order might be different than the traversal order, and when the generated code might have multiple execution paths.

Most constants appear as operands to the unary and binary operators, but constant folding makes it possible for an integer constant to appear as the first operand to the comparisons and hence to COND. For example, the statement

```
if (2.5) ...
```

causes conditional to build the expression 2.5 != 0.0, which simplify folds to a tree for the integer constant 1. ifstmt passes this tree to listnodes with a nonzero flab. For an integer CNST tree, listnodes generates a jump if tlab is nonzero and the constant is nonzero, or if flab is nonzero and the constant is zero:

⟨CNST 327⟩≡   327   318
```
    Type ty = unqual(tp->type);
    if (tlab || flab) {
        if (tlab && tp->u.v.i != 0)
            list(jump(tlab));
        else if (flab && tp->u.v.i == 0)
            list(jump(flab));
    }
```

For the example above, *nothing* is generated for the CNST tree, which is exactly what the programmer intended. A jump *is* generated for code like

```
    while (1) ...
```

Constants that don't appear in conditional contexts yield CNST nodes, unless their types dictate that they should be placed out of line:

⟨CNST 327⟩+≡   327   318
```
    else if (ty->u.sym->addressed)
        p = listnodes(cvtconst(tp), 0, 0);
    else
        p = node(tp->op, NULL, NULL, constant(ty, tp->u.v));
```

typeInit sets the addressed flag in a basic type's symbol-table entry to one if constants of that type cannot appear in instructions. Thus, a constant whose type's symbol has addressed set is placed in a variable and references to it are replaced by references to the rvalue of the variable. The constant 0.5 in Figure 1.2 (page 6) is an example; it appears in the tree, but ends up in a variable as shown in Figure 1.3. cvtconst generates the anonymous static variable, if necessary, and returns a tree for the rvalue of that variable:

⟨dag.c functions⟩+≡   323 337
```
    Tree cvtconst(p) Tree p; {
        Symbol q = constant(p->type, p->u.v);
        Tree e;

        if (q->u.c.loc == NULL)
            q->u.c.loc = genident(STATIC, p->type, GLOBAL);
        if (isarray(p->type)) {
            e = tree(ADDRG+P, atop(p->type), NULL, NULL);
            e->u.sym = q->u.c.loc;
        } else
            e = idtree(q->u.c.loc);
        return e;
    }
```

These variables are initialized when finalize calls doconst at the end of compilation.

12.4   Assignments

Nodes for assignments are always listed and return no value. Trees for assignments, however, mirror the semantics of assignment in C, which returns the value of its left operand. The listnodes case for assignment traverses the operands, and builds and lists the assignment node. It begins by processing the operands:

⟨ASGN 328⟩≡   328   318
```
    if (tp->kids[0]->op == FIELD) {
        ⟨l, r ← for a bit-field assignment 329⟩
    } else {
        l = listnodes(tp->kids[0], 0, 0);
        r = listnodes(tp->kids[1], 0, 0);
    }
    list(newnode(tp->op, l, r, NULL));
    forest->syms[0] = intconst(tp->kids[1]->type->size);
    forest->syms[1] = intconst(tp->kids[1]->type->align);
```

An ASGN's syms fields point to symbol-table entries for constants that give the size and alignment of the value (see page 83). Assignments to bit fields are described below.

An assignment invalidates nodes in the node table that depend on the previous value of the left operand. lcc handles just two cases:

⟨ASGN 328⟩+≡   328 329   318
```
    if (isaddrop(tp->kids[0]->op)
    && !tp->kids[0]->u.sym->computed)
        kill(tp->kids[0]->u.sym);
    else
        reset();
```

If the left operand is the address of a source-language variable or a temporary, the assignment kills only nodes for its rvalue. If the left operand is the address of a computed variable or a computed address, the assignment clears the node table. A computed variable represents the address of variable plus a constant, such as a field reference, and is generated by addrtree. Assignments to computed variables are like assignments to array elements — an assignment to a single element kills everything. Less drastic measures require more sophisticated analyses; those that offer the most benefit, like global common subexpression elimination, require data-flow analysis of the entire function, which lcc is not designed to accommodate.

The value of an assignment is the new value of the left operand, which is the possibly converted value of the right operand, so listnodes arranges for that node to annotate the ASGN tree:

⟨ASGN 328⟩+≡   3̂28   318
   p = listnodes(tp->kids[1], 0, 0);

tp->kids[1] has already been visited and annotated with the node that's assigned to r above. So p usually equals r, except for assignments to bit fields, which compute r differently and may not visit tp->kids[1] at all, as detailed below.

A FIELD tree as the left operand of ASGN tree identifies an assignment to a bit field. These assignments are compiled into the appropriate sequence of shifts and bitwise logical operations. Consider, for example, the multiple assignment w = x.amt = y where x is defined in Figure 11.1 on page 279 and w and y are global integers. The first assignment, x.amt = y, is compiled into the equivalent of

$$*\beta = ((*\beta)\&0xFFFFFF80) \mid (y\&0x7F);$$

where β denotes the address x+16. The word at x+16 is fetched, the bits corresponding to the field amt are cleared, the rightmost 7 bits of y are ORed into the cleared bits, and the resulting value is stored back into x+16. This expression isn't quite correct: The value of x.amt = y, which is assigned to w, is *not* y, it's the new value of x.amt. This value is equal to y unless its most significant bit is one, in which case that bit must be sign-extended if the result of the assignment is used. So, if y is 255, w becomes −1.

listnodes handles this case by building an ASGN tree whose right operand computes the correct value. For w = x.amt = y, it builds a right operand that's equivalent to (y<<25)>>25, which is what should appear in place of y in the assignment to $*\beta$ above. Figure 12.5 shows the complete tree for this multiple assignment.

The code for a bit-field assignment builds a tree for the expression shown above, and calls listnodes to traverse it.

⟨l, r ← *for a bit-field assignment* 329⟩≡   328
```
    Tree  x = tp->kids[0]->kids[0];
    Field f = tp->kids[0]->u.field;
    reset();
    l = listnodes(lvalue(x), 0, 0);
    if (fieldsize(f) < 8*f->type->size) {
        unsigned int fmask = fieldmask(f);
        unsigned int  mask = fmask<<fieldright(f);
        Tree q = tp->kids[1];
        ⟨q ← the r.h.s. tree 330⟩
        r = listnodes(q, 0, 0);
    } else
        r = listnodes(tp->kids[1], 0, 0);
```

The u.sym field of the FIELD tree tucked under the ASGN tree points to a field structure that describes the bit field. For the amt field, fmask and

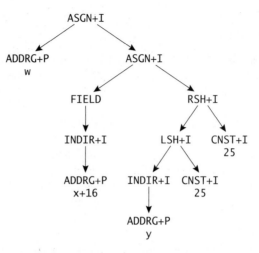

FIGURE 12.5   Tree for w = x.amt = y.

mask are both $7F_{16}$; the complement of mask is $FFFFFF80_{16}$. listnodes treats an assignment to a bit field like an assignment to an array element, and thus clears the node table.

There are two cases of assigning constants to bit fields that merit special treatment. If the constant is zero, the assignment clears the field, which can be done more simply by ANDing the word with the complement of mask:

⟨q ← *the r.h.s. tree* 330⟩≡   330   329

```
if (q->op == CNST+I && q->u.v.i == 0
|| q->op == CNST+U && q->u.v.u == 0)
    q = bittree(BAND, x, consttree(~mask, unsignedtype));
```

If the constant is equal to $2^s - 1$ where s is the size of the bit field, the assignment sets all of the bits in the field, which can be done by ORing the word with mask:

⟨q ← *the r.h.s. tree* 330⟩+≡   330 331   329

```
else if (q->op == CNST+I && (q->u.v.i&fmask) == fmask
||          q->op == CNST+U && (q->u.v.u&fmask) == fmask)
    q = bittree(BOR, x, consttree(mask, unsignedtype));
```

These improvements make assignments of constants to 1-bit fields as efficient as the more verbose logical operations. For example, x.used = 1 is compiled into the equivalent of

$$*\alpha = *\alpha \mid 0x8;$$

where α denotes the address x+12.

The general case requires the two ANDs and the OR shown in the assignment to $*\beta$ above.

⟨q ← *the r.h.s. tree* 330⟩+≡   330   329

```
  else {
    listnodes(q, 0, 0);
    q = bittree(BOR,
        bittree(BAND, rvalue(lvalue(x)),
            consttree(~mask, unsignedtype)),
        bittree(BAND, shtree(LSH, cast(q, unsignedtype),
            consttree(fieldright(f), inttype)),
            consttree(mask, unsignedtype)));
  }
```

Figure 12.6 shows the forest for the multiple assignment w = x.amt = y, which falls into this general case. In all three cases, q is the tree for the right-hand side of the assignment to the bit field, but tp->kids[1] is the tree that represents the value of the assignment. For example, it's the RSHI node in Figure 12.6 that annotates the bit-field ASGN+I tree in Figure 12.5, and is thus used as the right operand for the assignment to w.

The final else clause in ⟨q ← *the r.h.s. tree*⟩ rebuilds the rvalue of the word that holds the field because that word may have been changed by tp->kids[1]. For example, in

```
struct { int b:4, c:4; } x;
x.c = x.b++;
```

175	cast
193	consttree
66	fieldright
318	listnodes
169	lvalue
361	mask
169	rvalue
58	unsignedtype

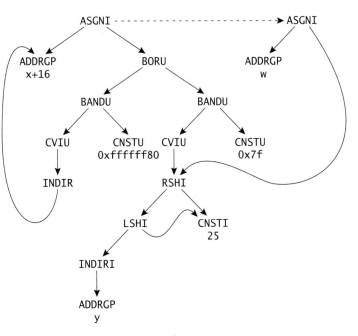

FIGURE 12.6 Forest for w = x.amt = y.

x.b++ changes the word that holds x.c. The tree returned by bittree's second argument, rvalue(lvalue(x)) in the fragment above, causes that word to be fetched again. If x were used instead, the assignment to x.c would use the value of the word *before* x.b is changed, and the new value of x.b would be lost.

12.5 Function Calls

Figure 12.7 shows the form of a CALL+B tree, which is the most general form of CALL. As explained in Section 9.3, the right operand is the address of a temporary to which the value returned is assigned. The other CALLs have only one operand.

CALL+B complicates the listnodes case for CALL, because if the interface wants_callb is zero, the right operand is passed as a hidden first argument and a CALLV node is used instead of a CALLB node. Another complication is that the ARG trees appear down in the CALL tree's left operand, but the corresponding nodes are listed, and the CALL node's left operand is the address of the function (see page 85). The interface flag left_to_right supplies the last complication: The arguments are evaluated left to right if that flag is one and right-to-left if it's zero. This evaluation order also applies to the hidden first argument when wants_callb is zero. Figure 12.8 shows the form of forest generated for the tree in Figure 12.7 when wants_callb is zero and left_to_right is one. The leading ARGP node is the hidden first argument.

firstarg 333
left_to_right 88
listnodes 318
wants_callb 88

The listnodes case for CALL is

⟨CALL 332⟩≡   318
    Tree save = firstarg;

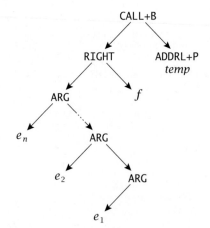

FIGURE 12.7 Tree for $f(e_1, e_2, \ldots, e_n)$ where f returns a structure.

FIGURE 12.8 Forest for $f(e_1, e_2, \ldots, e_n)$ where f returns a structure.

```
firstarg = NULL;
if (tp->op == CALL+B && !IR->wants_callb) {
    ⟨list CALL+B arguments 333⟩
    p = newnode(CALLV, 1, NULL, NULL);
} else {
    l = listnodes(tp->kids[0], 0, 0);
    r = listnodes(tp->kids[1], 0, 0);
    p = newnode(tp->op, 1, r, NULL);
}
list(p);
reset();
cfunc->u.f.ncalls++;
firstarg = save;
```

⟨*dag.c data*⟩+≡   314 343
```
    static Tree firstarg;
```

When necessary, `firstarg` carries the tree for the hidden first argument, as described below. It's saved, reinitialized to null, and restored so that arguments that include other calls don't overwrite it. A call is always listed, and it kills all nodes in the node table. The `ncalls` field in a symbol-table entry for a function records the number of CALLs that function makes. This value supplies the fourth argument to the interface procedure `function`, which is called from `funcdefn`.

As Figure 12.7 shows, `tp->kids[0]` is a RIGHT tree that holds both the arguments and the tree for the function address. Traversing this tree thus lists the arguments and returns the node for the function address, which becomes the left operand of the CALL node.

For CALL+B trees, the tree for the hidden first argument is assigned to `firstarg`:

⟨*list* CALL+B *arguments* 333⟩≡   333
```
    Tree arg0 = tree(ARG+P, tp->kids[1]->type,
        tp->kids[1], NULL);
    if (IR->left_to_right)
        firstarg = arg0;
    l = listnodes(tp->kids[0], 0, 0);
    if (!IR->left_to_right || firstarg) {
        firstarg = NULL;
```

```
        listnodes(arg0, 0, 0);
    }
```

If left_to_right is one, firstarg gets the tree for the hidden argument just before the arguments are visited, which occurs when listnodes traverses tp->kids[0], and the hidden argument will be listed before the other arguments. When left_to_right is zero, firstarg is unnecessary because the hidden argument is listed last anyway.

The last if statement in the fragment above also traverses the tree for the hidden argument when left_to_right is one and firstarg is nonnull. This case occurs for a call to a function that returns a structure but that has *no* arguments. For this case, the firstarg will *not* have been traversed by the ARG code below because tp->kids[0] contains no ARG trees for this call.

An ARG subtree is built as the arguments are parsed from left to right, and thus it always has the rightmost argument as the root, as shown in Figure 12.7. The ARG nodes can be listed left to right by visiting tp->kids[1] before tp->kids[0]; visiting the operands in the other order lists the ARG nodes right-to-left.

⟨ARG 334⟩≡   318
```
    if (IR->left_to_right)
        listnodes(tp->kids[1], 0, 0);
    if (firstarg) {
        Tree arg = firstarg;
        firstarg = NULL;
        listnodes(arg, 0, 0);
    }
    l = listnodes(tp->kids[0], 0, 0);
    list(newnode(tp->op, l, NULL, NULL));
    forest->syms[0] = intconst(tp->type->size);
    forest->syms[1] = intconst(tp->type->align);
    if (!IR->left_to_right)
        listnodes(tp->kids[1], 0, 0);
```

Like an ASGN node, the syms field of an ARG node points to symbol-table entries for constants that give the size and alignment of the argument.

The first time execution reaches the test of firstarg when the flag left_to_right is one is when the ARG for the first argument — the one for e_1 in Figure 12.7 — is traversed. If firstarg is nonnull, it's listed before the tree for the first argument and reset to null so that it's traversed only once.

12.6 Enforcing Evaluation Order

There are only a few operators for which the standard specifies an order of evaluation. It specifies short-circuit evaluation for AND and OR
and the usual if-statement evaluation for COND. The left operand of the
comma operator must be evaluated before its right operand. lcc represents e_1, e_2 with the tree (RIGHT e_1 e_2), so the listnodes case for
RIGHT evaluates the left operand first, then evaluates and returns the
right operand:

⟨RIGHT 335⟩≡   318
```
    if ((⟨tp is a tree for e++ 336⟩) {
       ⟨generate nodes for e++ 336⟩
    } else if (tp->kids[1]) {
       listnodes(tp->kids[0], 0, 0);
       p = listnodes(tp->kids[1], tlab, flab);
    } else
       p = listnodes(tp->kids[0], tlab, flab);
```

As Chapters 8 and 9 and this code suggest, RIGHT trees are used for
purposes other than the comma operator, and they may have one or two
operands. The value of a RIGHT tree is the value of its rightmost operand.

For example, RIGHT trees are used to unnest nested calls — those that
have calls as arguments. call hoists all such arguments into the left
operand of a RIGHT tree so that they are listed *before* the ARGs of the call
in which they appear. Figure 12.9 shows the tree for $f(e_1, g(e_2), e_3)$.

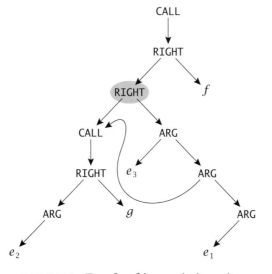

FIGURE 12.9 Tree for $f(e_1, g(e_2), e_3)$.

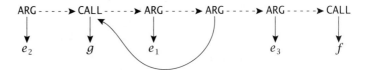

FIGURE 12.10   Forest for $f(e_1, g(e_2), e_3)$.

Compare this figure to Figure 12.7. The arguments in Figure 12.9 appear as the right operand of an *extra* RIGHT node, which is shaded, and the left operand of that node is the tree for the nested call $g(e_2)$. f's second ARG node refers to the value of the call to g.

listnodes traverses this tree in the code for CALL described in Section 12.5. When the left and only operand of the topmost CALL is traversed, the RIGHT trees cause the nested call to g to be traversed and listed before *any* of the arguments to f. Figure 12.10 shows the resulting forest.

RIGHT trees are also used to enforce the correct semantics for the expressions e++ and e--. Figure 12.11 shows the tree built by postfix for i++. The RIGHT nodes collaborate to return the value of i before it's incremented, but there's an additional complication. To enforce an evaluation order that evaluates the INDIR+I first, that tree must be traversed and its node listed in the forest *before* the assignment to i, and the node must annotate the RIGHT tree. Listing this INDIR node is what requires special treatment for the RIGHT idiom depicted by the lower RIGHT node in Figure 12.11.

⟨*tp is a tree for e++ 336*⟩≡   335
```
         tp->kids[0] && tp->kids[1]
     &&  generic(tp->kids[1]->op) == ASGN
     && (generic(tp->kids[0]->op) == INDIR
     && tp->kids[0]->kids[0] == tp->kids[1]->kids[0]
     || (tp->kids[0]->op == FIELD
     &&  tp->kids[0] == tp->kids[1]->kids[0]))
```

As this test indicates, for postincrement or postdecrement of a bit field, a FIELD node appears instead of an INDIR node, and this FIELD node is the target of the assignment.

When e is a not a bit field, the INDIR tree is traversed, and its node is listed before traversing the RIGHT tree's second operand:

⟨*generate nodes for e++ 336*⟩≡   337   335
```
     if (generic(tp->kids[0]->op) == INDIR) {
         p = listnodes(tp->kids[0], 0, 0);
         list(p);
         listnodes(tp->kids[1], 0, 0);
     }
```

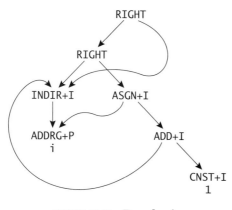

FIGURE 12.11   Tree for i++.

Figure 5.3 (page 87) shows the forest for the assignment i = *p++. The
INDIR node for p's rvalue appears before the assignment to p.

   Bit fields are problematic. listnodes can't list a FIELD node because there isn't one — FIELD operators appear only in trees. Instead,
listnodes must look below the FIELD tree to the INDIR tree that fetches
the word in which the bit field appears, traverse that tree, and list its
node:

⟨*generate nodes for e++* 336⟩+≡   ▲336 335

```
   else {
      list(listnodes(tp->kids[0]->kids[0], 0, 0));
      p = listnodes(tp->kids[0], 0, 0);
      listnodes(tp->kids[1], 0, 0);
   }
```

12.7   Driving Code Generation

Once the code list for a function is complete, funcdefn calls the interface procedure function to generate and emit the code. As described in
Section 5.10, this interface function makes two calls back into the front
end: It calls gencode to generate code, and it calls emitcode to emit the
code it generates. Each of these functions makes a pass over the code
list, calling the appropriate interface function for each code-list entry.

   funcdefn builds two arrays of pointers to symbol-table entries: The
callee array holds the parameters of the function as seen from within
the function, and caller holds the parameters as seen by any callers of
the functions. These arrays are passed to function, which passes them
to gencode:

⟨*dag.c functions*⟩+≡   ▲327 340
```
   void gencode(caller, callee) Symbol caller[], callee[]; {
```

```
Code cp;
Coordinate save;

save = src;
⟨generate caller to callee assignments 338⟩
cp = codehead.next;
for ( ; errcnt <= 0 && cp; cp = cp->next)
    switch (cp->kind) {
    case Address:   ⟨gencode Address 339⟩ break;
    case Blockbeg:  ⟨gencode Blockbeg 339⟩ break;
    case Blockend:  ⟨gencode Blockend 339⟩ break;
    case Defpoint:  src = cp->u.point.src; break;
    case Gen: case Jump:
    case Label:     ⟨gencode Gen,Jump,Label 340⟩ break;
    case Local:     (*IR->local)(cp->u.var); break;
    case Switch:    break;
    }
    src = save;
}
```

The assignments to `src` are made so that diagnostics issued during code generation will include the source coordinate of the offending expression.

Before making its pass through the code list, `gencode` inspects the symbols in `caller` and `callee`. For most functions, corresponding symbols in these arrays describe the same variable. For character and short parameters, however, the front end always promotes the argument to an integer or an unsigned; an example of this case is described in Section 5.5. When this promotion occurs, the types of the `caller` symbol and its corresponding `callee` symbol are different, and `gencode` must generate an assignment of the `caller` to the `callee`. This assignment must also occur if the storage classes of a `caller` and `callee` are different, which can occur, for example, when the back end changes the storage class of the `caller` or `callee` to conform to the target's calling convention.

These assignments change the code list, and they must be inserted *before* the first entry for the body of the function.

⟨*generate* caller *to* callee *assignments* 338⟩≡   338
```
{
    int i;
    Symbol p, q;
    cp = codehead.next->next;
    codelist = codehead.next;
    for (i = 0; (p = callee[i]) != NULL
            && (q = caller[i]) != NULL; i++)
```

```
      if (p->sclass != q->sclass || p->type != q->type)
         walk(asgn(p, idtree(q)), 0, 0);
   codelist->next = cp;
   cp->prev = codelist;
}
```

The manipulations of codehead and codelist before the loop collaborate to split the code list into two pieces: codelist points to the single Start entry and cp points to the rest of the code list. The call to walk appends each assignment to the code list pointed to by codelist, as usual. After the assignments are appended, the rest of the code list is reattached. These list manipulations are similar to those used in Section 10.7 and illustrated in Figure 10.2 to insert the selection code for the switch statement in the correct position.

The cases for Blockbeg and Blockend code-list entries announce the beginnings and ends of source-level compound statements.

⟨gencode Blockbeg 339⟩≡   338
```
   {
      Symbol *p = cp->u.block.locals;
      (*IR->blockbeg)(&cp->u.block.x);
      for ( ; *p; p++)
         if ((*p)->ref != 0.0)
            (*IR->local)(*p);
   }
```

⟨gencode Blockend 339⟩≡   338
```
   (*IR->blockend)(&cp->u.begin->u.block.x);
```

The interface functions blockbeg and blockend are passed the address of an Env value associated with the block. Back ends can use this value to save values that must be restored at the end of the block, such as sets of busy registers and frame offsets.

Blockbeg entries include an array of pointers to symbol-table entries for the locals declared in the block, and these are announced by the interface function local. Other locals, such as temporaries, appear in Local entries and are announced similarly, as shown above.

Address entries carry the information necessary to define symbols that depend on the addresses of locals or parameters and are created by addrtree. These symbols are announced by calling the interface function address:

⟨gencode Address 339⟩≡   338
```
   (*IR->address)(cp->u.addr.sym, cp->u.addr.base,
      cp->u.addr.offset);
```

For locals, these entries appear on the code list *after* the Blockbeg or Local entries that carry the symbols on which they depend. Once these latter symbols have been announced to the back end, the interface function `address` can be called to define the symbols in `Address` entries. These entries can also define symbols that depend on parameters, which have already been announced.

Gen, Jump, and Label entries carry forests that represent the code for expressions, jumps, and label definitions. These forests are passed to the interface function `gen`:

⟨gencode Gen,Jump,Label 340⟩≡   338
```
    if (!IR->wants_dag)
        cp->u.forest = undag(cp->u.forest);
    fixup(cp->u.forest);
    cp->u.forest = (*IR->gen)(cp->u.forest);
```

gen returns a pointer to a node. Usually, it annotates the nodes in forest, and perhaps reorganizes and returns the forest, but this interface permits gen to return something else that can represented by a pointer to a node. All of the back ends in this book return a pointer to a list of nodes for the instructions in the forest. If gen returns null, the corresponding call to the interface function emit, described below, is not made.

As detailed in previous sections, the forests in Gen entries can have nodes that are referenced more than once because they represent common subexpressions. If the interface flag wants_dag is one, gen is passed forests with these kinds of nodes. If wants_dag is zero, however, undag generates assignments that store common subexpressions in temporaries, and replaces references to the nodes that compute them by references to the temporaries. Section 12.8 reveals the details.

The syms[0] fields of nodes for the comparison operators and jumps point to symbol-table entries for labels. These labels might be synonyms for the real label, described in Section 10.9. fixup finds these nodes and changes their syms[0] fields to point to the real labels.

⟨dag.c functions⟩+≡   337 341
```
    static void fixup(p) Node p; {
        for ( ; p; p = p->link)
            switch (generic(p->op)) {
            case JUMP:
                if (p->kids[0]->op == ADDRG+P)
                    p->kids[0]->syms[0] =
                        equated(p->kids[0]->syms[0]);
                break;
            case EQ: case GE: case GT: case LE: case LT: case NE:
                p->syms[0] = equated(p->syms[0]);
            }
    }
```

When equatelab makes L_1 a synonym for L_2, it sets the u.1.equatedto field of the symbol-table entry for L_1 to the symbol-table entry for L_2.

equated follows the list of symbols formed by these fields, if there is one, to find the real label at the end:

⟨*dag.c functions*⟩+≡   340 341

```
static Symbol equated(p) Symbol p; {
    while (p->u.l.equatedto)
        p = p->u.l.equatedto;
    return p;
}
```

fixup need inspect only the root nodes in the forest, because JUMP and the comparison operators always appear as roots.

Once gencode returns, the interface procedure function has all the information it needs, such as the size of the frame and the number of registers used, to generate the function prologue. When it's ready to emit the generated code, it calls emitcode:

⟨*dag.c functions*⟩+≡   341 343

```
void emitcode() {
    Code cp;
    Coordinate save;

    save = src;
    cp = codehead.next;
    for ( ; errcnt <= 0 && cp; cp = cp->next)
        switch (cp->kind) {
        case Address: break;
        case Blockbeg: ⟨emitcode Blockbeg⟩ break;
        case Blockend: ⟨emitcode Blockend⟩ break;
        case Defpoint: ⟨emitcode Defpoint 341⟩ break;
        case Gen: case Jump:
        case Label:    ⟨emitcode Gen,Jump,Label 342⟩ break;
        case Local:    ⟨emitcode Local⟩ break;
        case Switch:   ⟨emitcode Switch 342⟩ break;
        }
    src = save;
}
```

217	Address
217	Blockbeg
217	Blockend
217	codehead
217	Code
38	Coordinate
217	Defpoint
92	emit
393	emit
46	equatedto
340	fixup
92	function
448	" (MIPS)
484	" (SPARC)
518	" (X86)
337	gencode
92	gen
217	Gen
402	gen
217	Jump
143	kind
217	Label
217	Local
217	Switch

⟨emitcode Defpoint 341⟩≡   341

```
    src = cp->u.point.src;
```

The cases for the code-list entries for Defpoint, Blockbeg, Blockend, and Local don't emit code. If lcc's -g option is specified, however, these cases call the stab interface functions to emit symbol-table information for debuggers.

Gen, Jump, and Label entries carry the forests returned by the interface function gen, and emitcode passes the nonnull forests to the interface function emit:

⟨emitcode Gen,Jump,Label 342⟩≡   341
```
  if (cp->u.forest)
     (*IR->emit)(cp->u.forest);
```

Switch code-list entries carry branch tables for switch statements generated by swcode. The u.swtch.values and u.swtch.labels arrays in these entries hold u.swtch.size value–label pairs that form the table. emitcode generates a global variable for the table whose symbol-table entry is in the u.swtch.table field, and initializes the table to the addresses specified by the labels.

⟨emitcode Switch 342⟩≡   341
```
  { int i;
     unsigned k = cp->u.swtch.values[0];
     defglobal(cp->u.swtch.table, LIT);
     for (i = 0; i < cp->u.swtch.size; i++, k++) {
        for ( ; k < (unsigned)cp->u.swtch.values[i]; k++)
           (*IR->defaddress)(equated(cp->u.swtch.deflab));
        (*IR->defaddress)(equated(cp->u.swtch.labels[i]));
     }
     swtoseg(CODE);
  }
```

The value–label pairs in u.swtch.values and u.swtch.labels are sorted in ascending order by value, but those values may not be contiguous. The default label in u.swtch.deflab is used for the missing values.

12.8 Eliminating Multiply Referenced Nodes

The front end builds trees, but some of those trees are dags. listnodes takes these trees and builds dags so that it can eliminate common subexpressions. This section describes undag, which takes dags and turns them back into proper trees, though they're still called dags. lcc's unfortunate abuse of proper terminology is perhaps best dealt with by remembering that "trees" refers to the intermediate representation built and manipulated by the front end, and "dags" refers to the intermediate representation passed to and manipulated by the back ends.

listnodes could be eliminated, but this would also sacrifice common-subexpression elimination, which contributes significantly to the quality of the generated code. The earliest versions of lcc did the opposite: the front end built dags directly. This approach was abandoned for the present scheme because dags made code transformations, like those done by simplify, much more complicated. Maintaining the reference counts, for example, was prone to error.

A node that represents a common subexpression is pointed to by the elements of the kids arrays in at least two other nodes in the same forest, and its count field records the number of those pointers. Back ends can generate code directly from the dags in each forest passed to the interface function gen, but these multiply referenced nodes complicate code generation in general and register allocation in particular. Some compilers thus eliminate these nodes, either in their front end or in their code generator. They generate code to assign their values to temporaries, and they replace the references to these nodes with references to their temporaries. As mentioned in Section 12.7, setting the interface flag wants_dag to zero causes lcc's front end to generate these assignments and thus eliminate multiply referenced nodes. If wants_dag is zero, the front end also generates assignments for CALLs that return values, even if they're referenced only once, because listing a CALL node will give it a hidden reference from the code list. All the code generators in this book set wants_dag to zero.

gencode calls undag with each forest in the code list before passing the forest to the interface function gen. undag builds and returns a new forest, adding the necessary assignments to the new forest as it visits each node in the old one.

⟨*dag.c data*⟩+≡   3̂33

```
static Node *tail;
```

⟨*dag.c functions*⟩+≡   3̂41 345
▼

```
static Node undag(forest) Node forest; {
    Node p;

    tail = &forest;
    for (p = forest; p; p = p->link)
        if (generic(p->op) == INDIR
        || iscall(p) && p->count >= 1)
            visit(p, 1);
        else {
            visit(p, 1);
            *tail = p;
            tail = &p->link;
        }
    *tail = NULL;
    return forest;
}
```

81	count
311	forest
337	gencode
92	gen
402	gen
344	iscall
87	mulops_calls
345	visit
89	wants_dag

The two arms of the if statement handle nodes that do not appear as roots in the new forest and those that do. Listed INDIR nodes and calls referenced by other nodes are replaced in the new forest by assignments of their values to temporaries. All other listed nodes, such as nodes for the comparisons, JUMP, LABEL, ASGN, and CALLs executed for side effect only, are appended to the new forest. Here, calls includes the multiplicative operators if the interface flag mulops_calls is one:

⟨*dag.c macros*⟩≡
```
#define iscall(p) (generic((p)->op) == CALL \
    || IR->mulops_calls \
    && ((p)->op==DIV+I || (p)->op==MOD+I || (p)->op==MUL+I \
    || (p)->op==DIV+U || (p)->op==MOD+U || (p)->op==MUL+U))
```

visit traverses a dag looking for nodes that are referenced more than once — those whose count fields exceed one. On the first encounter with each such node, visit generates a temporary, builds an assignment of the node to the temporary, and appends that assignment to the new forest. When that node is encountered again, either in the same dag or in a subsequent dag, visit replaces the reference to the node with a new node that references the appropriate temporary. The effect is that an assignment to a temporary appears in the new forest just *before* the root of the dag that first references it.

An example helps illustrate visit's details. The forest for the statement in

```
register int n, *q;
n = *q++ = f(n, n);
```

is shown in Figure 12.12. There are five common subexpressions and thus five multiply referenced nodes: The lvalues of q and n, the rvalues of q and n, and the call to f. Figure 12.13 shows the forest returned by undag. Only two of these common subexpressions have been replaced by temporaries: t2 is assigned the rvalue of q and t3 is assigned the value returned by the call to f. There are no temporaries for the lvalues of q and n because it's just as easy to recompute them, which is why there

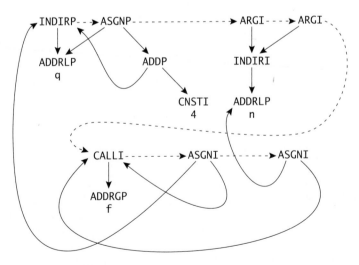

FIGURE 12.12   Forest for n = *q++ = f(n, n).

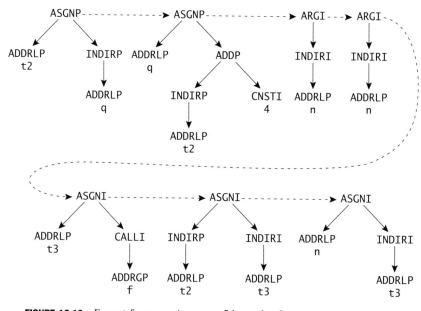

FIGURE 12.13   Forest for n = *q++ = f(n, n) when wants_dag is zero.

are two (ADDRLP q) nodes and three (ADDRLP n) nodes in Figure 12.13.
As detailed below, there's no temporary for the rvalue of n because n is
a register, so it's cheaper to replicate the INDIR node that references n,
which is why there are two (INDIRI (ADDRLP n)) dags in Figure 12.13.
The forest shown in Figure 12.13 is what might be generated if the statement above were written as

343 undag

```
register int n, *q, *t2, t3;
t2 = q;
q = *t2 + 1;
t3 = f(n, n);
*t2 = t3;
n = t3;
```

visit traverses the dag rooted at p and returns either p or a node for
the temporary that holds the value represented by p:

⟨*dag.c functions*⟩+≡   343 346
```
static Node visit(p, listed) Node p; int listed; {
    if (p)
        ⟨visit 346⟩;
    return p;
}
```

listed is one when undag calls visit, and it's zero when visit calls
itself recursively.

When `visit` generates a temporary for a node p, it stores the symbol-table entry for that temporary in `p->syms[2]`, which is not otherwise used by the front end. `visit` must also announce the temporary by calling the interface function `local` just as if there were a `Local` code-list entry for the temporary:

⟨p->syms[2] ← *a generated temporary* 346⟩≡   348
```
p->syms[2] = temporary(REGISTER, btot(p->op), LOCAL);
p->syms[2]->ref = 1;
p->syms[2]->u.t.cse = p;
(*IR->local)(p->syms[2]);
p->syms[2]->defined = 1;
```

⟨*temporaries* 346⟩≡   38
```
struct {
    Node cse;
} t;
```

Symbol-table entries for temporaries that hold common subexpressions are identified as such by having nonnull `u.t.cse` fields. These fields point to the nodes that represent their values. Back ends may use this information to identify common subexpressions that are cheaper to recompute than to burn a register for.

A nonnull `p->syms[2]` also marks p as a common subexpression, so references to p must be replaced by references to the temporary, which is `visit`'s first step:

⟨*visit* 346⟩≡   347   345
```
if (p->syms[2])
    p = tmpnode(p);
```

`tmpnode` builds and returns the dag (INDIR (ADDRLP p->syms[2])), which references the temporary's rvalue:

⟨*dag.c functions*⟩+≡   345 348
```
static Node tmpnode(p) Node p; {
    Symbol tmp = p->syms[2];

    if (--p->count == 0)
        p->syms[2] = NULL;
    p = newnode(INDIR + ⟨type suffix for tmp->type 346⟩,
        newnode(ADDRLP, NULL, NULL, tmp), NULL, NULL);
    p->count = 1;
    return p;
}
```

⟨*type suffix for* tmp->type 346⟩≡   346 348
```
(isunsigned(tmp->type) ? I : ttob(tmp->type))
```

`p->count` is the number of references to p. tmpnode decrements `p->count` for each reference and clears `p->syms[2]` on the last one. Setting the value of `p->syms[2]` to null reinitializes it for use by the back end.

For nodes that are referenced only once and calls made for side effect only, visit traverses and rewrites their operands:

⟨visit 346⟩+≡   346 347   345

```
else if (p->count <= 1 && !iscall(p)
||        p->count == 0 &&  iscall(p)) {
    ⟨visit the operands 347⟩
}
```

⟨visit the operands 347⟩≡   347 348

```
p->kids[0] = visit(p->kids[0], 0);
p->kids[1] = visit(p->kids[1], 0);
```

Calls that are referenced from other nodes are not processed here because they're replaced by assignments even if they have only one reference. They're treated as common subexpressions, as shown below.

As suggested above, temporaries are not generated for the addresses of locals and parameters because it's usually cheaper to recompute their addresses instead of using a register to save them. visit thus builds and returns a new node for *all* ADDRLP and ADDRFP nodes:

⟨visit 346⟩+≡   347 347   345

```
else if (p->op == ADDRLP || p->op == ADDRFP) {
    p = newnode(p->op, NULL, NULL, p->syms[0]);
    p->count = 1;
}
```

Similarly, it's usually wasteful to store the rvalue of a register variable in another register. It's better to build a new dag for each reference to the register's rvalue, as shown in Figure 12.13 for the two references to n. Figure 12.13 shows that q's rvalue *is* copied to a temporary. The two references to q's rvalue must *not* be duplicated because the INDIRP is listed, which indicates that the value must be copied, because q might be changed. visit thus looks for the pattern (INDIR (ADDR*x*P *v*)) where *v* is a register, but steers clear of those in which the INDIR is listed.

⟨visit 346⟩+≡   347 348   345

```
else if (generic(p->op) == INDIR && !listed
&& (p->kids[0]->op == ADDRLP || p->kids[0]->op == ADDRFP)
&&  p->kids[0]->syms[0]->sclass == REGISTER) {
    p = newnode(p->op, newnode(p->kids[0]->op, NULL, NULL,
        p->kids[0]->syms[0]), NULL, NULL);
    p->count = 1;
}
```

This case also reveals why undag can't be called earlier — for example, from walk. The storage class of locals and parameters isn't certain until the back end has seen the function. Once consumed, funcdefn calls checkref, which changes the storage class of frequently accessed locals and parameters to REGISTER. If undag were called from walk, it would generate temporaries for automatic locals and parameters that might later become registers.

The last two cases cover INDIRB nodes and nodes for common subexpressions. Registers can't hold structures, so there's no point in copying them to temporaries; visit just replicates the INDIRB node:

⟨visit 346⟩+≡   347   345

```
    else if (p->op == INDIRB) {
        --p->count;
        p = newnode(p->op, p->kids[0], NULL, NULL);
        p->count = 1;
        ⟨visit the operands 347⟩
    } else {
        ⟨visit the operands 347⟩
        ⟨p->syms[2] ← a generated temporary 346⟩
        *tail = asgnnode(p->syms[2], p);
        tail = &(*tail)->link;
        if (!listed)
            p = tmpnode(p);
    }
```

The else clause handles the first encounter with a common subexpression. After traversing the operands, visit generates a temporary, as described above, and calls

⟨dag.c functions⟩+≡   346

```
    static Node asgnnode(tmp, p) Symbol tmp; Node p; {
        p = newnode(ASGN + ⟨type suffix for tmp->type 346⟩,
            newnode(ADDRLP, NULL, NULL, tmp), p, NULL);
        p->syms[0] = intconst(tmp->type->size);
        p->syms[1] = intconst(tmp->type->align);
        return p;
    }
```

to generate an assignment to that temporary. It then appends the assignment to the new forest. This code is responsible for the assignments to t2 and t3 in Figure 12.13. If listed is zero, p is referenced from another node, so visit must return a reference to the temporary. Otherwise, p is referenced from the old forest, which isn't included in p->count and thus doesn't consume a reference to the temporary.

Further Reading

Using the code list to represent a function's code is idiosyncratic to lcc. A flow graph is the more traditional representation. As detailed in traditional compiler texts, such as Aho, Sethi, and Ullman (1986), the nodes in a flow graph are basic blocks and the edges represent branches from blocks to their successors. A flow graph is the representation usually used for optimizations that lcc doesn't do. Many intra-procedural optimization algorithms that discover and improve the code in loops use flow graphs, for example.

The bottom-up hashing algorithm used by node to discover common subexpressions is also known as *value numbering*, and it's been used in compilers since the late 1950s. The node numbers shown in Tables 12.1 and 12.2 are the value numbers of the nodes with which they are associated. Value numbering is also used in data-flow algorithms that compute information about available expressions in a flow graph. This information can be used to eliminate common subexpressions that are used in more than one basic block.

The scheme used in Section 12.3 to generate short-circuit code for the && and || operators is similer to the approach described by Logothetis and Mishra (1981). That approach and lcc's propagate true and false labels. Another approach, called *backpatching*, propagates lists of holes — the empty targets of jumps. Once the targets are known, these lists are traversed to fill the jumps. This approach works particularly well with syntax-directed translations in bottom-up parsers (Aho, Sethi, and Ullman 1986).

Most compilers generate code from trees, but some use dags; Aho, Sethi, and Ullman (1986) describe the relevant code-generation algorithms for trees and dags and weigh their pros and cons. Earlier versions of lcc included code generators that accepted dags. Instruction selection in these code generators was described with compact "programs" in a language designed specifically for generating code from lcc's dags (Fraser 1989). This language was used to write code generators for the VAX, Motorola 68030, SPARC, and MIPS. All the code generators in this book use trees.

Exercises

12.1 kill continues searching buckets for rvalues of p even after it's found and removed the first one. Give a C fragment that illustrates why there can be more than one kind of INDIR node for p in buckets at the same time. Hint: casts.

12.2 Implement ⟨OR⟩, the case in listnodes for the OR operator.

12.3 Draw the forest generated for the statement

```
while (a[i] && a[i]+b[i] > 0 && a[i]+b[i] < 10) ...
```

where a and b are integer arrays.

12.4 Implement ⟨RET⟩; RET nodes are always roots.

12.5 Implement ⟨DIV..MOD⟩; make sure your code handles the interface flag mulops_calls properly.

12.6 Implement unlist, which is described in Section 12.3.

12.7 Give an example of a conditional expression where the calls to equatelab and unlist in ⟨COND⟩ eliminate a branch to a branch. Hint: nested conditional expressions.

12.8 For code of the form

if (1) S_1 else S_2

lcc generates

$$
\begin{array}{ll}
 & S_1 \\
 & \text{goto } L+1 \\
L: & S_2 \\
L+1: &
\end{array}
$$

Revise lcc to omit the goto and the dead code S_2.

12.9 Figure 12.5 is the tree for the assignment w = x.amt = y; the lower ASGN+I tree is the tree for the single assignment x.amt = y. If the value of a bit-field assignment isn't used, asgntree's efforts in building a tree for the right operand that computes the correct result of the assignment are wasted and generate unnecessary code. Whenever the front end realizes that the value of a tree isn't used, it passes the tree to root and uses the tree returned in place of the original; see expr0 and expr for examples. Study root and extend it to simplify the right-hand sides of bit-field assignments when possible.

12.10 asgntree and the listnodes code in Section 12.4 collaborate to compute the result of a bit-field assignment by sign-extending or masking when necessary. Similar cases occur for other assignments. For example,

```
int i;
short s;
i = s = 0xFFFF;
```

sets i to −1 on targets that have 16-bit shorts and 32-bit integers. There's no special code for these kinds of assignments, but lcc generates the correct code for this assignment. Explain how.

12.11 Draw the forest for the tree shown in Figure 12.7 when the flag left_to_right is zero.

12.12 Draw the tree and the forest for the augmented assignment in

```
struct { int b:4, c:4; } x;
x.c += x.b++;
```

The bit fields b and c are in the same word, so that word is fetched twice and stored twice.

12.13 Managing labels and their synonyms is an instance of the union-find problem, which is described in Chapter 30 of Sedgewick (1990). Replace equatelab, fixup, and equated with versions that use the path-compression algorithm commonly used for solving union-find problems. Measure the improvement in lcc's execution time. If there's no significant improvement, explain why.

12.14 Why doesn't visit treat ADDRGP nodes like ADDRLP and ADDRFP nodes?

12.15 The code for ⟨AND⟩ begins by calling reset if depth is zero and incrementing depth, and this case ends by decrementing depth. The case for OR does the same. Thus, depth counts the number of nested AND or OR operators. The call to reset is needed for the same reason that it is needed in the case for COND, as explained on page 326. Show that without calling reset, lcc generates incorrect code for the assignment

```
x[i] = (n || (n=i), n);
```

Calling reset has no effect on the usual use of && and || as illustrated in Figure 12.3; explain why.

13
Structuring the Code Generator

The code generator supplies the front end with interface functions that find target-dependent instructions to implement machine-independent intermediate code. Interface functions also assign variables and temporaries to registers, to fixed cells in memory, and to stacks, which are also in memory.

A recurring priority throughout the design of 1cc's back end has been overall simplicity. Few compiling texts include *any* production code generators, and we present *three*. Typical modest handwritten code generators require 1,000–1,500 lines of C. Careful segregation of the target-specific material has cut this figure roughly in half. The cost is about 1,000 lines of machine-independent code, but we break even at two targets and profit from there on out; more important, it's easier to get a new code generator right if we use as much preexisting (i.e., machine-independent) code as possible.

print 18

1cc segregates some target-specific material by simply reorganizing mostly machine-independent functions into a large machine-independent routine that calls a smaller target-specific routine. It segregates other material by isolating it in tables; for example, 1cc's register allocator is largely machine-independent, and processes target-specific data held in structures that have a target-*independent* form. Finally, 1cc segregates some target-specific material by capturing it in languages specialized for concise expression of the material; for example, 1cc uses a language tailored for expressing instruction selectors, and this language includes a sublanguage for driving a code emitter.

To the machine-independent part of the code generator, target-specific operations are like hot coals; they must be handled indirectly, with "tongs." If a machine-independent routine must emit a store instruction, for example, it can't just call print. It must create an ASGN dag and generate code for it, or escape to a target-specific function that emits the instruction, or emit a predefined target-specific template. All these solutions need more code than a print call, but they can still pay off because they simplify retargeting. For example, a less machine-independent register spiller with target-dependent parts for each of three targets might take less code overall than 1cc's machine-independent spiller. But debugging spillers is hard, so it can save time to debug *one* machine-independent spiller instead of three simpler target-specific ones.

The next chapters cover instruction selection, register allocation, and the machine-specific material. This chapter describes the overall organization of the code generator and its data structures. It also treats a few loose ends that are machine-independent but don't fit cleanly under instruction selection or register allocation.

The rest of this book uses the term *tree* to denote a tree structure stored in node records, where the previous chapters use the term *dag* for structures built from nodes. To make matters worse, the previous chapters use the term *tree* for structures that multiply reference at least some nodes, so they aren't really trees. Changing terms in midstream is confusing, but the alternative is even worse. lcc originally used code generators that worked on dags, but the code generators in this book require trees; if subsequent text used "dag," it would be wrong, because some of the algorithms fail if the inputs are not pure trees. lcc still constructs dags in order to eliminate common subexpressions, but the code in this book clears wants_dag.

13.1 Organization of the Code Generator

Table 13.1 illustrates the overall organization of the back end by showing highlights from the call graph. Indentation shows which routines call which other routines. This table and section necessarily omit many details and even many routines. They'll simply orient us; they can't answer all questions.

Name of Routine	*Purpose*
function	emits the function prologue and epilogue and calls gencode
gencode	interprets the code list and passes trees to gen
gen	drives rewrite, prune, linearize, and ralloc
rewrite	drives prelabel, _label, and reduce
prelabel	changes the tree to cope with register variables and special targets
_label	labels tree with all plausible implementations
reduce	selects the cheapest implementation
prune	projects subinstructions out of the tree
linearize	orders instructions for output
ralloc	allocates registers
emitcode	interprets the code list and passes nodes to emit
emit	runs down the list of instructions and drives emitasm
requate	eliminates some register-to-register copies
moveself	eliminates instructions that copy a register to itself
emitasm	interprets assembler templates and emits most instructions
emit2	emits a few instructions too complex for templates

TABLE 13.1 Simplified back-end call tree.

The front end calls the interface procedure `function` to generate code for a routine. `function` decides how to receive and store the formals, then calls `gencode` in the front end. `gencode` calls `gen` in the back end for each forest in the code list. When `gencode` returns, the back end has seen the entire routine and has computed the stack size and registers used, so `function` emits the procedure prologue, then calls `emitcode` in the front end, which calls `emit` in the back end for each forest in the code list. When `emit` returns, `function` emits the epilogue and returns.

`gen` coordinates the routines that select instructions and allocate register temporaries for those instructions: `rewrite`, `prune`, `linearize`, and `ralloc`. `rewrite` selects instructions for a single tree. `prune` projects subinstructions — operations such as those computed by addressing modes — out of the tree because they don't need registers, and eliminating them now simplifies the register allocator. `linearize` orders for output the instructions that remain. `ralloc` accepts one node, allocates a target register for it, and frees any source registers that are no longer needed.

`rewrite` coordinates the routines that select instructions: `prelabel`, `_label`, and `reduce`. `prelabel` identifies the set of registers that suits each node, and edits a few trees to identify more explicitly nodes that read and write register variables. `_label` is automatically generated from a grammar that describes the target machine's instructions. It labels a tree with *all* plausible implementations that use the target instructions. `reduce` selects the implementation that's cheapest.

`emit` coordinates the routines that emit instructions and that identify some instructions that need not be emitted: `emitasm`, `requate`, and `moveself`. `requate` identifies some unnecessary register-to-register copies, and `moveself` identifies instructions that copy a register to itself. `emitasm` interprets assembler templates that are a bit like `printf` format strings. `emitasm` escapes to a target-specific `emit2` for a few instructions too complex for templates.

13.2 Interface Extensions

The material in the back end falls into two categories: target-specific versus machine-independent, and private to the back end versus visible to the front end. The two categories combine to divide the back end four ways. Here's a sample routine of each kind from Table 13.1:

Routine Name	Private?	Target-specific?
gen	no	no
function	no	yes
rewrite	yes	no
_label	yes	yes

Chapter 5 presents the public interface. This section summarizes the back end's private internal interface; Chapters 16–18 supply example implementations of this private interface, so they can help answer detailed questions.

Four routines in the public interface — blockbeg, blockend, emit, and gen — are target-independent. They could be moved into the front end, but that would complicate using the front end with different code-generation technologies. So one can retarget lcc by replacing all routines in the public interface *or* by replacing all but blockbeg, blockend, emit, and gen and implementing the private interface instead.

The Xinterface structure extends the interface record:

⟨*config.h* 355⟩≡   357
```
typedef struct {
    ⟨Xinterface 355⟩
} Xinterface;
```

This type collects all machine-specific data and routines that the target-independent part of the back end needs to generate code. It is to the target-independent part of this back end what the main body of the interface record is to the front end.

It starts with material that helps generate efficient code for ASGNB and ARGB, which copy blocks of memory. lcc generates loops to copy large blocks, but it unrolls short loops into straight-line code because loop overhead can swamp the cost of data movement for, say, an eight-byte block copy. The block-copy generator has machine-specific and machine-independent parts. The machine-specific material is a small integer and three procedures:

⟨Xinterface *initializer* 355⟩≡   379   432 464 498
```
blkfetch, blkstore, blkloop,
```

Code generators need not use the block-copy generator; for example, Chapter 18's code generator uses the X86 block-copy instructions, so it implements only stubs for the routines above.

The integer x.max_unaligned_load gives the maximum width in bytes that the target machine can load and store unaligned:

⟨Xinterface 355⟩≡   356   355
```
unsigned char max_unaligned_load;
```

For example, the SPARC architecture implements no unaligned loads, so its x.max_unaligned_load is one, because only load-byte instructions require no alignment. The MIPS architecture, however, does support unaligned 2- and 4-byte loads, so its x.max_unaligned_load is four.

The procedure x.blkfetch emits code to load a register from a given cell:

⟨Xinterface 355⟩+≡   355 356   355
   void (*blkfetch) ARGS((int size, int off, int reg, int tmp));

It emits code to load register `tmp` with `size` bytes from the address formed by adding register `reg` and the constant offset `off`. The procedure `x.blkstore` emits code to store a register into a given cell:

⟨Xinterface 355⟩+≡   356 356   355
   void (*blkstore) ARGS((int size, int off, int reg, int tmp));

It emits code to store `size` bytes from register `tmp` to the address formed by adding register `reg` and offset `off`.

The procedure `x.blkloop` emits a loop to copy a block in memory:

⟨Xinterface 355⟩+≡   356 356   355
```
   void (*blkloop)  ARGS((int dreg, int doff,
                          int sreg, int soff,
                          int size, int tmps[]));
```

`x.blkloop` emits a loop to copy `size` bytes in memory. The source address is formed by adding register `sreg` and offset `soff`, and the destination address is formed by adding register `dreg` and offset `doff`. `tmps` is an array of three integers that represent registers available to help implement the loop.

After the interface to the block-copy generator comes the interface to the instruction selector:

⟨Xinterface 355⟩+≡   356 356   355
   ⟨*interface to instruction selector* 379⟩

This fragment captures most of the target-specific code and data needed by the machine-independent `gen` and `emit`. It is generated automatically from a compact specification. The retargeter thus writes the specification instead of the interface code and data. Neither the specification nor the interface to the instruction selector can be described without preliminaries. The introduction to Chapter 14 elaborates.

`x.emit2` emits instructions that cannot be handled by emitting simple instruction templates:

⟨Xinterface 355⟩+≡   356 356   355
   void (*emit2) ARGS((Node));

Every machine — and many calling conventions — have a few idiosyncracies that can be hard to accommodate without `emit2`'s escape clause.

`x.doarg` computes the register or stack cell assigned to the next argument:

⟨Xinterface 355⟩+≡   356 357   355
   void (*doarg) ARGS((Node));

The back end makes several passes over the forest of trees. The first pass calls x.doarg as it encounters each ARG node. lcc needs doarg in order to emit code compatible with tricky calling conventions.

 x.target marks tree nodes that must be evaluated into a specific register:

⟨Xinterface 355⟩+≡   356 357   355
```
void (*target) ARGS((Node));
```

For example, return values must be developed into the return register, and some machines develop quotients and remainders into fixed registers. The mark takes the form of an assignment to the node's syms[RX], which records the result register for the node. Section 13.5 elaborates.

 x.clobber spills to memory and later reloads all registers destroyed by a given instruction:

⟨Xinterface 355⟩+≡   357   355
```
void (*clobber) ARGS((Node));
```

It usually takes the form of a switch on the node's opcode; each of the few cases calls spill, which is a machine-independent procedure that saves and restores a given set of registers.

13.3   Upcalls

Just as the back end uses some code and data in the front end, so the target-specific code in the back end uses some code and data in the machine-independent part of the back end. Most front-end routines reached by upcalls are simple and at or near leaves in the call graph, so it is easy for Chapter 5 to explain them. The back end's internal analogues are less simple and cannot, in general, be described out of context. They're summarized here so that retargeters can find them all in one spot; consult the page cited in the mini-index for the definition and — perhaps better yet — consult Chapters 16–18 for sample uses. Indeed, perhaps the best way to retarget lcc is to adapt one of the existing code generators; having a complete set of sample upcalls is one of the attractions.

⟨config.h 355⟩+≡   355 358
```
extern int     askregvar  ARGS((Symbol, Symbol));
extern void    blkcopy    ARGS((int, int, int,
                                int, int, int[]));
extern int     getregnum  ARGS((Node));
extern int     mayrecalc  ARGS((Node));
extern int     mkactual   ARGS((int, int));
extern void    mkauto     ARGS((Symbol));
```

```
extern Symbol   mkreg       ARGS((char *, int, int, int));
extern Symbol   mkwildcard  ARGS((Symbol *));
extern int      move        ARGS((Node));
extern int      notarget    ARGS((Node));
extern void     parseflags  ARGS((int, char **));
extern int      range       ARGS((Node, int, int));
extern void     rtarget     ARGS((Node, int, Symbol));
extern void     setreg      ARGS((Node, Symbol));
extern void     spill       ARGS((unsigned, int, Node));

extern int       argoffset, maxargoffset;
extern int       bflag, dflag;
extern int       dalign, salign;
extern int       framesize;
extern unsigned  freemask[], usedmask[];
extern int       offset, maxoffset;
extern Symbol    rmap[];
extern int       swap;
extern unsigned  tmask[], vmask[];
```

13.4   Node Extensions

The code generator operates mainly by annotating extensions to the front end's nodes. Annotations record such data as the instructions selected and the registers allocated. The extension field in the node structure is named x and has type Xnode:

⟨*config.h* 355⟩+≡   357 361

```
typedef struct {
    ⟨Xnode flags 359⟩
    ⟨Xnode fields 358⟩
} Xnode;
```

The instruction selector identifies the instructions and addressing modes that can implement the node, and it uses x.state to record the results:

⟨*Xnode fields* 358⟩≡   359   358

```
    void *state;
```

Chapter 14 elaborates on the information represented by the structure at which x.state points.

Nodes implemented by instructions can need registers, but those realized by addressing modes don't, so it is useful to distinguish these two classes once the instruction selector has identified them. The back end uses x.inst to mark nodes that are implemented by instructions:

⟨*Xnode fields* 358⟩ +≡   358 359   358
  short inst;

x.inst is nonzero if the node is implemented by an instruction. The value helps identify the instruction.

    The back end forms in x.kids a tree of the instructions:

⟨*Xnode fields* 358⟩ +≡   359 359   358
  Node kids[3];

The tree parallels the one in the front end's kids, but the nodes computed by subinstructions like addressing modes are projected out, as shown in Figure 1.5. That is, x.kids stores the solid lines in Figure 1.5 on page 9; kids stores *all* lines there.

    x.kids has three elements because lcc emits SPARC and X86 instructions that read up to three source registers, namely those that store one register to an address formed by adding two others. lcc once generated VAX code and used instructions with up to three operands that used up to two registers each — a base register and an index register — so that version of the compiler had six elements in its x.kids.

    At some point, the code generator must order the instructions for output. The back end traverses the projected instruction tree in postorder and forms in x.prev and x.next a doubly linked list of the instructions in this *execution order*:

```
                                                                  81  kids
                                                                  358 x.inst
```

⟨*Xnode fields* 358⟩ +≡   359 359   358
  Node prev, next;

For example, Figure 13.1 shows this list for Figure 1.5. It omits the trees threaded through kids and x.kids.

    The register allocator uses x.prevuse to link all nodes that read and write the same temporary:

⟨*Xnode fields* 358⟩ +≡   359 359   358
  Node prevuse;

Some calling conventions pass the first few arguments in registers, so the back end helps out by recording the argument number in the x.argno field of ARG nodes:

⟨*Xnode fields* 358⟩ +≡   359   358
  short argno;

    Each node extension holds several flags that identify properties of the node. Roots in the forest need some special treatment from, for example, the register allocator, so the back end flags them using x.listed:

⟨*Xnode flags* 359⟩ ≡   360   358
  unsigned listed:1;

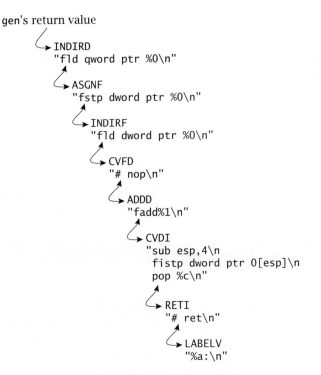

gen's return value

```
  INDIRD
  "fld qword ptr %0\n"

  ASGNF
  "fstp dword ptr %0\n"

  INDIRF
  "fld dword ptr %0\n"

  CVFD
  "# nop\n"

  ADDD
  "fadd%1\n"

  CVDI
  "sub esp,4\n
  fistp dword ptr 0[esp]\n
  pop %c\n"

  RETI
  "# ret\n"

  LABELV
  "%a:\n"
```

FIGURE 13.1   Figure 1.5 linearized.

The register allocator and the emitter can traverse some nodes more than once, but they must allocate a register and emit the node only at the first traversal, so they set x.registered and x.emitted to prevent reprocessing:

⟨*Xnode flags* 359⟩ +≡   359 360   358
```
unsigned registered:1;
unsigned emitted:1;
```

lcc rearranges some expression temporaries to eliminate instructions; to facilitate these optimizations, the back end uses x.copy to mark all instructions that copy one register to another, and it uses x.equatable to mark those that copy a register to a common-subexpression temporary:

⟨*Xnode flags* 359⟩ +≡   360 361   358
```
unsigned copy:1;
unsigned equatable:1;
```

Some common subexpressions are too cheap to deserve a register. To save such registers, the back end flags uses x.mayrecalc to mark nodes for computing common subexpressions that can be reevaluated safely.

⟨*Xnode flags* 359⟩+≡   360   358
```
    unsigned mayrecalc:1;
```

The back end adds two generic opcodes for node structures. LOAD represents a register-to-register copy. The back end inserts a LOAD node when a parent needs an input in one register and the child yields a different register. For example, if a function is called and its value is assigned to a register variable, then the child CALL yields the return register, and the parent needs a LOAD to copy it to the register variable.

If the back end assigns a local or formal to a register, it substitutes VREG for all ADDRFP or ADDRLP opcodes for the variable. Register and memory references need different code, and a different opcode tells us which to emit. There is sure to be an ASGN or INDIR node above the VREG; otherwise, the program computes the address of a register variable, which is forbidden. The INDIR is not torn out of the tree even though programs fetch register variables with no true indirection.

The target-independent Regnode structure describes a target-specific register:

⟨*config.h* 355⟩+≡   358 361
```
    typedef struct {
        Symbol vbl;
        short set;
        short number;
        unsigned mask;
    } *Regnode;
```

385 mayrecalc
315 node

If the register has been assigned to hold a variable — as opposed to a temporary value — vbl points to the symbol structure for that variable. set can handle a large number of register sets, but it handles all current targets with just IREG and FREG:

⟨*config.h* 355⟩+≡   361 362
```
    enum { IREG=0, FREG=1 };
```

IREG and FREG distinguish general registers from floating-point registers. number holds the register number; even if registers are identified by a name instead of a number (as in X86 assemblers) there is usually a companion numeric encoding used by binary emitters and debuggers. mask has ones in bit positions corresponding to the underlying hardware registers occupied. Most single-width registers have just a single one bit, and most double-width registers have exactly two. For example, the mask 1 identifies the single-width register 0, and the mask 6 identifies the double-width register that occupies single-width registers 1 and 2. The X86 architecture has one-, two-, and four-byte integer registers, so its masks have one, two, or four one-bits. This representation is general enough to describe most but not all register sets; see Exercise 13.2.

13.5   Symbol Extensions

The back end also extends `symbol` structures. The field is named x and has type Xsymbol:

⟨*config.h* 355⟩+≡   ▲ 361 362 ▼

```
typedef struct {
    char *name;
    int offset;
    ⟨fields for temporaries 362⟩
    ⟨fields for registers 362⟩
} Xsymbol;
```

x.name is what the back end emits for the symbol. For globals, it can equal `name` on some targets. For locals and formals, it is a digit string equivalent to x.offset, which is a stack offset. Offsets for local variables are always negative, but offsets for parameters can be positive, which explains why x.offset is signed.

　　If the symbol is a temporary in which the front end has stored a common subexpression, then the back end links all nodes that read or write the expression using x.lastuse, and it computes the number of such uses into x.usecount:

⟨*fields for temporaries* 362⟩≡   362

```
Node lastuse;
int usecount;
```

During initialization, the back end allocates one *register symbol* for each allocable register. It represents the register allocated to a node with a symbol so that the emitter can output register names and numbers using the same mechanism that emits identifiers and constants, which are also held in `syms`. These register symbols use two unique fields:

⟨*fields for registers* 362⟩≡   363 ▼ 362

```
Regnode regnode;
```

The back end points x.regnode at a structure that describes the register, and it sets x.name to the register's name or number. When it allocates a register to a node p, it stores the corresponding symbol in p->syms[RX]. The back end sets RX to two to avoid having to move the values that the front end passes it in syms[0] and syms[1]:

⟨*config.h* 355⟩+≡   ▲ 362 365 ▼

```
enum { RX=2 };
```

Once the front end calls `function`, however, *all* elements of `syms` become the property of the back end. The front end is done with them, and the back end can change them as it sees fit. Most of its changes are to the Xsymbol field and to syms[RX], but some changes are to other fields.

　　`mkreg` creates and initializes a register symbol:

⟨*gen.c functions*⟩≡   363 ▼
```
    Symbol mkreg(fmt, n, mask, set)
    char *fmt; int n, mask, set; {
        Symbol p;

        NEW0(p, PERM);
        p->x.name = stringf(fmt, n);
        NEW0(p->x.regnode, PERM);
        p->x.regnode->number = n;
        p->x.regnode->mask = mask<<n;
        p->x.regnode->set = set;
        return p;
    }
```

stringf is used to create a register name that includes the register number. For example, if i is 7, then mkreg("r%d", i, 1, IREG) creates a register named r7. A call like mkreg("sp", 29, 1, IREG) is used if register 29 is generally called sp instead of r29.

The back end also represents *sets* of registers; for example, if a node must be evaluated into a specific register, the back end marks the node with the register, but if the node can be evaluated into any one of a set of registers, then the mark is given a value that represents the set. The back end represents a *set* of registers by storing a vector of pointers to register symbols in the x.wildcard field of a special *wildcard symbol*:

⟨*fields for registers* 362⟩+≡   362   362
```
    Symbol *wildcard;
```

For example, the back end for a machine with 32 integer registers would allocate 32 register symbols and store them in a 32-element vector. Then it would allocate one wildcard symbol and store in its x.wildcard the address of the vector. mkwildcard creates a register-set symbol:

⟨*gen.c functions*⟩+≡   ▲363 365 ▼
```
    Symbol mkwildcard(syms) Symbol *syms; {
        Symbol p;

        NEW0(p, PERM);
        p->x.name = "wildcard";
        p->x.wildcard = syms;
        return p;
    }
```

The x.name "wildcard" should never appear in lcc's output, but x.name is initialized nonetheless, so that the emitter doesn't crash — and even emits a telling register name — when the impossible happens.

13.6   Frame Layout

A *procedure activation record*, or *frame*, holds all the state information needed for one invocation of a procedure, including the automatic variables, return address, and saved registers. A stack stores one frame for each active procedure invocation. The stack grows down, toward lower addresses. For example, if `main` calls `f`, and `f` calls itself recursively once, the stack resembles the illustration shown in Figure 13.2. The stack grows into the shaded area.

A logical *frame pointer* points somewhere into a stack frame. On all targets, the locals have negative offsets from the frame pointer. Formals and other data can be at positive or negative offsets, depending on the target's convention. Figure 13.3 shows a typical frame.

Some targets hold the frame pointer in a physical register; for example, Figure 18.1 shows that the X86 frame pointer is stored in register `ebp`, and it points at one of the registers saved in the frame. Other targets store only the stack pointer and represent the frame pointer as the sum of the stack pointer and a constant; the MIPS code generator, for example, does this. The virtual frame pointer for a routine with an 80-byte frame is the address `80($sp)` (80 plus the value of the stack pointer, `$sp`), and `-4+80($sp)` references the local assigned offset -4 (see Figure 16.1).

`offset` is the absolute value of the stack offset for the last automatic variable, and `mkauto` arranges aligned stack space for the next one:

mkauto 365

⟨*gen.c data*⟩ ≡   365
    `int offset;`

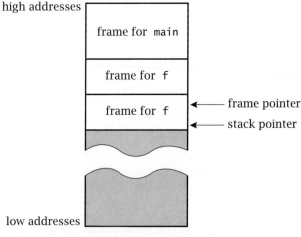

FIGURE 13.2   Three stack frames.

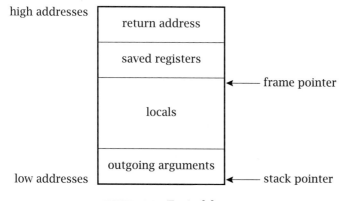

high addresses

low addresses

frame pointer

stack pointer

FIGURE 13.3 Typical frame.

⟨*gen.c functions*⟩+≡   363 365

```
void mkauto(p) Symbol p; {
   offset = roundup(offset + p->type->size, p->type->align);
   p->x.offset = -offset;
   p->x.name = stringd(-offset);
}
```

Using the absolute value avoids questions about rounding when dividing negative integers, and we don't assume that *all* offsets are negative
because for some formals, for example, they aren't.

   At the beginning of each block, the front end calls blockbeg to save
the current stack offset and allocation status of each register:

⟨*config.h* 355⟩+≡   362 377

```
typedef struct {
   int offset;
   unsigned freemask[2];
} Env;
```

⟨*gen.c functions*⟩+≡   365 365

```
void blockbeg(e) Env *e; {
   e->offset = offset;
   e->freemask[IREG] = freemask[IREG];
   e->freemask[FREG] = freemask[FREG];
}
```

blockend restores the saved values at the end of the block:

⟨*gen.c data*⟩+≡   364 366

```
int maxoffset;
```

⟨*gen.c functions*⟩+≡   365 366

```
void blockend(e) Env *e; {
```

```
        if (offset > maxoffset)
            maxoffset = offset;
        offset = e->offset;
        freemask[IREG] = e->freemask[IREG];
        freemask[FREG] = e->freemask[FREG];
    }
```

blockend also computes the maximum value of offset for the current routine. The interface procedure function sets framesize

⟨*gen.c data*⟩+≡   365 366

```
    int framesize;
```

to maxoffset — or more to save space to store data like registers that must be saved by the callee — and it emits a procedure prologue and epilogue that adjust the stack pointer by framesize to allocate and deallocate stack space for all blocks in the routine at once.

Each routine's stack frame includes an *argument-build area*, which is a block of memory for outgoing arguments, as shown in Figure 13.3. lcc can pass arguments by pushing them onto the stack; the push instructions allocate the block of memory implicitly. Current RISC machines, however, have no push instructions, and simulating them with multiple instructions is slow. On these machines, lcc allocates a block of memory and moves each argument into its cell in the block. It creates one block for each routine, making the block big enough for the largest set of outgoing arguments.

The code and data that compute the offsets and block size in the argument-build area resemble the ones above that manage automatics. argoffset is the next available block offset. mkactual rounds it up to a specified alignment, returns the result, and updates argoffset:

⟨*gen.c data*⟩+≡   366 366

```
    int argoffset;
```

⟨*gen.c functions*⟩+≡   365 367

```
    int mkactual(align, size) int align, size; {
        int n = roundup(argoffset, align);

        argoffset = n + size;
        return n;
    }
```

docall is invoked on the CALL node that ends each list of arguments. It clears argoffset for the next set of arguments, and computes in maxargoffset the size of the largest block of outgoing arguments:

⟨*gen.c data*⟩+≡   366 368

```
    int maxargoffset;
```

⟨*gen.c functions*⟩+≡   ▲ 366 367 ▼

```
static void docall(p) Node p; {
    p->syms[0] = intconst(argoffset);
    if (argoffset > maxargoffset)
        maxargoffset = argoffset;
    argoffset = 0;
}
```

`docall` records in `p->syms[0]` the size of *this* call's argument block, so that the caller can pop it off the stack if necessary. The X86 code generator illustrates this mechanism.

13.7 Generating Code to Copy Blocks

ASGNB and ARGB copy blocks of memory. `lcc` generates loops to copy large blocks, but it unrolls short loops into straight-line code because loop overhead can swamp the cost of data movement for, say, an eight-byte block copy.

`blkcopy` is the entry point into the block-copy generator. It is machine-independent and shares `blkloop`'s signature:

⟨*gen.c functions*⟩+≡   ▲ 367 368 ▼

```
void blkcopy(dreg, doff, sreg, soff, size, tmp)
int dreg, doff, sreg, soff, size, tmp[]; {
    ⟨blkcopy 367⟩
}
```

`blkcopy` emits code to copy `size` bytes in memory. The source address is formed by adding register `sreg` and offset `soff`, and the destination address is formed by adding register `dreg` and offset `doff`. `tmps` gives the numbers of three registers available for use as temporaries by the emitted code.

`blkcopy` calls `blkloop` for long blocks, but it unrolls the loops for blocks of 16 or fewer bytes; we chose this limit somewhat arbitrarily after determining what some other compilers used. `blkcopy` is recursive, so it starts by confirming that there's something left to copy:

⟨blkcopy 367⟩≡   367   367 ▼

```
if (size == 0)
    return;
```

If fewer than four bytes remain, `blkcopy` calls `blkunroll` to emit code to copy them:

⟨blkcopy 367⟩+≡   ▲ 367 368   367 ▼

```
else if (size <= 2)
    blkunroll(size, dreg, doff, sreg, soff, size, tmp);
```

```
else if (size == 3) {
    blkunroll(2, dreg, doff,   sreg, soff,   2, tmp);
    blkunroll(1, dreg, doff+2, sreg, soff+2, 1, tmp);
}
```

If the block has 4 to 16 bytes, blkcopy rounds size down to a multiple of four (using size&~3) and calls blkunroll to copy that number of bytes four at a time. It then calls itself recursively to handle the remaining zero to three bytes:

⟨blkcopy 367⟩+≡   367 368   367

```
else if (size <= 16) {
    blkunroll(4, dreg, doff, sreg, soff, size&~3, tmp);
    blkcopy(dreg, doff+(size&~3),
                  sreg, soff+(size&~3), size&3, tmp);
}
```

Loops copy blocks exceeding 16 bytes:

⟨blkcopy 367⟩+≡   368   367

```
else
    (*IR->x.blkloop)(dreg, doff, sreg, soff, size, tmp);
```

blkunroll shares a signature with blkcopy and blkloop, except for an extra leading integer k, which is the number of bytes to copy at a time and must be one, two, or four:

⟨gen.c functions⟩+≡   367 370

```
static void blkunroll(k, dreg, doff, sreg, soff, size, tmp)
int k, dreg, doff, sreg, soff, size, tmp[]; {
    int i;

    ⟨reduce k? 369⟩
    ⟨emit unrolled loop 369⟩
}
```

In a perfect world, blkunroll would interleave calls on blkfetch and blkstore to copy a block k bytes at a time. In *this* world, the alignments of the source or destination addresses may not be multiples of k, and some targets can't load or store k-byte units unless the address is a multiple of k. blkcopy's original caller sets globals salign and dalign to the alignment for the source and destination blocks:

⟨gen.c data⟩+≡   366 370

```
int dalign, salign;
```

If the compiler knows nothing about a source or destination alignment, then it sets salign or dalign to one, since all blocks have an address that's divisible by one. Using globals for dalign and salign is a trade-off: it would be cleaner to pass them as arguments, but the procedures have too many arguments already, and packaging the arguments as structures is a cure worse than the disease. blkunroll uses these values and x.max_unaligned_load to reduce k, and thus copy smaller chunks if k exceeds the maximum size for unaligned loads and the alignment of the source or destination:

⟨*reduce* k? 369⟩≡   368
```
    if (k > IR->x.max_unaligned_load
    && (k > salign || k > dalign))
        k = IR->x.max_unaligned_load;
```

So, a large block with, say, 32-bit alignment for the destination but only 16-bit alignment for the source gets copied 16 bits at a time. Copying the first 16 bits would give 32-bit alignment for the rest of the source, but it would drop the rest of the destination down to 16-bit alignment, so this step alone wouldn't help us generate better code; see Exercise 13.3.

blkunroll's other complication caters to machines that stall when a load comes right before an instruction that uses the value loaded. blkunroll cuts such stalls by emitting two loads and then two stores, so stores don't follow their companion loads immediately:

⟨*emit unrolled loop* 369⟩≡   369   368
```
    for (i = 0; i+k < size; i += 2*k) {
        (*IR->x.blkfetch)(k, soff+i,    sreg, tmp[0]);
        (*IR->x.blkfetch)(k, soff+i+k, sreg, tmp[1]);
        (*IR->x.blkstore)(k, doff+i,    dreg, tmp[0]);
        (*IR->x.blkstore)(k, doff+i+k, dreg, tmp[1]);
    }
```

Each trip through the for loop emits one pair. It quits when no pairs remain, and emits one last copy if the call requested an odd number:

⟨*emit unrolled loop* 369⟩+≡   369   368
```
    if (i < size) {
        (*IR->x.blkfetch)(k, i+soff, sreg, tmp[0]);
        (*IR->x.blkstore)(k, i+doff, dreg, tmp[0]);
    }
```

Figure 13.4 shows lcc generating MIPS code to copy a 20-byte structure with four-byte alignment of the source and destination. The first column traces the calls to the procedures above. The second shows the corresponding emitted code. tmps is initialized to $\{3, 9, 10\}$. Chapter 16 describes the MIPS instructions and the MIPS blkloop, blkfetch, and blkunroll. Its blkloop copies eight bytes at a time. It calls blkcopy recursively to copy the four bytes left over just *before* the loop.

```
blkcopy(25, 0, 8, 0, 20, {3,9,10})
 blkloop(25, 0, 8, 0, 20, {3,9,10})           addu  $8,$8,16
                                              addu  $10,$25,16

  blkcopy(10, 0, 8, 0, 4, {3,9,10})
   blkunroll(4, 10, 0, 8, 0, 4, {3,9,10})
    blkfetch(4, 0, 8, 3)                        lw  $3,0($8)
    blkstore(4, 0, 10, 3)                       sw  $3,0($10)
   blkcopy(10, 0, 8, 0, 0, {3,9,10})

                                             L.3:
                                              addu  $8,$8,-8
                                              addu  $10,$10,-8

  blkcopy(10, 0, 8, 0, 8, {3,9,10})
   blkunroll(4, 10, 0, 8, 0, 8, {3,9,10})
    blkfetch(4, 0, 8, 3)                        lw  $3,0($8)
    blkfetch(4, 4, 8, 9)                        lw  $9,4($8)
    blkstore(4, 0, 10, 3)                       sw  $3,0($10)
    blkstore(4, 4, 10, 9)                       sw  $9,4($10)
                                             bltu  $25,$10,L.3
```

FIGURE 13.4   Generating a structure copy.

13.8   Initialization

parseflags recognizes the command-line options that affect code generation. -d enables debugging output, which helps when retargeting lcc. This book omits the calls that emit debugging output, but they're on the companion diskette.

⟨*gen.c data*⟩+≡   368 371

```
int dflag = 0;
```

⟨*gen.c functions*⟩+≡   368 382

```
void parseflags(argc, argv) int argc; char *argv[]; {
    int i;

    for (i = 0; i < argc; i++)
        if (strcmp(argv[i], "-d") == 0)
            dflag = 1;
}
```

lcc can run on one machine — the host — and emit code for another — the target. One machine can be a big endian and the other a little endian, which subtly complicates emitting double constants, and is another matter that benefits from attention during initialization.

lcc assumes that it is running on and compiling for machines with IEEE floating-point arithmetic. The host and target machines need not be the same, but both must use IEEE floating-point arithmetic. This assumption was once constraining, but it sacrifices little now.

The discussion about the interface procedure defconst in Chapter 5 explained that code generators for C must encode floating-point numbers themselves. That is, they must emit equivalent hexadecimal constants and shun the assembler directives that convert a textual representation of a floating-point constant to its internal form.

lcc can emit a single word for each single-precision float, but it must emit two words for doubles. If lcc is running on a little endian *and* compiling for a little endian, or if both machines are big endian, then both encode doubles the same way, and the code generator can emit in order the two words that comprise the double. But if one machine is a big endian and the other a little endian, then one expects the high-order word first and the other expects the low-order word first. defconst must exchange the two halves as it emits them.

The interface flag little_endian classifies the target, but nothing in the interface classifies the host. lcc classifies the host automatically during initialization:

⟨*gen.c data*⟩+≡   ▲ 370 394 ▼

```
    int swap;
```

⟨*shared* progbeg 371⟩≡   433 466 498

```
    {
        union {
            char c;
            int i;
        } u;
        u.i = 0;
        u.c = 1;
        swap = (u.i == 1) != IR->little_endian;
    }
```

Little-endian machines define u.c on top of the *low* bits of u.i, so the assignment to u.c above sets u.i to 1. Big-endian machines define u.c on top of the *high* bits of u.i, so the assignment to u.c to sets u.i to 0x01000000 on lcc's 32-bit targets.

Further Reading

From this chapter on, it helps to be up to date on computer architecture. For example, blkunroll's load-load-store-store pattern makes little sense without an understanding of how loads and stores typically interact on current machines. Patterson and Hennessy (1990) surveys computer architecture.

Exercises

13.1 Parts of lcc assume that the target machine has at most two register sets. Identify these parts and generalize them to handle more register sets.

13.2 Parts of lcc assume that the target machine has at most N registers in each register set, where N is the number of bits in an unsigned. Identify these parts and generalize them to handle larger register sets.

13.3 The first column in Figure 13.4 gives a call trace for

blkcopy(25, 0, 8, 0, 20, {3, 9, 10})

when the source and destination addresses are divisible by four. Give the analogous trace when the source and destination addresses are divisible by two but not four.

13.4 lcc unrolls loops that copy structures of 16 or fewer bytes. This limit was chosen somewhat arbitrarily. Run experiments to determine if another limit suits your machine better.

blkcopy 367

14
Selecting and Emitting Instructions

The instruction selectors in this book are generated automatically from compact specifications by the program `lburg`, which is a *code-generator generator*. `lcc` has had other instruction selectors — some written by hand, some written by other code-generator generators — but none of them appear in this book. `lburg`'s code generators can misbehave if nodes are traversed more than once, so all back ends in this book clear `wants_dag` and act on trees, although the tree elements have type `struct node`, not `struct tree`.

`lburg` accepts a compact specification and emits a *tree parser* written in C that selects instructions for a target machine. Just as the front end's parser partitions its input into units like statements and expressions, a tree parser accepts a *subject tree* of intermediate code and partitions it into chunks that correspond to instructions on the target machine. The partition is called a *tree cover*. This chapter refers to the generated tree parser as BURM, but `lcc` needs one parser for each target machine, so it emits one BURM into each of `mips.c`, `sparc.c`, and `x86.c`.

The core of an `lburg` specification is a *tree grammar*. Like conventional grammars, a tree grammar is a list of rules, and each rule has a nonterminal on the left and a *pattern* of terminals — operators in the intermediate code — and nonterminals on the right.

Typical rules associate with each pattern an addressing mode or instruction that performs the operator that appears in the pattern. Conventional patterns are compared with a linear string, but tree patterns are compared with a structured tree, so tree patterns must describe the operators they match *and* the relative positions of those operators in the pattern. `lburg` specifications describe this structure with a functional notation and parentheses. For example, the pattern

    ADDI(reg, con)

matches a tree at an `ADDI` node if the node's first child recursively matches the nonterminal `reg` and the second child recursively matches the nonterminal `con`. The rule

    addr: ADDI(reg, con)

states that the nonterminal `addr` matches this sample pattern, and the rule

    stmt: ASGNI(addr, reg)

373

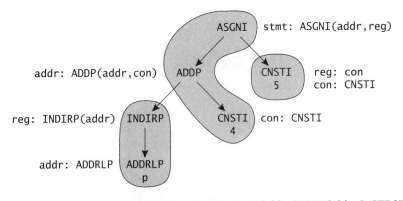

FIGURE 14.1   Cover for `ASGNI(ADDP(INDIRP(ADDRLP(p)),CNSTI(4)),CNSTI(5))`.

states that the nonterminal `stmt` matches each `ASGNI` node whose children recursively match the nonterminals `addr` and `reg`.

The generated code generator — that is, the output of the code-generator generator `lburg` — produces a tree cover, which completely covers each input tree with patterns from the grammar rules that meet each pattern's constraints on terminals and nonterminals. For example, Figure 14.1 gives a cover for the tree

`ASGNI(ADDP(INDIRP(ADDRLP(p)),CNSTI(4)),CNSTI(5))`

using the two rules above plus a few more shown in the figure. The rules to the side of each node identify the cover, and the shaded regions each correspond to one instruction on most machines.

Tree grammars that describe instruction sets are usually ambiguous. For example, one can typically increment a register by adding one to it directly, or by loading one into another register then adding the second register to the first. We prefer the cheapest implementation, so we augment each rule with a *cost*, and prefer the tree parse with the smallest total cost. Section 14.2 shows tree labels with costs.

A partial cover that looks cheap low in the tree can look more expensive when it's completed, because the cover from the root down to the partial cover can be costly. When matching a subtree, we can't know which matches will look good when it is completed higher in the tree, so the generated code generator records the best match for *every* nonterminal at each node. Then the higher levels can choose any available nonterminal, even those that don't look cheap at the lower levels. This technique — recording a *set* of solutions and picking one of them later — is called *dynamic programming*.

The generated code generator makes two passes over each subject tree. The first pass is a bottom-up *labeller*, which finds a *set* of patterns that cover each subtree with minimum cost. The second pass is a top-down *reducer*, which picks the cheapest cover from the set recorded by the labeller. It generates the code associated with the minimum-cost patterns.

14.1 Specifications

The following grammar describes `lburg` specifications. *term* and *non-term* denote identifiers that are terminals and nonterminals:

grammar:
   '%{' *configuration* '%}' { *dcl* } %% { *rule* } [%% C code]

dcl:
   %start *nonterm*
   %term { *term* = *integer* }

rule:
   nonterm : *tree template* [C expression]

tree:
   term ['(' *tree* [, *tree*] ')']
   nonterm

template:
   " { any character except double quote } "

`lburg` specifications are line oriented. The tokens %{, %}, and %% must appear alone in a line, and all of a *dcl* or *rule* must appear on a line. The *configuration* is C code. It is copied verbatim into the beginning of BURM. If there's a second %%, the text after it is also copied verbatim into BURM. at the end.

358 x.state

The configuration interfaces BURM and the trees being parsed. It defines NODEPTR_TYPE to be a visible type name for a pointer to a node in the subject tree. BURM uses the functions or macros OP_LABEL(p), LEFT_CHILD(p), and RIGHT_CHILD(p) to read the operator and children from the node pointed to by p.

BURM computes and stores a void pointer *state* in each node of the subject tree. The configuration section defines a macro STATE_LABEL(p) to access the state field of the node pointed to by p. A macro is required because `lburg` uses it as an lvalue. The other configuration operations may be implemented as macros or functions.

All `lburg` specifications in this book share one configuration:

⟨*lburg prefix* 375⟩ ≡   431 463 496

```
#include "c.h"
#define NODEPTR_TYPE Node
#define OP_LABEL(p) ((p)->op)
#define LEFT_CHILD(p) ((p)->kids[0])
#define RIGHT_CHILD(p) ((p)->kids[1])
#define STATE_LABEL(p) ((p)->x.state)
```

The %start directive names the nonterminal that the root of each tree must match. If there is no %start directive, the default start symbol is the nonterminal defined by the first rule.

The %term declarations declare terminals — the operators in subject trees — and associate a unique, positive integral opcode with each one. OP_LABEL(p) must return a valid opcode for node p. Each terminal has fixed arity, which lburg infers from the rules using that terminal. lburg restricts terminals to at most two children. lcc's terminal declarations, for example, include:

⟨*terminal declarations* 376⟩ ≡   431 463 496
```
%start stmt
%term ADDD=306 ADDF=305 ADDI=309 ADDP=311 ADDU=310
%term ADDRFP=279
%term ADDRGP=263
%term ADDRLP=295
%term ARGB=41 ARGD=34 ARGF=33 ARGI=37 ARGP=39
```

Figure 14.2 holds a partial lburg specification for lcc and a subset of the instruction set of most machines. The second and third lines declare terminals.

Rules define tree patterns in a fully parenthesized prefix form. Every nonterminal denotes a tree. A *chain rule* is a rule whose pattern is another nonterminal. In Figure 14.2, rules 4, 5, and 8 are chain rules.

OP_LABEL 375
stmt 403

The rules describe the instruction set and addressing modes offered by the target machine. Each rule has an assembler code *template*, which is a quoted string that specifies what to emit when this rule is used. Section 14.6 describes the format of these templates. In Figure 14.2, the templates are merely rule numbers.

Rules end with an optional cost. Chain rules must use constant costs, but other rules may use arbitrary C expressions in which a denotes the

```
%start stmt
%term ADDI=309 ADDRLP=295 ASGNI=53
%term CNSTI=21 CVCI=85 INDIRC=67
%%
con:    CNSTI                   "1"
addr:   ADDRLP                  "2"
addr:   ADDI(reg,con)           "3"
rc:     con                     "4"
rc:     reg                     "5"
reg:    ADDI(reg,rc)            "6"  1
reg:    CVCI(INDIRC(addr))      "7"  1
reg:    addr                    "8"  1
stmt:   ASGNI(addr,reg)         "9"  1
```

FIGURE 14.2 Sample lburg specification.

node being matched. For example, the rule

```
con: CNSTU  ""  (a->syms[0]->u.c.v.u < 256 ? 0 : LBURG_MAX)
```

notes that unsigned constants cost nothing if they fit in a byte, and have an infinite cost otherwise. All costs must evaluate to integers between zero and LBURG_MAX inclusive. LBURG_MAX is defined as the largest short integer:

⟨*config.h* 355⟩+≡   ▲365
```
#define LBURG_MAX SHRT_MAX
```

Omitted costs default to zero. The cost of a derivation is the sum of the costs for all rules applied in the derivation. The tree parser finds the cheapest parse of the subject tree. It breaks ties arbitrarily.

In Figure 14.2, con matches constants. addr matches trees that can be computed by address calculations, like an ADDRLP or the sum of a register and a constant. rc matches a constant or a reg, and reg matches any tree that can be computed into a register. Rule 6 describes an add instruction; its first operand must be in a register, its second operand must be a register or a constant, and its result is left in a register. Rule 7 describes an instruction that loads a byte, extends the sign bit, and leaves the result in a register. Rule 8 describes an instruction that loads an address into a register. stmt matches trees executed for side effect, which include assignments. Rule 9 describes an instruction that stores a register into the cell addressed by some addressing mode.

14.2 Labelling the Tree

BURM starts by labelling the subject tree. It works bottom-up and left-to-right, computing the rules that cover the tree with the minimum cost. Figure 14.3 shows the tree for the assignment in the fragment:

```
{ int i; char c; i = c + 4; }
```

The other annotations in Figure 14.3 describe the labelling. (N, C, M) indicates that the pattern associated with rule M with rule number N matches the node with cost C. Each C sums the costs of the nonterminals on the rule's right-hand side and the cost of the relevant pattern or chain rule.

For example, rule 2 of Figure 14.2 matches the node ADDRLP i with zero cost, so the node is labelled with $(2, 0, \text{addr} : \text{ADDRLP})$. Rule 8 says that anything that matches an addr also matches a reg — with an additional cost of one — so the node is also labelled with $(8, 1, \text{reg} : \text{addr})$. And rule 5 says that anything that matches a reg also matches an rc — at no extra cost — so the node is also labelled with $(5, 1, \text{rc} : \text{reg})$. As it happens, the next match higher in the tree needs an addr, so the chain

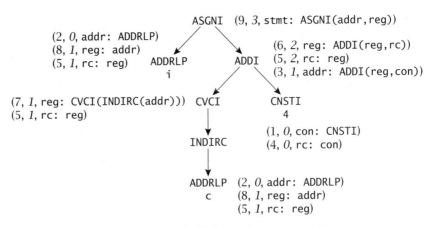

ASGNI (9, *3*, stmt: ASGNI(addr,reg))

(2, *0*, addr: ADDRLP)
(8, *1*, reg: addr)
(5, *1*, rc: reg)   ADDRLP   ADDI

(6, *2*, reg: ADDI(reg,rc))
(5, *2*, rc: reg)
(3, *1*, addr: ADDI(reg,con))

          i

(7, *1*, reg: CVCI(INDIRC(addr))) CVCI   CNSTI
(5, *1*, rc: reg)   4

                                    (1, *0*, con: CNSTI)
                        INDIRC   (4, *0*, rc: con)

                        ADDRLP (2, *0*, addr: ADDRLP)
                          c   (8, *1*, reg: addr)
                                (5, *1*, rc: reg)

FIGURE 14.3 Labelled tree for i = c + 4.

rules aren't needed here. They are needed for, say, the CNSTI node, which matches only con directly, but its parent needs rc, and only a chain rule records that every con is also an rc. A bottom-up tree matcher can't know which matches are needed at a higher level, so it records all of them and lets the top-down reduction pass select the ones required by the winner.

NODEPTR_TYPE 375

Patterns can specify subtrees beyond the immediate children. For example, rule 7 of Figure 14.2 refers to the grandchild of the CVCI node. No separate pattern matches the INDIRC node, but rule 7's pattern covers that node. The cost is the cost of matching the ADDRLP c as an addr (using rule 2) plus one.

Nodes are annotated with (N, C, M) only if C is less than all previous matches of the nonterminal in rule M. For example, the ADDI node matches a reg using rule 6; the total cost is 2. It also matches an addr using rule 3, so chain rule 8 gives a second match for reg, also at a total cost of 2. Only one of these matches for reg will be recorded. lburg breaks ties arbitrarily, so there's no easy way to predict which match will win, but it doesn't matter because they have the same cost.

lburg generates the function

⟨*BURM signature* 378⟩ ≡   379
    static void _label ARGS((NODEPTR_TYPE a));

which labels the entire subject tree pointed to by a. State zero labels unmatched trees; such trees may be corrupt or merely inconsistent with the grammar. lburg starts all generated names with an underscore to avoid colliding with names in BURM's C prologue and epilogue. The identifiers are declared static and their addresses are stored in an interface record so that lcc can include multiple code generators. One fragment collects the identifiers' declarations for a structure declarator:

⟨*interface to instruction selector* 379⟩ ≡   356
   void (*_label) ARGS((Node));

Another collects the names for the C initializer that records the names
of the statics:

⟨Xinterface *initializer* 355⟩ +≡   3̂55   432 464 498
  _label,

The other identifiers that lburg defines in BURM have corresponding entries in the two fragments above, but the text below elides them to cut
repetition.

14.3   Reducing the Tree

BURM's labeller traverses the subject tree bottom-up. It can't know which
rule will match at the next higher level, so it can't know which nonterminal that rule will require. So it uses dynamic programming and
records the best match for all nonterminals. The label encodes a vector
of rule numbers, one for each nonterminal. lburg creates a structure
type _state in which _label stores the best (N, C, M) for each nonterminal:

```
struct _state {
    short cost[MAX_NONTERMINALS];
    short rule[MAX_NONTERMINALS];
};
```

The cost vector stores the cost of the best match for each nonterminal,
and the rule vector stores the rule number that achieved that cost. (Part
of the declaration above is a white lie: lburg compresses the rule field
using bit fields, but lburg supplies functions to extract the fields, so we
needn't waste time studying the encoding.)
    lburg writes a function _rule, which accepts a tree's state label and
an integer representing a nonterminal:

⟨*BURM signature* 378⟩ +≡   3̂78 380
   static int _rule ARGS((void *state, int nt));

It extracts from the label's encoded vector of rule numbers the number
of the rule with the given nonterminal on the left. It returns zero if no
rule matched the nonterminal.
    BURM's second pass, or *reducer*, traverses the subject tree top-down,
so it has the context that the labeller was missing. The root must match
the start nonterminal, so the reducer extracts the best rule for the start
nonterminal from the vector of rule numbers encoded by the root's label. If this rule's pattern includes nonterminals, then they identify a new

frontier to reduce and the nonterminals that the frontier must match. The process begun with the root is thus repeated recursively to expose the best cover for the entire tree. The display below traces the process for Figure 14.3:

```
_rule(root, stmt) = 9
_rule(root->kids[0], addr) = 2
_rule(root->kids[1], reg) = 6
  _rule(root->kids[1]->kids[0], reg) = 7
    _rule(root->kids[1]->kids[0]->kids[0]->kids[0], addr) = 2
  _rule(root->kids[1]->kids[1], rc) = 5
  _rule(root->kids[1]->kids[1], con) = 1
```

Each rule's pattern identifies the subject subtrees and nonterminals for all recursive visits. Here, a subtree is not necessarily an immediate child of the current node. Patterns with interior operators cause the reducer to skip the corresponding subject nodes, so the reducer may proceed directly to grandchildren, great-grandchildren, and so on. On the other hand, chain rules cause the reducer to revisit the current subject node, with a new nonterminal, so x is also regarded as a subtree of x.

lburg represents the start nonterminal with 1, so nt for the initial, root-level call on _rule must be 1. BURM defines and initializes an array that identifies the values for nested calls:

_rule 379

⟨*BURM signature* 378⟩+≡   379 381

```
static short *_nts[];
```

_nts is an array indexed by rule numbers. Each element points to a zero-terminated vector of short integers, which encode the nonterminals for that rule's pattern, left-to-right. For example, the following code implements _nts for Figure 14.2:

```
static short _r1_nts[] = { 0 };
static short _r3_nts[] = { 4, 1, 0 };
static short _r4_nts[] = { 1, 0 };
static short _r5_nts[] = { 4, 0 };
static short _r6_nts[] = { 4, 3, 0 };
static short _r7_nts[] = { 2, 0 };
static short _r9_nts[] = { 2, 4, 0 };

short *_nts[] = {
    0,          /* (no rule zero) */
    _r1_nts,    /* con:  CNSTI */
    _r1_nts,    /* addr: ADDRLP */
    _r3_nts,    /* addr: ADDI(reg,con) */
    _r4_nts,    /* rc:   con */
    _r5_nts,    /* rc:   reg */
```

```
  _r6_nts,  /* reg:  ADDI(reg,rc) */
  _r7_nts,  /* reg:  CVCI(INDIRC(addr)) */
  _r7_nts,  /* reg:  addr */
  _r9_nts,  /* stmt: ASGNI(addr,reg) */
};
```

The user needs only _rule and _nts to write a complete reducer, but the redundant _kids simplifies many applications:

⟨*BURM signature* 378⟩+≡   380 389

```
static void _kids
    ARGS((NODEPTR_TYPE p, int rulenum, NODEPTR_TYPE kids[]));
```

It accepts the address of a tree p, a rule number, and an empty vector of pointers to trees. The procedure assumes that p matched the given rule, and it fills in the vector with the subtrees (in the sense described above) of p that must be reduced recursively. kids is not null-terminated.

The code below shows the minimal reducer. It traverses the best cover bottom-up and left-to-right, but it doesn't *do* anything during the traversal. parse labels the tree and then starts the reduction. reduce gets the number of the matching rule from _rule, the matching frontier from _kids, and the nonterminals to use for the recursive calls from _nts.

```
parse(NODEPTR_TYPE p) {
    _label(p);
    reduce(p, 1);
}
```

375 NODEPTR_TYPE
379 _rule

```
reduce(NODEPTR_TYPE p, int nt) {
    int i, rulenum = _rule(STATE_LABEL(p), nt);
    short *nts = _nts[rulenum];
    NODEPTR_TYPE kids[10];

    _kids(p, rulenum, kids);
    for (i = 0; nts[i]; i++)
        reduce(kids[i], nts[i]);
}
```

This particular reducer does nothing with any node. If the node were processed — for example, emitted or allocated a register — in preorder, the processing code would go at the beginning of the reducer. Postorder processing code would go at the end, and inorder code would go *between* reduce's recursive calls on itself. A reducer may recursively traverse subtrees in any order, and it may interleave arbitrary actions with recursive traversals.

Multiple reducers may be written, to implement multipass algorithms or independent single-pass algorithms. lcc has three reducers. One identifies the nodes that need registers, another emits code, and a third prints a tree cover to help during debugging. They all use `getrule`, which wraps `_rule` in some (elided) assertions and encapsulates the indirection through IR:

⟨*gen.c functions*⟩+≡   ▲ 370 382
                                                                   ▼

```
static int getrule(p, nt) Node p; int nt; {
    int rulenum;

    rulenum = (*IR->x._rule)(p->x.state, nt);
    return rulenum;
}
```

The first reducer prepares for register allocation. It augments the minimal reducer to mark nodes that are computed by instructions and thus may need registers:

⟨*gen.c functions*⟩+≡   ▲ 382 384
                                                                   ▼

```
static void reduce(p, nt) Node p; int nt; {
    int rulenum, i;
    short *nts;
    Node kids[10];
```

IR 306
reuse 384
_rule 379
x.inst 358
x.state 358

```
    p = reuse(p, nt);
    rulenum = getrule(p, nt);
    nts = IR->x._nts[rulenum];
    (*IR->x._kids)(p, rulenum, kids);
    for (i = 0; nts[i]; i++)
        reduce(kids[i], nts[i]);
    if (IR->x._isinstruction[rulenum]) {
        p->x.inst = nt;
        ⟨count uses of temporaries 384⟩
    }
}
```

lburg flags in `x.isinstruction` rules that emit instructions, in contrast to those that emit subinstructions like addressing modes; it does so by examining the assembler template, which Section 14.6 explains.

x.inst above is more than just a flag; it also identifies the nonterminal responsible for the mark. The register allocator linearizes the instruction tree, and the emitter reduces each instruction in isolation, so the emitter needs a record of the nonterminal used in the instruction's reduction.

reduce collaborates with reuse to reverse excessive common subexpression elimination. The front end assigns common subexpressions to temporaries and uses the temporaries to avoid recalculation, but this can increase costs in some cases. For example, MIPS addressing hardware adds a 16-bit constant to a register for free, so when such a sum is used only as an address (that is, by instructions that reference memory), putting it in a register would only add an instruction and consume another register.

So lburg extends the labeller to look for trees that read registers — INDIR*x* (VREGP). If the register holds a common subexpression, and if the expression may be profitably recalculated, the labeller augments the label with bonus matches equal to the set of all free matches of the expression assigned to the temporary.

For example, consider the code for p->b=q->b when, say, p is in register 23, q is in register 30, and the field b has offset 4. Figure 14.4 shows the trees of intermediate code.

The first tree copies the common subexpression 4 to a temporary register, and the second tree uses the temporary twice to complete the statement. The first label on the INDIRI node results from a typical pattern match, but the second is a bonus match. Without the bonus match, lcc's MIPS code generator would emit five instructions:

```
la  $25,4          load the constant 4 into register 25
add $24,$30,$25    compute the address of q->b into register 24
lw  $24,($24)      load value of q->b into register 24
add $25,$23,$25    compute the address of p->b into register 25
sw  $24,($25)      store the value of q->b into p->b
```

The bonus match enables several others, and together they save three instructions and one register:

384 reuse

```
lw  $24,4($30)     load value of i into register 24
sw  $24,4($23)     store register 24 into x[0]
```

lcc's reducers call reuse(p, nt) to see if the reduction of node p using nonterminal nt uses a bonus match. If so, reuse returns the common subexpression instead of p, and thus has the reducer reprocess the common subexpression and ignore the temporary:

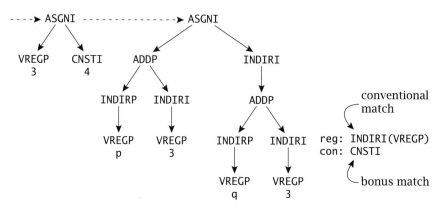

FIGURE 14.4 Excessive common subexpression elimination in p->b=q->b.

⟨*gen.c functions*⟩+≡   ▲ 382 385 ▼

```
static Node reuse(p, nt) Node p; int nt; {
    struct _state {
        short cost[1];
    };
    Symbol r = p->syms[RX];

    if (generic(p->op) == INDIR && p->kids[0]->op == VREG+P
    && r->u.t.cse && p->x.mayrecalc
    && ((struct _state*)r->u.t.cse->x.state)->cost[nt] == 0)
        return r->u.t.cse;
    else
        return p;
}
```

The first return effectively ignores the tree p and reuses the definition of common subexpression. If p uses a common subexpression, then the definition of that subexpression is guaranteed to have been labelled already, so the reducer that called reuse can't wander off into the wind. The cast and artificial _state above are necessary evils to access the labeller's cost of matching the tree to nonterminal nt. This book doesn't expose the form of the state record — except for here, it's needed only in code generated automatically from the lburg specification — though it's easy to understand if you examine the companion diskette's source code once you understand labelling. The length of the actual, target-specific cost vector can't be known here, but it isn't needed, so the declaration can pretend that the length is one.

reduce also counts the number of remaining uses for each temporary:

⟨*count uses of temporaries* 384⟩≡   382

```
if (p->syms[RX] && p->syms[RX]->temporary) {
    p->syms[RX]->x.usecount++;
}
```

If reuse leaves a temporary with no readers, the register allocator will eliminate the code that loads the temporary.

The initial version of reuse was implemented one type suffix at a time, which illustrates what really matters in at least some C programs. lcc comes with a testbed of 18 programs comprising roughly 9,000 lines. We store baseline assembler code for these programs, which we compare with the new code every time we change lcc. The first cut at reuse eliminated only free common subexpressions with the type suffix I. It saved the MIPS testbed 58 instructions. Adding the suffixes C, S, D, F, and B saved nothing, but adding P saved 382 instructions.

A common subexpression can't be recalculated if even one of its inputs has changed. Before allowing a bonus match, the labeller calls mayrecalc to confirm that the common subexpression can be reevaluated, and it records the answer in x.mayrecalc:

⟨gen.c functions⟩+≡   384 385
```
int mayrecalc(p) Node p; {
    Node q;

    ⟨mayrecalc 385⟩
}
```

mayrecalc fails if the node does not represent a common subexpression:

⟨mayrecalc 385⟩≡   385   385
```
if (!p->syms[RX]->u.t.cse)
    return 0;
```

It also fails if any tree earlier in the forest clobbers an input to the common subexpression:

⟨mayrecalc 385⟩+≡   385 385   385
```
for (q = head; q && q->x.listed; q = q->link)
    if (generic(q->op) == ASGN
    && trashes(q->kids[0], p->syms[RX]->u.t.cse))
        return 0;
```

If neither condition holds, then the common subexpression can safely be reevaluated:

⟨mayrecalc 385⟩+≡   385   385
```
p->x.mayrecalc = 1;
return 1;
```

trashes(p, q) traverses the common subexpression q and reports if the assignment target p is read anywhere in q:

⟨gen.c functions⟩+≡   385 386
```
static int trashes(p, q) Node p, q; {
    if (!q)
        return 0;
    else if (p->op == q->op && p->syms[0] == q->syms[0])
        return 1;
    else
        return trashes(p, q->kids[0])
            || trashes(p, q->kids[1]);
}
```

When reduce and its helpers are done, gen calls prune. It uses the x.inst mark to construct a tree of just instructions in the x.kids fields. The register allocator runs next, and only instructions need registers.

The rest of the nodes — for example, ADDP nodes evaluated automatically by addressing hardware — need no registers, so lcc projects them out of the tree that the register allocator sees. The original tree remains in the kids fields. The call to prune follows a reducer, but prune itself isn't a reducer.

⟨*gen.c functions*⟩+≡   385 388

```
static Node *prune(p, pp) Node p, pp[]; {
    ⟨prune 386⟩
}
```

pp points to an element of some node's x.kids vector, namely the next element to fill in. p points at the tree to prune. If p represents an instruction, prune stores the instruction into *pp and returns pp+1, which points at the next empty cell. Otherwise, prune stores nothing, returns pp, and does not advance.

If the tree p is empty, prune is done:

⟨prune 386⟩≡   386   386

```
if (p == NULL)
    return pp;
```

Otherwise, prune clears any trash in the node's x.kids fields:

kids 81
RX 362
temporary 50
x.inst 358
x.kids 359
x.usecount 362

⟨prune 386⟩+≡   386 386   386

```
p->x.kids[0] = p->x.kids[1] = p->x.kids[2] = NULL;
```

If p is not an instruction, prune looks for instructions in the subtrees, starting with the first child:

⟨prune 386⟩+≡   386 386   386

```
if (p->x.inst == 0)
    return prune(p->kids[1], prune(p->kids[0], pp));
```

Each recursive call can store zero or more instructions. Nesting the calls above ensures that prune returns the cumulative effect on pp.

If p is an instruction that sets a temporary, and if the temporary's x.usecount is less than two, then the temporary is set (by the instruction) but never used, the instruction is omitted from the tree, and the traversal continues as above:

⟨prune 386⟩+≡   386 387   386

```
else if (p->syms[RX] && p->syms[RX]->temporary
&& p->syms[RX]->x.usecount < 2) {
    p->x.inst = 0;
    return prune(p->kids[1], prune(p->kids[0], pp));
}
```

Recall that reduce just computed x.usecount.

If none of the conditions above are met, p is a necessary instruction. prune deposits it in *pp and returns the address of the next element to set. It also prunes the node's subtrees and deposits any instructions there into p's x.kids, because any instructions below this one must be children of p and not the higher node into which pp points.

⟨prune 386⟩+≡   386 386

```
else {
    prune(p->kids[1], prune(p->kids[0], &p->x.kids[0]));
    *pp = p;
    return pp + 1;
}
```

prune bumps pp and can later store another p into the addressed cell. This process can't overshoot, because x.kids has been made long enough to handle the maximum number of registers read by any target instruction, which is the same as the number of children that any instruction — and thus any node — can have. Ideally, prune would confirm this assertion, but checking would require at least one more argument that would be read only by assertions.

The dashed lines in Figure 14.5 show the x.kids that prune adds to the tree in Figure 14.3 if ASGNI, ADDI, and CVCI are instructions and the remaining nodes are subinstructions, which would be the case on many current machines: CVCI loads a byte and extends its sign, ADDI adds 4, and ASGNI stores the result. The solid lines are kids.

The display below tracks the calls on prune that are made as the dashed links are created, but it cuts clutter by omitting calls for which p is zero, and by naming the nodes with their opcodes:

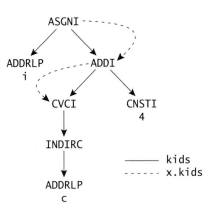

FIGURE 14.5 Figure 14.3 pruned.

```
prune(ASGNI, &dummy) called
 prune(ADDRLP, &ASGNI->x.kids[0]) called
 prune(ADDI, &ASGNI->x.kids[0]) called
  prune(CVCI, &ADDI->x.kids[0]) called
   prune(INDIRC, &ADDI->x.kids[0]) called
    prune(ADDRLP, &ADDI->x.kids[0]) called
  prune(CVCI, &ADDI->x.kids[0]) points the ADDI at the CVCI
  prune(CNSTI, &ADDI->x.kids[1]) called
 prune(ADDI, &ASGNI->x.kids[0]) points the ASGNI at the ADDI
prune(ASGNI, &dummy) points dummy at the ASGNI
```

gen calls prune and supplies a dummy cell to receive the pointer to the top-level instruction. A dummy cell suffices because the root is executed for side effect, so it must be an instruction, and gen knows where the roots are without examining dummy.

14.4 Cost Functions

Most of the costs in lburg specifications are constant, but a few depend on properties of the node being matched. For example, some instructions that add a constant to another operand are confined to constants that fit in a few bits. For nodes p that hold a constant — ADDRL and ADDRF nodes hold constant stack offsets, and CNST nodes hold numeric constants — range(p, lo, hi) determines whether the constant lies between integers lo and hi inclusive. If it does, range returns a zero cost; otherwise it returns a high cost, which forces the tree parser to use another match. In an lburg cost expression, a denotes the node being matched, namely the argument to _label when the cost expression is evaluated. A typical use is:

```
con8: CNSTI  "%a"  range(a, -128, 127)
```

The rule above matches all CNSTI nodes, but the cost is prohibitive if the constant doesn't fit in a signed 8-bit field. The implementation is:

⟨gen.c functions⟩+≡   386 389

```
    #define ck(i) return (i) ? 0 : LBURG_MAX

    int range(p, lo, hi) Node p; int lo, hi; {
        Symbol s = p->syms[0];

        switch (p->op) {
        case ADDRFP: ck(s->x.offset >= lo && s->x.offset <= hi);
        case ADDRLP: ck(s->x.offset >= lo && s->x.offset <= hi);
        case CNSTC:  ck(s->u.c.v.sc >= lo && s->u.c.v.sc <= hi);
        case CNSTI:  ck(s->u.c.v.i  >= lo && s->u.c.v.i  <= hi);
```

---

gen 92
gen 402
prune 386
x.offset 362

```
      case CNSTS:  ck(s->u.c.v.ss >= lo && s->u.c.v.ss <= hi);
      case CNSTU:  ck(s->u.c.v.u  >= lo && s->u.c.v.u  <= hi);
      case CNSTP:  ck(s->u.c.v.p  == 0  && lo <= 0 && hi >= 0);
      }
      return LBURG_MAX;
  }
```

For unsigned character constants, range should zero-extend with the value of u.c.v.uc, and not sign-extend with u.c.v.sc, but range's short-cut can't hurt because CNSTC nodes appear only as the right-hand side of an ASGNC, which ignores the extended bits anyway. Without this short-cut, we'd need signed and unsigned variants of CNSTC to distinguish the two cases. Unsigned short constants behave likewise.

14.5 Debugging

lburg augments the tree parser with an encoding of much of its input specification. This material is not strictly necessary, but it can help produce displays for debugging. For example, the vectors _opname and _arity hold the name and number of children, respectively, for each terminal:

⟨BURM signature 378⟩+≡   381 390

| 97 fprint |
| 306 IR |
| 388 range |

```
  static char *_opname[];
  static char _arity[];
```

They are indexed by the terminal's integral opcode. lcc uses them in dumptree, which prints the operator and any subtrees in parentheses and separated by commas:

⟨gen.c functions⟩+≡   388 390

```
  static void dumptree(p) Node p; {
      fprint(2, "%s(", IR->x._opname[p->op]);
      if (IR->x._arity[p->op] == 0 && p->syms[0])
          fprint(2, "%s", p->syms[0]->name);
      else if (IR->x._arity[p->op] == 1)
          dumptree(p->kids[0]);
      else if (IR->x._arity[p->op] == 2) {
          dumptree(p->kids[0]);
          fprint(2, ", ");
          dumptree(p->kids[1]);
      }
      fprint(2, ")");
  }
```

For leaves, dumptree adds p->syms[0] if it's present. It prints the tree in Figure 14.3 as:

```
ASGNI(ADDRLP(i), ADDI(CVCI(INDIRC(ADDRLP(c))), CNSTI(4)))
```

lcc uses dumptree, but this book omits the calls. They aren't interesting,
but dumptree itself is worth presenting to demonstrate lburg's debugging support.

The vector _string holds the text for each rule.

⟨*BURM signature* 378⟩+≡   ◣ 389 391 ◢

```
    static char *_string[];
```

It is indexed by a rule number. The reducer dumpcover extends the minimal reducer and uses _string to print a tree cover using indentation:

⟨*gen.c functions*⟩+≡   ◣ 389 391 ◢

```
    static void dumpcover(p, nt, in) Node p; int nt, in; {
        int rulenum, i;
        short *nts;
        Node kids[10];

        p = reuse(p, nt);
        rulenum = getrule(p, nt);
        nts = IR->x._nts[rulenum];
        fprint(2, "dumpcover(%x) = ", p);
        for (i = 0; i < in; i++)
            fprint(2, " ");
        dumprule(rulenum);
        (*IR->x._kids)(p, rulenum, kids);
        for (i = 0; nts[i]; i++)
            dumpcover(kids[i], nts[i], in+1);
    }

    static void dumprule(rulenum) int rulenum; {
        fprint(2, "%s / %s", IR->x._string[rulenum],
            IR->x._templates[rulenum]);
        if (!IR->x._isinstruction[rulenum])
            fprint(2, "\n");
    }
```

When compiling MIPS code for Figure 14.3, dumptree prints:

```
dumpcover(1001e9b8) = stmt: ASGNI(addr, reg) / sw $%2,%1
dumpcover(1001e790) =  addr: ADDRLP / %a($sp)
dumpcover(1001e95c) =  reg: addr / la $%c,%1
dumpcover(1001e95c) =   addr: ADDI(reg, con) / %2($%1)
dumpcover(1001e8a4) =    reg: CVCI(INDIRC(addr)) / lb $%c,%1
dumpcover(1001e7ec) =     addr: ADDRLP / %a($sp)
dumpcover(1001e900) =    con: CNSTI / %a
```

The next section explains x._templates and the assembler templates
after each rule.

14.6 The Emitter

lcc's emitter is what actually outputs assembler code for the target machine. The emitter is target-independent and driven by two arrays that capture the necessary machine-specific data. lburg emits into each BURM some C code that declares and initializes these arrays. Both arrays are indexed by a rule number. One yields the template for the rule:

⟨*BURM signature* 378⟩ +≡   390 391
```
    static char *_template[];
```

The other flags the templates that correspond to instructions, and thus distinguishes them from subinstructions like addressing modes:

⟨*BURM signature* 378⟩ +≡   391 406
```
    static char _isinstruction[];
```

lburg numbers the rules starting from one, and it reports matches by returning rule numbers, from which the templates may be found when necessary. If a template ends with a newline character, then lburg assumes that it is an instruction. If it ends with no newline character, then it's necessarily a *piece* of an instruction, such as an operand.

emitasm interprets the rule structure and its assembler code template:

⟨*gen.c functions*⟩ +≡   390 393
```
    static unsigned emitasm(p, nt) Node p; int nt; {
        int rulenum;
        short *nts;
        char *fmt;
        Node kids[10];

        p = reuse(p, nt);
        rulenum = getrule(p, nt);
        nts = IR->x._nts[rulenum];
        fmt = IR->x._templates[rulenum];
        ⟨emitasm 392⟩
        return 0;
    }
```

92	emit
393	emit
382	getrule
306	IR
384	reuse

emitasm is another reducer, but it processes a partially linearized tree. List elements are the roots of subtrees for instructions. emitasm calls itself recursively only to process subinstructions like address calculations. Its traversal starts with an instruction and ends when the recursion reaches the instructions that supply values to *this* instruction. That is, emitasm's reduction traces the *intra*-instruction tree parse, which corresponds to addressing modes and other computations inside a single instruction. emitasm's driver, emit, ensures that emitasm sees these instructions in the right order, which handles *inter*instruction ordering.

emit sets x.emitted to flag nodes as it emits them. When emitasm encounters an instruction that it has already emitted, it emits only the name of the register in which that instruction left its result. For all nodes that develop a value, the register allocator has recorded the target register in p->syms[RX]:

⟨emitasm 392⟩≡   392   391
```
    if (IR->x._isinstruction[rulenum] && p->x.emitted)
        outs(p->syms[RX]->x.name);
```

If the template begins with #, the emitter calls emit2, a machine-specific procedure:

⟨emitasm 392⟩+≡   392 392   391
```
    else if (*fmt == '#')
        (*IR->x.emit2)(p);
```

lcc needs this escape hatch to generate arbitrary code for tricky features like structure arguments. Otherwise, emitasm emits the template with a little interpretation:

⟨emitasm 392⟩+≡   392   391
```
    else {
        ⟨omit leading register copy? 393⟩
        for ((*IR->x._kids)(p, rulenum, kids); *fmt; fmt++)
            if (*fmt != '%')
                *bp++ = *fmt;
            else if (*++fmt == 'F')
                print("%d", framesize);
            else if (*fmt >= '0' && *fmt <= '9')
                emitasm(kids[*fmt - '0'], nts[*fmt - '0']);
            else if (*fmt >= 'a' && *fmt < 'a' + NELEMS(p->syms))
                outs(p->syms[*fmt - 'a']->x.name);
            else
                *bp++ = *fmt;
    }
```

bp is the pointer into the output buffer in the module output.c. %F tells emitasm to emit framesize, which helps emit local offsets that are relative to the size of the frame. Substrings of the form %*digit* tell it to emit recursively the subtree corresponding to the *digit*-th nonterminal from the pattern, counting from zero, left to right, and ignoring nesting. Substrings like %x tell emitasm to emit the node's p->syms['x'-'a']->x.name; for example, %c emits p->syms[2]->x.name. Table 14.1 summarizes these conventions.

So the emitter interprets the string "lw r%c,%1\n" by emitting "lw r", then the name (usually a digit string) of the target register, then a comma. Then it recursively emits p->kids[1] as an addr, if nts[1] holds the

Template	Emitted
%%	One percent sign
%F	`framesize`
%*digit*	The subtree corresponding to the rule's *digit*-th nonterminal
%*letter*	`p->syms[letter - 'a']->x.name`
any other character	The character itself
# (in position 1)	Call `emit2` to emit code
? (in position 1)	Skip the first instruction if the source and destination registers are the same

TABLE 14.1   Emitter template syntax.

integer that represents the nonterminal `addr`. Finally, `emitasm` emits a newline character.

Some targets have general three-operand instructions, which take two independent sources and yield an independent destination. Other targets save instruction bits by substituting two-operand instructions, which constrain the destination to be the first source. The first source might not be dead, so `lcc` uses two-instruction templates for opcodes like `ADDI`. The first instruction copies the first source to the destination, and second adds the second source to the destination. If the first source *is* dead, the register allocator usually arranges for the destination to share the same register, so the first instruction copies a register to itself and is redundant. These redundant instructions are most easily omitted at the last minute, in the emitter. Each specification flags such instructions with a leading question mark, and `emit` skips them if the source and destination registers are the same.

⟨*omit leading register copy?* 393⟩≡   392
```
if (*fmt == '?') {
    fmt++;
    if (p->syms[RX] == p->kids[0]->syms[RX])
        while (*fmt++ != '\n')
            ;
}
```

The interface procedure `emit` traverses a list of instructions and emits them one at a time:

⟨*gen.c functions*⟩+≡   ▲ 391 394 ▼
```
void emit(p) Node p; {
    for (; p; p = p->x.next) {
        if (p->x.equatable && requate(p) || moveself(p))
            ;
        else
```

```
            (*emitter)(p, p->x.inst);
        p->x.emitted = 1;
    }
}
```

Most interface routines have one implementation per target, but there's only one implementation of emit because the target-specific parts have been factored out into the assembler code templates.

The indirect call above permits lcc to call another emitter. For example, this feature has been used to replace this book's emitter with one that emits binary object code directly. emitter is initialized to emitasm:

⟨*gen.c data*⟩+≡   371 398

```
    unsigned (*emitter) ARGS((Node, int)) = emitasm;
```

emit implements two last-minute optimizations. moveself declines to emit instructions that copy a register on top of itself:

⟨*gen.c functions*⟩+≡   393 394

```
    static int moveself(p) Node p; {
        return p->x.copy
        && p->syms[RX]->x.name == p->x.kids[0]->syms[RX]->x.name;
    }
```

The equality test exploits the fact that the string module stores only one copy of each distinct string. x.copy is set by the cost function move, which is called by rules that select register-to-register moves:

⟨*gen.c functions*⟩+≡   394 394

```
    int move(p) Node p; {
        p->x.copy = 1;
        return 1;
    }
```

emit's other optimization eliminates some register-to-register copies by changing the instructions that use the destination register to use the source register instead. The register allocator sets x.equatable if p copies a register src to a temporary register tmp for use as a common subexpression. If x.equatable is set, then the emitter calls requate, which scans forward from p:

⟨*gen.c functions*⟩+≡   394 398

```
    static int requate(q) Node q; {
        Symbol src = q->x.kids[0]->syms[RX];
        Symbol tmp = q->syms[RX];
        Node p;
        int n = 0;
```

```
        for (p = q->x.next; p;  p = p->x.next)
            ⟨requate 395⟩
        for (p = q->x.next; p;  p = p->x.next)
            if (p->syms[RX] == tmp && readsreg(p)) {
                p->syms[RX] = src;
                if (--n <= 0)
                    break;
            }
        return 1;
}
```

The first for loop holds several statements that return zero; they cause the emitter to go ahead and emit the instruction, unless moveself intervenes. The emitter omits the register-to-register copy only if requate exits the first loop, falls into the second, and returns one. The second loop replaces all reads of tmp with reads from src; the first loop counts these reads in n.

If an instruction copies tmp back to src, it is changed so that moveself will delete it, and the loop continues to see if more changes are possible:

⟨requate 395⟩≡   395   395
```
    if (p->x.copy && p->syms[RX] == src
    &&  p->x.kids[0]->syms[RX] == tmp)
        p->syms[RX] = tmp;
```

Without this test, return f() would copy the value of f from the return register to a temporary and then back to the return register for the current function.

If the scan hits an instruction that targets src, if the instruction doesn't assign src to itself, and if the instruction doesn't merely *read* src, then requate fails because tmp and src do not, in general, hold the same value henceforth:

⟨gen.c macros⟩≡   413
```
    #define readsreg(p) \
        (generic((p)->op)==INDIR && (p)->kids[0]->op==VREG+P)
    #define setsrc(d) ((d) && (d)->x.regnode && \
        (d)->x.regnode->set == src->x.regnode->set && \
        (d)->x.regnode->mask&src->x.regnode->mask)
```

⟨requate 395⟩+≡   395 396   395
```
    else if (setsrc(p->syms[RX]) && !moveself(p) && !readsreg(p))
        return 0;
```

For example, c=*p++ generates the pseudo-instructions below when p is in register r1. Destinations are the rightmost operands.

```
move  r1,r2     save value of p
add   r2,1,r1   increment p
loadb (r2),r3   fetch character
storeb r3,c     store character
```

requate could change the add to use r1 instead of r2, but it can't change any subsequent instructions likewise, because r1 and r2 aren't equivalent after the add.

requate also quits if it encounters an instruction that spills tmp:

⟨requate 395⟩+≡   395 396   395
```
    else if (generic(p->op) == ASGN && p->kids[0]->op == ADDRLP
    && p->kids[0]->syms[0]->temporary
    && p->kids[1]->syms[RX]->x.name == tmp->x.name)
        return 0;
```

No explicit flag identifies the nodes that genspill inserts, but the condition above catches them.

requate also gives up if it hits a call, unless it ends the forest, because src might be a caller-saved register, which calls clobber.

⟨requate 395⟩+≡   396 396   395
```
    else if (generic(p->op) == CALL && p->x.next)
        return 0;
```

Usually, src is a callee-saved register variable, so requate might confirm that the register is caller-saved before giving up, but this check netted no gains in several thousand lines of source code, so it was abandoned as a gratuitous complication.

requate also gives up at each label, unless it ends the forest, because src might have a different value afterward:

⟨requate 395⟩+≡   396 396   395
```
    else if (p->op == LABEL+V && p->x.next)
        return 0;
```

If none of the tests above succeed, tmp and src hold the same value, so if this node reads tmp, it is counted and the loop continues to see if the rest of the uses of tmp can be replaced with src:

⟨requate 395⟩+≡   396 396   395
```
    else if (p->syms[RX] == tmp && readsreg(p))
        n++;
```

If a node writes tmp, or if requate runs out of instructions, then the forest is done with tmp, and requate's first loop exits:

⟨requate 395⟩+≡   396   395
```
    else if (p->syms[RX] == tmp)
        break;
```

Now requate's second loop replaces all reads of tmp with reads of src; then requate returns one, and the emitter omits the initial assignment to tmp.

At this point, the most common source of gratuitous register-to-register copies is postincrement in a context that uses the original value, such as c=*p++. lcc's code for these patterns starts with a copy, when some contexts could avoid it by reordering instructions. For example, a more ambitious optimizer could reduce the four pseudo-instructions above to

```
loadb (r1),r3    fetch character
add r1,1,r1      increment p
storeb r3,c      store character
```

Register-to-register moves now account for roughly 5 percent of the MIPS and SPARC instructions in the standard lcc testbed. In the MIPS code, about half copy a register variable or zero — which is a register-to-register copy using a source register hard-wired to zero — to a register variable or an argument or return register. Such moves are not easily deleted. Some but not all of the rest might be removed, but we're nearing the limit of what simple register-copy optimizations can do.

14.7 Register Targeting

Some nodes can be evaluated in any one of a large set of registers, but others are fussier. For example, most computers can compute integer sums into any of the general registers, but most calling conventions leave return values in only one register.

If a node needs a child in a fixed register, register *targeting* tries to compute the child into that register. If the child can't compute its value there, then the code generator must splice a register-to-register copy into the tree between the parent and child. For example, in

```
f(a, b) { return a + b; }
```

the return is fussy but the sum isn't, so the code can compute the sum directly into the return register. In contrast,

```
f() { register int i = g(); }
```

g generally returns a value in one register, and the register variable i will be assigned to another register, so a register-to-register copy can't be avoided.

The next chapter covers the actual allocation of registers to variables and temporaries, but the register-to-register copies are instructions. They can be handled just like all other instructions only if they are represented by nodes. To that end, prelabel makes a pass over the tree before labelling:

⟨*gen.c functions*⟩+≡   394 399

```
static void prelabel(p) Node p; {
    ⟨prelabel 398⟩
}
```

It marks each fussy node with the register on which it insists, and it marks the remaining nodes — at least those that yield a result instead of a side effect — with the `wildcard` symbol that represents the *set* of valid registers. It also inserts `LOAD` nodes where register-to-register copies might be needed.

`preload` starts by traversing the subtrees left to right:

⟨prelabel 398⟩≡   398   398

```
if (p == NULL)
    return;
prelabel(p->kids[0]);
prelabel(p->kids[1]);
```

Then it identifies the register class for nodes that leave a result in a register:

⟨prelabel 398⟩+≡   398 399   398

```
if (NeedsReg[opindex(p->op)])
    setreg(p, rmap[optype(p->op)]);
```

The `NeedsReg` test distinguishes nodes executed for side effect from those that need a register to hold their result. `NeedsReg` is indexed by a generic opcode and flags the opcodes that yield a value:

⟨*gen.c data*⟩+≡   394 402

```
static char NeedsReg[] = {
    0,                          /* unused */
    1,                          /* CNST */
    0, 0,                       /* ARG ASGN */
    1,                          /* INDIR  */
    1, 1, 1, 1,                 /* CVC CVD CVF CVI */
    1, 1, 1, 1,                 /* CVP CVS CVU NEG */
    1,                          /* CALL */
    1,                          /* LOAD */
    0,                          /* RET */
    1, 1, 1,                    /* ADDRG ADDRF ADDRL */
    1, 1, 1, 1, 1,              /* ADD SUB LSH MOD RSH */
    1, 1, 1, 1,                 /* BAND BCOM BOR BXOR */
    1, 1,                       /* DIV MUL */
    0, 0, 0, 0, 0, 0,           /* EQ GE GT LE LT NE */
    0, 0,                       /* JUMP LABEL    */
};
Symbol rmap[16];
```

rmap is indexed by a type suffix, and holds the wildcard that represents the set of registers that hold values of each such type. For example, rmap[I] typically holds a wildcard that represents the general registers, and rmap[D] holds the wildcard that represents the double-precision floating-point registers. Each register set is target-specific, so the target's progbeg initializes rmap. setreg records the value from rmap in the node to support targeting and register allocation:

⟨gen.c functions⟩+≡   398 400

```
void setreg(p, r) Node p; Symbol r; {
    p->syms[RX] = r;
}
```

It would be too trivial to merit a function if it hadn't been a useful spot for assertions and breakpoints in the past.

prelabel's call on setreg assigns the same wildcard to all opcodes with the same type suffix; prelabel corrects fussy nodes below.

Register variables can influence targeting, so prelabel next identifies nodes that read and write register variables. Front-end *symbols* distinguish between register and nonregister variables — the symbol's sclass field is REGISTER — but front-end *nodes* don't. The back end must generate different code to access these two storage classes, so prelabel changes some opcodes that access register variables. It replaces ADDRL and ADDRF with VREG if the symbol referenced is a register variable, and it replaces the wildcard in the INDIR above a VREG with the single register assigned to the variable:

⟨prelabel 398⟩+≡   398 400   398

```
switch (generic(p->op)) {
case ADDRF: case ADDRL:
    if (p->syms[0]->sclass == REGISTER)
        p->op = VREG+P;
    break;
case INDIR:
    if (p->kids[0]->op == VREG+P)
        setreg(p, p->kids[0]->syms[0]);
    break;
case ASGN:
    ⟨prelabel case for ASGN 399⟩
    break;
}
```

prelabel targets the right child of each assignment to a register variable to develop its value directly into the register variable whenever possible:

⟨prelabel case for ASGN 399⟩≡   399

```
if (p->kids[0]->op == VREG+P) {
```

```
        rtarget(p, 1, p->kids[0]->syms[0]);
}
```

Finally, `prelabel` calls a target-specific procedure that adjusts the register class for fussy opcodes:

⟨*prelabel* 398⟩+≡   399   398
```
  (IR->x.target)(p);
```

`rtarget(p, n, r)` guarantees that `p->kids[n]` computes its result directly into register `r`:

⟨*gen.c functions*⟩+≡   399   402
```
    void rtarget(p, n, r) Node p; int n; Symbol r; {
        Node q = p->kids[n];

        if (r != q->syms[RX] && !q->syms[RX]->x.wildcard) {
            q = newnode(LOAD + optype(q->op),
                q, NULL, q->syms[0]);
            if (r->u.t.cse == p->kids[n])
                r->u.t.cse = q;
            p->kids[n] = p->x.kids[n] = q;
            q->x.kids[0] = q->kids[0];
        }
        setreg(q, r);
}
```

If the child has already been targeted — to another a register variable or to something special like the return register — then `rtarget` splices a LOAD into the tree between parent and child, and targets the LOAD instead of the child. The code generator emits a register-to-register copy for LOADs. If the child has not been targeted already, then `q->syms[RX]` holds a wildcard; the final `setreg` is copacetic because `r` must be a member of the wildcard's set. If it weren't, then we'd be asking lcc to emit code to copy a register in one register set to a member of another register set, which doesn't happen without an explicit conversion node.

Figure 14.6 shows three sample trees before and after `rtarget`. They assume that r0 is the return register and r2 is a register variable. The first tree has an unconstrained child, so `rtarget` inserts no LOADI. The second tree has an INDIRI that yields r2 below a RETI that expects r0, so `rtarget` inserts a LOADI. The third tree has a CALLI that yields r0 below an ASGNI that expects r2, so again `rtarget` inserts a LOADI.

`prelabel` and `rtarget` use register targeting to fetch and assign register variables, so lcc's templates for these operations emit no code for either operation on any machine. All machines share the rules:

⟨*shared rules* 400⟩≡   403   431 463 496
```
    reg:  INDIRC(VREGP)      "# read register\n"
```

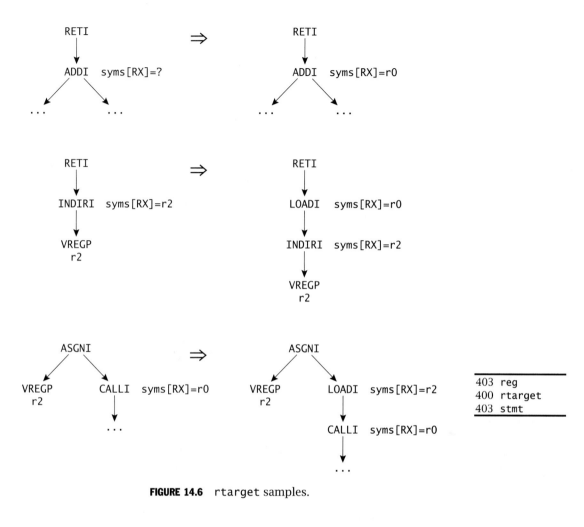

FIGURE 14.6 rtarget samples.

```
reg:   INDIRD(VREGP)        "# read register\n"
reg:   INDIRF(VREGP)        "# read register\n"
reg:   INDIRI(VREGP)        "# read register\n"
reg:   INDIRP(VREGP)        "# read register\n"
reg:   INDIRS(VREGP)        "# read register\n"
stmt:  ASGNC(VREGP,reg)     "# write register\n"
stmt:  ASGND(VREGP,reg)     "# write register\n"
stmt:  ASGNF(VREGP,reg)     "# write register\n"
stmt:  ASGNI(VREGP,reg)     "# write register\n"
stmt:  ASGNP(VREGP,reg)     "# write register\n"
stmt:  ASGNS(VREGP,reg)     "# write register\n"
```

The comment template emits no code, but it appears in debugging output, so the descriptive comments can help.

14.8   Coordinating Instruction Selection

Section 13.1 explained that rewrite and gen coordinate some of the processes described in this chapter. Now for the details. rewrite performs register targeting and instruction selection for a single tree:

⟨*gen.c functions*⟩+≡   ▲ 400 402 ▼

```
static void rewrite(p) Node p; {
    prelabel(p);
    (*IR->x._label)(p);
    reduce(p, 1);
}
```

The interface function gen receives a forest from the front end and makes several passes over the trees.

⟨*gen.c data*⟩+≡   ▲ 398 410 ▼

```
Node head;
```

⟨*gen.c functions*⟩+≡   ▲ 402 404 ▼

```
Node gen(forest) Node forest; {
    int i;
    struct node sentinel;
    Node dummy, p;

    head = forest;
    for (p = forest; p; p = p->link) {
        ⟨select instructions for p 402⟩
    }
    for (p = forest; p; p = p->link)
        prune(p, &dummy);
    ⟨linearize forest 414⟩
    ⟨allocate registers 415⟩
    return forest;
}
```

The first pass calls rewrite to select instructions, and the second prunes the subinstructions out of the tree. The first pass performs any target-specific processing for arguments and procedure calls; for example, it arranges to pass arguments in registers when that's what the calling convention specifies:

⟨*select instructions for p* 402⟩≡   402

```
if (generic(p->op) == CALL)
    docall(p);
else if (    generic(p->op) == ASGN
&& generic(p->kids[1]->op) == CALL)
```

```
    docall(p->kids[1]);
else if (generic(p->op) == ARG)
    (*IR->x.doarg)(p);
rewrite(p);
p->x.listed = 1;
```

Only doarg is target-specific. Within any one tree, the code generator is free to evaluate the nodes in whatever order seems best, so long as it evaluates children before parents. Calls can have side effects, so the front end puts all calls on the forest to fix the order in which the side effects happen. If the call returns no value, or if the returned value is ignored, then the call itself appears on the forest; the first if statement recognizes this pattern. Otherwise, the call appears below an assignment to a temporary, which is later used where the returned value is needed; the second if statement recognizes this pattern.

The first pass also marks listed nodes. Chapter 15 elaborates on this and on the rest of gen's passes.

14.9 Shared Rules

A few rules are common to all targets in this book. They are factored out in a target-independent fragment to save space and to keep them consistent as lcc changes. Some common rules match the integer constants:

⟨*shared rules* 400⟩+≡   400 403   431 463 496
```
con: CNSTC  "%a"
con: CNSTI  "%a"
con: CNSTP  "%a"
con: CNSTS  "%a"
con: CNSTU  "%a"
```

A convention shared by all lburg specifications in this book has the nonterminal reg match all computations that yield a result in a register and the nonterminal stmt match all roots, which are executed for some side effect, typically on memory or the program counter. The rule

⟨*shared rules* 400⟩+≡   403 403   431 463 496
```
stmt: reg   ""
```

is necessary when a node that yields a register appears as a root. A CALLI is such a node when the caller ignores its value.

The following rules note that no current lcc target requires any computation to convert an integral or pointer type to another such type of the same size:

⟨*shared rules* 400⟩+≡   403   431 463 496
```
reg: CVIU(reg)   "%0"   notarget(a)
```

```
reg: CVPU(reg)   "%0"   notarget(a)
reg: CVUI(reg)   "%0"   notarget(a)
reg: CVUP(reg)   "%0"   notarget(a)
```

The cost function `notarget` makes a zero-cost match in most cases, but if register targeting has constrained the node to yield a fixed register — that is, the destination register is no longer a wildcard that represents a set of registers — then a register-to-register copy may be required, so `notarget` returns a cost that aborts this rule:

⟨*gen.c functions*⟩+≡   402 410

```
int notarget(p) Node p; {
    return p->syms[RX]->x.wildcard ? 0 : LBURG_MAX;
}
```

Each specification includes parallel rules that generate a unit-cost register copy, which is used when the node has a fixed target register.

14.10 Writing Specifications

Chapters 16–18 show some complete `lburg` inputs. Perhaps the easiest way to write an `lburg` specification is to start by adapting one explained in this book, but a few general principles can help. Page 436 illustrates several of these guidelines.

Write roughly one rule for each instruction and one for each addressing mode that you want to use. The templates give the assembler syntax, and the patterns describe the effect of the instruction using a tree of intermediate-language operators.

Replicate rules for equivalent operators. For example, a rule for ADDI usually requires a similar rule for ADDU and ADDP.

Write extra rules for each tree operator that can be implemented as a special case of some more general operation. For example, ADDRLP can often be implemented by adding a constant to the frame pointer, so whenever you write a rule that matches the sum of a constant and a register, write a variant of the rule that matches ADDRLP.

Write an extra rule for each degenerate case of a more general operation. For example, if some addressing mode matches the sum of a constant and a register, then it can also perform simple indirect addressing, when the constant is zero.

Write an extra rule that emits multiple instructions for each operator in the intermediate language that no single instruction implements. For example, many machines have no instruction that implements CVCI directly, so their specifications implement a rule whose template has two shift instructions. These instructions propagate the sign bit by shifting the byte left logically or arithmetically, then right arithmetically.

Use one nonterminal to derive all trees that yield a value. Use this nonterminal wherever the instruction corresponding to a rule pattern reads a register. This book uses the nonterminal reg this way. A variant that can catch a few more errors uses one nonterminal for general-purpose registers and another for floating-point registers (e.g. freg). For example, rules that use only one register nonterminal can silently accept corrupt trees like NEGF(INDIRI(...)). This particular error is rare.

Similarly, use one nonterminal to derive all trees executed only for side effect. Examples include ASGN and ARG. This book uses stmt for side-effect trees. It is possible to write lburg specifications that combine reg and stmt into one large class, but the register allocator assumes that the trees with side effects are roots, and trees with values are interior nodes or leaves; it can silently emit incorrect code — the worst nightmare for compiler writers — if its assumptions are violated. Separating reg from stmt makes the code generator object if these assumptions are ever violated.

Ensure that there's at least one way to generate code for each operation in the intermediate language. One easy way to do so is to write one register-to-register rule for each operator:

```
reg:   LEAF
reg:   UNARY(reg)
reg:   OPERATOR(reg,reg)
```

403 reg
403 stmt

Such rules ensure that lcc can match each node at least one way and emit assembler code with one instruction per node.

Scan your target's architecture manual for instructions or addressing modes that perform multiple intermediate-code operations, and write rules with patterns that match what the instructions compute. Rules 3 and 7 in Figure 14.2 are examples. If you have a full set of register-to-register rules, these bigger rules won't be necessary, but they typically emit code that is shorter and faster. Skip instructions and addressing modes so exotic that you can't imagine a C program — or a C compiler — that could use them.

Use nonterminals to factor the specification. If you find you're repeating a subpattern often, give it a rule and a nonterminal name of its own.

Further Reading

lcc's instruction selector is based on an algorithm originally described by Aho and Johnson (1976). The interface was adapted from burg (Fraser, Henry, and Proebsting 1992) and the implementation from the compatible program iburg (Fraser, Hanson, and Proebsting 1992). iburg performs dynamic programming at compile time. burg uses BURS theory (Pelegrí-Llopart and Graham 1988; Proebsting 1992) to do its dynamic programming when processing the specification, so it is faster but somewhat less flexible.

The retargetable compiler gcc (Stallman 1992) displays another way to select instructions. It uses a naive code generator and a thorough retargetable peephole optimizer that is driven by a description of the target machine. Davidson and Fraser (1984) describe the underlying method.

Exercises

14.1 What would break if we changed the type of costs from short to int?

14.2 _kids is not strictly necessary. Describe how you'd implement a reducer without it.

14.3 lburg represents each nonterminal with an integer in a compact range starting at one, which represents the start nonterminal. The zero-terminated vector _ntname is indexed by these numbers and holds the name of the corresponding nonterminal:

⟨*BURM signature* 378⟩+≡   391
```
    static char *_ntname[];
```

Use it to help write a procedure void dumpmatches(Node p) to display a node p and *all* rules that have matched it. Typical output might be

```
    dumpmatches(0x1001e790)=ADDRLP(i):
        addr: ADDRLP / %a($sp)
        rc: reg / $%1
        reg: addr / la $%c,%1
```

dumpmatches is *not* a reducer.

14.4 Tree parsers misbehave on dags. Does the labelling pass misbehave? Why or why not? Does the reducer misbehave? Why or why not?

14.5 Use the -d or -Wf-d option to compile

```
    f(i) { return (i-22)>>22; }
```

for any machine. The lines from dumpcover identify themselves. Which correspond to reuse's bonus matches? Which correspond to subsequent matches enabled by bonus matches?

14.6 How many instructions does the moveself optimization save when compiling lcc on your machine?

14.7 One measure of an optimization is whether it pays off compiling the compiler. For example, the `requate` optimization takes time. Can you detect how much time it takes on your machine? When the optimization is used to compile `lcc` with itself, it can save time by generating a faster compiler. Can you measure this improvement on your machine? Did `requate` pay off?

394 requate

15
Register Allocation

Register allocation can be viewed as having two parts: *allocation* decides which values will occupy registers, and *assignment* assigns a particular register to each value. Instruction selection commits certain subexpressions to registers and thus implicitly allocates *temporaries*, or *intermediate values*, but the allocation for register variables and the assignment of all registers has been left to this chapter.

Like all register allocators, lcc's has several tasks. It must keep track of which registers are free and which are busy. It must allocate a register at the beginning of the lifetime of a variable or an intermediate value, and it must free the register for other use at the end of that lifetime. Finally, when the register allocator runs out of registers, it must generate code to spill a register to memory and to reload it when the spilled value is needed again later.

lcc provides register variables, and it assigns some variables to registers even without explicit declarations, but this is the extent of its global register allocation. It does no interprocedural register allocation, and allocates temporaries only locally, within a forest.

More sophisticated register allocators are available, but this one yields code that is satisfactory and competitive with other compilers in wide use. lcc's spiller is particularly modest. Typical compilations spill so seldom that it seemed more effective to invest tuning effort elsewhere. A more ambitious register allocator would keep more values in registers over longer intervals, which would increase the demand for registers and thus would increase the number of spills. lcc's register allocator is simple, so its companion spiller can be simple too.

A top priority in the design of lcc's register allocator was that it have enough flexibility to match existing conventions for register usage, because we wanted lcc's code to work with common existing ANSI C libraries. That is, we didn't want to write, maintain, or compile with an lcc-specific library.

The second priority was overall simplicity, particularly minimizing target-specific code. These goals can conflict. For example, lcc's spiller is target independent, and thus must construct indirectly the instructions to spill and reload values. That is, it creates intermediate-code trees and passes them through the code generator; this is complicated by the fact that we're already in the middle of the code generator and out of registers to boot. A target-specific spiller would be simpler because it could simply emit target instructions to spill and reload the register, but we'd have to write and debug a new spiller for each target. Even with a simple spiller like lcc's, spills are rare, which means that good test cases for spillers are complex and hard to find, and spillers are thus hard to debug. One target-specific spiller would be simpler than lcc's, but the savings would've been lost over the long run.

15.1   Organization

Table 15.1 illustrates the overall organization of the register allocator by showing highlights from the call graph. Indentation shows who calls whom. This material is at a high level and is meant to orient us before we descend to the low levels.

After the back end has selected instructions and projected the subinstructions out of the tree — in the tree linked through the x.kids array — linearize traverses the projected tree in postorder and links the instructions in the order in which they will ultimately execute. gen walks down this list and passes each instruction to ralloc, which normally calls just putreg to free the registers no longer used by its children, and getreg to allocate a register for itself. For temporaries, ralloc allocates a register at the first assignment, and frees the register at the last use.

If getreg finds no free register that suits the instruction, it calls spillee to identify the most distantly used register. Then getreg calls spill to generate code to spill this register to memory and reload the value again later. genspill generates the spill, and genreload replaces all not-yet-processed uses of the register with nodes that load the value from memory. genreload calls reprune to reestablish the relationship between kids and x.kids that prune established before spilling changed the forest.

411	askfixedreg
411	askreg
92	gen
402	gen
426	genreload
424	genspill
412	getreg
81	kids
413	linearize
386	prune
410	putreg
417	ralloc
426	reprune
422	spillee
427	spill
423	spillr
359	x.kids

Name of Routine	Purpose
linearize	orders for output one instruction tree
ralloc	frees and allocates registers for one instruction
putreg	frees a busy register
getreg	finds and allocates a register
askreg	finds and allocates a free register
askfixedreg	tries to allocate a given register
spillee	identifies a register to spill
spill	spills one or more registers
spillr	spills one register
genspill	generates code to spill a register
genreload	generates code to reload a spilled value
reprune	updates kids after genreload updates x.kids

TABLE 15.1   Back-end call tree (simplified).

ralloc is not the only entry point for these routines. clobber calls spill directly to spill and reload such registers as those saved across calls by the caller. Also, each target's interface procedure local can reach askreg via askregvar, which tries to allocate a register for a register variable.

15.2 Tracking the Register State

Masks record which registers are free and which have been used during the routine being compiled. freemask tracks which registers are free; it tells the register allocator which registers it can allocate. usedmask tracks all registers that have been used by the current routine; it tells function which registers must be saved in the procedure prologue and restored in the epilogue. Both masks are vectors with one element for each register set.

⟨*gen.c data*⟩+≡   402 410

```
    unsigned freemask[2];
    unsigned usedmask[2];
```

Each target's function interface procedure initializes the masks to record that no registers have been used and all are free:

⟨*clear register state* 410⟩≡   448 485 519

```
    usedmask[0] = usedmask[1] = 0;
    freemask[0] = freemask[1] = ~(unsigned)0;
```

Each progbeg sets the parallel masks tmask and vmask. tmask identifies the registers to use for temporary values. vmask identifies the registers that may be allocated to register variables.

⟨*gen.c data*⟩+≡   410

```
    unsigned tmask[2];
    unsigned vmask[2];
```

Unallocable registers — the stack pointer, for instance — belong in neither tmask nor vmask.

The values of freemask and usedmask are maintained by the low-level routines putreg, getreg, askreg, and askregvar, which allocate and free individual registers. putreg frees the register represented by symbol r. Only freemask distinguishes busy registers from free ones, so putreg need change nothing else.

⟨*gen.c functions*⟩+≡   404 411

```
    static void putreg(r) Symbol r; {
        freemask[r->x.regnode->set] |= r->x.regnode->mask;
    }
```

askfixedregr allocates a fixed register r if possible. If the register is busy, askfixedreg returns null. Otherwise, it adjusts the record of the register state and returns r.

⟨gen.c functions⟩+≡   410 411

```
static Symbol askfixedreg(s) Symbol s; {
    Regnode r = s->x.regnode;
    int n = r->set;

    if (r->mask&~freemask[n])
        return NULL;
    else {
        freemask[n] &= ~r->mask;
        usedmask[n] |=  r->mask;
        return s;
    }
}
```

askreg accepts a symbol that represents one fixed register or a wild-card symbol that represents a set of registers. askreg's second argument is a mask that can limit the wildcard. If the register is fixed, askreg simply calls askfixedreg. Otherwise, it looks for a free register acceptable to the mask and the set of registers represented by the wildcard:

⟨gen.c functions⟩+≡   411 412

```
static Symbol askreg(rs, rmask)
Symbol rs; unsigned rmask[]; {
    int i;

    if (rs->x.wildcard == NULL)
        return askfixedreg(rs);
    for (i = 31; i >= 0; i--) {
        Symbol r = rs->x.wildcard[i];
        if (r != NULL
        && !(r->x.regnode->mask&~rmask[r->x.regnode->set])
        && askfixedreg(r))
            return r;
    }
    return NULL;
}
```

The use of register masks places an upper bound on the number of reg-isters in a register set; the upper bound is the number of bits in an unsigned integer mask on the machine that hosts the compiler. This number has been 32 for every target to date, so fixing askregvar's loop to 32 iterations seemed tolerable at first. But lcc's latest code generator — for the X86 — would compile faster if we could define smaller register sets, and machines exist that have bigger ones. There are now machines with thirty-two 64-bit integer registers, which undermines the motive behind the shortcut. If we were doing it over, we'd represent register sets with a structure that could accommodate sets of variable sizes.

getreg *demands* a register. If askreg can't find one, then spillee selects one to spill, and spill edits the forest to include instructions that store it to memory and reload it when it's needed. The second askreg is thus guaranteed to find a register.

⟨*gen.c functions*⟩+≡   411 412

```
static Symbol getreg(s, mask, p)
Symbol s; unsigned mask[]; Node p; {
    Symbol r = askreg(s, mask);
    if (r == NULL) {
        r = spillee(s, p);
        spill(r->x.regnode->mask, r->x.regnode->set, p);
        r = askreg(s, mask);
    }
    r->x.regnode->vbl = NULL;
    return r;
}
```

If a register is allocated to a variable, x.regnode->vbl points to the symbol that represents the variable; getreg's default assumes that the register is not allocated to a variable, so it clears the vbl field.

askregvar tries to allocate a register to a local variable or formal parameter. It returns one if it succeeds and zero otherwise:

⟨*gen.c functions*⟩+≡   412 413

```
int askregvar(p, regs) Symbol p, regs; {
    Symbol r;

    ⟨askregvar 412⟩
}
```

askregvar declines to allocate a register if the variable is an aggregate, or if it doesn't have the register storage class:

⟨askregvar 412⟩≡   413 412

```
if (p->sclass != REGISTER)
    return 0;
else if (!isscalar(p->type)) {
    p->sclass = AUTO;
    return 0;
}
```

If u.t.cse is set, then the variable is a temporary allocated to hold a common subexpression, and askregvar postpones allocation until the register allocator processes the expression:

⟨askregvar 412⟩+≡   412 413   412
```
  else if (p->temporary && p->u.t.cse) {
      p->x.name = "?";
      return 1;
  }
```

Waiting helps lcc use one register for more than one temporary. To help distinguish such variables when debugging the compiler, askregvar temporarily sets the x.name field of such temporaries to a question mark.

If none of the conditions above is met, askregvar asks askreg for a register. If one is found, the symbol is updated to point at the register:

⟨askregvar 412⟩+≡   413 413   412
```
  else if ((r = askreg(regs, vmask)) != NULL) {
      p->x.regnode = r->x.regnode;
      p->x.regnode->vbl = p;
      p->x.name = r->x.name;
      return 1;
  }
```

Otherwise, the variable is forced onto the stack:

⟨askregvar 412⟩+≡   413   412
```
  else {
      p->sclass = AUTO;
      return 0;
  }
```

15.3 Allocating Registers

Register allocation starts by picking the order in which to execute the instructions. linearize(p, next) linearizes the instruction tree rooted at p. The list is doubly linked through the x.next and x.prev fields. The parameter next points to a sentinel at the end of the list formed so far. linearize adds the dotted lines that turn Figure 14.5 into Figure 15.1.

⟨gen.c macros⟩+≡   395
```
  #define relink(a, b) ((b)->x.prev = (a), (a)->x.next = (b))
```

⟨gen.c functions⟩+≡   412 417
```
  static void linearize(p, next) Node next, p; {
      int i;

      for (i = 0; i < NELEMS(p->x.kids) && p->x.kids[i]; i++)
          linearize(p->x.kids[i], next);
      relink(next->x.prev, p);
```

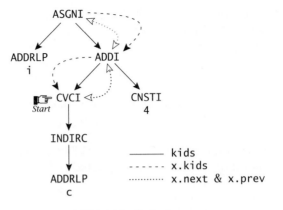

FIGURE 15.1   Ordering uses.

```
        relink(p, next);
    }
```

linearize traverses the tree in preorder, so it starts by processing
the subtrees recursively. Then it appends p to the growing list, which
amounts to inserting it between next and its predecessor. The first
relink points next's predecessor forward to p and p back at next's predecessor. The second relink does the same operation for p and next
themselves.

gen calls relink to initialize the list to a circular list holding only the
sentinel:

⟨*linearize forest* 414⟩≡   414   402
    relink(&sentinel, &sentinel);

Then it runs down the forest, linearizing each listed tree, and linking the
trees into the growing list before the sentinel:

⟨*linearize forest* 414⟩+≡   414 414   402
    for (p = forest; p; p = p->link)
        linearize(p, &sentinel);

At the end of the loop, gen sets forest to the head of the list, which is
the node *after* the sentinel in the circular list:

⟨*linearize forest* 414⟩+≡   414 414   402
    forest = sentinel.x.next;

Finally, it clears the first x.prev and the last x.next to break the circle:

⟨*linearize forest* 414⟩+≡   414   402
    sentinel.x.next->x.prev = NULL;
    sentinel.x.prev->x.next = NULL;

The register allocator makes three passes over the forest. The first builds a list of all the nodes that use each temporary. This list identifies the last use and thus when the temporary should be freed, and identifies the nodes that must be changed when a temporary must be spilled to memory. If p->syms[RX] points to a temporary, then the value of p->syms[RX]->x.lastuse points to the last node that uses p; that node's x.prevuse points to the previous user, and so on. The list includes nodes that read *and* write the temporary:

⟨*allocate registers* 415⟩≡   415   402

```
for (p = forest; p; p = p->x.next)
    for (i = 0; i < NELEMS(p->x.kids) && p->x.kids[i]; i++) {
        if (p->x.kids[i]->syms[RX]->temporary) {
            p->x.kids[i]->x.prevuse =
                p->x.kids[i]->syms[RX]->x.lastuse;
            p->x.kids[i]->syms[RX]->x.lastuse = p->x.kids[i];
        }
    }
}
```

The fragment uses nested loops — first the instructions, then the children of each instruction — to visit the uses in the order in which they'll be executed. A single unnested loop over the forest is tempting but wrong:

```
for (p = forest; p; p = p->x.next)
    if (p->syms[RX]->temporary) {
        p->x.prevuse = p->syms[RX]->x.lastuse;
        p->syms[RX]->x.lastuse = p;
    }
}
```

311	forest
19	NELEMS
362	RX
50	temporary
359	x.kids
362	x.lastuse
359	x.next
359	x.prevuse

It would visit the same uses, but the order would be wrong for some inputs. For example, a[i]=a[i]-1 uses the address of a[i] twice and thus assigns it to a temporary. This incorrect code would visit the INDIR that fetches the temporary for the left-hand side first, so the INDIR that fetches the temporary for the right-hand side would appear to be the last use. The temporary would be freed after the load and reused to hold the difference, and the subsequent store would use a corrupt address. Figure 15.2 shows the effect of the loop nesting on the order of the x.prevuse chain for this example.

The second pass over the forest eliminates some instructions that copy one register to another, by targeting the expression that computed the source register to use the destination register instead. If the source is a common subexpression, we use the destination to hold the common subexpression if the code between the two instructions is straight-line code and doesn't change the destination:

⟨*allocate registers* 415⟩+≡   415 417   402

```
for (p = forest; p; p = p->x.next)
```

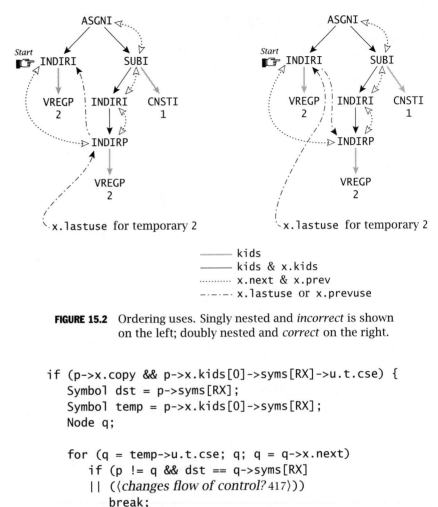

FIGURE 15.2   Ordering uses. Singly nested and *incorrect* is shown on the left; doubly nested and *correct* on the right.

```
if (p->x.copy && p->x.kids[0]->syms[RX]->u.t.cse) {
    Symbol dst = p->syms[RX];
    Symbol temp = p->x.kids[0]->syms[RX];
    Node q;

    for (q = temp->u.t.cse; q; q = q->x.next)
        if (p != q && dst == q->syms[RX]
        || (⟨changes flow of control? 417⟩))
            break;
    if (!q)
        for (q = temp->x.lastuse; q; q = q->x.prevuse)
            q->syms[RX] = dst;
}
```

The first inner loop scans the rest of the forest and exits early if the destination is set anywhere later in the block or if some node changes the flow of control. It could quit looking when the temporary dies, but the extra logic cut only five instructions out of 25,000 in one test, so we discarded it. If no other node sets the destination, then it's safe to use that register for the common subexpression. The second inner loop changes all instances of the common subexpression to use the destination instead. Once the common subexpression is computed into dst, the original register-to-register copy copies dst to itself. The emitter and moveself collaborate to cut such instructions.

Calls are deemed a break in straight-line code only if the destination isn't a register variable, because calls don't change register variables:

⟨*changes flow of control?* 417⟩≡   416
```
q->op == LABELV || q->op == JUMPV || generic(q->op)==RET ||
generic(q->op)==EQ || generic(q->op)==NE ||
generic(q->op)==LE || generic(q->op)==LT ||
generic(q->op)==GE || generic(q->op)==GT ||
(generic(q->op) == CALL && dst->sclass != REGISTER)
```

The last pass over the forest finally allocates a register for each node. rmap is a vector indexed by a type suffix; each element is the register wildcard that represents the set of registers that suit untargeted nodes of the corresponding type.

⟨*allocate registers* 415⟩+≡   ▲415   402
```
for (p = forest; p; p = p->x.next) {
    ralloc(p);
    if (p->x.listed && NeedsReg[opindex(p->op)]
    && rmap[optype(p->op)]) {
        putreg(p->syms[RX]);
    }
}
```

Registers are freed when the parent reaches ralloc, but a few nodes, like CALLI, can allocate a register and have no parent, if the value goes unused. The if statement above frees the register allocated to such nodes. Existing targets use this code only for CALLs and LOADs.

ralloc(p) frees the registers no longer needed by p's children, then allocates a register for p, if p needs one and wasn't processed earlier. Finally, it calls the target's clobber to spill any registers that this node clobbers:

⟨*gen.c functions*⟩+≡   ▲413 422▼
```
static void ralloc(p) Node p; {
    int i;
    unsigned mask[2];

    mask[0] = tmask[0];
    mask[1] = tmask[1];
    ⟨free input registers 418⟩
    if (!p->x.registered && NeedsReg[opindex(p->op)]
    && rmap[optype(p->op)]) {
        ⟨assign output register 418⟩
    }
    p->x.registered = 1;
    (*IR->x.clobber)(p);
}
```

If a child yields a register variable, or if the register holds a common subexpression for which other uses remain, then its register must not be freed. The if statement below catches exactly these exceptions:

⟨*free input registers* 418⟩≡   417
```
    for (i = 0; i < NELEMS(p->x.kids) && p->x.kids[i]; i++) {
        Node kid = p->x.kids[i];
        Symbol r = kid->syms[RX];
        if (r->sclass != REGISTER && r->x.lastuse == kid)
            putreg(r);
    }
```

r->x.lastuse points to r's last use. For most expression temporaries, there is only one use, but temporaries allocated to common subexpressions have multiple uses.

Now ralloc allocates a register to this node. prelabel has stored in p->syms[RX] a register or wildcard that identifies the registers that p will accept. Again, common subexpressions complicate matters because askregvar has pointed their p->syms[RX] at a register variable that hasn't yet been allocated. So we need to use two values: sym is p->syms[RX], and set is the set of registers that suit p:

⟨*assign output register* 418⟩≡   418   417
```
    Symbol sym = p->syms[RX], set = sym;
    if (sym->temporary && sym->u.t.cse)
        set = rmap[optype(p->op)];
```

If p needs no register, then ralloc is done. Otherwise, it asks getreg for a register and stores it in the node or nodes that need it:

⟨*assign output register* 418⟩+≡   418   417
```
    if (set->sclass != REGISTER) {
        Symbol r;
        ⟨mask out some input registers 419⟩
        r = getreg(set, mask, p);
        ⟨assign r to nodes 419⟩
    }
```

ralloc frees the input registers before allocating the output register, which allows it to reuse an input register as the output register. This economy is always safe when the node is implemented by a single instruction, but it can be unsafe if a node is implemented by a sequence of instructions: If the output register is also one of the input registers, and if the sequence changes the output register before reading the corresponding input register, then the read fetches a corrupt value. We take care that all rules that emit instruction sequences set their output register only after they finish reading all input registers. Most templates emit just one instruction, so this assumption is a good default, but it does require considerable care with multi-instruction sequences.

This rule is impractical for instructions that *require* the output register to be one of the input registers. For example, the X86 add instructions take only two operands; they add the second to the first and leave the result in the first. If the first operand isn't dead yet, the generated code must form the sum into a free register, and it must start by copying the first operand to this free register. The code template is thus generally two instructions: the first copies the first operand to the destination register, and the second computes the sum. For example, the X86 add template is:

```
reg: ADDI(reg,mri1)   "mov %c,%0\nadd %c,%1\n"   2
```

Such templates change the output register *before* reading all input registers, so they violate the rule above.

To handle two-operand instructions, we mark their code templates with a leading question mark. That is, the complete form of the rule above is:

```
reg: ADDI(reg,mri1)   "?mov %c,%0\nadd %c,%1\n"   2
```

When ralloc sees such a rule, it edits mask to prevent reallocation of all input registers but the first, which is why the loop below starts at one instead of zero:

⟨*mask out some input registers* 419⟩≡   418

```
if (*IR->x._templates[getrule(p, p->x.inst)] == '?')
    for (i = 1; i < NELEMS(p->x.kids) && p->x.kids[i]; i++) {
        Symbol r = p->x.kids[i]->syms[RX];
        mask[r->x.regnode->set] &= ~r->x.regnode->mask;
    }
```

The code generators must take care that no node targets the same register as any of its children except the first.

Once the register is allocated, ralloc stores the allocated register into the nodes that use it:

⟨*assign r to nodes* 419⟩≡   418

```
if (sym->temporary && sym->u.t.cse) {
    Node q;
    r->x.lastuse = sym->x.lastuse;
    for (q = sym->x.lastuse; q; q = q->x.prevuse) {
        q->syms[RX] = r;
        q->x.registered = 1;
        if (q->x.copy)
            q->x.equatable = 1;
    }
}
```

```
    } else {
        p->syms[RX] = r;
        r->x.lastuse = p;
    }
```

If the node is not a common subexpression, the else clause stores r into
p->syms[RX] and notes the single use in r->x.lastuse. If sym is a common subexpression, x.lastuse already identifies the users, so the fragment runs down the list, storing r and marking the node as processed
by the register allocator. It also notes in x.equatable if the common
subexpression is already available in some other register.

15.4 Spilling

When the register allocator runs out of registers, it generates code to
spill a busy register to memory, and it replaces all not-yet-processed
uses of that register with nodes that *reload* the value from memory.
More ambitious alternatives are available — see Exercises 15.6 and 15.7
— but lcc omits them. Spills are rare, so lcc's spiller has been made as
simple as possible without sacrificing target independence. It would be
wasteful to tune code that is seldom used, and test cases are hard to find
and hard to isolate, so it would be hard to test a complex implementation
thoroughly.

When the register allocator runs out of registers, it spills to memory
the most distantly used register, which is the optimal choice. The spiller
replaces all not-yet-processed uses of that register with nodes that load
the value from memory, and it frees the register to satisfy the current
request.

Several routines collaborate to handle spills: spillee identifies the
best register to spill, and spillr calls genspill to insert the spill code
and genreload to insert the reloads. Figure 15.3 illustrates their operation on the program

```
    int i;
    main() { i = f() + f(); }
```

which is the simplest program that spills on most targets. It spills the
value of the first call from the return register so that it won't be destroyed
by the second call.

The figure's first column shows the forest before code generation; that
is, the forest from the front end after prelabel substitutes VREGs for
ADDRLs that reference (temporary) register variables and injects LOADs to
write such registers. The second column shows the forest after lineariza-
tion; it assumes that the nodes linked by arcs with open arrowheads are

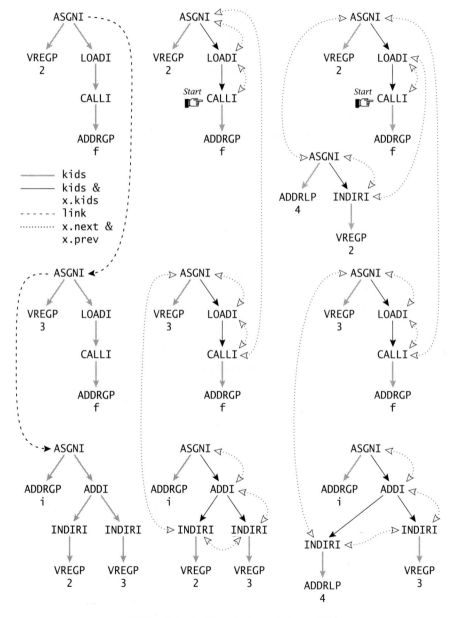

FIGURE 15.3 Spilling in i = f() + f().

instructions — although INDIR and ASGN nodes that read and write registers are typically just comment instructions — and the rest are subinstructions like address calculations. The last column shows the injected
spill and reload, which use ADDRLP(4). The dark arrows in the last two
columns show kids and x.kids, which are the links that remain when
subinstructions are projected out of the tree.

When getreg runs out of registers, it calls spillee (set,here) to
identify the register in set that is used at the greatest distance from
here:

⟨*gen.c functions*⟩+≡   417 422

```
static Symbol spillee(set, here) Node here; Symbol set; {
    Symbol bestreg = NULL;
    int bestdist = -1, i;

    if (!set->x.wildcard)
        return set;
    for (i = 31; i >= 0; i--) {
        Symbol ri = set->x.wildcard[i];
        if (ri != NULL && ri->x.lastuse
        && ri->x.regnode->mask&tmask[ri->x.regnode->set]) {
            Regnode rn = ri->x.regnode;
            Node q = here;
            int dist = 0;
            for (; q && !uses(q, rn->mask); q = q->x.next)
                dist++;
            if (q && dist > bestdist) {
                bestdist = dist;
                bestreg = ri;
            }
        }
    }
    return bestreg;
}
```

If set is not a wildcard, then it denotes a single register; only that register
will do, so spillee simply returns it. Otherwise, set denotes a proper
set of registers, and spillee searches for an element of that set with the
most distant use. spillee calls uses to see if node p reads one given
register:

⟨*gen.c functions*⟩+≡   422 423

```
static int uses(p, mask) Node p; unsigned mask; {
    int i;
    Node q;
```

```
        for (i = 0; i < NELEMS(p->x.kids)
            && (q = p->x.kids[i]) != NULL; i++)
            if (q->x.registered
            && mask&q->syms[RX]->x.regnode->mask)
                return 1;
        return 0;
    }
```

spillr(r, here) spills register r and changes each use of r after here to use a reload instead:

⟨*gen.c functions*⟩+≡　　　　　　　　　　　　　　　　　　　　422 424

```
    static void spillr(r, here) Symbol r; Node here; {
        int i;
        Symbol tmp;
        Node p = r->x.lastuse;
        ⟨spillr 423⟩
    }
```

spillr spills the register to memory. It is sometimes possible to spill to another register, but this complicates the logic because it risks another spill and thus infinite recursion. spillr finds the first use — the x.prevuse chain *ends* with the first use — which is the assignment that establishes the value in r:

⟨spillr 423⟩≡　　　　　　　　　　　　　　　　　　　423　　423

```
    while (p->x.prevuse)
        p = p->x.prevuse;
```

r can hold a simple expression temporary with a single use or a common subexpression with multiple uses, but both are assigned by exactly one instruction. spillr finds it and sends it to genspill, which stitches a spill into the forest at the assignment:

⟨spillr 423⟩+≡　　　　　　　　　　　　　　　　　　423 423　　423

```
    tmp = newtemp(AUTO, optype(p->op));
    genspill(r, p, tmp);
```

The spill could be done anywhere between the assignment and here, but the site of the assignment is a good safe place for it, which explains why the spill in Figure 15.3 is in the last column's first tree.

Next, spillr changes all remaining nodes that read r to load the spill cell instead; it concludes by freeing r:

⟨spillr 423⟩+≡　　　　　　　　　　　　　　　　　　　423　　423

```
    for (p = here->x.next; p; p = p->x.next)
        for (i = 0; i < NELEMS(p->x.kids) && p->x.kids[i]; i++) {
            Node k = p->x.kids[i];
```

```
        if (k->x.registered && k->syms[RX] == r)
            genreload(p, tmp, i);
    }
    putreg(r);
```

The scan for nodes that read r starts with here->x.next instead of here for reasons that are subtle. here can spill one of its own kids. For example, the code (*f)() might load the value of the pointer into a caller-saved register and then use an indirect call instruction, which clobber must spill. Most instruction templates hold just one instruction, so they finish reading their input registers before clobbering anything; the indirect call, for example, doesn't clobber the address register until after it's done with the value, unless the address register is used again by an instruction *after* the call, which is at or after here->x.next.

Also, genreload doesn't call ralloc to allocate registers for the nodes that it inserts. genreload stitches each reload into the list of instructions just before the instruction that uses the reloaded value. Such instructions had referenced the spilled value at or before here, but genreload edits them to use reloads that are *after* here. We simply postpone register allocation for the new instructions until ralloc encounters them on the list of remaining instructions.

genspill(r, last, tmp) spills to tmp the assignment of r at last:

⟨*gen.c functions*⟩+≡   423 426
```
    static void genspill(r, last, tmp)
    Symbol r, tmp; Node last; {
        Node p, q;
        Symbol s;
        unsigned ty;

        ⟨genspill 424⟩
    }
```

genspill synthesizes a register variable of the appropriate type to use in the spill:

⟨genspill 424⟩≡   425   424
```
    ty = optype(last->op);
    if (ty == U)
        ty = I;
    NEW0(s, FUNC);
    s->sclass = REGISTER;
    s->x.name = r->x.name;
    s->x.regnode = r->x.regnode;
    s->x.regnode->vbl = s;
```

The register being spilled is not a register variable, but pretending it is ensures that no instructions will be generated to compute the value to be spilled, because INDIR*x* (VREGP) emits nothing. The value has been computed already, and we want no additional instructions. Next, genspill creates nodes to spill the register to memory:

⟨genspill 424⟩+≡   424 425   424

```
q = newnode(ADDRLP, NULL, NULL, s);
q = newnode(INDIR + ty, q, NULL, NULL);
p = newnode(ADDRLP, NULL, NULL, tmp);
p = newnode(ASGN + ty, p, q, NULL);
```

Now genspill selects instructions, projects out the subinstructions, and linearizes the resulting instruction tree:

⟨genspill 424⟩+≡   425 425   424

```
rewrite(p);
prune(p, &q);
q = last->x.next;
linearize(p, q);
```

Finally, it passes the new nodes through the register allocator:

⟨genspill 424⟩+≡   425   424

```
for (p = last->x.next; p != q; p = p->x.next) {
    ralloc(p);
}
```

If the call on genspill originated because ralloc ran out of registers, these calls risk infinite recursion if they actually try to allocate a register. We must take care that the code generator can spill a register without allocating another register. Spills are stores, which usually take just one instruction and thus need no additional register, but some machines have limits on the size of the constant part of address calculations and thus require two instructions and a temporary register to complete a store to an arbitrary address. Therefore we must ensure that these stores use a register that is not otherwise allocated by ralloc. The MIPS R3000 architecture has such restrictions, but the assembler handles the problem using a temporary register reserved for the assembler. The SPARC target is the only one so far that requires attention from the code generator; Section 17.2 elaborates.

genspill's ralloc calls above must allocate no register, but it calls ralloc anyway, since ralloc is responsible for more than just allocating a register. It also calls, for example, the target's clobber. It is unlikely that a simple store would cause clobber to do anything, but some future target could do so, so genspill would hide a latent bug if it didn't call ralloc. The back end sends all other nodes through rewrite, prune, linearize, and ralloc, so it seems unwise to omit any of these steps for spill nodes.

genreload(p, tmp, i) changes p->x.kids[i] to load tmp instead of reading a register that has now been spilled:

⟨*gen.c functions*⟩+≡   424 426
                                                                            ▼
```
static void genreload(p, tmp, i)
Node p; Symbol tmp; int i; {
    Node q;
    int ty;

    ⟨genreload 426⟩
}
```

It changes the target node to a tree that loads `tmp`, selects instructions
for it, and projects out the subinstructions:

⟨genreload 426⟩≡   426   426
                                                                      ▼
```
ty = optype(p->x.kids[i]->op);
if (ty == U)
    ty = I;
q = newnode(ADDRLP, NULL, NULL, tmp);
p->x.kids[i] = newnode(INDIR + ty, q, NULL, NULL);
rewrite(p->x.kids[i]);
prune(p->x.kids[i], &q);
```

Next, `genreload` linearizes the reloading instructions, as is usual after
pruning, but we need two extra steps first:

⟨genreload 426⟩+≡   ▲
                                                                     426   426
```
reprune(&p->kids[1], reprune(&p->kids[0], 0, i, p), i, p);
prune(p, &q);
linearize(p->x.kids[i], p);
```

In most cases, each entry in `x.kids` was copied from some entry in some
`kids` by `prune`, but `genreload` has changed `x.kids[i]` without updat-
ing the corresponding entry in any `kids`. The emitter uses `kids`, so
`genreload` must find and update the corresponding entry. The call on
`reprune` above does this, and the second call on `prune` makes any similar
changes to the node at which `p` points.

   `reprune(pp, k, n, p)` is called to reestablish the connection between
`kids` and `x.kids` when `p->x.kids[n]` has changed. That is, `reprune` must
do whatever is necessary to make it look like the reloads were in the forest from the beginning. `reprune` is thus an incremental version of `prune`:
`prune` establishes a correspondence between `kids` and `x.kids` for a complete tree, and `reprune` reestablishes this correspondence after a change
to just one of them, namely the one corresponding to the reload. Figure 15.4 shows how `reprune` repairs the final tree shown in Figure 15.3.

   The initial, root-level call on `reprune` has a pointer, `pp`, that points to
the first `kids` entry that might need change.

⟨*gen.c functions*⟩+≡   ▲
                                                                    426 427
                                                                          ▼
```
static int reprune(pp, k, n, p) Node p, *pp; int k, n; {
    struct node x, *q = *pp;
```

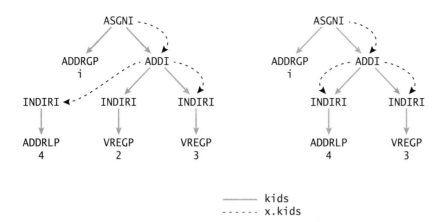

———— kids
------ x.kids

FIGURE 15.4 Figure 15.3's reload before and after reprune.

```
if (q == NULL || k > n)
    return k;
else if (q->x.inst == 0)
    return reprune(&q->kids[1],
        reprune(&q->kids[0], k, n, p), n, p);
if (k == n) {
    *pp = p->x.kids[n];
    x = *p;
    (IR->x.target)(&x);
}
return k + 1;
}
```

kids link the original tree, and x.kids link the instruction tree. The second is a projection of the first, but an arbitrary number of nodes have been projected out, so finding the kids entry that corresponds to p->x.kids[i] requires a recursive tree search. reprune's recursive calls track prune's recursive calls. They bump k, which starts out at zero, and advance p in exactly those cases where prune finds an instruction and sets the next entry in x.kids. So when k reaches n, reprune has found the kids entry to update, and x confines the change to the reload.

getreg and each target's clobber call spill(mask, n, here) to spill all busy registers in register set n that overlap the registers indicated by mask. A typical use is for CALL nodes, because calls generally corrupt some registers, which must be spilled before the call and reloaded afterward. spill marks the registers as used and runs down the rest of the forest looking for live registers that need spilling. It economizes by first confirming that there are registers that need spilling:

⟨gen.c functions⟩+≡   426▲

```
void spill(mask, n, here) unsigned mask; int n; Node here; {
```

```
    int i;
    Node p;

    usedmask[n] |= mask;
    if (mask&~freemask[n])
        for (p = here; p; p = p->x.next)
            ⟨spill 428⟩
}
```

The inner loop below identifies the live registers that need spilling and calls spillr to spill them:

```
⟨spill 428⟩≡                                                          428
    for (i = 0; i < NELEMS(p->x.kids) && p->x.kids[i]; i++) {
        Symbol r = p->x.kids[i]->syms[RX];
        if (p->x.kids[i]->x.registered && r->x.regnode->set == n
        && r->x.regnode->mask&mask)
            spillr(r, here);
    }
```

Spill gives lcc caller-saved registers for free, as a special case of a mechanism that is needed for oddball instructions that clobber some fixed set of registers.

Further Reading

Execution ordering determines the order of the instruction in the output. Most languages are only partially constrained. For example, ANSI specifies that we must evaluate assignment statements in order, but it doesn't care which operand of an assignment is computed first. linearize uses one fixed order, but better alternatives exist. For example, *Sethi-Ullman numbering* (Aho, Sethi, and Ullman 1986) can save registers by evaluating first the children that need the most registers.

Instruction scheduling interacts with register allocation. It helps to start slow instructions long before their result is needed, but this ties up the result register longer and thus uses more registers. Proebsting and Fischer (1991) solve one class of trade-offs compactly. Krishnamurthy (1990) surveys some of the literature in instruction scheduling.

Many ambitious register allocators use graph coloring. The compiler builds a graph in which the values computed are the nodes, and it links two nodes if and only if the two values are ever live at the same time, which means that they can't share a register or, equivalently, a graph color. Chaitin et al. (1981) describe the process.

Selecting a register to spill is related to page replacement in operating systems. Virtual memory systems can't know the most distantly used page, but spillers can determine the most distantly used register (Freiburghouse 1974).

Exercises

15.1 Section 15.3 describes an optimization abandoned because it saved only 5 instructions out of 25,000 in one test. Implement the optimization and see if you can find useful programs that the optimization improves more.

15.2 Adapt lcc to use Sethi-Ullman numbering. How much faster does it make lcc's code for your programs?

15.3 Construct some input programs that exercise the spiller.

15.4 Change `spillee` to spill the least recently used register. Using timings, can you detect any difference in compilation rate or quality of the generated code for some useful programs?

15.5 The simplest compilers omit spillers and die uttering a diagnostic instead. Remove lcc's spiller. You'll have to change `clobber`. How much simpler is the new compiler? How many of your favorite C programs do you need to compile before one is rejected? How does this number change if you change CALLs to copy the result register to an arbitrary register, thus avoiding the spill in f()+f()?

357	clobber
435	" (MIPS)
468	" (SPARC)
502	" (X86)
422	spillee

15.6 Some spills occur when registers are still available. For example, the expression f()+f() must spill the first return value from the return register because the second call needs the same register, but other registers might be free. Change lcc's spiller to spill to another register when it can. How much does this change improve the code for your favorite C programs? Was it worth the effort?

15.7 lcc generates one reload for each reference processed after the spill, but fewer reloads can suffice. Change lcc's spiller to avoid gratuitous reloads. How much does this change improve the code for your favorite C programs? Was it worth the effort?

16
Generating MIPS R3000 Code

The MIPS R3000 architecture and the companion R3010 floating-point unit comprise a RISC. They have 32 32-bit registers each, a compact set of 32-bit instructions, and one addressing mode. They access memory only through explicit load and store instructions. The calling convention passes some arguments in registers.

We might begin this chapter with a complete description of the MIPS assembler language, but describing the add instruction in isolation and then giving it again in the rule for ADDI later would be repetitious, so we begin not with a reference manual but rather with a few sample instructions, as shown in Table 16.1. Our aim here is to appreciate the general syntax of the assembler language — the appearance and position of registers, addresses, opcodes, and assembler directives. This understanding, plus the templates and the text that describes the rules, plus the parallel construction of repetitive rules, tell us what we need to know about the target machine.

The file `mips.c` collects all target-specific code and data for the MIPS

Assembler	Meaning
move $10,$11	Set register 10 to the value in register 11.
subu $10,$11,$12	Set register 10 to register 11 minus register 12.
subu $10,$11,12	Set register 10 to register 11 minus the constant 12.
lb $10,11($12)	Set register 10 to the byte at the address 11 bytes past the address in register 12.
sub.d $f12,$f14,$f16	Set register 12 to register 14 minus register 16. Use double-precision floating-point registers and arithmetic.
sub.s $f12,$f14,$f16	Set register 12 to register 14 minus register 16. Use single-precision floating-point registers and arithmetic.
b L1	Jump to the instruction labelled L1.
j $31	Jump to the address in register 31.
blt $10,$11,L1	Branch to L1 if register 10 is less than register 11.
.byte 0x20	Initialize the next byte in memory to hexadecimal 20.

TABLE 16.1 Sample MIPS assembler input lines.

code generator. It's an `lburg` specification with the interface routines after the grammar:

⟨`mips.md` 431⟩≡
```
%{
```
⟨*mips.c macros*⟩
⟨*lburg prefix* 375⟩
⟨*interface prototypes*⟩
⟨*MIPS prototypes*⟩
⟨*MIPS data* 433⟩
```
%}
```
⟨*terminal declarations* 376⟩
```
%%
```
⟨*shared rules* 400⟩
⟨*MIPS rules* 436⟩
```
%%
```
⟨*MIPS functions* 433⟩
⟨*MIPS interface definition* 431⟩

The last fragment configures the front end and points to the MIPS code and to data in the back end. Most targets have just one interface record, but MIPS machines can be configured as either big or little endian, so `lcc` needs two interface records for them:

79 Interface

⟨*MIPS interface definition* 431⟩≡   431
```
    Interface mipsebIR = {
```
⟨*MIPS type metrics* 431⟩
```
        0, /* little_endian */
```
⟨*shared interface definition* 432⟩
```
    }, mipselIR = {
```
⟨*MIPS type metrics* 431⟩
```
        1, /* little_endian */
```
⟨*shared interface definition* 432⟩
```
    };
```

Systems from Digital Equipment run the Ultrix operating system, are little endians, and use `mipselIR`. Systems from Silicon Graphics run the IRIX operating systems, are big endians, and use `mipsebIR`. The systems share the same type metric:

⟨*MIPS type metrics* 431⟩≡   431
```
    1, 1, 0,  /* char */
    2, 2, 0,  /* short */
    4, 4, 0,  /* int */
    4, 4, 1,  /* float */
    8, 8, 1,  /* double */
    4, 4, 0,  /* T * */
    0, 1, 0,  /* struct */
```

They also share the rest of interface record:

⟨*shared interface definition* 432⟩≡   431
```
    0,  /* mulops_calls */
    0,  /* wants_callb */
    1,  /* wants_argb */
    1,  /* left_to_right */
    0,  /* wants_dag */
    ⟨interface routine names⟩
    0, 0, 0, stabinit, stabline, stabsym, 0,
    {
        4, /* max_unaligned_load */
        ⟨Xinterface initializer 355⟩
    }
```

Some of the symbol-table handlers are missing. lcc, like many compilers, assumes that all data for the debugger can be encoded using assembler directives. MIPS compilers encode file names and line numbers this way, but information about the type and location of identifiers is encoded in another file, which lcc does not emit. MIPS debuggers can thus report the location of an error in an executable file from lcc, but they can't report or change the values of identifiers; see Exercise 16.5.

stabinit 80
stabline 80
stabsym 80

16.1 Registers

The MIPS R3000 processor has thirty-two 32-bit registers, which are known to the assembler as $i. The MIPS R3010 floating-point coprocessor adds thirty-two more 32-bit registers, which are usually treated as sixteen even-numbered 64-bit registers and are known to the assembler as fi$.

The hardware imposes only a few constraints — register $0 is always zero, and the jump-and-link instruction puts the return address in $31 — but lcc observes many more conventions used by other compilers, in order to interoperate with the standard libraries and debuggers. Table 16.2 enumerates the conventions.

The assembler reserves $1 to implement pseudo-instructions. For example, the hardware permits only 16-bit offsets in address calculations, but the assembler permits 32-bit offsets by injecting extra instructions that form a large offset using $1. lcc uses some pseudo-instructions, but it forgoes others to simplify adaptations of lcc that emit binary object code directly.

The convention reserves $2–$3 and $f0–$f2 for return values, but lcc uses only the first half of each. The second half is for Fortran's complex arithmetic type. C doesn't have this type, but C compilers respect the convention to interoperate with Fortran code.

Registers	Use
$0	zero; unchangeable
$1	reserved for the assembler
$2-$3	function return value
$4-$7	first few procedure arguments
$8-$15	scratch registers
$16-$23	register variables
$24-$25	scratch registers
$26-$27	reserved for the operating system
$28	global pointer; also called $gp
$29	stack pointer; also called $sp
$30	register variable
$31	procedure return address
$f0-$f2	function return value
$f4-$f10	scratch registers
$f12-$f14	first two procedure arguments
$f16-$f18	scratch registers
$f20-$f30	register variables

TABLE 16.2 MIPS register conventions.

progend does nothing for this target. progbeg encodes Table 16.2 in the register allocator's data structures.

⟨*MIPS functions* 433⟩≡   435   431
```
static void progbeg(argc, argv) int argc; char *argv[]; {
    int i;

    ⟨shared progbeg 371⟩
    print(".set reorder\n");
    ⟨parse -G flag 458⟩
    ⟨initialize MIPS register structures 434⟩
}
```

First, it emits a harmless directive — the MIPS assembler objects to empty inputs — and parses a target-specific flag. Then it initializes the vectors of register symbols:

⟨*MIPS data* 433⟩≡   434   431
```
static Symbol ireg[32], freg2[32], d6;
```

Each element of `ireg` represents one integer register, and `freg2` represents pairs of adjacent floating-point registers. `d6` represents the pair $6-$7.

Actually, the machine has only 31 register pairs of each type, but the declaration supplies 32 to keep `askreg`'s inelegant loop bounds valid.

411 askreg
458 gp
 89 progend
466 " (SPARC)
502 " (X86)

⟨*initialize MIPS register structures* 434⟩≡   434   433

```
for (i = 0; i < 31; i += 2)
    freg2[i] = mkreg("%d", i, 3, FREG);
for (i = 0; i < 32; i++)
    ireg[i]  = mkreg("%d", i, 1, IREG);
ireg[29]->x.name = "sp";
d6 = mkreg("6", 6, 3, IREG);
```

mkreg assigns numeric register names. It renames the stack pointer — $29 — to use the assembler mnemonic $sp. We don't need the mnemonic $gp, or we'd rename $28 too.

rmap stores the wildcard that identifies the default register class to use for each type:

⟨*initialize MIPS register structures* 434⟩+≡   434 434   433

```
rmap[C] = rmap[S] = rmap[P] = rmap[B] = rmap[U] = rmap[I] =
    mkwildcard(ireg);
rmap[F] = rmap[D] = mkwildcard(freg2);
```

tmask identifies the scratch registers, and vmask the register variables:

⟨*mips.c macros*⟩≡   443

```
#define INTTMP 0x0300ff00
#define INTVAR 0x40ff0000
#define FLTTMP 0x000f0ff0
#define FLTVAR 0xfff00000
```

⟨*initialize MIPS register structures* 434⟩+≡   434 434   433

```
tmask[IREG] = INTTMP; tmask[FREG] = FLTTMP;
vmask[IREG] = INTVAR; vmask[FREG] = FLTVAR;
```

ARGB and ASGNB need not just source and destination addresses but also three temporary registers to copy a block. $3 is always available for temporary use, but we need two more, and all five registers must be distinct. An easy way to enforce this rule is to target the source register to a register triple: $8 for the source and $9 and $10 for the two temporaries. tmpregs lists the three temporaries — $3, $9, and $10 — for blkcopy:

⟨*MIPS data* 433⟩+≡   433 434   431

```
static int tmpregs[] = {3, 9, 10};
```

blkreg is the source register triple:

⟨*MIPS data* 433⟩+≡   434 458   431

```
static Symbol blkreg;
```

⟨*initialize MIPS register structures* 434⟩+≡   434   433

```
blkreg = mkreg("8", 8, 7, IREG);
```

Name	What It Matches
acon	address constants
addr	address calculations for instructions that read and write memory
ar	labels and addresses in registers
con	constants
rc	registers and constants
rc5	registers and constants that fit in five bits
reg	computations that yield a result in a register
stmt	computations done for side effect

TABLE 16.3 MIPS nonterminals.

The third argument to mkreg is a mask of three ones, which identifies $8, $9, and $10. The emitted code takes care to use $8 as the source register and the other two as temporaries.

target calls setreg to mark nodes that need a special register, and it calls rtarget to mark nodes that need a child in a special register:

⟨*MIPS functions* 433⟩+≡   433 435   431

```
static void target(p) Node p; {
    switch (p->op) {
    ⟨MIPS target 437⟩
    }
}
```

If an instruction clobbers some registers, clobber calls spill to save them first and restore them later.

⟨*MIPS functions* 433⟩+≡   435 444   431

```
static void clobber(p) Node p; {
    switch (p->op) {
    ⟨MIPS clobber 443⟩
    }
}
```

363	mkreg
400	rtarget
399	setreg
427	spill

The cases missing from target and clobber above appear with the germane instructions in the next section.

16.2 Selecting Instructions

Table 16.3 summarizes the nonterminals in lcc's lburg specification for the MIPS code generator. It provides a high-level overview of the organization of the tree grammar.

Some assembler instructions have a suffix that identifies the data type on which the instruction operates. The suffixes s and d identify single- and double-precision floating-point instructions, and b, h, and w identify

8-, 16-, and 32-bit integral instructions, respectively. The optional suffix u flags some instructions as unsigned. If it's omitted, the operation is signed.

Constants and identifiers represent themselves in assembler:

⟨*MIPS rules* 436⟩≡   436   431

```
acon: con      "%0"
acon: ADDRGP   "%a"
```

The instructions that access memory use address-calculation hardware that adds an instruction field and the contents of an integer register. The assembler syntax is the constant followed by the register in parentheses:

⟨*MIPS rules* 436⟩+≡   436 436   431

```
addr: ADDI(reg,acon)   "%1($%0)"
addr: ADDU(reg,acon)   "%1($%0)"
addr: ADDP(reg,acon)   "%1($%0)"
```

Degenerate sums — with a zero constant or $0 — supply absolute and indirect addressing. The zero field may be omitted:

⟨*MIPS rules* 436⟩+≡   436 436   431

```
addr: acon   "%0"
addr: reg    "($%0)"
```

%F 392
reg 403

The hardware permits only 16-bit offsets in address calculations, but the assembler uses $1 and extra instructions to synthesize larger values, so lcc can ignore the hardware restriction, at least on this machine.

ADDRFP and ADDRLP add a constant offset to the stack pointer:

⟨*MIPS rules* 436⟩+≡   436 437   431

```
addr: ADDRFP   "%a+%F($sp)"
addr: ADDRLP   "%a+%F($sp)"
```

%a emits p->syms[0]->x.name, and %F emits the size of the frame. $sp is decremented by the frame size when the routine starts, so the %F($sp) part recreates $sp's initial value. Locals have negative offsets, so they're below the initial $sp. Formals have positive offset, so they're just above, in the caller's frame. Section 16.3 elaborates.

addr illustrates several guidelines from Section 14.10. It includes rules for each of the addressing modes, plus rules for degenerate cases, rules replicated for equivalent operators, and rules that implement operators that are special cases of a more general computation. It also factors the specification to avoid replicating the material above for each rule that uses addr.

The pseudo-instruction la performs an address calculation and leaves the address in a register. For example, la $2,x($4) adds $4 to the address x and leaves the result in $2:

⟨*MIPS rules* 436⟩+≡   ▲436 437   431
```
   reg: addr   "la $%c,%0\n"   1
```

`%c` emits `p->syms[RX]->x.name`. A con is an addr, so lcc uses `la` whenever it needs to load a constant into a register. Zero is always available in `$0`, so we need no instruction to compute zero:

⟨*MIPS rules* 436⟩+≡   ▲437 437   431
```
   reg: CNSTC   "# reg\n"   range(a, 0, 0)
   reg: CNSTS   "# reg\n"   range(a, 0, 0)
   reg: CNSTI   "# reg\n"   range(a, 0, 0)
   reg: CNSTU   "# reg\n"   range(a, 0, 0)
   reg: CNSTP   "# reg\n"   range(a, 0, 0)
```

Recall that cost expressions are evaluated in a context in which a denotes the node being labelled, which here is the constant value being tested for zero. `target` arranges for these nodes to return `$0`:

⟨*MIPS* target 437⟩≡   443   435
```
   case CNSTC: case CNSTI: case CNSTS: case CNSTU: case CNSTP:
      if (range(p, 0, 0) == 0) {
         setreg(p, ireg[0]);
         p->x.registered = 1;
      }
      break;
```

Allocating `$0` makes no sense, so `target` marks the node to preclude register allocation.

    The instructions `l` and `s` load from and store into memory. They take a type suffix, an integer register, and an addr. For example, `sw $4,x` stores the 32-bit integer in `$4` into the memory cell labelled x. `sb` and `sh` do likewise for the low-order 8 and 16 bits of the register. `lb`, `lh`, and `lw` reverse the process and load an 8-, 16-, or 32-bit value:

⟨*MIPS rules* 436⟩+≡   ▲437 438   431
```
   stmt: ASGNC(addr,reg)   "sb $%1,%0\n"   1
   stmt: ASGNS(addr,reg)   "sh $%1,%0\n"   1
   stmt: ASGNI(addr,reg)   "sw $%1,%0\n"   1
   stmt: ASGNP(addr,reg)   "sw $%1,%0\n"   1
   reg:  INDIRC(addr)      "lb $%c,%0\n"   1
   reg:  INDIRS(addr)      "lh $%c,%0\n"   1
   reg:  INDIRI(addr)      "lw $%c,%0\n"   1
   reg:  INDIRP(addr)      "lw $%c,%0\n"   1
```

`lb` and `lh` propagate the sign bit to fill the top part of the register, so they implement a free CVCI and CVSI. `lbu` and `lhu` fill with zeroes instead, so they implement a free CVCU and CVSU:

⟨*MIPS rules* 436⟩+≡   4̂37 438   431
```
    reg: CVCI(INDIRC(addr))   "lb $%c,%0\n"   1
    reg: CVSI(INDIRS(addr))   "lh $%c,%0\n"   1
    reg: CVCU(INDIRC(addr))   "lbu $%c,%0\n"  1
    reg: CVSU(INDIRS(addr))   "lhu $%c,%0\n"  1
```

These rules illustrate another guideline from Section 14.10: when instructions evaluate more than one intermediate-language opcode, write a rule that matches multiple nodes.

l. and s. load and store floating-point values. All floating-point instructions separate the opcode and type suffix with a period:

⟨*MIPS rules* 436⟩+≡   4̂38 438   431
```
    reg:  INDIRD(addr)        "l.d $f%c,%0\n"   1
    reg:  INDIRF(addr)        "l.s $f%c,%0\n"   1
    stmt: ASGND(addr,reg)     "s.d $f%1,%0\n"   1
    stmt: ASGNF(addr,reg)     "s.s $f%1,%0\n"   1
```

All integer-multiplicative instructions accept two source registers and leave a result in a destination register. The left and right operands follow the source register. For example, div $4,$5,$6 divides $5 by $6 and leaves the result in $4.

⟨*MIPS rules* 436⟩+≡   4̂38 438   431

reg 403
stmt 403
```
    reg: DIVI(reg,reg)   "div $%c,$%0,$%1\n"    1
    reg: DIVU(reg,reg)   "divu $%c,$%0,$%1\n"   1
    reg: MODI(reg,reg)   "rem $%c,$%0,$%1\n"    1
    reg: MODU(reg,reg)   "remu $%c,$%0,$%1\n"   1
    reg: MULI(reg,reg)   "mul $%c,$%0,$%1\n"    1
    reg: MULU(reg,reg)   "mul $%c,$%0,$%1\n"    1
```

The remaining binary integer instructions also have an immediate form, in which the right operand may be a constant instruction field:

⟨*MIPS rules* 436⟩+≡   4̂38 439   431
```
    rc:  con             "%0"
    rc:  reg             "$%0"

    reg: ADDI(reg,rc)    "addu $%c,$%0,%1\n"    1
    reg: ADDP(reg,rc)    "addu $%c,$%0,%1\n"    1
    reg: ADDU(reg,rc)    "addu $%c,$%0,%1\n"    1
    reg: BANDU(reg,rc)   "and $%c,$%0,%1\n"     1
    reg: BORU(reg,rc)    "or $%c,$%0,%1\n"      1
    reg: BXORU(reg,rc)   "xor $%c,$%0,%1\n"     1
    reg: SUBI(reg,rc)    "subu $%c,$%0,%1\n"    1
    reg: SUBP(reg,rc)    "subu $%c,$%0,%1\n"    1
    reg: SUBU(reg,rc)    "subu $%c,$%0,%1\n"    1
```

Immediate shift instructions, however, require constants between zero and 31:

⟨*MIPS rules* 436⟩ +≡   438 439   431

```
rc5: CNSTI            "%a"               range(a,0,31)
rc5: reg              "$%0"

reg: LSHI(reg,rc5)    "sll $%c,$%0,%1\n"  1
reg: LSHU(reg,rc5)    "sll $%c,$%0,%1\n"  1
reg: RSHI(reg,rc5)    "sra $%c,$%0,%1\n"  1
reg: RSHU(reg,rc5)    "srl $%c,$%0,%1\n"  1
```

Only register forms are available for the unary instructions:

⟨*MIPS rules* 436⟩ +≡   439 439   431

```
reg: BCOMU(reg)    "not  $%c,$%0\n"    1
reg: NEGI(reg)     "negu $%c,$%0\n"    1
reg: LOADC(reg)    "move $%c,$%0\n"    move(a)
reg: LOADS(reg)    "move $%c,$%0\n"    move(a)
reg: LOADI(reg)    "move $%c,$%0\n"    move(a)
reg: LOADP(reg)    "move $%c,$%0\n"    move(a)
reg: LOADU(reg)    "move $%c,$%0\n"    move(a)
```

Recall that move returns one but also marks the node as a register-to-register move and thus a candidate for some optimizations.

The floating-point instructions also have only register forms:

⟨*MIPS rules* 436⟩ +≡   439 439   431

394	move
388	range
403	reg

```
reg: ADDD(reg,reg)  "add.d $f%c,$f%0,$f%1\n"  1
reg: ADDF(reg,reg)  "add.s $f%c,$f%0,$f%1\n"  1
reg: DIVD(reg,reg)  "div.d $f%c,$f%0,$f%1\n"  1
reg: DIVF(reg,reg)  "div.s $f%c,$f%0,$f%1\n"  1
reg: MULD(reg,reg)  "mul.d $f%c,$f%0,$f%1\n"  1
reg: MULF(reg,reg)  "mul.s $f%c,$f%0,$f%1\n"  1
reg: SUBD(reg,reg)  "sub.d $f%c,$f%0,$f%1\n"  1
reg: SUBF(reg,reg)  "sub.s $f%c,$f%0,$f%1\n"  1
reg: LOADD(reg)     "mov.d $f%c,$f%0\n"       move(a)
reg: LOADF(reg)     "mov.s $f%c,$f%0\n"       move(a)
reg: NEGD(reg)      "neg.d $f%c,$f%0\n"       1
reg: NEGF(reg)      "neg.s $f%c,$f%0\n"       1
```

Few instructions are specialized to convert between types. CVCI and CVSI sign-extend by shifting first left and then right. CVCU and CVSU zero-extend by "anding out" the top part of the register:

⟨*MIPS rules* 436⟩ +≡   439 440   431

```
reg: CVCI(reg)  "sll $%c,$%0,24; sra $%c,$%c,24\n"   2
reg: CVSI(reg)  "sll $%c,$%0,16; sra $%c,$%c,16\n"   2
reg: CVCU(reg)  "and $%c,$%0,0xff\n"                 1
reg: CVSU(reg)  "and $%c,$%0,0xffff\n"               1
```

These rules illustrate another guideline from Section 14.10: When no instruction directly implements an operation, write a rule that pieces the operation together using other instructions.

The rest of the conversions, which involve only integer and pointer types, do nothing. Conversions to narrower types like CVIC need not clear the top of the register because the front end never builds trees that use the upper bits of a narrow value. The shared rules and the rules below generate nothing if the existing register will do:

⟨*MIPS rules* 436⟩ +≡   ▲439 440   431
```
reg: CVIC(reg)  "%0"  notarget(a)
reg: CVIS(reg)  "%0"  notarget(a)
reg: CVUC(reg)  "%0"  notarget(a)
reg: CVUS(reg)  "%0"  notarget(a)
```

More expensive rules generate a register-to-register copy if a specific register has been targeted:

⟨*MIPS rules* 436⟩ +≡   ▲440 440   431
```
reg: CVIC(reg)  "move $%c,$%0\n"  move(a)
reg: CVIS(reg)  "move $%c,$%0\n"  move(a)
reg: CVIU(reg)  "move $%c,$%0\n"  move(a)
reg: CVPU(reg)  "move $%c,$%0\n"  move(a)
reg: CVUC(reg)  "move $%c,$%0\n"  move(a)
reg: CVUI(reg)  "move $%c,$%0\n"  move(a)
reg: CVUP(reg)  "move $%c,$%0\n"  move(a)
reg: CVUS(reg)  "move $%c,$%0\n"  move(a)
```

cvt.d.s converts a float to a double, and cvt.s.d reverses the process:

⟨*MIPS rules* 436⟩ +≡   ▲440 440   431
```
reg: CVDF(reg)  "cvt.s.d $f%c,$f%0\n"  1
reg: CVFD(reg)  "cvt.d.s $f%c,$f%0\n"  1
```

cvt.d.w converts an integer to a double. The integer must be in a floating-point register, so CVID starts with a mtc1, which copies a value from the integer unit to the floating-point unit:

⟨*MIPS rules* 436⟩ +≡   ▲440 441   431
```
reg: CVID(reg)  "mtc1 $%0,$f%c; cvt.d.w $f%c,$f%c\n"  2
```

It sets the target register twice: first to the unconverted integer and then to the equivalent double. See Exercise 16.6.

The trunc.w.d instruction truncates a double and leaves the integral result in a floating-point register, so lcc follows up with a mfc1, which copies a value from the floating point unit to the integer unit, where the client of the CVDI expects it:

move 394
notarget 404
reg 403

⟨*MIPS rules* 436⟩+≡   440 441   431

```
  reg: CVDI(reg)    "trunc.w.d $f2,$f%0,$%c; mfc1 %%c,$f2\n"   2
```

It needs a floating-point scratch register to hold the converted value, so it uses $f2, which the calling convention reserves as a secondary return register, but which lcc does not otherwise use.

A label is defined by following it with a colon:

⟨*MIPS rules* 436⟩+≡   441 441   431

```
  stmt: LABELV   "%a:\n"
```

The b instruction jumps unconditionally to a fixed address, and the j instruction jumps unconditionally to an address from a register:

⟨*MIPS rules* 436⟩+≡   441 441   431

```
  stmt: JUMPV(acon)    "b %0\n"    1
  stmt: JUMPV(reg)     "j $%0\n"   1
```

Switch statements implemented using branch tables need j. All other unconditional branches use b.

The integer conditional branches compare two registers and branch if the named condition holds:

⟨*MIPS rules* 436⟩+≡   441 442   431

```
  stmt: EQI(reg,reg)    "beq $%0,$%1,%a\n"     1
  stmt: GEI(reg,reg)    "bge $%0,$%1,%a\n"     1
  stmt: GEU(reg,reg)    "bgeu $%0,$%1,%a\n"    1
  stmt: GTI(reg,reg)    "bgt $%0,$%1,%a\n"     1
  stmt: GTU(reg,reg)    "bgtu $%0,$%1,%a\n"    1
  stmt: LEI(reg,reg)    "ble $%0,$%1,%a\n"     1
  stmt: LEU(reg,reg)    "bleu $%0,$%1,%a\n"    1
  stmt: LTI(reg,reg)    "blt $%0,$%1,%a\n"     1
  stmt: LTU(reg,reg)    "bltu $%0,$%1,%a\n"    1
  stmt: NEI(reg,reg)    "bne $%0,$%1,%a\n"     1
```

403 reg
403 stmt

The hardware does not implement all these instructions directly, but the assembler compensates. For example, hardware instructions for GE, GT, LE, and LT assume that the second comparand is zero, but the assembler synthesizes the pseudo-instructions above by computing a difference into $1 if necessary. Also, only the j instruction accepts a full 32-bit address, but the pseudo-instructions above assemble arbitrary addresses from the hardware's more restricted addresses. When lcc uses pseudo-instructions, it can't know exactly what real instructions the assembler emits, so the costs above are necessarily approximate, but there's only one way to generate code for these intermediate-language operators anyway, so the inaccuracies can't hurt the quality of the emitted code.

The floating-point conditional branches test a condition flag set by a separate comparison instruction. For example, c.lt.d $f0,$f2 sets the flag if the double in $f0 is less than the double in $f2. bc1t branches if the flag is set, and bc1f branches if the flag is clear.

⟨*MIPS rules* 436⟩ += 441 442 431

```
stmt: EQD(reg,reg)  "c.eq.d $f%0,$f%1; bc1t %a\n"  2
stmt: EQF(reg,reg)  "c.eq.s $f%0,$f%1; bc1t %a\n"  2
stmt: LED(reg,reg)  "c.le.d $f%0,$f%1; bc1t %a\n"  2
stmt: LEF(reg,reg)  "c.le.s $f%0,$f%1; bc1t %a\n"  2
stmt: LTD(reg,reg)  "c.lt.d $f%0,$f%1; bc1t %a\n"  2
stmt: LTF(reg,reg)  "c.lt.s $f%0,$f%1; bc1t %a\n"  2
```

Floating-point comparisons implement only less-than, less-than-or-equal, and equal, so lcc implements the rest by inverting the sense of the relation and following it with a bc1f:

⟨*MIPS rules* 436⟩ += 442 442 431

```
stmt: GED(reg,reg)  "c.lt.d $f%0,$f%1; bc1f %a\n"  2
stmt: GEF(reg,reg)  "c.lt.s $f%0,$f%1; bc1f %a\n"  2
stmt: GTD(reg,reg)  "c.le.d $f%0,$f%1; bc1f %a\n"  2
stmt: GTF(reg,reg)  "c.le.s $f%0,$f%1; bc1f %a\n"  2
stmt: NED(reg,reg)  "c.eq.d $f%0,$f%1; bc1f %a\n"  2
stmt: NEF(reg,reg)  "c.eq.s $f%0,$f%1; bc1f %a\n"  2
```

For example, it can't use

```
c.gt.d $f0,$f2
bc1t L
```

reg 403
stmt 403

so instead it uses

```
c.le.d $f0,$f2
bc1f L
```

The jal instruction saves the program counter in $31 and jumps to an address stored in a constant instruction field or in a register.

⟨*MIPS rules* 436⟩ += 442 442 431

```
ar:   ADDRGP     "%a"

reg:  CALLD(ar)  "jal %0\n"  1
reg:  CALLF(ar)  "jal %0\n"  1
reg:  CALLI(ar)  "jal %0\n"  1
stmt: CALLV(ar)  "jal %0\n"  1
```

CALLV yields no result and thus matches stmt instead of reg. Most calls jump to a label, but indirect calls like (*p)() need a register form:

⟨*MIPS rules* 436⟩ += 442 443 431

```
ar: reg    "$%0"
```

Some device drivers jump to addresses at fixed numeric addresses. jal insists that they fit in 28 bits:

⟨*MIPS rules* 436⟩+≡   442 443   431
```
ar: CNSTP  "%a"   range(a, 0, 0x0fffffff)
```

If the constant won't fit in 28 bits, then lcc falls back on more costly rules that load an arbitrary 32-bit constant into a register and that jump indirectly using that register. The MIPS assembler makes most of the decisions that require checking ranges, but at least some versions of the assembler leave this particular check to the compiler.

The front end and the routines function and target collaborate to get return values into the return register, and return addresses into the program counter, so RET nodes produce no code:

⟨*MIPS rules* 436⟩+≡   443 444   431
```
stmt: RETD(reg)  "# ret\n"  1
stmt: RETF(reg)  "# ret\n"  1
stmt: RETI(reg)  "# ret\n"  1
```

CALLDs and CALLFs yield $f0, and CALLIs yield $2. Each RET has its child compute its value into the corresponding register.

⟨*MIPS target* 437⟩+≡   437 445   435
```
case CALLD: case CALLF: setreg(p, freg2[0]);    break;
case CALLI:             setreg(p, ireg[2]);     break;
case RETD: case RETF:   rtarget(p, 0, freg2[0]); break;
case RETI:              rtarget(p, 0, ireg[2]);  break;
```

Recall that setreg sets the result register for the node in hand, and that rtarget sets the result register for a child of the node. rtarget exists because simply calling setreg on the child could clobber something of value. The material on rtarget elaborates.

The scratch and return registers are not preserved across calls, so any live ones must be spilled and reloaded, except for the return register used by the call itself:

⟨*mips.c macros*⟩+≡   434
```
#define INTRET 0x00000004
#define FLTRET 0x00000003
```

⟨*MIPS clobber* 443⟩≡   435
```
case CALLD: case CALLF:
    spill(INTTMP | INTRET, IREG, p);
    spill(FLTTMP,          FREG, p);
    break;
case CALLI:
    spill(INTTMP,           IREG, p);
    spill(FLTTMP | FLTRET, FREG, p);
    break;
case CALLV:
```

```
        spill(INTTMP | INTRET, IREG, p);
        spill(FLTTMP | FLTRET, FREG, p);
        break;
```

Floating-point values return in the double register $f0, and all other values return in $2. target and clobber collaborate. Consider CALLI; target arranges for it to yield register $2, and clobber asks spill to save all other caller-saved registers before the call and to restore them afterward.

The rules to transmit arguments require collaboration between target and emit2:

⟨*MIPS rules* 436⟩+≡   443 446   431
```
    stmt: ARGD(reg)    "# arg\n"    1
    stmt: ARGF(reg)    "# arg\n"    1
    stmt: ARGI(reg)    "# arg\n"    1
    stmt: ARGP(reg)    "# arg\n"    1
```

⟨*MIPS functions* 433⟩+≡   435 444   431
```
    static void emit2(p) Node p; {
        int dst, n, src, ty;
        static int ty0;
        Symbol q;

        switch (p->op) {
        ⟨MIPS emit2 446⟩
        }
    }
```

The MIPS calling convention passes the first four words of arguments (including gaps to satisfy alignments) in registers $4-$7, except that if the first argument is a float or a double, it is passed in $f12, and if the first argument is passed in $f12 and the second argument is a float or a double, the second argument is passed in $f14. argreg implements these rules:

⟨*MIPS functions* 433⟩+≡   444 445   431
```
    static Symbol argreg(argno, offset, ty, ty0)
    int argno, offset, ty, ty0; {
        if (offset > 12)
            return NULL;
        else if (argno == 0 && (ty == F || ty == D))
            return freg2[12];
        else if (argno == 1 && (ty == F || ty == D)
        && (ty0 == F || ty0 == D))
            return freg2[14];
        else if (argno == 1 && ty == D)
```

```
          return d6;   /* Pair! */
     else
          return ireg[(offset/4) + 4];
}
```

argno is the argument number. offset and ty are the offset and type of an argument. ty0 is the type of the *first* argument, which can influence the placement the second argument. If the argument is passed in a register, argreg returns the register. Otherwise, it returns null.

gen calls doarg to compute argno and offset for argreg:

⟨*MIPS functions* 433⟩+≡   ▲444 447   431

```
     static void doarg(p) Node p; {
          static int argno;
          int size;

          if (argoffset == 0)
               argno = 0;
          p->x.argno = argno++;
          size = p->syms[1]->u.c.v.i < 4 ? 4 : p->syms[1]->u.c.v.i;
          p->syms[2] = intconst(mkactual(size,
               p->syms[0]->u.c.v.i));
     }
```

docall clears argoffset at each CALL, so a zero there alerts doarg to reset its static argument counter. mkactual uses the argument size and alignment — rounded up to 4 if necessary, because smaller arguments are widened — and returns the argument offset.

target uses argreg and rtarget to compute the children of ARG nodes into the argument register, if there is one:

⟨*MIPS* target 437⟩+≡   ▲443 447   435

```
     case ARGD: case ARGF: case ARGI: case ARGP: {
          static int ty0;
          int ty = optype(p->op);
          Symbol q;

          q = argreg(p->x.argno, p->syms[2]->u.c.v.i, ty, ty0);
          if (p->x.argno == 0)
               ty0 = ty;
          if (q &&
          !((ty == F || ty == D) && q->x.regnode->set == IREG))
               rtarget(p, 0, q);
          break;
     }
```

The fragment also remembers the type of the first argument to help determine the register for later arguments. The long conditional omits targeting if the argument is floating point but passed in an integer register.

lcc assumes that floating-point opcodes yield floating-point registers, so no tree can develop an unconverted floating-point value into an integer register. emit2 must handle these oddballs and the arguments that travel in memory:

⟨*MIPS* emit2 446⟩≡   446   444

```
case ARGD: case ARGF: case ARGI: case ARGP:
    ty = optype(p->op);
    if (p->x.argno == 0)
        ty0 = ty;
    q = argreg(p->x.argno, p->syms[2]->u.c.v.i, ty, ty0);
    src = getregnum(p->x.kids[0]);
    if (q == NULL && ty == F)
        print("s.s $f%d,%d($sp)\n", src, p->syms[2]->u.c.v.i);
    else if (q == NULL && ty == D)
        print("s.d $f%d,%d($sp)\n", src, p->syms[2]->u.c.v.i);
    else if (q == NULL)
        print("sw $%d,%d($sp)\n", src, p->syms[2]->u.c.v.i);
    else if (ty == F && q->x.regnode->set == IREG)
        print("mfc1 $%d,$f%d\n", q->x.regnode->number, src);
    else if (ty == D && q->x.regnode->set == IREG)
        print("mfc1.d $%d,$f%d\n", q->x.regnode->number, src);
    break;
```

If argreg returns null, then the caller passes the argument in memory, so emit2 stores it, using the offset that doarg computed. The last two conditionals above emit code for floating-point arguments transmitted in integer registers. mfc1 x, y copies a single-precision value from floating-point register y to integer register x. mfc1.d does likewise for doubles; the target is a register pair.

emit2 and target also collaborate to emit block copies:

⟨*MIPS rules* 436⟩+≡   444   431

```
stmt: ARGB(INDIRB(reg))        "# argb %0\n"        1
stmt: ASGNB(reg,INDIRB(reg))   "# asgnb %0 %1\n"    1
```

emit2's case for ASGNB sets the globals that record the alignment of the source and destination blocks, then lets blkcopy do the rest:

⟨*MIPS* emit2 446⟩+≡   446 447   444

```
case ASGNB:
    dalign = salign = p->syms[1]->u.c.v.i;
    blkcopy(getregnum(p->x.kids[0]), 0,
        getregnum(p->x.kids[1]), 0,
        p->syms[0]->u.c.v.i, tmpregs);
    break;
```

The call trace shown in Figure 13.4 starts in this case. tmpregs holds the numbers of the three temporary registers, which form the triple register that progbeg assigned to blkreg. ARGB and ASGNB target their source-address register to reserve blkreg:

⟨*MIPS* target 437⟩+≡   ▲445   435

```
    case ASGNB: rtarget(p->kids[1], 0, blkreg); break;
    case ARGB:  rtarget(p->kids[0], 0, blkreg); break;
```

This source comes from a grandchild because the intervening child is a pro forma INDIRB. emit2's case for ARGB is similar to the case for ASGNB:

⟨*MIPS* emit2 446⟩+≡   ▲446   444

```
    case ARGB:
        dalign = 4;
        salign = p->syms[1]->u.c.v.i;
        blkcopy(29, p->syms[2]->u.c.v.i,
            getregnum(p->x.kids[0]), 0,
            p->syms[0]->u.c.v.i, tmpregs);
        n   = p->syms[2]->u.c.v.i + p->syms[0]->u.c.v.i;
        dst = p->syms[2]->u.c.v.i;
        for ( ; dst <= 12 && dst < n; dst += 4)
            print("lw $%d,%d($sp)\n", (dst/4)+4, dst);
        break;
```

dalign differs because the stack space for the outgoing argument is always aligned to at least a multiple of four, which is the most that blkcopy and its helpers can use. The first argument is 29 because the destination base register is $sp, and the second argument is the stack offset for the destination block, which doarg computed. If the ARGB overlaps the first four words of arguments, then the for loop copies the overlap into the corresponding argument registers to conform with the calling convention.

16.3   Implementing Functions

The front end calls local to announce each new local variable:

⟨*MIPS* functions 433⟩+≡   ▲445 448   431 ▼

```
    static void local(p) Symbol p; {
        if (askregvar(p, rmap[ttob(p->type)]) == 0)
            mkauto(p);
    }
```

Machine-independent routines do most of the work. askregvar allocates a register if it's appropriate and one is available. Otherwise, mkauto assigns a stack offset; Figure 16.1 shows the layout of the MIPS stack frame.

    The front end calls function to announce each new routine. function drives most of the back end. It calls gencode, which calls gen, which

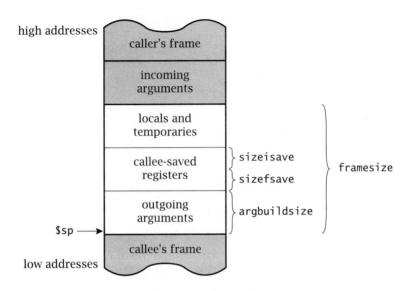

high addresses

$sp →

low addresses

FIGURE 16.1   MIPS stack frame.

calls the labeller, reducer, linearizer, and register allocator. function also calls the front end's emitcode, which calls the back end's emitter.

⟨*MIPS functions* 433⟩+≡   447 455   431

```
static void function(f, caller, callee, ncalls)
Symbol f, callee[], caller[]; int ncalls; {
    int i, saved, sizefsave, sizeisave, varargs;
    Symbol r, argregs[4];

    ⟨MIPS function 448⟩
}
```

The front end passes to function a symbol that represents a routine, vectors of symbols representing the caller's and callee's view of the arguments, and a count of the number of calls made by the routine. It starts by freeing all registers and clearing the variables that track the frame and that track the area into which the outgoing arguments are copied:

⟨*MIPS function* 448⟩≡   448   448
```
    ⟨clear register state 410⟩
    offset = maxoffset = maxargoffset = 0;
```

Then it determines whether the routine is variadic, because this attribute influences some of the code that we're about to generate:

⟨*MIPS function* 448⟩+≡   448 449   448
```
    for (i = 0; callee[i]; i++)
```

```
;
varargs = variadic(f->type)
    || i > 0 && strcmp(callee[i-1]->name, "va_alist") == 0;
```

By convention on this machine, there must be a prototype, or the last argument must be named va_alist. function needs it to determine the location of some incoming arguments:

⟨*MIPS* function 448⟩+≡   448 451   448
```
for (i = 0; callee[i]; i++) {
    ⟨assign location for argument i 449⟩
}
```

Recall that the first four words of arguments (including gaps to satisfy alignments) are passed in registers $4-$7, except the first argument is passed in $f12 if it is a float or a double, and the second argument is passed in $f14 if it is a float or a double and the first argument is passed in $f12. This calling convention complicates function, particularly the body of the loop above. It starts by assigning a stack offset to the argument:

⟨*assign location for argument* i 449⟩≡   449   449
```
Symbol p = callee[i];
Symbol q = caller[i];
offset = roundup(offset, q->type->align);
p->x.offset = q->x.offset = offset;
p->x.name = q->x.name = stringd(offset);
r = argreg(i, offset, ttob(q->type), ttob(caller[0]->type));
if (i < 4)
    argregs[i] = r;
offset = roundup(offset + q->type->size, 4);
```

Even arguments that arrive in a register and remain in one have a reserved stack slot. Indeed, the offset helps argreg determine which register holds the argument. argregs[i] records for use below argreg's result for argument i. All arguments to variadic routines are stored in the stack because the code addresses them indirectly:

⟨*assign location for argument* i 449⟩+≡   449 450   449
```
if (varargs)
    p->sclass = AUTO;
```

If the argument arrived in a register and the routine makes no calls that could overwrite it, then the argument can remain in place if it is neither a structure, nor accessed indirectly, nor a floating-point argument passed in an integer register.

⟨*leave argument in place?* 449⟩≡   450
```
r && ncalls == 0 &&
!isstruct(q->type) && !p->addressed &&
!(isfloat(q->type) && r->x.regnode->set == IREG)
```

⟨*assign location for argument* i 449⟩+≡   449 450   449

```
   else if (⟨leave argument in place? 449⟩) {
      p->sclass = q->sclass = REGISTER;
      askregvar(p, r);
      q->x = p->x;
      q->type = p->type;
   }
```

askregvar is guaranteed to succeed because r can't have been allocated for any other purpose yet; a hidden assertion confirms this claim. Conforming the type and sclass fields prevents the front end from generating code to copy or convert the argument. Finally, we allocate a register for the argument that doesn't have one or can't stay in the one that it has:

⟨*assign location for argument* i 449⟩+≡   450   449

```
   else if (⟨copy argument to another register? 450⟩) {
      p->sclass = q->sclass = REGISTER;
      q->type = p->type;
   }
```

The conditional succeeds if and only if the argument arrives in one register and must be moved to another one. For example, if an argument arrives in $4 but the routine makes calls, then $4 is needed for outgoing arguments. If the incoming argument is used enough to belong in a register, the code above arranges the copy. A floating-point argument could have arrived in an integer register, which is an operation that the front end can't express, so the code above conforms the type and sclass to tell the front end to generate nothing, and the fragment ⟨*save argument in a register*⟩ on page 453 generates the copy.

The conditional in the last else-if statement above tests up to three clauses. First, askregvar must allocate a register to the argument:

⟨*copy argument to another register?* 450⟩≡   451   450

```
   askregvar(p, rmap[ttob(p->type)])
```

If askregvar fails, then the argument will have to go in memory. If it's not already there, the fragment ⟨*save argument in stack*⟩ on page 454 will put it there. In this case, the two sclass fields are already conformed, but we don't want to conform the two type fields because a conversion might be needed. For example, a new-style character argument needs a conversion on big endians; it is passed as an integer, so its value is in the least significant bits of the argument word, but it's going to be accessed as a character, so its value must be moved to the most significant end of the word on big endians.

The second condition confirms that the argument is already in a register:

⟨*copy argument to another register?* 450⟩+≡   450 451   450
&& r != NULL

If this condition fails, then the argument arrived in memory and needs to
be loaded into the register that askregvar found. For example, such an
argument might be the last of five integer arguments, which means that
it's passed in memory and thus should be loaded into a register now, if
it's used heavily. askregvar sets p->sclass to REGISTER; q->sclass is
never REGISTER, so falling through with the differing values causes the
front end to generate the load.

The third and last condition confirms that no conversion is needed:

⟨*copy argument to another register?* 450⟩+≡   451   450
&& (isint(p->type) || p->type == q->type)

For example, if q (the caller) is a double and p is a float, then a CVDF is
needed. In this case, the sclass and type fields differ, so falling through
causes the front end to generate a conversion.

After assigning locations to all arguments, function calls gencode to
select code and allocate registers for the body of the routine:

⟨*MIPS* function 448⟩+≡   449 451   448
    offset = 0;
    gencode(caller, callee);

When gencode returns, usedmask identifies the registers that the routine touches. function adds the register that holds the return address
— unless the routine makes no calls — and removes the registers that
the caller must have saved:

⟨*MIPS* function 448⟩+≡   451 451   448
    if (ncalls)
        usedmask[IREG] |= ((unsigned)1)<<31;
    usedmask[IREG] &= 0xc0ff0000;
    usedmask[FREG] &= 0xfff00000;

function then completes the computation of the size of the argument-
build area:

⟨*MIPS* function 448⟩+≡   451 452   448
    maxargoffset = roundup(maxargoffset, 4);
    if (maxargoffset && maxargoffset < 16)
        maxargoffset = 16;

The calling convention requires that the size of the outgoing argument
block be divisible by four and at least 16 bytes unless it's empty. Then
function computes the size of the frame and the blocks within it needed
to save the floating-point and integer registers.

⟨*MIPS* function 448⟩+≡   451 452   448

```
sizefsave = 4*bitcount(usedmask[FREG]);
sizeisave = 4*bitcount(usedmask[IREG]);
framesize = roundup(maxargoffset + sizefsave
    + sizeisave + maxoffset, 8);
```

bitcount counts the ones in an unsigned integer. Figure 16.1 illustrates these values. The convention keeps the stack aligned to double words.

Now function has the data it needs to start emitting the routine. The prologue switches to the code segment, ensures word alignment, and emits some boilerplate that starts MIPS routines:

⟨*MIPS* function 448⟩+≡   452 452   448

```
segment(CODE);
print(".align 2\n");
print(".ent %s\n", f->x.name);
print("%s:\n", f->x.name);
i = maxargoffset + sizefsave - framesize;
print(".frame $sp,%d,$31\n", framesize);
if (framesize > 0)
    print("addu $sp,$sp,%d\n", -framesize);
if (usedmask[FREG])
    print(".fmask 0x%x,%d\n", usedmask[FREG], i - 8);
if (usedmask[IREG])
    print(".mask 0x%x,%d\n",  usedmask[IREG],
        i + sizeisave - 4);
```

lcc's code uses only the label and addu, which allocates a frame for the routine. The rest of the directives describe the routine to other programs like debuggers and profilers. .ent announces a procedure entry point; .frame declares the stack pointer, frame size, and return-address register; and .fmask and .mask identify the registers saved and their locations in the stack, respectively.

The prologue continues with code to store the callee-saved registers, as defined in Table 16.2:

⟨*MIPS* function 448⟩+≡   452 453   448

```
saved = maxargoffset;
for (i = 20; i <= 30; i += 2)
    if (usedmask[FREG]&(3<<i)) {
        print("s.d $f%d,%d($sp)\n", i, saved);
        saved += 8;
    }
for (i = 16; i <= 31; i++)
    if (usedmask[IREG]&(1<<i)) {
        print("sw $%d,%d($sp)\n", i, saved);
        saved += 4;
    }
```

Then it saves arguments that arrive in registers:

⟨*MIPS* function 448⟩+≡   452 453   448

```
for (i = 0; i < 4 && callee[i]; i++) {
    r = argregs[i];
    if (r && r->x.regnode != callee[i]->x.regnode) {
        ⟨save argument i 453⟩
    }
}
```

For variadic routines, lcc saves the rest of the integer argument registers too, because the number used varies from call to call:

⟨*MIPS* function 448⟩+≡   453 454   448

```
if (varargs && callee[i-1]) {
    i = callee[i-1]->x.offset + callee[i-1]->type->size;
    for (i = roundup(i, 4)/4; i <= 3; i++)
        print("sw $%d,%d($sp)\n", i + 4, framesize + 4*i);
}
```

This loop picks up where its predecessor left off and continues until it has stored the last integer argument register, $7.

For nonvariadic routines, the prologue saves only those argument registers that are used and that can't stay where they are:

⟨*save argument* i 453⟩≡   453

```
Symbol out = callee[i];
Symbol in  = caller[i];
int rn = r->x.regnode->number;
int rs = r->x.regnode->set;
int tyin = ttob(in->type);

if (out->sclass == REGISTER
&& (isint(out->type) || out->type == in->type)) {
    ⟨save argument in a register 454⟩
} else {
    ⟨save argument in stack 454⟩
}
```

93	callee
93	caller
366	framesize
92	function
448	" (MIPS)
484	" (SPARC)
518	" (X86)
60	isint
361	number
80	REGISTER
19	roundup
361	set
73	ttob
362	x.offset
362	x.regnode

It distinguishes arguments assigned to some other register from those assigned to memory. The clause after the **&&** matches the one in ⟨*leave argument in place?*⟩ on page 449, which determined what we should generate here.

If a register was allocated for an argument that arrives in a register, and if the argument can't remain where it is, then function emits code to copy an incoming argument register to another register:

⟨*save argument in a register* 454⟩ ≡   453
```
    int outn = out->x.regnode->number;
    if (rs == FREG && tyin == D)
        print("mov.d $f%d,$f%d\n", outn, rn);
    else if (rs == FREG && tyin == F)
        print("mov.s $f%d,$f%d\n", outn, rn);
    else if (rs == IREG && tyin == D)
        print("mtc1.d $%d,$f%d\n", rn,    outn);
    else if (rs == IREG && tyin == F)
        print("mtc1 $%d,$f%d\n",    rn,    outn);
    else
        print("move $%d,$%d\n",     outn, rn);
```

If the argument has been assigned to memory, then the prologue stores it into the procedure activation record:

⟨*save argument in stack* 454⟩ ≡   453
```
    int off = in->x.offset + framesize;
    if (rs == FREG && tyin == D)
        print("s.d $f%d,%d($sp)\n", rn, off);
    else if (rs == FREG && tyin == F)
        print("s.s $f%d,%d($sp)\n", rn, off);
    else {
        int i, n = (in->type->size + 3)/4;
        for (i = rn; i < rn+n && i <= 7; i++)
            print("sw $%d,%d($sp)\n", i, off + (i-rn)*4);
    }
```

The loop in the last arm usually executes only one iteration and stores a single integer argument, but it also handles floats that arrived in an integer register, and the loop generalizes to handle double and structure arguments, which can occupy multiple integer registers. It terminates when it runs out of arguments or argument registers, whichever comes first.

After emitting the last of the procedure prologue, function emits the procedure body:

⟨*MIPS function* 448⟩ +≡   453 454   448
```
    emitcode();
```

The epilogue reloads the callee-saved registers, first the floating-point registers:

⟨*MIPS function* 448⟩ +≡   454 455   448
```
    saved = maxargoffset;
    for (i = 20; i <= 30; i += 2)
        if (usedmask[FREG]&(3<<i)) {
            print("l.d $f%d,%d($sp)\n", i, saved);
```

```
        saved += 8;
    }
```

and then the general registers:

⟨*MIPS* function 448⟩+≡   454 455   448
```
    for (i = 16; i <= 31; i++)
        if (usedmask[IREG]&(1<<i)) {
            print("lw $%d,%d($sp)\n", i, saved);
            saved += 4;
        }
```

Now it can pop the frame off the stack:

⟨*MIPS* function 448⟩+≡   455 455   448
```
    if (framesize > 0)
        print("addu $sp,$sp,%d\n", framesize);
```

and return:

⟨*MIPS* function 448⟩+≡   455   448
```
    print("j $31\n");
    print(".end %s\n", f->x.name);
```

16.4   Defining Data

defconst emits assembler directives to allocate a scalar and initialize it
to a constant:

⟨*MIPS* functions 433⟩+≡   448 456   431
```
    static void defconst(ty, v) int ty; Value v; {
        switch (ty) {
        ⟨MIPS defconst 455⟩
        }
    }
```

The cases for the integer types emit a size-specific directive and the appropriate constant field:

⟨*MIPS* defconst 455⟩≡   456   455
```
    case C: print(".byte %d\n",    v.uc); return;
    case S: print(".half %d\n",    v.ss); return;
    case I: print(".word 0x%x\n",  v.i);  return;
    case U: print(".word 0x%x\n",  v.u);  return;
```

The case for numeric address constants treats them like unsigned integers:

366	framesize
361	IREG
410	usedmask
47	Value
362	x.name

⟨*MIPS* defconst 455⟩ +≡   455 456   455

```
case P: print(".word 0x%x\n", v.p); return;
```

defaddress handles symbolic address constants:

⟨*MIPS functions* 433⟩ +≡   455 456   431

```
static void defaddress(p) Symbol p; {
    print(".word %s\n", p->x.name);
}
```

The assembler's .float and .double directives can't express floating-point constants that result from arbitrary expressions (e.g., with casts), so defconst emits floating-point constants in hexadecimal:

⟨*MIPS* defconst 455⟩ +≡   456 456   455

```
case F: print(".word 0x%x\n", *(unsigned *)&v.f); return;
```

The two halves of each double must be exchanged if lcc is running on a little endian and compiling for a big endian, or vice versa:

⟨*MIPS* defconst 455⟩ +≡   456   455

```
case D: {
    unsigned *p = (unsigned *)&v.d;
    print(".word 0x%x\n.word 0x%x\n", p[swap], p[!swap]);
    return;
}
```

Barring this possible exchange, this code assumes that the host and target encode floating-point numbers identically. This assumption is not particularly constraining because most targets use IEEE floating point now.

defstring emits directives for a series of bytes:

⟨*MIPS functions* 433⟩ +≡   456 456   431

```
static void defstring(n, str) int n; char *str; {
    char *s;

    for (s = str; s < str + n; s++)
        print(".byte %d\n", (*s)&0377);
}
```

It finds the end of the string by counting because ANSI C escape codes permit strings with embedded null bytes.

export uses an assembler directive to make a symbol visible in other modules:

⟨*MIPS functions* 433⟩ +≡   456 457   431

```
static void export(p) Symbol p; {
    print(".globl %s\n", p->x.name);
}
```

import uses a companion directive to make a symbol from another module visible in this one:

⟨*MIPS functions* 433⟩ +≡   4̂56 45̲7   431

```
static void import(p) Symbol p; {
    if (!isfunc(p->type))
        print(".extern %s %d\n", p->name, p->type->size);
}
```

MIPS compiler conventions omit such directives for functions.

The front end calls defsymbol to announce a new symbol and cue the back end to initialize the x.name field:

⟨*MIPS functions* 433⟩ +≡   4̂57 45̲7   431

```
static void defsymbol(p) Symbol p; {
    ⟨MIPS defsymbol 457⟩
}
```

defsymbol generates a unique name for local statics to keep from colliding with other local statics with the same name:

⟨*MIPS* defsymbol 457⟩ ≡   457   45̲7

```
if (p->scope >= LOCAL && p->sclass == STATIC)
    p->x.name = stringf("L.%d", genlabel(1));
```

By convention, such symbols start with an L and a period. If the symbol is generated but not covered by the rule above, then the name field already holds a digit string:

⟨*MIPS* defsymbol 457⟩ +≡   4̂57 45̲7   457

```
else if (p->generated)
    p->x.name = stringf("L.%s", p->name);
```

Otherwise, the front- and back-end names are the same:

⟨*MIPS* defsymbol 457⟩ +≡   4̂57   457

```
else
    p->x.name = p->name;
```

80	EXTERN
50	generated
45	genlabel
38	GLOBAL
60	isfunc
38	LOCAL
37	scope
80	STATIC
99	stringf
362	x.name
362	x.offset

Many UNIX assemblers normally omit from the symbol table symbols that start with L, so compilers can save space in object files by starting temporary labels with L.

address is like defsymbol for symbols that represent some other symbol plus a constant offset.

⟨*MIPS functions* 433⟩ +≡   4̂57 45̲8   431

```
static void address(q, p, n) Symbol q, p; int n; {
    q->x.offset = p->x.offset + n;
    if (p->scope == GLOBAL
    || p->sclass == STATIC || p->sclass == EXTERN)
        q->x.name = stringf("%s%s%d", p->x.name,
            n >= 0 ? "+" : "", n);
```

```
        else
            q->x.name = stringd(q->x.offset);
    }
```

For variables on the stack, address simply computes the adjusted offset. For variables accessed using a label, it sets x.name to a string of the form *name* ± *n*. If the offset is positive, the literal "+" emits the operator; if the offset is negative, the %d emits it.

MIPS conventions divide the globals to access small ones faster. MIPS machines form addresses by adding a register to a signed 16-bit instruction field, so developing and accessing an arbitrary 32-bit address takes multiple instructions. To reduce the need for such sequences, translators put small globals into a special 64K bytes sdata segment. The dedicated register $gp holds the base address of sdata, so up to 64K bytes of globals can be accessed in one instruction. The -G*n* option sets the threshold gnum:

⟨*MIPS data* 433⟩ +≡   434 459   431

```
    static int gnum = 8;
```

⟨*parse -G flag* 458⟩ ≡   433

```
    parseflags(argc, argv);
    for (i = 0; i < argc; i++)
        if (strncmp(argv[i], "-G", 2) == 0)
            gnum = atoi(argv[i] + 2);
```

The front end calls the interface procedure global to announce a new global symbol:

⟨*MIPS functions* 433⟩ +≡   457 459   431

```
    static void global(p) Symbol p; {
        if (p->u.seg == BSS) {
            ⟨define an uninitialized global 459⟩
        } else {
            ⟨define an initialized global 458⟩
        }
    }
```

global puts small initialized globals into sdata and the rest into data:

⟨*define an initialized global* 458⟩ ≡   458

```
    if (p->u.seg == DATA
    && (p->type->size == 0 || p->type->size > gnum))
        print(".data\n");
    else if (p->u.seg == DATA)
        print(".sdata\n");
    print(".align %c\n", ".01.2...3"[p->type->align]);
    print("%s:\n", p->x.name);
```

`p->type->size` is zero when the size is unknown, which happens when certain array declarations omit bounds. This path through `global` winds up by emitting an alignment directive and the label. `".01.2...3"[x]` is a compact expression for the logarithm to the base 2 of an alignment x, which is what this `.align` directive expects.

The directives for uninitialized globals implicitly define the label, reserve space, and choose the segment based on size:

⟨*define an uninitialized global* 459⟩≡   458

```
    if (p->sclass == STATIC || Aflag >= 2)
        print(".lcomm %s,%d\n", p->x.name, p->type->size);
    else
        print( ".comm %s,%d\n", p->x.name, p->type->size);
```

`.comm` also exports the symbol and marks it so that the loader generates only one common global even if other modules emit `.comm` directives for the same identifier. `.lcomm` takes neither step. lcc uses it for statics to avoid the export, and the scrupulous double `-A` option uses it to have the loader object when multiple modules define the same global. Pre-ANSI C permitted multiple definitions, but ANSI C technically expects exactly one definition; other modules should use `extern` declarations instead.

`cseg` tracks the current segment:

⟨*MIPS data* 433⟩+≡   ▲458   431

```
    static int cseg;
```

Since symbols in the DATA and BSS segments do their own segment switching, `segment` emits directives for only the text and literal segments:

⟨*MIPS functions* 433⟩+≡   ▲458 459▼   431

```
    static void segment(n) int n; {
        cseg = n;
        switch (n) {
        case CODE: print(".text\n");  break;
        case LIT:  print(".rdata\n"); break;
        }
    }
```

`space` emits a directive that reserves a block of memory unless the symbol is in the BSS segment, because `global` allocates space for BSS symbols:

⟨*MIPS functions* 433⟩+≡   ▲459 460▼   431

```
    static void space(n) int n; {
        if (cseg != BSS)
            print(".space %d\n", n);
    }
```

`.space` clears the block, which the standard requires of declarations that use it.

16.5 Copying Blocks

blkloop emits a loop to copy size bytes from a source address — formed by adding register sreg and offset soff — to a destination address — formed by adding register dreg and offset doff. Figure 13.4 shows blkloop, blkfetch, and blkstore in action.

⟨*MIPS functions* 433⟩+≡   ▲459 460   431
                                                             ▼

```
static void blkloop(dreg, doff, sreg, soff, size, tmps)
int dreg, doff, sreg, soff, size, tmps[]; {
    int lab = genlabel(1);

    print("addu $%d,$%d,%d\n", sreg, sreg, size&~7);
    print("addu $%d,$%d,%d\n", tmps[2], dreg, size&~7);
    blkcopy(tmps[2], doff, sreg, soff, size&7, tmps);
    print("L.%d:\n", lab);
    print("addu $%d,$%d,%d\n", sreg, sreg, -8);
    print("addu $%d,$%d,%d\n", tmps[2], tmps[2], -8);
    blkcopy(tmps[2], doff, sreg, soff, 8, tmps);
    print("bltu $%d,$%d,L.%d\n", dreg, tmps[2], lab);
}
```

tmps names three registers to use as temporaries. Each iteration copies eight bytes. Initial code points sreg and tmps[2] at the end of the block to copy. If the block's size is not a multiple of eight, then the first blkcopy copies the stragglers. Then the loop decrements registers sreg and tmps[2], calls blkcopy to copy the eight bytes at which they now point, and iterates until the value in register tmps[2] reaches the one in register dreg.

blkfetch emits code to load register tmp with one, two, or four bytes from the address formed by adding register reg and offset off:

⟨*MIPS functions* 433⟩+≡   ▲460 461   431
                                                             ▼

```
static void blkfetch(size, off, reg, tmp)
int size, off, reg, tmp; {
    if (size == 1)
        print("lbu $%d,%d($%d)\n",  tmp, off, reg);
    else if (salign >= size && size == 2)
        print("lhu $%d,%d($%d)\n",  tmp, off, reg);
    else if (salign >= size)
        print("lw $%d,%d($%d)\n",  tmp, off, reg);
    else if (size == 2)
        print("ulhu $%d,%d($%d)\n",  tmp, off, reg);
    else
        print("ulw $%d,%d($%d)\n",  tmp, off, reg);
}
```

If the source alignment, as given by `salign`, is at least as great as the size of the unit to load, then `blkfetch` uses ordinary aligned loads. Otherwise, it uses assembler pseudo-instructions that load unaligned units. For byte loads, alignment is moot. `blkstore` is the dual of `blkfetch`:

⟨*MIPS functions* 433⟩ +≡   ▲460   431

```
static void blkstore(size, off, reg, tmp)
int size, off, reg, tmp; {
    if (size == 1)
        print("sb $%d,%d($%d)\n",  tmp, off, reg);
    else if (dalign >= size && size == 2)
        print("sh $%d,%d($%d)\n",  tmp, off, reg);
    else if (dalign >= size)
        print("sw $%d,%d($%d)\n",  tmp, off, reg);
    else if (size == 2)
        print("ush $%d,%d($%d)\n", tmp, off, reg);
    else
        print("usw $%d,%d($%d)\n", tmp, off, reg);
}
```

Further Reading

Kane and Heinrich (1992) is a reference manual for the MIPS R3000 series. lcc's MIPS code generator works on the newer MIPS R4000 series, but it doesn't exploit the R4000 64-bit instructions.

Exercises

16.1 Why can't small global arrays go into `sdata`?

16.2 Why must all nonempty argument-build areas be at least 16 bytes long?

16.3 Explain why the MIPS calling convention can't handle variadic routines for which the first argument is a float or double.

16.4 Explain why the MIPS calling convention makes it hard to pass structures reliably in the undeclared suffix of variable length argument lists. How could this problem be fixed?

16.5 Extend lcc to emit the information about the type and location of identifiers that your debugger needs to report and change the values of identifiers. The symbolic back end that appears on the companion diskette shows how the stab functions are used.

16.6 Page 418 describes `ralloc`'s assumption that all templates clobber no target register before finishing with all source registers. `lcc`'s MIPS template for CVID on page 440 satisfies this requirement in two ways. Describe them.

16.7 Using the MIPS code generator as a model, write a code generator for another RISC machine, like the DEC Alpha or Motorola PowerPC. Read Section 19.2 first.

`ralloc` 417

17

Generating SPARC Code

The SPARC architecture is another RISC. It has 32 32-bit general registers, 32 32-bit floating-point registers, a compact set of 32-bit instructions, and two addressing modes. It accesses memory only through explicit load and store instructions.

The main architectural differences between the MIPS and SPARC involve the SPARC *register windows*, which automatically save and restore registers at calls and returns. The associated calling convention changes `function` a lot. For a truly simple `function`, see the X86 `function`.

`lcc`'s target is, however, the assembler language, not the machine language, and the MIPS and SPARC assemblers differ in ways that exaggerate the differences between the code generators. Most RISC machines can, for example, increment a register by a small constant in one instruction, but larger constants take more instructions. They develop a full 32-bit constant into a temporary, which they then add to the register. The MIPS assembler insulates us from this feature; that is, it lets us use arbitrary constants almost everywhere, and it generates the multi-instruction implementation when necessary. The SPARC assembler is more literal and requires the code generator to emit different code for large and small constants. Similarly, the MIPS assembler schedules instructions, but the SPARC assembler does not.

92	function	
448	"	(MIPS)
484	"	(SPARC)
518	"	(X86)

SPARC assembler instructions list source operands before the destination operand. A % precedes register names. Table 17.1 describes enough sample instructions to get us started.

The file `sparc.c` collects all code and data specific to the SPARC architecture. It's an `lburg` specification with the interface routines after the grammar:

⟨sparc.md 463⟩≡
```
%{
⟨lburg prefix 375⟩
⟨interface prototypes⟩
⟨SPARC prototypes⟩
⟨SPARC data 467⟩
%}
⟨terminal declarations 376⟩
%%
⟨shared rules 400⟩
⟨SPARC rules 469⟩
%%
```

Assembler	Meaning
mov %i0,%o0	Set register o0 to the value in register i0.
sub %i0,%i1,%o0	Set register o0 to register i0 minus register i1.
sub %i0,1,%o0	Set register o0 to register i0 minus one.
ldsb [%i0+4],%o0	Set register o0 to the byte at the address four bytes past the address in register i0.
ldsb [%i0+%i4],%o0	Set register o0 to the byte at the address equal to the sum of registers i0 and i4.
fsubd %f0,%f2,%f4	Set register f4 to register f0 minus register f2. Use double-precision floating-point arithmetic.
fsubs %f0,%f2,%f4	Set register f4 to register f0 minus register f2. Use single-precision floating-point arithmetic.
ba L1	Jump to the instruction labelled L1.
jmp [%i0]	Jump to the address in register i0.
cmp %i0,%i1	Compare registers i0 and i1 and record results in the condition flags.
bl L1	Branch to L1 if the last comparison recorded less-than.
.byte 0x20	Initialize the next byte in memory to hexadecimal 20.

TABLE 17.1   Sample SPARC assembler input lines.

⟨*SPARC functions* 466⟩
⟨*SPARC interface definition* 464⟩

The last fragment configures the front end and points to the SPARC routines and data in the back end:

⟨*SPARC interface definition* 464⟩≡   464

```
Interface sparcIR = {
    ⟨SPARC type metrics 465⟩
    0,  /* little_endian */
    1,  /* mulops_calls */
    1,  /* wants_callb */
    0,  /* wants_argb */
    1,  /* left_to_right */
    0,  /* wants_dag */
    ⟨interface routine names⟩
    stabblock, 0, 0, stabinit, stabline, stabsym, stabtype,
    {
        1,  /* max_unaligned_load */
        ⟨Xinterface initializer 355⟩
```

```
      }
   };
```

⟨*SPARC type metrics* 465⟩≡   464
```
   1, 1, 0,   /* char */
   2, 2, 0,   /* short */
   4, 4, 0,   /* int */
   4, 4, 1,   /* float */
   8, 8, 1,   /* double */
   4, 4, 0,   /* T * */
   0, 1, 0,   /* struct */
```

mulops_calls is one because some SPARC processors implement the multiplication and division with code instead of hardware.

The SPARC and MIPS conventions for structure arguments and return values are duals. The MIPS conventions use ARGB but no CALLB, and the SPARC conventions use CALLB but no ARGB.

The symbol-table emitter is elided but complete. The two zeros in the stab routines correspond to routines that need emit nothing on this particular target. The other stab names above are #defined to zero when building the SPARC code generator into a cross-compiler on another machine because the elided code includes headers and refers to identifiers that are known only on SPARC systems.

87 mulops_calls

17.1   Registers

The SPARC assembler language programmer sees 32 32-bit general registers. Most are organized as a stack of overlapping *register windows*. Most routines allocate a new window to store locals, temporaries, and outgoing arguments — the calling convention passes some arguments in registers — and free the window when they return.

The general registers have at least two names each, as shown in Table 17.2. One is r0-r31, and the other encodes a bit more about how the register is used and where it goes in a register window. g0 is hard-wired to zero. Instructions can write it, but the change won't take. When they read it, they read zero.

Basic Name	Equivalent Name	Explanation
r0-r7	g0-g7	Fixed global registers. Not stacked.
r8-r15	o0-o7	Outgoing arguments. Stacked.
r16-r23	l0-l7	Locals. Stacked.
r24-r31	i0-i7	Incoming arguments. Stacked.

TABLE 17.2   SPARC general registers.

FIGURE 17.1 main calls f.

greg 467

The machine arranges the register windows so that the physical registers called o0–o7 in each caller are the same registers referred to as i0–i7 in the callee. Figure 17.1 shows the register windows for

```
main() { f(); }
f() { return; }
```

just before f returns. There are 32 general registers, but each call consumes only 16, because g0–g7 aren't stacked, and the shading shows that the caller's o0–o7 are the same physical registers as the callee's i0–i7.

The interface procedure progend does nothing for this target. progbeg parses the target-specific flags -p and -pg, which have lcc emit code for the SPARC profilers, but which this book omits. progbeg also initializes the structures that describe the register set:

⟨*SPARC functions* 466⟩ ≡   468   464
```
    static void progbeg(argc, argv) int argc; char *argv[]; {
        int i;

        ⟨shared progbeg 371⟩
        ⟨parse SPARC flags⟩
        ⟨initialize SPARC register structures 467⟩
    }
```

progbeg causes each element of greg to describe one general register:

⟨*SPARC data* 467⟩≡   467   463
```
    static Symbol greg[32];
    static Symbol *oreg = &greg[8], *ireg = &greg[24];
```

The initialization code parallels Table 17.2:

⟨*initialize SPARC register structures* 467⟩≡   467   466
```
    for (i = 0; i < 8; i++) {
        greg[i +  0] = mkreg(stringf("g%d", i), i +  0, 1, IREG);
        greg[i +  8] = mkreg(stringf("o%d", i), i +  8, 1, IREG);
        greg[i + 16] = mkreg(stringf("l%d", i), i + 16, 1, IREG);
        greg[i + 24] = mkreg(stringf("i%d", i), i + 24, 1, IREG);
    }
```

The machine also has 32 32-bit floating-point registers, f0-f31 in assembler language. These are conventional registers and involve nothing like the general-register stack. Even-odd register pairs may be used as double-precision floating-point registers. progbeg causes each element of freg to describe one single-precision floating-point register, and each even numbered element of freg2 to describe one double-precision floating-point register:

⟨*SPARC data* 467⟩+≡   467 487   463
```
    static Symbol freg[32], freg2[32];
```

⟨*initialize SPARC register structures* 467⟩+≡   467 467   466
```
    for (i = 0; i < 32; i++)
        freg[i]  = mkreg("%d", i, 1, FREG);
    for (i = 0; i < 31; i += 2)
        freg2[i] = mkreg("%d", i, 3, FREG);
```

rmap stores the wildcard that identifies the default register class to use for each type:

⟨*initialize SPARC register structures* 467⟩+≡   467 468   466
```
    rmap[C] = rmap[S] = rmap[P] = rmap[B] = rmap[U] = rmap[I] =
        mkwildcard(greg);
    rmap[F] = mkwildcard(freg);
    rmap[D] = mkwildcard(freg2);
```

lcc puts no variables or temporaries in g0-g7, i6-i7, o0, or o6-o7. The calling convention does not preserve g0-g7 across calls. o6 is used as the stack pointer; it's sometimes termed sp. i6 is used as the frame pointer; it's sometimes termed fp. Each caller puts its return address in its o7, which is known as i7 in the callee (see Figure 17.1). A function returns its value in its i0, which its caller knows as o0. A routine that calls other routines expects its callees to destroy its o0-o7. Floating-point values return in f0 or f0-f1.

That leaves general registers i0-i5, l0-l7, and o1-o5. lcc will put temporaries in any of these registers:

⟨*initialize SPARC register structures* 467⟩+≡   467 468   466
    tmask[IREG] = 0x3fff3e00;

lcc will put register variables in about half of them, namely 14–17 and
i0–i5:

⟨*initialize SPARC register structures* 467⟩+≡   468 468   466
    vmask[IREG] = 0x3ff00000;

Recall that tmask identifies the registers that may serve as temporaries
while evaluating expressions, and vmask identifies those that may hold
register variables. The dividing line between temporaries and register
variables is somewhat arbitrary. Ordinarily, the two sets are mutually
exclusive: registers for variables are spilled in the routine's prologue to
avoid spilling all live register variables at all call sites, but temporaries
can be spilled at the call sites because it's easy for the register allocator to identify the few that are typically live. The SPARC register stack,
however, automatically saves many registers when it enters a routine, so
we may as well permit temporaries in all of them. We restrict variables
to about half of the registers because they get first crack at the register,
and if we leave too few temporaries, then we can get a lot of spills or
hamstring the register allocator altogether.

The calling convention preserves no floating-point registers across
calls. lcc uses them only for temporaries:

⟨*initialize SPARC register structures* 467⟩+≡   468   466
    tmask[FREG] = ~(unsigned)0;
    vmask[FREG] = 0;

target calls setreg to mark nodes that need a special register, and it
calls rtarget to mark nodes that need a child in a special register:

⟨*SPARC functions* 466⟩+≡   466 468   464
```
static void target(p) Node p; {
    switch (p->op) {
    ⟨SPARC target 473⟩
    }
}
```

If an instruction clobbers some registers, clobber calls spill to save
them first and restore them later.

⟨*SPARC functions* 466⟩+≡   468 469   464
```
static void clobber(p) Node p; {
    switch (p->op) {
    ⟨SPARC clobber 477⟩
    }
}
```

The cases missing from target and clobber above appear with the germane instructions in the next section.

17.2 Selecting Instructions

Table 17.3 summarizes the nonterminals in lcc's lburg specification for the SPARC code generator. It provides a high-level overview of the organization of the tree grammar.

The use of percent signs in the SPARC assembler language interacts unattractively with lcc's use of percent sign as the template escape character. For example, the set pseudo-instruction sets a register to a constant integer or address, so the rule for ADDRGP is:

⟨*SPARC rules* 469⟩≡   470   463
```
reg: ADDRGP  "set %a,%%%c\n"  1
```

The template substring %% emits one %, and the template substring %c emits the name of the destination register, so the template substring %%%c directs the emitter to precede the register name with a percent sign in the generated code. It isn't pretty, but it's consistent with print and printf, and if we'd picked a different escape character, it would probably have needed quoting on some other target.

SPARC instructions with an immediate field store a signed 13-bit constant, so several instructions use the target-specific cost function imm, which returns a zero cost if p's constant value fits and a huge cost if it doesn't:

⟨*SPARC functions* 466⟩+≡   468 477   464

| 18 print |
| 388 range |
| 403 reg |

```
static int imm(p) Node p; {
    return range(p, -4096, 4095);
}
```

For example, if 13 bits are enough for the signed offset of an ADDRFP or ADDRLP node, then one instruction can develop the address into a register:

Name	What It Matches
addr	address calculations for instructions that read and write memory
addrg	ADDRG nodes
base	addr minus the register+register addressing mode
call	operands to call instructions
con	constants
con13	constants that fit in 13 signed bits
rc	registers and constants
reg	computations that yield a result in a register
stk	addresses of locals and formals
stk13	addresses of locals and formals that fit in 13 signed bits
stmt	computations done for side effect

TABLE 17.3 SPARC nonterminals

⟨*SPARC rules* 469⟩ +≡   469 470   463 ▼

```
stk13: ADDRFP  "%a"                        imm(a)
stk13: ADDRLP  "%a"                        imm(a)
reg:   stk13   "add %0,%%fp,%%%c\n"  1
```

Otherwise, it takes more instructions:

⟨*SPARC rules* 469⟩ +≡   470 470   463 ▼

```
stk: ADDRFP  "set %a,%%%c\n"                    2
stk: ADDRLP  "set %a,%%%c\n"                    2
reg: ADDRFP  "set %a,%%%c\nadd %%%c,%%fp,%%%c\n"  3
reg: ADDRLP  "set %a,%%%c\nadd %%%c,%%fp,%%%c\n"  3
```

set is a pseudo-instruction that generates two instructions if the constant can't be loaded in just one, and if one instruction would do, then stk13 will take care of it. We might have done something similar in the MIPS code generator, but the MIPS assembler can hide constant size-checking completely, so we might as well use this feature. The SPARC assembler leaves at least part of the problem to the programmer or compiler, so we had no choice this time.

The four rules above appear equivalent to

```
stk: ADDRFP  "set %a,%%%c\n"       2
stk: ADDRLP  "set %a,%%%c\n"       2
reg: stk     "add %0,%%fp,%%%c\n"  1
```

but the shorter rules fail because they ask reduce to store two different values into one x.inst. Recall that a node's x.inst records as an instruction the nonterminal that identifies the rule that matches the node, if there is one. The problem with the short rules above is that the x.inst field for the ADDRLP or ADDRFP can't identify both stk and reg.

The nonterminal con13 matches small integral constants:

⟨*SPARC rules* 469⟩ +≡   470 470   463 ▼

```
con13: CNSTC  "%a"  imm(a)
con13: CNSTI  "%a"  imm(a)
con13: CNSTP  "%a"  imm(a)
con13: CNSTS  "%a"  imm(a)
con13: CNSTU  "%a"  imm(a)
```

The instructions that read and write memory cells use address calculation that can add a register to a 13-bit signed constant:

⟨*SPARC rules* 469⟩ +≡   470 471   463 ▼

```
base: ADDI(reg,con13)  "%%%0+%1"
base: ADDP(reg,con13)  "%%%0+%1"
base: ADDU(reg,con13)  "%%%0+%1"
```

If the constant is zero or the register g0, the sum degenerates to a simple indirect or direct address:

⟨*SPARC rules* 469⟩ +≡   470 471   463
```
base: reg    "%%%0"
base: con13  "%0"
```

If the register is the frame pointer, then the sum yields the address of a
formal or local:

⟨*SPARC rules* 469⟩ +≡   471 471   463
```
base: stk13  "%%fp+%0"
```

The address calculation hardware can also add two registers:

⟨*SPARC rules* 469⟩ +≡   471 471   463
```
addr: base            "%0"
addr: ADDI(reg,reg)   "%%%0+%%%1"
addr: ADDP(reg,reg)   "%%%0+%%%1"
addr: ADDU(reg,reg)   "%%%0+%%%1"
addr: stk             "%%fp+%%%0"
```

Most loads and stores can use the full set of addressing modes above:

⟨*SPARC rules* 469⟩ +≡   471 471   463
```
reg:   INDIRC(addr)     "ldsb [%0],%%%c\n"   1
reg:   INDIRS(addr)     "ldsh [%0],%%%c\n"   1
reg:   INDIRI(addr)     "ld [%0],%%%c\n"     1
reg:   INDIRP(addr)     "ld [%0],%%%c\n"     1
reg:   INDIRF(addr)     "ld [%0],%%f%c\n"    1
stmt:  ASGNC(addr,reg)  "stb %%%1,[%0]\n"    1
stmt:  ASGNS(addr,reg)  "sth %%%1,[%0]\n"    1
stmt:  ASGNI(addr,reg)  "st %%%1,[%0]\n"     1
stmt:  ASGNP(addr,reg)  "st %%%1,[%0]\n"     1
stmt:  ASGNF(addr,reg)  "st %%f%1,[%0]\n"    1
```

```
469 imm
403 reg
403 stmt
```

The `ldd` and `std` instructions load and store a double, but only at addresses divisible by eight. The conventions for aligning arguments and
globals guarantee only divisibility by four, so `ldd` and `std` suit only locals:

⟨*SPARC rules* 469⟩ +≡   471 472   463
```
addr1: ADDRLP          "%%%fp+%a"           imm(a)

reg:   INDIRD(addr1)    "ldd [%0],%%f%c\n"   1
stmt:  ASGND(addr1,reg) "std %%f%1,[%0]\n"   1
```

The pseudo-instructions `ld2` and `st2` generate instruction pairs to load
and store doubles aligned to a multiple of four, but some SPARC assemblers silently emit incorrect code when the address is the sum of two
registers, so the rules for these pseudo-instructions use the nonterminal
`base`, which omits register-plus-register addressing:

⟨*SPARC rules* 469⟩+≡   ▲471 472   463
▼

```
    reg:  INDIRD(base)     "ld2 [%0],%%f%c\n"   2
    stmt: ASGND(base,reg)  "st2 %%f%1,[%0]\n"   2
```

But for this assembler bug, the rules defining base and addr could be combined and define a single nonterminal.

The spiller needs to generate code that can store a register when all allocable registers are busy. When the offset doesn't fit in a SPARC immediate field, the ASGN rules above generate multiple instructions, and the instructions need a register to communicate, which violates the spiller's assumption. lcc corrects this problem with a second copy of the ASGN rules. They use the unallocable register g1 to help store locals — lcc spills only to locals — that are not immediately addressable:

⟨*SPARC rules* 469⟩+≡   ▲472 472   463
▼

```
    spill:  ADDRLP               "%a"  !imm(a)

    stmt: ASGNC(spill,reg)  "set %0,%%g1\nstb %%%1,[%%fp+%%g1]\n"
    stmt: ASGNS(spill,reg)  "set %0,%%g1\nsth %%%1,[%%fp+%%g1]\n"
    stmt: ASGNI(spill,reg)  "set %0,%%g1\nst %%%1,[%%fp+%%g1]\n"
    stmt: ASGNP(spill,reg)  "set %0,%%g1\nst %%%1,[%%fp+%%g1]\n"
    stmt: ASGNF(spill,reg)  "set %0,%%g1\nst %%f%1,[%%fp+%%g1]\n"
    stmt: ASGND(spill,reg)  "set %0,%%g1\nstd %%f%1,[%%fp+%%g1]\n"
```

The rules have an artificially low cost of zero so that they'll win when they match, which isn't often. These rules can apply to stores that aren't spills, but using a cost of zero in those cases is harmless. See Exercise 17.7.

ldsb and ldsh extend the sign bit of the cell that they load, so they implement a CVCI and CVSI for free. ldub and lduh clear the top bits, so they include a free CVCU and CVSU.

⟨*SPARC rules* 469⟩+≡   ▲472 472   463
▼

```
    reg: CVCI(INDIRC(addr))   "ldsb [%0],%%%c\n"   1
    reg: CVSI(INDIRS(addr))   "ldsh [%0],%%%c\n"   1
    reg: CVCU(INDIRC(addr))   "ldub [%0],%%%c\n"   1
    reg: CVSU(INDIRS(addr))   "lduh [%0],%%%c\n"   1
```

The integral conversions to types no wider than the source can also generate a register-to-register move instruction. Recall that move returns one and marks the node for possible optimization by requate and moveself.

⟨*SPARC rules* 469⟩+≡   ▲472 473   463
▼

```
    reg: CVIC(reg)   "mov %%%0,%%%c\n"   move(a)
    reg: CVIS(reg)   "mov %%%0,%%%c\n"   move(a)
    reg: CVIU(reg)   "mov %%%0,%%%c\n"   move(a)
    reg: CVPU(reg)   "mov %%%0,%%%c\n"   move(a)
    reg: CVUC(reg)   "mov %%%0,%%%c\n"   move(a)
```

```
reg: CVUI(reg)    "mov %%%0,%%%c\n"   move(a)
reg: CVUP(reg)    "mov %%%0,%%%c\n"   move(a)
reg: CVUS(reg)    "mov %%%0,%%%c\n"   move(a)
```

If the node targets no special register, it can generate nothing at all:

⟨*SPARC rules* 469⟩+≡   472 473   463
```
reg: CVIC(reg)    "%0"   notarget(a)
reg: CVIS(reg)    "%0"   notarget(a)
reg: CVUC(reg)    "%0"   notarget(a)
reg: CVUS(reg)    "%0"   notarget(a)
```

This second list looks shorter than the one above it, but the target-independent fragment ⟨*shared rules*⟩ on page 400 makes up the difference.

LOADs also generate register copies:

⟨*SPARC rules* 469⟩+≡   473 473   463
```
reg: LOADC(reg)   "mov %%%0,%%%c\n"   move(a)
reg: LOADI(reg)   "mov %%%0,%%%c\n"   move(a)
reg: LOADP(reg)   "mov %%%0,%%%c\n"   move(a)
reg: LOADS(reg)   "mov %%%0,%%%c\n"   move(a)
reg: LOADU(reg)   "mov %%%0,%%%c\n"   move(a)
```

It would be nice to share *these* rules too, but the templates are machine-specific.

Register g0 is hard-wired to hold zero, so integral CNST nodes with the value zero generate no code:

⟨*SPARC rules* 469⟩+≡   473 474   463
```
reg: CNSTC   "# reg\n"   range(a, 0, 0)
reg: CNSTI   "# reg\n"   range(a, 0, 0)
reg: CNSTP   "# reg\n"   range(a, 0, 0)
reg: CNSTS   "# reg\n"   range(a, 0, 0)
reg: CNSTU   "# reg\n"   range(a, 0, 0)
```

Recall that cost expressions are evaluated in a context in which a denotes the node being labelled, which here is the constant value being tested for zero. target arranges for these nodes to return g0:

⟨*SPARC* target 473⟩≡   476   468
```
case CNSTC: case CNSTI: case CNSTS: case CNSTU: case CNSTP:
    if (range(p, 0, 0) == 0) {
        setreg(p, greg[0]);
        p->x.registered = 1;
    }
    break;
```

Allocating g0 makes no sense, so target marks the node to preclude register allocation.

The set pseudo-instruction can load any constant into a register:

⟨*SPARC rules* 469⟩+≡   4̂73 474   463
  reg: con   "set %0,%%%c\n"   1

set generates one instruction if the constant fits in 13 bits and two otherwise. The assembler insulates us from the details.

    Most binary instructions that operate on integers can accept a register
or a 13-bit constant as the second source operand:

⟨*SPARC rules* 469⟩+≡   4̂74 474   463
  rc: con13   "%0"
  rc: reg   "%%%0"

The first operand and the result must be registers:

⟨*SPARC rules* 469⟩+≡   4̂74 474   463
```
    reg: ADDI(reg,rc)    "add %%%0,%1,%%%c\n"   1
    reg: ADDP(reg,rc)    "add %%%0,%1,%%%c\n"   1
    reg: ADDU(reg,rc)    "add %%%0,%1,%%%c\n"   1
    reg: BANDU(reg,rc)   "and %%%0,%1,%%%c\n"   1
    reg: BORU(reg,rc)    "or %%%0,%1,%%%c\n"    1
    reg: BXORU(reg,rc)   "xor %%%0,%1,%%%c\n"   1
    reg: SUBI(reg,rc)    "sub %%%0,%1,%%%c\n"   1
    reg: SUBP(reg,rc)    "sub %%%0,%1,%%%c\n"   1
    reg: SUBU(reg,rc)    "sub %%%0,%1,%%%c\n"   1
```

range 388
reg 403

Shift instructions, however, can't accept constant shift operands less
than zero or greater than 31:

⟨*SPARC rules* 469⟩+≡   4̂74 474   463
  rc5: CNSTI   "%a"   range(a, 0, 31)
  rc5: reg   "%%%0"

The first operand and the result must be registers:

⟨*SPARC rules* 469⟩+≡   4̂74 474   463
```
    reg: LSHI(reg,rc5)   "sll %%%0,%1,%%%c\n"   1
    reg: LSHU(reg,rc5)   "sll %%%0,%1,%%%c\n"   1
    reg: RSHI(reg,rc5)   "sra %%%0,%1,%%%c\n"   1
    reg: RSHU(reg,rc5)   "srl %%%0,%1,%%%c\n"   1
```

The three Boolean operators have variants that complement the second
operand:

⟨*SPARC rules* 469⟩+≡   4̂74 475   463
```
    reg: BANDU(reg,BCOMU(rc))   "andn %%%0,%1,%%%c\n"   1
    reg: BORU(reg,BCOMU(rc))    "orn %%%0,%1,%%%c\n"    1
    reg: BXORU(reg,BCOMU(rc))   "xnor %%%0,%1,%%%c\n"   1
```

The unary operators work on registers only:

⟨*SPARC rules* 469⟩+≡   474 475   463
```
    reg:  NEGI(reg)    "neg %%%0,%%%c\n"    1
    reg:  BCOMU(reg)   "not %%%0,%%%c\n"    1
```

The conversions that widen a signed character or a signed short do so by shifting left and then right arithmetically to extend the sign bit:

⟨*SPARC rules* 469⟩+≡   475 475   463
```
    reg:  CVCI(reg)   "sll %%%0,24,%%%c; sra %%%c,24,%%%c\n"   2
    reg:  CVSI(reg)   "sll %%%0,16,%%%c; sra %%%c,16,%%%c\n"   2
```

The unsigned conversions use and instructions to clear the top bits:

⟨*SPARC rules* 469⟩+≡   475 475   463
```
    reg:  CVCU(reg)   "and %%%0,0xff,%%%c\n"                 1
    reg:  CVSU(reg)   "set 0xffff,%%g1; and %%%0,%%g1,%%%c\n"  2
```

CVSU needs a 16-bit mask, which won't fit in the instruction as CVCU's does.

All SPARC unconditional jumps and conditional branches have a one-instruction *delay slot*. The instruction *after* the jump or branch — which is said to be "in the delay slot" — is always executed, just as if it had been executed *before* the jump or branch. For the time being, we'll fill each delay slot with a harmless nop. The ba instruction targets constant addresses, and the jmp instruction targets the rest, namely the ones needed for switch statements.

403 reg
403 stmt

⟨*SPARC rules* 469⟩+≡   475 475   463
```
    addrg:  ADDRGP            "%a"
    stmt:   JUMPV(addrg)      "ba %0; nop\n"    2
    stmt:   JUMPV(addr)       "jmp %0; nop\n"   2
    stmt:   LABELV            "%a:\n"
```

The integral relationals compare one register to another register or to a constant:

⟨*SPARC rules* 469⟩+≡   475 476   463
```
    stmt:  EQI(reg,rc)   "cmp %%%0,%1; be %a; nop\n"    3
    stmt:  GEI(reg,rc)   "cmp %%%0,%1; bge %a; nop\n"   3
    stmt:  GEU(reg,rc)   "cmp %%%0,%1; bgeu %a; nop\n"  3
    stmt:  GTI(reg,rc)   "cmp %%%0,%1; bg %a; nop\n"    3
    stmt:  GTU(reg,rc)   "cmp %%%0,%1; bgu %a; nop\n"   3
    stmt:  LEI(reg,rc)   "cmp %%%0,%1; ble %a; nop\n"   3
    stmt:  LEU(reg,rc)   "cmp %%%0,%1; bleu %a; nop\n"  3
    stmt:  LTI(reg,rc)   "cmp %%%0,%1; bl %a; nop\n"    3
    stmt:  LTU(reg,rc)   "cmp %%%0,%1; blu %a; nop\n"   3
    stmt:  NEI(reg,rc)   "cmp %%%0,%1; bne %a; nop\n"   3
```

The call instruction targets a constant address or a computed one:

⟨*SPARC rules* 469⟩+≡   4̂75 476   463

```
call: ADDRGP              "%a"
call: addr                "%0"
reg:  CALLD(call)         "call %0; nop\n"            2
reg:  CALLF(call)         "call %0; nop\n"            2
reg:  CALLI(call)         "call %0; nop\n"            2
stmt: CALLV(call)         "call %0; nop\n"            2
stmt: CALLB(call,reg)     "call %0; st %%%1,[%%sp+64]\n"  2
```

CALLB transmits the address of the return block by storing it into the stack. The store instruction occupies the delay slot.

The front end follows each RET node with a jump to the procedure epilogue, so RET nodes generate no code and serve only to help the back end target the return register:

⟨*SPARC rules* 469⟩+≡   4̂76 477   463

```
stmt: RETD(reg)   "# ret\n"   1
stmt: RETF(reg)   "# ret\n"   1
stmt: RETI(reg)   "# ret\n"   1
```

Functions return values in f0, f0-f1, or o0, which is known as i0 in the callee. target arranges compliance with this convention:

⟨*SPARC* target 473⟩+≡   4̂73 476   468

```
case CALLD: setreg(p, freg2[0]);     break;
case CALLF: setreg(p, freg[0]);      break;
case CALLI:
case CALLV: setreg(p, oreg[0]);      break;
case RETD:  rtarget(p, 0, freg2[0]); break;
case RETF:  rtarget(p, 0, freg[0]);  break;
```

The case for RETI marks the node to prevent register allocation and avoid an apparent contradiction:

⟨*SPARC* target 473⟩+≡   4̂76 477   468

```
case RETI:
    rtarget(p, 0, ireg[0]);
    p->kids[0]->x.registered = 1;
    break;
```

If a routine's first argument is integral, it resides in i0. If a function returns an integer, i0 must hold the return value too. lcc's register allocator can spill temporaries but not formals, so the register allocator will fail if we ask it to allocate i0 to a RETI. Formals are, however, dead at returns, so we simply mark the node allocated, which awards i0 to the RETI and prevents the register allocator from doing anything, including spilling the formal.

The register stack automatically saves and restores the general registers at calls, so only the floating-point registers, minus the return register, need to be explicitly saved and restored:

⟨*SPARC* clobber 477⟩≡   479   468
```
  case CALLB: case CALLD: case CALLF: case CALLI:
    spill(~(unsigned)3, FREG, p);
    break;
  case CALLV:
    spill(oreg[0]->x.regnode->mask, IREG, p);
    spill(~(unsigned)3, FREG, p);
    break;
```

Recall that `ralloc` calls the target's `clobber` after allocating a register to the node.

`doarg` stores in each ARG node's `syms[RX]` an integer constant symbol equal to the argument offset divided by four, which names the outgoing o-register for most arguments:

⟨*SPARC functions* 466⟩+≡   469 478   464
```
  static void doarg(p) Node p; {
    p->syms[RX] = intconst(mkactual(4,
        p->syms[0]->u.c.v.i)/4);
  }
```

ARG nodes are executed for side effect, so they don't normally use `syms[RX]`, but the SPARC calling convention implements ARG nodes with register targeting or assignment, so using RX is natural.

Targeting arranges to compute the first 24 bytes of arguments into the registers for outgoing arguments. `target` calls `rtarget` to develop the child into the desired o-register, and then it changes the ARG into a LOAD into the same register, which `emit` and `moveself` optimize away:

⟨*SPARC* target 473⟩+≡   476 480   468
```
  case ARGI: case ARGP:
    if (p->syms[RX]->u.c.v.i < 6) {
      rtarget(p, 0, oreg[p->syms[RX]->u.c.v.i]);
      p->op = LOAD+optype(p->op);
      setreg(p, oreg[p->syms[RX]->u.c.v.i]);
    }
    break;
```

Calls with too many arguments for these registers pass the rest in memory. To pass an argument in memory, the assembler template undoes the division and adds 68:

⟨*SPARC rules* 469⟩+≡   476 478   463
```
  stmt: ARGI(reg)  "st %%%0,[%%sp+4*%c+68]\n"  1
  stmt: ARGP(reg)  "st %%%0,[%%sp+4*%c+68]\n"  1
```

sp points at 16 words — 64 bytes — in which the operating system can store the routine's i- and l-registers when the register windows are exhausted and some must be spilled. The next word is reserved for the

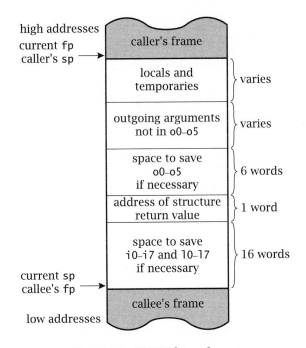

FIGURE 17.2 SPARC frame layout.

reg 403
stmt 403

address of the structure return block, if there is one. The next words are for the outgoing arguments; space is reserved there for even those that arrive in i0–i5. So the argument at argument offset n is at %sp+n+68, which explains the template above. Figure 17.2 shows a SPARC frame.

The code for variadic routines can look in only one spot for, say, the argument at offset 20, so even floating-point arguments must travel in o0–o5; note the parallel with the MIPS calling convention. lcc assumes that floating-point opcodes yield floating-point registers, so no tree can develop an unconverted floating-point value into an integer register. emit2 must handle these odd ARGs:

⟨*SPARC rules* 469⟩+≡ 477 480 463
```
stmt: ARGD(reg)   "# ARGD\n"   1
stmt: ARGF(reg)   "# ARGF\n"   1
```

⟨*SPARC functions* 466⟩+≡ 477 483 464
```
static void emit2(p) Node p; {
    switch (p->op) {
    ⟨SPARC emit2 479⟩
    }
}
```

ARGF must get a value from a floating-point register into an o-register or

onto the stack. A stack slot is reserved for each outgoing argument, and
the only path from a floating-point register to a general register is via
memory, so emit2 copies the floating-point register into the stack, and
then loads the stack slot into the o-register, unless we're past o5:

⟨*SPARC* emit2 479⟩≡   479   478

```
case ARGF: {
    int n = p->syms[RX]->u.c.v.i;
    print("st %%f%d,[%%sp+4*%d+68]\n",
        getregnum(p->x.kids[0]), n);
    if (n <= 5)
        print("ld [%%sp+4*%d+68],%%o%d\n", n, n);
    break;
}
```

ARGD is similar, but it needs two stores and up to two loads:

⟨*SPARC* emit2 479⟩+≡   479 482   478

```
case ARGD: {
    int n = p->syms[RX]->u.c.v.i;
    int src = getregnum(p->x.kids[0]);
    print("st %%f%d,[%%sp+4*%d+68]\n", src, n);
    print("st %%f%d,[%%sp+4*%d+68]\n", src+1, n+1);
    if (n <= 5)
        print("ld [%%sp+4*%d+68],%%o%d\n", n, n);
    if (n <= 4)
        print("ld [%%sp+4*%d+68],%%o%d\n", n+1, n+1);
    break;
}
```

If a double argument is preceded by, say, five integers, then its first
half travels in o5 and its second half on the stack. Splitting the double
seems strange, but variadic routines leave no alternative, and procedure
prologues reunite the two halves.

It seems unwise to ask the register allocator to allocate a general register to a floating-point node, so clobber calls spill to ensure that any
live value in the argument register is saved before the floating-point ARG
and restored later:

⟨*SPARC* clobber 477⟩+≡   477 480   468

```
case ARGF:
    if (p->syms[2]->u.c.v.i <= 6)
        spill((1<<(p->syms[2]->u.c.v.i + 8)), IREG, p);
    break;
case ARGD:
    if (p->syms[2]->u.c.v.i <= 5)
        spill((3<<(p->syms[2]->u.c.v.i + 8))&0xff00, IREG, p);
    break;
```

The MIPS code generator avoided this step because it never allocated the argument registers for any other purpose, but the SPARC convention uses o1–o5 for temporaries when they aren't holding outgoing arguments.

The first SPARC systems offered no instructions to multiply, divide, or find remainders, so the standard library supplied equivalent functions. It is perhaps premature to abandon these systems, so lcc sets mulops_calls and sticks with the functions even on newer machines that offer multiplicative instructions (see Exercise 17.1):

⟨*SPARC rules* 469⟩ +≡   478 480   463

```
reg: DIVI(reg,reg)    "call .div,2; nop\n"     2
reg: DIVU(reg,reg)    "call .udiv,2; nop\n"    2
reg: MODI(reg,reg)    "call .rem,2; nop\n"     2
reg: MODU(reg,reg)    "call .urem,2; nop\n"    2
reg: MULI(reg,reg)    "call .mul,2; nop\n"     2
reg: MULU(reg,reg)    "call .umul,2; nop\n"    2
```

target arranges to pass the operands in o0 and o1, and to receive the result in o0:

⟨*SPARC* target 473⟩ +≡   477   468

```
case DIVI: case MODI: case MULI:
case DIVU: case MODU: case MULU:
    setreg(p, oreg[0]);
    rtarget(p, 0, oreg[0]);
    rtarget(p, 1, oreg[1]);
    break;
```

The library functions allocate no new register window, and instead destroy o1–o5:

⟨*SPARC* clobber 477⟩ +≡   479   468

```
case DIVI: case MODI: case MULI:
case DIVU: case MODU: case MULU:
    spill(0x00003e00, IREG, p); break;
```

The binary floating-point instructions accept only registers:

⟨*SPARC rules* 469⟩ +≡   480 481   463

```
reg: ADDD(reg,reg)    "faddd %%f%0,%%f%1,%%f%c\n"    1
reg: ADDF(reg,reg)    "fadds %%f%0,%%f%1,%%f%c\n"    1
reg: DIVD(reg,reg)    "fdivd %%f%0,%%f%1,%%f%c\n"    1
reg: DIVF(reg,reg)    "fdivs %%f%0,%%f%1,%%f%c\n"    1
reg: MULD(reg,reg)    "fmuld %%f%0,%%f%1,%%f%c\n"    1
reg: MULF(reg,reg)    "fmuls %%f%0,%%f%1,%%f%c\n"    1
reg: SUBD(reg,reg)    "fsubd %%f%0,%%f%1,%%f%c\n"    1
reg: SUBF(reg,reg)    "fsubs %%f%0,%%f%1,%%f%c\n"    1
```

Most floating-point unary operators are similar:

IREG	361
mulops_calls	87
oreg	467
reg	403
rtarget	400
setreg	399
spill	427
target	357
(MIPS) "	435
(SPARC) "	468
(X86) "	502

⟨*SPARC rules* 469⟩+≡   480 481   463
```
   reg: NEGF(reg)    "fnegs %%f%0,%%f%c\n"   1
   reg: LOADF(reg)   "fmovs %%f%0,%%f%c\n"   1
   reg: CVDF(reg)    "fdtos %%f%0,%%f%c\n"   1
   reg: CVFD(reg)    "fstod %%f%0,%%f%c\n"   1
```

The conversions between doubles and integers need three instructions each because the necessary conversion instructions use only floating-point registers even for the integral operand. `fdtoi` converts a double into an integer, but leaves the result in a floating-point register. The parent of the CVDI expects a general register, so the template copies the result to a general register via a temporary cell in memory, which is the only available path:

⟨*SPARC rules* 469⟩+≡   481 481   463
```
   reg: CVDI(reg)   "fdtoi %%f%0,%%f0; st %%f0,[%%sp+64]; _
        ld [%%sp+64],%%%c\n"   3
```

CVID reverses the process:

⟨*SPARC rules* 469⟩+≡   481 481   463
```
   reg: CVID(reg)   "st %%%0,[%%sp+64]; ld [%%sp+64],%%f%c; _
        fitod %%f%c,%%f%c\n"   3
```

CVDI and CVID use the spot reserved for the address of the structure return block for any callees. The spot is unused except between the branch delay slot of a `call` instruction and the callee's prologue instruction that allocates a new stack frame. No CVDI or CVID can appear in any such interval.

403 reg
403 stmt

The floating-point comparisons have one delay slot after the branch, and another after the comparison:

⟨*SPARC rules* 469⟩+≡   481 482   463
```
   rel: EQD(reg,reg)    "fcmped %%f%0,%%f%1; nop; fbue"
   rel: EQF(reg,reg)    "fcmpes %%f%0,%%f%1; nop; fbue"
   rel: GED(reg,reg)    "fcmped %%f%0,%%f%1; nop; fbuge"
   rel: GEF(reg,reg)    "fcmpes %%f%0,%%f%1; nop; fbuge"
   rel: GTD(reg,reg)    "fcmped %%f%0,%%f%1; nop; fbug"
   rel: GTF(reg,reg)    "fcmpes %%f%0,%%f%1; nop; fbug"
   rel: LED(reg,reg)    "fcmped %%f%0,%%f%1; nop; fbule"
   rel: LEF(reg,reg)    "fcmpes %%f%0,%%f%1; nop; fbule"
   rel: LTD(reg,reg)    "fcmped %%f%0,%%f%1; nop; fbul"
   rel: LTF(reg,reg)    "fcmpes %%f%0,%%f%1; nop; fbul"
   rel: NED(reg,reg)    "fcmped %%f%0,%%f%1; nop; fbne"
   rel: NEF(reg,reg)    "fcmpes %%f%0,%%f%1; nop; fbne"

   stmt: rel   "%0 %a; nop\n"   4
```

A few opcodes can't be implemented by any fixed assembler template, and must be saved for `emit2`. No SPARC instruction copies one double-precision register to another, so `lcc` emits two single-precision instructions for each LOADD:

⟨*SPARC rules* 469⟩+≡   481 482   463
```
    reg:   LOADD(reg)    "# LOADD\n"   2
```

⟨*SPARC* `emit2` 479⟩+≡   479 482   478
```
    case LOADD: {
        int dst = getregnum(p);
        int src = getregnum(p->x.kids[0]);
        print("fmovs %%f%d,%%f%d; ", src,   dst);
        print("fmovs %%f%d,%%f%d\n", src+1, dst+1);
        break;
    }
```

NEGD is similar. One instruction copies the first word and changes the sign bit in transit. The other instruction copies the second word:

⟨*SPARC rules* 469⟩+≡   482 482   463
```
    reg:   NEGD(reg)    "# NEGD\n"   2
```

⟨*SPARC* `emit2` 479⟩+≡   482 482   478
```
    case NEGD: {
        int dst = getregnum(p);
        int src = getregnum(p->x.kids[0]);
        print("fnegs %%f%d,%%f%d; ", src,   dst);
        print("fmovs %%f%d,%%f%d\n", src+1, dst+1);
        break;
    }
```

Finally, `emit2` calls `blkcopy` to generate code to copy a block of memory:

⟨*SPARC rules* 469⟩+≡   482   463
```
    stmt:  ASGNB(reg,INDIRB(reg))   "# ASGNB\n"
```

⟨*SPARC* `emit2` 479⟩+≡   482   478
```
    case ASGNB: {
        static int tmpregs[] = { 1, 2, 3 };
        dalign = salign = p->syms[1]->u.c.v.i;
        blkcopy(getregnum(p->x.kids[0]), 0,
                getregnum(p->x.kids[1]), 0,
                p->syms[0]->u.c.v.i, tmpregs);
        break;
    }
```

Figure 13.4 traces the block-copy generator in action for the MIPS target, but the SPARC code differs only cosmetically. The SPARC instruction set has no unaligned loads or stores, but this is moot here because the example in the figure doesn't use the MIPS unaligned loads and stores anyway. Recall that `salign`, `dalign`, and `x.max_unaligned_load` collaborate to copy even unaligned blocks, so the target-specific code can ignore this complication. The g-registers aren't being used, so the emitted code can use g1–g3 as temporaries; the MIPS code was trickier because the conventions there made it harder to acquire so many registers at once.

emit2 omits the usual case for ARGB because `wants_argb` is zero on this target.

17.3 Implementing Functions

The front end calls `local` to announce new local variables. Like its counterpart for the other targets, the SPARC `local` calls `askregvar` to assign the local to a register if possible, and it calls `mkauto` if `askregvar` can't comply:

⟨*SPARC functions* 466⟩+≡   478 484   464
```
static void local(p) Symbol p; {
    ⟨structure return block? 484⟩
    ⟨put even lightly used locals in registers 483⟩
    if (askregvar(p, rmap[ttob(p->type)]) == 0)
        mkauto(p);
}
```

The front end won't switch a local to use `sclass` REGISTER unless it estimates that the variable will be used three or more times. This cutoff leaves in memory locals used too little to justify spilling a register in the procedure prologue and reloading it in the epilogue. SPARC register windows, however, make some general registers available for locals automatically, so our code might as well use them even if the local is used only once or twice:

⟨*put even lightly used locals in registers* 483⟩≡   483
```
if (isscalar(p->type) && !p->addressed && !isfloat(p->type))
    p->sclass = REGISTER;
```

The SPARC code generator sets `wants_callb` so that it can match the SPARC convention for returning structures. When `wants_callb` is set, the front end takes three actions:

1. It generates CALLB nodes to reach functions that return structures.

2. It sets the second child of each CALLB to a node that computes the address of the block into which the callee must store the structure that it's returning.

3. It precedes each return with an ASGNB that copies the block addressed by the child of the return into the block addressed by the first local.

The front end announces this local like any other, and the back end arranges for it to address the stack slot reserved for the location of structure return blocks:

⟨*structure return block?* 484⟩ ≡   483

```
if (retstruct) {
    p->x.name = stringd(4*16);
    p->x.offset = 4*16;
    retstruct = 0;
    return;
}
```

function sets retstruct to one if the current function returns a structure or union.

The front end calls the interface procedure function to announce each new routine. function drives most of the back end. It calls gencode, which calls gen, which calls the labeller, reducer, linearizer, and register allocator. function also calls the front end's emitcode, which calls the back end's emitter. The front end passes to function a symbol that represents a routine, vectors of symbols representing the caller's and callee's views of the arguments, and a count of the number of calls made by the routine:

⟨*SPARC functions* 466⟩ +≡   483 489   464

```
static void function(f, caller, callee, ncalls)
Symbol f, callee[], caller[]; int ncalls; {
    int autos = 0, i, leaf, reg, varargs;

    ⟨SPARC function 484⟩
}
```

leaf flags simple leaf routines, varargs flags variadic routines, and autos counts the parameters in memory, which helps compute leaf. Only varargs can be computed immediately:

⟨*SPARC function* 484⟩ ≡   485   484

```
for (i = 0; callee[i]; i++)
    ;
varargs = variadic(f->type)
    || i > 0 && strcmp(callee[i-1]->name,
        "__builtin_va_alist") == 0;
```

The SPARC convention either declares the routine variadic or uses a macro that names the last argument __builtin_va_alist.

function clears the back end's record of busy registers:

⟨*SPARC* function 484⟩+≡   484 485   484
  ⟨*clear register state* 410⟩
  for (i = 0; i < 8; i++)
    ireg[i]->x.regnode->vbl = NULL;

The for loop above has no counterpart in the MIPS code generator. lcc allocates no variables to MIPS argument registers, but it *does* allocate variables to SPARC argument registers, so x.regnode->vbl can hold trash from the last routine compiled by the SPARC code generator.

   offset initially holds the frame offset of the next formal parameter in this routine. function initializes it to record the fact that each frame includes at least one word to hold the address of the target block for functions that return a structure, plus 16 words in which to store i0–i7 and l0–l7 if the register window must be spilled:

⟨*SPARC* function 484⟩+≡   485 485   484
  offset = 68;

maxargoffset holds the size of the stack block for outgoing arguments. function reserves space for at least o0–o5:

⟨*SPARC* function 484⟩+≡   485 485   484
  maxargoffset = 24;

Procedure prologues store incoming floating-point arguments into this space because little can be done with them in the i-registers, and variadic callees like printf store all incoming argument registers in this space, because they must use a procedure prologue that works for an unknown number of arguments, and they must access those arguments using addresses calculated at runtime, not register numbers fixed at compile time.

   function determines the i-register or stack offset for each incoming argument. At the beginning of each iteration of the for loop below, offset holds the stack offset reserved for the next parameter, and reg holds the number of the register or register pair for the next parameter, if the parameter arrives in a register. The stack needs 4-byte alignment, so we round the parameter size up to a multiple of four before doing anything with it. This parameter chews up size bytes of stack space and thus size/4 registers, except for structure arguments, which are passed by reference and thus chew up only one i-register.

⟨*SPARC* function 484⟩+≡   485 487   484
  reg = 0;
  for (i = 0; callee[i]; i++) {
    Symbol p = callee[i], q = caller[i];
    int size = roundup(q->type->size, 4);
    ⟨*classify SPARC parameter* 486⟩
    offset += size;
    reg += isstruct(p->type) ? 1 : size/4;
  }

function can confine its attention to scalar formals because `wants_argb` is zero.

If the parameter is a floating-point value or past the end of the argument registers, then it goes in memory, and this routine needs a frame in memory to store this parameter:

⟨*classify SPARC parameter* 486⟩≡   486   485

```
if (isfloat(p->type) || reg >= 6) {
    p->x.offset = q->x.offset = offset;
    p->x.name = q->x.name = stringd(offset);
    p->sclass = q->sclass = AUTO;
    autos++;
}
```

In the first case, function must generate code itself to store the parameter if it arrived in a register; the front end can't help because lcc's intermediate code gives it no way to store the floating-point value from an integer register.

If the parameter is integral and arrived in an i-register, it still belongs in memory if its address is taken or if the routine is variadic:

⟨*classify SPARC parameter* 486⟩+≡   486 486   485

```
else if (p->addressed || varargs)
    ⟨arrives in an i-register, belongs in memory 486⟩
```

⟨*arrives in an i-register, belongs in memory* 486⟩≡   486

```
{
    p->x.offset = offset;
    p->x.name = stringd(p->x.offset);
    p->sclass = AUTO;
    q->sclass = REGISTER;
    askregvar(q, ireg[reg]);
    autos++;
}
```

function sets the callee's and caller's `sclass` to differing values so the front end will generate an assignment to store the register.

The parameter can remain in a register if it arrived in one, if it's integral, if its address isn't taken, and if the routine isn't variadic:

⟨*classify SPARC parameter* 486⟩+≡   486   485

```
else {
    p->sclass = q->sclass = REGISTER;
    askregvar(p, ireg[reg]);
    q->x.name = p->x.name;
}
```

Now to call gencode in the front end, which calls gen in the back end. First, function clears offset to record that no locals have been assigned to the stack yet, it clears maxoffset to track the largest value of offset, and it flags each function that returns an aggregate because local must treat its first local specially:

⟨*SPARC data* 467⟩+≡   ▲467 492   463
```
static int retstruct;
```

⟨*SPARC function* 484⟩+≡   ▲485 487   484
```
offset = maxoffset = 0;
retstruct = isstruct(freturn(f->type));
gencode(caller, callee);
```

When gencode completes the first code-generation pass and returns, function can compute the size of the frame and of the argument-build block, in which the outgoing arguments are marshaled. The size of the argument-build area must be a multiple of four, or some stack fragments will be unaligned. The frame size must be a multiple of eight, and includes space for the locals, the argument-build area, 16 words in which to save i0-i7 and 10-17, and one word to store the address of any aggregate return block:

⟨*SPARC function* 484⟩+≡   ▲487 487   484
```
maxargoffset = roundup(maxargoffset, 4);
framesize = roundup(maxoffset + maxargoffset + 4*(16+1), 8);
```

function emits code that saves time by allocating no new frame or register window for routines that don't need them:

⟨*SPARC function* 484⟩+≡   ▲487 488   484
```
leaf = (⟨is this a simple leaf function? 487⟩);
```

The constraints are many. The routine must make no calls:

⟨*is this a simple leaf function?* 487⟩≡   487   487
```
!ncalls
```

It must have no locals or formals in memory:

⟨*is this a simple leaf function?* 487⟩+≡   ▲487 487   487
```
&& !maxoffset && !autos
```

It must not return a structure, because such functions use a frame pointer in order to access the cell that holds the location of the return block:

⟨*is this a simple leaf function?* 487⟩+≡   ▲487 488   487
```
&& !isstruct(freturn(f->type))
```

It must save no registers:

⟨*is this a simple leaf function?* 487⟩+≡   487   487
```
&& !(usedmask[IREG]&0x00ffff01)
&& !(usedmask[FREG]&~(unsigned)3)
```

which means that it must confine itself to the incoming argument registers o0–o7. The routine must also require neither debugging nor profiling, but those checks are omitted from this book. If all these conditions are met, then the routine can make do with no frame.

All prologues start with a common boilerplate:

⟨*SPARC* function 484⟩+≡   487 488   484
```
print(".align 4\n.proc 4\n%s:\n", f->x.name);
```

Most continue with a save instruction, which allocates a new register window and adds a register or constant to a register. Most uses of save add a negative constant to sp, which allocates a new frame on the downward-growing stack:

⟨*SPARC* function 484⟩+≡   488 489   484
```
if (leaf) {
    ⟨emit leaf prologue 488⟩
} else if (framesize <= 4095)
    print("save %%sp,%d,%%sp\n", -framesize);
else
    print("set %d,%%g1; save %%sp,%%g1,%%sp\n", -framesize);
```

If the constant won't fit in a SPARC immediate field, then the prologue first computes it into register g1.

Routines eligible for the leaf optimization require no prologue, but the code generator has used the i-registers for arguments and, for that matter, for the locals and temporaries. Now we've decided to generate no frame or register window, so we must use the corresponding o-registers instead. lcc's back end was not designed with wholesale register renaming in mind, so even the best solution is clunky: function temporarily changes the structures that store the name and number of each i-register to name an o-register instead. It starts with its caller argument vector. function's initial for loop copied the name of an i-register into the argument's x.name field, so now function must correct that field:

⟨*emit leaf prologue* 488⟩≡   488
```
for (i = 0; caller[i] && callee[i]; i++) {
    Symbol p = caller[i], q = callee[i];
    if (p->sclass == REGISTER && q->sclass == REGISTER)
        p->x.name = greg[q->x.regnode->number - 16]->x.name;
}
rename();
```

The procedure rename makes the remaining changes:

⟨*SPARC functions* 466⟩ +≡   484 490   464
```
  #define exch(x, y, t) (((t) = x), ((x) = (y)), ((y) = (t)))

  static void rename() {
     int i;

     for (i = 0; i < 8; i++) {
        char *ptmp;
        int itmp;
        if (ireg[i]->x.regnode->vbl)
           ireg[i]->x.regnode->vbl->x.name = oreg[i]->x.name;
        exch(ireg[i]->x.name, oreg[i]->x.name, ptmp);
        exch(ireg[i]->x.regnode->number,
           oreg[i]->x.regnode->number, itmp);
     }
  }
```

rename *exchanges* the name and number from corresponding i- and o-registers, so that another exchange at the end of function will restore normality. If the register allocator has assigned the register to a variable, rename also corrects the name recorded in the symbol structure for that variable. Exchanges implement rename's changes because they must be undone at the end of the current routine, but simple assignments implement the changes to caller and register variables because they don't outlive the current routine.

    function next emits prologue code to save any arguments that arrived in registers but can't remain there. Variadic routines must save all of i0–i5 because their prologue code can't know how many of them actually hold arguments:

⟨*SPARC* function 484⟩ +≡   488 490   484
```
  if (varargs)
     for (; reg < 6; reg++)
        print("st %%i%d,[%%fp+%d]\n", reg, 4*reg + 68);
  else
        ⟨spill floats and doubles from i0-i5 489⟩
```

Prologues also save floating-point values that arrive in general registers because instructions can't do much with them there.

⟨*spill floats and doubles from* i0-i5 489⟩ ≡   489
```
  offset = 4*(16 + 1);
  reg = 0;
  for (i = 0; caller[i]; i++) {
     Symbol p = caller[i];
     if (isdouble(p->type) && reg <= 4) {
        print("st %%r%d,[%%fp+%d]\n",
```

```
                        ireg[reg++]->x.regnode->number, offset);
                  print("st %%r%d,[%%fp+%d]\n",
                        ireg[reg++]->x.regnode->number, offset + 4);
            } else if (isfloat(p->type) && reg <= 5)
                  print("st %%r%d,[%%fp+%d]\n",
                        ireg[reg++]->x.regnode->number, offset);
            else
                  reg++;
            offset += roundup(p->type->size, 4);
      }
```

isfloat succeeds for floats and doubles, so the first else arm above saves not just floats but also the first half of any double that arrives in i5; the second half will be in memory already, courtesy of the caller.

Finally, function emits some profiling code (not shown), the body of the current routine, and the epilogue. The general epilogue is a ret instruction, which jumps back to the caller, and a restore instruction in the ret's delay slot, which undoes the prologue's save instruction. If the routine does without a register window and stack frame, there's no save to undo, but another rename is needed to restore normality to the names and numbers of the i-registers:

⟨*SPARC* function 484⟩ +≡   489   484

```
      ⟨emit profiling code⟩
      emitcode();
      if (!leaf)
            print("ret; restore\n");
      else {
            rename();
            print("retl; nop\n");
      }
```

ret and retl are both pseudo-instructions that emit an indirect branch using the register that holds the return address. They need different names because ret uses i7, and retl uses o7 to name the same register because no register stack frame was pushed.

17.4 Defining Data

The SPARC defconst, defaddress, defstring, and address are the same as their MIPS counterparts. See Chapter 16 for the code.

The front end calls export to expose a symbol to other modules, which is the purpose of the SPARC assembler directive .global:

⟨*SPARC functions* 466⟩ +≡   489 491   464

```
      static void export(p) Symbol p; {
```

```
    print(".global %s\n", p->x.name);
}
```

The front end calls `import` to make visible in the current module a symbol defined in another module. The SPARC assembler assumes that undefined symbols are external, so the SPARC `import` has nothing to do:

⟨*SPARC functions* 466⟩+≡   ▲ 490 491   464
```
    static void import(p) Symbol p; {}
```

The front end calls `defsymbol` to announce a new symbol and cue the back end to initialize the `x.name` field. The SPARC conventions generate a name for local statics and use the source name for the rest. The SPARC link editor leaves symbols starting with L out of the symbol table, so `defsymbol` prefixes L to generated symbols. It prefixes an underscore to the rest, following another SPARC convention:

⟨*SPARC functions* 466⟩+≡   ▲ 491 491   464
```
    static void defsymbol(p) Symbol p; {
        if (p->scope >= LOCAL && p->sclass == STATIC)
            p->x.name = stringf("%d", genlabel(1));
        else
            p->x.name = p->name;
        if (p->scope >= LABELS)
            p->x.name = stringf(p->generated ? "L%s" : "_%s",
                p->x.name);
    }
```

91	BSS
91	CODE
459	cseg (MIPS)
492	" (SPARC)
501	" (X86)
91	DATA
50	generated
45	genlabel
38	LABELS
91	LIT
38	LOCAL
37	scope
92	space
459	" (MIPS)
492	" (SPARC)
524	" (X86)
80	STATIC
99	stringf
362	x.name

Statics at file scope retain their names. Statics at deeper scope get numbers to avoid colliding with other statics of the same name in other routines.

The interface routine `segment` emits the `.seg "name"`, which switches to a new segment:

⟨*SPARC functions* 466⟩+≡   ▲ 491 492   464
```
    static void segment(n) int n; {
        cseg = n;
        switch (n) {
        case CODE: print(".seg \"text\"\n"); break;
        case BSS:  print(".seg \"bss\"\n");  break;
        case DATA: print(".seg \"data\"\n"); break;
        case LIT:  print(".seg \"text\"\n"); break;
        }
    }
```

`segment` tracks the current segment in `cseg` for the interface procedure `space`, which emits the SPARC `.skip` assembler directive to reserve n bytes of memory for an initialized global or static:

⟨*SPARC data* 467⟩+≡   487 463
```
static int cseg;
```

⟨*SPARC functions* 466⟩+≡   491 492 464
```
static void space(n) int n; {
    if (cseg != BSS)
        print(".skip %d\n", n);
}
```

`.skip` arranges to clear the space that it allocates, which the standard requires.

If we're in the BSS segment, then the interface procedure `global` can define the label and reserve space in one fell swoop, using `.common` for external symbols and `.reserve` for the rest:

⟨*SPARC functions* 466⟩+≡   492 492 464
```
static void global(p) Symbol p; {
    print(".align %d\n", p->type->align);
    if (p->u.seg == BSS
    && (p->sclass == STATIC || Aflag >= 2))
        print(".reserve %s,%d\n", p->x.name, p->type->size);
    else if (p->u.seg == BSS)
        print(".common %s,%d\n",  p->x.name, p->type->size);
    else
        print("%s:\n", p->x.name);
}
```

It also emits an alignment directive and, for initialized globals, the label. `.common` also exports the symbol and marks it so that the loader generates only one common global even if other modules emit `.common` directives for the same identifier. `.reserve` takes neither step. Statics use it to avoid the export, and the scrupulous double -A option uses it to have the loader complain when multiple modules define the same global. Pre-ANSI C permitted multiple definitions, but ANSI C technically expects exactly one definition; other modules should use `extern` declarations instead.

17.5 Copying Blocks

`blkfetch` emits code to load register `tmp` with k bytes from the address formed by adding register `reg` and offset `off`. k is 1, 2, or 4:

⟨*SPARC functions* 466⟩+≡   492 493 464
```
static void blkfetch(k, off, reg, tmp)
int k, off, reg, tmp; {
    if (k == 1)
```

```
        print("ldub [%%r%d+%d],%%r%d\n", reg, off, tmp);
    else if (k == 2)
        print("lduh [%%r%d+%d],%%r%d\n", reg, off, tmp);
    else
        print("ld [%%r%d+%d],%%r%d\n",   reg, off, tmp);
}
```

No SPARC instructions load unaligned values, so blkfetch needn't decide between aligned and unaligned loads, which the MIPS blkfetch does. blkunroll has used x.max_unaligned_load to pick a block size and guarantee that the alignment is no smaller than the block size. blkfetch need only choose between loading an 8-bit byte, a 16-bit halfword, or a 32-bit word. blkstore mirrors blkfetch:

⟨*SPARC functions* 466⟩ +≡   ▲ 492 493   464
                                              ▼

```
    static void blkstore(k, off, reg, tmp)
    int k, off, reg, tmp; {
        if (k == 1)
            print("stb %%r%d,[%%r%d+%d]\n", tmp, reg, off);
        else if (k == 2)
            print("sth %%r%d,[%%r%d+%d]\n", tmp, reg, off);
        else
            print("st %%r%d,[%%r%d+%d]\n",  tmp, reg, off);
    }
```

All SPARC blk procedures use generic register names like r9. If we tried to use the g, i, l, and o names that we use elsewhere, we'd need to change the interface between the blk procedures to pass symbolic register names instead of integral register numbers, which would complicate adapting lcc to emit binary object code directly, for example.

blkloop emits a loop to copy size bytes from a source address — formed by adding register sreg and offset soff — to a destination address — formed by adding register dreg and offset doff:

⟨*SPARC functions* 466⟩ +≡   ▲ 493   464

```
    static void blkloop(dreg, doff, sreg, soff, size, tmps)
    int dreg, doff, sreg, soff, size, tmps[]; {
        ⟨SPARC blkloop 494⟩
    }
```

tmp names three registers to use as temporaries. Each iteration copies eight bytes. Initial code points sreg to the end of the source block and tmp[2] to the end of the target block. This fragment has two arms. Block sizes that fit in a signed 13-bit field are processed directly. Larger block sizes are computed into register tmps[2], and the register is added to the incoming source and destination addresses.

⟨*SPARC* blkloop 494⟩≡   494   493

```
  if ((size&~7) < 4096) {
      print("add %%r%d,%d,%%r%d\n", sreg, size&~7, sreg);
      print("add %%r%d,%d,%%r%d\n", dreg, size&~7, tmps[2]);
  } else {
      print("set %d,%%r%d\n", size&~7, tmps[2]);
      print("add %%r%d,%%r%d,%%r%d\n", sreg, tmps[2], sreg);
      print("add %%r%d,%%r%d,%%r%d\n", dreg, tmps[2], tmps[2]);
  }
```

If the block's size is not divisible by eight, then an initial blkcopy copies the stragglers:

⟨*SPARC* blkloop 494⟩+≡   494 494   493

```
  blkcopy(tmps[2], doff, sreg, soff, size&7, tmps);
```

The loop decrements registers sreg and tmp[2] by eight for each iteration. It does tmp[2] immediately, but pushes sreg's decrement forward to fill the branch delay slot at the end of the loop:

⟨*SPARC* blkloop 494⟩+≡   494 494   493

```
  print("1: dec 8,%%r%d\n", tmps[2]);
```

blkcopy 367

The loop next calls blkcopy to copy eight bytes from the source to the destination. The source offset is adjusted to account for the fact that sreg should've been decremented by now:

⟨*SPARC* blkloop 494⟩+≡   494 494   493

```
  blkcopy(tmps[2], doff, sreg, soff - 8, 8, tmps);
```

Finally, the loop continues if more bytes remain:

⟨*SPARC* blkloop 494⟩+≡   494   493

```
  print("cmp %%r%d,%%r%d; ", tmps[2], dreg);
  print("bgt 1b; ");
  print("dec 8,%%r%d\n", sreg);
```

Further Reading

The SPARC reference manual elaborates on the architecture of this machine (SPARC International 1992). Patterson and Hennessy (1990) explain the reasons behind delay slots. Krishnamurthy (1990) surveys the literature in instruction scheduling, which fills delay slots.

Exercises

17.1 Add a flag that directs the back end to emit instructions instead of calls to multiply and divide signed and unsigned integers.

17.2 Adapt lcc's SPARC code generator to make better use of g1–g7 and to keep some floating-point variables in floating-point registers. Recall that the calling convention and thus all previously compiled library routines preserve none of these registers.

17.3 Find some use for at least some of the delay slots after unconditional jumps. For example, the slot after an unconditional jump can be filled with a copy of the instruction at the jump target, and the jump can be rewritten to target the next instruction. Some optimizations require buffering code and making an extra pass over it. The MIPS R3000 architecture has such delay slots too, but the standard assembler reorders instructions to fill them with something more useful, so we could ignore the problem there.

17.4 Find some use for at least some of the delay slots after conditional branches. It may help to exploit the *annul bit*, which specifies that the instruction in the delay slot is to have no effect unless the branch is conditional and taken. Set the annul bit by appending ,a to the opcode (e.g., be,a L4).

17.5 Some SPARC chips stall for at least one clock cycle when a load instruction immediately precedes an instruction that uses the value loaded. The object code would run just as fast with a single nop after the load, though it would be one word longer. Reorder the emitted assembler code to eliminate at least some of these stalls. Proebsting and Fischer (1991) describe one solution.

17.6 Some leaf routines need no register window, but still lose the leaf optimization because they need a frame pointer. For example, some functions that return structures need no window, but do use a frame pointer. Change lcc to generate a frame but no register window for such routines.

17.7 The SPARC code generator includes idiosyncratic code to ensure that the spiller can emit code to store a register when no allocable registers are free. Devise a short test program that exercises this code.

18
Generating X86 Code

This book uses the name X86 for machines compatible for the purposes of code generation with the Intel 386 architecture, which include the Intel 486 and Pentium architectures, plus clones from manufacturers like AMD and Cyrix. The lburg specification uses approximate Intel 486 cycle counts for costs, which often but not always gives the best result for compatibles. Some costs are omitted because they aren't needed. For example, if only one rule matches some operator, there is no need for costs to break ties between derivations.

The X86 architecture is a CISC, or complex instruction set computer. It has a large set of variable-length instructions and addressing modes. It has eight 32-bit largely general registers and eight 80-bit floating-point registers organized as a stack.

There are many C compilers for the X86, and their conventions (e.g., for calling functions and returning values) differ. The code generator in this chapter uses the conventions of Borland C++ 4.0. That is, it interoperates with Borland's standard include files, libraries, and linker. Using lcc with other X86 environments may require a few changes; documentation on the companion diskette elaborates.

There are many X86 assemblers, and they don't all use the same syntax. lcc works with Microsoft's MASM 6.11 and Borland's Turbo Assembler 4.0. That is, it emits code in the intersection of the languages accepted by these two assemblers. Both have instructions that list the destination operand before the source operand. The registers have names instead of numbers. Table 18.1 describes enough sample instructions to get us started.

The file x86.c collects all X86-specific code and data. It's an lburg specification with the interface routines after the grammar:

```
⟨x86.md 496⟩ ≡
    %{
    ⟨X86 macros 498⟩
    ⟨lburg prefix 375⟩
    ⟨interface prototypes⟩
    ⟨X86 prototypes⟩
    ⟨X86 data 499⟩
    %}
    ⟨terminal declarations 376⟩
    %%
    ⟨shared rules 400⟩
```

Assembler	Meaning
mov al,byte ptr 8	Set register al to the byte at address 8.
mov dword ptr 8[edi*4],1	Set to one the 32-bit word at the address formed by adding eight to the product of register edi and four.
subu eax,7	Subtract seven from register eax.
fsub qword ptr x	Subtract the double-precision floating-point value in the memory cell labelled x from the top of the floating-point stack.
jmp L1	Jump to the instruction labelled L1.
cmp dword ptr x,7	Compare the 32-bit word at address x with seven and record the results in the condition flags.
jl L1	Branch to L1 if the last comparison recorded less-than.
dword 020H	Initialize the next 32-bit word in memory to hexadecimal 20.

TABLE 18.1   Sample X86 assembler input lines.

⟨*X86 rules* 503⟩
%%   79 Interface
⟨*X86 functions* 498⟩
⟨*X86 interface definition* 497⟩

The last fragment configures the front end and points to the X86-specific routines and data in the back end:

⟨*X86 interface definition* 497⟩≡   497
```
    Interface x86IR = {
        1, 1, 0,  /* char */
        2, 2, 0,  /* short */
        4, 4, 0,  /* int */
        4, 4, 1,  /* float */
        8, 4, 1,  /* double */
        4, 4, 0,  /* T * */
        0, 4, 0,  /* struct; so that ARGB keeps stack aligned */
        1,        /* little_endian */
        0,        /* mulops_calls */
        0,        /* wants_callb */
        1,        /* wants_argb */
        0,        /* left_to_right */
        0,        /* wants_dag */
        ⟨interface routine names⟩
        ⟨symbol-table emitters 498⟩
```

```
    {1, ⟨Xinterface initializer 355⟩}
};
```

The MIPS and SPARC conventions evaluate arguments left to right, but the X86 conventions evaluate them right to left, which is why the interface flag left_to_right is zero.

X86 conventions offer no standard way for compilers to encode symbol tables in assembler code for debuggers, so lcc's X86 back end includes no symbol-table emitters:

⟨*symbol-table emitters* 498⟩≡   497
```
    0, 0, 0, 0, 0, 0, 0,
```

18.1   Registers

The X86 architecture includes eight general registers. Assemblers typically refer to them by a name — eax, ecx, edx, ebx, esp, ebp, esi, and edi — rather than by a number. lcc's register allocator needs a number to compute shift distances for register masks, so lcc borrows the encoding from the binary representation of some instructions:

⟨*X86 macros* 498⟩≡   496
```
    enum { EAX=0, ECX=1, EDX=2, EBX=3, ESI=6, EDI=7 };
```

Conventions reserve ebp for the frame pointer and esp for the stack pointer, so lcc doesn't allocate them.

progbeg builds the structures that describe the registers:

⟨*X86 functions* 498⟩≡   501   497
```
    static void progbeg(argc, argv) int argc; char *argv[]; {
        int i;

        ⟨shared progbeg 371⟩
        parseflags(argc, argv);
        intreg[EAX] = mkreg("eax", EAX, 1, IREG);
        intreg[EDX] = mkreg("edx", EDX, 1, IREG);
        intreg[ECX] = mkreg("ecx", ECX, 1, IREG);
        intreg[EBX] = mkreg("ebx", EBX, 1, IREG);
        intreg[ESI] = mkreg("esi", ESI, 1, IREG);
        intreg[EDI] = mkreg("edi", EDI, 1, IREG);
        ⟨X86 progbeg 499⟩
    }
```

Assembler code uses different names for the full 32-bit register and its low order 8- and 16-bit subregisters. For example, assembler code uses eax for the first 32-bit register, ax for its bottom half, and al for its bottom byte. This rule requires initializing separate register vectors for shorts and characters:

⟨*X86 data* 499⟩≡   501   496
    `static Symbol charreg[32], shortreg[32], intreg[32];`
    `static Symbol fltreg[32];`

⟨*X86* progbeg 499⟩≡   499   498
```
shortreg[EAX] = mkreg("ax", EAX, 1, IREG);
shortreg[ECX] = mkreg("cx", ECX, 1, IREG);
shortreg[EDX] = mkreg("dx", EDX, 1, IREG);
shortreg[EBX] = mkreg("bx", EBX, 1, IREG);
shortreg[ESI] = mkreg("si", ESI, 1, IREG);
shortreg[EDI] = mkreg("di", EDI, 1, IREG);
```

⟨*X86* progbeg 499⟩+≡   499 500   498
```
charreg[EAX]  = mkreg("al", EAX, 1, IREG);
charreg[ECX]  = mkreg("cl", ECX, 1, IREG);
charreg[EDX]  = mkreg("dl", EDX, 1, IREG);
charreg[EBX]  = mkreg("bl", EBX, 1, IREG);
```

No instructions address the bottom byte of esi or edi, so there is no byte version of those registers. Byte instructions can address the top half of each 16-bit register, but lcc does without these byte registers because using them would complicate code generation. For example, CVCI would need to generate one sequence of instructions when the operand is in the low-order byte and another sequence when the operand is next door. Table 18.2 summarizes the allocable registers.

498 EAX
498 EBX
498 ECX
498 EDI
498 EDX
498 ESI
361 IREG
363 mkreg

The floating-point registers are organized as a stack. Some operands of some instructions can address an arbitrary floating-point register — from the top down — but some crucial instructions effectively assume a stack. For example, all variants of floating-point addition require at least one operand to be atop the stack. The assembler operand st denotes the top of the stack, and st(1) denotes the value underneath it. Pushing a value on the stack causes st to denote a new cell and st(1) to denote the cell previously denoted by st.

lcc was tailored for registers with fixed names, not names that change as a stack grows and shrinks. The X86 floating-point registers violate

Int	Short	Char
eax	ax	al
ecx	cx	cl
edx	dx	dl
ebx	bx	bl
esi	si	
edi	di	

TABLE 18.2 Allocable X86 registers.

these assumptions, so lcc disables its register allocator for the X86
floating-point registers and lets the instructions manage the registers.
For example, a load instruction pushes a value onto the stack and thus effectively allocates a register; an addition pops two operands and pushes
their sum, so it effectively releases two registers and allocates one.

The register allocator can't be disabled by simply clearing the entries
in rmap for floats and doubles. If a node yields a value, then the register allocator assumes that it needs a register, and expects the node's
syms[RX] to give a register class. So we need a representation of the
floating-point registers, but the representation needs to render the register allocator harmless. One easy way to do this is to create registers
with zero masks, which causes getreg to succeed always and to change
no significant compiler state:

⟨*X86* progbeg 499⟩+≡   499 500   498

```
for (i = 0; i < 8; i++)
    fltreg[i] = mkreg("%d", i, 0, FREG);
```

This dodge permits lcc's register allocator to work, but it can't do a very
good job. This problem exemplifies a trade-off common in retargetable
compilers. We move as much code as seems reasonable into the machine-
independent parts of the compiler, but then those parts are fixed, and
code generators for targets with features not anticipated in the design
require idiosyncratic work-arounds and emit suboptimal code.

rmap stores the wildcard that identifies the default register class to
use for each type:

⟨*X86* progbeg 499⟩+≡   500 500   498

```
rmap[C] = mkwildcard(charreg);
rmap[S] = mkwildcard(shortreg);
rmap[P] = rmap[B] = rmap[U] = rmap[I] = mkwildcard(intreg);
rmap[F] = rmap[D] = mkwildcard(fltreg);
```

tmask and vmask identify the registers to use for temporaries and to allocate to register variables. The X86 gives lcc only six general registers,
and some of these are spilled by calls, block copies, and other special instructions or sequences of instructions. If there are too many common
subexpressions, lcc's simple register allocator can emit code that does
to the registers what thrashing does to pages of virtual memory. The
conservative solution thus reserves all six general registers for temporaries and allocates no variables to registers.

⟨*X86* progbeg 499⟩+≡   500 501   498

```
tmask[IREG] = (1<<EDI) | (1<<ESI) | (1<<EBX)
            | (1<<EDX) | (1<<ECX) | (1<<EAX);
vmask[IREG] = 0;
```

lcc does likewise for the floating-point registers.

⟨*X86* progbeg 499⟩+≡   500 501   498
```
tmask[FREG] = 0xff;
vmask[FREG] = 0;
```

progbeg also emits some boilerplate required to assemble and link the emitted code:

⟨*X86* progbeg 499⟩+≡   501 501   498
```
print(".486\n");
print(".model small\n");
print("extrn __turboFloat:near\n");
print("extrn __setargv:near\n");
```

The references to external symbols direct the linker to arrange a particular floating-point package and code to set argc and argv in each main routine.

To switch from one segment to another requires two directives: an ends that names the current segment, and a segment that names the new one:

⟨*X86 data* 499⟩+≡   499 509   496
```
static int cseg;
```

⟨*X86 functions* 498⟩+≡   498 502   497
```
static void segment(n) int n; {
    if (n == cseg)
        return;
    if (cseg == CODE)
        print("_TEXT ends\n");
    else if (cseg == DATA || cseg == BSS || cseg == LIT)
        print("_DATA ends\n");
    cseg = n;
    if (cseg == CODE)
        print("_TEXT segment\n");
    else if (cseg == DATA || cseg == BSS || cseg == LIT)
        print("_DATA segment\n");
}
```

export needs a directive that must appear between segments. CODE, DATA, LIT, and BSS are all positive, so export can use segment(0) to close the active segment without opening a new one.

progbeg clears cseg, which records that the back end is between segments:

⟨*X86* progbeg 499⟩+≡   501 509   498
```
cseg = 0;
```

progend emits boilerplate that closes the current segment and the entire assembler program:

⟨*X86 functions* 498⟩ +≡   501 502   497
```
static void progend() {
    segment(0);
    print("end\n");
}
```

target records that an operator needs a specific register, and clobber calls spill to spill and reloads busy register that are overwritten by a few operators:

⟨*X86 functions* 498⟩ +≡   502 502   497
```
static void target(p) Node p; {
    switch (p->op) {
    ⟨X86 target 508⟩
    }
}

static void clobber(p) Node p; {
    static int nstack = 0;

    nstack = ckstack(p, nstack);
    switch (p->op) {
    ⟨X86 clobber 513⟩
    }
}
```

The cases missing above appear with the instructions for the germane operators in the next section. clobber tracks in nstate the height of the stack of floating-point registers. When progbeg disabled allocation of these registers, it also disabled the spiller, so the X86 code generator must cope with floating-point spills itself. ckstack adjusts nstate to record the result of the current instruction:

⟨*X86 functions* 498⟩ +≡   502 507   497
```
#define isfp(p) (optype((p)->op)==F || optype((p)->op)==D)

static int ckstack(p, n) Node p; int n; {
    int i;

    for (i = 0; i < NELEMS(p->x.kids) && p->x.kids[i]; i++)
        if (isfp(p->x.kids[i]))
            n--;
    if (isfp(p) && p->count > 0)
        n++;
    if (n > 8)
        error("expression too complicated\n");
    return n;
}
```

The for loop pops the source registers, and the subsequent if statement pushes any result. Floating-point instructions done for side effect — such as assignments and conditional branches — push nothing. ckstack directs the programmer to simplify the expression to avoid the spill. lcc merely reports the error because such spills are rare, so reports are unlikely to irritate users. If lcc ignored the problem completely, however, it would silently emit incorrect code for some programs, which is unacceptable. Exercises 18.8 and 18.9 explore related matters.

18.2 Selecting Instructions

Table 18.3 summarizes the nonterminals in lcc's lburg specification for the X86. It provides a high-level overview of the organization of the tree grammar.

Integer and address constants denote themselves:

⟨*X86 rules* 503⟩≡   504   497
    acon: ADDRGP   "%a"
    acon: con   "%0"

A base address may be an ADDRGP or the sum of an acon and one of the

502 ckstack

Name	What It Matches
acon	address constants
addr	address calculations for instructions that read and write memory
addrj	address calculations for instructions that jump
base	unindexed address calculations
cmpf	floating-point comparands
con	constants
con1	the integer constant 1
con2	the integer constant 2
con3	the integer constant 3
flt	floating-point operands
index	indexed address calculations
mem	memory cells used by general-purpose operators
memf	memory cells used by floating-point operators
mr	memory cells and registers
mrc0	memory cells, registers, and constants whose memory cost is 0
mrc1	memory cells, registers, and constants whose memory cost is 1
mrc3	memory cells, registers, and constants whose memory cost is 3
rc	registers and constants
rc5	register cl and constants between 0 and 31 inclusive
reg	computations that yield a result in a register
stmt	computations done for side effect

TABLE 18.3 X86 nonterminals.

general registers. The assembler syntax puts the register name in square brackets:

⟨*X86 rules* 503⟩+≡   5̂03 504   497
```
    base: ADDRGP          "%a"
    base: reg             "[%0]"
    base: ADDI(reg,acon)  "%1[%0]"
    base: ADDP(reg,acon)  "%1[%0]"
    base: ADDU(reg,acon)  "%1[%0]"
```

If the register is the frame pointer, the same operation computes the address of a formal or local:

⟨*X86 rules* 503⟩+≡   5̂04 504   497
```
    base: ADDRFP   "%a[ebp]"
    base: ADDRLP   "%a[ebp]"
```

Some addresses use an index, which is a register scaled by one, two, four, or eight:

⟨*X86 rules* 503⟩+≡   5̂04 504   497
```
    index: reg "%0"
    index: LSHI(reg,con1)   "%0*2"
    index: LSHI(reg,con2)   "%0*4"
    index: LSHI(reg,con3)   "%0*8"

    con1:  CNSTI  "1"  range(a, 1, 1)
    con1:  CNSTU  "1"  range(a, 1, 1)
    con2:  CNSTI  "2"  range(a, 2, 2)
    con2:  CNSTU  "2"  range(a, 2, 2)
    con3:  CNSTI  "3"  range(a, 3, 3)
    con3:  CNSTU  "3"  range(a, 3, 3)
```

range 388
reg 403

Recall that cost expressions are evaluated in a context in which a denotes the node being labelled, which here is the constant value being compared with small integers. The unsigned shifts to the left are equivalent to the integer shifts:

⟨*X86 rules* 503⟩+≡   5̂04 504   497
```
    index: LSHU(reg,con1)   "%0*2"
    index: LSHU(reg,con2)   "%0*4"
    index: LSHU(reg,con3)   "%0*8"
```

A general address may be a base address or the sum of a base address and an index. The front end puts index operations on the left; see Section 9.7.

⟨*X86 rules* 503⟩+≡   5̂04 505   497
```
    addr: base                "%0"
```

```
addr: ADDI(index,base)   "%1[%0]"
addr: ADDP(index,base)   "%1[%0]"
addr: ADDU(index,base)   "%1[%0]"
```

If the base address is zero, the sum degenerates to just the index:

⟨*X86 rules* 503⟩+≡   504 505   497
```
addr: index   "[%0]"
```

Many instructions accept an operand in memory. Assemblers for many machines encode the datatype in the instruction opcode, but here the operand specifier does the job. word denotes a 16-bit operand, and dword a 32-bit operand.

⟨*X86 rules* 503⟩+≡   505 505   497
```
mem: INDIRC(addr)   "byte ptr %0"
mem: INDIRI(addr)   "dword ptr %0"
mem: INDIRP(addr)   "dword ptr %0"
mem: INDIRS(addr)   "word ptr %0"
```

Some instructions accept a register or immediate operand, some accept an operand in a register or memory, and some accept all three:

⟨*X86 rules* 503⟩+≡   505 505   497
```
rc:    reg  "%0"
rc:    con  "%0"

mr:    reg  "%0"
mr:    mem  "%0"

mrc0:  mem  "%0"
mrc0:  rc   "%0"
```

403 reg

Some instructions in the last class access memory without cost; others suffer a penalty of one cycle, and still others a penalty of three cycles:

⟨*X86 rules* 503⟩+≡   505 505   497
```
mrc1: mem  "%0"  1
mrc1: rc   "%0"

mrc3: mem  "%0"  3
mrc3: rc   "%0"
```

The lea instruction loads an address into a register, and the mov instruction loads a register, constant, or memory cell:

⟨*X86 rules* 503⟩+≡   505 506   497
```
reg: addr      "lea %c,%0\n"  1
reg: mrc0      "mov %c,%0\n"  1
```

```
reg: LOADC(reg)    "mov %c,%0\n"    move(a)
reg: LOADI(reg)    "mov %c,%0\n"    move(a)
reg: LOADP(reg)    "mov %c,%0\n"    move(a)
reg: LOADS(reg)    "mov %c,%0\n"    move(a)
reg: LOADU(reg)    "mov %c,%0\n"    move(a)
```

mov incurs no additional penalty for its memory access, so it uses mrc0. Recall that the cost function move returns one but also marks the node as a register-to-register copy; emit, requate, and moveself collaborate to remove some marked instructions.

Integral addition and subtraction incur a one-cycle penalty when accessing memory, so they use mrc1:

⟨*X86 rules* 503⟩+≡   505 506   497

```
reg: ADDI(reg,mrc1)    "?mov %c,%0\nadd %c,%1\n"    1
reg: ADDP(reg,mrc1)    "?mov %c,%0\nadd %c,%1\n"    1
reg: ADDU(reg,mrc1)    "?mov %c,%0\nadd %c,%1\n"    1
reg: SUBI(reg,mrc1)    "?mov %c,%0\nsub %c,%1\n"    1
reg: SUBP(reg,mrc1)    "?mov %c,%0\nsub %c,%1\n"    1
reg: SUBU(reg,mrc1)    "?mov %c,%0\nsub %c,%1\n"    1
```

The bitwise instructions are similar:

⟨*X86 rules* 503⟩+≡   506 507   497

```
reg: BANDU(reg,mrc1)    "?mov %c,%0\nand %c,%1\n"    1
reg: BORU(reg,mrc1)     "?mov %c,%0\nor %c,%1\n"     1
reg: BXORU(reg,mrc1)    "?mov %c,%0\nxor %c,%1\n"    1
```

Recall that a leading question mark in the assembler template tells emit to omit the first instruction in the template if the current instruction reuses the first kid's destination register. That is, if %c is eax, %0 is ebx and %1 is ecx, then the SUBU template above emits

```
mov eax,ebx
sub eax,ecx
```

but if %c is eax, %0 is eax, and %1 is ecx, the same template emits

```
sub eax,ecx
```

The binary instructions clobber their first operand, so the general implementation must start by copying their first operand into the destination register, but the copy is redundant in many cases. The costs above are estimates, because lcc doesn't determine whether the mov is needed until it allocates registers, which is too late to help select instructions. This is a classic phase-ordering problem: the compiler must select instructions to allocate registers, but it must allocate registers to compute instruction costs accurately.

The binary operators above have a variant that modifies a memory cell. Some fix the other operand to be one. For example, the instruction

```
inc dword ptr i
```

bumps i by one.

⟨*X86 rules* 503⟩+≡   506 507   497
```
    stmt: ASGNI(addr,ADDI(mem,con1))   "inc %1\n"   memop(a)
    stmt: ASGNI(addr,ADDU(mem,con1))   "inc %1\n"   memop(a)
    stmt: ASGNP(addr,ADDP(mem,con1))   "inc %1\n"   memop(a)
    stmt: ASGNI(addr,SUBI(mem,con1))   "dec %1\n"   memop(a)
    stmt: ASGNI(addr,SUBU(mem,con1))   "dec %1\n"   memop(a)
    stmt: ASGNP(addr,SUBP(mem,con1))   "dec %1\n"   memop(a)
```

The lone operand identifies the source operand *and* the destination.
memop confirms that the tree has the form $\text{ASGN}a(x,b(\text{INDIR}(x),c))$:

⟨*X86 functions* 498⟩+≡   502 507   497
```
    static int memop(p) Node p; {
       if (generic(p->kids[1]->kids[0]->op) == INDIR
       && sametree(p->kids[0], p->kids[1]->kids[0]->kids[0]))
          return 3;
       else
          return LBURG_MAX;
    }
```

memop confirms the overall shape of the tree, and sametree confirms that   ─────────────
the destination is the same as the first source operand: 403 stmt
                                                                                  ─────────────

⟨*X86 functions* 498⟩+≡   507 511   497
```
    static int sametree(p, q) Node p, q; {
       return p == NULL && q == NULL
       || p && q && p->op == q->op && p->syms[0] == q->syms[0]
          && sametree(p->kids[0], q->kids[0])
          && sametree(p->kids[1], q->kids[1]);
    }
```

Other variants on the binary operators permit the second operand to be
a register or constant:

⟨*X86 rules* 503⟩+≡   507 508   497
```
    stmt: ASGNI(addr,ADDI(mem,rc))    "add %1,%2\n"   memop(a)
    stmt: ASGNI(addr,ADDU(mem,rc))    "add %1,%2\n"   memop(a)
    stmt: ASGNI(addr,SUBI(mem,rc))    "sub %1,%2\n"   memop(a)
    stmt: ASGNI(addr,SUBU(mem,rc))    "sub %1,%2\n"   memop(a)

    stmt: ASGNI(addr,BANDU(mem,rc))   "and %1,%2\n"   memop(a)
    stmt: ASGNI(addr,BORU(mem,rc))    "or %1,%2\n"    memop(a)
    stmt: ASGNI(addr,BXORU(mem,rc))   "xor %1,%2\n"   memop(a)
```

Each integral unary operator clobbers its lone operand:

⟨*X86 rules* 503⟩+≡   507 508   497
```
reg: BCOMU(reg)    "?mov %c,%0\nnot %c\n"   2
reg: NEGI(reg)     "?mov %c,%0\nneg %c\n"   2

stmt: ASGNI(addr,BCOMU(mem))   "not %1\n"   memop(a)
stmt: ASGNI(addr,NEGI(mem))    "neg %1\n"   memop(a)
```

The shift instructions are similar to the other binary integral instructions, except that the shift distance must be constant or in byte register cl, which is the bottom of register ecx:

⟨*X86 rules* 503⟩+≡   508 509   497
```
reg: LSHI(reg,rc5)   "?mov %c,%0\nsal %c,%1\n"   2
reg: LSHU(reg,rc5)   "?mov %c,%0\nshl %c,%1\n"   2
reg: RSHI(reg,rc5)   "?mov %c,%0\nsar %c,%1\n"   2
reg: RSHU(reg,rc5)   "?mov %c,%0\nshr %c,%1\n"   2

stmt: ASGNI(addr,LSHI(mem,rc5))   "sal %1,%2\n"   memop(a)
stmt: ASGNI(addr,LSHU(mem,rc5))   "shl %1,%2\n"   memop(a)
stmt: ASGNI(addr,RSHI(mem,rc5))   "sar %1,%2\n"   memop(a)
stmt: ASGNI(addr,RSHU(mem,rc5))   "shr %1,%2\n"   memop(a)
```

```
rc5: CNSTI   "%a"   range(a, 0, 31)
rc5: reg     "cl"
```

We take care to emit no shifts by constants less than zero or greater than 31. There are many X86 assemblers, so we can't be sure that some won't issue a diagnostic for undefined shifts. rtarget arranges to compute into cl all shift counts that aren't constants between zero and 31 inclusive:

⟨*is* p->kids[1] *a constant common subexpression?* 508⟩≡   508
```
      generic(p->kids[1]->op) == INDIR
&& p->kids[1]->kids[0]->op == VREG+P
&& p->kids[1]->syms[RX]->u.t.cse
&& generic(p->kids[1]->syms[RX]->u.t.cse->op) == CNST
```

⟨*X86* target 508⟩≡   509   502
```
case RSHI: case RSHU: case LSHI: case LSHU:
    if (generic(p->kids[1]->op) != CNST
    && !(⟨is p->kids[1] a constant common subexpression? 508⟩)) {
        rtarget(p, 1, intreg[ECX]);
        setreg(p, intreg[EAX]);
    }
    break;
```

The call on setreg above ensures that *this* node doesn't target ecx. If it did, the mov instruction that starts the template would clobber ecx and thus cl before its value has been used. eax is not the only acceptable register, but non-constant shift amounts were rare in our tests, so it wasn't worth tailoring a wildcard without ecx for these shifts.

The imul instruction multiplies signed integers. One variant multiplies a register by a register, constant, or memory cell:

⟨*X86 rules* 503⟩+≡   508 509 497
```
    reg: MULI(reg,mrc3)    "?mov %c,%0\nimul %c,%1\n"    14
```

Another variant takes three operands and leaves in a register the product of a constant and a register or memory cell:

⟨*X86 rules* 503⟩+≡   509 509 497
```
    reg: MULI(con,mr)      "imul %c,%1,%0\n"    13
```

The remaining multiplicative instructions are more constrained. The mul instruction multiples unsigned integers.

⟨*X86 rules* 503⟩+≡   509 510 497
```
    reg: MULU(reg,mr)   "mul %1\n"    13
```

It expects its first operand in eax and leaves its result in the double register edx-eax; eax holds the low-order bits, which is the result of the operation, unless the operation overflows, in which case ANSI calls the result undefined, so eax is as good a result as any:

⟨*X86* target 508⟩+≡   508 510 502
```
    case MULU:
        setreg(p, quo);
        rtarget(p, 0, intreg[EAX]);
        break;
```

498	EAX
498	EDX
361	IREG
361	mask
363	mkreg
403	reg
400	rtarget
399	setreg
362	x.regnode

quo and rem denote the eax–edx register pair, which hold a product after an unsigned multiplication and a dividend before a division. After a division, eax holds the quotient and edx the remainder.

⟨*X86 data* 499⟩+≡   501 496
```
    static Symbol quo, rem;
```

⟨*X86* progbeg 499⟩+≡   501 498
```
    quo = mkreg("eax", EAX, 1, IREG);
    quo->x.regnode->mask |= 1<<EDX;
    rem = mkreg("edx", EDX, 1, IREG);
    rem->x.regnode->mask |= 1<<EAX;
```

The div instruction divides integers. It expects its first argument in the edx-eax double register, and it leaves the quotient in eax and the remainder in edx:

⟨*X86* target 508⟩+≡   509 512   502

```
case DIVI: case DIVU:
    setreg(p, quo);
    rtarget(p, 0, intreg[EAX]);
    rtarget(p, 1, intreg[ECX]);
    break;
case MODI: case MODU:
    setreg(p, rem);
    rtarget(p, 0, intreg[EAX]);
    rtarget(p, 1, intreg[ECX]);
    break;
```

An xor instruction clears edx to prepare for an unsigned division:

⟨*X86 rules* 503⟩+≡   509 510   497

```
reg: DIVU(reg,reg)   "xor edx,edx\ndiv %1\n"
reg: MODU(reg,reg)   "xor edx,edx\ndiv %1\n"
```

The cdq instruction propagates eax's sign bit through edx to prepare for a signed division:

⟨*X86 rules* 503⟩+≡   510 510   497

```
reg: DIVI(reg,reg)   "cdq\nidiv %1\n"
reg: MODI(reg,reg)   "cdq\nidiv %1\n"
```

EAX	498
ECX	498
emit2	356
(MIPS) "	444
(SPARC) "	478
(X86) "	511
move	394
quo	509
reg	403
rem	509
rtarget	400
setreg	399

The first instruction clobbers edx, so it's vital that that the divisor be elsewhere. Targeting it into ecx above is one solution. It's gratuitously restrictive, but integer division and modulus are not particularly common.

The conversions between integral and pointer types are vacuous and thus implemented by mov instructions. move marks them as such in hopes of eliminating them:

⟨*X86 rules* 503⟩+≡   510 510   497

```
reg: CVIU(reg)   "mov %c,%0\n"   move(a)
reg: CVPU(reg)   "mov %c,%0\n"   move(a)
reg: CVUI(reg)   "mov %c,%0\n"   move(a)
reg: CVUP(reg)   "mov %c,%0\n"   move(a)
```

movsx and movzx are like mov, but they sign- or zero-extend to widen the input:

⟨*X86 rules* 503⟩+≡   510 511   497

```
reg: CVCI(INDIRC(addr))   "movsx %c,byte ptr %0\n"   3
reg: CVCU(INDIRC(addr))   "movzx %c,byte ptr %0\n"   3
reg: CVSI(INDIRS(addr))   "movsx %c,word ptr %0\n"   3
reg: CVSU(INDIRS(addr))   "movzx %c,word ptr %0\n"   3
```

movsx and movzx can also operate on registers, but they require help from emit2, because the source operand must name the 8- or 16-bit sub-register:

⟨*X86 rules* 503⟩+≡   510 511   497
```
    reg: CVCI(reg)    "# extend\n"    3
    reg: CVCU(reg)    "# extend\n"    3
    reg: CVSI(reg)    "# extend\n"    3
    reg: CVSU(reg)    "# extend\n"    3
```

⟨*X86 functions* 498⟩+≡   507 512   497
```
    static void emit2(p) Node p; {
        ⟨X86 emit2 511⟩
    }
```

⟨*result* 511⟩≡   511
```
    p->syms[RX]->x.name
```

⟨*X86* emit2 511⟩≡   511   511
```
    #define preg(f) ((f)[getregnum(p->x.kids[0])]->x.name)

    if (p->op == CVCI)
        print("movsx %s,%s\n", ⟨result 511⟩, preg(charreg));
    else if (p->op == CVCU)
        print("movzx %s,%s\n", ⟨result 511⟩, preg(charreg));
    else if (p->op == CVSI)
        print("movsx %s,%s\n", ⟨result 511⟩, preg(shortreg));
    else if (p->op == CVSU)
        print("movzx %s,%s\n", ⟨result 511⟩, preg(shortreg));
```

403 reg
362 RX
359 x.kids
362 x.name

The integral narrowing conversions also require special treatment:

⟨*X86 rules* 503⟩+≡   511 512   497
```
    reg: CVIC(reg)    "# truncate\n"    1
    reg: CVIS(reg)    "# truncate\n"    1
    reg: CVUC(reg)    "# truncate\n"    1
    reg: CVUS(reg)    "# truncate\n"    1
```

The template "?mov %c,%0\n" and cost move(a) would move the input to the output and omit the move when the source and destination are the same, but mov expects both its source and target to be the same size, so when a mov is necessary, emit2 emits one but uses the 16-bit version of the source and target registers, which mollifies the assembler and copies enough bits for all integral narrowing conversions:

⟨*X86* emit2 511⟩+≡   511   511
```
    else if (p->op == CVIC || p->op == CVIS
            || p->op == CVUC || p->op == CVUS) {
        char *dst = shortreg[getregnum(p)]->x.name;
        char *src = preg(shortreg);
        if (dst != src)
```

```
        print("mov %s,%s\n", dst, src);
    }
```

The mov instruction stores as well as loads:

⟨*X86 rules* 503⟩+≡   5̂11 5̲1̲2   497

```
    stmt: ASGNC(addr,rc)    "mov byte ptr %0,%1\n"    1
    stmt: ASGNI(addr,rc)    "mov dword ptr %0,%1\n"   1
    stmt: ASGNP(addr,rc)    "mov dword ptr %0,%1\n"   1
    stmt: ASGNS(addr,rc)    "mov word ptr %0,%1\n"    1
```

ARGI and ARGP are analogous to ASGNI and ASGNP, but their target is a new cell atop the stack. They use the push instruction, which pushes an argument onto the stack:

⟨*X86 rules* 503⟩+≡   5̂12 5̲1̲3   497

```
    stmt: ARGI(mrc3)    "push %0\n"    1
    stmt: ARGP(mrc3)    "push %0\n"    1
```

The mrc3 above is correct, if counter-intuitive. push 0 takes four cycles even though

```
    mov eax,0
    push eax
```

takes only two.

doarg calls mkactual, which computes the stack offset for the next actual argument and updates maxargoffset. Unlike lcc's RISC targets, the X86 has a push instruction that obviates any need for mkactual's stack offset, but doarg still calls mkactual to compute maxargoffset, which docall stores in CALL nodes because the call instructions need it to pop the actual arguments off the stack after the call.

⟨*X86 functions* 498⟩+≡   5̂11 5̲1̲3   497

```
    static void doarg(p) Node p; {
        mkactual(4, p->syms[0]->u.c.v.i);
    }
```

ASGNB copies a block of memory. The movsb instruction copies a byte from the address in esi to the address in edi, then adds one to each of those registers. The rep string-instruction prefix repeats the suffix instruction ecx times, so the combination rep movsb copies ecx bytes from the address in esi to the address in edi. target arranges to compute the source and destination addresses into esi and edi:

⟨*X86* target 508⟩+≡   5̂10 5̲1̲3   502

```
    case ASGNB:
        rtarget(p, 0, intreg[EDI]);
        rtarget(p->kids[1], 0, intreg[ESI]);
        break;
```

The template for ASGNB copies the size of the block into ecx and issues the rep movsb:

⟨*X86 rules* 503⟩+≡   5̂12 513   497
   stmt: ASGNB(reg,INDIRB(reg)) "mov ecx,%a\nrep movsb\n"

ARGB is similar. The source is the ARGB's lone child:

⟨*X86* target 508⟩+≡   5̂12 5̌17   502
   case ARGB:
      rtarget(p->kids[0], 0, intreg[ESI]);
      break;

The destination is fixed to be the top of the stack, so the template starts by allocating a block atop the stack and pointing `edi` at it:

⟨*X86 rules* 503⟩+≡   5̂13 513   497
   stmt: ARGB(INDIRB(reg)) "sub esp,%a\nmov edi,esp\n_
                     mov ecx,%a\nrep movsb\n"

`rep` clobbers `ecx` and `movsb` clobbers `esi` and `edi`:

⟨*X86* clobber 513⟩≡   5̌17   502
   case ASGNB: case ARGB:
      spill(1<<ECX | 1<<ESI | 1<<EDI, IREG, p);
      break;

The `blk` procedures aren't needed:

⟨*X86 functions* 498⟩+≡   5̂12 5̌18   497
   static void blkfetch(k, off, reg, tmp)
   int k, off, reg, tmp; {}
   static void blkstore(k, off, reg, tmp)
   int k, off, reg, tmp; {}
   static void blkloop(dreg, doff, sreg, soff, size, tmps)
   int dreg, doff, sreg, soff, size, tmps[]; {}

498	ECX
498	EDI
498	ESI
361	IREG
403	reg
400	rtarget
427	spill
403	stmt
497	x86IR

The fragment ⟨*interface routine names*⟩ expects static `blk` procedures and appears in x86IR, so we must define the routines, but they don't have to do anything because nothing calls them.

   The floating-point instructions use a stack of eight 80-bit registers. All temporary values are 80 bits; ANSI C allows calculations to use extra precision, so the code generator need not compensate.

   Some floating-point instructions take an operand from memory. The operand, not the operator, specifies the type:

⟨*X86 rules* 503⟩+≡   5̂13 514   497
   memf: INDIRD(addr)   "qword ptr %0"
   memf: INDIRF(addr)   "dword ptr %0"
   memf: CVFD(INDIRF(addr)) "dword ptr %0"

The `fld` instruction loads a floating-point value from memory and pushes it onto the floating-point stack:

⟨*X86 rules* 503⟩ +≡   5̂13 514   497
  reg: memf   "fld %0\n"   3

fstp pops the floating-point stack and stores the result in memory:

⟨*X86 rules* 503⟩ +≡   5̂14 514   497
  stmt: ASGND(addr,reg)   "fstp qword ptr %0\n"   7
  stmt: ASGNF(addr,reg)   "fstp dword ptr %0\n"   7
  stmt: ASGNF(addr,CVDF(reg))   "fstp dword ptr %0\n"   7

Floating-point arguments travel on the memory stack, so a subtraction allocates space for them, and an fstp fills the space:

⟨*X86 rules* 503⟩ +≡   5̂14 514   497
  stmt: ARGD(reg)   "sub esp,8\nfstp qword ptr [esp]\n"
  stmt: ARGF(reg)   "sub esp,4\nfstp dword ptr [esp]\n"

The unary operators change the element atop the floating-point stack. For example, the fchs instruction negates the top of the stack:

⟨*X86 rules* 503⟩ +≡   5̂14 514   497
  reg: NEGD(reg)   "fchs\r
  reg: NEGF(reg)   "fchs\n"

The binary operators work on the top two elements of the floating-point stack or on the top element and an operand from memory:

reg 403
stmt 403

⟨*X86 rules* 503⟩ +≡   5̂14 514   497
  flt: memf   " %0"
  flt: reg   "p st(1),st"

For example, the instruction

    fsubp st(1),st

subtracts the top of the stack (st) from the element one (st(1)) underneath it and pops (the p suffix) the stack once, discarding the value subtracted. The instruction

    fsub qword ptr x

subtracts the 64-bit value of x from the top of the stack. The p suffix is missing, so the height of the floating-point stack doesn't change. The other binary operators are similar:

⟨*X86 rules* 503⟩ +≡   5̂14 515   497
  reg: ADDD(reg,flt)   "fadd%1\n"
  reg: ADDF(reg,flt)   "fadd%1\n"
  reg: DIVD(reg,flt)   "fdiv%1\n"
  reg: DIVF(reg,flt)   "fdiv%1\n"
  reg: MULD(reg,flt)   "fmul%1\n"
  reg: MULF(reg,flt)   "fmul%1\n"
  reg: SUBD(reg,flt)   "fsub%1\n"
  reg: SUBF(reg,flt)   "fsub%1\n"

The conversion from float to double does nothing to a floating-point register, because the register is already 80 bits wide and thus needs no further widening. CVFD's widening has thus already been done:

⟨*X86 rules* 503⟩+≡   514 515   497
  reg: CVFD(reg) "# CVFD\n"

No instruction directly narrows a double to a float, so we must store the value into a temporary float, which narrows the value. Then we reload the value, which widens it again, but the extra precision is gone:

⟨*X86 rules* 503⟩+≡   515 515   497
  reg: CVDF(reg) "sub esp,4\nfstp dword ptr 0[esp]\n_
                       fld dword ptr 0[esp]\nadd esp,4\n" 12

The conversion from double to integer is similar. The instruction `fistp` pops the floating-point stack, converts the value to an integral value, and stores it in memory:

⟨*X86 rules* 503⟩+≡   515 515   497
  stmt: ASGNI(addr,CVDI(reg)) "fistp dword ptr %0\n" 29

If the code needs the integral result in a (general) register, then we'll create, use, and free a temporary on the stack in memory:

⟨*X86 rules* 503⟩+≡   515 515   497
  reg: CVDI(reg) "sub esp,4\n_
                fistp dword ptr 0[esp]\npop %c\n" 31

61	ptr
403	reg
403	stmt

The `fild` instruction loads an integer, converts it to an 80-bit floating-point value, and pushes it onto the floating-point stack:

⟨*X86 rules* 503⟩+≡   515 515   497
  reg: CVID(INDIRI(addr)) "fild dword ptr %0\n" 10

If the operand comes from a (general) register, then we create, use, and free another temporary on the stack in memory:

⟨*X86 rules* 503⟩+≡   515 515   497
  reg: CVID(reg) "push %0\n_
             fild dword ptr 0[esp]\nadd esp,4\n" 12

The `jmp` instruction jumps unconditionally. It accepts a label, register, or memory cell:

⟨*X86 rules* 503⟩+≡   515 516   497
  addrj: ADDRGP "%a"
  addrj: reg   "%0" 2
  addrj: mem   "%0" 2

```
stmt:   JUMPV(addrj)   "jmp %0\n"   3
stmt:   LABELV         "%a:\n"
```

The conditional branches compare two values and branch when the condition is met. The `cmp` instruction does the comparisons and has several variants. One compares a memory cell with a register or constant. The signed integers have all six relationals:

⟨*X86 rules* 503⟩+≡   515 516   497

```
stmt: EQI(mem,rc)   "cmp %0,%1\nje %a\n"    5
stmt: GEI(mem,rc)   "cmp %0,%1\njge %a\n"   5
stmt: GTI(mem,rc)   "cmp %0,%1\njg %a\n"    5
stmt: LEI(mem,rc)   "cmp %0,%1\njle %a\n"   5
stmt: LTI(mem,rc)   "cmp %0,%1\njl %a\n"    5
stmt: NEI(mem,rc)   "cmp %0,%1\njne %a\n"   5
```

The unsigned integers have only four because `EQI` and `NEI` work for unsigned integers too:

⟨*X86 rules* 503⟩+≡   516 516   497

```
stmt: GEU(mem,rc)   "cmp %0,%1\njae %a\n"   5
stmt: GTU(mem,rc)   "cmp %0,%1\nja  %a\n"   5
stmt: LEU(mem,rc)   "cmp %0,%1\njbe %a\n"   5
stmt: LTU(mem,rc)   "cmp %0,%1\njb  %a\n"   5
```

reg 403
stmt 403

Another variant of `cmp` compares a register to a constant, a memory cell, or another register, so we repeat the signed and unsigned rules above with this combination of operands:

⟨*X86 rules* 503⟩+≡   516 516   497

```
stmt: EQI(reg,mrc1)   "cmp %0,%1\nje %a\n"    4
stmt: GEI(reg,mrc1)   "cmp %0,%1\njge %a\n"   4
stmt: GTI(reg,mrc1)   "cmp %0,%1\njg %a\n"    4
stmt: LEI(reg,mrc1)   "cmp %0,%1\njle %a\n"   4
stmt: LTI(reg,mrc1)   "cmp %0,%1\njl %a\n"    4
stmt: NEI(reg,mrc1)   "cmp %0,%1\njne %a\n"   4

stmt: GEU(reg,mrc1)   "cmp %0,%1\njae %a\n"   4
stmt: GTU(reg,mrc1)   "cmp %0,%1\nja %a\n"    4
stmt: LEU(reg,mrc1)   "cmp %0,%1\njbe %a\n"   4
stmt: LTU(reg,mrc1)   "cmp %0,%1\njb %a\n"    4
```

The instruction `fcomp` x pops one element from the floating-point stack and compares it with the operand x in memory. The `fcompp` variant pops both comparands from the floating-point stack. The nonterminal `cmpf` allows one rule to emit both variants:

⟨*X86 rules* 503⟩+≡   516 517   497

```
cmpf: memf   " %0"
cmpf: reg    "p"
```

The similar nonterminal flt, which is defined on page 514, won't do, because the assembler requires a st(1),st on binary operators but curiously forbids it on fcomp. fcomp stores the result of the comparison in some machine flags. The instruction fststw ax stores the flags in the bottom of eax, and the instruction sahf loads them into the flags tested by the conditional branch instructions:

⟨*X86 rules* 503⟩+≡   516 517   497

```
stmt: EQD(cmpf,reg)    "fcomp%0\nfststw ax\nsahf\nje %a\n"
stmt: GED(cmpf,reg)    "fcomp%0\nfststw ax\nsahf\njbe %a\n"
stmt: GTD(cmpf,reg)    "fcomp%0\nfststw ax\nsahf\njb %a\n"
stmt: LED(cmpf,reg)    "fcomp%0\nfststw ax\nsahf\njae %a\n"
stmt: LTD(cmpf,reg)    "fcomp%0\nfststw ax\nsahf\nja %a\n"
stmt: NED(cmpf,reg)    "fcomp%0\nfststw ax\nsahf\njne %a\n"

stmt: EQF(cmpf,reg)    "fcomp%0\nfststw ax\nsahf\nje %a\n"
stmt: GEF(cmpf,reg)    "fcomp%0\nfststw ax\nsahf\njbe %a\n"
stmt: GTF(cmpf,reg)    "fcomp%0\nfststw ax\nsahf\njb %a\n"
stmt: LEF(cmpf,reg)    "fcomp%0\nfststw ax\nsahf\njae %a\n"
stmt: LTF(cmpf,reg)    "fcomp%0\nfststw ax\nsahf\nja %a\n"
stmt: NEF(cmpf,reg)    "fcomp%0\nfststw ax\nsahf\njne %a\n"
```

clobber records that the floating-point conditional branches destroy eax:

⟨*X86* clobber 513⟩+≡   513 518   502

```
case EQD: case LED: case GED: case LTD: case GTD: case NED:
case EQF: case LEF: case GEF: case LTF: case GTF: case NEF:
    spill(1<<EAX, IREG, p);
    break;
```

The call instruction pushes on the stack the address of the next instruction and jumps to the address specified by its operand:

⟨*X86 rules* 503⟩+≡   517 518   497

```
reg:  CALLI(addrj)  "call %0\nadd esp,%a\n"
stmt: CALLV(addrj)  "call %0\nadd esp,%a\n"
```

The add instruction pops the arguments off the stack after the call. The front end points each call node's syms[0] at a symbol equal to the number of bytes of actual arguments. The %a causes this number to be emitted. The return value arrives in eax:

⟨*X86* target 508⟩+≡   513   502

```
case CALLI: case CALLV:
    setreg(p, intreg[EAX]);
    break;
case RETI:
    rtarget(p, 0, intreg[EAX]);
    break;
```

Floating-point functions return a value in the top of the stack of floating-point registers:

⟨*X86 rules* 503⟩+≡   517 518   497
```
reg: CALLF(addrj)   "call %0\nadd esp,%a\n"
reg: CALLD(addrj)   "call %0\nadd esp,%a\n"
```

⟨*X86* clobber 513⟩+≡   517   502
```
case CALLD: case CALLF:
    spill(1<<EDX | 1<<EAX, IREG, p);
    break;
```

Return nodes exist, as usual, more to guide register targeting than to emit code:

⟨*X86 rules* 503⟩+≡   518   497
```
stmt: RETI(reg)   "# ret\n"
stmt: RETF(reg)   "# ret\n"
stmt: RETD(reg)   "# ret\n"
```

18.3   Implementing Functions

The front end calls local to announce a local variable, including the temporaries that it generates. The code generator assigns no floating-point locals — not even temporaries — to registers, so local starts by forcing them onto the stack:

⟨*X86 functions* 498⟩+≡   513 518   497
```
static void local(p) Symbol p; {
    if (isfloat(p->type))
        p->sclass = AUTO;
    if (askregvar(p, rmap[ttob(p->type)]) == 0)
        mkauto(p);
}
```

Floating-point and integral locals are handled asymmetrically because integral temporaries *are* assigned to registers. Other locals aren't, but progbeg cleared vmask[IREG], which directs askregvar to keep bona fide variables out of registers.

The front end calls the interface procedure function to announce a new routine:

⟨*X86 functions* 498⟩+≡   518 520   497
```
static void function(f, caller, callee, n)
Symbol f, callee[], caller[]; int n; {
    int i;
```

⟨*X86* function 519⟩
}

It emits the procedure prologue, which includes a label and instructions to save ebx, esi, edi, and ebp:

⟨*X86* function 519⟩≡   519   519
```
print("%s:\n", f->x.name);
print("push ebx\n");
print("push esi\n");
print("push edi\n");
print("push ebp\n");
print("mov ebp,esp\n");
```

The prologue code also updates ebp. Figure 18.1 shows an X86 frame.

Next, function clears the state of the register allocator and calculates the stack offset for each incoming argument. The first resides 20 bytes from ebp: 16 bytes save registers and four more save the return address.

⟨*X86* function 519⟩+≡   519 520   519
```
⟨clear register state 410⟩
offset = 16 + 4;
for (i = 0; callee[i]; i++) {
    ⟨assign offset to argument i 520⟩
}
```

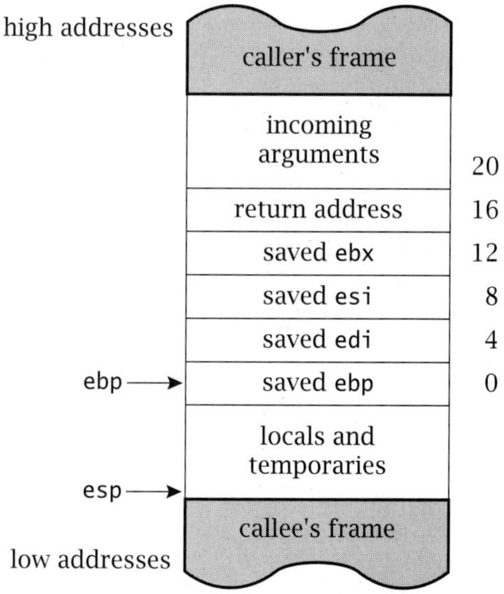

FIGURE 18.1   A frame for the X86.

offset gives the offset from ebp to the next argument. It determines
the x.offset and x.name fields of the callee and caller views of the arguments:

⟨*assign offset to argument* i 520⟩≡   519
```
    Symbol p = callee[i];
    Symbol q = caller[i];
    p->x.offset = q->x.offset = offset;
    p->x.name = q->x.name = stringf("%d", p->x.offset);
    p->sclass = q->sclass = AUTO;
    offset += roundup(q->type->size, 4);
```

The sclass fields are set to record that no arguments are assigned to
registers, and offset is adjusted for the next argument and to keep the
stack aligned.

function then calls gencode to process the body of the routine. It
first resets offset and maxoffset to record that no locals have yet been
allocated:

⟨*X86* function 519⟩+≡   519 520   519
```
    offset = maxoffset = 0;
    gencode(caller, callee);
    framesize = roundup(maxoffset, 4);
    if (framesize > 0)
        print("sub esp,%d\n", framesize);
```

When gencode returns, maxoffset is the largest value that offset took
on during the lifetime of gencode, so code to allocate the rest of the
frame can now be emitted into the prologue. Then function calls
emitcode to emit the body of the routine, and it calls print directly
to emit the epilogue, which merely undoes the prologue:

⟨*X86* function 519⟩+≡   520   519
```
    emitcode();
    print("mov esp,ebp\n");
    print("pop ebp\n");
    print("pop edi\n");
    print("pop esi\n");
    print("pop ebx\n");
    print("ret\n");
```

18.4 Defining Data

The front end calls defsymbol to announce each new symbol:

⟨*X86 functions* 498⟩+≡   518 521   497
```
    static void defsymbol(p) Symbol p; {
```

⟨*X86* defsymbol 521⟩
}

Static locals get a generated name to avoid other static locals of the same name:

⟨*X86* defsymbol 521⟩≡   521   521
  if (p->scope >= LOCAL && p->sclass == STATIC)
    p->x.name = stringf("L%d", genlabel(1));

Generated symbols already have a unique numeric name. defsymbol simply prefixes a letter to make a valid assembler identifier:

⟨*X86* defsymbol 521⟩+≡   521 521   521
  else if (p->generated)
    p->x.name = stringf("L%s", p->name);

Conventions for exported globals prefix an underscore to the name:

⟨*X86* defsymbol 521⟩+≡   521 521   521
  else if (p->scope == GLOBAL || p->sclass == EXTERN)
    p->x.name = stringf("_%s", p->name);

Hexadecimal constants must be reformatted. Where the front end uses 0xff, the X86 assembler expects 0ffH:

⟨*X86* defsymbol 521⟩+≡   521 521   521
  else if (p->scope == CONSTANTS
  && (isint(p->type) || isptr(p->type))
  && p->name[0] == '0' && p->name[1] == 'x')
    p->x.name = stringf("0%sH", &p->name[2]);

The front end and back ends share the same name for the remaining symbols, such as decimal constants and static globals:

⟨*X86* defsymbol 521⟩+≡   521   521
  else
    p->x.name = p->name;

The interface procedure address does for symbols that use offset arithmetic, like _up+28, what defsymbol does for ordinary symbols:

⟨*X86 functions* 498⟩+≡   520 522   497
  static void address(q, p, n) Symbol q, p; int n; {
    if (p->scope == GLOBAL
    || p->sclass == STATIC || p->sclass == EXTERN)
      q->x.name = stringf("%s%s%d",
        p->x.name, n >= 0 ? "+" : "", n);
    else {
      q->x.offset = p->x.offset + n;

```
          q->x.name = stringd(q->x.offset);
      }
  }
```

For variables on the stack, address simply computes the adjusted offset. For variables accessed using a label, it sets x.name to a string of the form *name* ± *n*. If the offset is positive, the literal "+" emits the operator; if the offset is negative, the %d emits it.

The front end calls defconst to emit assembler directives to allocate and initialize a scalar to a constant. The argument ty identifies the proper member of the union v:

⟨*X86 functions* 498⟩+≡   521 523   497

```
  static void defconst(ty, v) int ty; Value v; {
      switch (ty) {
          ⟨X86 defconst 522⟩
      }
  }
```

Most cases simply emit the member into an assembler directive that allocates and initializes a cell of the type ty:

⟨*X86* defconst 522⟩≡   522   522

```
  case C: print("db %d\n",    v.uc); return;
  case S: print("dw %d\n",    v.ss); return;
  case I: print("dd %d\n",    v.i ); return;
  case U: print("dd 0%xH\n", v.u ); return;
  case P: print("dd 0%xH\n", v.p ); return;
```

The assembler's real4 and real8 directives are unusable because they can't express floating-point constants that result from arbitrary expressions (e.g., with casts), so defconst emits floating-point constants in hexadecimal:

⟨*X86* defconst 522⟩+≡   522 522   522

```
  case F:
      print("dd 0%xH\n", *(unsigned *)&v.f);
      return;
```

The two halves of each double must be exchanged if lcc is running on a little endian and compiling for a big endian, or vice versa:

⟨*X86* defconst 522⟩+≡   522   522

```
  case D: {
      unsigned *p = (unsigned *)&v.d;
      print("dd 0%xH,0%xH\n", p[swap], p[1 - swap]);
      return;
  }
```

The interface procedure defaddress allocates space for a pointer and initializes it to a *symbolic* address:

⟨*X86 functions* 498⟩ +≡   522 5̲2̲3̲   497

```
static void defaddress(p) Symbol p; {
    print("dd %s\n", p->x.name);
}
```

defconst's switch case for pointers initializes a pointer to a *numeric*
address.

The interface procedure defstring emits directives that initialize a
series of bytes:

⟨*X86 functions* 498⟩ +≡   523 5̲2̲3̲   497

```
static void defstring(n, str) int n; char *str; {
    char *s;

    for (s = str; s < str + n; s++)
        print("db %d\n", (*s)&0377);
}
```

It finds the end of the string by counting, because ANSI C escape codes
permit strings with embedded null bytes.

The front end calls export to expose a symbol to other modules. The
public assembler directive does just that:

⟨*X86 functions* 498⟩ +≡   523 5̲2̲3̲   497

```
static void export(p) Symbol p; {
    print("public %s\n", p->x.name);
}
```

The extern directive makes visible in the current module a symbol exported by another module, but it may not appear inside a segment, so
the interface procedure import temporarily switches out of the current
segment:

⟨*X86 functions* 498⟩ +≡   523 5̲2̲4̲   497

```
static void import(p) Symbol p; {
    int oldseg = cseg;

    if (p->ref > 0) {
        segment(0);
        print("extrn %s:near\n", p->x.name);
        segment(oldseg);
    }
}
```

The near directive declares that the external can be addressed directly.
The flat memory model and its 32-bit addresses permit direct addresses
for *everything*, so it's unnecessary to understand near and the related
directives unless one is generating segmented code, which is harder.

lcc's implementation of segment for the X86 takes care that the call segment(0) switches out of the current segment but not into any new segment. import checks the symbol's ref field to emit the directives only if the symbol is used, because some X86 linkers object to gratuitous extrns.

The front end calls the interface procedure global to define a new global. If the global is initialized, the front end next calls defconst, so global allocates space only for uninitialized globals, which are in the BSS segment:

⟨*X86 functions* 498⟩+≡   523 524   497

```
static void global(p) Symbol p; {
    print("align %d\n",
        p->type->align > 4 ? 4 : p->type->align);
    print("%s label byte\n", p->x.name);
    if (p->u.seg == BSS)
        print("db %d dup (0)\n", p->type->size);
}
```

The front end calls the interface procedure space to define a block of global data initialized to zero:

⟨*X86 functions* 498⟩+≡   524   497

```
static void space(n) int n; {
    if (cseg != BSS)
        print("db %d dup (0)\n", n);
}
```

Further Reading

Various reference manuals elaborate on the architecture of this machine (Intel Corp. 1993). The assembler manuals that come with Microsoft's MASM and Borland's Turbo Assembler elaborate on the assembler language in general and the directives that control the various memory models in particular.

Exercises

18.1 Scan the X86 reference manual for instructions that lcc could use but doesn't. Add rules to emit these instructions. Benchmark the compiler before and after each change to determine which changes pay off.

18.2 Some of lcc's opcodes commute, which means that for every rule like

```
reg: ADDI(reg,mrcl)    "mov %c,%0\nadd %c,%1\n"   2
```

we might also have a rule

```
reg: ADDI(mrcl,reg)    "mov %c,%1\nadd %c,%0\n"   2
```

Experiment with adding some commuted rules. Which ones make a significant difference? Which *can't* make a difference because the front end never generates them?

18.3 Some noncommutative operations have a dual that exchanges their operands. For example, the rule

```
stmt: GTI(reg,mrcl)    "cmp %0,%1\njg %a\n"   2
```

has the dual

```
stmt: GTI(mrcl,reg)    "cmp %1,%0\njl %a\n"   2
```

because $x > y$ if and only if $y < x$. Try to find some X86 dual rules that pay off.

18.4 `rep movsb` copies `ecx` bytes one at a time. `rep movsw` copies `ecx` 16-bit units about twice as fast, and `rep movsd` copies `ecx` 32-bit units another rough factor of two faster. Change the block-copy code to exploit these instructions when it can.

---
502 `ckstack`

18.5 `lcc`'s function prologues and epilogue save and restore `ebx`, `esi`, and `edi` even if the routine doesn't touch them. Correct this blemish and determine if it was worth the effort.

18.6 Reserve one general register and assign it to the most promising local. Measure the improvement. Repeat the experiment for more registers. Which number of register variables gives the best result?

18.7 `lcc` emits `lea edi,1[edi]` for the addition in `f(i+1)`. We'd prefer `inc edi`, but it's hard to adapt the X86 code generator to emit that code for this particular case. Explain why.

18.8 Construct a small C program that draws `ckstack`'s diagnostic.

18.9 Revise the X86 code generator to spill and reload floating-point registers without help from the programmer. See the discussion of `ckstack`.

19
Retrospective

lcc is *one* way to build a C compiler. Hundreds of technical decisions were made during lcc's design and implementation, and there are viable alternatives for many of them. The exercises in the previous chapters suggest some alternatives. This chapter looks back at lcc's design and discusses some of the global design alternatives that would most affect the current implementation. These alternatives are the ones that, with the benefit of hindsight, we might now prefer.

Many of the programming techniques used in lcc, such as Chapter 2's storage allocator and the string management described in Section 2.5, are useful in a wide range of applications. The symbol-table module, described in Chapter 3, is specific to lcc, but can be easily adapted to other applications that need similar functions, and the input module in Section 6.1 can be used anywhere high-speed input is important.

The parsing techniques detailed in Chapter 8 are useful in applications that must parse and evaluate expressions, such as spreadsheets. Even lburg has applications beyond its use for selecting instructions, as described in Chapter 14. The matchers lburg generates know little about lcc's nodes and they can be used for problems that boil down to matching patterns in trees. The approach epitomized by lburg — generating a program from a compact specification of its salient attributes — has wide applicability. Other compilers routinely use this approach for generating lexical analyzers and parsers with tools like LEX and YACC, for example.

19.1 Data Structures

Sharing data structures between the front end and the code generator is manageable because there are few such structures. A disadvantage of this approach, however, is that the structures are more complex than they might be in other designs, which compromises simplicity. For example, symbols represent all identifiers across the interface. Symbols have many fields, but some are relevant only to the front end, and access to them can be regulated only by convention. Some symbols use only a few of the fields; labels, for example, use only the name field and the fields in u.1. A data structure tailored to labels would be much less cluttered.

C shares the blame for this complexity: Specifying all of the possibilities requires a type system richer than C's. Some of the complexity might be avoided by defining separate structures — for example, one for each kind of symbol and another for private front-end data — but doing so increases the data-structure vocabulary and hence complexity. Type systems with inheritance simplify defining variants of a structure without also complicating uses of those variants. The type systems in object-oriented languages, such as Oberon-2, Modula-3, and C++, have the necessary machinery. In these languages, we would define a base symbol type with only the fields common to all symbols, and separate types for each kind of symbol. These types would use inheritance to extend the base type with symbol-specific fields.

In Modula-3, for example, the base type might be defined simply as

```
TYPE Symbol = OBJECT
    name: TEXT
END;
```

which defines an object type with one field, name, that holds a string. A type for labels would add fields specific to labels:

```
TYPE Label = Symbol OBJECT
    label: INTEGER;
    equatedto: Label
END;
```

which defines Label to be an object type with all of Symbol's fields plus the two label-specific fields. Procedures that manipulate Symbols can also manipulate Labels, because a Label is also a Symbol.

The same mechanism could be used for the other data structures, such as types, trees, and nodes. The back-end extensions — the x fields of symbols and nodes — would be unnecessary because the back end could define additional types that extend front-end types with target-specific fields.

Object-oriented languages also support methods, which are procedures that are associated with and operate on values of a specific type. Methods would replace some of the interface functions, and they would eliminate switch statements like the ones in the implementations of defconst, because the methods would be applied to only specific types.

91	defconst
455	" (MIPS)
490	" (SPARC)
522	" (X86)
315	node
37	symbol

19.2 Interface

lcc's code-generation interface is compact because it omits the inessential and makes simplifying assumptions. These omissions and assumptions do, however, limit the interface's applicability to other languages and machines.

The interface assumes that signed and unsigned integers and long integers all have the same size. This assumption lets lcc make do with nine type suffixes and 108 type-specific operators, but it complicates full use of some 64-bit machines. If we had it to do over again, we might use distinct type suffixes for signed and unsigned characters, shorts, integers, and long integers, and for floats, doubles, and long doubles. We've even considered backing such types into lcc, though it's hard to be enthusiastic about the chore. For example, adding a suffix for just long doubles would add at least 19 operators and code in both the front and back ends to handle them. This change wouldn't need a lot of additional code in a few places; it would need a few lines of code in many places. Another alternative is for the suffixes to denote only datatype, not size, and to add separate suffixes for each size. For example, ADDI2 and ADDI4 would denote addition of 2-byte and 4-byte integers. The sizes could also be carried elsewhere in a node instead of being encoded in the operator names.

The interface assumes that all pointers have the same representation. This assumption complicates targeting word-addressed machines, where pointers to units smaller than a word — like characters — need extra bits to identify a unit within the word. Differentiating between character and word pointers would add another suffix and at least 13 more operators. We don't regret this assumption yet, but we haven't targeted a word-addressed machine yet either.

The operator repertoire omits some operators whose effect can be synthesized from simpler ones. For example, bit fields are accessed with shifting and masking instead of specific bit-field operators, which may complicate thorough exploitation of machines with bit-field instructions. On the other hand, the front end special-cases one-bit fields and generates efficient masking dags, which often yields better code than code that uses bit-field instructions.

The interface has gone through several revisions and has been simplified each time by moving functionality into the front end or by pruning the interface vocabulary. For example, earlier versions had an interface function and an operator to implement switches. Each revision made the back ends smaller, but blemishes remain.

On one hand, we may have moved too much into the front end. For example, there were once operators for such holes in the opcode × type matrix as INDIRU, RETP, and CVUD; cutting the redundancy saved a little code, but a more regular operator set would be easier to learn. As another example, the back end doesn't see the code list and can traverse it only via gencode and emitcode. Several people have used lcc to study global optimizations, and some found that they needed finer control over the traversals. To get this control, they had to expose the code list to the back end — that is, have the code list *be* the interface — and move more ambitious versions of gencode and emitcode into the target-independent part of the back end. This change replaces interface functions like local with the equivalent code-list entry. An interface that exposed the code list — or a flow graph — together with standard implementations of gencode and emitcode would permit clients to choose between simplicity and flexibility.

On the other hand, the interface could be simpler yet. For example, ASGN and CALL have type-specific variants that take different numbers of operands. This variability complicates decisions that otherwise could be made by inspecting only the generic operation. Operators that always generate trivial target code are another example. A few operators generate nothing on *some* targets, but some, like CVUI and CVIU, generate nothing on *all* current or conceivable targets. Production back ends, like those described in this book, take pains to avoid generating vacuous register-to-register moves for these operators. Similarly, the narrowing conversions CV{UI} × {CS} are vacuous on all targets and might well be omitted.

Several interface conventions, if not obeyed, can cause subtle errors. For example, the interface functions local and function, and the code for the operator CALLB collaborate to generate code for functions that return structures. Three sites in the back end must cooperate perfectly, or the compiler will silently generate incorrect code. The front end *could* deal with such functions completely and thus eliminate the interface flag wants_callb, but this would exclude some established calling sequences. Similar comments apply to ARGB and the flag wants_argb. The trade-off for generating compatible calling-sequence code is a more complex code-generation interface.

lcc's interface was designed for use in a monolithic compiler in which the front end and back ends are linked together into a single program. This design complicates separating the front and back ends into separate programs. Some of the interaction is two-way; the upcalls from the interface function function to gencode and emitcode are examples. These upcalls permit the front end to generate conversion code required at function entry. The back end examines few fields in the source-language type representation; it uses front-end functions like isstruct to query types. To make the back end a separate program, type data must be transmitted to answer such queries, and the back end might have to implement the function entry conversions.

19.3 Syntactic and Semantic Analyses

lcc interleaves parsing and semantic analyses. This approach is typical of many compilers based on the classical design for recursive-descent parsers that has been used widely since the early 1960s. It's easy to understand and to implement by hand, and it yields fast compilers.

Many languages, such as C, were designed for one-pass compilation, in which code is emitted as the source program is consumed, as in lcc.

Most languages have a declaration-before-use rule: They insist that identifiers be declared before they are used, except in specific contexts, and they provide mechanisms that help programmers comply. For example, the C declaration

```
extern Tree (*optree[])(int, Tree, Tree);
```

declares, but does not define, optree so that it can be used before it's defined. Other examples include the forward structure declaration described on page 276 and Pascal's forward declaration. The sole purpose of these kinds of declarations is to make one-pass compilation possible.

Modern languages, such as Modula-3 and ML, have no such rules. In Modula-3, for example, declarations are definitions; they introduce names for constants, types, variables, exceptions, and procedures, and they can appear in *any* order. The order in which they appear affects only the order in which initializations are executed. This flexibility can be confusing at first, but Modula-3 has *fewer* linguistic rules and special cases than does C, which makes it easier to understand in the long run.

Languages with these kinds of features demand multiple-pass compilers because the entire source must be consumed in order to resolve the dependencies between declarations, for example. These compilers separate syntax analysis from semantic analysis because they must. The first pass usually builds an AST (abstract syntax tree) for the entire source program, and subsequent passes traverse the AST adding pass-specific annotations. For example, the declarations pass in a Modula-3 compiler analyzes only declarations, builds symbol tables, and annotates the nodes in the AST with pointers to symbol-table entries. The code generation passes might visit procedure nodes and their descendants, generate code, and annotate procedure nodes with the equivalent of lcc's code lists.

lcc's one-pass approach has its advantages. It consumes less memory than ASTs require, and it can be faster because simple constructs don't pay for the time overhead associated with building and traversing ASTs. Initializations of large arrays exemplify these advantages; lcc compiles them in space proportional to only their largest single initializer, and can thus handle initializations of any size. Compilers that use ASTs usually build a tree for an entire list of initializers, and thus may limit the maximum size of an initialization in order to avoid excessive memory use.

On modern computers, however, the time and space efficiency of one-pass compilers is no longer as important as the flexibility of the AST approach. Separating the various compilation passes into AST traversals can simplify the code for each pass. This approach would simplify lcc's modules that parse and analyze declarations, expressions, and statements, and it would make the corresponding chapters in this book easier to understand.

Using ASTs would also make it easier to use 1cc for other purposes. Parts of 1cc have been used to build browsers, front ends for other back ends, back ends for other front ends, and link-time and run-time code generators, and it has been used to generate code from within an interpreter and a debugger. 1cc's design did not anticipate some of these uses, and at least some of these projects would have been easier if 1cc had built ASTs and let clients traverse and annotate them.

19.4   Code Generation and Optimization

Code generation requires trade-offs. Ambitious optimizers emit better code, but they're bigger and slower. A bigger compiler would've taken us longer and wouldn't have fit in a book, and a slower compiler would cost time for us and for all programmers, for whom compilation time is often a bottleneck. So 1cc emits satisfactory code, but other compilers can beat it on this score.

1cc's instruction selection is optimal for each tree in isolation, but the boundaries between the code for adjacent trees may be suboptimal. 1cc would benefit from a final peephole optimization pass to clean up such problems. Of the various optimizations that one might add, however, this one is probably the simplest, but our past experience suggests it would yield the least.

92	function
448	" (MIPS)
484	" (SPARC)
518	" (X86)
92	gen
402	gen

1cc's interface is designed to support only code generation; it has no direct support for building a flow graph or other structures that facilitate global optimization. More elaborate versions of function and gen could collaborate to build the relevant structures, perform optimizations, and invoke the simpler gen, but generating flow graphs from ASTs is a more general solution.

1cc's register allocator is rudimentary. It allocates some variables and local common subexpressions to registers, but in all other respects it is minimal. A modern graph-coloring register allocator would do better. We resisted a more ambitious register allocator mainly because we estimated that it would add over 1,000 lines, or roughly 10%, to the compiler, and we already had to omit parts of the compiler from this book.

1cc's SPARC code needs instruction scheduling now, and other targets are likely to need scheduling in the future. Ideally, scheduling interacts with register allocation, but a postpass scheduler would probably be simpler and would thus fit 1cc better.

19.5   Testing and Validation

This book's companion diskette includes some programs that we use to test 1cc at every change. This first-level testing compares the emitted assembler code and the output of the assembled program with saved baseline assembler code and output. Sometimes we expect the assembler code to change, so the first comparison can tell us nothing, but it's worth doing because sometimes it fails unexpectedly and thus tells us that a change to the compiler went overboard.

We also test, though somewhat less often, using the language conformance section of the Plum-Hall Validation Suite for ANSI C compilers and with a large set of numeric programs translated from Fortran. The numeric programs have more variables, longer expressions, and more common subexpressions than the other tests, which strains the register allocator and thus tests the spiller better. Spills are rare, so spillers are often hard to test.

lcc's test suite includes material that came to us as bug reports, but we wish we'd saved more. lcc has been in use at AT&T Bell Laboratories and Princeton University since 1988 and at many other sites since then. Many errors have been reported, diagnosed, and corrected. Electronic news summarized each repair for users at Bell Laboratories and Princeton, so that users might know if they needed to discard old binaries. We recorded all the news messages, but next time we'd record more.

First, we'd record the shortest possible input that exposes each bug. Just finding this input can be half the battle. Some bug reports were nothing more than a note that lcc's code for the program gave a wrong answer and a pointer to a directory full of source code. It's hard to find a compiler error when all you have is a large, unknown source program and thousands of lines of object code. We usually start by trimming the program until another cut causes the bug to vanish. Almost all bugs have, in the end, been demonstrated by sample code of five lines or fewer. Next time, we'd save these programs with sample input and output, and create a test harness that would automatically recheck them. One must resist the temptation to omit bugs deemed too arcane to reoccur. We've sometimes reintroduced an old bug when fixing a new one, and thus had to track and fix the old one a second time. A test harness would probably pay for itself after one or two reintroduced bugs.

We'd also link at least some bugs with the code that corrects them. lcc was not originally written as a literate program; the English here was retrofitted to the code. In this, we encountered several compiler fragments that we could no longer explain immediately. Most of them turned out to repair bugs, but we'd have saved time if we'd kept more sample bugs — that is, the source code and sample input and output — nearby in comments or, now, in possibly elided fragments of the literate program.

Another kind of test suite would help retargeters. When writing a back end for a new target, we don't implement the entire code generator before we start testing. Instead, we implement enough to compile, say, the trivial program

```
main() {
    printf("Hello world\n");
}
```

When we get lcc to compile that correctly, we trust — perhaps naively — all simple function calls and use them to test another primitive feature that is needed for most other testing. Integer assignment is a typical second step:

```
main() {
    int i = 0;
    printf("%d\n", i);
}
```

We continue testing with a series of similar programs. Each is simple, tests exactly one new feature, and uses as few other features as possible, in order to minimize the amount of assembler code and compiler traces we must read if the test program fails. We never took the time to collect the tiny test programs as a guide for future retargetings, but doing so would have saved us time in the long run, and it would save you time when you write an lcc back end for your favorite computer.

Further Reading

Schreiner and Friedman (1985) describe how to use LEX (Lesk 1975) and YACC (Johnson 1975) by building a toy compiler for a small language. Holub (1990) and Gray et al. (1992) describe more modern variants of these compiler tools and how to implement them.

Budd (1991) is a gentle introduction to object-oriented programming and object-oriented programming languages; he describes SmallTalk, C++, Object Pascal, and Objective-C. The reference manuals for C++ (Ellis and Stroustrup 1990), Oberon-2 (Mössenböck and Wirth 1991), and Modula-3 (Nelson 1991) are the definitive sources for those languages.

Ramsey (1993) adapted lcc to be an expression server for the retargetable debugger ldb. The server accepts a C expression entered during debugging and a symbol table, compiles the expression as if it appeared in a context described by the supplied symbol table, and evaluates it. Ramsey wrote a back end that emits PostScript instead of assembler language, and ldb's embedded PostScript interpreter evaluates the generated code and thus evaluates the expression. He also modified lcc to emit ldb symbol tables.

Appel (1992) describes a research compiler for ML that builds ASTs and makes more than 30 passes over them during compilation.

Our paper describing an earlier version of lcc (Fraser and Hanson 1991b) compares lcc's size and speed and the speed of its generated code with the vendor's compilers and with gcc on the VAX, Motorola

68020, SPARC, and MIPS R3000. lcc generated code that was usually better than the code generated by the commercial compiler without optimization enabled. A companion paper gives measurements that support our intuition that register spills are rare (Fraser and Hanson 1992).

Lamb (1981) describes a typical peephole optimizer. The peephole optimizer copt is about the simplest possible; it is available by anonymous ftp from ftp.cs.princeton.edu in pub/lcc/contrib. Davidson and Fraser (1984) describe a peephole optimizer driven by a formal description of the target machine.

Chaitin et al. (1981) describe register allocation by graph coloring, and Krishnamurthy (1990) surveys some of the literature in instruction scheduling. Proebsting and Fischer (1991) describe one of the simplest integrations of register allocation and instruction scheduling.

Bibliography

Aho, A. V., and S. C. Johnson. 1974. LR parsing. *ACM Computing Surveys* 6(2), 99-124.

———. 1976. Optimal code generation for expression trees. *Journal of the ACM* 23(3), 488-501.

Aho, A. V., R. Sethi, and J. D. Ullman. 1986. *Compilers: Principles, Techniques, and Tools.* Reading, MA: Addison Wesley.

American National Standards Institute, Inc. 1990. *American National Standard for Information Systems, Programming Language C ANSI X3.159-1989.* New York: American National Standards Institute, Inc.

Appel, A. W. 1991. Garbage collection. In P. Lee, Ed., *Topics in Advanced Language Implementation Techniques*, 89-100. Cambridge, MA: MIT Press.

———. 1992. *Compiling with Continuations.* Cambridge: Cambridge University Press.

Baskett, F. 1978. The best simple code generation technique for while, for, and do loops. *SIGPLAN Notices* 13(4), 31-32.

Bernstein, R. L. 1985. Producing good code for the case statement. *Software—Practice and Experience* 15(10), 1021-1024.

Boehm, H.-J., and M. Weiser. 1988. Garbage collection in an uncooperative environment. *Software—Practice and Experience* 18(9), 807-820.

Budd, T. A. 1991. *An Introduction to Object-Oriented Programming.* Reading, MA: Addison Wesley.

Bumbulis, P., and D. D. Cowan. 1993. RE2C: A more versatile scanner generator. *ACM Letters on Programming Languages and Systems* 2(1-4), 70-84.

Burke, M. G., and G. A. Fisher. 1987. A practical method for LR and LL syntactic error diagnosis. *ACM Transactions on Programming Languages and Systems* 9(2), 164-197.

Chaitin, G. J., M. A. Auslander, A. K. Chandra, J. Cocke, M. E. Hopkins, and P. W. Markstein. 1981. Register allocation via coloring. *Journal of Computer Languages* 6, 47-57.

Cichelli, R. J. 1980. Minimal perfect hash functions made simple. *Communications of the ACM* 23(1), 17-19.

Clinger, W. D. 1990. How to read floating-point numbers accurately. *Proceedings of the SIGPLAN'90 Conference on Programming Language Design and Implementation, SIGPLAN Notices* 25(6), 92-101.

Davidson, J. W., and C. W. Fraser. 1984. Code selection through object code optimization. *ACM Transactions on Programming Languages and Systems* 6(4), 505-526.

Davie, A. J. T., and R. Morrison. 1981. *Recursive Descent Compiling.* New York: John Wiley & Sons.

Ellis, M. A., and B. Stroustrup. 1990. *The Annotated C++ Reference Manual.* Reading, MA: Addison Wesley.

Fischer, C. N., and R. J. LeBlanc, Jr. 1991. *Crafting a Compiler with C.* Redwood City, CA: Benjamin/Cummings.

Fraser, C. W. 1989. A language for writing code generators. *Proceedings of the SIGPLAN'89 Conference on Programming Language Design and Implementation, SIGPLAN Notices* 24(7), 238-245.

Fraser, C. W., and D. R. Hanson. 1991a. A code generation interface for ANSI C. *Software—Practice and Experience* 21(9), 963-988.

———. 1991b. A retargetable compiler for ANSI C. *SIGPLAN Notices* 26(10), 29-43.

———. 1992. Simple register spilling in a retargetable compiler. *Software—Practice and Experience* 22(1), 85-99.

Fraser, C. W., D. R. Hanson, and T. A. Proebsting. 1992. Engineering a simple, efficient code-generator generator. *ACM Letters on Programming Languages and Systems* 1(3), 213-226.

Fraser, C. W., R. R. Henry, and T. A. Proebsting. 1992. BURG—Fast optimal instruction selection and tree parsing. *SIGPLAN Notices* 27(4), 68-76.

Freiburghouse, R. A. 1974. Register allocation via usage counts. *Communications of the ACM* 17(11), 638-642.

Gray, R. W., V. P. Heuring, S. P. Levi, A. M. Sloane, and W. M. Waite. 1992. Eli: A complete, flexible compiler construction system. *Communications of the ACM* 35(2), 121-131.

Griswold, R. E. 1972. *The Macro Implementation of SNOBOL4.* San Francisco: W. H. Freeman.

Hansen, W. J. 1992. Subsequence references: First-class values for substrings. *ACM Transactions on Programming Languages and Systems* 14(4), 471–489.

Hanson, D. R. 1974. A simple technique for representing strings in Fortran IV. *Communications of the ACM* 17(11), 646–647.

———. 1983. Simple code optimizations. *Software—Practice and Experience* 13(8), 745–763.

———. 1985. Compact recursive-descent parsing of expressions. *Software—Practice and Experience* 15(12), 1205–1212.

———. 1990. Fast allocation and deallocation of memory based on object lifetimes. *Software—Practice and Experience* 20(1), 5–12.

Harbison, S. P., and G. L. Steele, Jr. 1991. *C: A Reference Manual* (third edition). Englewood Cliffs, NJ: Prentice Hall.

Hennessy, J. L., and N. Mendelsohn. 1982. Compilation of the Pascal case statement. *Software—Practice and Experience* 12(9), 879–882.

Heuring, V. P. 1986. The automatic generation of fast lexical analyzers. *Software—Practice and Experience* 16(9), 801–808.

Holub, A. I. 1990. *Compiler Design in C.* Englewood Cliffs, NJ: Prentice Hall.

Holzmann, G. J. 1988. *Beyond Photography.* Englewood Cliffs, NJ: Prentice Hall.

Intel Corp. 1993. *Intel486 Microprocessor Family Programmer's Reference Manual.* Intel Corp.

Jaeschke, G., and G. Osterburg. 1980. On Cichelli's minimal perfect hash function method. *Communications of the ACM* 23(12), 728–729.

Johnson, S. C. 1975. YACC—Yet another compiler compiler. Technical Report 32, Murray Hill, NJ: Computing Science Research Center, AT&T Bell Laboratories.

———. 1978. A portable compiler: Theory and practice. In *Conference Record of the ACM Symposium on Principles of Programming Languages*, Tucson, AZ, 97–104.

Kane, G., and J. Heinrich. 1992. *MIPS RISC Architecture.* Englewood Cliffs, NJ: Prentice Hall.

Kannan, S., and T. A. Proebsting. 1994. Correction to 'producing good code for the case statement'. *Software—Practice and Experience* 24(2), 233.

Kernighan, B. W., and R. Pike. 1984. *The UNIX Programming Environment*. Englewood Cliffs, NJ: Prentice Hall.

Kernighan, B. W., and D. M. Ritchie. 1988. *The C Programming Language* (second edition). Englewood Cliffs, NJ: Prentice Hall.

Knuth, D. E. 1973a. *The Art of Computer Programming: Volume 1, Fundamental Algorithms* (second edition). Reading, MA: Addison Wesley.

———. 1973b. *The Art of Computer Programming: Volume 3, Searching and Sorting*. Reading, MA: Addison Wesley.

———. 1984. *The TeXBook*. Reading, MA: Addison Wesley.

———. 1992. *Literate Programming*. CSLI Lecture Notes Number 27. Stanford, CA: Center for the Study of Language and Information, Stanford University.

Krishnamurthy, S. M. 1990. A brief survey of papers on scheduling for pipelined processors. *SIGPLAN Notices* 25(7), 97-106.

Lamb, D. A. 1981. Construction of a peephole optimizer. *Software—Practice and Experience* 11(12), 639-648.

Lesk, M. E. 1975. LEX—A lexical analyzer generator. Technical Report 39, Murray Hill, NJ: Computing Science Research Center, AT&T Bell Laboratories.

Logothetis, G., and P. Mishra. 1981. Compiling short-circuit Boolean expressions in one pass. *Software—Practice and Experience* 11(11), 1197-1214.

McKeeman, W. M., J. J. Horning, and D. B. Wortman. 1970. *A Compiler Generator*. Englewood Cliffs, NJ: Prentice Hall.

Mössenböck, H., and N. Wirth. 1991. The programming language Oberon-2. *Structured Programming* 12(4), 179-195.

Nelson, G. 1991. *Systems Programming with Modula-3*. Englewood Cliffs, NJ: Prentice Hall.

Patterson, D. A., and J. L. Hennessy. 1990. *Computer Architecture: A Quantitative Approach*. San Mateo, CA: Morgan Kaufmann.

Pelegrí-Llopart, E., and S. L. Graham. 1988. Optimal code generation for expression trees: An application of BURS theory. In *Conference Record of the ACM Symposium on Principles of Programming Languages*, San Diego, CA, 294-308.

Proebsting, T. A. 1992. Simple and efficient BURS table generation. *Proceedings of the SIGPLAN'92 Conference on Programming Language Design and Implementation, SIGPLAN Notices* 27(6), 331–340.

Proebsting, T. A., and C. N. Fischer. 1991. Linear-time, optimal code scheduling for delayed-load architectures. *Proceedings of the SIGPLAN'91 Conference on Programming Language Design and Implementation, SIGPLAN Notices* 26(6), 256–267.

Ramsey, N. 1993. *A Retargetable Debugger.* Ph.D. diss., Princeton University, Princeton, NJ.

———. 1994. Literate programming simplified. *IEEE Software* 11(5), 97–105.

Ramsey, N., and D. R. Hanson. 1992. A retargetable debugger. *Proceedings of the SIGPLAN'92 Conference on Programming Language Design and Implementation, SIGPLAN Notices* 27(7), 22–31.

Richards, M., and C. Whitby-Strevens. 1979. *BCPL—The Language and Its Compiler.* Cambridge: Cambridge University Press.

Ritchie, D. M. 1993. The development of the C language. *Preprints of the Second ACM SIGPLAN History of Programming Languages Conference (HOPL-II), SIGPLAN Notices* 28(3), 201–208.

Sager, T. J. 1985. A polynomial time generator for minimal perfect hash functions. *Communications of the ACM* 28(5), 523–532.

Schreiner, A. T., and H. G. Friedman, Jr. 1985. *Introduction to Compiler Construction with UNIX.* Englewood Cliffs, NJ: Prentice Hall.

Sedgewick, R. 1990. *Algorithms in C.* Reading, MA: Addison Wesley.

Sethi, R. 1981. Uniform syntax for type expressions and declarators. *Software—Practice and Experience* 11(6), 623–628.

SPARC International. 1992. *The SPARC Architecture Manual, Version 8.* Englewood Cliffs, NJ: Prentice Hall.

Stallman, R. M. 1992. Using and porting GNU CC. Technical report, Cambridge, MA: Free Software Foundation.

Steele, Jr., G. L., and J. L. White. 1990. How to print floating-point numbers accurately. *Proceedings of the SIGPLAN'90 Conference on Programming Language Design and Implementation, SIGPLAN Notices* 25(6), 112–126.

Stirling, C. 1985. Follow set error recovery. *Software—Practice and Experience* 15(3), 239–257.

Tanenbaum, A. S., H. van Staveren, and J. W. Stevenson. 1982. Using peephole optimization on intermediate code. *ACM Transactions on Programming Languages and Systems* 4(1), 21–36.

Ullman, J. D. 1994. *Elements of ML Programming.* Englewood Cliffs, NJ: Prentice Hall.

Waite, W. M. 1986. The cost of lexical analysis. *Software—Practice and Experience* 16(5), 473–488.

Waite, W. M., and L. R. Carter. 1993. *An Introduction to Compiler Construction.* New York: Harper Collins.

Waite, W. M., and G. Goos. 1984. *Compiler Construction.* New York: Springer-Verlag.

Weinstock, C. B., and W. A. Wulf. 1988. Quick fit: An efficient algorithm for heap storage management. *SIGPLAN Notices* 23(10), 141–148.

Wilson, P. R. 1994. Uniprocessor garbage collection techniques. *ACM Computing Surveys* 27, to appear.

Wirth, N. 1976. *Algorithms + Data Structures = Programs.* Englewood Cliffs, NJ: Prentice Hall.

———. 1977. What can be done about the unnecessary diversity of notation for syntactic definitions? *Communications of the ACM* 20(11), 822–823.

Index

Bold page numbers refer to definitions. For a fragment or an identifier, roman numbers refer to its uses in code, and italic numbers refer to its uses in the text. Fragments and identifiers without definitions identify those omitted from this book.

How to Obtain lcc

The complete source code for lcc is available free of charge to the purchaser of this book. All distributions include the source code for the front end, the code generators for the SPARC, MIPS R3000 and Intel 386, the source code for the code-generator generator, and documentation that gives instructions for installing and running lcc on a variety of platforms. lcc runs on UNIX systems and on PCs with a 386 processor or its successor running DOS 6.0 or Windows 3.1.

There is an electronic lcc mailing list. To subscribe, send a e-mail message with the one-line body

    subscribe lcc

to majordomo@cs.princeton.edu. This line must appear in the message body; "Subject:" lines are ignored. Additional information about lcc is also available on the Wide World Web via Mosaic and other Web browsers. The universal resource locator is

    http://www.cs.princeton.edu/software/lcc

lcc may be obtained from the sources listed below.

Internet

The distribution is available for downloading via anonymous ftp from ftp.cs.princeton.edu (128.112.152.13) in the directory pub/lcc. To retrieve information about the distribution, ftp to ftp.cs.princeton.edu; for example, on UNIX systems, use the command

    ftp ftp.cs.princeton.edu

Log in as anonymous, and use your e-mail address as your password. Once connected, change to the lcc directory with the command

    cd pub/lcc

The file named README gives instructions for retrieving the distribution with ftp and information about lcc since this book went to press. The command

    get README

will retrieve this file. Follow the instructions therein for retrieving the distribution in the form that is appropriate for your system.

Diskette

The distribution is available free of charge on a 3.5", high-density diskette to the original purchaser of this book. To obtain your copy, fill in the coupon on the next page and return it to Addison-Wesley.

lcc is an active research compiler and will continue to change over time. Thus, the diskette version cannot be as up to date as the online versions.

To obtain a free 3.5" diskette containing the 1cc distribution, fill in the coupon below, carefully remove this entire page from the book, fold the page so that the Addison-Wesley Publishing Company address, printed on the reverse side, is visible, attach appropriate postage, and mail. Allow two weeks from receipt of this coupon for delivery.

Only an original of this page can be redeemed for a diskette; photocopies are not accepted.

Please send me my free 3.5" diskette containing the 1cc distribution, ISBN 0-8053-1672-8.

Name _____

Street/Box _____

City/State/Country _____

Postal Code _____

Computer Science Editoral Department
Addison-Wesley Publishing Company
390 Bridge Parkway
Redwood City, CA 94065

Attention: 1cc Disk Fulfillment